The World Transformed

1945 TO THE PRESENT

Michael H. Hunt

The University of North Carolina at Chapel Hill

BEDFORD / ST. MARTIN'S   Boston   ◆   New York

For Bedford/St.Martin's

Publisher for History: Patricia A. Rossi
Director of Development for History: Jane Knetzger
Developmental Editor: Louise Townsend
Production Editor: Bridget Leahy
Marketing Manager: Jenna Bookin Barry
Editorial Assistant: Molly Minturn
Copyeditor: Alice Vigliani
Indexer: Katharyn Dunham
Cover Design: Donna Lee Dennison
Cover Art: A Chinese woman makes a phone call between barbed wires and paramilitary officers in Beijing, China. AP/Wide World Photos.
Composition: Pine Tree Composition
Printing and Binding: R.R. Donnelley & Sons Company

President: Joan E. Feinberg
Editorial Director: Denise B. Wydra
Director of Marketing: Karen Melton Soeltz
Director of Editing, Design, and Production: Marcia Cohen
Managing Editor: Elizabeth M. Schaaf

Library of Congress Control Number: 2003101700

9 8 7
f e d

For information, write: Bedford/St. Martin's, 75 Arlington Street, Boston, MA 02116 (617-399-4000)

ISBN-10: 0–312–24583–1
ISBN-13: 978–0–312–24583–2

Acknowledgments

Hanan Ashrawi. Poem (p. 89) from *This Side of Peace* by Hanan Ashrawi. Copyright © 1995 by Hanan Mikhail-Ashrawi. Reprinted with the permission of Simon & Schuster.

Pablo Neruda. "In Guatemala." Poem from *Song of Protest* by Pablo Neruda and translated by Miguel Algarín. English translation copyright © 1976 by Miguel Algarín. Reprinted by permission of HarperCollins Publishers, Inc.

Lyrics to "Born in the U.S.A" (4 lines) by Bruce Springsteen. Copyright © 1984 Bruce Springsteen. All rights reserved. Reprinted by permission.

PREFACE

Preparing this text has been a prolonged and delightful exercise in self-indulgence from which, I hope, others will benefit. I was born a few years before the dropping of the first atomic bomb. I grew up overseas, a witness to Japan's struggle to recover from war and to other countries' search for a way to true independence and a better life. My family and I benefited from amazing economic and technological progress during the postwar years, and marveled at the accumulation of power in our own country. I was too young when the postwar era dawned to predict its trajectory, and few of the pundits at the time got it right. Looking back, I am amazed at how much has changed, often for the better, but also how many difficulties remain. My hope is that readers will come to share my sense of the drama and importance of contemporary history and my faith in the social utility of history as a powerful discipline essential to understanding the place humans have created for themselves.

This retrospective exercise began in earnest in a course surveying the post-1945 world that I have taught along with colleagues at the University of North Carolina at Chapel Hill since the 1980s. That course has proven popular for its historical immediacy and its relevance—as a vehicle for filling in the background on the world that students inherit and the issues that they, as part of an informed electorate, will have to address. Experience with that course, along with growing immersion in the new global history, deepened my interest in figuring out what the last half-century has meant. Informal class notes slowly turned into a text after I found no published survey that did justice to my notion of what has transpired over the past sixty years.

Two challenges faced me. One was to move away from international relations, which most surveys used as the chief organizing theme. The explosion of global history scholarship helped here, as did new literature on a wide variety of discrete topics. Combing through bibliographies and library shelves has left me in awe of the cumulative achievements of scholars around the world, especially in recent decades. The other challenge was to see the developments of the post-1945 era in relation to the dramatic changes over the last dozen years, beginning with the collapse of European and Russian socialism, continuing with the decade of global economic expansion and growing global awareness, and finally the reverberations set off by the events of September 11, 2001. All of us unavoidably see the past through the prism of the present. The historian's task is to strike a balance, avoiding on the one hand a past that does not speak to the world in which the reader lives and, on the other, a past that is robbed of its richness by presentist concerns.

THEMES

The premise on which this text rests is that 1945 is best understood not as a new phase in a long or short twentieth century. It marks rather a major watershed in its own right in the history of the modern world—the beginnings of a distinct, profoundly transformative epoch. The defining features of the world of 1945 would within a half-century fade from view, to be replaced by new ones that few in 1945 would have predicted or could even have imagined. Hence the title that this volume carries: *The World Transformed*. To make this case for fundamental change is hard enough for a single country or region. It is especially daunting when an entire world is the subject. Peter Stearns has observed perceptively that if history may seem to some like "one damn thing after another," then world history will feel like "an unusual number of damn things."[1] Any broad claim about change on a global scale badly needs discrete interpretive threads that will give order and coherence to the argument. This text has three: the themes of international relations, the international economy, and the developing world."

The transformation most likely to come first to the mind of most readers occurred in interstate relations. The emergence of a sharp and unusually ideological rivalry between two fresh forces on the world scene, the United States and the Soviet Union, dominated much of the postwar era. And then this unusual bipolar distribution of international power gave way to an even more unusual condition—an American hegemony that promises to persist well into the twenty-first century.

The second point of post-1945 distinctiveness is to be found in the international economy. A world in shambles as the war drew to a close managed some spectacular wealth creation over the next half-century while also generating adverse effects, including unparalleled environmental stress and widening gaps between the rich and poor. Whether for good or for ill, this globe-encircling system of production, finance, and consumption has had a far-reaching social and cultural influence over lives everywhere.

The struggles in that part of the world that was either colonial or semicolonial in 1945 mark a third major area of change. Those struggles provide insight on the aspirations and conditions of most of the earth's people as they embarked on what many at the time imagined would be a path-breaking course of liberation and development. Launched into independence with shared high hopes and bound together by a common set of problems and historical experiences, those countries increasingly took divergent paths toward century's end. Some made notable headway toward realizing their early aspirations, while others found themselves mired in poverty and dissension over their country's future course.

ORGANIZATION

In a world of simultaneous, multilevel communication, it should be possible to clearly convey the complex, evolving interrelationships among these three strands in a seamless fashion. But this kind of "virtual reality" presentation is impossible to get on the printed page and equally impossible to absorb. With a bow to these limits, this account offers a chronological treatment laid out in three parts. Each part corresponds to a major phase in the unfolding of the postwar era. Each part opens with a vignette meant to highlight a defining moment in the postwar period, and each contains a chapter on the Cold War, the international economy, and the third or developing world. While each chapter tackles one of the three major themes, connections are continually made to the other two themes, thus creating a more integrated picture of history in the reader's mind. Finally, an introductory essay and comprehensive conclusion provide crucial background and analysis to help students make sense of the post-1945 world.

By focusing on the three themes one at a time in the introduction, in the chapters within the three major parts of the text, and in the conclusion, this account can better convey a sense of the major contours and key developments defining the contemporary world. This interpretative strategy easily accommodates to courses organized along either chronological or topical lines. While instructors wanting to proceed in more or less chronological fashion can assign the three parts consecutively, those preferring a more topical approach will find it easy to pick and choose. For example, my own preference has been to put before students the most familiar topic first—that is, the Cold War from origins to end. I thus begin with Chapters 1, 4, and 7. I follow with the third world (Chapters 3, 6, and 9) and then go to global economic issues (Chapters 2, 5, and 8). The Conclusion provides an appropriate cap whether the course is taught chronologically or topically. It offers a "Where are we now?" survey of the last decade in light of trends over the last half-century.

APPROACH

In tracing the evolving postwar world, I have made several carefully considered choices about my approach.

I have first of all emphasized the role of personality. Individuals have an out-sized influence on events as will become repeatedly evident in cases from Joseph Stalin to Rachel Carson to Morita Akio. That individuals are also shaped by their times and that individual ambitions can take surprising and sometimes disap-pointing turns seem to me especially important points for students to grasp as they develop a sense of their own potentials and limits. People around the world have over the last half-century faced complex choices. That they did not all reach the same decisions and that their choices could evolve are also important points for students to understand as they confront the problems of a still diverse world. Finally, I have wanted to show the way in which prominent individuals and guid-ing ideas operate within a social and cultural setting that can be both enabling and restrictive. Popular needs and preferences regarding issues ranging from gender roles to market forces are essential to understand each of the major sets of transformations discussed. This emphasis on individuals, both elite and ordinary, makes possible the introduction into the text of enlivening vignettes, anecdotes, and voices. These, along with the biographical sketches, help to bring history alive for students by humanizing it.

A second major set of choices has shaped my approach to what is referred to here as the third or developing world. I have opted for in-depth case studies that serve to highlight landmarks and patterns in what for many students is murky terrain. A limited number of carefully selected cases can avoid an overload of information while conveying a sense of the commonalties as well as the variations within the general pattern. These case studies thus serve as an invitation to exercise the skills of historical comparison. Instructors wanting to add their own favorite cases through lectures, supplementary readings, and assignments on the World Wide Web should find here a good basis on which to build.

A third area of concern has been to strike the right balance in the attention given the United States. I have been mindful of the dangers of ethnocentrism—of priveleging the country with which most readers of this volume identify. Such prominent placement runs the risk of encouraging the notion that the rest of the world is like us or wants to be like us. It may also promote the equally mistaken idea that the United States can reshape the world regardless of the preference of others. On the other hand, a close examination of the post-1945 world reveals American fingerprints everywhere. Not only did the United States maintain a clear edge throughout the Cold War, U.S. victory in that conflict resulted in a true political and military hegemony. If the Cold War is the most obvious manifestation of American prominence, economic and cultural globalization comes a close second. The way in which Americanization is conventionally used interchangeably with Westernization and modernization attests to a recognition of strong, pervasive U.S. influence. Finally, the United States has had a pronounced impact throughout the third world—whether as patron, model, or foe. It is difficult to find the case where there has not been some substantial sort of American mark. That the United States looms large may at first blush seem to flatter the national pride of many students, but they will encounter here an often-unsettling perspective on their country's past.

While I made these choices with the needs of a history survey course primarily in mind, my hope is that this text will provide coverage adaptable to a variety of disciplinary needs. Those teaching in political science, international relations, and international/global studies with a contemporary focus should find this volume suitable as a main or supplementary reading. Those in search of supplementary materials are invited to look at the documentary collection, *The World Transformed, 1945 to the Present: A Documentary Reader.* This reader, which serves as a companion to the main text, offers a wealth of primary sources on the pivotal events that shaped the post-1945 world. Its ten chapters provide a wide-ranging selection of documents—from Joseph Stalin on Soviet ideology and Hiroshima victims' memories to a U.S. marine's experiences in Vietnam and

Mexican critics debating NAFTA. Like the main text, this reader demonstrates the fundamental interdependence among developments in the Cold War, the international economy, and the third world.

FEATURES

To assist students in their grasp of post-1945 world history and engage them in the process of learning, *The World Transformed* offers the following pedagogic features:

The comprehensive introduction explains the significance of the watershed year 1945 and sets the stage for the material to come with an overview of the main events in the history of international politics, the global economy, and the colonial system both pre and post-1945. Drawing students into the text, each part introduction opens with a vignette that embodies some of the most significant themes of that part, followed by an overview of the topics to come. Chapter conclusions offer students the opportunity to review the chapter's main themes. Because making sense of recent history can be especially hard for students, the conclusion, "Globalization Ascendant: The 1990s and Beyond," offers a summing up of major trends and events and provides some observations about the nature and impact of globalization and its prospects.

A striking photo program with detailed captions strengthens students' understanding of history through images from the period under discussion. Plentiful maps, tables, and graphs help students in comprehending world geography and drawing conclusions based on statistics. Throughout the text, brief "spot" chronologies provide a handy review of significant events and prominent organizations and personalities for the period or country under discussion. Students wanting to pursue a particular topic will find annotated "Recommended Resources" at the close of each chapter directing them to a range of sources, from general works to titles on specific topics. They include novels, memoirs, and films. The Bedford/St. Martin's History Links Library (www.bedfordstmartins .com/historylinks/) contains continually updated and annotated links to pedagogically useful sites.

Now more than ever I realize that any textbook and especially one with a global focus has to be selective. It has to emphasize some points and neglect or even omit others—not randomly or arbitrarily but guided by some interpretive framework. As a historian who has grappled with synthesis has sensibly pointed out, "A textbook is not an encyclopaedia, and can hardly be judged in terms of how exhaustive it is, but should be evaluated from the point of view of its structural coherency, and its ability to stimulate the reader's interest."[2] Here is the test—accessibility, breadth, and coherence—that I want this survey to pass. My hope is that in making my choices about which parts of the past to capture and how to treat them I have created a balanced, focused account. If I have succeeded, instructors will find this text easy to supplement at some points and fruitful to challenge at others. Even more important, students will gain a better understanding of how their world came into being and what sorts of challenges they face as citizens and moral agents.

Acknowledgments

I could not have explored the highways and byways that this volume travels and then prepared my trip report without the help of many people. The readers secured by Bedford/St. Martin's for drafts of this text—Michael Adas (Rutgers University), Brian Bonhomme (University of Central Arkansas), Charles Bright (University of Michigan), Jürgen Buchenau (University of North Carolina at Charlotte), Susan Carruthers (University of Wales, Great Britain), Andrew F. Clark (University of North Carolina at Wilmington), Kenneth Curtis (California State University at Long Beach), Gary Darden (Rutgers University), Carole Fink (Ohio State University), Jeff Hornibrook (State University of New York at Plattsburgh), Caroline Kennedy-Pipe (Durham University, Great Britain), Paul Gordon Lauren (University of Montana), Steven I. Levine (University of North Carolina at Chapel Hill), Michelle Mannering (Butler University), Melvin E. Page (East Tennessee State University), George Schuyler (University of Central Arkansas), Gerald Surh (North Carolina State University), Alexander Sydorenko (Arkansas State University), David S. Trask (Guilford Technical Community College), and Marilyn Young (New York University)—gave good counsel that I hope they find at least substantially reflected in this edition.

Katherine Kurzman at Bedford Books saw potential in this project, and after her Patricia Rossi and Jane Knetzger have kept it moving smoothly ahead. Among the supportive, professional team at Bedford, Louise Townsend, a skilled editor, stands out for the way she has patiently and adroitly guided me through the development process. Bridget Leahy was the good shepherd through the process of bookmaking—thoughtful, meticulous, in control, and full of good humor. Donna Dennison came up with a brilliant solution to the cover puzzle. Robin Raffer adroitly handled the complexities of art and text research, while Sandy Schechter did the same with permissions. Editorial assistant Molly Minturn cheerfully helped out with numerous editorial tasks. Alice Vigliani proved a skillful copyeditor, while Katharyn Dunham adroitly handled the special challenges of indexing this volume. For assembling this talented team and making it available for this project, I have to thank Joan Feinberg, Denise Wydra, and Chuck Christensen. Their collective effort has made the final product a great deal better than I had originally imagined it.

The University of North Carolina at Chapel Hill provided a supportive environment in which to undertake this project. I am grateful to the graduate students who over the last decade taught and studied with me and in the process helped sharpen and broaden my thinking on what to include and how to present it. I owe special thanks in this regard to Christopher Endy, Matthew Jacobs, Alan McPherson, Leah Potter, Nathaniel Smith, and Odd Arne Westad for their interest and assistance. Specialists and especially department colleagues were unfailing responsive to my requests for guidance. I am especially grateful to Judith Bennett, Peter Coclanis, W. Miles Fletcher, Donald Raleigh, Donald Reid, Anne Richards, Sarah Shields, and Wyatt Wells. The Reynolds Fund, the Institute for Arts and Humanities, and the Department of History—all at UNC—gave me the gift of time to work on this project.

Paula Hunt has kept me grounded, listened patiently, and emphatically perked up when matters relating to Italy, peace, and social justice came into view. Once more I have a chance to express my deep gratitude to her.

More errors than I would like to contemplate doubtless remain despite all those who have tried to set me straight. Those flaws have to be set against my name.

CONTENTS

Part Three
FROM COLD WAR TO GLOBALIZATION, 1968–1991   297

INTRODUCTION:
THE 1945 WATERSHED

An attentive reader of a good daily newspaper in August 1945, just as World War II reached its end, would have sensed a world damaged and disrupted. Beginning in 1937 in Asia and in 1939 in Europe, warfare had spread over broad stretches of the globe. Fighting, together with genocide and privation, brought death to sixty million people (about two-thirds civilians) and left countless others wounded or displaced. Nothing captured better the awful destructive power of wartime than one of its final images: a mushroom cloud rising above Hiroshima, Japan. In an instant that city had become rubble, joining the many others not only in Japan but also in China, the Soviet Union, and continental Europe flattened by more conventional bombing or ground combat. Debris—once homes, schools, and churches—spread out in great vistas. This orgy of destruction mocked the achievements of the old European-dominated international order, humbling once-powerful states, tearing apart societies, arresting international trade and finance, and leaving distant colonies in ferment.

But our reader would also have glimpsed the first signs of a world rebuilding, animated by hopes for a new era of peace and prosperity. Newspapers had already reported the defeat of Germany's aggressive and genocidal regime in May and the launching of a fresh international initiative, the United Nations, to bring the world community together in a new spirit of collective security and commitment to human welfare. Even before the Japanese surrender in August, reporters noted that the U.S. economy, the largest in the world and the only major one undamaged by the war, was beginning to shift production back to civilian goods. This transition was cheering news, especially for people overseas facing the arduous task of reconstruction after years of economic depression and military conflict. To judge from the press, the colonial world might seem stable, but a careful reader would have noticed reports of Indian and Vietnamese calls for independence and might have guessed that self-determination was becoming a burning question that these and other peoples under foreign control were no longer willing to postpone.

Our attentive newspaper reader, whether in Shanghai, Chicago, Rome, or Accra, would not have found this text's premise surprising—that the year 1945 was a watershed date. It marked a distinct shift in contemporary global history, the

MONSOON FAILS TO HALT PURSUITS OF WAR AND PEACE

A British patrol crosses on a dry ridge in Burma while a native tiller works his flooded field

The New York Times (British Official)

A Cameo of the Postwar Forces in Play

In this photo published in the *New York Times* on August 8, 1945, British soldiers on patrol in Burma represent the authority of a tottering colonial order. The soldiers were cultural worlds away from the peasant plowing his ricefield behind a pair of oxen. He had grown up within an intimate set of village relations that defined status, obligations, and rights. But global economic forces had altered those relations, creating a highly competitive market for rice. Producers for that market, such as the man pictured here, would have been mainly concerned about the price at harvest time, whereas questions of independence from Britain preoccupying the Burmese political elite would have seemed relatively remote. (The New York Times)

ending of one era and the beginning of another. But our reader could not have begun to guess how the changes already in motion in August 1945 would play out. The economic power and missionary sense of the United States would propel it to a position of dominance, first evident in the contest with the Soviet Union and then accentuated after the Soviet rival faltered and finally collapsed. Individual states within the global economy recovered; but more significant, the most productive of them—all on the U.S. side of the Cold War line—embraced variations on the model of the free market (where supply and demand determined price) and set off on a relentless integration that by degrees encompassed the entire world. While the world's economic output soared, so too did the number of people with a claim on that output and the level of environmental stress with increasingly serious global as well as local effects. Finally, the challenge to the colonial system proved irresistible. As it rapidly gained momentum and support, it sparked international crises and spawned heady (albeit ultimately disappointed) hopes for a new, more equitable global order. These pronounced and interacting postwar trends would produce broad and fundamental transformations over the latter half of the twentieth century. Our 1945 newspaper reader, however perceptive and far-sighted, could not have imagined how these trends would combine by the twenty-first century to produce a world barely recognizable in its main features.

INTERNATIONAL POLITICS RECONFIGURED

The most obvious break in 1945 occurred in the realm of international politics. A system that had long consisted of multiple powers with shifting ties gave way after World War II to a bipolar rivalry between the world's two most powerful states, the Soviet Union and the United States.

This shift is best appreciated against the backdrop of international struggle centering on the major powers of Europe. The British and the French embarked on a rivalry in the late seventeenth and eighteenth centuries. Their long and costly contest drew in other, lesser powers such as Spain, Holland, Austria, and Russia, but it also reached well outside of Europe. London and Paris each sought control of land and resources in the Americas and maritime Asia and began building rival colonial empires. This accelerating pattern of imperialism into which virtually all the European powers would be drawn began to bind the globe into a single integrated economy. The French Revolution of 1789 and the ambitions of Napoleon I ignited the last round in the long Anglo-French contest. In 1815 Great Britain emerged as the victor—and established its dominance among the major powers, which included France, Austria, and Russia. By the late nineteenth century Germany and Italy had joined the great-power club, followed soon thereafter by the United States and Japan.

But mounting tensions among the powers would strain and finally destroy this multipolar state system. A popular Japanese song from the 1880s captured the anxiety inherent in this loose, competitive arrangement of states:

> There is a Law of Nations, it is true,
> but when the moment comes, remember,
> the Strong eat up the Weak.[1]

A newly united Germany sought dominance on the European continent and began a naval buildup that threatened British supremacy on the high seas. Alarmed by the German threat, Britain and France put aside their rivalry and joined with Russia to form an alliance known as the Triple Entente. Germany's reaction was to consolidate political and military ties with Austria-Hungary and the Ottoman Empire to create the Central Powers. The stage was set for conflict when in 1914 a minor crisis in the Balkans spun out of control. The resulting war, which dragged on for over four years, was the first blow to European power. The incredible carnage of 1914–1918 was finally brought to an end by exhaustion and by U.S. intervention in 1917 on the side of the Entente. Though the Entente triumphed, the war left ten million dead and European societies and economies reeling.

Wilson and Lenin as Rival Visionaries

In 1917 two distinct visions were emerging that pronounced bankrupt the international system that had plunged Europe into war. One of these visions issued from U.S. president Woodrow Wilson; the other came from Vladimir Lenin, the leader of the revolution that year in the Russian empire (soon renamed the Soviet Union). Both denounced the costly military rivalry, the repression of popular sentiment, and the accumulation of colonies that had come to characterize the leading European states. Both leaders called for nothing less than a basic overhaul of the international regime. Each was in his own way championing a program of sweeping liberation that would become part of the official creed of his country. Each associated his cause with the future welfare of humankind. Thus each at a fundamental ideological level challenged not just the European-dominated international system but also the legitimacy of states organized around other political, economic, and social principles. But fatefully, whatever the similarities, these were mutually incompatible—indeed, directly antagonistic—outlooks.

President Wilson took his country into the deadlocked European war in 1917 calling for "a world made safe for democracy." He then constructed a fourteen-point program for a post–World War I world that in his view advanced a fundamental American commitment, as old as the nation itself, to "show mankind the way to liberty." Wilson sought to promote free trade, halt the arms race, banish secret diplomacy with its alliances and terrible carnage, pull down empires, and promote self-determination throughout Europe. Out of the popular unrest after World War I, he hoped to see emerge moderate, democratic, constitutional regimes in Germany, Russia, and the nations newly liberated from the Austro-Hungarian Empire. At the heart of Wilson's program was an organization of democratic states, a League of Nations committed to peace and security and determined to bring an end to the tyranny and aggression that lay at the roots of the world war. His program spoke, as he put it, to the "universal unrest" of all peoples seeking justice and had the support "of forward looking men and women everywhere, of every modern nation, of every enlightened community." His principles were, in short, "the principles of mankind."[2]

Wilson's belief—one that would become the pivot of much subsequent U.S. foreign policy—was that the internal composition of countries bore a critical relationship both to the rights and well-being of their citizens and to harmony within the international community. To the degree that democracy prevailed, peace and prosperity would also prevail both within countries and internationally. Where autocracies, dictatorships, militarism, and imperialism held sway, the free flow of goods and ideas would give way to political repression and international conflict.

As leader of the revolutionary Bolshevik party, Lenin championed a no less fundamental reshaping of the global system. As a proponent of his own version of Marxism, he built on the writings of Karl Marx and Friedrich Engels, above all their *Communist Manifesto* of 1848, and on their premise that material conditions, specifically the prevailing economic system, shaped who people are and what they think. Marx put the matter succinctly: "The mode of production in material life determines the general character of the social, political, and spiritual processes of life. It is not the consciousness of men that determine their existence, but, on the contrary, their social existence determines their consciousness."[3] Engels put this essential idea more concretely: "Mankind must first of all eat, drink, have shelter and clothing, before it can pursue politics, science, art, religion, etc."[4] In this conception of society and history, changing systems of economic production drove and defined human development. New systems gave rise to new social classes at odds with the established ones. The most recent of those systems to arise was capitalism (an industrial economy commanded by a bourgeois class). Capitalism had eclipsed feudalism (an agricultural economy with peasant producers at the bottom of a social hierarchy). But capitalism would in time fall to the working class (an exploited proletariat) that was growing within its industrial centers. The Communist Party would lead the transition to worker domination. As the guide of the new revolutionary class, the party first had to overthrow capitalism and then establish in its place socialism, representing a higher stage of economic development and human freedom.

Lenin made his own contribution to this ideology by elaborating on how the transition from capitalism to socialism was to occur. His *Imperialism,* published in 1916, identified the three fundamental flaws within global capitalism that spelled its imminent doom. First was the contradiction within advanced capitalist economies. Sharpening exploitation of the working class had saved those economies from a crisis of overproduction for a time. But as overproduction increased, capitalists looked abroad for cheap raw materials and new markets for the sale of goods. The result was an economically driven imperialism. As the advanced capitalist countries became ever more dependent on overseas markets, they had to ensure their own prosperity by securing control, either informal or formal, over them. The second contradiction was among the major capitalist countries as they increasingly collided over control of world markets. This rivalry had (in Lenin's view) precipitated World War I. He was confident that other wars would follow, each further weakening the major powers. The third contradiction pitted the advanced capitalist states against the greater part of the world's population living in colonial and dependent countries. As the imperialists sought to exploit weaker peoples, they would not only arouse nationalist resentments but also spawn an industrial working class on the economic periphery. As capitalism developed and these three contradictions sharpened, revolutionary outbreaks would eventually begin among the working classes in advanced capitalist countries and then radiate out to the rest of the world.

Lenin imagined his Bolshevik revolution of 1917 as the first break in the capitalist chain of control then encircling the globe. That revolution would serve as an inspiration and model for others. Above all, it demonstrated what Lenin had earlier argued—the capacity of a tightly knit, dedicated, ideologically united revolutionary party to accelerate the victory of socialism. The prime task of this "Leninist" or vanguard party was to instill in the working class (or proletariat) a deeper sense of its identity and historical mission to bring capitalism down. Once it was victorious, the party would run the new workers' state, control the means of production in the name of the workers, and end economic exploitation. Increasing material abundance would eventually pave the way for the transition from socialism to communism and the final withering away of the state itself.

But after World War I and throughout the 1920s, neither Washington nor Moscow seemed about to remake the world. The former Entente powers, together with Japan, devoted themselves to combating the Bolsheviks, who found their only friend in an equally ostracized Germany. The U.S. government shared the aversion of its wartime allies to Bolshevism, but Americans were also in a cautious mood. In fact, national leaders and the public turned against Wilson's democratic crusade. In 1919–1920 the Senate rejected membership in the League of Nations, and the postwar Republican presidents kept Old World politics at arm's length.

World War II and the Onset of the Cold War

During the 1930s resurgent nationalism destabilized the postwar settlement and doomed Europe to its second major conflict in barely two decades, World War II. Germany's Adolf Hitler promoted an ideology of national revenge and racial purification, while Benito Mussolini in Italy and a military-dominated Japan were gripped by dreams of empire. Those three powers joined in a coalition known as the Axis. By bringing Germany together with its two foes from World War I, the Axis provided an illustration of the continuing fluidity of the alliance system. By 1939 Britain and France had aligned against the Axis. At first, Joseph Stalin, Lenin's successor as head of the Soviet Union, stood aside, while the American president, Franklin Roosevelt, showed increasing sympathy for the Anglo-French cause.

The second major war of the twentieth century, like the first, centered on Europe, but it proved more global and more destructive as the belligerents mobilized ever more formidable resources and technology against their foes. In 1939, after secretly agreeing with Stalin to divide Poland in a nonaggression pact, Hitler invaded that country (thereby snuffing out a state resurrected only twenty years earlier to keep Germany and Russia apart). The next year German forces rolled over France. In 1941 Germany directed a surprise attack against the Soviet Union, pushing Stalin to the side of the emerging Anglo-American alliance. In East Asia, Japan's imperial ambitions had collided with rising Chinese nationalist sentiment, most overtly beginning in 1931 when Japan seized China's northeastern provinces (known in the West as Manchuria). A formal state of war came in 1937. The Japanese attack on Pearl Harbor in December 1941 turned the European and Asian battle zones into a single global conflict. The United States at once declared war on Japan. Hitler, already fighting the Americans in the Atlantic, quickly closed the circle of hostilities by declaring war on the United States. The country that had sought to avoid the fighting now stood against the Axis in both Europe and the Pacific.

The main players in World War II reflected the decline of European predominance on the international stage. Japan, the Soviet Union (a Eurasian power), and the United States (a Pacific as well as an Atlantic power) were all to have

FROM WORLD WAR I TO WORLD WAR II

1914	World War I breaks out between the Entente and the Central Powers
1917	President Wilson intervenes on the side of the Entente; Bolsheviks led by Lenin take power in Russia
1918	World War I ends with Entente victory
1919–1920	Wilson presses fourteen-point peace plan on Entente partners; the U.S. Senate rejects participation in the League of Nations
1931	Japan invades China's northeastern provinces (Manchuria)
1937	Japan and China go to war
1939	Germany and the Soviet Union sign nonaggression pact; German invasion of Poland plunges Europe into war
1940	German invasion of France
1941	Germany invades the Soviet Union; Japanese attack on Pearl Harbor brings the United States formally into World War II

prominent roles, and the latter two carried the burden of the conflict on the ultimately victorious Allied side. Soviet and American might, already evident in wartime, was to bring an end to the era of multipolarity and give rise to a new bipolar world. No longer could the old contenders for advantage within the European sphere—Britain, France, Germany, and Italy—keep up with the two new global giants. These Old World powers had spent down their wealth and exhausted their will. That other relative newcomer, Japan, lay in ruins.

The postwar bipolar system spawned a Cold War that locked the United States and the Soviet Union in an intense, far-reaching rivalry spanning four decades. Like the two world wars earlier in the century, this contest began in Europe, with the war-weary region split by what was then called an "Iron Curtain" into U.S. and Soviet areas of influence. The contest then gradually spread, igniting distant, proxy wars and ultimately leaving no people or point of the globe untouched. However, the rivals would avoid the trauma of a direct clash of arms (hence the designation "Cold War"). The development of nuclear weapons helped set limits by making the prospect of such a clash especially fearsome. Though on the whole cautiously managed, this superpower rivalry would prove enormously costly. By one estimate, Americans alone would pay out $12 trillion before the contest came to a definitive close.

But hardly had Cold War mindsets taken hold in Washington and Moscow than they began in the 1950s to soften. The divisions between the blocs would become increasingly difficult to delineate in the 1960s as superpower clients grew restive and superpower leaders began talking to each other. Flux increasingly characterized the latter stages of the Cold War. It came to a sudden and surprising end in 1989 with the rapid collapse of socialist regimes in eastern Europe followed two years later by the demise of the Soviet Union itself. While this outcome represented the victory of ideals championed by the United States, the extent of the victory remained in doubt. Indeed, the relationship between the United States and its two old rivals, Russia and China, was plagued by uncertainty, and Americans had to face knotty questions about what role they could or should play in an international system that they alone now dominated militarily.

The Role of Nationalism

The era of interstate rivalry spanning the nineteenth and early twentieth centuries and culminating in the Cold War had a basic animating faith—nationalism. Wonderfully malleable, this ideology had at its core a belief in a shared sense of identity among a group of people that entitled them to statehood and obliged them to sacrifice, even die, for their common cause. It made its first appearance during the American and French revolutions as a claim to emancipation from oppressive rule made by those who wished no longer to be subjects but rather citizens determining their own destiny. By the end of the nineteenth century, this nationalist faith had a firm grip in all the great powers, reshaping established states such as Britain and France and giving rise to new ones, notably Italy and Germany in 1870–1871.

The nationalist notions that had taken such deep root on both sides of the Atlantic came to constitute a state ideology. Agents of the state played a pivotal role in planting in the imagination of many a loyalty to a single, overarching political community grounded in a common language, ethnicity, and history. These agents included the primary school teacher charged with mass education, the drill sergeant conducting compulsory military training, the postal clerk presiding over a dense communications network, and the bureaucrat fitting all citizens to the same requirements. Thanks to their efforts, nationalist refrains could be found at every turn—in religious sermons, popular songs, political speeches, public rituals, and schoolbooks. The resulting popular loyalty had broad and powerful implications. It facilitated the state's claim over the lives and economic resources of its citizens, helped integrate large populations in the midst of rapid and often disruptive industrial and social change, and fueled enthusiasm for military strength and overseas empire. This role of the state as agent and benefactor of nationalism was critical. Without a state, nationalism was merely a struggling and frustrated political or intellectual movement. Once the state existed, nationalists had the power to impose cultural uniformity, craft sustaining historical myths, silence dissenters, and reach for greatness.

Euro-American nationalisms fed off each other as they sought to prove their superiority whether measured by industrial output, naval power, or colonial holdings. The resulting rivalries easily led nationalists into superheated discussions drawing damning distinctions between good and evil people, superior and inferior cultures. The examples are legion—including the long-standing British contempt for the French, the German envy of the British, and the Russian fear of the Germans. This collective sense of a dangerous difference among peoples— infused with a strong moral dimension—gave nationalism a frightening intensity. It fed the ambitions and fears sustaining the rival alliances that pitched Europe into a frenzy of killing between 1914 and 1918. It also could turn collections of other humans into a virus, a plague, and even vermin—to be destroyed or at least removed, subordinated, or quarantined. Hitler's genocidal campaign against Jews and others outside the national pale was only the most extreme example of a commonplace nationalist tendency toward murderous intolerance.

Far from discrediting nationalism, World War I accentuated its appeal. Nationalist ambitions guided those who negotiated the peace terms ending the war just as nationalist movements set about dismembering the empires of Austria-Hungary and the Ottomans on the way to creating new Polish, Serbian, Czech, Bulgarian, and other states. In Germany and Italy, insecurity and resentment combined with economic turmoil to feed a bitter nationalism that made possible the rise of the dictators Hitler and Mussolini. By the interwar years, nationalism had transcended its North Atlantic origins to become a nearly universal ideology. In Japan a state-sponsored faith in the making since the late nineteenth century flared in the face of what appeared to be Anglo-American cultural contempt and strategic encirclement. Within the colonial world, nationalism's message of liberation had already won an enthusiastic following. The vigorous political activity in such places as Egypt, Ghana, India, China, and Vietnam signaled a major upheaval in the making.

It is a tribute to the power of nationalist ideas that a second world conflict far more destructive than the first ended with nationalism exercising a more powerful and pervasive influence than ever. A sharp sense of national mission drove the United States after 1945 to stand up to the communist challenge. At the same time, national pride survived in that bastion of internationalism, the Soviet Union, in both popular and elite thinking and in both its Russian core and its peripheral lands. Western Europeans still clung to the old nation-state even as they began to explore supranational integration, while Japanese, shorn of territorial empire, went to work with determination and pride on a new economic empire. Elsewhere nationalism would intensify anti-colonial feelings, speed the rapid triumph of liberation movements, and inspire some of the major revolutions of the postwar era, including China's and Cuba's.

Even today, nationalism remains one of the world's most potent belief systems, with a grip on peoples in widely scattered places and diverse circumstances. It remains a prominent force among the well-established states such as China, Russia, and the United States just as it is still a preoccupation of the stateless such as the Chechens in Russia, the Basques in Spain, and the French Canadians in Quebec. Even in a time of transnational forces unleashed by globalization, there is good reason to think that nationalism will remain a major source of group identity, state legitimacy, ethnic discontent and oppression, and international contention.

THE GLOBAL ECONOMY IN TRANSITION

Along with the emergence of a new constellation of international power, 1945 also brought significant changes in the international economy. The architects of the post-1945 economic system rejected the practices that had prevailed during the interwar period and instead took as their model the achievements of a great wave of economic globalization spanning the late nineteenth and early twentieth centuries. In this sense the post-1945 period followed a back-to-the-future scenario. This redirection of economic activity gave rise to a second phase of modern globalization with enormous implications for countries great and small all around the world over the following half-century.

The victors of World War II were quick to focus their energy and resources on economic reconstruction and equally quick to split into two competing blocs. Each promised to outperform the other. The bloc led by the Soviet Union included the parts of eastern Europe occupied by the Red Army during its advance against Germany. China would link up with the Soviet bloc in 1949 following the triumph of Communist forces. This bloc was united by the belief that the global system of capitalism was a spent force. In contrast to the economic exploitation and social disruption associated with capitalism, socialists called for an egalitarian system in which the working class was properly rewarded for its labor, given respect, and protected from abuse. Instead of an economy driven by the random effects of supply and demand playing out within the market, the socialist economy would be centrally and rationally planned. A strong state run by a Communist party and speaking in the name of the working class could better serve the broad public rather than the narrow interests of the privileged few. Such a state could, moreover, focus national energies on a strategy of efficient economic development, minimizing waste and avoiding the sharp ups and downs that characterized the capitalist system.

Far larger and ultimately more influential was the market-oriented international system shaped by Anglo-American initiatives in an effort to rescue the damaged world economy. These initiatives arose from the conviction that the free exchange of goods would make for a more prosperous world. Each country would specialize, engaging in the kind of economic activity for which it was best suited by natural resources or skills. The free flow of goods on a global scale presupposed free domestic markets and would promote (so its advocates claimed) international interdependence and understanding and ultimately eliminate the curse of war. The experience of the nineteenth century inspired these hopes. International trade had grown, bringing greater prosperity and a long era of relative peace among the great powers.

The First Phase of Globalization, 1870s–1914

The economic system toward which this rescue effort was directed had behind it several hundred years of industrialization and commercialization that laid the groundwork for post-1945 developments. The closing decades of the nineteenth century and the beginning of the twentieth—a time of considerable economic vitality within trans-Atlantic economies and the extension of its web of trade and investment outward to other regions—was on the minds of many as they contemplated what the end of World War II would yield.

The steadily accumulating economic momentum in the middle of the nineteenth century had caught the attention of two perceptive observers, best known as the fathers of communism. Writing in 1848, Karl Marx and Friedrich Engels foresaw the imminent rise of global capitalism. In strikingly clear terms, they described a world market that would soon shape production and consumption virtually everywhere. Driving the change would be new industries "whose products are consumed, not only at home, but in every quarter of the globe. In place of the old wants, satisfied by the productions of the country, we find new wants, requiring for their satisfaction the products of distant lands and climes. In place of the old local and national seclusion and self-sufficiency, we have intercourse in every direction, universal inter-dependence of nations."[5]

The process that made this vision of an integrating global economy a reality had begun in Britain, spread across western Europe and to the United States, and then drew in Japan and Russia. In each case, overseas trade expanded as a byproduct of the industrial revolution. First in Britain from the middle of the eighteenth century and then in the later industrializers in the course of the nineteenth century, the steam engine made possible dramatically higher levels of production, a rising surplus available for export, and the low-cost transport essential to distribute factory-made goods to consumers at home and abroad. Manufactured goods as well as raw materials moved in greater volume, first within Europe but increasingly on a broader world stage. The value of international trade registered a fifteen-fold jump between the mid-nineteenth century and 1910, and it represented a rapidly increasing although still small proportion of production around the world. International investments also rose sharply. The acceptance of gold as the standard of international value facilitated both trade and investment.

As new centers of industrial and agricultural production sprang up around the world, migrants looking for better jobs moved by the millions (perhaps close to ten percent of the world's population between 1870 and 1914). Nearly fifty million Europeans left their homelands between the 1840s and the onset of World War I. Most headed toward the Americas—Argentina, Brazil, Canada, and above all the United States (the destination for two-thirds of these immigrants). A massive movement of people from China into Southeast Asia was occurring simultaneously and in the process transforming not just the ethnic makeup but also the economy of colonies within the region. Overall, the sheer number of those traveling, often long distances, in search of better economic opportunity at the turn of the twentieth century probably exceeded anything seen since.

This dynamic, increasingly international economy bore three important features. First, it was sustained by a system of finance that underwrote overseas trade and supplied investment needs in both newly industrializing countries (such as the United States) and colonies rich in raw materials (such as French Indochina with its rubber plantations and Belgian Congo with its mines). London was the chief financial center until loans made by U.S. bankers during World War I established New York as a serious rival. The second feature was the appearance of the first multinational corporations in manufacturing and marketing and in the extraction of raw materials. These multinationals, so called because they had headquarters in one country but operated in many, would come to dominate global markets. Finally, new technology played a critical role in creating a truly global pattern of trade and finance by the turn of the twentieth century. The steam engine driving trains and ships provided cheap and rapid transport, while the telegraph made possible quick trans-continental and trans-oceanic communication. These two technological innovations were critical to the unfolding of this first wave of global economic integration.

Along with its vitality, the new trend toward globalization demonstrated a propensity toward troubling downswings, for example during the 1890s. Excess production forced factories to close, swelling the ranks of the unemployed and generating social and political tensions. The global economy was also vulnerable to disruption by international conflict. World War I marked the beginning of the end of the first phase of globalization. It was followed at once by a drop in production and by protectionist measures such as tariffs on imports that raised barriers to foreign trade in major markets. The financial crash of 1929 on New York City's Wall Street sent economies around the world into the most serious downward spiral of the twentieth century. By 1931 financial markets were in crisis. Britain abandoned the gold standard. Germany and Austria imposed controls over exchange of their currencies. They and others were acting to insulate their economies from the outside pressures dragging them down. The resulting Great Depression hit the industrial states first. In Europe industrial production dropped by one-third, and in Germany alone it fell by 40 percent. This slump caused foreign trade to further fall off, thereby making the depression global. By 1933 international trade overall was down by one-third. Some countries such as Japan, where exports had fallen by half, were especially hard hit. The economic pain felt by national communities opened the door to strong leaders in Europe, Japan, and the United States championing state intervention and shared sacrifice. This authoritarian trend arising from economic hard times facilitated the march to war in East Asia and Europe between 1937 and 1945—and to still more punishment to economies already damaged by prolonged depression.

Globalization Reborn, 1945 to the Present

As World War II drew to a close, U.S. and British leaders set about repairing the shattered international economy. Their handiwork would bear striking similarities to the earlier phase of globalization. As earlier, the system of finance had its prominent centers: New York (overshadowing London) and, in time, Tokyo and Bonn. Multinational corporations would continue to dominate the production and international distribution of goods and services, even if they bore new names such as Disney, Sony, and Volkswagen. Finally, technology now as then figured critically in driving and defining the new phase of global economic activity, with the telephone, the airplane, and the Internet only the most prominent products of an era of innovation.

The efforts of the Americans and the British would prove over the long haul an enormous success. The new framework for trade and finance brought unrivaled prosperity to Americans, and it soon restored prosperity to western Europe and Japan. It made deep inroads in countries on the margins of the international economy. Even newly independent states with a socialist bias had to confront the fact that the global market economy was the most promising outlet for their exports and the best source for technology and capital. Peasants from the interior of Central America to western Africa watched as crops grown for sale overseas increasingly dominated the land. The accompanying disruption was in some cases new, but in most cases it was an extension of a process that had begun in the nineteenth century or earlier.

This global market-oriented system of production and investment not only had a wide and deep impact but also began demonstrating its appeal. As early as the 1950s, it set a standard against which citizens as well as leaders in the bastions of socialism came to measure the performance of their own system. By the early 1980s China was succumbing to the temptations of the market; eastern Europe, Russia, and other successor states to the Soviet Union would follow soon thereafter. By the 1990s the competitive, market-oriented rules and organizations put in place in the mid-1940s had become the basis for a genuinely global system. Socialism was on the defensive; free market principles seemed well on their way to becoming the world's governing economic faith.

This increasingly international economy exercised extraordinary power over ordinary lives. In developed economies, it surrounded consumers with a wondrous array of goods, many of foreign origin. At the same time it placed workers there in keen competition with others around the world and made education and a productive workplace the key to making a good living. The international economy left business managers as well as investors vulnerable to rapid, unforeseeable developments in distant markets. In developing economies, the impact of outside economic forces could be benign, providing opportunities for attracting new industry that could no longer operate competitively in developed economies and for gaining access to rich markets for agricultural and basic manufactured goods. But the international market economy could also be harsh, driving peasants from the land as the wealthy consolidated land holdings to implement more efficient farming methods. The now redundant labor emptied out of villages, tearing the fabric of community while filling cities with the poor who were desperate for work. Foreign markets, once alive with promise, could suddenly close; foreign capital, once the engine of local development, could flee. The effects on small economies could be instantaneous and disastrous.

Finally, the international economy presented citizens with a broad range of new challenges that were profoundly altering their lives. The social dynamism promoted by the market set gender roles in question, pitted a newly assertive individualism against the good of the group, and gave rise to far-reaching migrations that affected not only those who went abroad looking for opportunity but also the societies where they came to settle. It was becoming impossible to escape the international flow of information and entertainment with its powerful cultural impact. And the same economic forces that carried manufactured goods, immigrant laborers, and popular culture also carried diseases such as HIV/AIDS rapidly over long distances and sustained far-reaching networks of terrorism that gave the few a remarkable power to frighten the many. More ominous for the long term, the international economy by its very productivity created serious threats to the natural environment that in turn imperiled plants, animals, and human health and welfare—even perhaps the survival of the human species.

Key Economic Terms

Despite its importance, the international economy is not well or easily understood by the public. Part of the reason is that economic phenomena can be complex to the point of obscurity. The British writer H. G. Wells lamented that economics "hangs like a gathering fog in a valley, a fog which begins nowhere and goes nowhere." His countryman George Bernard Shaw ridiculed its practitioners for their irrelevance: "If all the economists in the world were laid end to end, they still wouldn't reach a conclusion." It is true that economics cannot be reduced to simple generalizations, but mastering the following basic terms (to appear repeatedly in the chapters to follow) is an important first step toward functional economic literacy.

constant dollars: A recalculation of value that takes account of the effects of inflation, which over time diminishes what a dollar or other currency can actually purchase. Constant dollars thus allow more realistic comparisons between GNP, GDP, or per capita income statistics over different periods because the dollars at each point represent the same purchasing power.

gross national product (GNP) and **gross domestic product (GDP):** Closely related measures of overall economic activity and economic growth. Both GNP and GDP represent the value of all goods and services produced by a country in a given year. GNP includes income earned abroad by citizens of that country and excludes income earned by foreigners from domestic production. GDP includes only the output that occurs within a country. The practical difference between the two terms is usually negligible.

inflation: A gauge of a currency's declining purchasing power. Inflation is usually the result of a scarcity of goods or of government printing money too freely. Either way, a market imbalance develops that raises the prices of goods while diminishing the purchasing power of money. High levels of inflation are associated with wartime or political upheaval.

infrastructure: Those public investments essential to economic activity, including roads, airports, telecommunications, electrical power, and health and educational programs. Usually the more developed a country's infrastructure, the more favorable its conditions for economic growth.

laissez faire: A French phrase meaning "let (people) do as they wish" but taken in economics to stand for the doctrine formulated in the eighteenth century that stated markets worked best when freed from government interference. The doctrine inspired support in the nineteenth and twentieth centuries for expanding free trade and the sphere of individual choice.

per capita income: Derived by dividing GNP or GDP by the total population of a country or a region. The result is an average, indicating what portion of the total output each person would claim if it were equally shared. It thus serves as a rough general measurement of the standard of living.

protectionism: A policy of shielding producers of goods and services in one country from competition by those in other countries. Devices for limiting or cutting off access to the home market include a charge on imports (a tariff), import quotas, and regulatory measures difficult for foreign producers to meet. Critics argue that the benefits of protectionism to a few local producers are offset by losses to the much larger number of local consumers, who must pay more or receive less than in a free trade system in which each country specializes in what it can produce most efficiently.

Yet even as the global economy fixed its grip on the lives of people every-where, the way that economy functioned within one country or another remained culturally conditioned. National economies from Indonesia to Iceland and from Kazakhstan to Nigeria continued to reflect widely varying but firmly held preferences on fundamental issues. These issues can be expressed in the fol-lowing questions: How important are individualism and individual opportunity? Should group solidarity or social stability take precedence? How large a gap between the richest and poorest in a society is permissible? Are economic rights inextricably tied to political rights, and if so, how broadly defined should eco-nomic rights be? Finally, and perhaps most important, how large a role in the economy should the state play, and precisely what should that role be? Answers vary significantly from one market economy to another, suggesting the impor-tance of being alert to what might be called "economic culture." In an integrated global system of production and consumption a diversity of beliefs and practices could survive, even flourish.

THE COLONIAL SYSTEM ON THE BRINK

Before 1945 much of the world—roughly half the surface of the globe and some 70 percent of its population—had fallen under colonial administration or infor-mal great-power control. The process of subjugation occurred in two successive waves as Europeans laid claim to mastery over other lands and peoples. The first expansionist thrust came between the sixteenth and eighteenth centuries with the main targets the Americas, the Indian subcontinent, and parts of the Pacific. The second imperial impulse came in the late nineteenth century (coincident with state nationalism and economic globalization). At that time the major Euro-pean powers, joined by Japan and the United States, established new colonies in Africa, Southeast Asia, the Pacific, and the Caribbean. Britain was the clear front-runner in the colonial race. By the early part of the twentieth century it exercised authority over roughly two-thirds of all colonized peoples. China resisted out-right colonization but fell under the sway of multiple states, and Central America and parts of the Caribbean came under informal U.S. dominion.

This subjugation of vast and distant territories and the maintenance of con-trol there depended on the imperial powers' possession of superior technology. Indeed, the application of science to the concerns of everyday life made possible material wealth and military might that were previously unimaginable. This technology took a striking variety of forms—potent weapons of war, rapid trans-portation and communications, and improved public health that helped Euro-pean troops, administrators, and settlers withstand otherwise deadly tropical diseases. The intruders' technical skills often impressed non-European peoples with their own inferiority and prompted some to seek cooperation with these outsiders.

The process of subjugation was also driven, as Marx and Engels argued, by the needs of thriving industrial economies for a secure supply of foodstuffs and raw materials such as rubber, minerals, and timber as well as an outlet for manufac-tured goods. The growing stake created by trade and investment often led to a

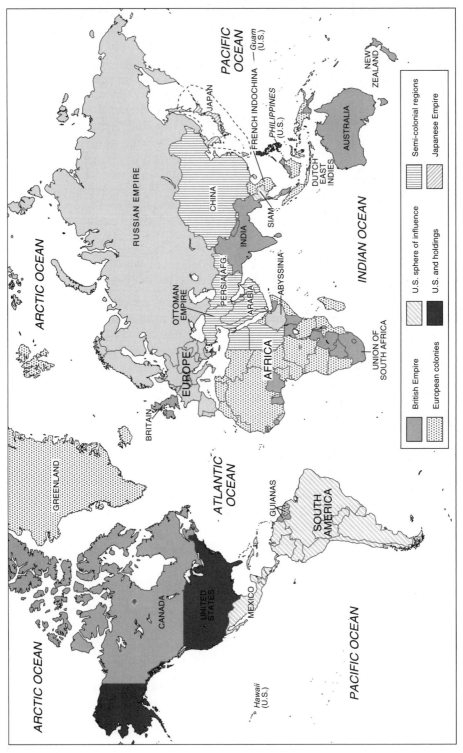

decision to secure direct political control. By firmly tying foreign lands to the home market, producers in one country could be certain of meeting their own needs and, if necessary, denying the needs of international rivals. The great China market, for example, fixated Europeans and Americans at the turn of the century. And so began an international tussle over dividing that weakened empire into spheres of influence. Colonial administrations had the additional benefit of ensuring that valued raw materials, along with the labor needed to work mines and fields, could be had at extremely low cost. One of the most extreme examples was Belgian Congo, the personal possession of Belgium's king, which became a vast graveyard of those worked to death to ensure a steady supply of low-cost minerals. But conditions in the cotton fields of British Uganda and the rubber plantations in French Indochina were only marginally better.

Finally, nationalism played a major role in this subjugation. Expansionist Europeans, soon followed by Americans and Japanese, argued that national standing depended on conquest. The richer and larger the prizes a country could claim, the higher its international prestige. Nationalism inspired popular support critical to financing and manning imperial armies and administrations. But it also sharpened rivalries among nations at the end of the nineteenth century as each raced to win territory abroad.

Vulnerabilities of Empire

The impressive structure of imperial control was not to last. By 1945, within roughly half a century of its apogee, it teetered on the brink of collapse. Almost at once after World War II the march from formal subordination to formal independence began, and the pace accelerated in the 1960s. By the early 1970s, colonies were increasingly rare. New states swelled the ranks of the United Nations. By 1970 it had grown to 127 members, up from the 51 charter members in 1945, and more were waiting in the wings. What accounts for this rapid collapse of empire?

One reason is to be found in the conflicts of the first half of the twentieth century that demoralized and weakened Europe. Driven by nationalist passions, the imperial countries went to war against each other using ever more destructive technology. Each round of conflict dealt body blows to all the combatants and made more difficult the maintaining of control over distant colonies. In any case the losers had to surrender their overseas possessions. After World War I, Germany's colonies in sub-Saharan Africa and the Pacific went as spoils to the victors. The Ottoman Empire fell, opening an opportunity for the French and British to extend their control into such places in the Middle East as Iraq and Syria. What World War I began, World War II completed. Japan's war machine drove the Europeans and Americans from East and Southeast Asia, discrediting foreign mastery in Asia. And then following their defeat, Italy and Japan forfeited

◄MAP I.1
Western Domination on the Eve of World War I

their imperial holdings. Even as victorious British, French, Dutch, and American forces reclaimed old possessions throughout Southeast Asia including Malaya, Indochina, the East Indies, and the Philippines, it was already apparent that the old order was under siege. The imperial collapse was to accelerate during the period of American-Soviet struggle as each superpower dismissed a declining European colonial presence as outmoded and ineffective, preferring instead to assemble its own stable of Cold War clients.

The other explanation for this rapid imperial collapse is to be found in the capacity of subjugated peoples to turn the ideological weapons of the West to their own ends. In country after country, an educated, politically engaged minority, usually from relatively privileged backgrounds, mixed indigenous values with imported ideas. The resulting amalgam provided the vision that gave order and direction to the independence struggles and programs of domestic renovation that dominated the first decades after independence.

Nationalism was the most significant of the imports that would help subvert the colonial order. As in Europe, the United States, and Japan, so too in the countries they dominated, nationalists worked to create a body of unifying myths and values that would overcome internal divisions and lay the groundwork for ending foreign control. New nation builders in places as far-flung as Guatemala, Algeria, and Ghana turned to the methods that European nationalists had developed to build mass support—print and other communications technologies, education, and promotion of an official language.

The other Western ideology with a strong appeal to anti-colonial leaders was Marxism-Leninism. For leaders and intellectuals from Cuba to Cambodia, it proved appealing as a tool for scientifically analyzing societies troubled by internal weakness and poverty. It seemed also to offer an explanation for foreign domination at the same time that it promised liberation from a morally corrupt and economically declining capitalism. Finally, it made an attractive case for the effectiveness of a loyal, determined, and ideologically united party in fighting for liberation from foreign control and creating a new, better society. The achievements of the Communist Party in the Soviet Union seemed to strengthen the case for Marxism as a guide to revolution and development.

By 1945, the ideological tide was flowing strongly against the colonial status quo. The winning side in two world wars had set the stage by promoting the principle of self-determination trumpeted by Woodrow Wilson and Vladimir Lenin in the immediate aftermath of World War I. In 1919 representatives of restive colonial peoples had pressed the victors of World War I to honor that principle. That same year, Lenin's new Bolshevik regime in Moscow organized the Communist International (Comintern) on the premise that the Western ideology of Marxism would find eager converts in the colonial world. Soviet emissaries were soon reaching out to restive peoples eager to throw off foreign control, encouraging the organization of local Communist parties, and providing support in the form of money, advisors, and schooling. Moscow thus demonstrated in the 1920s and 1930s that it alone among the world powers was genuinely committed to the principle of liberation. World War II brought the United States and Britain (nominally at least) back to that position in a conflict that they claimed was about freedom. By the mid-twentieth century Western colonial control had become suspect on the basis of its own ideologies of nationalism and Marxism. Unable to match the nationalist and revolutionary energies of subjugated people, colonial powers such as France and Britain had to rely on their superior wealth and technology to maintain an increasingly fragile grip. The imperial game for them was all but over.

The Appearance of the "Third World"

Third world was the term that came to be widely applied to newly emerging countries. In the nineteenth or early twentieth centuries arrogant European colonizers would have described those lands as "uncivilized" or "barbaric." The term *third world,* first used in France in 1952 and then adopted in the United States, was a less offensive way to refer to peoples who had to be located within a world already divided two ways by the Cold War. The United States and its allies in western Europe and Japan became the *first world.* The socialist bloc—the USSR, its eastern European satellites, and its Asian allies (North Vietnam, North Korea, and for a time China)—was the *second world,* leaving the rest as the *third*

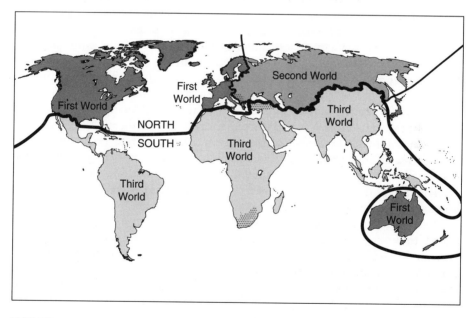

MAP I.2
How to Carve Up the Post-1945 World?
This map delineates two answers that found widespread acceptance. The lighter line traces what during the Cold War became the critical line of division between the first and second worlds of capitalism and communism, leaving the rest as the "third world." The darker line indicates an alternative geography that came into vogue in the latter part of the twentieth century. Here the developed north is set against the underdeveloped south. The three countries marked with dots—Yugoslavia, South Africa, and Turkey—have resisted easy classification under either the Cold War notion of three worlds or its north-south alternative.

world. More recently, the term of choice has become *the developing world* or even *the south* (to distinguish areas generally below the equator still marked by poverty from the more affluent and economically developed countries that are for the most part in the north).

The difficulties in finding a blanket term for the regions engaged in struggles for independence and development are insurmountable if the line of division is thought of as simple and all-encompassing. The decolonization that followed World War II was characterized by enormous variation from region to region and even within regions. Some countries such as Vietnam and Iran gravitated toward strong state authority; others such as India, the Philippines, and Guatemala resisted that course. Some such as Egypt began with a relatively homogenous ethnic and linguistic population, whereas others such as Algeria and South Africa were fragmented or even violently divided. Some such as China had experienced the turmoil of civil war and revolution; others such as India and Ghana enjoyed a relatively peaceful transition to independence. Is there anything that Chinese, Guatemalans, Egyptians, and South Africans had in common that might make any blanket term useful?

Even if every one of the newly independent states has a unique story of dramatic changes to tell, they do share some important traits. For the first three decades of the postwar era, the term *third world* has some value, though it has to be used not in terms of Cold War alignments but in relation to a set of features that created a sense of community among countries around the world and gave rise to shared hope and identity. It included countries such as China, Cuba, and Vietnam that were for a time aligned with the Soviet Union but not dominated by it. As we will see, increasingly toward century's end countries in the third world set off on divergent developmental trajectories, rendering less and less relevant the preoccupations they had formerly shared. From the 1970s onward, the terms *developed* and *developing* are more appropriate for their focus on varying levels of economic productivity and prosperity that increasingly became the marker of international status at a time of global economic integration.

The first of the features that gave reality to the third world during the early postwar decades was the experience of foreign domination by Europeans and, to a lesser degree, by Americans and Japanese. All members of the third world ultimately took up the struggle to end foreign dominance and win independence. Early in the twentieth century, advocates of independence—a minority with foreign education and a sense of the broader world—began to make their appearance. After World War II in country after country, subjugated peoples moved to organize political movements to overthrow foreign masters wounded or vanquished in two world wars. By the 1960s formal colonial control had become an anachronism, and much of the third world was launched on a new phase—the post-independence struggle for economic development and for national identity and unity.

The second feature that gave reality to the third world was the need to make choices about post-independence political and economic development in light of what foreigners, usually Europeans, had wrought. In colonies such as Ghana, Algeria, and the Philippines, they had imposed political systems and introduced their own political values. They created state boundaries in some cases (notably in sub-Saharan Africa) and often played favorites, offering education and political advancement to some at the expense of others. They reshaped economies by linking them to outside markets and promoting foreign investment. Even countries such as China and Cuba not under direct colonial control felt the far-reaching cultural as well as economic effects of these outside initiatives. Time and again, those attempting to get out from under foreign domination had to face the question of which of these legacies was worth keeping and which should be discarded. In grappling with that question, they encountered another: How were strong indigenous values, institutions, and practices to be reconciled with these foreign legacies? These related questions were in part practical. For example, no one could ignore the efficacy of Western military arms and organization. But there was also a large psychological dimension to these questions involving nothing less than identity and pride after a time of confusion and humiliation. Different third-world peoples came to different answers, but everyone had to wrestle with the same questions.

The struggle for independence and the subsequent search for an appropriate development path unfolded against the backdrop of the Cold War. Indeed, U.S.-Soviet rivalry brought unwanted pressures and blatant intervention but also the prospect of generous aid and invaluable protection. All in the third world had to deal with the superpowers as best they could. This shared preoccupation by weaker countries led to the emergence of the non-aligned movement in the 1950s. Beginning with the first meeting in Bandung, Indonesia, in 1955, newly independent states pressed for an end to colonialism, attacked racism, opposed great-power intervention, and resisted pressure from the Cold War rivals to commit to one side or the other. Participants in the movement, led by India, Egypt, and Yugoslavia, called for an international order in which political self-determination and economic development took precedence over the Cold War military and ideological rivalry.

A final feature that the third world had in common during the early postwar decades was a heavily peasant population, typically 70 to 80 percent right after the war. That the specific conditions governing peasant life differed from country to country should not obscure qualities of social and political life that were widely shared. To begin with, the life of most rural dwellers was hard. Most peasants lived with uncertainty on the economic margin and under conditions of poverty attended by such woes as high infant mortality, low educational levels, poor health, and short life spans. The caloric intake of villagers in any year could vary enormously depending on what rainfall, disease, or warfare did to crop yields. The problem was especially acute for those dependent on growing their own food (subsistence farmers), whose condition a British economic historian described as "like that of a man permanently up to his neck in water, so that even a ripple might drown him."[6] Bad years could bring hunger and perhaps death to weaker members of the village.

The combination of adversity and isolation had long put a premium on social solidarity expressed through local traditions, rites, and myths and organized typically within villages and around kinship. Though weakening in the nineteenth and early twentieth centuries, shared community values still served to govern *and* constrain peasant behavior. They sanctioned maintenance of communal land and sharing of food in hard times. Solidarity also meant placing the interest of the group over the interest of individuals or particular families. Those who prospered but did not share were criticized and even excluded from community life. Fellow villagers who became plantation overseers or went to work in the city might well encounter suspicion from those who stayed at home. This sense of solidarity often created an attachment to the status quo that was puzzling to outsiders. Giving up tried-and-true methods of farming might disrupt production or village harmony. A new seed strain, for example, might promise greater yield or disease resistance. But the peasant had to wonder if it was suited to local growing conditions and to worry that buyers might steer clear of unfamiliar, untested produce. Why take a risk that might create the ripple that drowns families or entire villages barely clinging to survival?

The forces of globalization effected a quiet revolution in rural life, weakening solidarity and disrupting society. This process in most places began well before 1945. As the rising capitalist powers began to create a global market, their economies penetrated ever deeper into remote rural communities. Those who were not caught up by the time of the first wave of globalization in the late nineteenth and early twentieth centuries were engulfed by the second, post-1945 wave. The timing varied considerably. Some regions, such as China's Yangzi Valley, had peasants producing for distant markets well before European trade intruded, whereas regions of Guatemala were still largely isolated into the 1960s. Regardless of the precise timing, peasant production everywhere increasingly was not for local consumption but for cash sales and for shipment to distant markets. As the well-to-do consolidated control of land, trade, and finance, they fundamentally redefined social relations within villages. When a food crisis developed, landlords were no longer obliged to supply food, waive rents, or mobilize community resources. No longer would they have to display their generosity by sponsoring lavish celebrations and giving generously to local shrines, temples, and schools. Ambitious, profit-maximizing landlords worked to break down peasant landholdings and turn former owners or tenants into low-cost seasonal laborers. Colonial officials hastened this rural transformation by demanding tax payments in cash rather than in goods. Unless peasants began producing crops for the market where they could make cash sales, they could not pay their taxes and thus risked losing their most prized possession, their land. The bonds of solidarity long critical to survival within rural communities further eroded as the young and able-bodied left to look for work in the cities or on new agricultural frontiers, leaving behind women, children, and old people.

Some peasants reacted to rising market forces in an entrepreneurial spirit. They wanted to escape subsistence agriculture and to reap the rewards for those who could produce more and better in response to the market with its changing levels of supply and demand. The industrious and the innovative could get ahead. But those who followed the entrepreneurial path also found themselves subject to the vagaries of distant markets. For example, overproduction of rice in Southeast Asia could mean ruin for peasants in China growing rice for that same, now glutted international market. Whether world commodity prices were high or low, taxes had to be paid; the family fed until the next harvest; and certain necessities purchased such as cloth and tools. Moneylenders would supply the funds to get peasants through hard times, but at rates that were exorbitant (sometimes 8 to 10 percent per *month*). Once in debt, peasants often could not extricate themselves. Some might become virtually hired hands working their own, now heavily mortgaged property. Others would have to sell land and livestock to cover their debt.

Peasants passing through this economic and social transformation engaged in a kind of politics peculiar to rural conditions. Regardless of the resentments they felt, peasants were notably reluctant to risk a confrontation. An Ethiopian proverb urged dissembling even by those with grievances: "When the great lord passes[,] the wise peasant bows deeply and silently farts."[7] But sufficiently provoked, peasant communities would resort to a range of public, collective, sometimes even desperate actions to protect their way of life, keep their land, and ensure the survival of their families. Angry peasants might begin by trying to shame powerful locals guilty of seizing public lands or cheating tenants. If songs, stories, dances, or plays mocking them had no effect, then peasants might become bolder, for example, withholding their labor from abusive landlords by feigning illness, committing arson, or spoiling crops. In extreme situations, peasants might attack tax, rent, or debt collectors, resort to banditry, or even stage an armed uprising (as with the Huks in the Philippines or more recently with the Indians in Mexico's Chiapas region). These desperate measures usually failed. Linguistic, ethnic, and regional differences prevented peasants in one area from forming alliances with other peasants. Insurgent forces lacked arms, discipline, and experienced leadership. They risked starvation if military or political activities disrupted food production. For all these reasons, government and landlord-controlled forces easily crushed rebellious peasants, often massacring whole families and seizing their lands. The exceptions to this generalization can be found in modern-day China, Vietnam, the Philippines, and Guatemala. In these cases (to be discussed in the upcoming chapters), reformers or revolutionaries from outside the village convinced the locals to support programs that would improve their security and livelihood. These programs had to knit local discontents into a broad, organized, sustainable movement and to target abuses that peasants deeply resented. Thus these programs attacked exploitative landlords and moneylenders, merchants who sought to establish monopolies and fix prices, and corrupt colonial officials who took more in taxes and bribes than they returned in benefits such as health care, education, or roads to market.

Even though the experience of foreign domination, the challenge of liberation and development, and the conditions of a large peasantry buffeted by powerful outside forces created commonalities among a group of countries called the third world, that sense of sharing a similar fate did not endure. It reached its peak in the 1960s and thereafter began to fade. The era of domination meant less to a younger generation who knew it only secondhand. Socialism as a developmental model lost its luster. Elites, earlier advocates of radical change, became more cautious and experimented with increasingly diverse practices attended by widely varying success.

Finally, rural conditions underwent a major alteration. The consolidation of land into larger, more efficient holdings meant fewer opportunities for work even as the rural population increased as a result of better medical care. With increased migration to the cities, urban populations exploded and village life atrophied. This process was as familiar to Egyptian, Iranian, and Indian villages as it was to settlements in rural Mexico, Nicaragua, and Brazil. This exodus reduced the peasantry as a portion of the total population throughout the last half of the twentieth century as industry and service work began to catch up with and in some cases overtake the agricultural sector. By the late 1990s the downward trend had played out in strikingly different degrees in countries formerly part of the third world. In places such as China, Guatemala, and Ghana those making their living from the soil were still half or more, while in the Philippines, Cuba, Iran, and Egypt agriculture accounted for only 25 to 40 percent of the workforce (still high compared with no more than 5 percent in Germany, Japan, and the United States at century's end). Even those left behind were transformed as they became more tied to city ways through better roads, radios, television, higher literacy, and contact with those who had migrated. Thus as the proportion of peasants shrank so too did their distinctive isolation and wariness fade.

By the late twentieth century, so diverse had become its members that the term *third world* had outlived its usefulness. But whatever we choose to call these countries, be it *developing nations* or *the south,* the importance of understanding the greater part of humankind cannot be understated. Africa's population is one and a half times as large as Europe's. The peoples of Asia combined are ten times more numerous than those in North America. China alone is almost five times more populous than the United States. Among these large populations have occurred some of the most horrific events of the post-1945 era that outsiders find difficult to understand. China's leader, Mao Zedong, sought to improve rural conditions by bringing industry to the countryside in the late 1950s, and as a result millions upon millions died from starvation and disease. Peasants in sub-Saharan Africa have in recent decades come face to face with the scourges—often cruelly combined—of deteriorating land conditions, soaring birth rates, explosive ethnic antagonisms, and HIV/AIDS sweeping through households and villages. Precisely because we still know so little about so many, we have the most to gain by stretching our imagination and exercising our empathy. But beyond the moral weight of our common humanity, there are practical reasons for cultivating an awareness of the broader world. We are bound by a complicated economic network of competition and cooperation. Local financial crises can now travel rapidly, becoming international literally overnight. Immigrants move vast distances with effects on host countries that are cultural as well as economic. Global warming may have some of its sources in distant developments—for example, the loss of tropical forests or the multiplication of cars in newly wealthy countries—but everyone, no matter how distant, feels the environmental effects. A terrorist's resentment may find expression thousands of miles from where it originally formed. Infectious diseases cross continents as easily aboard aircraft as their human hosts do.

The themes sketched here unfold in greater detail in the pages that follow. The story of the post-1945 world begins with the rise of a dangerously competitive

Cold War order. Between 1945 and 1953, the Soviet Union and the United States embarked on a struggle that both overshadowed international economic reform and implicated the third world. (This is the subject of Part One.) Between 1953 and 1968, that Cold War order gained a modicum of stability. On the one side, stability facilitated economic revival in the developed world, but on the other side it faced unexpected challenges—not only from rising discontents within the decolonizing world but also from a new generation of youth raised under conditions of peace and affluence. (These developments are treated in Part Two.)

From the 1970s through the 1980s, the Cold War order eroded. Superpower rivalry imposed heavy costs on its Soviet and American protagonists. At the same time an increasingly intrusive international economy exerted competitive constraints on the behavior of all countries. Nowhere did that economy have a greater impact than on the third world, creating striking differences among countries earlier marked by strong commonalities. (Part Three covers these events.) A new post–Cold War international regime emerged in the course of the 1990s. It was defined by the interplay between strong globalizing forces (both economic and cultural) on the one side and, on the other, strong states as well as vital local cultures seeking to brake or bend globalization to their own needs. (These trends and what they portend are treated in the book's conclusion.)

In covering this half-century, the reader should gain some sense of the world as our imagined newspaper reader knew it in 1945 and experience the surprises, hardships, fear, joy, and disappointments known to those who lived during the decades that followed. Along the way the reader should gain a better grasp of the origins of the world we inhabit and of the other cultures that share that world with us. This kind of historical knowledge is not, for better or worse, free of controversy. A French philosopher once said that whoever "writes the history of his own time must expect to be attacked for everything he has said, and for everything he has not said."[8] The risks are more than offset by the gains. A sense of the past is essential to acting as responsible moral agents and as citizens well enough informed to understand, debate, and decide critical issues. By exposing us to the diversity of cultures around the world, that knowledge also sharpens our sense of self, both as individuals and as members of national and transnational communities. Finally, the past teaches what is durable and difficult to change and helps us distinguish between problems beyond our control and those where the application of our energy and imagination might make a difference. In all these ways, understanding the history of this or any era remains a critical part of the equipment of an educated person.

RECOMMENDED RESOURCES

On **world historical geography,** a good general reference is Richard Overy, ed., *Hammond Atlas of the 20th Century* (1996). The online map collection maintained by the Perry-Castañeda Library at the University of Texas at Austin <www.lib.utexas.edu/maps> is a rich resource. Martin W. Lewis and Kären E. Wigen, *The Myth of Continents: A Critique of Metageography* (1997), and Edward W. Said, *Orientalism* (rev. ed., 1994), reveal how each era has bent the world into shapes that fit its own particular assumptions.

The post-1945 period is richly blessed with **documentary footage.** The close of the century coming hard on the heels of the end of the Cold War inspired a spate of retrospectives. The most thoughtful series are *The People's Century,* produced by WGBH in Boston and the BBC; and *The Pacific Century* (ten hour-long parts; 1992; series project dir. Frank Gibney; dir. and ed. Marc Levin; prod. Al Levin; Corporation for Public Broadcasting).

On the role of **the great powers and trans-Atlantic capitalism** in both creating globalization and bringing its first phase to an end, see the lively and coherent four-volume history of the modern era by E. J. Hobsbawm, especially *The Age of Empire, 1875–1914* (1987) and *Age of Extremes: The Short Twentieth Century, 1914–1991* (1994); Paul Kennedy, *The Rise and Fall of the Great Powers: Economic Change and Military Conflict from 1500 to 2000* (1987); Harold James, *The End of Globalization: Lessons from the Great Depression* (2001); and Gerhard L. Weinberg, *A World at Arms: A Global History of World War II* (1994). On the ideas associated with Wilson and Lenin that would challenge the European system, see Michael H. Hunt, *Ideology and U.S. Foreign Policy* (1987), and the introduction to the classic text by Karl Marx and Friedrich Engels, *The Communist Manifesto,* ed. John E. Toews (1999).

Good places to begin on **nationalism** are Benedict Anderson's influential *Imagined Communities: Reflections on the Origin and Spread of Nationalism* (rev. ed., 1991), and E. J. Hobsbawm's spirited economic interpretation, *Nations and Nationalism since 1780: Programme, Myth, Reality* (rev. ed., 1992). Geoff Eley and Ronald Grigor Suny, eds., *Becoming National: A Reader* (1996), and John Hutchinson and Anthony D. Smith, eds., *Nationalism* (1994), both provide a good sample from a large body of literature.

On **global economic trends,** consult Angus Maddison, *The World Economy: A Millennial Perspective* (2001), for an invaluable collection of authoritative data that updates his *Monitoring the World Economy, 1820–1992* (1995); Peter N. Stearns, *Consumerism in World History: The Global Transformation of Desire* (London: Routledge, 2001); Gilbert Rist, *The History of Development: From Western Origins to Global Faith,* trans. Patrick Camiller (1997); and Immanuel Wallerstein, "The Rise and Future Demise of the World Capitalist System," in his *The Capitalist World-Economy* (1979), pp. 1–36, a summary of an influential interpretation.

On **imperialism and colonialism,** Philip D. Curtin, *The World and the West: The European Challenge and the Overseas Response in the Age of Empire* (2000), is especially helpful in identifying types of Western expansion and forms of counter-responses. Mike Davis, *Late Victorian Holocausts: El Niño Famines and the Making of the Third World* (2001), makes a provocative case for climate change compounding stress in colonial societies. See also Alfred W. Crosby, *Ecological Imperialism: The Biological Expansion of Europe, 900–1900* (1986); Daniel R. Headrick, *Tools of Empire: Technology and European Imperialism in the Nineteenth Century* (1981); Headrick, *The Tentacles of Progress: Technology Transfer in the Age of Imperialism, 1850–1940* (1988); and Michael Adas, *Machines as the Measure of Men: Science, Technology, and Ideologies of Western Dominance* (1989).

On **peasant life,** see Teodor Shanin, ed., *Peasants and Peasant Societies: Selected Readings* (rev. ed., 1987); E. J. Hobsbawm, *Primitive Rebels: Studies in Archaic Forms of Social Movement in the 19th and 20th Centuries* (1959); and David Arnold, *Famine: Social Crisis and Historical Change* (1988). For a critical introduction to a controversy over peasant outlook and motivation, see Jonathan Lieberson, *Peasant Values and Rural Development: An Unresolved Controversy* (1981). Eric R. Wolf, *Peasant Wars of the Twentieth Century* (1969), takes the side of that controversy stressing peasants' attachment to village solidarity.

On **revolutionary change,** Theda Skocpol, *States and Social Revolutions: A Comparative Analysis of France, Russia, and China* (1979), is a classic study. Theodore Hamerow, *From the Finland Station: The Graying of Revolution in the Twentieth Century* (1990), traces the fairly regular stages through which revolutions in Russia, China, Vietnam, and Cuba passed on their way to eventual decline. Jonathan Glover, *Humanity: A Moral History of the Twentieth Century* (2000), reflects on revolutionary mayhem and other manifestations of human brutality.

PART ONE

HOPES AND FEARS CONTEND
1945 – 1953

Shortly after eight in the morning of August 6, 1945, Mr. Katsutani finished his breakfast and was about to light a cigarette. He suddenly saw, he later recalled, "a white flash" followed by "a tremendous blast," and then "a big black cloud" filled the sky. What he had seen was a nuclear device dropped by a U.S. Air Force bomber, the *Enola Gay*. This single bomb had detonated about two thousand feet above the ground. One of the bomber crew described the city of Hiroshima below turning into "a big mess of flame and dust." Another saw "a pot of bubbling tar." The co-pilot noted in his log simply, "My God!"[1]

The ensuing impressions cut deep into the memory of the survivors of Hiroshima as they began searching through the ruins for relatives. Katsutani recalled averting his gaze from the bomb victims. The features of their heads—eyes, noses, mouths, ears—had all been burned away. "They were all so badly injured. I could not bear to look into their faces. They smelled like burning hair." He remembered all the victims begging for water and children crying for their mothers. The scene was "a living hell." Fujie Ryōso strapped her infant on her back and went looking for her husband, who had that morning set off to work in the city. For seven days she picked through piles of charred bodies pulled from the river, from incinerated streetcars, and from collapsed, burnt buildings. Empty-handed, the thirty-five-year-old Ryōso finally returned to her farm and children, clinging to the hope that somehow her husband had survived. She confessed in a 1981 interview that she still waited. "If I hear a noise outside in the middle of the night, my heart starts pounding, thinking that he's come back." With personal trauma and family loss went new political attitudes. Ryōso drummed into the heads of her grandchildren the constant message: "War is really cruel; it's really cruel. Never make war!" Ikuko Wakasa, a five-year-old on August 6, confessed six years later that she still trembled to recall that fateful day in Hiroshima. Any reference to war, even in movie newsreels, made her shudder.[2]

The terrifying impact on the ground that day would cast a moral cloud over the balance of the century. In 1942 President Franklin D. Roosevelt had set in motion the large-scale, top-secret effort known as the Manhattan Project to develop a nuclear weapon, the first of which was successfully tested in July 1945. Three weeks later the second bomb, known as "Little Boy," exploded with the strength of 13,500 tons of TNT on Hiroshima. Some 100,000 residents died at once—and several tens of thousands more perished later as a result of blast, fire, and radiation, bringing the total to 130–150,000. This devastation set off a chain of events that would bring World War II in the Pacific to a rapid conclusion. On August 8 the Soviet Union declared war against Japan. The next day the U.S. Air Force, following the established plan to use the remaining bomb—"Fat Man"— as soon as operationally possible, flattened the city of Nagasaki and killed a total of 60–80,000 people. On August 14, following these two devastating bombings and Soviet entry into the war, Japan surrendered and the war in the Pacific officially ended. As the Japanese Emperor delicately put it in a radio announcement to his awe-struck subjects, "The war situation has developed not necessarily to Japan's advantage."[3]

The American scientists who had turned theoretical notations into searing heat and crushing, deafening blast began to realize the ominous implications of their handiwork. The preeminent physicist Albert Einstein came to lament, "The unleashed power of the atom has changed everything save our modes of thinking, and thus we drift toward unparalleled catastrophe." J. Robert Oppenheimer, the director of the Los Alamos research facility where the first atomic bombs were made, had at the first test in July 1945 watched a ball of light burst and swell in the desert dawn. Oppenheimer later recalled that the foreboding line from one of the Hindu classics had jumped into his mind: "Now I have become death, the destroyer of worlds." These men's comments were prophetic even if the scale of the destruction and the toll of civilian life did not surpass conventional wartime firebombing of Dresden in Germany or Japan's capital, Tokyo.[4]

The broad reaction within the United States to the nuclear dawn was at first euphoric. The *New York Times* reported the Hiroshima blast with banner headlines, stressing the extraordinary power of the new American weapon. Publicly President Harry S. Truman warned Japan of a "rain of ruin" while also welcoming "a new era in man's understanding of nature's forces," thus linking this triumph of science to promising peacetime uses. When Japan surrendered, he shared the joy of the troops gathering for the invasion of Japan. They would not

Hiroshima's City Center Showing the Effects of the Atomic Bomb
The small figures of people on the road give a sense of the scale of the destruction. (Photo: Shigeo Hayashi. Courtesy Hiroshima Peace Museum)

have to endure an attack that would have cost many lives. Public opinion polls in the United States indicated a widespread view of nuclear weapons as a godsend. Two weeks after Hiroshima, 85 percent approved dropping the bomb. The "good" atom quickly entered U.S. popular culture in a light-hearted way through songs and popular new phrases—such as "anatomic bomb" applied to a starlet a few weeks after Hiroshima.[5]

For those in 1945 peering into the immediate future, the bomb posed the grave question of how states would use their power. Would they apply their imagination and resources to rebuilding a world battered by economic collapse and the second major war of the twentieth century? Or would they stumble amidst the ruins, blinded by fear and enmity, until the next cycle of bloodshed and destruction? All over the world those first postwar years witnessed a battle between hope and fear.

Nowhere was it more tempting to imagine better times ahead than in an emerging third world in the grip of independence fever. Allied propaganda, most notably the Atlantic Charter proclaimed by Franklin D. Roosevelt and Winston Churchill in 1941, had depicted World War II as a battle for freedom, and so third-world proponents of a new postwar order gladly saw it. Thus encouraged, they entertained dreams of rapidly realizing national liberation and social justice. Many were ready to turn their backs on the world of political anarchy, material deprivation, foreign domination, and battlefield carnage. They wanted badly to believe that colonialism was over and that something better was within reach of their peoples. The leader of the Chinese Communist movement, Mao Zedong, concluded that Soviet-American cooperation signified nothing less than "the opening of a new stage in the history of the world"—one conducive to peace and reform in China. Ho Chi Minh as the leader of a struggling anti-colonial movement in Vietnam quoted from the American Declaration of Independence in August 1945 while proclaiming an end to French colonial control. Independence sentiment gripped India, where a weakened Britain struggled to maintain control, as well as the Philippines, which the United States had already declared a readiness to free. In the General Assembly of the newly organized United Nations, the head of the Indian delegation rose in December 1946 to protest religious and racial discrimination in the name of "millions of voiceless people" in Asia and Africa. "It is only on the foundation of justice that we can create a new world order," she cautioned.[6]

Popular hopes for peace and reconstruction also took shape within the societies of the major belligerents after an exhausting war. Throughout Europe voices called for focusing national attention and resources on social and political betterment after the upheaval and destruction that had turned Europe from the showcase of civilization into an exhibit for human folly. Surely two world wars in thirty years was enough. In 1942 British historian E. H. Carr noticed especially among the younger generation a revulsion against "a bad and mad world" and a conviction that "almost everything in it needs to be uprooted and replanted." In the Soviet Union the population longed for a respite from the society-wide mobilization campaigns that their leaders had imposed on them, first to collectivize agriculture and build up the economy and then to repulse the German invaders. One Soviet veteran recalled how as the war approached its end, soldiers dwelt on the promise of postwar life. "We pictured things in rainbow colors." Though spared the direct effects of fighting on their own soil, Americans, too, longed to put the pinch of depression and the sacrifice of war behind them. In 1943 the poet Archibald MacLeish looked out from his wartime office in Washington and thought that he saw forming not only in his own country but around the world a determination to turn the sacrifice of war into "something admirable, something of human worth and human significance."[7]

But an undercurrent of fear was already building as the war came to an end. Nuclear weapons at once injected a dangerous new dynamic into the U.S.-Soviet relationship. They would figure as a major impetus for the Cold War and one of its defining features. Adding to the fear was a dark Cold War vision of moral struggle that promised more sacrifice and danger—looming tests on the battlefield, a race for nuclear advantage, and the specter of internal subversion. Hardly had the war ended than those fears began to shape U.S. and Soviet foreign policy and spill over into their respective societies. With the U.S. and Soviet leaders—Harry Truman and Joseph Stalin—as the presiding presences, the Cold War began to etch a line across the globe.

As hopes gave way to fears, Cold War concerns increasingly informed superpower plans for the war-wounded countries of Europe and Asia. In Japan and western Europe it was the United States that prevailed in collaboration with conservative elites operating through center-right parties, while in eastern Europe the Soviets exerted strong control, making genuine self-determination as problematic as in any traditional sphere of great-power influence. With superpower political influence also went the promotion of a way of life—"coca-colonization" on one side of the Cold War divide and socialist education on the other.

The miasma of Cold War fears gradually engulfed the third world, throwing a major obstacle in the way of impatient liberators and destroying their sanguine expectations for the postwar period. Washington listened anxiously to the rising call for decolonization and reacted with outright hostility to radical programs at odds with the American political and economic model or with U.S. Cold War interests. Stalin, for whom suspicion was second nature, was only marginally more receptive to third-world voices. Here, as in general, he was cautious in dealing with states and situations that he could not control. And he was anxious not to provoke the United States or waste scarce resources on distant and dubious causes. The superpowers thus in combination made the inherently difficult path toward national independence and domestic renovation more arduous, prolonged, and dangerous.

For witnesses to the immediate postwar years—whatever their vantage point on the surface of the globe—every step forward seemed matched in these turbulent times by a step back. Hopes for peace barely survived in the face of rising Cold War tensions and even a limited war in Korea. Hopes for prosperity struggled through a time of economic adjustment and reconstruction with little sense of the long-term benefit of the global system of trade and investment then beginning to take shape. Science and technology, which were also critical to delivering higher living standards, showed their most destructive face in the American Manhattan Project and its Soviet counterpart. Finally, hopes for independence among those under foreign domination quickly ran up against the tenacity of colonial powers, the intrusion of the Cold War rivals, and often deeply divergent views about the future within countries charting a fresh course. In retrospect we can see the first years after 1945 marked the beginning of a new era. But it was far less clear to people at the time. Did these events that buffeted their lives add up to something better or worse for them and their children?

CHAPTER 1

THE COLD WAR: TOWARD SOVIET-AMERICAN CONFRONTATION

The United States and the USSR emerged from World War II the dominant powers. They looked out on a devastated world. Except for the United States, all the major participants in the war were economically wounded. American leaders could see the potential for chaos that might in turn invite communist subversion or invasion. Just as plausibly, Soviet leaders had good reason to suspect that the United States might exploit its unrivaled economic power to extend its influence. Guided by their competing political and economic views, those two powers not surprisingly collided over postwar arrangements—above all for Europe.

That collision produced the Cold War. Wartime cooperation turned into a decades-long rivalry in part because of the simple bipolar division of international power created by World War II and the ideological antagonisms taking shape as early as World War I (both noted in the Introduction). The personalities of Soviet and American leaders in the mid-1940s and the sudden intrusion of the nuclear issue into the Soviet-American relationship also played an important part in generating tension. Taken together, these ingredients proved a potent combination. Soon on both sides mobilization for the Cold War would begin, with effects that would reverberate throughout both societies and increasingly around the world. But the Soviet Union and the United States avoided a direct military contest. Both preferred to do their fighting through proxies, avoid the risks of nuclear war, but otherwise pursue their rivalry in every imaginable way. "Cold War" was a fitting name.

ORIGINS OF THE RIVALRY

Controversy has long surrounded the opening phase of the Cold War. The debate began during the late 1940s, revived in the 1960s with the publication of official U.S. documents, and picked up again in the 1990s following the opening of Soviet records. The controversy has consistently turned on the question of responsibility for initiating the struggle. Do we conclude that both Americans and Soviets overreacted and exaggerated the threat from the other side? Or do we place primary blame on one side—or not place blame at all? These questions remain worthy of debate, but arriving at convincing answers requires first a basic understanding of the steps that carried the two powers to their historic confrontation. We then need to see that series of steps from the distinct perspectives of American leaders Franklin D. Roosevelt and Harry S. Truman and their Soviet counterpart, Joseph Stalin.

From Cooperation to Conflict

The Soviet-American rivalry began with the two powers' involvement in World War II. Germany launched a surprise attack against the Soviet Union in June 1941. That attack pushed leaders in Washington and Moscow from wariness of each other toward alliance against a common foe. The Japanese attack on Pearl Harbor the following December completed the process of alliance formation by bringing the United States fully into the global war. A United States eager to keep Russians fighting while the American war machine got into high gear entered into a working relationship with an embattled USSR. (Britain and China were the other major partners in this coalition.) In early 1943 Soviet forces turned back the German invaders and began their drive to Germany's capital, Berlin, and in the middle of the next year American and British forces landed in France to open a second front against Germany. The Allies had thus only begun their march on Germany, whereas Soviet forces were occupying eastern Europe. The Soviet military advance would give Stalin a distinct advantage in negotiating the postwar settlement. At the same time, Roosevelt was asking for Soviet participation in what was expected to be the last bloody phase of the war against Japan.

By 1945 the Soviet-American alliance had passed its high point of cooperation and entered a time of strain. The first notable signs of tension appeared in February at Yalta (a Crimean resort on the Black Sea), where Joseph Stalin hosted Roosevelt and British prime minister Winston Churchill. While Stalin reassured Roosevelt with the promise that Soviet forces would intervene in the war against Japan soon after the defeat of Germany, the leaders otherwise sparred over the postwar settlement in Europe. The most divisive issue was the political future of Poland.

Germany's surrender in May and the obvious weakening of Japan intensified the pressure to reach agreement on peace terms. To that end the Big Three of the alliance (the USSR, the United States, and Britain) met in July 1945 at Potsdam on the outskirts of Berlin. This was the occasion for the first and only meeting between Stalin and Roosevelt's successor, Harry S. Truman. A month later the final act of the global war played out in a rush with the dropping of the two U.S. atomic bombs on Japan, the entry of Soviet forces into the Pacific War, and Japan's surrender. Despite the welcome peace, terms of the postwar settlement remained a sensitive issue among the former allies. Through 1946 Moscow and Washington maintained a publicly civil stance, but privately the acid of suspicion on both sides was corroding the relationship. Soviet troops that had entered China's northeast provinces (Manchuria) and northern Iran during the war were becoming a particular source of irritation in Washington. Even more worrisome was Moscow's tightening grip on Poland, Czechoslovakia, Hungary, Romania, and Bulgaria. Thanks to the presence of the Soviet army and Moscow's support, Communist parties in those countries began imposing themselves despite their minority status. The future of an occupied Germany remained unsettled, with the lines of division hardening between the Soviet-controlled zone and the rest where the Americans, British, and French were in control.

The end of the road on the way to the Cold War came in 1947 as American and Soviet leaders publicly proclaimed the world divided into two antagonistic blocs. Americans took the lead. In March in a speech to Congress, Truman proposed a program of assistance to Greece and Turkey. This speech announced what would become known as the Truman Doctrine, a commitment by the United States to take a stand against what the president described as the global threat posed by communism to free peoples everywhere. A few months later Truman's secretary of state, George C. Marshall, announced a fresh initiative—an ambitious program that became known as the Marshall Plan to help rebuild and stabilize European economies and preempt any popular turn toward communist programs.

Stalin was close behind in endorsing the view of a fundamentally divided world. He responded with alarm to the Marshall Plan and called for a meeting of

FROM WORLD WAR TO COLD WAR		
1945	Feb.	Roosevelt, Stalin, and Churchill meet at Yalta
	Apr.	Roosevelt's death puts Truman in the White House
	May	Germany surrenders
	July 16	First U.S. A-bomb tested while Truman and Stalin spar over the future of eastern Europe at the Potsdam conference
	Aug. 6	A-bomb dropped on Hiroshima
	Aug. 8	Soviet Union declares war on Japan
	Aug. 9	A-bomb dropped on Nagasaki
	Aug. 14	Japan surrenders
1946	Spring	U.S.-Soviet tensions develop over Soviet troops in northeast China and Iran and over Communist party control in eastern Europe
1947	Mar.	Truman uses proposal for aid to Greece and Turkey to declare Truman Doctrine
	June	Marshall Plan proposed for European economic recovery
	Sept.	Stalin sees collapse of cooperation with the United States and organizes Cominform as first step toward tightening grip on eastern Europe

Europe's major Communist parties for September to create a coordinating body, the Communist Information Bureau (Cominform). The Soviet delegates set the tone at that meeting with their call to European Communists and "progressive forces" around the world to rally against an expansionist United States.

These two emergent rivals both claimed superpower status, but they did not in fact stand on an equal footing. The United States enjoyed a number of important advantages over the USSR. Americans had suffered relatively little from World War II. There had been no fighting on their soil, and U.S. involvement in combat had come relatively late and under favorable conditions. American casualties came to only 300,000, while the Soviet Union had lost heavily at the hands of the German army as it marched deep into Soviet territory (including the death of roughly 25 million, civilians as well as military). Moreover, the United States enjoyed the advantage of an undamaged economy that had more than doubled in the value of gross national product (or GNP; see "key economic terms" on p. 14) in the course of the war. The Soviet economy had by contrast suffered serious destruction. Finally, the United States came out of the war with a marked military advantage. Washington commanded the only major navy and air force and held a monopoly on nuclear weapons. Although the Soviets had the largest ground force at the end of the war, peace brought a steep and rapid demobilization.

U.S. Policy in Transition

U.S. foreign policy underwent a major transformation during the period leading up to the Cold War. Roosevelt and then Truman were responsible for managing that policy, especially the sensitive relationship with the Soviet Union. They had contrasting backgrounds and personalities and thus saw international developments and shaped U.S. policy along different lines. In making any comparison, however, it is important to keep in mind the differing contexts in which they operated. Roosevelt was president at the height of wartime cooperation among the Allies, whereas Truman took charge in the midst of the rocky transition to peace.

FDR's Diplomacy of Accommodation. Roosevelt, a New York patrician, had enjoyed the best private schooling, including a Harvard education. He had taken as his political model none other than his own cousin, Theodore Roosevelt, a two-term president and larger-than-life public figure early in the twentieth century. During World War I while serving as an assistant secretary of the navy, FDR had warmly embraced President Woodrow Wilson's dream of the United States playing a larger role in ordering the world, and he stayed true to that dream while running unsuccessfully in 1920 as the Democratic Party's vice-presidential nominee. Despite crippling polio, he stayed in politics and in 1932 tried for the presidency—and won.

Once in office, Roosevelt focused on the deep economic depression gripping the country and sought to stay clear of international entanglements. Like many Americans, he believed that participation in World War I had been a serious mistake. Pushing Wilson's plans for international reform had come to seem a bad idea. But by 1937 the Wilsonian in Roosevelt revived as he watched the rise of two international outlaws, Japan in Asia and Germany in Europe. He cautiously led the country toward greater support for China, Britain, and the USSR in their respective contests with Japan and Germany. Even before the Japanese attack on Pearl Harbor pushed the United States fully into World War II, he publicly tied the Allied cause to the distinctly Wilsonian aims of creating a new international order. The Atlantic Charter, an agreement signed by Churchill and Roosevelt in August 1941, enshrined the goals of this new order. The postwar world was to be governed by the principles of self-determination and support for democracy, collective security through what was to become the United Nations, and the freedom to trade and travel the high seas. Once in the war, Roosevelt made clear that he would settle for nothing less than the unconditional surrender of Germany and Japan, clearing the way for sweeping internal reforms in both countries so that they would become respectable members of international society.

The United Nations was the most prominent symbol of this return to Wilson's program. The League of Nations had been the centerpiece of his plans for a peaceful, democratic world (see the Introduction, p. 4). But the Senate and seemingly the electorate in the 1920 presidential vote had rejected the League along with Wilson's overall peace plan. With the onset of a new world war, Roosevelt resolved to make a second attempt at creating a League. When the fifty-one nations fighting the Axis met in San Francisco in spring 1945 to form the new international organization, they divided it into two bodies. A Security Council was to consist of the big-five states of the time (the United States, the USSR, France, Britain, and China), together with a rotating group of other states. Each of the big five was to have veto power over UN action. The General Assembly was to contain all member states. It would make its decisions by majority vote, and those decisions would be nonbinding. Unlike Wilson, Roosevelt won overwhelming Senate support for U.S. membership in this new league, and as a sign of his country's commitment he arranged to place the UN headquarters in the United States.

Privately, however, FDR's thinking about the immediate postwar period revealed him a wary Wilsonian. In a letter in 1943 he claimed to see ahead "a trial or transition period after the fighting stops—we might call it even a period of trial and error." He favored setting aside difficult international issues for two to four years while "shell shocked" societies around the world recovered. To keep the peace during this transitional period, Roosevelt wanted Russia, China, Britain, and the United States to work together—in effect to "act as sheriffs for the maintenance of order." These "four policemen" would control Japan and Germany, preside over the UN, and generally maintain the peace. Rigid, universal principles should not get in the way of reconciling the divergent interests among the Allies, so Roosevelt reasoned. This goal of maintaining a working relationship among the Allies meant in concrete terms Roosevelt accepting, for the time being at least, Moscow's ambitions along the Soviet periphery as well as the continued existence of the British empire.[1]

Churchill, Roosevelt, and Stalin at Yalta, February 1945
Though it is posed and formal, this photo highlights the vigor of the British and Soviet leaders
in contrast to the American president, whose face is sagging, eyes dark and hollow, jaw slack, and
hands drooping. These signs of declining health foreshadow the president's death only a few
months later and would subsequently raise questions among Roosevelt's critics about his effectiveness in dealing with Stalin at this critical moment as the war in Europe drew to a close.
(Franklin D. Roosevelt Library)

At Yalta, his last major meeting with Stalin, Roosevelt hewed to this middle
way. He conceded the Soviet Union's special interests along its border (reflecting
his view that great powers had to respect the influence that each wielded within
its own region). At the same time he pushed Stalin to respect self-determination
in Poland and neighboring countries occupied by the Red Army. He realized,
however, that the implementation of self-determination would have to be gradual and that continued cooperation among the powers (each secure in its interests) was the best way to create a better world. More immediately cooperation
served to keep the coalition together through the final phase of World War II and
into the period of peacemaking.

Truman Takes a Hard Line.   In April 1945, with the German Third Reich in
ruins and Japan under constant aerial bombardment, Roosevelt died at age sixty-
three. His death put Vice President Harry S. Truman, just two years FDR's jun-

ior, in the White House. Truman could with justification call himself a "man of the people." He was raised in Independence, Missouri, a town whose pace and mores epitomized middle America. He was not born to wealth, and he had little formal education. After fighting in France during World War I and then struggling in business after the war, Truman joined the Missouri Democratic political machine and in 1934 advanced to the U.S. Senate. In 1944 FDR plucked Truman from relative obscurity to play the role of the bland vice-presidential candidate needed on the Democratic ticket.

On the afternoon of April 12, 1945, Vice President Truman had finished presiding over a routine session of the Senate when he was called to the White House. Tight-jawed, Truman arrived to hear the newly widowed Eleanor Roosevelt say, "Harry, the president is dead." After a hastily called meeting with the Roosevelt cabinet, Truman was sworn in. Throughout that terrible day, it dawned on the new president how difficult his situation was. The next day he asked some reporters to pray for him. Roosevelt's death had left him feeling "like the moon, the stars, and all the planets had fallen on me."[2]

Truman was ill prepared to bear the daunting responsibility for the last phase of the war and for the peacemaking challenge. He was dogged by self-doubt. He would have to act in the shadow of the great man and beloved leader. But having seen Roosevelt only eight times in his last year, Truman had to act with arguably less insight on Roosevelt's wartime strategy and commitments than anyone else in the upper levels of the administration. To make matters worse, Truman was unversed in international affairs and the making of foreign policy.

With little time for preparation, a president in need of guidance fell back on his own general views. At the core of those views was a fairly stark, pugnaciously held Wilsonian faith. Truman believed deeply in the principle of self-determination and the duty of the United States to lead a community of free peoples. He looked back with pride on his country's sacrifice in World War I. Whereas others had developed second thoughts about Wilson's crusade, Truman had held rock steady. He welcomed participation in World War II as an opportunity for the country to play a constructive role in world affairs. Truman's view of what U.S. foreign policy should be was also informed by his reading of history as an ongoing contest between civilization and barbarism waged by a succession of major powers. The United States had in his day emerged as the foremost of the civilized countries, and now it had to fulfill its duty to prevent aggression and discipline wrongdoers.

Truman also depended on advisers inherited from the Roosevelt administration. They offered him contradictory guidance, beginning with the sensitive issue of Soviet influence in Poland. On one side was a set of political conservatives and anti-Soviet diplomats previously ignored by FDR. They argued for taking a firm line toward the USSR. Specifically, they contended that Poland was a test case of Soviet intentions toward the postwar world and of the American commitment to self-determination. Some even warned the new president that he faced a "barbarian invasion of Europe." On the other side was a group that had worked closely with Roosevelt throughout the war. They questioned the wisdom of a hard-line policy on Poland, a country right on the Soviet border. Secretary of War Henry L. Stimson wondered if "the Russians perhaps were being more real-

MAP 1.1
Europe after World War II

istic than we were in regard to their own security." He and others argued that a diplomacy of compromise was essential to the final phase of the war against Japan and could sustain good relations with Stalin into the postwar period.[3]

From the start the new president tilted sharply to the side of the hard-liners. They offered clear-cut advice that was consistent with Truman's general outlook as well as his desire to show himself, despite his inexperience, a tough, decisive policymaker. He assured them of his intention "to be firm with the Russians and make no concessions from American principles or traditions" to win them over.[4] A marked shift in the tone of high-level discussions on Soviet policy became strikingly evident in the first meetings that Truman held in late April. While the hard-liners were to stay on as his chief advisers, some former FDR intimates began to leave, dismayed by the new, increasingly belligerent tone.

Policy toward the Soviet Union vacillated through the balance of 1945. Truman was not yet certain in his get-tough views and in any case was unready to translate those views into a policy of confrontation. He still needed Soviet support in imposing unconditional surrender on Japan, and the public wanted peace and demobilization, not a renewal of international conflict. In talks with the Soviets in London and Moscow late in the year, Truman's new secretary of state, James F. Byrnes, expressed Washington's resentment over the Soviet breach of the principle of self-determination in eastern Europe but finally agreed to recognize the Soviet-backed governments there. Meanwhile, the Pentagon demobilized the armed forces. Standing forces would fall from 12.1 million in 1945 to 1.6 million in 1947, and the military budget would drop between those years from $81 billion to $13 billion. At the same time the Pentagon set up military bases around the world to ensure that no enemy would be able to strike suddenly across the Atlantic or Pacific in the way that Japan had. Despite calls to seek an international agreement on nuclear arms, Truman was not about to compromise his monopoly of a weapon that had helped bring Japan to its knees and that gave the United States a distinct edge over the Soviet Union. In the fall of 1945 he rejected Secretary of War Stimson's proposal to consult with the Soviets on nuclear issues in order to establish an atmosphere of trust. The next year the Truman administration as well as the Soviets offered plans to forestall a nuclear arms race, but they failed to find common ground. The nuclear genie was permanently out of the bottle.

In the course of 1946 Truman ended his vacillation over which road to take. In January the angry president privately denounced what he now saw clearly as Stalin's aggressive intent, charging Russia with reaching out for Iran, for Turkey, and for the Dardanelles (the narrow passage that provided Soviet ships an outlet from the Black Sea to the Mediterranean) just as it had gone after the Baltic states of Latvia, Estonia, and Lithuania in 1940 and Poland after the war. "Unless Russia is faced with an iron fist and strong language[,] another war is in the making. Only one language do they understand—'How many divisions have you?'" Truman's response now was to play hardball. He would refuse to recognize Soviet-dominated Romania and Bulgaria. He would defend Iran and China's northeast provinces against Soviet troops that had entered during the war and had stayed beyond the deadline for their withdrawal. He would assert control over Japan and the entire Pacific and make sure that China and South Korea had strong central governments able to resist communism. He concluded, "I'm tired babying the Soviets."[5]

Truman's private fears over aggressive Soviet intentions were soon confirmed by the analysis of Soviet expert George F. Kennan serving in the Moscow embassy. Responding to a speech delivered by Stalin in February 1946 generally perceived in the United States as a declaration of hostility, Kennan offered an interpretation of Soviet policy that was at once embraced in official circles. He explained that the Kremlin suffered from a "neurotic view of world affairs," rooted in the "traditional and instinctive Russian sense of insecurity." It was further distorted by a Marxist ideology that "is seemingly inaccessible to considerations of reality in its basic reactions." The result was "a political force committed fanatically to the belief that with US there can be no permanent *modus vivendi*, that it is desirable and necessary that the internal harmony of our society be disrupted, our traditional way of life be destroyed, the international authority of our

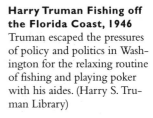

Harry Truman Fishing off the Florida Coast, 1946
Truman escaped the pressures of policy and politics in Washington for the relaxing routine of fishing and playing poker with his aides. (Harry S. Truman Library)

state be broken, if Soviet power is to be secure."[6] But, he stressed, Soviet leaders were sensitive to the logic of force. If the United States and its allies stood firm in the face of attempted Soviet expansion, then it would be possible to hold the line and in the long term force internal changes in the Soviet system. This formulation by Kennan evolved into a policy known as "containment." It stipulated that Soviet pressure at any point would be met by U.S. counter-force. Containment became the master doctrine for U.S. Cold War policy, the touchstone for guiding the competition with the Soviet Union down to the very end of the Cold War.

Truman's bottled-up concerns over the Soviet threat began bubbling over. In June, he fulminated in his diary, "Get plenty of Atomic Bombs on hand— drop one on Stalin, put the United Nations to work and eventually set up a free world." Finally, Soviet pressure on Turkey and apparent Soviet sponsorship of a leftist insurgency in Greece pushed Truman to make his views public. The Truman Doctrine proclaimed in March 1947 effectively declared that the United States was embarked on a Cold War. More important than the call for aid to Greece and Turkey was the president's stark picture of a world divided between two ways of life—one defined by the path toward freedom and the other toward totalitarian control. The United States would now take as its fundamental policy "to support free peoples who are resisting attempted subjugation by armed minorities or by outside pressures." In the monumental struggle now looming, free countries and peoples around the world looked to the United States. "If we falter in our leadership," Truman warned, "we may endanger the peace of the world—and we shall surely endanger the welfare of this Nation."[7]

Some within the administration criticized the speech for committing the United States to a cause for which it still lacked funding, while public critics doubted the inherent wisdom of so bold a stance. But Truman stuck to his promise to defend threatened countries everywhere, even on the periphery of American global interests and even where American forces could not reach without leaving Europe vulnerable. The announcement a few months later of the Marshall Plan to rebuild the European economies revealed his determination to make good on this commitment beginning with the region judged the highest priority in the emerging rivalry with the USSR.

Stalin's Pursuit of Territory and Security

Joseph Stalin dominated the Soviet scene to a degree unequaled in the United States by Truman or even Roosevelt. Stalin was born in the Russian empire's southern province of Georgia in 1879. He began studying for the priesthood but was thrown out of seminary for revolutionary activity and (some accounts say) laziness. After the 1917 Bolshevik revolution he climbed to prominence in the new ruling Communist Party thanks to his administrative skills and adroit political maneuvering. As party general secretary he demonstrated patience, avoided controversy, and built up a following of supporters.

Following Lenin's death in 1924, Stalin made himself the dominant figure in the party. The concentration of power at the top made it easy for Stalin to fully consolidate his control by 1929 and to make the party-state serve as an extension of his will and vision for almost a quarter-century. Within this highly centralized political system lower-level committees formed the mass base of the party pyramid (about 4 percent of the population in the Stalin years). Near the top was a central committee elected by what were supposed to be regular party congresses. The top ten or so central committee members stood at the apex of the pyramid. As members of the Politburo (short for Political Bureau), their task was to guide the party, direct the operations of the state, and take their cues from Stalin.

The "Genius Leader." Stalin brought to his era of unchallenged control a variety of striking personality traits. He was provincial in his outlook and thus markedly at odds with the cosmopolitan group that had surrounded Lenin and taken a leading role in the founding of the Soviet state. Stalin was neither intellectually cultivated nor well traveled. He was a domineering leader who insisted on making the final decision on a wide range of issues. Comrades either turned into servile courtiers full of praise for the "genius leader" or fell victim to his mistrust.

What Stalin's successors would come to call a dangerous cult of personality reflected not just his drive to dominance but also a terrible suspicion of others. Paranoia drove him to fix blame for errors that he regarded as serious whether in family matters or party and national affairs. Almost invariably the blame came to rest on one person or class of people even if the likelihood of their responsibility was highly improbable. He rejected explanations that involved abstract forces, bad luck, or a complex combination of events. He wanted a clear villain to hold accountable. For example, when the Germans captured his son during World War II, he inexplicably blamed the son's wife and had her arrested. Once he had found a scapegoat, he was an implacable avenger impervious to appeals from the "guilty" party, relatives and friends, and respected colleagues. In the world Stalin controlled, one serious mistake could prove disastrous for an individual, a family, or a whole class of people. This paranoia, sometimes manipulated by Stalin's underlings to their own advantage, injected fear and mistrust into elite Soviet political and intellectual circles and spelled misery, even death, for millions whom he judged a threat to him or his program.

In the late 1940s, just as Cold War tensions sharpened, an increasingly frail Stalin grew more suspicious, finding enemies all around him. First it was the Communist Party organization in Leningrad. He had it purged in 1949 and had six of its leaders executed in 1950. Lesser purges followed in Moscow, Estonia, and Georgia. He became obsessed with the idea that Soviet Jews, abetted by British and American intelligence, were plotting against him. His suspicions finally settled in November 1952 on the doctors, predominantly Jewish, assigned to the Kremlin. Under torture, they admitted to conspiring to kill the leadership. Stalin showed the confessions to his colleagues and lamented, "You are like blind kittens; what will happen without me? The country will perish because you don't know how to recognize enemies." As the circle of suspicion narrowed, Stalin wondered aloud if close colleagues were also working for Western intelligence agencies. Those at Stalin's side well knew that a personal misstep or a rival's slander might plant the seeds of deadly suspicion in their master's mind. They were thus "temporary people," as future Soviet leader Nikita Khrushchev chillingly put it. "As long as he trusted us to a certain degree, we were allowed to go on living and working. But the moment he stopped trusting you, Stalin would start to scrutinize you until the cup of his distrust overflowed. Then it would be your turn to follow those who were no longer among the living."[8]

Stalin's handling of his relationship with the United States was to some degree conditioned by his personality. But arguably more important was his fixation from the late 1930s onward with a surprisingly traditional set of territorial aims. Acting like a latter-day czar, he focused relentlessly on restoring the land once attached to the Russian empire stretching across Eurasia. He also gave priority (as had the czars) to promoting influence in areas along the Russian periphery, especially in eastern Europe but also in East Asia. Where the old empire had been dominant, Stalin wanted to be dominant. Where territory and privileges had been lost, Stalin wanted them back. In his devotion to these goals, Stalin played the diplomat—shrewd, hard bargaining, cautious, and opportunistic. His achievements in this regard were formidable, evident in gains all along the Soviet border.

Stalin might talk the language of Lenin and even see the world through the prism of Marxist-Leninist concepts, but he had long since abandoned early Bolshevik hopes for world revolution. As he saw it, a strong and secure Soviet Union was the best guarantee of socialism's ultimate global victory. Already in the interwar period he had put the Soviet Union first. In keeping with the priority he gave security along the Soviet border, Stalin treated the international

Communist movement as an instrument of Soviet foreign policy and, where necessary, sacrificed Communist parties in other lands to advance Soviet goals.

Stalin and the Allies. In contrast to a consistent policy on border areas, Stalin's policy toward the United States moved by zigs and zags toward Cold War enmity. In large measure this was the result of his understanding of what made capitalist powers such as the United States tick. Stalin's own training as a disciple of Marx and Lenin led him in two distinct directions. The official orthodoxy pushed him toward suspicion of their intentions, reinforcing a tendency that also derived from Stalin's paranoia and historical sense of Russian vulnerability. But he also believed that capitalist states, however malign their intentions, were not formidable threats. Like other Marxists, he was confident that their maturing capitalist economies faced crises that would sooner or later precipitate an internal collapse or a debilitating war among them over markets. Whichever course it took, capitalism was a doomed system that grew weaker while the Soviet Union grew stronger. Out of the debris of capitalist collapse, socialist states would arise to cooperate with the USSR in constructing a new world order. Time was on the Soviet side.

Initially Stalin had good reason for suspicion of the United States. Shortly after the Bolshevik revolution, U.S. as well as British, French, and Japanese forces had intervened militarily against it. In the 1930s they had refused to cooperate with the Soviet Union against Hitler. Stalin then shifted to appeasement of Adolf Hitler and sought to extract the best bargain possible. Their 1939 nonaggression pact (see the Introduction, p. 6) laid the basis for Soviet control over parts of Poland. The surprise German attack in June 1941 betrayed Stalin's calculations. Badly shaken, a dejected Soviet leader moaned, "Lenin left us a state and we have turned it to shit."[9] The only bright spot was that the disaster would put Washington behind Moscow against their new common enemy.

Stalin entered the alliance from a position of weakness. Overrun by German forces, he desperately needed supplies and the prompt opening of a second European front that would draw away German divisions. FDR was forthcoming with the supplies, but repeated delays in launching Anglo-American military operations on the European continent left Stalin fuming. In November 1942 American and British troops finally went into action in North Africa and moved into Italy in 1943; however, the overdue cross-channel invasion of France did not take place until June 1944. In the meantime, the war devastated the Soviet land, and millions of Soviet citizens were dying. Bearing the brunt of the struggle against Germany, the USSR would lose over six million soldiers and some twenty million civilians.

Stalin complained about British and American military passivity but otherwise put the best face on the situation. In November 1943 he pronounced his alliance with the two major capitalist powers in good shape despite their "different ideologies and social systems."[10] At the same time, he associated himself with the broad Anglo-American war aims such as national self-determination. That same year he formally disbanded the Comintern (see the Introduction, p. 18) a symbol of the Soviet commitment to world revolution, as a goodwill gesture to his capitalist allies.

By 1944 Stalin's military position was quite strong. Soviet forces were advancing on Germany. When the Allies met at Yalta early in 1945, Stalin agreed to enter the Pacific War within three months after the end of the European war. In return he secured his claim to territory lost to Japan in 1905 and during World War I (the Kuril Islands and the southern half of Sakhalin) and to the former Russian sphere of influence in China's northeast region (including the Chinese Eastern Railway and bases at Dairen and Port Arthur; see Map 1.3 on p. 57). Exactly three months after Germany's surrender in May 1945, Stalin made good on his promise to join the fight against Japan. The Soviet declaration of war, together with the American atomic bombing, quickly forced Japan's surrender. The end of the war found the Soviet Union the dominant power across Eurasia.

Two interrelated concerns regarding the shape of the postwar settlement were already preoccupying Stalin by late 1944. One was the prospect for maintaining the Soviet-American partnership on a mutually advantageous basis. The Marxist theoretician in Stalin told him that the postwar American economy would need markets to absorb its excess production and surplus capital. Stalin could help Roosevelt hold economic crisis at bay and at the same time speed Soviet reconstruction by opening the USSR to American goods and capital. Cooperation would gain time for the USSR to rebuild and consolidate its wartime gains while securing international acceptance of the Red Army's recovery of territory from Japan and Russia's dominance in eastern Europe. In practical terms this last consideration was probably the most important in Stalin's dealings with the United States.

Stalin's most immediate concern was the future of Poland. That country had served as an invasion route into Russia three times—by Napoleon in 1812, by Germany in 1914, and by Germany again in 1941. Each time the invaders had penetrated deeply into Russian territory and left behind appalling destruction. Stalin had already tried to bar this strategic Polish door to Russia when in 1939 he agreed with Hitler on a partition—but he had gotten instead an invasion. Once the Red Army had turned the Germans back, Stalin seized his second chance to solve this strategic problem. He agreed with his alliance partners on restoring an independent Poland, but he also wanted that new Poland to be pro-Soviet and to give up land in the east to the USSR in exchange for German land in the west. When the conservative Polish government in exile in London rejected a deal, Stalin turned to the Polish Communist Party. That weak and divided party needed the Red Army to gain and maintain power, and thus it was ready to subordinate itself on the territorial issue as on other matters.

Stalin's unilateral decision to deal with the Communist-controlled Polish provisional government based in Lublin did not sit well with his British and American partners. At the Yalta conference Stalin defended his action on the grounds of immediate wartime necessity and long-term Soviet security interests. The advancing Red Army, he explained, required a friendly administration in its rear area, and the Soviet Union needed to be sure that Poland did not serve again as Germany's invasion route. FDR conceded the legitimacy of Stalin's concerns while at the same time pressing for an Allied agreement on self-determination that would give the London Poles a role in a reorganized, broad-based government. Churchill was even more emphatic in defense of self-determination, flatly denying the legitimacy of the Lublin government. The Yalta conference closed with a declaration on liberated Europe pledging respect for democratic forms and providing a diplomatic mechanism for constituting a generally acceptable Polish government. The declaration made no reference to Soviet security interests, but Stalin would not (as it turned out) let go of what his army had won for him. He spelled out this basic principle several months later: "Whoever occupies a territory also imposes on it his own social system. Everyone imposes his own system as far as his army can reach."[11]

Stalin and the Postwar Settlement

Once Truman took over the White House, Stalin faced additional challenges and slights from the Americans. Immediately after victory in Europe and despite the Soviet commitment to join in the war against Japan, the Truman administration made an abrupt and awkwardly executed decision to cut off aid to the Soviets and followed a policy toward eastern Europe that made no allowance for Soviet interests. The ill omens continued. Truman surrounded the U.S. atomic bomb project with secrecy (just as Roosevelt had), and at Potsdam he informed Stalin of the first successful test in only the most terse and casual terms. Then, despite the Soviet Union's intervention in the Pacific War, Stalin found himself effectively excluded from a real role in the postwar occupation of Japan. Finally, by early 1946 Washington was beginning to apply pressure to get Soviet troops out of China and Iran.

Truman's off-handed announcement of the first U.S. nuclear test set off alarm bells even though Stalin had reacted with feigned indifference. He was already aware of a top-secret U.S. nuclear weapons program thanks to his intelligence services, and indeed in 1942 he had initiated a parallel Soviet program. By the time Stalin left Potsdam, he had resolved to accelerate that program, giving it the highest priority. The bombing of Hiroshima, he later observed, "has shaken the world. The balance has been destroyed."[12]

Stalin's reaction to the ominous developments in U.S. policy was otherwise surprisingly restrained. He maintained a rough-edged working relationship with the Truman administration, seeking an understanding that would ratify Soviet territorial gains and win acceptance of Soviet standing as a leading power in the postwar world. Though irritated by U.S. policy, he couched his comments to the Americans in the language of hardheaded bargaining and accommodation of mutual interests.

Following Japan's surrender, a fatigued Stalin (now sixty-five) took a long vacation on the Black Sea. He could take satisfaction from the way heavy Soviet sacrifices in the war had paid off in major gains in territory and influence along the Soviet periphery. He had in 1940 seized the Baltic states of Estonia, Latvia, and Lithuania. He had extended the Soviet border westward at the expense of Finland, Poland, Czechoslovakia, Hungary, and Romania. Thanks to the Red Army, he controlled part of Germany and Austria and exercised a strong political influence throughout eastern Europe. He had regained Russian privileges in

China's northeastern provinces, recovered influence in Korea lost a half-century earlier, and redeemed territory lost to Japan. These were by any standard impressive achievements. Having repaired the breaches suffered by the Russian empire, Stalin was determined to hold his advanced positions. (See Maps 1.1 and 1.3.)

Stalin expressed at least in public a hopeful view about the prospects for cooperation. In the February 1946 speech that George Kennan and other American policymakers had found so alarming, Stalin focused not on international dangers but on the tasks of rebuilding at home. He balanced a vaguely worded injunction to raise production over the next two decades—so that "our homeland will be guaranteed against all possible accidents"—with a reference linking the United States and Britain to the Soviet Union as "freedom-loving" states. The next month the Soviet leader decried warmongering by British leader Winston Churchill, while in September insisting that cooperation was still possible between countries with different ideologies.[13]

To calm U.S. policymakers increasingly agitated by evidence of Soviet expansion, Stalin also staged a series of retreats. He pulled his forces out of northeastern China, Iran, and several points in Scandinavia, and he dropped demands for changing the rules for passage of ships through the Dardanelles. Military spending continued to fall from its wartime high, while the steep demobilization of his 11.3 million wartime force continued apace.

But in the course of 1947 Stalin's hopes for avoiding estrangement gradually evaporated. In March Truman laid down his doctrine drawing an ideological line around the world, and a few months later he endorsed the Marshall Plan. Stalin's reaction was somewhat mixed. For example, an insurgency in Greece launched in late 1944 and led by the Greek Communist Party proved an inconvenience to Stalin's management of relations with his old capitalist allies, so he pressed Yugoslavia, Albania, and Bulgaria to terminate their support for the insurgents. Moreover, he did not immediately reject the Marshall Plan and even went so far as to send a delegation to explore its details. But after deciding that the United States was trying to use its economic power to tighten its grip on Europe, he withdrew his delegation and took his European clients with him.

The Marshall Plan finally moved Stalin to accept the idea of a Cold War dividing line between the two rival blocs, and he began to take a tougher stance on his side. As mentioned earlier, to counter rising U.S. influence in Europe, in September he pulled nine European communist parties more tightly under his control through the new coordinating body, the Cominform. He wanted to make sure that the large and influential parties in France and Italy were on a short leash.

Addresses by Politburo members Andrei Zhdanov and Vyacheslav Molotov delivered at the inauguration of the Cominform emphasized the American drive toward world domination. According to this new and more pessimistic public Soviet reading of the international situation, the Americans wanted nothing less than control of the industrially advanced areas of western Europe along with Japan, penetration of the colonial world, and creation of a ring of bases around the USSR. The world was now sharply divided, Zhdanov and Molotov contended, into two ideological camps—one "imperialist and anti-democratic" and the other "anti-imperialist and democratic."[14]

FROM EUROPE TO THE PERIPHERY

When in the course of 1947 U.S. and Soviet leaders declared the Cold War begun, they set in motion developments with consequences they themselves could not control or foresee. The overriding concern in both Washington and Moscow was maximizing their influence in Europe. But at the same time they began to look far beyond Europe with an eye to recruiting allies and winning friends. Examining the early globalization of the Cold War helps explain the origins of "limited wars," the small-scale conflicts into which both rivals became drawn but during which they avoided a direct collision. Fear that small wars might spread in scale and escalate in destructiveness (possibly even set off an exchange of nuclear weapons) worried policymakers in Washington and Moscow. These limited wars played out at points distant from Europe—first in Korea and later in Vietnam, the Middle East, and Afghanistan. More broadly, Cold War rivalry led to a costly arms race with nuclear weapons and missile technology the main areas of competition. The widening competition, rising fears, and growing costs would shake people's lives not just in the Soviet Union and the United States but at virtually every point around the world for decades to come.

Drawing the Line in Europe

By 1950 the Cold War had deeply and intractably divided Europe. Suspicions spawned by disputes at the end of World War II soon gave rise to what Churchill would call in 1946 an "iron curtain" falling across Europe. Once leaders on both sides gave private fears public voice in the course of 1947, the process accelerated, and by 1950 Truman and Stalin had completed cutting Europe in two (see Map 1.1).

The Truman administration effort began in earnest in 1948 when Marshall Plan assistance started reaching western European economies and helped reverse political inroads by local Communist parties. The two senior Communist parties in western Europe at the end of World War II had grown rapidly—the French party to one million members and the Italian party to two million—thanks to their prominent role in wartime resistance against the Germans and the promise of their postwar programs of popular welfare. By 1950 the Marshall Plan and other forms of U.S. aid intended to stabilize the situation had risen to $10 billion and had contributed to the beginnings of economic recovery. U.S. political pressure had encouraged Christian Democratic parties occupying a center-right position on the political spectrum to consolidate their hold on power. They would remain the predominant political presence throughout most of western Europe during the Cold War. (The European perspective on these developments is covered in Chapter 2.) The final step in the process of strategic consolidation came in 1949 with the formation of the North Atlantic Treaty Organization (NATO), committing the United States to the defense of western Europe. The charter members of NATO were Britain, France, Italy, Belgium, the Netherlands, Denmark, Norway, Portugal, and Luxembourg as well as the United States, Canada, and Iceland. Greece and Turkey joined in 1952, followed by West Germany in 1955 (see Map 1.1).

Stalin pursued a roughly parallel strategy on his side of the line. As the Red Army had swept through eastern Europe, Moscow-aligned Communist parties had followed close behind. One by one they took power—in Poland, Hungary, East Germany, Romania, Bulgaria, and Albania. By 1948 Stalin had good reason to further tighten Soviet control. As we have seen, the military balance was not favorable. American estimates at the time made the Soviets seem more formidable than they were. In fact, the U.S. armed forces together with the British were roughly equal to the Soviets in numbers alone, and they had in addition an atomic monopoly and an unrivaled strategic bombing capability.

Stalin lacked the economic resources available to the United States to win and shore up European clients. Indeed, his country had just emerged from a terrible food shortage stemming from the war. So in the new, tougher mood of 1948, Stalin resorted to straightforward repression to snuff out the last sparks of independence in his zone of control. Czechoslovakia, which had retained both its traditionally strong economic ties westward and its democracy, was made to submit. Stalin's demands that the Czechs not participate in the Marshall Plan marked the beginning of the end for this Czech middle way. In February Communists carried out a coup there, completing the process of assimilation into the Soviet bloc. By the end of 1948 Poland had become a one-party state. Stalin had the head of the Polish Communist Party, Władysław Gomułka, arrested. To ensure that his satellites remained responsive to Soviet direction, Stalin assigned each of his colleagues in the Politburo a country to supervise. To coordinate trade and investment, he imposed a regional economic mechanism (COMECOM, short for the Council for Mutual Economic Assistance) in 1949. But he would leave to his successors the task of creating a military alliance (the Warsaw Pact) as a counter to NATO.

At one point—in Tito's Yugoslavia—Stalin's crackdown backfired. Unlike the leaders of other socialist regimes in Eastern Europe, Josip Broz, who went by the name Tito, had fought his own way to power during World War II and insisted on national independence within the Soviet-led bloc. Tensions developed in early 1948 as a result of Tito pursuing an independent regional policy in defiance of Stalin's wishes. Along with Bulgaria and Albania, Tito had offered support to the Greek Communist insurgents even though Stalin wanted the Greek struggle closed down. Tito favored close ties with Albania, and he sought to deal directly with neighboring Bulgaria rather than go through Moscow. This dogged independence angered Stalin. He is supposed to have growled, "I will shake my little finger—and there will be no more Tito."[15] But the Soviet leader lacked the tools available to him elsewhere in the region to enforce his will—an occupying Red Army and a significant body of loyalists within the local Communist Party. Unwilling to risk an invasion for fear it might trigger a broader war, Stalin's only recourse was to expel Yugoslavia from the Cominform in June 1948 and impose an economic embargo.

Germany, which had been divided at the end of the war into U.S., British, French, and Soviet zones, was the last point of division to be resolved between the superpowers. Negotiations among the occupiers on terms for uniting Germany had dragged on inconclusively as Cold War frictions intensified. Frustrated

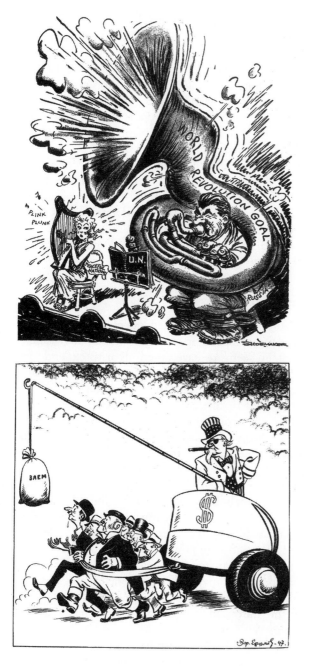

A Brutish Stalin Threatens World Peace and "American Motor of the Latest Type"

These two early Cold War cartoons—one American and one Soviet—reveal the antagonisms tearing apart the wartime alliance.

The first, published in a Chicago newspaper in mid-1946, represents an early expression of the anti-Soviet feeling that would soon sweep over the country. Stalin blasts away on his tuba of "world revolution" to the distress of the "peaceful nations." The "UN" marked on the music sheet suggests that this discordance makes a mockery of international cooperation. Like any successful cartoon, this one exploits popular stereotypes. Stalin as Russia is depicted as a "Slavic" type: a ham-fisted, gross-featured peasant wearing hobnail boots. The disconcerted young woman trying to play the delicate harp is by contrast "civilized"—European-looking and demure. These gender and ethnic stereotypes raise the question: What will happen if the beautiful damsel is left alone to face the big brute?

The Soviet cartoon appeared a year later in the popular humor magazine *Krokodil,* published by the Communist Party paper. It depicts the Marshall Plan, which so alarmed Stalin, as an insidious attempt by Uncle Sam to harness western Europe to the chariot of American capitalism. Desperate European leaders pursue a bag of money marked "loan" in hopes of saving their economies from crisis and their capitalist societies from revolution. The cartoon uses familiar stereotypes to portray the capitalists: They wear top hats, bow ties, formal jackets, and vests to convey privilege, and Uncle Sam arrogantly smokes a cigar. The cartoon reveals the Soviet assumption that foreign policy was about class interest—in this case, the American capitalists dominating European economies while avoiding an economic crisis at home that might promote mass discontent or even imperil their mastery. (Vaughn Shoemaker, *The Chicago Daily News; Krokodil,* August 20, 1947, New York Public Library, Slavic and Baltic Division)

British, American, and French authorities finally launched efforts to integrate their western zones of occupation economically and politically. This was a clear step toward establishing the basis for a distinct West German government located in Bonn and tied to the rest of western Europe. Stalin responded in June 1948 by imposing a blockade on Berlin, which itself had been divided into separate occupation zones among the four powers. (See Map 1.1.) By sealing off Berlin he hoped not just to oust his former allies from that divided city but to create a rift among the Western powers that would derail their unification plans. When an American airlift nullified his blockade, Stalin abandoned crude pressure in May 1949 in favor of a return to negotiations. As the United States moved toward the creation of NATO and sponsored West German membership, he countered with his own proposal for a united but demilitarized Germany—but to no avail. He would have to settle for an East German state (the German Democatic Republic) under his sway. Like Europe as a whole, Germany was now split. As Germany's old capital and leading city, Berlin remained divided, a flashpoint of Cold War tensions and a playground for spies.

The Nuclear Arms Race Accelerates

These mounting tensions over Europe had broad consequences. One was a sharp boost to Soviet and American military spending. Congress raised the military budget by a third in 1948, and Stalin seems to have raised his arms expenditures either that same year or shortly thereafter. Military spending quickly became a heavy burden on a Soviet economy that was smaller than the American and still struggling to recover from wartime destruction. By 1950, according to one recent estimate, a quarter of Soviet national income was going to military and police forces and the bureaucracies in charge of aviation, shipbuilding, and atomic weapons. The United States made the next major move. In April 1950 an alarmist and influential Truman administration policy review known as National Security Council study 68 (NSC 68) called for tripling the defense budget. The call was prompted by the 1949 Soviet atomic bomb test (breaking the U.S. nuclear monopoly) and the victory of Communist forces in China. Reflecting Washington's alarm, NSC 68 warned, "The assault on free institutions is world-wide now, and in the context of the present polarization of power a defeat of free institutions anywhere is a defeat everywhere." Truman formally endorsed the study's dire findings but not the higher taxes needed to pay for global containment until the outbreak of war in Korea in June overcame public and congressional resistance.

The other consequence of the European standoff was to accelerate nuclear weapons research and production. With arms control dead, the Cold War very much alive, and the military budget tight, nuclear weapons assumed an important place in the U.S. arsenal. Totaling no more than twenty-nine in July 1947, the number of warheads had grown to fifty by late spring 1948. Without the funds to build up a conventional force that could stop the Soviets in western Europe, the Mediterranean, the Middle East, or Northeast Asia, the U.S. military planners developed plans for an atomic air offensive designed to "kill a nation" by destroying its industries and urban centers. Some in the military were skeptical about the nuclear panacea. They predicted that a campaign of atomic bombing would destroy only about one-third of Soviet industrial capacity while arousing popular patriotism in Russia. American conventional forces would still face the difficult task of recovering the territory of western Europe, which the Red Army would have easily seized during the opening months of any war. Despite these inadequacies of a nuclear strategy, there were no military alternatives that would work within the budget limits Truman had imposed. And so in the spring of 1949 Truman formally accepted atomic bombs as the principal weapon against the USSR.

These American strategic calculations suffered a major blow in 1949 when the Soviet Union tested its first nuclear device. Responding to Stalin's mandate, Soviet scientists had worked furiously in their own isolated research centers, determined to show that their country's science was up to world-class standards and to safeguard their country's security. One recalled, "The feeling of defenselessness increased particularly after Hiroshima and Nagasaki. For all who realized the realities of the new atomic era, the creation of our own atomic weapons, the restoration of equilibrium became a categorical imperative." When a twenty-kiloton nuclear device exploded on the steppes of Kazakhstan on August 29, 1949, one project scientist described what was becoming a familiar scene on the planet's surface: "The fireball, rising and revolving, turned orange, red. Then dark streaks appeared. Streams of dust, fragments of brick and board were drawn in after it, as into a funnel." After a time the shock wave "reached us like the roar of an avalanche." The Soviet team had produced the bomb in four years of all-out effort—about the same time taken by the Manhattan Project.[16]

The successful Soviet test surprised U.S. policymakers, alarmed the public, and pushed the president to order accelerated production to cover a longer list of Soviet targets. Some American scientists argued for developing a new, far more powerful weapon, the hydrogen bomb. Although some scientific advisers, including J. Robert Oppenheimer, warned that a hydrogen weapon would prove so powerful that it could become an instrument of genocide, the public and most political leaders favored forging ahead on the new weapon. In January 1950 Truman approved the H-bomb development project after only seven minutes of discussion with his advisers and without having read their recommendations. He had once more shown that he was tough and decisive.

In November 1952 the U.S. H-bomb proved itself, producing an explosion over seven hundred times more powerful than the Hiroshima blast. The following August the Soviets tested their own H-bomb. In the decades ahead the Soviet and American arsenals would not only grow rapidly in numbers of nuclear warheads but also improve dramatically in sophistication. The technological imperative to develop, manufacture, and deploy whatever new devices scientists dangled before policymakers would continue to govern. Its logic was irresistible to Soviet no less than American leaders: New technology might provide an edge over the enemy, and if one side hesitated, then the other might acquire the new weapon first, thereby gaining a significant, perhaps decisive, advantage. This nuclear arms race not only raised the risk of devastation for both sides but also exacerbated mounting tensions between the superpowers, who were anxiously eyeing each other across a divided Europe.

Opening a Front in the Third World

Despite the tensions generated by the nuclear buildup and deepening Soviet and American suspicions of each other, the superpowers settled into an acceptance of the political division of Europe. Neither was prepared to go to war to improve its position there. Thus increasingly each side looked elsewhere for opportunities to press its advantage and weaken its rival. Most of the contested sites were strategically peripheral to both powers. Yet neither was prepared to duck a challenge or accept losses that might create the impression that the tide of history was running the other way.

The U.S. concern with the periphery was already apparent as World War II came to an end. While the U.S. military built a global system of bases, it also controlled Japan, which increasingly figured as a strong point in the effort to contain the Soviet Union along its Asian borders. (Chapter 2 contains an account of Japan's occupation and recovery.) The list of U.S. commitments along the periphery lengthened considerably during the late 1940s and the 1950s as Washington moved to shore up the long containment line stretching around the Soviet Union and China and to forestall a communist leap over that line into Latin America, the Middle East, or Africa.

U.S. policymakers engaged in the battle against communism worried deeply about the third world, especially when the currents of change ran strong— toward ending foreign control, promoting democracy and social justice at home, and reducing great-power domination of the international system. Washington reacted in a time-honored and distinctly paternalistic way to the prospect that apparently "immature" third-world peoples would mishandle their affairs, creating not only instability but also an irresistible opportunity for Soviet intrigue. George Kennan, the intellectual father of containment, reported after touring Latin America in 1950 that he was unable to imagine "a more unhappy and hopeless background for the conduct of human life" than he found in those "confused and unhappy societies." The American ambassador to Egypt surveyed the Middle East in 1954 and concluded that the United States "must to a certain extent adopt the attitude of an intelligent parent faced with a 'problem child.'" To get the child to accept guidance, he warned, would require parental "circumspection and finesse." To counter communist penetration in the contested third world, policymakers sought to find nationalists and democrats with whom they could work to block Soviet influence. But when effective centrists could not be found, Washington did not hesitate to make allies of military and other authoritarian regimes.[17]

In pursuing its interests in the third world, Washington worked with three basic tools. It could offer military and economic aid (to total $175 billion between the inception of the Cold War and the late 1970s). At particularly imperiled points Washington could also raise the ante by concluding defense agreements. In fact, one wit described Washington's frenzy of treaty signing during the early Cold War as "pactomania." Where the lure of American aid or the promise of U.S. military backing was not enough to keep third-world countries in the free-world camp, Washington resorted to a third option: CIA-sponsored

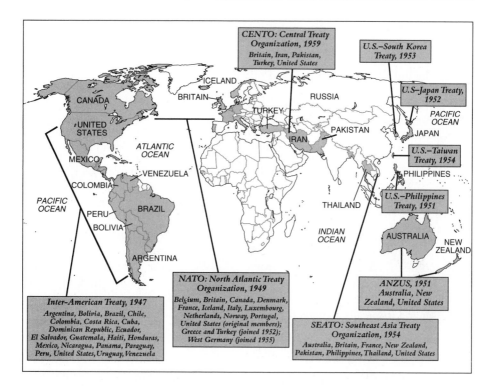

MAP 1.2
"Pactomania": U.S. Cold War Alliances around the World, 1947–1959
NATO, concluded in 1949, was the most important but only one part of a far-flung U.S. system of alliances that served to encircle the Soviet bloc. These military agreements began by covering Latin America (Inter-America Treaty of 1947) even before the conclusion of NATO. The western Pacific took center stage during the early 1950s (separate treaties with Japan in 1951, Australia and New Zealand in 1951, South Korea in 1953, and Taiwan in 1954). In 1954 Southeast Asia became part of the alliance network (Southeast Asia Treaty Organization, or SEATO). Finally, in 1959 the Middle East fell into place (Central Treaty Organization, or CENTO). With these alliances went the grant of bases for U.S. forces and the dispatch of new equipment and advisory groups to train host-country forces and coordinate planning.

covert operations. The most notable of these were directed against regimes that resisted taking sides in the Cold War (for example, the Iranian government, overthrown in 1953) and against leftist governments moving toward the Soviet side (for example, the Guatemala government, toppled in 1954, or Fidel Castro's Cuba, made a target in 1960). (All three of these cases are treated in Chapter 6.)

The Soviet Union also looked to the third world, albeit cautiously as long as Stalin lived. He wanted to avoid provoking the United States into a costly military collision. He wanted to concentrate on building up the USSR and let the contradictions mounting within the capitalist camp intensify. A crisis between the blocs might retard the developing divisions among the capitalist powers.

Moreover, he distrusted Communist leaders such as Mao Zedong in China and Ho Chi Minh in Vietnam who had won power on their own and whose nationalist impulses made them less responsive to Soviet direction. Reflecting his doubts, he did not include these and other non-European Communist parties in the Cominform.

Even so, Stalin did make some important contributions of his own to a globalized Cold War in the volatile East Asian region. Although he had consistently doubted the capacity of the Chinese Communists to win power, he did begin funneling small amounts of aid to them after they launched a major military campaign from their stronghold in China's northeastern provinces in 1946. The victory of the Chinese Communists in 1949 and their establishment that same year of a People's Republic of China prompted Stalin to send more advisers and aid. In early 1950 Stalin received Mao in Moscow, where they concluded an alliance. At the same time Stalin granted diplomatic recognition to Ho Chi Minh's revolutionary movement (the Viet Minh) fighting the French in Vietnam, and he urged the Chinese to provide the Vietnamese assistance. (See Chapter 3 for a fuller account of the first stages of the revolution in China and Vietnam.) In a divided Korea, Stalin exercised the most influence of anywhere in East Asia and ironically managed there to lose control of events.

Limited War in Korea

The crisis that hit Korea in 1950 made it the scene of the first of the Cold War's limited wars. That crisis was rooted in events of 1945. Having liberated the country from Japanese colonial control, the representatives of the Soviet Union and the United States were suddenly confronted with the question of Korea's future. Ultimately, they agreed on a temporary division along the 38th parallel, with Soviet troops in control north of that line and U.S. forces to the south. For nationalist Korean leaders, the defeat of Japan meant something quite different— not foreign military occupation, but the end of Japanese rule on the peninsula going back to 1910 and the prospect of full independence. One of those nationalists was Syngman Rhee. He had been educated by Christian missionaries in Korea, and later as a nationalist in exile he had looked to the United States as Korea's patron. In 1945 the seventy-year-old Rhee finally came home behind the arriving U.S. military. Rhee's political nemesis, Kim Il Sung, came from the other end of the Korean nationalist spectrum. As a relatively junior member of the Korean Communist Party, he had commanded guerrillas across the Korean border in China and then served during World War II in the Soviet army. He was only thirty-three years old when he returned home with the Soviet forces.

The provisional dividing line gradually hardened between 1945 and 1948, thanks to growing international tensions between the two dominant powers on the peninsula. Kim consolidated his authority in the north with the backing of the Soviet occupation authorities. Preoccupied with national unity, he sought Stalin's support for a military initiative against the South. Stalin was not at first interested in a confrontation. He cautioned Kim, "The Americans will never agree to be thrown out of there and because of that, to lose their reputation as a

MAP 1.3
Northeast Asia in the Wake of World War II

great power. The Soviet people would not understand the necessity of a war in Korea, which is a remote place outside the sphere of the USSR's vital interests."[18] On the other side Rhee took control, abetted by the American military governor, who feared losing the South to Moscow. Like Kim, Rhee was keen on reunification by force if necessary. But Truman was equally cool to his client's military schemes.

The situation changed dramatically in the course of 1950. Stalin made a fateful shift in January—about the same time as he allied with Mao and offered diplomatic backing to Ho. The previously skeptical Soviet leader agreed to back an invasion, persuaded by Kim's argument that North Korean forces could quickly seize the South without provoking the United States into sending in its own troops. The American-created regime looked weak, and the Truman administration had indicated publicly that it lacked the forces to defend this strategically marginal area. Kim and Stalin interpreted Washington's reluctance to take a strong stand on Korea's defense as a green light.

The stage was now set for the first major superpower crisis in the third world. With the guarded blessings of Stalin as well as Mao and reinforced by Soviet arms and Korean forces that had fought with the Chinese Communists, Kim attacked in late June, driving deep into South Korea. Truman took the attack as a classic case of aggression that spoke directly to the historical lessons his generation had just painfully learned. He recalled "how each time that the democracies failed to act it had encouraged the aggressors to keep going ahead. Communism was acting in Korea just as Hitler, Mussolini, and the Japanese had acted." Truman and his advisers were also influenced by growing alarm over the first Soviet atomic test and the loss of China to Communist forces. The aroused president blustered, "By God[,] I'm going to let them have it."[19]

Now galvanized, Truman swung into action. He ordered U.S. forces deployed from Japan to Korea to resist the invasion. He told his advisors to make preparations for an atomic strike on the Soviet Union in case it were to enter the conflict. He expanded the CIA's overseas operations. And he set about raising the defense budget (as recommended in April by NSC 68)—from $15.5 billion in August to $42 billion by December. By the end of 1951 annual military spending had reached almost $70 billion. Truman did not seek a congressional declaration of war, calling the commitment in Korea a "police action." He did, however, move quickly to secure UN backing. By 1950 Truman had turned the United Nations into an instrument of U.S. Cold War policy. As a result of U.S. dominance, the Soviet Union was regularly exercising its veto power on the Security Council. However, when the Korean War erupted, the Soviets were boycotting its proceedings in protest over the refusal to admit to membership the new Communist government in China. The UN command would be led and financed by Washington.

The June surprises by Kim and then Truman were followed by a Chinese surprise in the fall. Beijing watched anxiously as the UN commander, U.S. general Douglas MacArthur, reversed the tide of battle late in the summer and began a march northward to unify Korea by force. With their Korean adventure turning into a disaster, Stalin and Kim now appealed to Mao to bail them out. After some hesitation, Mao resolved to stop the Americans, who were rapidly advancing toward the Yalu River and Chinese territory. The sudden appearance of Chinese forces once more reversed the fortunes of war, driving stunned UN forces southward. An equally stunned Truman spoke publicly of using atomic weapons, and he declared a national state of emergency.

Once begun, the Korean War was not easily ended even though by spring 1951 the battle lines had stabilized not far from the 38th parallel. Peace talks, begun in July 1951, bogged down, and Truman faced public discontent with this stalemated war and Republican attacks on his no-win strategy. Frustrated, he repeatedly entertained proposals for expanding the scope of the war or bringing nuclear weapons into play. But caution prevailed on both sides, and finally

THE SUPERPOWER RIVALRY INTENSIFIES AND SPREADS	
1948	**On the Soviet side:** Stalin tightens grip on eastern Europe, beginning with coup in Czechoslovakia, and cuts off West Berlin to halt the formation of a West German state; Tito-Stalin split drives Yugoslavia from the Soviet orbit
	On the U.S. side: Congress approves Marshall Plan; North Atlantic Treaty Organization (NATO) formed; Inter-America treaty concluded as first of regional tools of U.S. Cold War policy
1949	Soviet Union imposes Council for Mutual Economic Assistance on European clients, ends Berlin blockade, and tests its first A-bomb; Communists win in China
1950	Stalin and Mao conclude alliance; NSC 68 calls for tripling U.S. military budget; Korean War begins; U.S. and then Chinese forces intervene in Korean conflict
1952	The United States tests first hydrogen bombs (followed by USSR less than a year later)

in mid–1953 an armistice brought the fighting to a halt. The war had in the meantime devastated the Korean peninsula and resulted in the deaths of some four million Koreans (combatants and civilians from both sides) along with some 380,000 Chinese soldiers. Korea would remain divided, each side deeply hostile toward the other. The autocratic Rhee would survive in power until 1960. Kim outlasted him, retaining power until his death in 1994 and making his son Kim Jong Il his successor.

The Korean War is sometimes seen as a watershed in the development of the Cold War. An alternative, more compelling view is that the conflict served to accelerate trends already gaining impetus. In general, lines already hardening in 1948 and 1949 grew harder. Suspicions of the enemy mounting since 1945 and fears of traitors within reached phobic proportions in the Soviet Union, the United States, and China. Beijing and Moscow grew closer. Mao consolidated his party's control in China. Washington, for its part, decided to expand its commitments in Asia (notably in the Philippines and Vietnam) and other parts of the third world and to further toughen its policy toward China. The war also convinced U.S. leaders to elevate even higher Japan's geopolitical importance and to give even more attention to rearmament in Europe.

SUPERPOWER SOCIETIES IN AN UNQUIET TIME

Wars have a major impact on the societies that fight them. The Cold War was no exception. From the start of the Soviet-American rivalry, leaders in both countries asked fresh sacrifices of their citizens in the name of national security and international prestige. Those sacrifices can be measured in material terms— investments made on defense and foreign aid that could have gone to the civilian sector. But they can also be measured in terms of the ideological chill both countries experienced. The boundaries of political tolerance narrowed as em-battled officials settled into a knee-jerk defense of the domestic status quo while keeping vigilant watch for enemies within.

Domestic mobilization meant different things for the Soviet Union and the United States. For the Soviets, the Cold War hindered recovery from wartime destruction as military spending in the late 1940s took more and more out of an economy never geared to civilian production and considerably smaller than that of the United States. The Cold War also gave Stalin an excuse for denying the hopes entertained by many that the postwar period would bring a political and cultural thaw. Americans entered the postwar with similar hopes for an end to tensions, and the Cold War brought instead for them too a renewal of military preparations and repression in the face of a global threat so powerful that it seemed to have even subverted elements of American society. For U.S. citizens, however, the sacrifices associated with the Cold War were softened by the vital-ity of the American economy. Its quick conversion back to civilian production and rapid growth made possible alongside an ambitious military program the abundant output on which revived consumer expectations depended. Ameri-cans, unlike Soviet citizens, could have both "guns and butter"—that is, sustain a major military effort while also enjoying domestic abundance. (See Chapters 2 and 5 for treatment of the good times that the postwar years would bring for an increasing number of Americans.)

Soviet Society under Stress

Postwar Soviet society was in large measure a prewar creation that bears the name of its principal architect, Joseph Stalin. Whereas Vladimir Lenin fomented the Bolshevik revolution and consolidated it before his death in 1924, it was Stalin who gave the Soviet domestic system its shape. "Stalinism" is the label applied by foreign observers and by Russians after Stalin's lifetime to describe what Stalin and his lieutenants created as they went about "building socialism."

The collapse of socialism in the Soviet Union as well as in its European satel-lites between 1989 and 1991 makes it tempting to dismiss Stalinism as a bankrupt experiment run by immoral men fully deserving the harsh verdict commonly laid on them abroad and even in their own countries. But any sweeping con-demnation obscures two important historical points. First, Stalin should be seen in the context of a recurrent modernizing impulse in Russian history. Like his predecessors, he followed a pattern of forced, often brutal, state-guided modern-ization, first evident with Czar Peter the Great in the 1680s and reappearing in the nineteenth and early twentieth centuries as the imperial government eman-cipated the serfs and spurred industrialization. The goal was to bring the country to the front ranks of the great Western powers by creating an advanced military, acquiring cutting-edge technology, achieving high levels of literacy, and develop-ing a base of heavy industry and efficient communications and transport systems. Second, Communist leaders were not moved by simple malevolence but rather by the faith that a new, highly centralized system could transform Russia into a superpower as well as create a better life for many under Soviet sway.

The Stalinist System. It is impossible to understand postwar Soviet society without understanding the contours that the Stalinist system had already assumed in the 1930s. When the Bolsheviks took power in 1917, Russia's social and economic circumstances were closer to the third world than a modern great power. This depressing condition and the determination to change it make it easier to understand the mixture of hope, envy, hatred, and fear that drove Stalinism. Its proponents entertained a utopian vision of an essentially peasant Russian society overcoming its backwardness and catching up with the West. They would catapult their country into a new age of enlightenment and development. In this leap they imagined the forces of history and the sympathy of most ordinary peoples around the world on their side. Arrayed against them were powerful capitalists eager to frustrate Soviet ambitions and destroy the Soviet experiment. Faced by the capitalist West's campaign of encirclement, the Soviet Union had a simple choice, Stalin is supposed to have observed in 1931: Either catch up in industrial capacity in ten years, or be crushed by stronger powers to the west. At home the regime imagined another menace—resistance from the remnants of the old order. These included nationalist groups hostile to central control, class enemies in hiding, spies, intellectuals promoting reactionary ideas, peasants wedded to their land, and ideologically tainted party members.

Stalin pursued his ambitious program through a powerful, party-controlled state apparatus. It was totalitarian in the sense that it was supposed to be able to shape every facet of Soviet life. A large centralized bureaucracy was indispensable to running an all-encompassing command economy in which the state owned farm and factory, staffed leading administrative positions, and elaborately planned production. Putting the state in charge and having one coherent vision seemed the only way to make the most of limited resources. In December 1929 the senior party planner articulated the widely shared vision of a great united economic effort: "We need to organise a social and political mechanism with which 150 million people will act, guided by a single plan, a single concept, a single will, a single effort to accomplish what is laid down by the plan."[20] Maintaining popular enthusiasm and imposing popular sacrifice was accordingly a critical state function. That state was also to have the task of social engineering, expunging objectionable traces of the old society and nurturing socialist values throughout a vast and varied population. Directing the arts, the media, and science along approved lines thus became a central concern of the Soviet state. Finally, the state had to keep the Bolshevik experiment safe by repressing internal class enemies. Although in Marxist theory the socialist era was ultimately to bring the withering away of the state, in point of fact the opposite tendency was evident during Stalin's time and thereafter.

The Stalinist program left an enduring mark in three critical areas of Soviet life. First, it dramatically expanded and controlled the industrial sector. Stalin pressed between 1928 and 1939 (through two five-year economic plans) for the rapid buildup of Soviet industry and succeeded in making the USSR a major industrial economy. Stalin's program was also of lasting importance for driving the peasantry into collectivized agriculture. The Communists were determined to end private land holdings and bring agricultural production under state control and at the same time transform the rural sector from backward, small-scale farming into an efficient, modern, large-scale enterprise. This factory system in the countryside was in effect to remake the peasantry into a rural proletariat, while at the same make it possible for Soviet economic planners to extract from agriculture the resources essential to building industry.

Second, Stalin launched agricultural collectivization in 1929–1930. When some of the 100 million targeted peasants resisted, he struck back in brutal fashion—especially against prosperous peasants (*kulaks*), whom he regarded as a dangerous capitalist influence in the countryside. Millions were expropriated and deported. The disruption that attended collectivization resulted in food shortages in 1932–1933 that created urban hardship and rural starvation. But Stalin had his way. By the end of the 1930s the collective system covered most of the countryside. On most collectives (*kolkhozy*) peasant-workers received a share of whatever production was left over after meeting all state requirements. They retained only a small private plot and some livestock. (The exception was the state-run collectives, where peasants gave up all land and received a wage in return for their work.)

In the economic sphere—in both industry and agriculture—what in theory looked efficient and rational proved in practice not so. Central bureaucrats exercised imperfect control over a vast landmass. Their plans imposed high costs not just in lives but also in terms of industrial pollution, social disruption, and popular alienation. And planners themselves were hostage to the vagaries of the top leadership, as today's plan might be arbitrarily modified by tomorrow's order. Below them were a sullen peasantry and a lethargic industrial workforce, both ingenious at finding ways to frustrate the stream of directives calling for ever-higher output.

The third major feature of Stalin's program was a strong domestic security force, a succession of agencies best known by their initials (GPU, OGPU, NKVD, and KGB). Their target was broadly defined to include any anti-Soviet ideas or actions. The security apparatus made arrests without legal restraints and either executed class enemies or dispatched them to brutal labor camps, where many died. At the local level the process of purging often got out of control of central authorities as ambitious subordinates denounced their superiors or vengeful rivals evened old scores. The "liquidation of the kulaks" was the first broad-scale "cleansing" operation. Throughout the 1930s Stalin's suspicions fell on other suspected counter-revolutionaries—in the party, in the army, and among intellectuals. These purges reached their peak between 1936 and 1938 and included party leaders Sergei Kirov (assassinated in 1934) and Nikolai Bukharin (put on trial and executed in 1938). One credible estimate of those arrested as enemies of the Soviet state in the Stalin years (1929–1953) is about 20 million people, though that figure may well prove too high.

Socially, the Stalinist system generated an entrenched, privileged class. This group, known as the *nomenklatura,* consisted of those members of the Communist Party appointed to posts at the top of the party and state bureaucracy as well as the military. They lived above the mass of the population and were attached to the status quo in a way that would in time make them allergic to economic or political reform. The *nomenklatura* enjoyed special access to housing, education, medical care, food, and other consumer goods. They used their power over economic resources to benefit clients and family members.

Postwar Soviet Recovery. In its last years Stalin's rule was conservative socially as well as politically. After the upheaval of the war, many in the Soviet Union longed for an end to heroic exertion and personal sacrifice. But the postwar period brought hardly any relaxation of tensions and certainly no alteration of the system. The new five-year plan, prepared in fall 1945 and announced by Stalin in February 1946, continued the emphasis on heavy industry. Soon the rising military budget was claiming a substantial hunk of the economic output. The hunger for consumer goods would have to wait.

The domestic security forces remained vigilant. They packed returning prisoners of war off to labor camps on suspicion of collaboration with the Germans, while "pacifying" the westernmost part of the Soviet Union (especially recently annexed parts of Ukraine) where anti-Soviet groups had formed during the war and remained a threat into 1948. By 1950 labor camps contained 2.8 million

Russia in Ruins
This is one of many scenes of destruction that awaited civilians and soldiers returning home at war's end. The fighting had engulfed territory where nearly half of the Soviet population had lived. (Sovfoto/ Eastfoto)

prisoners, incarcerated for all types of "crimes." Stalin insisted on ideological conformity, not just in politics but also in literature, science, and the social sciences—with himself the ultimate arbiter. The ideological vise tightened as the Cold War took shape and as official campaigns took aim at elements within Soviet society supposedly infected by decadent Anglo-American values.

Most people in the Soviet Union experienced the first few years of peace as a time nearly as trying as war. In cities through which the German army had swept, many homes and factories had been reduced to rubble and public facilities destroyed. With housing in short supply, some lived in dugouts or in the open air throughout the bitterly cold winter. Basic goods such as food, clothes, and shoes were all scarce. Soldiers returning home were shocked by the conditions, and some two million invalid veterans found only limited care waiting for them. The streets were filled with beggars and with vagabond youth orphaned or otherwise cut loose from family. Crime became rampant, with bands robbing and killing with seeming impunity.

The low point came during 1946–1947 when drought combined with the lingering effects of wartime disruptions to produce the lowest harvest in a century. The ensuing famine caused some two million deaths from malnutrition between 1946 and 1948. Loud complaints could be heard on the street about food aid rumored to be going to France as well as to eastern Europe. One citizen angrily observed, "We feed the bourgeois while we ourselves starve."[21] As hunger worsened, the discontented looked to Stalin to save them. After all, they reasoned, as the good ruler he could not wish his people ill. The popular plight must be the fault of corrupt and incompetent officials who were conspiring to keep Stalin in the dark.

Recovery finally came in 1948. By then industrial production had regained prewar levels, the demobilization of the armed forces had been completed, and the wartime rationing system had ended. Even so, conditions remained difficult. Occasional rumors of war with the West ignited panic buying, quickly stripping the shelves of provisions. Discontent festered within groups ill-treated during the war, including minorities deported from their homelands and workers assigned to distant factories. Perhaps most ominous for the long term was the discontent among pockets of urban youth who had been swept up in the war. In informal discussions they focused on the gap between party propaganda and the reality of peacetime hunger and other kinds of deprivation and questioned whether the party had turned exploitative.

A powerful, pervasive Stalin cult steered such subversive musings away from the leader. The Communist Party's central bureaucracy promoted and monitored the cult, while the popular media dutifully celebrated Stalin as a poor man from a backwater region who had proven himself a friend of Lenin and a hero during the revolution and civil war. Following Lenin's death, he had assumed the role of the fearless, all-knowing leader who had industrialized the country, looked after the welfare of its hardworking, ordinary people, beaten back the German invader, and won international respect. The cult made Stalin into a demi-god in the eyes of many, even those whose families had felt the sting of loss from war or purges. The news of Stalin's death on March 6, 1953, plunged the Soviet Union into shock and mourning. The outpouring of grief revealed how deeply the cult had taken hold. "What will become of us now[?]" people asked as crowds pressed forward to pay respects to the embalmed body lying in state.[22] In the press of tearful mourners, some were literally crushed to death.

Peasants, Workers, and Intellectuals. Of all those experiencing hardship and discontent in the postwar period, the rural majority—some 100 million people, comprising 60 percent of the population in 1945—led the way. Country folk lived in poor backwaters, frightened by change and waiting for higher-ups to resolve the problems of their hopelessly inefficient system of agriculture. The collectives, the product of Stalin's drive to remake the countryside, were as unpopular as ever after the war. Meanwhile, Moscow continued to make such heavy demands on the collectives that rural people were virtually working for the state without pay. Resentment focused on the heads of the collectives, who had to meet assigned quotas and who sometimes ran the collective like a private fiefdom. One demoralized peasant woman complained in mid-1946, "We work on the collective farm as we used to work for the landlords in the days of serfdom. They drive us to work, and they neither feed nor pay us."[23] Villagers responded as they had in the past by investing more time on their own small private plots and trying to expand private holdings at the expense of the collective.

Compounding the quiet crisis in the countryside was a sharp decline in numbers of able-bodied males available for agricultural work resulting from wartime levies and casualties and flight from rural hardship by those with education and initiative. And the number continued to decline under the lure of better living conditions in the cities. With only one man left in the villages after the war for every three women, women were left to bear the brunt of care for children, the infirm, and the elderly as well as meet state-imposed production quotas and wring a subsistence from their own private plots. The famine of 1946–1947 added to their burden by draining foodstuffs to feed the cities. One woman appealed from the countryside, "Our children are living like animals—constantly angry and hungry."[24]

Discontent and alienation also persisted among the industrial workforce. In theory, the working class was the group in whose name the Bolshevik party functioned. But in practice, Stalin's effort in the 1930s to harness the workforce to his ambitious industrialization plans had strained the relationship. Managers sharply limited the autonomy that workers had carved out for themselves in previous decades on the factory floors of Russia's nascent industries. In expressing their resentments workers learned to "speak Bolshevik," turning the political rhetoric of their bosses back on them. Workers regarded managers and specialists above them as a new exploiting class who lived a markedly better life thanks to the toil of the common man. They complained of incompetence, speculation, and privilege of these higher-ups and responded by "liberating" collective goods under their control for sale or personal use. They resented the boring meetings with their empty slogans. "A lot of chatter and little business. I go to the meetings, but the waste of time makes me angry," fumed one worker.[25]

Despite their discontents, workers generally fared better than peasants. Material conditions were superior in urban areas, and the shortage of labor gave workers the option of leaving for a better post elsewhere. A manager who lost workers would have a hard time meeting quotas assigned by the economic authorities above him. In the resulting accommodation, management avoided punishing such forms of worker indiscipline as drunkenness and absenteeism and tended to tolerate low productivity. This pact built lasting inefficiencies into the system of production. Defective products and inefficient use of raw materials and fuel would permanently plague Soviet industry.

The educated were the smallest but also the most closely monitored part of the population. In a society that Stalin thought should run like a machine, writers, painters, teachers, and scientists had a critical long-term influence as (in his words) "engineers of human souls." Their work would create the new socialist man. Some intellectuals gladly embraced the role, for example, by publicly celebrating Stalin as an all-knowing and inspiring leader. He was everywhere watching and evaluating the work his people did. As one poet expressed it, "You work badly—his brows lower / But when good, he smiles in his moustache."[26]

But to an impressive degree, intellectuals and artists proved stubbornly independent and outspoken even as Stalin cowed workers and peasants into submission. After the repression of the 1930s, the war brought more tolerant times in which patriotic unity displaced class suspicion. Many loyal intellectuals—from scientists to philosophers to economists to artists—hoped for liberalization in the postwar period. A more open, creative atmosphere would allow the country to deal with past mistakes, especially persistent economic problems. The rigidly conservative atmosphere in Stalin's last years would, however, disappoint them, while the campaign from 1947 onward against "worshipping foreign cultures" and "kowtowing before the West" would intimidate scientists, philosophers, and others with professional links to the outside world.

Composer Dmitri Shostakovich illustrates the perseverance of the intellectual class in the face of official pressure and blasted hopes for a humane revolutionary path. He had gotten into trouble in 1937 for music that Stalin and the cultural commissars thought too "complex" and "dark." At the same time, a purge in Leningrad was proceeding at full tilt against friends and colleagues, while his patron in Moscow (a senior army general) had just been executed on espionage charges. Shostakovich still found a way in his next composition—his famous, brooding fifth symphony—to communicate what he and his audience of Leningraders felt but could not openly express: their grief for relatives and friends lost in the purges, the fear for their own lives, the resentment at the pompous, domineering leader who controlled their destiny, and the failure of a revolutionary ideal. By the third, slow movement of the symphony many in the audience were in tears. The standing ovation at the end lasted over forty minutes, longer than the musical performance itself. Shostakovich got away with this piece of surreptitious resistance and survived to become one of the stars in Stalin's cultural firmament during the war and beyond. Before his death in 1975, he was finally able to talk openly about how much his music stood as

THE STALIN ERA

1924	Lenin's death
1929	Stalin consolidates grip on power, presses industrialization, and collectivizes agriculture
1935–1939	Stalin purges party, military, and intellectual elites
1939	USSR signs nonaggression pact with Germany, dividing Poland between them
1941	Germany launches surprise attack on the Soviet Union, providing basis for alliance with United States and Britain
1943	Battle of Stalingrad marks the turning point of war against Germany
1945	Red Army marches into eastern Germany
1946	Stalin's reconstruction plan emphasizes heavy industry
1946–1947	Massive famine in war-torn areas results in two million deaths
1947	Cominform is organized to strengthen Soviet control over European Communist parties; Stalin begins crackdown in eastern Europe
1948	Soviet economy regains prewar levels
1953	Stalin's death

"tombstones" to those lost to political oppression. "Too many of our people died and were buried in places unknown to anyone, not even their relatives. It happened to many of my friends." He added, "I think constantly of those people, and in almost every major work I try to remind others of them."[27]

Stalin's domestic program left a mixed legacy. Its most notable achievement is tied to the two five-year plans (1929–1939) that built industry, promoted urbanization, and created a better-educated society. This rapid, state-directed economic and social development transformed a "backward," peasant society into a modern one in which many enjoyed a better, longer life and greater geographical and social mobility. That economic transformation had also made possible Soviet successes in international affairs after 1939—the defeat of the German invaders, the extension of control into eastern Europe, the sponsorship of junior partners in Asia (China, North Korea, and Vietnam), and the rise to the status of a superpower rival to the United States. Stalin's critics, on the other hand, recoiled from the terrible cost in lives and wondered if the achievements of those years required such human sacrifice. How to create a humane socialism—one that brought modernization in a less ruthless fashion—would be the central problem to confront Stalin's successors, Nikita Khrushchev (see Chapter 4) and Mikhail Gorbachev (see Chapter 7).

The U.S. Anti-Communist Consensus

While the Cold War reinforced Stalin's repressive instincts and the priority he had given to heavy industry and the military over civilian needs, in the United States rising international tensions led to fears of radicals and subversives not seen since the last Red Scare in the immediate aftermath of World War I. This growing alarm over the dangerous inroads of an alien ideology promoted by the Soviet Union had a pervasive impact on domestic society and political culture, and it created the basis for a potent anti-communist consensus at home critical to waging the Cold War abroad. But the effects of anti-communism were buffered by a popular preoccupation with enjoying the fruits of postwar prosperity (treated in Chapter 2). Anti-communism thus in some ways had to compete with consumerism and in other ways had to accommodate to it.

The Hunt for Subversives. This preoccupation with communist subversion is usually associated with the figure of Joseph McCarthy. This small-town Wisconsin lawyer had served in the Pacific during World War II and won a Senate seat as a Republican in 1946. Worried about reelection in 1952, he sought a winning issue. He found it in charges of communist subversion and Democratic Party betrayal. He jumped into the public spotlight in February 1950 when he announced that he had a long list of U.S. government officials secretly working for the USSR. His main target was a State Department "thoroughly infested with Communists" and "the bright young men [there] who are born with a silver spoon in their mouths." He called for a clean sweep of "the whole sorry mess of twisted, warped thinkers" who had reduced the United States to its current "position of impotence."[28] McCarthy's charges exploded in the press, making him the most visible pursuer of "Communists and queers" in high places. He brought to subsequent Senate hearings raw energy and a gift for the sensational.

McCarthy quickly overreached himself. President Dwight D. Eisenhower disapproved of his reckless charges and his disruptive intrusions into the affairs of the executive branch but refused to "get into the gutter with that guy."[29] Fellow senators also grew uncomfortable and launched an investigation of McCarthy's methods. In December 1954 the Senate voted to censure him. By the time of his death in 1957, McCarthy had come to epitomize a hysterical fear of communist subversion and a disposition to root out communists and communist sympathizers by means of inquisitorial congressional investigations and public accusations.

In fact, the pressures for ideological conformity unleashed by the Cold War were bigger than this one man. Fear of communism had deep roots. During the late nineteenth century, radicals in the labor movement, in immigrant communities, and elsewhere stirred fears of socialism and anarchism undermining American institutions and values. The Bolshevik revolution precipitated another eruption of fear at the end of World War I. With communist contagion seemingly spreading into Europe and threatening to infect the United States, the Wilson administration and local governments were gripped by a "Red Scare." They launched programs to eliminate "dangerous" dissenters, and universities dismissed faculty with "radical" views. The American Left revived during the

Depression and the wartime alliance with the Soviet Union. But already by the late 1930s a backlash was building. Congressional investigators began looking for subversives, and the FBI under its long-time leader, J. Edgar Hoover, targeted U.S. citizens and foreign residents thought to be in the service of the Soviet Union.

Conservatives suspicious of the Soviets and mistrustful of Roosevelt's judgment began to raise their voices as World War II drew to a close. The march of communism across Europe, along with revolutionary stirrings around the world, deepened the sense of alarm. The internal security issue had become especially attractive to Republicans after their party's frustrating loss of the 1948 presidential election. They charged "twenty years of treason" under the Democrats. The welfare and regulatory policies developed by the Roosevelt administration to fight the Depression seemed to them akin to communist ideas promoted by Moscow, and leftist inroads, they argued, had created conditions conducive to subversion now so threatening in the context of the Cold War struggle. These charges became a galvanizing issue for a wide range of organizations, including the American Legion, the Catholic Church, and conservatives within the American Federation of Labor.

The crucial development that gave resources and legitimacy—and thus great impetus—to the postwar anti-Red drive was the support of the federal government. Hoover wanted action, and he enjoyed support from his nominal boss, Truman's attorney general, who warned that communists were everywhere—"in factories, offices, butcher shops, on street corners, in private business, and each carries in himself the germs of death for society." Truman finally swung over in 1947. In late March he put into effect a loyalty program targeting communists and sympathizers within the federal government. Hoover underlined the importance of Truman's security measures by warning of the vulnerability, especially of labor and liberals, to the "virus of communism," which was a "disease that spreads like an epidemic and like an epidemic a quarantine is necessary to keep it from infecting the Nation."[30]

Truman was motivated in part by domestic political calculations. The Republicans had taken control of Congress in 1946. The 1948 presidential election found him facing opposition from former vice president Henry Wallace, running as a third-party candidate decrying the growing anti-communist hysteria and enjoying the support of the U.S. Communist Party as well as left-leaning Democrats. By taking a strong anti-communist stance, Truman could blunt the inroads of his Republican challenger, Thomas Dewey, while discrediting Wallace. His surprise election in 1948 seemed to vindicate that strategy.

But genuine alarm over foreign crises and spy revelations also moved the president as it did others. Dramatic communist gains in 1949 and 1950—the first Soviet A-bomb test, the resounding defeat of the U.S.-backed government in China, and the North Korean invasion—alarmed many Americans. A string of highly publicized spy cases further added to the atmosphere of anxiety. State Department official Alger Hiss, pursued for espionage by ambitious Republican representative Richard Nixon, was convicted in early 1950 of the lesser charge of perjury. At the same time British authorities arrested Klaus Fuchs, who had worked on the Manhattan Project, for helping Moscow acquire atomic secrets.

He in turn pointed to Julius and Ethel Rosenberg as atomic spies. They were convicted in March 1951 and later executed. The presiding judge handed down a death sentence as a warning to "traitors in our midst."[31]

Between 1947 and 1950—in parallel with the international struggle against the Soviet Union—federal efforts to deal with disloyal Americans turned into a crusade. In Congress, the Senate Internal Security Subcommittee and the House Un-American Activities Committee gained new prominence and legitimacy. Within the executive branch, Truman and his successor, Dwight D. Eisenhower, made it easier to fire government employees under suspicion. The accused could not confront their accusers and had no right to know the source of the information on which charges were based. Security measures became a prime concern of such federal agencies as the Post Office, the Internal Revenue Service, the Immigration and Naturalization Service, and the National Security Agency, each of which used its power to identify and intimidate those with tainted pasts or "un-American" views. State and local bureaucracies and office holders in turn took their cue from federal actions.

Dissenters Silenced. At the center of the anti-communist bull's eye was the U.S. Communist Party with its forty to fifty thousand members. It had channeled the bulk of its energy into the union cause, civil rights, and peace rallies in the face of what it charged was an increasingly expansionist U.S. foreign policy. As if these positions did not give its enemies enough ammunition, the party also operated in a secretive fashion with no real internal democracy and with close but veiled links to the Soviet Union. The Red hunters got the party leaders arrested in July 1948 for conspiring to overthrow the U.S. government. In 1951 the Supreme Court upheld their conviction by a 6–2 vote. By then the party was well on its way to collapse. Legal battles exhausted its treasury and its leadership while media attacks and administrative harassment beat down the rank and file.

The political chill produced by this anti-communist campaign proved far-reaching. Businesses fired employees suspected of radical sympathies. Hollywood blacklisted those who did not cooperate with congressional investigators. Left-wing unions fell under suspicion and either capitulated or collapsed, while universities expelled suspected communists from their faculties. African American leaders split between those such as the writer W. E. B. Du Bois and the singer and actor Paul Robeson, who were opposed to letting anti-communism dominate the black agenda, and those such as Walter White of the old-line National Association for the Advancement of Colored People (NAACP), who reasoned that embracing the Cold War crusade would help blacks gain freedom and that, in any case, defiance would cost civil rights popular support. Dissent became dangerous in the press, and when academics or journalists appealed their right to freedom of speech, the courts generally sidestepped the issue, giving "national security" precedence over constitutionally protected civil liberties. Those merely accused of communist beliefs and associations often had their lives shattered. They faced the overwhelming costs of defending themselves; they lost their jobs and were entered on blacklists; their privacy was destroyed; and their good names were impugned without means of redress.

The figures on those affected can only be approximated. The government internal security probes between 1947 and 1956 prompted some 12,000 simply to resign rather than engage in a costly fight without access to the evidence against them. Some 2,700 fought and then suffered formal dismissal. Jobs lost outside government—for example, in corporations, foundations, and schools—are hard to estimate with any accuracy. Many were caught in the net of guilt by association when organizations to which they belonged appeared on the attorney general's list of 197 subversive organizations.

Some examples give a sense of the broad impact. Despite his accomplishments on the atomic bomb project, J. Robert Oppenheimer had his security clearance revoked in 1954 on the basis of his prewar left-wing political associations and his decision to protect a friend who had approached him in 1943 on behalf of the Soviet Union. Owen Lattimore, an accomplished and outspoken authority on China at Johns Hopkins University, fell afoul of Republican investigators determined to cast him as the "architect" of a U.S. policy designed to help the Communists to victory in China. A perjury conviction in 1952 quickly fell apart, but Lattimore's professional reputation was so damaged that he moved to England. The State Department revoked both Du Bois' and Robeson's passports so that they could no longer speak or perform abroad, and both men became self-imposed exiles. A postal clerk faced charges in 1954 that included having communist literature and art in his home. He explained that the literature was from a college course and that the art included works by Picasso and Renoir. He sought without avail to see the sources on which the charges were based. The Civil Service Commission ended a year of appeals by making the dismissal definitive.

The Legacy of the Anti-Communist Crusade. The effects of this anti-communist fervor were long-lasting. It convinced many Americans that their country could not deal with the global communist monolith except by eradicating the enemy within. The anti-communist campaign pushed the center of American political and intellectual life noticeably to the right, leaving the high ground to anti-communist liberals and even more anti-communist conservatives. Foreign policy specialists in the State Department and academe, above all those charged with helping to "lose China," were intimidated into silence at a time when such eminently debatable Cold War issues as intervention in Vietnam were beginning to take shape. On domestic issues as well, anti-communism was a handy stick to silence critics and hold back change. For example, campaigns to unionize factories and to dismantle the system of racial segregation in the South met charges that those involved were communists or communist dupes—and either way, un-American.

Just as policymaking was a man's domain, the battle against communism at home was couched in terms of manliness and vigor. A strong, vigilant America could resist communism's insidious inroads, McCarthy and others argued, only if the vulnerable points—the overeducated, the effeminate, the gay community, and foreign-born citizens who pretended loyalty the better to betray—were properly monitored. A tabloid reported in 1950 that "more than ninety twisted twerps in trousers had been swished out of the state department" but that "at least 6,000 homosexuals [were still] on the government payroll." In the State Department itself, George Kennan, the influential Soviet analyst, worried that American society was becoming soft and passive as the disintegration of family, local neighborhoods, and other groups left individuals adrift. He welcomed the Soviet challenge; it gave Americans a chance at "pulling themselves together and accepting the responsibilities of moral and political leadership that history plainly intended them to bear." Out of this image of the Cold War struggle came a long-lasting language of toughness that took competition with the Soviets as the yard-stick of the nation's and its leaders' virility. The language was as likely to appear in presidential addresses as in such popular media as *Reader's Digest*.[32]

This campaign to restore masculine values in public life had broad implications for gender roles in society. From the mid-1910s to the mid-1940s, the United States had gone through two wartime economic mobilizations, a bout of liberating prosperity, and a dislocating depression. The cumulative effect was to unsettle established notions of the proper place of men and women in ordinary life. Worried by the mounting threat to the stable, male-dominated nuclear family, social conservatives pounced on Cold War fears to press their case. Social stability at home no less than national security abroad, they argued, depended on men and women assuming their "traditional" roles. While strong men took responsibility outside the home and the homeland, women were supposed to turn their energies to domestic affairs. Working women were thus guilty of evading their obligations and betraying their men, confusing their children, and ultimately weakening their nation in its time of testing. For social conservatives, strong men and subservient women were as important to family health as muscular political leadership was to national survival.

This look at McCarthyism suggests comparisons with the ideological strait-jacket that Stalin fastened on his country. As there, so too in the United States, the courts, the legislature, and the executive at all levels imposed a more restrictive social and political atmosphere. In the United States, as in the Soviet Union, the easiest way to discredit challengers to the status quo was to link them somehow to the foreign enemy and thus make them appear unpatriotic, even dangerously subversive. McCarthyism reminds us of the unpleasant paradox that attended the American side of the Cold War struggle. Americans went crusading in foreign lands in the name of freedom even as those freedoms significantly narrowed at home. That those who fell victim to McCarthyism lost their jobs and reputations and not their lives and that their numbers were far fewer than those exiled to Soviet labor camps or executed serves to qualify, not invalidate, the comparison and to extenuate, not excuse, the betrayal of fundamental American political values.[33]

CONCLUSION

The first years of the Cold War constituted a dark moment for many people around the world, but especially for those in the United States and the Soviet Union. Cold War fears and dangers rapidly displaced the hopes for peace and prosperity for a combination of reasons. The completeness of the Allied triumph during World War II placed the fate of the postwar world to a large extent in the hands of the two leading Allied powers. Moscow and Washington had to confront a wide range of complex issues amidst the confusion and desperation of a world recently torn by war. Those two leading powers brought to the task strongly divergent worldviews that spawned mistrust as well as misunderstanding. Sharply accentuating the potential for conflict were marked differences in the styles and outlooks of the two leaders who happened to be at the helm between 1945 and 1953. Truman was inexperienced, impatient, and insecure—not the best combination of traits for resolving complicated issues thrust upon him following Roosevelt's death. Stalin, on the other hand, brought to his postwar tasks personal paranoia and skill at dissembling and maneuver honed in Soviet domestic and foreign policy over decades. These qualities combined to make his approach both cautious and opaque. Of all the circumstances leading to the rise of the Cold War, the personalities of the superpowers' leaders may be both the most critical but also the most easily overlooked. The postwar period was bound to be contentious; these personal differences helped turn differences into a deep and disruptive rivalry that would last for decades.

The mounting Soviet-American tensions of the early postwar period might have risen higher, leading to another world war with destruction on a magnitude previously unimagined. But in early 1953 Truman and Stalin disappeared from the center of power, marking the end of the worst of the Cold War peril and the first glimmers of a thaw. The efforts by their successors to limit the rivalry bore fruit in the 1950s and 1960s. Promoting this trend were the increasingly apparent costs of waging the Cold War, growing popular discontent on both sides, and above all the ever clearer realization of nuclear war's suicidal potential. Nikita Khrushchev and Dwight Eisenhower would begin what would prove a long, meandering path toward accommodation and ultimately the end of the Cold War some forty years after its start (see Chapter 4).

RECOMMENDED RESOURCES

General Works on the Cold War
John W. Young, *Cold War and Détente, 1941–91* (1993), is a handy guide to key terms, personalities, and events. On the developing nuclear arms race, see Marek Thee's provocative *Military Technology, Military Strategy, and the Arms Race* (1986).

The United States during the Cold War
General surveys include Michael S. Sherry, *In the Shadow of War: The United States since the 1930s* (1995); William H. Chafe, *The Unfinished Journey: America since World War II* (3rd ed., 1995); Norman L. Rosenberg and Emily S. Rosenberg, *In Our Times: America since World War II* (5th ed., 1995); and James T. Patterson, *Grand Expectations: The United States, 1945–1974* (1996). On **U.S. foreign policy,** see Walter LaFeber, *America, Russia, and the Cold War, 1945–2000* (9th ed., 2002), which offers an overview; Melvyn P. Leffler, *The Specter of Communism: The United States and the Origins of the Cold War, 1917–1953* (1994), for the best brief treatment of the coming of the Cold War; Arnold A. Offner, *Another Such Victory: President*

Truman and the Cold War, 1945–1953 (2002), a good interpretive counterpoint to Leffler; and John Lewis Gaddis, *We Now Know: Rethinking Cold War History* (1997), which attempts to update the story of how the Cold War began in light of new Soviet materials. Robert Divine, *Roosevelt and World War II* (1969), portrays a controversial figure in balanced, generally sympathetic terms. Robert Dallek, *Franklin D. Roosevelt and American Foreign Policy, 1932–1945* (1979), is a fuller, authoritative account. William E. Pemberton, *Harry S. Truman: Fair Dealer and Cold Warrior* (1989), is an accessible and informative political biography. See also Alonzo L. Hamby, *Man of the People: The Life of Harry S. Truman* (1995). *Truman* (writ. and prod. David Grubin; 1997; 270 min.), a documentary prepared for the *American Experience* series on PBS, nicely evokes the challenges facing the first Cold War president. On **McCarthyism in American society and culture**, see Ellen Schrecker, *The Age of McCarthyism: A Brief History with Documents* (1994), a first-rate, fresh overview. See also her fuller account, *Many Are the Crimes: McCarthyism in America* (1998), as well as Richard M. Fried, *Nightmare in Red: The McCarthy Era in Perspective* (1990). Stephen J. Whitfield, *The Culture of the Cold War* (2nd ed., 1996), an engaging treatment of the late 1940s and 1950s, stresses the way anti-communism narrowed cultural as well as political expression. *Point of Order* (dir. Emile de Antonio; 1964; 107 min.) is a documentary that captures the drama of the McCarthy investigations.

The Soviet Union

General treatments include Robert Service's balanced text, *A History of Twentieth-Century Russia* (1998). Stephen F. Cohen, *Rethinking the Soviet Experience: Politics and History since 1917* (1985); Alec Nove, ed., *The Stalin Phenomenon* (1993); and Martin Malia, *The Soviet Tragedy: A History of Socialism in Russia, 1917–1991* (1994), articulate competing interpretations of Bolshevism. Robert V. Daniels, ed., *A Documentary History of Communism in Russia: From Lenin to Gorbachev* (1993), and Daniels, ed., *A Documentary History of Communism and the World* (3rd ed., 1994), gather important original sources. **Insights on Stalin** emerge from Robert C. Tucker's widely respected biography: *Stalin as Revolutionary, 1879–1929: A Study in History and Personality* (1973) and *Stalin in Power: The Revolution from Above, 1928–1941* (1990). Dimitri Volkogonov, *Stalin: Triumph and Tragedy*, ed. and trans. Harold Shukman (1991), and Eduard Radzinsky, *Stalin*, trans. H. T. Willetts (1997), make use of newly available materials. For insights on Stalin's lieutenants, see *Molotov Remembers: Inside Kremlin Politics—Conversations with Felix Chuev*, trans. and ed. Albert Resis (1993); and Amy Knight, *Beria: Stalin's First Lieutenant* (1993). Studies on **Soviet foreign policy** drawing on new sources include Vladislav Zubok and Constantine Pleshakov, *Inside the Kremlin's Cold War: From Stalin to Khrushchev* (1996); Vojtech Mastny, *The Cold War and Soviet Insecurity: The Stalin Years* (1996); and Jeffrey Burds, *The Cold War in Soviet West Ukraine, 1944–1948* (2001). Insights on the Polish Communists who worked closely with the Soviets emerge from a set of probing interviews in Teresa Torańska, *Them: Stalin's Polish Puppets*, trans. Agnieszka Kolakowska (1987), and in the deft sketches of former Communist associates by Czeslaw Milosz, *The Captive Mind*, trans. Jane Zielonko (1953). **The domestic system Stalin created** is treated in John Channon, ed., *Politics, Society, and Stalinism in the USSR* (1998), reflecting the insights afforded by newly available source materials. Serge Schmemann, *Echoes of a Native Land: Two Centuries of a Russian Village* (1997), re-creates the life of a single village while also telling the tale of dispossession and exile suffered by the author's own well-to-do family.

The Beginning of the Nuclear Age

On **the U.S. atomic bomb project**, Richard Rhodes, *The Making of the Atomic Bomb* (1986); and Martin Sherwin, *A World Destroyed: The Atomic Bomb and the Grand Alliance* (1975), are standard accounts. Michael B. Stoff, et al., eds., *The Manhattan Project: A Documentary Introduction to the Atomic Age* (1991), and Gene Dannen at <http://www.peak.org/~danneng/decision> supply accessible collections of original documents. The **Japanese perspective** was first widely disseminated in John Hersey, *Hiroshima* (1946). This first-hand account by a distinguished observer treats the lives of a half dozen survivors of atomic warfare. There is a large body of Japanese oral histories, including Michihiko Hachiya, *Hiroshima Diary: The Journal of a Japanese Physician, August 6–September 30, 1945*, trans. and ed. Warner Lee Wells (1995); Arata Osada, ed., *Children of Hiroshima* (1982); and Mikio Kanda, ed., *Widows of Hiroshima: The Life Stories of Nineteen Peasant Wives*, trans. Taeko Midorikawa (1989). The emergence of **the Soviet nuclear program** is treated in David Holloway, *Stalin and the Bomb: The Soviet Union and Atomic Energy, 1939–1956* (1994).

The Korean War

Steven Hugh Lee, *The Korean War* (2001), provides a concise, up-to-date international overview with documents. See also Burton I. Kaufman, *The Korean War: Challenges in Crisis, Credibility, and Command* (2nd ed., 1997); William Stueck, *The Korean War: An International History* (1994); and Callum A. MacDonald, *Korea: The War before Vietnam* (1986).

CHAPTER 2

THE INTERNATIONAL ECONOMY: OUT OF THE RUINS

At the end of World War II the United States stood as the premier economic power. It accounted for half of all manufacturing around the world and held two-thirds of the world's gold reserves. U.S. dominance was enhanced by the wartime destruction that had spared none of the other economic powers. American goods, capital, and leadership were the main source of hope for recovery in other lands. With its vast scale married to considerable military, political, and cultural clout, the United States entered the postwar era at the peak of its power. It had the capacity to give a significant boost to a market-oriented system of trade and finance. Quick to use that capacity, the United States had an incredible impact as a global economic reformer, as a rescuer of capitalism in stricken western Europe and Japan, and as a fount of goods and dreams for foreign no less than American consumers.

In knitting together an international economy devastated by depression and war, the United States by necessity had to work with others, especially in the developed world where the Cold War stakes were highest and where the potential for a rapid recovery of production and living standards was greatest. Though drained by two world wars, the British government worked closely with Washington on international economic reforms. In western Europe, Catholic politicians determined to block Communist electoral advances looked to the United States for relief supplies and capital critical to meeting popular demands for food, fuel, and housing. In a Japan exhausted by war and devastated by bombing, a new generation of leaders emerged who, like their European counterparts, were anticommunist, bent on reconstruction, and dependent on the United States for assistance. The popular dreams for a better life in both Europe and Japan, to which democratic politicians had to be attuned, took on a strong U.S. flavor. Even before World War II, U.S. cultural imports had planted in the minds of the working and middle classes images of a lifestyle of comfort and pleasure. The postwar presence of American soldiers, films, and advertising intensified the taste for a level of consumption made possible only by an economy of abundance.

Americanization, the codeword for this pervasive U.S. economic and cultural influence, was for many a welcome social reality but for cultural elites a source of alarm.

ANGLO-AMERICAN REMEDIES FOR AN AILING SYSTEM

The revival of a battered international economic system was a project undertaken jointly by leaders in Washington and London during wartime and the early postwar years. Both powers knew that the United States would dominate the postwar scene. London and the British pound, formerly central to trade and investment, had lost their pivotal role as a result of the damage that two wars had done to the British economy. No longer the premier international power, Britain could hope to maintain a modicum of influence only in collaboration with the ascendant United States. Now, both parties recognized, was the time to write new rules and create new institutions that would promote international trade and investment. Through this collaboration, the Americans and British would set their stamp on the international system and lay the foundation for the second phase of the great age of globalization.

They took as an article of faith that a revival of the global economy held the best hope for bringing a better life for all people. The late nineteenth- and early twentieth-century economic record offered ample argument for the gains that would flow from the free movement of goods and capital. The more recent interwar past also offered a powerful warning of how excessive state interference in the market, including protecting home markets from foreign producers and restricting currency exchange, could not only plunge the world economy into depression but also derange the entire system. Above all, traders and investors needed the promise of a stable international environment for the profitable and predictable conduct of their business. But restoration of beneficial market forces—at least the removal of trade barriers and the implementation of a mechanism to facilitate the international flow of capital—would not happen automatically. Paradoxically, the achievement of these free market goals would take state initiative, regulation, even intervention.

Keynesian Economics and a Design for Prosperity

A mischievous bit of verse scribbled by a British participant in talks with the Americans on postwar economic arrangements claimed, "It's true *they* have the money bags / But *we* have all the brains."[1] John Maynard Keynes was the British brains.

Born in 1883 into modest circumstances, Keynes was raised and educated in Cambridge, England. Within the insulated, clubby atmosphere of that university, he developed economic ideas that proved stunningly original, even revolutionary. In London Keynes led another life. He lived within the iconoclastic Bloomsbury circle devoted to the arts, good food, and stimulating conversation while also serving as an influential adviser to the British government. In his spare time he made a personal fortune trading on the currency and stock markets. Although homosexual, he courted and married the beautiful Russian ballerina Lydia Lopokova in the early 1920s in what would prove a lasting and mutually supportive match. He was loyal to his friends and colleagues, yet he was the master of the cutting remark and the rude putdown. He was at once a social and political conservative and an unorthodox thinker, religious agnostic, and proponent of popular welfare. In 1946, shortly before his death, he was honored by elevation to the House of Lords.

Keynes once observed as though anticipating his own influential place in postwar history: "The ideas of economists and political philosophers, both when they are right and when they are wrong, are more powerful than is commonly understood."[2] Keynes's idea that ultimately gained wide political acceptance was that the free market internationally as well as domestically would perform better if subject to constant state oversight and periodic intervention. He laid the foundation for this point by demonstrating in his interwar writings the exaggerated faith that economists since the eighteenth century had put in the impersonal operations of the market. Supply and demand sometimes failed to balance out and thus could not be counted on to produce optimum economic efficiency and growth. The widespread deprivation brought on by the Great Depression cast serious doubt on the old market faith and led Keynes and his colleagues to an intense search not only for an explanation for this failure of the economy to right itself but also for possible solutions. As Keynes came to see it, the doctrine of government non-interference in the marketplace (known as *laissez faire;* see p. 14) failed to take account of the ways savings and investment could fall out of synch and disrupt the economy at both the bottom and the top of the range of economic performance. At the bottom, savings dried up, making investment that might revive the economy difficult. At the top, savings might multiply beyond the capacity of investors to prudently place them, making speculation and collapse almost inevitable.

Having concluded that the hidden hand of the market did not always work, Keynes substituted intervention by the state at those moments when the economy threatened to plunge or languish. To bring investment and savings into line and thereby smooth out the economic cycles, Keynes proposed a greater role for government than either British or American practice sanctioned before the 1930s. To get a stalled economy going, he would have the government make public investments. These investments would prime the economic pump by restoring investor and consumer confidence. If the economy was reaching the peak of its capacity, the government could redistribute income. Producers would then expect higher levels of demand and would undertake new investments, thereby sustaining prosperity. Keynes's advocacy of government intervention did not make him a socialist. Committed to the capitalist system, he did not want a planned economy, nor did he favor states taking from firms the fundamental decisions about what to produce and how much.

Taken in broader terms, Keynes pointed toward a new age of capitalism in which the state would play a prominent role. From quite early on he was moved by the belief that the survival of democracy depended on attending to the liveli-hood of its citizens. If democracy did not function humanely as well as efficiently, the consequences could be fearsome, as Keynes himself had seen in his own life-time in Hitler's Germany and Stalin's Soviet Union. Keynes's advocacy of a larger state role in economic affairs ran up against a general American preference for the free operation of the market subject to only the most minimal state interven-tion. On the other hand, on the European continent Keynes reinforced a propensity across a broad spectrum of political opinion to look to the state to tend to the common economic welfare. Interwar governments in Germany and Italy had intervened deeply to promote prosperity and development, and even though Mussolini and Hitler were discredited, their economic policies retained popularity. On the postwar Left, socialists committed to a democratic way advo-cated extensive state intervention, and they found a measure of agreement with conservative Christian Democratic parties guided by a strong Catholic tradition of social justice.

Seen in this second context, Keynes stood for a middle way between Soviet state planners and Americans suspicious of centralized power. In 1926 he wrote of the mix of values that informed his hybrid views. In his opinion, economic efficiency and individual liberty were important but not by themselves sufficient. Social justice, which he associated with "an unselfish and enthusiastic spirit, which loves the ordinary man," was an indispensable part of the mix.[3] Keynes had no illusions about the brutality of the Soviet system of state planning and consistently rejected it as a negation of all the values that he cherished. The ulti-mate goal as Keynes saw it was to save the capitalist system and, with it, much of the free market by according a regulatory role to a humanely activist state.

During World War II Keynes made his main contribution to the support of that middle way by leading the British delegation in talks with the Americans on economic issues. He could not have found a better partner than the Roosevelt administration. Americans, usually fundamentalist in their devotion to the free market and rugged individualism, had been shaken by the Great Depression and also impressed by how state intervention could alleviate suffering. The president and his influential secretary of the treasury, Henry Morgenthau, shared Keynes's belief in the inherent good of the free market and certitude in the necessity of state intervention to avert another economic disaster.

Keynes was perhaps even more important in the long term for the way his justification of state intervention drew the lines of the most important economic debate of the last half of the twentieth century. The proposition Keynes articu-lated would divide economists in an ongoing battle over a fundamental question: Did the dangers posed by an activist state exceed any good that it might do? The role of the state would also increasingly divide Americans inclined to favor indi-vidual opportunity over state control from western Europeans and Japanese, who took Keynes's ideas as common sense, the only debatable point being not *whether* but *how* the state would intervene in the economy. Europeans saw the state as the guarantor of individual and group interests against the workings of an impersonal market. Europeans took for granted the "welfare state." The Japanese tendency, on the other hand, was to see the state as the leader in making the economy competitive and the people prosperous. Thus "guided capitalism" emerged as the prevailing East Asian approach. The increasing integration of the international economy would in time make the state's role in the free market a matter of contention among the leading economic powers (see Chapters 5 and 8).

The Bretton Woods Agreements

Keynes joined his American counterpart, the Treasury Department's Harry Dexter White, at Bretton Woods, New Hampshire, in July 1944. The U.S. government had called the conference to hammer out the basis for the postwar economic system. Forty-four countries sent representatives (although the Soviet Union did not). The British and the Americans were fully in charge, represented by Keynes and White, who took the lead in designing the institutional framework in which the postwar economy would function and evolve. When twenty-eight nations signed the Bretton Woods agreements in late 1945, they were approving the Keynes-White handiwork.

Their major achievement was to lay down a new system for capital flow that took the place of the gold standard, abandoned at the outset of the Great Depression. The U.S. dollar became the pivotal currency. With its value set at $35 for an ounce of gold, the dollar became the basis for establishing the value of all other currencies. The United States agreed to exchange dollars presented by foreign governments for gold at the fixed rate. Those governments for their part agreed to keep their currencies in a stable relationship to the dollar.

The IMF and the World Bank. A currency exchange system had to be not only free but also predictable if it was to facilitate trade. To meet these criteria, Bretton Woods established two institutions to serve as stabilizers and facilitators of international economic activity. The International Monetary Fund (IMF), created with a reserve of $8.8 billion, provided a mechanism for preserving currency convertibility and avoiding government-imposed exchange controls. It was to lend funds to ensure that trading countries would be able in the short term to pay for their imports and sustain their economic development. The other major, long-lived Bretton Woods institution was the World Bank, initially called the International Bank for Reconstruction and Development to reflect its first mission of promoting the recovery of war-ravaged economies. Launched with a fund of $9.1 billion, the bank first focused primarily on Europe but then in the 1950s shifted to addressing the needs of newly independent countries lacking infrastructure (see key economic terms on p. 14).

Far from constituting a bold return to the pre-1931 open, liberal international financial order, the Bretton Woods blueprint explicitly gave states control over capital flows. Keynes and White agreed that speculative capital movements had created turmoil and threatened to deprive states of the control of their economies critical to serving popular welfare. It was the responsibility of elected leaders, not distant bankers, to select the policies that best served their country. State control of capital movements made possible interest rate differentials from country to country. Otherwise, capital would move to countries with the highest returns and leave low-interest countries starved for funds. Moreover, state control would prevent the wealthy from evading welfare legislation by moving capital beyond the reach of their governments. Finally, state control was good for trade, which was easily disrupted by speculative capital movements. Stable exchange rates would mean a more predictable economic environment encouraging greater trade and discouraging unproductive currency speculation. In the Keynes-White plan the state role was to be exercised at two levels: All states retained the right to control capital moving across their borders, and the leading economic powers had an additional say through such international institutions as the IMF and World Bank. Representatives from the major economies dominated the governing boards of those institutions and, as the source of much of their funding, the United States commanded the largest bloc of votes.

In both the United States and Britain a coalition of government, industrial, and labor leaders supported the Bretton Woods reforms against the preferences of bankers for a restoration of the open, unregulated international financial system that had prevailed during an earlier era of globalization. The New York financial community, eager to secure its international dominance, had opposed the drift toward what it saw as a "welfare state" under the New Deal, and now it saw the IMF as an extension of that trend to the global economy. Those eager free marketers wanted the western European countries to remove restrictions on currency exchange. Let the international market decide the value of each nation's currency, they argued. This approach threatened upheaval for countries already grappling with enormous problems of postwar recovery. One problem was the disruptive flight of capital to the United States. Investors worried by the heavy clouds hanging over Europe shifted their money to an economy where the returns were good and the investment secure. A second problem involved serious trade deficits. Europeans had little to export but were heavily dependent on imports to rebuild the economy and restart production. How were they to pay off the resulting deficits? If capital flight and deficits persisted, Europe would suffer more economic pain and even risk dangerous social strains.

To the disappointment of strict free market advocates, the Truman administration finally intervened. It supported restrictions on capital flight, while Marshall Plan transfers helped to close trade deficits and boost reconstruction. These decisions, taken in the course of 1947, provided the basis for a new consensus within the United States behind the Bretton Woods arrangements. Cold War fears of instability were beginning to trump the free market principles favored by New York bankers and conservative Republicans.

GATT and the Question of Free Trade. Free-market principles also suffered a setback in negotiations over postwar trade. The Roosevelt administration had launched those talks guided by a strong faith in international free trade. If each country specialized by producing and exporting what it was best at doing, international exchange would keep prices low and quality high to everyone's benefit. For example, a country that produced expensive agricultural goods but also made cheap, well-made cars would shift out of the former to focus its resources on the latter, the product that was most competitive on the international market. As tariff and other protectionist barriers fell, so the argument went, international trade would gain a fresh stimulus and bring prosperity to all. The lessons that American leaders drew from the recent past reinforced their belief that long-term political stability depended on an open, stable system of international trade. According to this common wisdom, the economic crash of 1929 had been brought on by shortsighted protectionism (see key economic terms on p. 14) that ignored economic interdependency. Once the crash had occurred, a difficult situation was made worse as each country turned inward, trying to solve its economic crisis independently and rejecting the cooperation that was the surest road to an international recovery. The result, according to this reading of the recent past, was social and political unrest in Germany, Italy, and Japan; the rise of Hitler, Mussolini, and the Tokyo militarists; and ultimately aggressive policies that brought on World War II. Secretary of State Cordell Hull, the staunchest of the free traders in the Roosevelt administration, observed that "unhampered trade dovetailed with peace; high tariffs, trade barriers, and unfair economic competition with war."[4]

The Bretton Woods conference anticipated the free movement of goods in the postwar economy, but when Washington got down to the details of the free-trade regime, it ran into trouble. Ambitious provisions for rapidly dismantling trade barriers provoked Britain and its imperial partners such as Australia and South Africa, which were determined to protect their close, exclusive trade relationship. Within the United States, wool producers, independent oil firms, dairy farmers, and others vulnerable to foreign competition had steadfast supporters among Republicans in Congress and were sure to defeat any agreement.

By 1950, when the Truman administration abandoned any plans for a major makeover of the trade system, an alternative, more modest mechanism for promoting free trade had taken shape. The General Agreement on Tariffs and Trade (GATT), concluded in Geneva in 1947, proved the sleeper amidst the ambitious designs and major negotiations of the period. Originally part of an overall U.S. free-trade initiative, GATT provided an informal method for negotiating multilateral arrangements for tariff reductions. Without a permanent secretariat, however, GATT seemed of limited importance, and to get the agreement approved, the United States had to open its market to its trading partners and effect sharp cuts on U.S. tariffs on foreign imports. By making one-sided concessions and turning their back on protectionism, U.S. officials hoped to enshrine the principle of ever-freer trade in international discussions and at the same time give access to the large and prosperous U.S. market for producers in countries who were allied to the United States in the Cold War struggle and whose growing prosperity would create a rising demand for American goods. Promoting postwar recovery in Japan and western Europe thus made both political and economic sense.

However modest its early achievements, GATT would prove over the decades an important vehicle for gradually but dramatically lowering trade barriers all around the world. GATT would also come to serve as an important forum where its members could define and adjudicate the rules for their increasingly complex and interdependent trade relationships. By the 1960s GATT had established itself alongside the IMF and the World Bank as an institutional pillar for the international economy.

THE U.S. RESCUE OPERATION

In the immediate postwar years Japan and the states of western Europe began a remarkable economic recovery. As they did so, they fundamentally rethought their national goals. After years of devoting their economic resources to external expansion and military rivalry, these states now experienced a major paradigm shift. Putting aside the old preoccupation with blood and soil, Japanese and western European leaders took instead internal economic development as their chief concern, and they made the chief measure of success rising per capita income (see key economic terms on p. 14). If there was any international rivalry in this new era, it was over who had the highest popular standard of living, and the results were adjudicated not on the battlefield or in diplomatic confrontations but by citizen-consumers in regular national elections. Leaders who did not deliver did not stay in office.

The United States played an important role in both speeding economic recovery and encouraging the new national goals. It was a source of scarce hard currency and food. It exported industrial goods essential to restarting production. It unilaterally opened its home market to imports from struggling European and Japanese producers. U.S. leaders acted from a mixture of motives—a humanitarian impulse to help former allies, a missionary desire to convert former enemies, the Cold War imperative to preempt Soviet influence, and a selfish conviction that U.S. prosperity depended on economic revival elsewhere. A world floundering in misery was likely to be neither democratic nor immune to communist appeals. The impact of the American role was most pronounced in Japan, where U.S. occupation authorities exercised direct control for the first seven postwar years. In Europe, American control was direct only in its quarter of occupied Germany. Elsewhere on the continent the United States dealt with sovereign states, but their desperate economic straits left them vulnerable to American pressure even if they did not have to take American orders.

In assessing this U.S. impact, it is important to keep in mind the considerable assets that survived the war in both western Europe and Japan. The workforce was educated and experienced, and a sophisticated management was ready to take charge of what remained of productive capacity. In this atmosphere state authorities quickly turned their hand to recovery. Above all, participants in the reconstruction effort were familiar with the organizational forms and practices that had worked for them in the past and could be tailored to new conditions. These indigenous endowments were critical to postwar recovery, and without them U.S. recovery efforts might have failed.

Occupation and Recovery in Japan

Japan, which was to emerge as one of the leading economic powers of the late twentieth century, boasts two economic success stories. The first one spanned the first third of the twentieth century. By 1900 Japan was emerging as a prominent participant in the first phase of globalization. With its labor-intensive industries such as textiles and the merchant marine developing rapidly, the country prospered through World War I and the 1920s. The Great Depression dealt Japan a major blow as other countries closed off their markets. A victim of this trend toward protectionism, Japan sought late in the 1930s to extend its political and military control across a broad sweep of East Asia in a desperate bid to secure raw materials and markets. This imperial enterprise provoked resistance not only in the region but also from the British and the Americans, resulting in war and another major blow to Japan's economy. The second miracle would not begin until the 1950s (see Chapter 5). But the period of economic recovery immediately after the war prepared the way.

Recovering from war posed a major economic challenge. Bombing had done extensive damage to housing stocks and production facilities. Factories still intact had to be converted back to civilian production. Eighty percent of the merchant fleet critical to supplying the resource-poor collection of islands that the Japanese called home lay on the ocean floor. Twenty billion dollars in overseas investments were gone. Inflation (see key economic terms on p. 14), a wartime problem, persisted. The future was further clouded by the threat of having to pay massive reparations claimed by neighboring countries devastated by Japan's war machine.

The war had also devastated Japanese society. Nearly three million people had died. The survivors lived at near subsistence level. Per capita income was only half of what it had been in the mid-1930s before Japan had embarked on its disastrous experiment in expansion overseas. Some 6.5 million soldiers, sailors, and civilians overseas at war's end began to trickle back empty handed to a land that offered little opportunity or hope. One soldier returning home in May 1946 reported grimly what he found, "My house was burned, my wife and children missing. What little money I had quickly was consumed by the high prices, and I was a pitiful figure. Not a single person gave me a kind word. Rather, they cast hostile glances my way."[5] Women left without support turned to prostitution; orphans scavenged for food and shelter. Families sold off their possessions in a desperate race between a dwindling stock of goods and rising food prices. Starvation became shockingly commonplace. Only black marketeers seemed to flourish amidst the privation and despondency.

Economic Turnaround. By April 1952 when the U.S. occupation came to an end, Japan was back on its feet. Production was rising. Per capita income had nearly regained prewar levels, and inflation would soon be mastered. That the Japanese were able to overcome a dire situation was partially the result of the policies of the American-dominated military occupation headed by General Douglas MacArthur.

But even more important were the assets that Japan carried over from war to peace. The imperial bureaucracy had survived the war and continued to operate with American toleration, even encouragement. This respected and experienced elite had a strong faith in government economic planning and social direction as the best path to restore Japan's standing in the world. Their lifetime tenure made them confident and knowledgeable. The economic institutions—from major corporations to the dominant business associations—were also tested and commanded respect. Finally, the productivity and discipline of the workforce were at an all-time high. Technical schools as well as company training had improved worker skills even as their numbers increased dramatically from 1930 onward. While companies took the first steps toward treating workers as part of the family, the government had initiated welfare measures, including the beginnings of medical insurance and pension plans, and celebrated loyalty to the firm and sacrifice for the country. Firms could also turn to a cadre of scientists and engineers active in wartime research and ready to exploit advances in such areas as electronics and petrochemicals.

The initial impetus for this economic turnaround came from basic reforms initiated during the first several years of the occupation. Some were projects that career bureaucrats had conceived earlier, and now with the ultra-nationalist and military elites gone, they had a freer hand to press ahead. For example, on the critical matter of land reform, wartime government agencies had made an important start by intervening directly into food production and distribution. This step cut the ties between the exploitative landlord class and their tenants, reducing rural poverty and discontent.

Other reforms issued from the headquarters of the American occupation force. MacArthur took up his duties at the end of a long and distinguished military career. The latter stages had seen him lead the Allied advance across the southwest Pacific. MacArthur ran the occupation through several thousand American military and civilian officials, who in turn supervised a revived Japanese bureaucracy. The Truman administration left him considerable latitude to follow his own design, and he was virtually unchallengable until the added duties of commanding UN forces in Korea embroiled him in difficulty with Truman and precipitated his recall in April 1951. The occupation, on which he had by then left a major mark, had only a year to go.

From the start MacArthur was confident that he understood "the oriental mind," and he acted on a missionary-like determination to turn a militaristic Japan toward modern civilization. Compared to Anglo-Saxons, the Japanese were (as he put it after leaving Japan) "like a boy of twelve."[6] The task of the occupation was to help that youth become a responsible adult. MacArthur's aloof bearing and his idealistic commitment to creating a new Japan cleansed of its discredited past won him popularity in a country taught by wartime propaganda to expect the worst from the "American-English demons." He began with the goal of demilitarizing Japan—making it into what he called the "Switzerland of Asia." Japan's new constitution, drafted by the Americans, renounced war as an instrument of national policy. Japan could maintain only a limited self-defense force that was forbidden to operate beyond Japanese waters.

MacArthur also proceeded with a series of steps toward democratization that cumulatively had a major impact on the economy. One of his most consequential decisions was to push further on the land reform already begun by the bureaucracy. He took hold of an agricultural system in which nearly half of all land had been tenanted. By the time he was finished with redistribution, only 10 percent of the land was worked by non-owners. As a result of this dramatic increase in independent farmers, the countryside became more politically stable and economically productive. Labor found the Americans supportive of the right to organize and bargain collectively for better working conditions and pay, while employers with dangerous or unsanitary working conditions were called to account. Finally, in a distinctly American move without support among Japan's bureaucrats, the occupation turned to breaking up the large, family-controlled business conglomerates known as *zaibatsu* that had dominated the economy. One of these conglomerates might have had hundreds of thousands of employees (in one case, almost two million at home and abroad) and controlled hundreds of companies. American reformers implicated these conglomerates in the earlier policy of aggression and argued that democracy and free markets in Japan required their destruction. As an influential American economic mission asserted after surveying Japan just after the war, "Unless the Zaibatsu are broken up, the Japanese have little prospect of ever being able to govern themselves as free men."[7]

The "Reverse Course" in Occupation Policy. The Cold War provided an additional impetus to recovery. As U.S.-Soviet tensions mounted, occupation policy underwent in 1947–1948 what is known as the "reverse course." Washington had begun the occupation with political and economic reform uppermost in mind, but it increasingly saw Japan as an important anti-communist bastion in Asia. The American occupiers, now working closely with conservative Prime Minister Yoshida Shigeru, took steps to control the political Left and to blunt labor activism. At the same time growing U.S. commitments overseas were making it difficult for Washington to continue to bear the costs of occupying and rehabilitating Japan. Under pressure to speed economic recovery, the occupation took a more kindly view of industrial concentration. Large Japanese corporations began to form "enterprise groups" (*keiretsu*) in which members with diverse lines of production—for example, chemicals, automobiles, iron and steel, and electrical machinery—joined in a long-term partnership anchored by a major bank. One major *keiretsu* brought the Mitsubishi Bank, the Mitsubishi Corporation, Mitsubishi Heavy Industries, and Mitsubishi Motors into close affiliation. Like much else in postwar Japan, the leading enterprise groups—Mitsui and Sumitomo along with Mitsubishi—were based on relationships going back to wartime and earlier.

The outbreak of war in neighboring Korea in mid-1950 capped the process of recovery. Japan served as a staging area for U.S. forces fighting on the nearby peninsula. Earnings from a broad range of goods and services underlined the close trade ties that had developed with the United States and provided the first hints of postwar prosperity. In 1952 with Korea still in conflict, Washington and Tokyo concluded a treaty that brought the occupation to an end and that carried important economic as well as political consequences. It placed Japan under the U.S. defense umbrella, allowing Tokyo to keep its military budget low and concentrate its resources on the civilian economy. U.S. bases located on Japanese soil not only gave substance to this defense commitment but also served as an important source of economic stimulation. The treaty minimized reparations due to neighbors victimized during wartime, thus calming Japanese business interests worried about the loss of already scarce resources available to restart production.

By the latter stages of the occupation the rough outlines of a unique Japanese economic model were beginning to form. Joseph Dodge, a U.S. banker sent to advise on the Japanese economy in 1948, came to a predictable if mistaken conclusion: "The fundamental problem of the Japanese nation can be expressed in the simple terms of too many people, too little land and too few natural resources." An official in the Finance Ministry quickly replied that the same point could be made about Manhattan![8] One Japanese solution to ensure prosperity for those crowded islands called for government planning, but both U.S. officials and Prime Minister Yoshida were staunchly opposed. The alternative that prevailed was a coordinated public-private approach that brought government direction and resources to bear on economic development but that left business to make the best market decisions within this benign environment. From this collaboration would emerge a kind of guided capitalism.

In the first modest exercise of its leadership the Yoshida government focused in 1947 on the revival of the coal and steel industries. It used loans, price subsidies, tariffs to hold back imports, and allocation of scarce resources to stimulate recovery. The government would move on in the early 1950s to "rationalize" key industrial sectors—encouraging investment in modern new facilities that would reduce production costs. It began with steel and coal once more and then moved on to electrical power and shipbuilding, among others. Here too it used incentives, including special tax treatment, interest subsidies, loans, and "administrative guidelines." This flexible approach would make the "Switzerland of Asia" also its Manhattan.

Recovery in Western Europe

Like Japan, the European economies in the immediate aftermath of war were in a desperate condition. Unlike World War I when the civilian population had largely escaped destruction, bombing and fighting during World War II had brought the conflict home. This time half the deaths had been noncombatants (some eighteen million), and facilities for production, transport, and communication had suffered heavy damage. Much of what industry remained had yet to be converted back to civilian use and to find suppliers and markets within new postwar boundaries. Whole cities lay in ruins. Defeated Germany and Italy had suffered especially heavy losses as a result of bombing and invasion. For example, more than half of the housing stock in Germany was gone. The prospects for recovery looked grim. Everywhere coal for heating and power for production were alarmingly scarce. Food supplies were equally precarious. Livestock was gone, and fertilizer was nowhere to be found. Dollars to pay for imports, even of such essentials as food and coal, were in desperately short supply. The winter of 1946–1947 proved the harshest in memory. Soon rising Soviet-American tensions would further dampen hope and inhibit investment.

In contrast to Japan just after the war, general social breakdown in western Europe seemed a real possibility. Demobilized soldiers were coming home hoping to find work. The refugee problem assumed massive proportions as thirty million people (mostly Germans) fled before the Red Army, were displaced by redrawn frontiers in eastern Europe, or were freed from prisoner of war, forced labor, or concentration camps. These "displaced" were, an American journalist noted at the end of 1945, "desperate and homeless . . . milling east and west, north and south, across the continent." Disrupted transport systems and a shortage of food and shelter left many in dire straits and uncertain where to turn. One refugee driven from fire-bombed Dresden found a world in which the word *unimaginable* had lost its meaning: "This nightmare of destruction, dust, the Americans' speeding vehicles, of lack of everything and, above all, of absolute uncertainty, unreliability, vagueness—this terrible jelly, both literally and metaphorically, of debris, rubble, and dust." Workers angry over continuing hardships that neither governments nor business leaders could solve went on strike, while street demonstrations drew the cold and hungry.[9]

Food shortages had intensified during the war. Young hostesses in France assigned to escort American liberators to cultural sites recalled viewing these young soldiers with ready access to food "with their eyes in their stomachs. Each soldier, however ugly, was worth his weight in chocolate, protein, glucose, and like Pavlov's dogs, each girl began to salivate at the sight of a uniform." To everyone's dismay, conditions did not rapidly improve with the end of the war in May 1945. Rather, they further deteriorated. Even as late as the summer of 1946 a hundred million Europeans were down to 1,500 calories or less per day—the level at which health suffers and work becomes difficult if not impossible. Another forty million were just a shade above this dangerous level. Hit hardest by war and displacement, Germans were the worst off. In early 1946 those in the French, American, and British zones of occupation were at a daily caloric intake that hovered around 1,000, and by 1947 the average weight for German men and women had fallen to around 93 pounds. A German politician recalled some forty

German Woman Rebuilding amidst the Rubble of War
Grim determination was critical to family survival and physical reconstruction at a time when men were scarce. In Germany, images like this one highlighted the suffering the war had brought ordinary Germans (significantly women) and turned attention away from the destruction aggressive Germans (men) had inflicted on others. Now hard work would usher in a new era of prosperity and peace. Despite praise for their sacrifices and labor during these difficult years, German women did not win expanded postwar occupational opportunities. (Bundesbildstelle Berlin Bild-Nr: 105 886 Fotograff(in): Puck)

years later how those hard times had taught him "what hunger really meant and how it feels, how it looks when the last slice of bread is shared amongst five members of the family."[10]

The Marshall Plan. Back in Washington, the Truman administration was slow to grasp the full magnitude of the European crisis. It had supported humanitarian aid administered by the UN as a stopgap measure, but Washington insisted on closing down that program at the end of 1946 because some benefits were going to countries under Soviet sway. Finally in 1947 with the Marshall Plan, the Truman administration embraced a more ambitious effort to replace destroyed industry and restart production. By then, growing concern with the Soviet threat had made Washington more receptive to calls for helping western Europe and especially heavily damaged Germany. In theory the Marshall Plan had allowed for aid to the Soviet Union and the Soviet-aligned states of eastern Europe, but Washington's task was greatly simplified when Stalin pulled his delegation out of preliminary consultations in mid-1947 and took his clients with him. Washington proceeded to work out a recovery plan with the western European states and then made available grants that would total some $12 billion through 1952 (about half of the total U.S. aid to Europe since the end of the war; see Table 2.1). To ensure that this altruism benefited the U.S. economy, Congress stipulated that roughly 70 percent of the aid be spent on American-made goods.

U.S. assistance had a significant impact economically, even though by the time it began to arrive in 1948 conditions were already improving. That year the average level of real earnings of western European workers had already exceeded the level for 1938 by 20 percent. Agricultural production and industrial output were rising, transport problems were easing, and spending by firms as well as by ordinary people on goods and services began to increase for the first time. Still, housing and food remained in short supply. Thanks to the Marshall Plan, conditions continued to improve. By 1952 industrial and agricultural production had climbed to 35 percent above the prewar point. Western European economies had turned the corner.

More broadly, the Marshall Plan provided an opportunity to promote American economic and political values in an Old World that had seemingly lost its way. American planners on the scene and their superiors in Washington pushed regional economic integration as a first step toward creating a union of states. U.S. officials were also determined to protect the free market from disruption by

TABLE 2.1 Marshall Plan Aid to Major Western European Recipients	
	(in billions of dollars)
Britain	3.2
France	2.7
Benelux states (Belgium, the Netherlands, and Luxembourg)	1.6
Italy	1.5
West Germany	1.4

Communist-led unions and from state schemes to redistribute wealth, certain that such measures would undermine production and sharpen social tensions without solving Europe's economic problems. Finally, American representatives in Europe opposed rapidly increasing consumption. Rather, they favored "productionism,"—market-driven economic growth through investment in production—confident that this was the surest way to defuse class tensions and restore prosperity and stability while also promoting exports that would integrate European economies into the global trading system. A Marshall Plan brochure that circulated in Italy in 1949 promised "a higher standard of living for the entire nation" and "maximum employment for workers and farmers," but it linked these good things to "greater production."[11]

The substantial U.S. aid program gave Washington less leverage than the planners had expected, however. As one wit has put it, Europe in effect said to the Americans that "we want to be dominated, but on our own terms."[12] U.S. planners had first of all to face rising popular pressure for an immediate improvement in welfare and consumption rather then deferring them in favor of investment and production with the promise of long-term benefits. Governments that did not listen to their citizens clamoring for immediate improvements in food and housing and for jobs risked losing votes. U.S. planners had also to take into account the agenda of centrist conservative politicians at the head of Christian Democratic parties, especially important in France, West Germany, and Italy after the political Right had been discredited by its wartime policies of aggression and collaboration. These conservatives were favorably disposed to the United States—and ready to play on U.S. fears of communism to extract economic and trade concessions from American cold warriors who had nowhere else to turn.

Communist parties in the early postwar period were especially large and influential in France and Italy. Both had strong labor support and popularity derived from wartime resistance to the Germans. But Washington worried that the ties of those parties to Moscow made them a dangerously subversive force if allowed inside any governing coalitions. Christian Democrats, happy to see their rivals out of favor in Washington, cooperated in the exclusion of Communists from power. In France, for example, in spring 1947 the governing coalition dropped its Communist partners. U.S. policy also sought with considerable success to drive a wedge between left-wing and centrist unions, in effect destroying the unity of the European labor movement within countries as well as across the continent.

By marginalizing the Left and by cultivating conservative European elites, the Marshall Plan helped pave the way for economic cooperation as well as the formation of NATO. Christian Democratic parties would in the bargain secure a prolonged period of dominance in European politics while also defending sovereignty and protecting their own economic preferences in the face of demands for a national remake on American lines. Christian Democratic leaders were strikingly traditional in their commitment to preserving state authority and making it serve social stability but also popular welfare. Although favorably disposed to a greater degree of regional cooperation, they were not about to give up national power to a united Europe. And although they were inclined to rely on the market in economic matters, they were not prepared to leave it unchecked and disregard issues of social justice.

The West German Road to Recovery. For West Germany the Marshall Plan signaled a great turnaround in U.S. policy. Initially the Roosevelt administration was determined to render Germany impotent so that it could not precipitate Europe into war for a third time in the twentieth century. As a Jew, Henry Morgenthau, FDR's influential secretary of the treasury, was deeply offended by Nazi anti-Semitism. Germany seemed to him militaristic to the core. He was sure that it would inevitably pose a threat to the peace if not crushed and controlled more decisively than after World War I. Morgenthau's plan was to break Germany up as a political entity and to weaken its economy by "pastoralizing"— destroying industry, exporting industrial equipment as reparations, and leaving only an agricultural base. Ordinary Germans as accomplices of their criminal leaders should be forced to live on a subsistence diet, so Morgenthau contended. FDR's own moral revulsion made him equally vindictive.

The Morgenthau plan set off public controversy as well as dissension within the U.S. government. Secretary of State Hull and Secretary of War Henry L. Stimson recalled that the vindictive peace of 1919 following World War I had spurred German desire for revenge and thus planted the seeds for World War II. They saw reconciliation as the more promising basis for peace. Roosevelt started softening occupation policy, and Truman continued the trend after becoming president. In May 1945 he announced his policy toward the now vanquished Germans. It called for denazification, demilitarization, and a living standard no higher than the lowest elsewhere in Europe, and it embraced the idea that democratization would head off any impulse toward renewed aggression. Truman left the details of the new approach to the commanders of the American, Russian, British, and French forces each occupying a zone of Germany along with a section of Berlin (see Map 1.1).

Between 1946 and 1955 the former enemy became an ally with the emergence of a separate West German state closely linked to western Europe politically and economically. In June 1948 the territorial pieces of what would become the new West German state came together when France, Britain, and the United States merged their zones and introduced a new currency. This step provoked Stalin late in the month to institute his Berlin blockade (see p. 52) in a doomed attempt to avert a permanent division. The blockade hardened American resolve to hold on to western Germany and confirmed anti-Soviet prejudices. The Truman administration moved in fairly short order to create a single West German state (the Federal Republic of Germany, with its capital in Bonn) in May 1949, just two weeks after the end of the Soviet blockade of Berlin.

The Christian Democratic Union won the parliamentary majority that year in the first postwar elections in West Germany. Its leader, the seventy-three-year-old Konrad Adenauer, became chancellor. An opponent of the Hitler regime, he had emerged from prison only to find the Soviets reaching deep into Europe— indeed, into Germany itself. Adenauer reacted with repugnance to this alien force embodying "Asian spirit and power."[13] He accepted the painful division of his country with the hope of saving the non-Soviet portion by aligning it with countries to the west. That meant making peace with the long-time enemy France, seeking economic and military integration within western Europe, and accepting the United States as the ultimate guarantor of German economic recovery and security. These principles would form the basis of his long authoritarian rule. Until 1963 he would support economic cooperation within the European community and make West Germany a full member of NATO.

The Adenauer government and its successors shaped economic policy within the framework of the "social market." This German model stressed free-market competition rather than government management. It gave preference to investment-led and export-oriented growth strategies. It practiced tight monetary policy inspired by memories of the harm soaring inflation had done to fledgling German democracy in the 1920s. These features of the German model were congruent with American preferences. But other prominent features were not. The social market approach promoted a paternalistic welfare system with roots in the late nineteenth century. It tolerated, even encouraged, industrial concentration and cooperation among firms.

Italy's Sturdy Economic Establishment. Italy presents a different pattern, highlighting the diversity of the Marshall Plan impact. Because Italy came out of the war with a post-fascist government acceptable to the British and the Americans, it escaped military occupation. But, as in much of the rest of western Europe, the country's dependence on American assistance gave Washington considerable influence over the government in Rome. That influence was reinforced by the covert activities of the CIA and the overt participation of American labor organizations in the shaping of the postwar Italian labor movement. The Truman administration used these resources to force Italy's large Communist Party out of the coalition government in mid-1947 (at about the same time that the French party suffered its expulsion) and to drive a wedge between Communist and other labor unions. Washington won these victories in close collaboration with an influential center-right Christian Democratic Party headed by Alcide de Gasperi.

But collaboration was a two-way street. Although loyal to Washington on Cold War issues, Rome maintained considerable autonomy in charting its domestic economic course. It presided over an economy defined by concentrated power and a tangled web of public and private interests shaped during the Mussolini era and even earlier. The Christian Democratic government was allied with a tightly knit business elite based in the Piedmont-Lombard region of northern Italy. That elite controlled the country's major private industry located in a triangle defined by the cities of Turin, Milan, and Genoa and articulated its interests through Confindustria, the official association of Italian industry founded in 1919.

The state itself played a major direct economic role. The Institute for Industrial Reconstruction (IRI), a huge bank and industrial holding company that had given the interwar Italian government control of a share of economic activity second only to the Soviet Union, remained a major presence on the postwar scene. A socialist adviser to Mussolini, Alberto Beneduce, had created IRI and

MENDING THE INTERNATIONAL ECONOMY

1929	Financial crash leads to Great Depression
1930s	Industrial economies resort to inward-looking, protectionist policies
1939–1945	World War II devastates production worldwide
1944	Bretton Woods conference makes the dollar the pivotal currency and establishes the International Monetary Fund and the World Bank as oversight institutions for the international economy
1945	The United States accounts for one-third of all global production and two-thirds of world gold reserves
1947	Marshall Plan proposes to revive European economies; U.S. occupation policy in Japan is reversed in favor of economic recovery; General Agreement on Tariffs and Trade is concluded, beginning a gradual reduction in trade barriers
1952	U.S. occupation of Japan ends; Japanese and western European economies approach prewar levels

run it until his death at the end of the war. His son-in-law, Enrico Cuccia (married to Beneduce's aptly named daughter Idea Socialista), then took over. A press-shy Sicilian, Cuccia also headed the influential Milan-based Mediobanca. Created at the end of World War II, it would be Italy's only merchant bank until the 1980s. Funded and majority owned by the state, the bank served firms belonging to the northern business elite and acted as a guarantor of stability within the industrial sector by blocking brash interlopers and dubious mergers. The bank exercised its influence through its minority stake in Italy's major corporations such as Fiat (cars), Pirelli (tires), and Olivetti (office machines) and through its power to open or close the funding spigot for these capital-hungry firms.

This economic establishment carried forward the nationalist and modernizing impulse that had governed Italy's development policy since the turn of the century. That policy gave priority to encouraging foreign trade, protecting the home market, and promoting industrial cooperation, with labor and the state as partners with business. The public-private coalition resorted to a wide range of measures to maintain a high rate of investment essential to achieving these basic goals. Those measures included compression of wages, exploitation of agriculture, and promotion of emigration for the remittances it generated. To the dismay of Americans, advocates of the free market had no more influence in the postwar Italian order than they had had earlier.

THE AMERICAN ECONOMIC POWERHOUSE

The fact that the United States emerged as the impresario of the postwar system of trade and finance was more than a matter of a benevolent national impulse to save the world or Cold War fears that hard times in capitalist countries might work to communist advantage. It also took an American economy that was moving to unprecedented levels of output in the late 1940s and that was unmatched among all the economies of the world. Without its strength, American leaders would have been nearly impotent in the face of profound postwar challenges, and the American public would likely have been loath to direct resources overseas. Because of its strength, that economy could not only meet the needs of government and consumers but also have a deep impact on other countries. American resources and leadership hastened the recovery of western Europe and Japan and offered a vision of a consumer society that many found attractive in the wake of prolonged depression and war. But others, articulating criticisms that would echo into the twenty-first century, charged the U.S. economic giant with intimidating its competitors and forcing them to play by its rules. They also contended that U.S. exports threatened local cultures and eroded a younger generation's national identity.

Good Times Return

The economic might that was critical to making the United States a postwar leader with a global reach had built rapidly from the late nineteenth century. By 1914 the United States was the largest and most homogenous market in the world and had the largest industrial output. For example, already by 1900 American steel output had surpassed that of Britain and Germany combined. Americans had the highest standard of living of any people in the world. And they had the highest level of labor productivity, made possible by sizable capital investments in innovative technology, equipment, and production processes. World War I further elevated the U.S. position, converting it from a net debtor who had borrowed heavily on European capital markets. It was now banker to the world. The U.S. economy had put on an impressive performance with striking growth between 1870 and 1929 in both per capita income and gross domestic product (or GDP; see the key economic terms on p. 14 and Figure 2.1 on p. 97). Already the United States stood as the exemplar of what a modern economy could deliver.

As the largest and most vital of the world's economies, the United States had played a prominent role in bringing the long period of growth to a halt. By closing off the home market during the 1920s and refusing to cooperate with Britain and other economic powers once the Great Depression began to hammer global trade and finance, Washington helped create and then prolong the global downswing. Like others around the world, Americans suffered. In 1933, the grimmest year of the depression, total output had fallen by over a quarter from its high point in 1929, and at least one out of every four workers was unemployed.

While Europe and Japan suffered destruction during wartime and then in the early postwar years struggled with the essentials of survival, Americans watched their economy begin to improve in what turned into a dramatic resurgence. The turnaround began in 1939. In that year GDP recovered to 1929 levels, and by 1944 it had more than doubled, thanks to the stimulus imparted by wartime mobilization.

The first years after the war proved turbulent, though without hardships comparable to what other countries engulfed by war were going through. GDP dropped by a quarter between 1944 and 1947 as the economy made the transition to peacetime. Some eleven million demobilized men returned to the workforce. Savings accumulated by workers during wartime rationing chased too few goods and unleashed inflation. Industries struggling with converting back to civilian production could not keep up with the heavy consumer demand. Inflation coming on top of wartime restraints on wages left organized labor restive. Strike activity began in 1944 and continued to the end of the decade, prompting Republicans in Congress to retaliate by imposing restrictions on labor unions. By 1947 Cold War commitments were adding fresh economic pressures. The Marshall Plan was the first hint of the costs associated with the overseas anticommunist struggle. As we have seen, Truman tried to hold the military budget down, but after the outbreak of the Korean War he put into effect his advisers' proposal for a tripling of defense spending. This dramatic hike set off a fresh bout of inflation, and Truman declared a state of emergency in December 1950 following the Chinese intervention in the war.

Social change set in motion by the war created immediate postwar tensions that were harbingers of major upheavals to come. The shortage of wartime labor had drawn women and African Americans into the mainstream economy. Three out of four women in the workforce remained there after the war, although they were often forced into lower-paying jobs by homecoming veterans. African Americans had migrated out of the South to fill openings in the war industry, and black soldiers returned looking for the freedom at home that their government had asked them to defend abroad. They also wanted economic opportunities to build a better life for their families.

Hanging over these years was the shadow of Keynes. Many economists were convinced that the U.S. economy was approaching maturity and that as it did so, the prospects for growth would dim and the chances of another major downturn would rise. To avert this outcome and extract from the economy its best performance, the American Keynesians prescribed government intervention in the form of counter-cyclical spending—boosting government outlays to stimulate a slowing economy and reducing outlays when the economy was on the rise and employment and industrial capacity were approaching their peak. The new philosophy, born of a determination to avoid another traumatic depression, was embodied in the Full Employment Act of 1946, committing the government to act in order to maximize the potential for economic growth and keep that growth steady.

The fear of renewed depression that haunted the first few postwar years dissipated, though the belief in economic management had become an orthodoxy that survived through the boom time ahead. The economy's immediate problem proved the reverse of what economists had anticipated: not an excess of goods but rather insufficient production to meet demand. But then factories completed their transition from wartime to civilian goods, once scarce raw materials became more available, and so production steadily expanded to meet high demand, inflation dropped, and the standard of living climbed impressively. Though they made

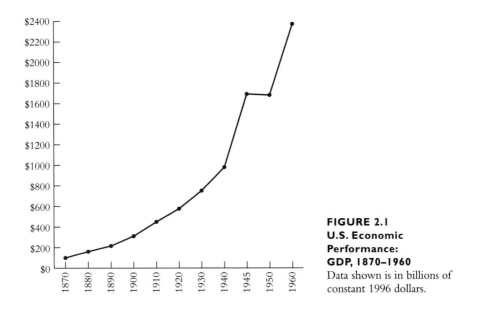

FIGURE 2.1
U.S. Economic
Performance:
GDP, 1870–1960
Data shown is in billions of
constant 1996 dollars.

up only six percent of the world's population, by the mid-1950s Americans were producing a third of the global output. American industry was unchallenged in aircraft and aerospace, electrical appliances, chemical synthetics, automobiles, and lightweight metals, and it was developing new technology with a great future. For example, the first photocopy machine appeared on the market in 1947. IBM sold the first computer in 1953. Television, developed from wartime technology, was proving wildly popular. By 1953 half of all U.S. families owned a set.

The rapid spread of television highlights a broader postwar trend—the capacity of Americans to consume what they produced with such ingenuity and in such abundance. Postwar America witnessed a flowering of consumerism that citizens of all developed countries today take for granted but that at the time was a marvel. Americans led the way in creating a consumer regime, in which much of an individual's daily life as well as the broader culture and economy revolved around the pleasurable acquisition and use of a diverse range of nonessential goods and services. So intense was this engagement in consumption that it helped define personal identity and shape national culture.

The postwar flowering was the culmination of long-term trends. By the end of the twentieth century rising incomes, especially in cities, a growing population, and the development of industry had created a new society edging toward mass consumption. Providing the critical element in this transformation, U.S. industry took the pioneering steps toward mass-produced goods. Rising family incomes began easily to cover basic food and housing, leaving ample funds to spend on nonessential goods and services. By the 1920s many Americans were able to purchase new consumer products such as the telephone, radio, phonograph, and automobile and to afford various forms of entertainment such as

Consumerism and the American Family
Print advertisements put heavy stress in their graphics on domesticity and convenience. This example from 1953 has all the family members in their proper
gender role. The primly attired women in the family admire the adjustable
shelves, the roominess, and the automatic defrosting features of this General
Electric refrigerator. The contented husband looks on, while the boys rough
house outside. Advertisements like this one were part of a sophisticated system of industrial mass production in which the American economy pio-
neered. High output kept prices low. The task of advertising was to get
ordinary Americans to keep buying. Here GE offers encouragement by
offering easy credit terms of $4.36 a week (with vague reference to a
"small down payment" in finer print). (Gaslight Advertising Archives)

movies and vacations. These goods and diversions were coming to define how
substantial numbers of Americans even below the middle class defined the good
life.

Although the Depression of the 1930s checked the development of consumer
culture and wartime rationing further delayed its return, in the postwar years it
revived with a surprising vigor. The return of economic growth intersected with
two closely related trends: the rise of the suburbs and a surge in family formation.
Marriage and birth rates jumped as soldiers and prosperity returned after the war.
Housing sprang up, primarily in the suburbs and mostly owner occupied.
Between 1947 and 1953 some nine million Americans relocated to those
outlying developments where they could purchase a home, often in low-cost real

estate developments. Low down payments and tax deductions for mortgages provided an incentive to buy. Once purchased, homes needed furnishings, and far-flung suburbs made a car essential to get to work and shopping. Mortgage and auto payments came to dominate the family budget. But there was still enough left for weekly diversions as well as an annual vacation. Even a trip to Europe came within reach of ordinary Americans by the early 1950s.

Advertising—from radio jingles to roadside billboards to magazine and newspapers—helped to inspire and shape this outpouring of consumption by celebrating individual choice ("consumer sovereignty") and immediate gratification ("buy now, pay later") and by feeding dreams of ever-greater abundance. Tums appealed to sufferers from indigestion with a catchy jingle: "Night and day, at home or away, always carry TUMS FOR THE TUMMY!" For the busy family, Borden promised the convenience of hot chocolate that "you can make right in the cup!" Listerine asked wives, "Do inhibitions (doubts) threaten married love?"—and offered reassurance in the form of a mouthwash. A lithe, confident skater drew viewers into a fantasy world: "I dreamed I went skating in my Maidenform bra."[14] The advent of television provided a potent new means of reaching the whole family, even children with their growing allowances. Catchy jingles heard often enough—such as "double your pleasure, double your fun" (touting Doublemint chewing gum)—could now enter into an entire generation's collective memory.

Focused on the good life at home, Americans responded coolly when asked to foot the Cold War bill. In the late 1940s Truman needed to raise taxes to cover his multiplying overseas commitments. But Congress, reflecting popular sentiment, was resistant. Truman's war in Korea prompted the same popular impatience as taxes and inflation rose and veterans got the call to return to service. Consumers were proving reluctant crusaders. They wanted instead to relax in the warm glow of prosperity and enjoy the abundance of goods that were beginning to cascade from the American economic cornucopia.

Disney and the U.S. Economic Edge

American corporations looking for business abroad had powerful advantages in the early postwar period. Some of the advantages were temporary. Wartime destruction had badly hurt overseas competitors, and the U.S. government used its dominant position to open foreign markets for U.S. companies. But other advantages, more fundamentally economic and long-lasting, had to do with the fact that American goods came out of the world's most advanced economy geared to mass production for a mass market. Those goods embodied the most recent technology in a country that prided itself on scientific and technical innovation. They carried costs lower than their foreign competitors in part because of their efficient mode of production but also because the home market—the largest output in the world with the highest per capita income—helped reduce the cost of each item in the overall production run. U.S. firms could have a large sales volume, produce on a standardized, assembly-line basis, and thus keep output high and the company growing. Finally, to win and keep buyers, the masters of the new science of advertising exploited market research and insights on the psychology of the consumer. This combination of market scale and technological and advertising skill helped U.S. firms such as IBM in office machines, Kodak in film stock, Du Pont in chemicals, and Boeing in aircraft hold a competitive advantage in postwar international markets.

The American entertainment and communications industry was among the most visible and vigorous part of the export drive, and U.S. filmmakers were its leaders. Already in the interwar period four major producers—Paramount, Fox, Loew's (later MGM), and Warner Brothers—had established their international dominance by building on a strong, centralized American film business. They had worked out cartel arrangements among themselves to limit competition. They also enjoyed the backing of the government. Tariffs protected them from foreign competition from 1920 onward, while the U.S. Commerce Department helped them with overseas marketing and breaching tariff barriers imposed by other countries trying to promote their own film industries.

The Walt Disney enterprise illustrates the international economic edge enjoyed by U.S. business generally and by the burgeoning entertainment industry sector in particular. Though by comparison with the big studios it was an entrepreneurial upstart, Disney was, like them, in an ideal position to exploit postwar opportunities to sell abroad by drawing on a tried-and-true formula applied to consistently innovative, entertaining products. Born in 1901 in Chicago, Disney had begun his career as a cartoonist in his late teens. In 1928 he created the single most important Disney character, Mickey Mouse. This creature combined the personality and voice of Walt Disney with the cartooning skills of Disney's associate, Ubbe Iwerks. Already in 1929 with five short films out, this star of the Disney stable had inspired a craze, filling theaters and creating fan clubs.

To win and keep a broad audience, Disney lavished attention on packaging a product that gave customers what they wanted—chiefly, action and escapist stories. He summed up his unabashedly commercial philosophy in comments to some French cartoonists whose artsy approach left him cold: "Don't go for the *avant garde* stuff. Be commercial. What is art, anyway? It's what people like. So give them what they like. There's nothing wrong with being commercial."[15] Before the release of a film, he would gauge audience reaction to a preview screening and identify last-minute improvements. His carefully worked out public relations strategy relied heavily on good marketing, and he zealously protected his brand name with its promise of a quality, standardized product. He wanted no consumer confusion about what Disney productions meant.

Sensitivity to his audience led Disney to keep his changing political values out of his commercial productions. Growing up on a Missouri farm in the first decades of the century, Disney had picked up from his father what he later called a "socialistic" outlook and a sympathy for the ordinary working man. During the Great Depression he supported Roosevelt's New Deal effort, but success as a filmmaker brought out Disney's conservative side. In 1941, with his payroll climbing to 1,100 employees and a state-of-the-art studio under construction, he suddenly found himself facing serious labor unrest. The resulting strike began turning him to the political right. The anti-communist atmosphere in

Hollywood during the early Cold War completed the shift. He joined the hunt for subversives in the film industry late in the decade and went on to become a conservative Republican who worried about the threat posed by big unions and big government at home and communists abroad. But those who consumed Disney products had little sense of his emergence as a Cold War conservative.

His production process followed widely practiced industrial techniques. Disney projects operated on a tight schedule with work broken into specialized components and under the close supervision of financial specialists. Into this process of mass production for mass consumption, Disney was constantly introducing technological innovations to maintain the novelty of his products and keep one step ahead of the competition. Already in the 1930s he had seen the possibilities of integrating new sound technology to create musical cartoons (in the *Silly Symphony* series culminating in the movie *Fantasia*), the addition of color, and the invention of the multi-plane camera (a fourteen-foot-high mechanical contraption that gave cartoons depth). Other innovations followed after the war—notably big screens (cinema-scope) and stereo sound.

Disney's success in the large and diverse U.S. market made his and other American firms a natural to succeed in foreign markets. The size of that market alone gave him an advantage. Domestic earnings on most films were so great that they would recoup the production costs, thus making overseas income almost pure and sometimes handsome profit. Indeed, overseas sales accounted for almost half of Disney's revenue until the outbreak of World War II disrupted that part of his business. The diversity of the home market also helped by forcing him no less than other producers of consumer goods to design products so that they would appeal to all customers despite the fact that those customers were divided along ethnic, regional, and class lines, each with its own tastes. This challenge of finding a common denominator at home gave his creations a distinct advantage abroad. Mickey Mouse with his universally appealing character led the way overseas as he had at home. The secret to the mouse's international appeal was an ambiguous identity. His age, nationality, and income status were anyone's guess. Only his gender was clear—and that only from his name. That Mickey Mouse and other cartoon characters such as Pluto, Goofy, and Donald Duck did little talking helped as well. By letting the picture tell the story, Disney could limit the dialogue and the distraction of subtitles or voice-overs.

At the end of the war, Disney joined other U.S. export giants in forging ahead. The demand was great, especially from audiences eager to forget the nightmare of depression and war. Disney products quickly regained and then surpassed their former popularity in Europe while making inroads in Asia. Japanese learned to love the Mouse during the American occupation and proved themselves devoted Disney consumers. Merchandise such as watches, toys, comic books, and clothes bearing the image of the famous, adorable rodent, already popular overseas in the late 1920s, remained a bestseller in the postwar period, appearing almost everywhere around the world and assuming a kaleidoscopic array of guises. Building on past strengths, Disney set about to systematically diversify his business, using the large U.S. market as the proving ground and springboard for products that would sell abroad. He moved first into profitable feature-length films and then into television, producing for the home market and then reselling the same material abroad. In Disney's last years he opened the famous theme parks—Disneyland in 1955 and Disney World in 1971. Within a decade of Disneyland's opening, an estimated quarter of the U.S. population had come for a visit. With its appeal established, the Disney theme park model would appear first in Japan and then in France, with China next in line. Following Disney's death in 1966, the company continued to grow and diversify, starting a chain of retail stores to merchandise Disney-related products and acquiring a major television network, ABC. An imaginary mouse had given birth to a distinctly American, globe-girdling corporate enterprise devoted to the sale of pleasant distractions.

"Coca-Colonization" and the Mass Consumption Model

As Mickey Mouse and the Disney theme parks suggest, patterns of consumption indulged in by Americans exercised an appeal well beyond American shores. This global reach has been dubbed "Coca-colonization" after the soft drink originating in Atlanta in the 1880s. Coca-Cola would become the symbol of an international expansion of American popular culture and American-style consumerism throughout the postwar period. It demonstrated how advertising could create broad demand, even for a drink with no nutritional value. Coke, which its president once described as containing "the essence of capitalism," first turned to the export market in the 1920s.[16] By the 1930s the company was operating in twenty-eight countries through franchise arrangements. The parent company provided advertising, quality control, and of course the concentrate with its secret formula. Wherever American troops and, later, tourists arrived in the 1940s and 1950s, Coke was close behind. Advertising promised that with every sip of the sugary beverage went the spirit of adventure, freedom, modernity, and prosperity.

Foreigners gravitated to Coke and other uniquely American products precisely because they were appealing symbols of a way of life ("Americanization"). In Europe, young people were often the first and most fervent in embracing things American and thus claiming a symbolic liberation from their own country's or parents' codes. Consuming Coke represented a vote for a different kind of life vaguely imagined from Hollywood westerns, knock-offs of American comic books, or the fluid, improvisational nature of American jazz. Even though American dominance and interference in European affairs could irritate some among the broader public and many among the intellectual elite, Europeans were in general drawn to consumer goods and mass culture and admired the modernity, economic abundance, and technical virtuosity that the United States represented. As economies recovered and incomes climbed, Europeans acquired the products that defined the new consumer lifestyle: kitchen appliances, vacuum cleaners, washers and dryers, radios and televisions, cameras and film, cosmetics, detergents, pre-processed food, and even cars.

As a marker of Americanization, however, Coke took second place to Hollywood, whose products were already flooding foreign cinemas in the interwar period. U.S. films proved a strong draw in the European market with its relatively high per capita income and especially in cities among women and workers. They liked fast-paced, escapist stories. They were transfixed by images of fantastic wealth playing on the screen. And they found appealing Hollywood's democratic impulse to parody authority and celebrate personal choice and mobility. Hollywood was also moving into the emerging markets of Latin America and Asia.

After World War II, Hollywood exports retained their strong position in foreign markets. Defeated Japan and the U.S. portion of occupied Germany were fully open to "tinsel town" products. Italy, which came out of the war with a still vital film industry and an avid movie-going public, proved an especially rich market. Of the 850 films Italians watched in 1946, 600 were American. Only 65 were locally made. In 1948, U.S.-made films climbed to 668 and claimed 75 percent of what Italians spent on movies. By contrast, Italian-made films had fallen to 54 and accounted for only 13 percent of theater revenue. The data for other international markets told the same story of Hollywood strength eclipsing local productions.

Film exports after World War II took up the theme first sounded so forcefully by interwar films—the possibilities of a new lifestyle. Popular films such as *The Wizard of Oz, Bambi, Zorro's Fighting Legion, Gone with the Wind*, and *Drums along the Mohawk* (to take just a sample from the early 1950s) celebrated individualism and freedom. They provided a new definition of glamour and physical beauty quickly adopted by fashion-conscious women. They pictured the abundant lifestyle that Americans had achieved (or at least saw within reach). These packaged dreams reinforced by the new art of advertising and by Cold War propaganda helped shape postwar aspirations among ordinary people, especially in western Europe and Japan. Ordinary people could have a home of their own with adequate room for all the family, a kitchen filled with appliances, washing and drying machines to take away domestic drudgery, a car for convenience and mobility, and regular vacation trips to new and interesting places. Reinforcing Hollywood's messages were American GIs with their slang and casual ways indifferent to class. U.S. military stores in Europe were themselves amazing advertisements for American comfort and abundance. Out of those stores poured food, liquor, cigarettes, candy, cosmetics, and nylons, which became either gifts or sale items on the black market. Even literature assumed new prominence as a window on the world of a rich and romantic country. For example, in occupied Japan during 1949 and 1950, the 1936 novel *Gone with the Wind* topped the bestseller list. Americans had become models even for transcending defeat.

European Resistance to "Americanization"

In Europe, U.S. cultural influence was at a transitional point in the early postwar years. It was regaining ground it had won early in the century, especially in the 1920s. But its scope and impact were still limited. Many Europeans were struggling to feed, clothe, and house themselves, putting consumer dreams out of practical reach for the moment. Vested economic interests proved another obstacle to doing business American style. U.S. companies and their trade groups joined Marshall planners in pressing for new distribution methods that would get goods to consumers in the most direct way at the lowest cost. But small shop-keepers, who had enjoyed traditional political protection throughout Europe, successfully fought back. They were determined to protect their livelihoods from the threat of department stores and chain-managed stores that prevailed in the U.S. market. More broadly, the immediate hopes for a single market with a homogenous taste—again, the American model—was frustrated by the persistence of strong differences between urban and rural Europe, among Europeans of different classes, and among regions even within the same country.

Adding to the resistance to U.S. cultural and economic incursion were outspoken elites. They had already developed elaborate critiques of American influence in reaction against inroads earlier in the century. Fascist regimes and Communist parties alike had denounced things American as degenerate and doomed. They claimed that U.S. influence represented materialism, crude mass culture, and rule by an ignorant public or by corrupt political bosses. Cultural nationalists in Nazi Germany saw U.S. films promoting crass values and bad racial influences antithetical to their goal of a purified people. In the Nazi indictment Hollywood was run by Jews, and Mickey Mouse along with jazz were condemned as parts of a "negroized" popular culture. In interwar France the Right also led the resistance to American films and other products. They found particularly objectionable the depiction of social freedom that seemed to them to border on anarchy. The French government took action to preserve national identity and social order by, for example, subsidizing the French film industry.

After the war the Left, especially the continent's Communist parties, became vocally anti-American, while intellectuals and politicians affiliated with the Catholic Church sometimes seconded their complaints. The Left bristled over the penetration of American capital and the presumed influence that U.S. corporations and government wielded over European life. That influence was particularly worrisome in the context of the emerging Cold War. Socialists and Communists saw this cultural penetration along with the Marshall Plan and NATO as part of a broad American effort to integrate Europe into a U.S.-dominated bloc. Catholic-inspired commentators and critics shared with the Americans a firm anti-communism but still deplored the acquisitive individualism and obsession with market values associated with an encroaching American way.

The Case of France. France was the hotbed of European anti-Americanism throughout the early postwar years and beyond. Critics made frequent attacks on American influence and the spiritually empty and culturally stunted American lifestyle. American methods of mass production and mass consumption promoted conformism and a fixation with efficiency that would overwhelm France's humanistic values and undermine French conceptions of a balanced economy (mixing state and free market) and traditional ways of production, sales, savings, and spending. American economic, military, and political dominance at the end of the war reinforced those prejudices. How could a declining France operate under the shadow of this superpower and still retain its proud national identity? That Americans were guided by a dangerously rigid anti-communism and were ignorant of the Europe that they pretended to lead only made the situation more upsetting.

The main source of this French anti-Americanism was the French Communist Party. It was joined by a substantial, influential segment of the intellectual class, including artists such as the painter Pablo Picasso, the existentialist philosophers Jean-Paul Sartre and Albert Camus, and the influential *Le Monde* newspaper whose editors favored a separate European path and rejected any control by the two superpowers. All these groups perceived a major American invasion under way. An essay in *Le Monde* complained, "Chryslers and Buicks speed down our roads; American tractors furrow our fields; Frigidaires keep our food cold; stockings 'made by Du Pont' sheathe the legs of our stylish women."[17]

As during the interwar period, Hollywood films drew fire as dangerous vehicles for spreading American values. The French Left denounced Hollywood's films as capitalist propaganda. These banal, escapist, profit-driven products created a standardized taste for the endless pursuit of consumer goods. If given free rein, Hollywood would make the French what the Americans already had become— slaves to their movie magazines, household appliances, automobiles, or whatever advertisers were pushing. The French Left thus called, just as the Right had earlier, for state intervention to protect national values from this foreign plague. The first governmental attempt to restrict American films came in 1946, and this official effort to limit the U.S. "cultural invasion" would continue to century's end even as audiences flocked to cinemas showing Hollywood's creations.

The most dramatic moment in the French struggle against American inroads came in the late 1940s with Coke rather than Hollywood the target. Coke had had only one bottler in France before the outbreak of war, but it planned on generally expanding its European operations in the postwar period. It had made a good start during the war by setting up bottling plants close enough to the front lines to supply U.S. troops. When the postwar expansion got started, Coke encountered opposition throughout Europe but nowhere more vociferously than in France. In 1948 the finance ministry took a stand against the U.S. bottler on the grounds that its operation would bring no fresh capital to help with French recovery and, worse yet, was likely to drain profits back to the parent company in the United States. Threatened domestic interests—notably producers of wine, fruit juice, mineral water, cider, and beer—lobbied the government for protection while publicly charging that Coke was "a poison." In their view, it was, like other addictive substances such as drugs and tobacco, a threat to public health. The French Communist Party, standing at the forefront of this attack on "the Coca-Cola invasion," launched a sustained and highly polemical assault. It warned that this "American trust" would leave France poorer and even suggested that its distribution system would double as an espionage network.[18]

Coke's lawyers and lobbyists fought back, while its management got the State Department and the U.S. embassy in Paris to lean on the French government. The U.S. media, which closely followed the attack on this national icon, joined Coke spokesmen in framing the issue in terms of French gratitude for wartime sacrifices and loyalty in the Cold War struggle. The head of the Coke export drive chided the French for their ingratitude: "Coca-Cola was not injurious to the health of the Americans who liberated France from the Nazis." A U.S. newspaper editorial invoked the anti-communist preoccupations of the time when it stated

Coca-Cola Embraces the World
The May 15, 1950, cover of *Time,* the popular U.S. weekly magazine, shows a kindly Coke bottle cap helping a thirsty world to a long, cooling drink. Critics in France and elsewhere saw something less benign in the friendly embrace—a campaign to displace local cultures with "the American way of life." (TimePix)

confidently, "You can't spread the doctrines of Marx among people who drink Coca-Cola."[19]

The controversy over the soft drink finally abated in 1950. France's National Assembly had decided to leave the final decision to public health experts. They told the government that Coke posed no threat. Finally, in 1953 a lingering legal battle ended in favor of the Americans. The Communists had wrung all the propaganda they could from the issue. Centrist cabinets tied to NATO and dependent on Marshall Plan support had reluctantly lined up against Coke. They were glad to see the issue go away. The French establishment—parliamentarians, high civil servants, academics, business managers, and other professionals—were in general also glad to see the furor disappear. This entrenched elite was uneasy over the encroachment of what it regarded as an immature, uncivilized American culture but, unlike the Left, was more sympathetic to American political and economic influence and thus less alarmed by Coke's expansion plans. Finally, domestic producers were feeling less threatened. Polls suggested that 61 percent of the population thoroughly disliked Coke. This response set the postwar pattern in which France would lag behind all the rest of Europe in per capita consumption of the quintessentially American beverage. It was for the tourists to drink. As one French pundit put it, his countrymen would proudly back national tradition, sticking with wine and rejecting the drinks of the superpowers, whether vodka or Coke.

The Impact of the U.S. Consumer Model. Were these early critics right to attack Coke and other American exports and, more broadly, American economic domination? One way to think about this question—one that remains pertinent today—is in counterfactual ("What if?") terms. If there had been no United States to wield its influence in the immediate postwar years, how different would the emerging economic order have looked? The U.S. role was probably indispensable to mending the tears in the system. It joined Britain in quickly putting the international economy on a solid footing. It supplied the funds to restore the western European economies. And it took in hand the reform of the Japanese economy.

It is less clear how to appraise the impact of the American consumer model that spread through the medium of popular culture. Was the United States by dint of its leadership and resources transforming the world in its own image? Some would say that the U.S. model sent the lives and imagination of peoples in the advanced economies off in new directions. It is true that Americans were setting the pace in regard to industrial mass production and mass consumption. These trends in production and consumption were in turn associated with urbanization, rising levels of literacy and technological skills, the shift to a nuclear family, and increasing personal mobility at the expense of community.

But rather than seeing the United States creating these trends in other countries, it might be more revealing to think of the United States both as a leading indicator of where other advanced industrial countries were likely to go and as an example encouraging those trends. Perhaps it would be more accurate to see the United States, western Europe, and Japan all following parallel trajectories, all driven by similar technological and social forces, and all moving toward a modernity that would look largely but not entirely alike. In attacking the United States, critics were perhaps more fundamentally attacking features of modern life that they found homogenizing and dehumanizing without also counting the considerable gains in standards of living that went with new conditions. Were homes without electricity, indoor plumbing, and labor-saving appliances really so wonderfully quaint that they should remain unchanged? Could Mickey Mouse and Coke really transform the outlook of unwary consumers, or did those products answer to new tastes made possible by higher incomes and more discretionary spending? Comfortable intellectual and political elites might have doubts, but for ordinary Europeans the chance for a family to go out for a light entertainment and perhaps a quick snack and then return to comfortable quarters was not optional or debatable; it was becoming a right in the new postwar social order.

CONCLUSION

U.S. economic initiatives had proven extraordinarily successful on a broad front in a short time. It was no small feat to set the international economy on a new foundation, thus making possible a new phase in the process of globalization.

Closely related was the U.S. contribution to hastening the recovery of western Europe while at the same time rehabilitating former foes in West Germany and Japan. Thanks to the vitality of the U.S. economy, American leaders could do all these things despite the high costs of the global war just ended and of the Cold War commitments just beginning.

For all its efforts at reconstruction, the United States would (as Chapter 5 will show) reap rewards: participation in international economic growth spanning the 1950s and 1960s, an enhanced reputation as an effective leader of the anti-communist coalition, and allies in Europe and Japan whose prosperity made them assets rather than liabilities in the Cold War. But success also bred problems (as Chapter 5 will also show). Europe and Japan participated in the American-led international economy without fully accepting American notions of how that economy should work. National cultural values, often with roots in the premodern period, would prove surprisingly persistent. They would inform economic behavior even in an age of increasing global exchange and turn seemingly universal economic and social trends in regionally distinct directions that would bedevil American leaders. Alongside contending views on how the free market should operate arose sharp criticism of flaws in its practical effects. Rapid, heedless growth, however welcome in the short term, imposed environmental costs that were dangerous in the long term. Women in the United States and Europe demanded greater opportunities to participate in and benefit from the new prosperity through enhanced educational and job opportunities and family-friendly government policies. Finally, out of the developing world came a sharp critique of the promise that the new international economy would benefit all and close the gap between rich and poor countries.

RECOMMENDED RESOURCES

The international economy

For **a general overview of the postwar economy,** turn to Daniel Yergin and Joseph Stanislaw, *The Commanding Heights: The Battle for the World Economy* (rev. ed., 2002), sprightly and impressionistic. **John Maynard Keynes,** so influential in shaping postwar reforms, is well served by D. E. Moggridge, *Keynes* (3rd ed., 1993) and Robert J. A. Skidelsky, *Keynes* (1996)—both brief introductions prepared by Keynes's two foremost biographers. The contributors to Peter A. Hall, ed., *The Political Power of Economic Ideas: Keynesianism across Nations* (1989), do an excellent job of tracing Keynes's worldwide impact.

The U.S. economy

For **general treatments:** Robert M. Collins, *More: The Politics of Economic Growth in Postwar America* (2000), is an essential overview on a critical theme for the entire last half of the twentieth century. See also Tom Kemp, *The Climax of Capitalism: The U.S. Economy in the Twentieth Century* (1990), which stresses inherent instabilities; and Richard Holt, *The Reluctant Superpower: A History of America's Global Economic Reach* (1995), which makes the case for a belated, qualified, and brief U.S. leadership role. On **the flowering of postwar consumer culture,** see Daniel Horowitz, *The Morality of Spending: Attitudes toward the Consumer Society in America, 1875–1940* (1985); Susan Strasser, *Satisfaction Guaranteed: The Making of the American Mass Market* (1989); and Olivier Zunz, *Why the American Century?* (1998), especially important on the rise of a consumer society during the interwar period. For print advertisements revealing changing social styles and tastes from the 1940s onward, go to the archives at <http:www.adflip.com>. On **Disney and Coke,** the most helpful works are Richard Schickel, *The Disney Version: The Life, Times, Art, and Commerce of Walt Disney* (rev. ed., 1986); Steven Watts, *The Magic Kingdom: Walt Disney and the American Way of Life* (1997); and Mark Pendergrast, *For God, Country, and Coca-Cola: The Definitive History of the World's Most Popular Soft Drink* (rev. ed., 2000).

Postwar Europe

For **overviews**, see J. Robert Wegs and Robert Ladrech, *Europe since 1945: A Concise History* (4th ed., 1996); Walter Laqueur, *Europe in Our Time: A History, 1945–1992* (1992); and Robert O. Paxton, *Europe in the Twentieth Century* (3rd ed., 1997). All are balanced, wide-ranging accounts that define their subject broadly to include the Soviet Union. On **the recovery from wartime devastation,** see David W. Ellwood, *Rebuilding Europe: Western Europe, America, and Postwar Reconstruction* (1992); Jean-Pierre Rioux, *The Fourth Republic, 1944–1958*, trans. Godfrey Rogers (1987); and Paul Ginsborg, *A History of Contemporary Italy: Society and Politics, 1943–1988* (1990).

Japan's recovery

John Dower, *Embracing Defeat: Japan in the Wake of World War II* (1999), the product of a lifetime of research, is the place to begin. See also his *Empire and Aftermath: Yoshida Shigeru and the Japanese Experience, 1878–1954* (1979). The trauma and upheaval that Japanese experienced through wartime and American occupation become clear in Haruko Taya Cook and Theodore Cook, *Japan at War: An Oral History* (1992), and Sodei Rinjirō, *Dear General MacArthur: Letters from the Japanese during the American Occupation*, ed. John Junkerman and trans. Shizue Matsuda (2001). Andrew Gordon, ed., *Postwar Japan as History* (1993), contains a fine collection of essays, as does *The Cambridge History of Japan*, vol. 6: *The Twentieth Century*, ed. Peter Duus (1988).

Americanization

The impact of American mass media and values in Europe has attracted considerable attention of late. Richard H. Pells, *Not Like Us: How Europeans Have Loved, Hated, and Transformed American Culture since World War II* (1997), and Richard F. Kuisel, *Seducing the French: The Dilemma of Americanization* (1993), highlight the differences among scholars on the depth of American influence. Victoria de Grazia, "Mass Culture and Sovereignty: The American Challenge to European Cinemas, 1920–1960," *Journal of Modern History* 61 (March 1989): 53–87, is a gem that underlines the degree to which postwar Americanization built on earlier inroads. For insights on U.S. influence outside the heavily studied trans-Atlantic context, see Gilbert M. Joseph et al., eds., *Close Encounters of Empire: Writing the Cultural History of U.S.–Latin American Relations* (1998).

CHAPTER 3

THE THIRD WORLD: FIRST TREMORS IN ASIA

Asian lands underwent a profound transformation after World War II. The region extending from Korea, through China, Vietnam, and maritime Southeast Asia (including Indonesia and the Philippines), and then on to Burma and India became the most turbulent part of the third world from the late 1940s through the 1960s. The reasons that Asia led the way during the early and middle phases of the Cold War are clear. Nowhere was the old colonial order weaker. Elite-led nationalist movements were organizing in these regions even before the Pacific War began. During the war Japanese forces drove Americans and Europeans from much of the region, and in some places the Japanese occupation actively encouraged anti-colonial sentiment. Only in India did the British retain control in the face of advancing Japanese forces and restive subjects. The sudden end of the Pacific War in August 1945 and the collapse of Japanese authority created confusion that independence-minded Asian leaders were often able to exploit to their advantage. Subject peoples were no longer prepared to accept foreign control as the natural order of things.

At the very time that their grip on Asian possessions was weakening, Europeans who had once ruled vast sweeps of the globe faced other problems. At home they staggered under the devastation of World War II, while internationally they had to accept their own eclipse before rising Soviet and American powers intent on harnessing decolonization to their own ends. As we have already seen, U.S. cold warriors worried about instability at peripheral Asian points but feared diverting scarce resources from the critical European front. From the perspective of the Kremlin, Asia offered opportunities to win friends and isolate the United States but also posed dangers, as opportunistic nationalists and impetuous Communists proved hard to control.

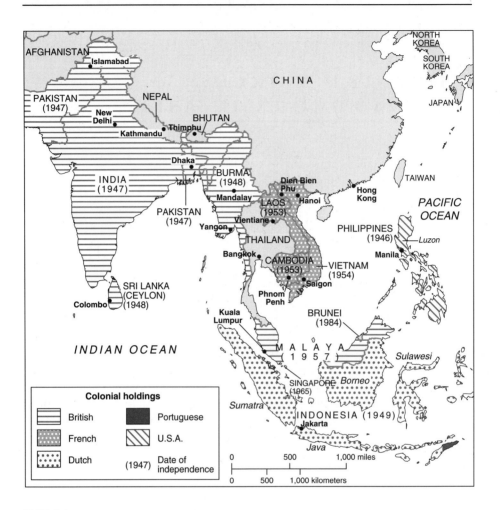

MAP 3.1
South and Southeast Asia on the Eve of Independence

THE APPEAL OF REVOLUTION
AND THE STRONG STATE

In parts of Asia the immediate postwar years were marked by tumult and some-times by violence. Korea was liberated by Japan's defeat only to be divided by Soviet and American forces of occupation and then wracked by conflict when the Soviet-backed northern regime attacked the U.S.-supported South in a bid to reunite the country (see Chapter 1). Three years of fighting, drawing in both U.S. and Chinese forces, ended in stalemate. Korea was battered and the political division became permanent. But it is to China and Indochina (the French pos-session out of which the states of Vietnam, Cambodia, and Laos would emerge by 1954) that we must turn for the most notable upheavals of the first decade following World War II. The Chinese and Vietnamese revolutions stand in their scope, their ambitions, and their ultimate travails on a par with any of the major revolutions of the twentieth century, including Russia's. They reshaped the lives of nearly a quarter of the world's peoples, convulsed the region, raised the temperature of the global Cold War, and both inspired and frightened foreign observers.

The Chinese Communist Triumph

China's revolution had enormous ramifications, changing the lives of a population totaling about half a billion at mid-century. It both built on and tried to alter a long and unbroken cultural tradition. And it preserved China's great territorial expanse—the only major empire to survive to the end of the twentieth century and beyond.

Applied to China, the word *revolution* carries a variety of meanings. In its narrowest sense it points to the Communist seizure of power in 1949, made possible by the defeat of its Nationalist foes and the ensuing effort by the Communist leader Mao Zedong to fundamentally remake China's culture and politics. Taken in its broadest meaning, China's revolution refers to a century-long effort to save a country in decline and to restore its power and prestige. China's loss of sovereignty began in the 1830s with Britain's victory over the Qing dynasty in the Opium War and the conclusion of the first unequal treaties giving foreigners a wide range of special rights and privileges. A long rain of blows followed, including having the capital, Beijing, twice occupied by foreign troops and the empire's vast territory carved up by the major powers into informal spheres of influence. Finally in 1912 the last of the dynasties, the Qing, collapsed and in its place appeared a weak republic.

Already in the late nineteenth century Chinese political leaders were seeking the secret of the wealth and power enjoyed by an ascendant West and an energized Japan. That search carried those leaders toward an ever more radical agenda. They focused at first on acquiring basic technology, mastering modern weapons, and learning foreign languages. By the turn of the century, impatient reformers were exploring foreign political systems—first constitutional monarchy, then democracy, and finally fascism and socialism—as the cure-all for China's woes. Even after the Chinese Communist Party (CCP) won power, the search continued, with Mao's vision of a permanent revolution at odds with the bureaucratically controlled, specialist-dominated planning favored by some of his colleagues. Finally, in the late 1970s Mao's successors experimented with a free-market economy functioning within an authoritarian political system. (The post-1949 phases of the revolution are covered in Chapters 6 and 8.) "Wealth and power," a phrase coined in the nineteenth century, remained to the end of the twentieth century and beyond a core aspiration of Chinese nationalism and a driving concern of Chinese engaged in this revolutionary makeover of their country.

Mao and the Making of China's Revolution. Mao Zedong's central place in this revolution and the shadow he cast long after his death offer another reminder of the important impact strong personalities can have in human affairs. He was the father of one revolution, and his successors would have to carry out a second, market-oriented revolution in order to escape the political and economic constraints that the Mao era had created. Looking through the prism of Mao's life can help us see the stages through which China's revolution unfolded and the concerns that drove it.

Mao grew up in a period marked by the first stirrings of reform and then revolutionary activity among political elites. He was born in 1893 in the interior province of Hunan into a rich peasant family. The young Mao staged his first revolution against his father, whom he regarded as domineering and exploitative. He went away to study in foreign-influenced schools in the capital city of his province, and he served briefly in the republican army that toppled the imperial dynasty in 1912. He worked for a time as a librarian in Beijing University and got caught up in the intellectual and political ferment that was gripping educated youth during the late 1910s.

Like other young intellectuals of the time, Mao was outraged by nearly a century of foreign aggression, and he was desperate to save China from the humiliations foreigners had inflicted on a proud people with a glorious history and culture. His earliest years had coincided with the loss of Korea (then a Chinese protectorate) and Taiwan (a frontier territory), the second occupation of Beijing, the repeated payment of indemnities to foreign powers, and the informal Russo-Japanese partition of the northeastern provinces (known to foreigners as Manchuria), so all these events were fresh in mind. Sometime around 1910–1911, Mao (then in his late teens) read a political pamphlet lamenting China's imminent dismemberment. It so impressed him that years later he could still recall its opening line—"Alas, China will be subjugated."—and his own feeling of depression "about the future of my country" and the dawning realization "that it was the duty of all people to help save it."[1]

As a social critic and advocate of reform, Mao sought to understand why China had lost its way. He blamed a feudal society for holding China back. As a young man he bristled at arranged marriages, lamented neglect of the public good in the name of family and profit, and attacked popular superstition. He wanted a strong Chinese state that could create a modern, united country and secure respect on the international stage. Mao's concerns with social renovation and national salvation came together in 1919. Writing in a magazine that he edited, Mao made the fervid prediction for his country that

> the more profound the oppression, the greater its resistance. . . . [O]ne day, the reform of the Chinese people will be more profound than that of any other people, and the society of the Chinese people will be more radiant than that of any other people. . . .
> We must all exert ourselves! We must all advance with the utmost strength! Our golden age, our age of glory and splendour, lies before us.[2]

True to his faith in China's greatness, he joined other students in 1919 in a nationwide protest (known as the May Fourth Movement) against Japanese aggression in China and against the warlords and traitors who helped keep China weak. The students called for the creation of a new culture that was vigorous, scientific, and democratic. They were measuring China's deficiencies against Western achievements.

These concerns led Mao, like many educated youth of his generation, to take a growing interest in the Bolshevik revolution and Marxist theory. They saw in revolutionary Russia a model applicable to China and an inspiration to a weak and poor country seeking to regain its independence and rid itself of a corrupt and enfeebled ruling class. The Marxist ideology that guided the Bolsheviks appealed strongly to those angry over foreign ("imperialist") domination and exploitation and determined to move China from feudalism to a higher level of development. Marxism in its Russian form (Leninism) offered a tool of analysis and a guide to action. Few Chinese thoroughly understood these imported ideas, but Mao and others were certain that they had found a body of thought that could carry China to a new era of national unity, wealth, power, and justice.

Mao was a founding member of the Chinese Communist Party, formally organized in 1921 with only fifty members. The CCP drew on its members' patriotism and readiness to sacrifice, while providing a Leninist party organization and formal ideology, both critical for collective action. Mao remained active through its difficult early years. Guided by emissaries from Moscow, the CCP entered into a one-sided alliance with the Nationalist Party and was nearly wiped out when the leader of that party, Chiang Kai-shek, turned on the Communists in 1927. Chiang was bent on bringing central control and order to a country torn by civil war among regional authorities ever since the fall of the last imperial dynasty. The Communists threatened his program, and he regarded Soviet support for the CCP as another case of imperialist meddling in China's domestic affairs.

Mao fled to the countryside and began to act on his growing conviction that the secret to revolution in China was to be found not in the urban proletariat but in the peasantry. Mao's discovery, critical to the survival and ultimate triumph of the CCP, was that peasants had aspirations and discontents that the CCP could tap and channel to its own benefit. Peasants wanted land, reduced interest on debts, lower rents, and freedom from oppressive taxes. Peasants might have a narrow horizon, but they could be politically mobilized if the CCP addressed these immediate, concrete concerns.

Mao's reliance on peasant support developed by stages. His own rural roots had introduced him to the harsh realities of life in the countryside. During his early years in the party he had given peasants a prominent place in his reflections on revolutionary strategy even if party leaders and their Soviet advisers scoffed at the notion of the party of the proletariat vesting its hopes in the most backward, feudal social element. After he personally conducted studies of rural conditions with an eye to their revolutionary potential, Mao declared in 1927 that peasants could "rise like a tornado or tempest—a force so extraordinarily swift and violent that no power, however great, will be able to suppress it."[3] Mao first applied his insights in a remote rural area (known as the Jiangxi Soviet) where the CCP had carved out a base of operations among peasants and peasants-turned-bandits. In 1934 the Jiangxi Soviet collapsed under relentless Nationalist military pressure, and some ninety thousand Communists fled, beginning what came to be

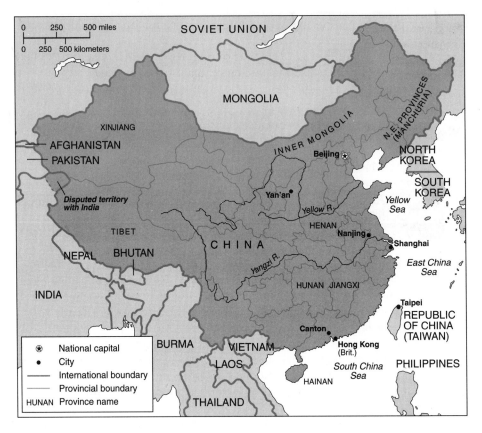

MAP 3.2
China and Its Neighbors, 1949
China's international boundaries depicted here reflect territorial claims advanced by the People's Republic of China and realized within its first few years. Mao's regime claimed Taiwan but, much to his frustration, the island remained under the control of the rival Nationalist government.

known as the "Long March." Only five thousand with Mao in the lead would reach the new center of party activity in a remote and impoverished area of China's northwest (the region around Yanan). Once more, it was to peasants that he would have to turn to make his revolution.

Between 1935 and 1949 Mao took control of the CCP and guided it down what would prove a tortuous and dangerous road to victory. By the late 1930s the elements for a successful revolution had come together. Mao had assembled a leadership team with a clear program, an effective party organization, and a skilled guerrilla army. The relocation to Yanan, distant from Nationalist centers of power, brought Mao's CCP an unprecedented degree of safety. There Mao honed his skills as a political tactician and military strategist. But even this combination of favorable circumstances might not have been enough to bring the CCP victory had not the Japanese invaded China in 1937, further weakening and distracting the Nationalists. The ensuing war against Japan would devastate the eastern portion of the country and kill an estimated fifteen million Chinese. Only the Soviet Union had greater losses during World War II. The CCP called almost at once for united national resistance against the invaders and used the ensuing anti-Japanese struggle to expand its area of influence and to attract to its ranks patriotic young people.

The war years engendered in Mao a marked optimism about the postwar situation. Like a broad spectrum of political leaders, he saw China as a semi-colonial country in need of liberation and renovation. Allied promises to end the old international system that had done such harm to China appealed powerfully to him. He was heartened by the Anglo-American meeting in August 1941 that produced the Atlantic Charter commitment to a new world order and expressions of Anglo-American interest in cooperating with the embattled Soviet Union. America's entry into the war several months later struck him as a guarantee not only of an anti-fascist victory but also of a lasting international alignment favorable to peace and change within China.

By early 1945 Mao was in even higher spirits. In the benign national and international environment produced by Allied cooperation, he expected that he could force the Nationalists to accept a power-sharing arrangement. The longer-term prospects were, in his estimate, even brighter. Although the United States seemed for the moment economically vital, Mao held to the orthodox Marxist view that ultimately, within a decade perhaps, that country would find itself in the grip of a shattering crisis. The Soviet Union would then come into unchallenged preeminence, and fundamental change within nations and within the global system would be assured. Mao held to this optimistic view well into 1946. But by then the Cold War chill was beginning to reach China. The Nationalists were not interested in power sharing, and Washington backed the Nationalists as the best counter to growing Communist influence.

With political reform blocked, Mao fell back on the rural base-area strategy that had earlier proven its worth. Acting on his insight that peasants offered the CCP its broadest and staunchest support, Mao and his colleagues had demonstrated a commitment to dealing with rural problems such as landlessness and extortionate interest rates. Their efforts had won the party military recruits, a supply of food, intelligence, hiding places, and a stream of sympathizers and, ultimately, members. Thanks to the resilience of these base areas, Mao had been able to survive before 1945 in the face of far stronger Japanese and Nationalist forces. Now in 1946 with civil war looming, Mao looked to base areas as the key to ultimate victory. Though initially outnumbered and facing a Nationalist army generously supported by the United States, his forces finally managed to take the offensive thanks primarily to peasant support as well as superior morale and leadership and some assistance from the Soviet Union.

Given the diversity of China's countryside, there was no single peasant perspective on the CCP appeal. One example—Houhua village in northernmost Henan province in north central China—offers a sense of the grim and precarious conditions that many of the rural poor were desperate to escape. Good years provided barely enough to get by, and bad years could be disastrous. A folk saying in the area captured the daily struggle to stay alive:

> In Spring the land is white with salt
> In Summer floodwaters rush in
> In Autumn locusts fill the air
> In Winter wind kicks up the sand
> In normal years we are cold and hungry
> For only half the year is there enough grain.[4]

Bad years could be horrendous, as 1942 demonstrated. It began with drought that left the land parched and crops dying. Prayers for rain had no effect. Then swarms of locusts hit, stripping away whatever vegetation was left. With no relief coming from outside, 125 out of Houhua's 800 inhabitants starved to death. Ninety percent of all families had to sell their land and flee to other areas to look for work and food. Nearby markets were soon selling women and female children. Even human flesh began appearing for sale. One village resident recalled this "sorrowful period of our history"—how an uncle had had to sell both his daughters for about twenty gallons of grain and how his grandfather had handed over the family's three-room brick house for the same amount. The family's precious acre of farming land had gone too.

In Houhua as elsewhere, peasant desperation presented an opportunity for local CCP organizers to win support. A handful of party members in a nearby village began secretly recruiting poor peasants by convincing them that it was possible to organize to resist land grabs and other abuses by rich households. Peasant associations thus took shape, and from the most active and effective participants, the CCP recruited new members. Influence within many villages like Houhua gave the CCP the resources essential to ensuring its survival and making itself a national force.

New China Sets Its Course. By 1948, CCP victory was assured; by the end of 1949, most of China was under party control. In October 1949, standing before an enthusiastic crowd filling the square in central Beijing, Mao proudly proclaimed the creation of the People's Republic of China (PRC). China, so long humiliated, had at last stood up. "Our nation will never again be an insulted nation," he had declared a short time earlier. Looking ahead, he defined the ultimate task of the CCP to exploit the potential of the Chinese revolution to "change everything." He promised "before long there will arise a new China with a big population and a great wealth of products, where life will be abundant and culture will flourish."[5]

Mao continued to work alongside other party leaders with whom he had closely collaborated during the Yanan years. Zhou Enlai, a worldly, well-traveled figure from an elite background who had once seemed destined to lead the party, would serve as premier of the PRC as well as Mao's all-too-loyal aide. Liu Shaoqi, who had directed the CCP's work outside the rural base areas, emerged as Mao's successor and, along with the more junior Deng Xiaoping, an influen-

Land Reform in the Late 1940s
Typically, a party-appointed work team would arrive within a village to
initiate land reform. The team would form a peasant union, with poor peasants as the core group. Landlords would then have to face the entire village to
listen to accusations of exploitation and abuse—a critical moment captured
in this photo. These "struggle sessions" not only discredited the dominant
figures in the village but also gave the poor a new sense of confidence and
control. The final steps consisted of working out the economic status of each
family and then redistributing goods (household items as well as land) from
the privileged to the poor. (New China Pictures/Sovfoto)

tial voice in both party and government affairs. These men exercised their power
through a political structure modeled on that of the Soviets. The party's Central
Committee, nominally elected by periodic national party congresses, served as a
rubber stamp wielded by the smaller and more powerful Politburo, which contained its own still more elite Standing Committee entrusted with the supervision of day-to-day policy. Mao stood at the pinnacle of power as the chairman of
the CCP as well as the head of state and head of the party's military affairs
commission.

    Mao and his comrades had won the struggle for power; what would they now
do with that power? They were in agreement on foreign affairs. By 1949 the
CCP had already taken sides in the Cold War. The Truman administration had
supported the Nationalists to the bitter end of the civil war, and even after their

defeat it had continued hostile to the Chinese revolution. Responding to Washington's attempt to isolate his country, Mao unceremoniously abrogated the old unequal treaties imposed by the powers on a weak China and began to develop a broad-based relationship with the Soviet Union. He regarded the United States as strong on the surface but plagued by underlying weaknesses—foremost an economic system with a pronounced tendency to throw itself into crisis and set off social tumult at home and conflicts with allies. "American imperialism is sitting on this volcano," he observed in 1947.[6] As insurance against possible U.S. military intervention, Mao himself traveled to Moscow to negotiate a defense treaty with the USSR. In early 1950 he got from Stalin the treaty as well as some economic aid and the help of Soviet advisers.

The leaders of the CCP agreed in broad terms on the next step: regaining territory lost during the last imperial dynasty's waning years. As soon as it came to power, the CCP set in motion military efforts that recovered Tibet and Xinjiang along with part of Mongolia (Inner Mongolia). And in 1959 the Chinese used that military power to put down a revolt in Tibet. When in 1962 India refused to negotiate a border dispute, China's military again acted, this time driving Indian forces back from rugged, sparsely populated territory (see Map 3.2).

Only in regard to Taiwan was the CCP frustrated. The island had been settled by Chinese and incorporated into the Chinese empire only to be lost to Japan in 1895. China's allies during World War II had endorsed Taiwan's return. By the time of the creation of the PRC, the defeated Nationalists had dug in on the island and soon gained U.S. support capped by a defense treaty in 1954. Mao denounced this land grab and pressed China's claim by saber rattling, first in 1954

Mao with His Son, Mao Anying, 1949
The son died a year later while serving with Chinese forces in Korea. (New China Pictures/Sovfoto)

and then in 1958, on both occasions provoking crises with Washington. But he lacked both the naval force needed for an invasion and the firm Soviet backing critical to going to the brink with the Americans.

Restoring the old imperial borders was not enough. Mao's ultimate foreign policy goal was to raise China into the ranks of the major world powers—as a regional force for revolutionary change, as a model for change in the third world generally, and as a nuclear power commanding the respect of the other major powers. In its first years the PRC publicly signaled its support for Vietnamese revolutionaries (in 1949), launched a major aid program to help them defeat the French (in 1950), and during the Korean War between 1950 and 1953 (described in Chapter 1) drove back U.S. forces and (as Mao put it) "beat American arrogance."[7] Mao thus asserted China's influence along its border just as strong dynasties had earlier. The difference was that Mao determined his clients on the basis of their revolutionary credentials.

On domestic policy China's new leaders were initially in rough agreement on the importance of restoring stability and production after over a decade of chaos and destruction. In the countryside, where most Chinese still lived, the CCP focused on bringing some uniformity to agricultural policy. Some places, especially in southern China where the CCP presence was not well entrenched until the early 1950s, had yet to see even the most rudimentary changes in the land system. In the northern part of the country where most base areas had developed, moderate reforms had taken hold consisting of redistributing land from landlords who had actively resisted the CCP to poor peasants and the landless, reducing the rent on land, and cutting back on interest paid on loans. As the

THE RISE OF REVOLUTIONARY CHINA	
1919	May Fourth Movement marks culmination of a period of intellectual ferment among politicized, educated youth
1921	Chinese Communist Party organized
1931	Japanese invade China's Northeast (Manchuria)
1935	Mao emerges as CCP leader after Long March from Jiangxi to Yanan
1937	Sino-Japanese War begins, with the United States supporting Chiang's Nationalist government
1946– 1949	Civil war ends in CCP victory over U.S.-backed Nationalists, who take refuge on Taiwan
1949	People's Republic of China created; moderate domestic policy proclaimed
1950	Sino-Soviet alliance concluded; Chinese forces stop American advance in Korea
1959	China puts down revolt in Tibet
1962	Sino-Indian border clashes

CCP consolidated rural control, it applied this moderate program to the rest of the country. This task was completed by the early 1950s, but Mao's effort to remake life in the countryside had only just begun.

In the modern urban sector the CCP was prepared to work with the capitalist class to speed economic recovery and thus facilitate an eventual transition to socialism. The CCP's initial goal was, as Mao explained in 1949, "to regulate capitalism, not to destroy it."[8] Faced with the awesome enterprise of extending party control from the rural bases into the cities and organizing the new CCP-dominated state, party leaders also hoped to tap the talents of intellectuals. In the cities as in the countryside, moderation would, however, soon succumb to an assertive Mao driven by his own, highly personal vision of China's future.

Vietnam's Revolutionary Struggle

The story of the Vietnamese revolution, which closely parallels that in China, had begun to unfold long before serious U.S. involvement in Vietnam in the 1950s (see Chapter 1). This story goes back to the early nineteenth century when imperial Vietnam confronted French intruders. The French launched a successful drive to take over Vietnam along with Cambodia and Laos. Behind that drive was the resolve to promote and protect Catholic missionaries, the desire for a base for expanding trade into China, and the hunger for national prestige. In pursuing their colonial ambitions the French enjoyed advantages familiar from other colonial enterprises. They had superior technology such as cannons, steamships, and telegraph that were critical in war and in administration. They had a nationalist faith in France's special civilizing mission. And they had organizational advantages—an ability to focus limited resources on the region at decisive moments but otherwise administer the colony and police it at low cost with the help of Vietnamese—both elite collaborators and peasant military recruits.

In the face of steady French encroachment throughout the middle of the nineteenth century, the Vietnamese engaged in sporadic and largely ineffectual opposition. The ruling dynasty, which had expelled the Chinese and reunited the country in 1802, could not decide on whether to appease or oppose these new invaders. By the 1880s France had imposed direct rule over Cochinchina (the French name for the southernmost part of Vietnam that included the Mekong Delta) and protectorates over Annam (the central region) and Tonkin (the northernmost section including the densely populated Red River Delta). These three regions, together with the neighboring protectorates of Cambodia and Laos, constituted French Indochina, which was controlled by a single governor general.

By the 1890s the French had crushed armed resistance. Regional peasant armies—ill armed and ill organized—had proven no match for French forces. The morale among the elite that supported the Vietnamese state soon collapsed, and some accepted service in the colonial administration and army, while others continued in the old imperial bureaucracy, now firmly under French supervision. Yet others exploited new opportunities for profit from plantation agriculture (especially large estates producing rubber) and trade opened by French capital. Training in French schools became for this new class the ticket to advancement and the badge of their modernity.

French influence, particularly in the south, accentuated regional differences that remain important even today. Cochinchina, a late-settled frontier zone not integrated politically with the rest of Vietnam until early in the nineteenth century, would undergo profound social and economic change. Even before the French conquest, those in the north, the home of Vietnamese civilization, looked down on southerners as crude and culturally backward. The deepening colonial impact in Cochinchina and the widespread collaboration there accentuated the contempt felt by northerners, whose strong sense of patriotism had been forged through two millennia of resistance to Chinese domination. This antipathy, fully reciprocated by southerners, would only increase in the twentieth century.

Ho Chi Minh and the Path to Liberation. Ho Chi Minh was the charismatic leader who would set this conquered and divided land on the road to independence and unity. The many aliases that Ho would use during his revolutionary career are revealing of his motives. Named by his family Nguyen Tat Thanh (meaning Nguyen Who Will Be Victorious), he later called himself Nguyen O Phap (Nguyen Who Hates the French) and Nguyen Ai Quoc (Nguyen Who Loves His Country) before picking up in 1945 the name that stuck, Ho Chi Minh (Ho Who Aspires to Enlightenment).

Born in the early 1890s in the northern Annam region into the local gentry, he had grown up steeped in the rich patriotic tradition of Vietnam. His father was eligible to serve in the imperial bureaucracy but refused because it was under the heel of the French. The province in which Ho came to maturity was noted for its stubborn opposition to foreign rule even after organized resistance had died. Exposed to both Chinese classical and French education, Ho decided in 1911 to study the West at first hand. Once settled in Paris, he sought in 1919 support for his country's cause from the victors of World War I with their liberal peace program. Ignored by them, he turned to the French Socialist Party only to discover it was tainted by colonial ambitions. Even the French Communist Party, which Ho helped found, did not extend its professed solicitude for the downtrodden to France's colonial subjects: Liberating exploited Western workers was one thing, granting independence to half-civilized Vietnamese was altogether another.

In the early 1920s Ho had become a Communist. He vividly recalled the ecstatic moment of his conversion. While living in Paris, he had stumbled on a work by Lenin dealing with nationalism in colonial countries. Ho found in it "political terms that were difficult to understand. But by reading them again and again finally I was able to grasp the essential part. What emotion, enthusiasm, enlightenment and confidence they communicated to me! I wept for joy. Sitting by myself in my room, I would shout as if I were addressing large crowds: 'Dear martyr compatriots! This is what we need, this is our path to liberation!'"[9]

Ho soon moved to Moscow and then served in the 1920s and 1930s as a Comintern operative in China and Thailand. He also helped found the Indochinese Communist Party (ICP). Originating in 1925 as a nine-man cell, it was formally organized in Hong Kong in 1930 by uniting rival communist groups. This Communist party would operate like others. The center of decision-making was the Politburo, made up of roughly ten to fifteen of the most senior leaders. The general secretary occupied the guiding (though not necessarily the determining) role in its discussions. Below the Politburo was the Central Committee, made up of some 50 to 100 members who nominally elected the Politburo. At the base of the pyramid of power were the party members around the country. Like Mao and his colleagues, Ho and a generation of even younger Vietnamese were drawn to the Leninist party organization. Disciplined, centralized with a mass base and ideological coherence, it gave them a tool to carry forward the formidable task of restoring indigenous political authority against a well-entrenched colonial power.

Only in 1941 did Ho return home. The Japanese occupation of Indochina that year, the first step toward invasion of the rest of Southeast Asia, created an opportunity for patriotic Vietnamese to align their anti-colonial cause with the gathering Allied coalition preaching self-determination. Ho arrived as the head of the newly created Viet Minh (a shortened version of its full name, the Vietnamese Independence League). The Viet Minh was a united-front organization. Though organized and controlled by the Communist Party, it was designed to appeal to Vietnamese from all walks of life—from urban intellectuals to peasants. This particular organizational form enabled the Communists to marshal the popular support that was indispensable for a small, still weak political party, while at the same time soothing any fears about party domination or anxiety about its ultimate goals. The Viet Minh established itself as the only organized, staunchly anti-French and anti-Japanese resistance group, and it remained organizationally central to the resistance down to the French defeat in 1954. Ho was already well on his way to capturing the nationalist banner. Other political forces lacked strong organization and a substantial base of popular support, and some were even tainted by collaboration with the French.

When the Japanese surrendered in August 1945, the Viet Minh moved quickly to exploit the opportunity to take power. It had initially operated in the remote, mountainous region in northernmost Vietnam along the Chinese border and then in the last stage of the Pacific War extended its influence and operations into the Red River Delta. In what became known as the August Revolution, Viet Minh forces marched into Hanoi and established an independent Vietnamese state, the Democratic Republic of Vietnam (DRV) ruled by a coalition government with Ho as head of state. The Communist Party was firmly in control, even though it had at least nominally disbanded that fall. (In 1951 the party was formally revived and renamed the Vietnamese Workers' Party to allow room for the development of separate Cambodian and Laotian Communist parties.)

Realizing its weakness, the new government pursued a moderate policy. It downplayed radical domestic goals to win maximum popular support and reassure French residents as well as the United States. It expressed a willingness to negotiate with France on phased steps toward full independence, and it asked the victorious Allies for support. Its September 1945 declaration of independence quoted from the U.S. Declaration of Independence: "We hold [as] truths that all men are created equal, that they are endowed by their Creator with certain unalienable Rights, among these are Life, Liberty and the pursuit of Happiness." The declaration concluded with an appeal meant as much for foreign as Vietnamese ears: "A people which has so stubbornly opposed the French domination for more than 80 years, a people who, during these last years, so doggedly ranged itself and fought on the Allied side against Fascism, such a people has the right to be free, such a people must be independent."[10]

Moderation, however, proved a fruitless strategy—at least on the international scene. Ho failed to convince the French to agree to even a gradual withdrawal from Vietnam. French nationals who had made their lives in Indochina understood all too well that their privileged existence depended on their continued political and economic domination. Ho also failed in his appeals to the victorious Allies for support on the basis of a presumed common commitment to the principles of liberty and self-determination. Ho had favorably impressed the U.S. intelligence teams operating in northern Vietnam during the war. But President Truman, to whom Ho wrote directly, made no response.

By December 1946 Ho's negotiations with the French had collapsed and armed conflict had begun in earnest in what would come to be called the first Indochina War (1946–1954). Ho abandoned Hanoi, returned to the countryside, and resumed his war of resistance. The Viet Minh avoided major military engagements in the first years of the conflict, stressing instead political mobilization of the peasantry and expansion of the party. Membership, no more than twenty thousand in 1946, had increased by 1950 to 700,000 (5 percent of the population). The Viet Minh concentrated its efforts in the north, but its activists managed gradually to gain a foothold in roughly half the south.

Ho's forces, aided by advisors and supplies from the new Communist government in China, gradually wore the French down despite rising levels of U.S. assistance to the colonial forces. The war was eating up 10 percent of France's national budget, pushing the casualty totals on the French side toward 55,000,

ANTI-COLONIAL RESISTANCE IN VIETNAM

1802	Vietnam expels Chinese invaders and achieves unity under the Nguyen dynasty
1880s	France completes takeover of Vietnam; resistance subsides
1919	Ho asks World War I victors meeting in Paris to support independence; he then turns to the French Socialists and Communists and finally the Comintern
1930	Indochinese Communist Party established
1941	Japanese troops occupy Indochina; Viet Minh (led by Ho) founded as vehicle for united-front resistance
1945	"August Revolution" results in creation of the Democratic Republic of Vietnam headed by Ho
1946	Viet Minh begins armed struggle against France
1954	Viet Minh scores a victory at Dien Bien Phu; Geneva conference divides Vietnam

Ho (center) Discussing Attack on Dien Bien Phu
In this November 1953 planning session, Ho is flanked by his long-time lieutenants Le Duan, Pham
Van Dong, Truong Chinh, and Vo Nguyen Giap (from left to right). (Vietnam News Agency)

and generating popular protests. Ho's colleague in charge of military affairs, Vo
Nguyen Giap, dealt the final blow to colonial hopes in early 1954 by encircling
and then forcing the surrender of a French garrison at Dien Bien Phu. Certain of
victory if only the Vietnamese would stand and fight, the French had underesti-
mated the effectiveness of a popular, well-organized, if low-tech resistance force.
France and its Cold War allies agreed to sit down with the Communist powers at
Geneva and work out a compromise. Under pressure from his Soviet and Chinese patrons, Ho finally in July 1954 accepted a bargain—temporary partition of
his country with the promise of national elections in 1956 to reunify it.

Patriotism, Peasantry, and the Viet Minh. What accounts for the rise of
Ho's independence movement and his unexpected success against the French?
External factors noted earlier, including a weakened, war-weary France and
superpowers with little or no sympathy for the French effort, are part of the
answer. No less important are internal forces—above all the concerns of politically engaged Vietnamese intellectuals arrayed against the French and soon to
rally against the United States.

Perhaps the single most powerful idea sustaining the Vietnamese was the
patriotic tradition of resistance to foreign intervention. They saw themselves as
the descendants of those who had fought and died for independence, first during
the epic struggle against Chinese control spanning two thousand years and then
against the French colonizers. Ho and his colleagues in the Communist leader-

ship brought a stubborn determination to the cause of liberation that issued from the keen memory of this long history of patriotic resistance. Their popular appeals could tap a capacity for struggle and sacrifice that antedated the imported Western ideas of nationalism and whose strength Paris and Washington (already resolved by 1950 to block further communist inroads in Indochina) never understood.

A national literature of struggle and sacrifice kept this self-image alive for those who came to political consciousness in the first half of the twentieth century. They honored those who in the thirteenth century had resisted the Mongol invaders coming down from China and in the nineteenth century had fought the French. An 1864 poem that concluded with a call for sacrifice to expel the French sounded a familiar theme: "Life has fame, death too has fame. Act in such a way that your life and your death will be a fragrant ointment to your families and to your country." Even the lullabies sung to nodding children asked them "What do we love more than our country?" and pointed to the generations past whose labor "is now seen in each foot of river, each inch of mountain, each melon's pith, and each silkworm's innards." Little wonder that many would respond to Ho's call to work with the Communists and by devoting themselves to redeeming their country to take their place in the long line of dedicated and self-sacrificing patriots.[11]

No less important than patriotism in sustaining Vietnamese resistance was Communist success in attracting the peasantry into the resistance. The parallels with the Chinese Communist experience are striking. Like their Chinese counterparts, Vietnamese party organizers searching for a proletarian spearhead for their movement learned early that urban centers were inhospitable, even dangerous. Forced to take refuge in the countryside where four-fifths of their countrymen lived, they had to make a virtue of necessity—winning the support of peasants. They learned that the primary enemy of the rural people was less the humiliating foreign occupation preoccupying the well educated from privileged backgrounds than the grinding poverty of everyday life. Beginning in the 1940s, the Viet Minh promised peasants a new order and took some practical steps toward its realization, above all by redistributing land and ending exploitatively high interest rates on loans and high rents on land. Ho's forces thus secured their influence in northern Vietnam, aided in the final months of World War II by their effectiveness in battling famine.

Interviews with peasants in the Red River Delta testify to the success of the Viet Minh. Tuan Doanh, who became a Viet Minh activist, recalled, "[The Viet Minh's] seizure of rice for public use finally removed the peasants' uncertainties about the revolution." He looked back to August 1945 with its promise of "independence and freedom. The mood of the country was unbelievable: people were burning with enthusiasm. I shall never forget those times." From this beginning the Viet Minh was able to build a solid base of support in Doanh's home region. Villages provided shelter and offered bases for night raids on enemy outposts. A poor and less politically engaged peasant, Doan Van Hoc, recalled the same process of political mobilization in terms that were perhaps more typical. In 1945 when the Viet Minh showed up for the first time in his village, "I didn't really know what the Vietminh was. Also, I was scared: I was chary of joining them because I couldn't see what good they would do us." By 1947 Viet Minh performance, not propaganda, had brought him around and into a supporting role in the anti-French struggle. Hoc recalled particularly the front's role in combating famine: "They seized the rice and shared it out among the neediest." By 1947, he recalled, "I had seen the light, and I did my bit by becoming a village security agent, checking people's papers, tracking down poultry thieves, that kind of thing. I wasn't treated to a lot of propaganda: I just noticed how different they [the Viet Minh] were from the Japanese."[12]

The Viet Minh presence in rural areas opened opportunities for women. They were in Ho Chi Minh's phrase "long-haired warriors" who had much to contribute to their country's liberation and building an egalitarian society. Organizers entering a village looked first to women along with poor peasants and youth for support. Women carried out tasks that might bring suspicion on men such as visiting relatives in jail, carrying messages, distributing propaganda, and spying for guerrilla units. But they were also trained as combatants and nurses.

Nguyen Thi Dinh illustrates the role peasant women assumed in the resistance and the hardships that activist women had to bear. Dinh was born in 1920 into a peasant family in a Mekong Delta province. Vietnam's Communist Party had established a presence there during the 1930s. It was then that Dinh, a teenager, joined the resistance. She had been influenced by her activist brother but also by Confucian and village notions of social justice. She recalled, "I hated those in the old days who abused their power, position and wealth to harm honest people." A simple hatred for abusive landlords and local bullies had been enough to get her to take her first political risks. "I did not understand anything more than that the Communists loved the poor and opposed the officials in the village." The French figured only secondarily in her pantheon of villains. Dinh became active in passing out publications and leaflets, organizing local women, and carrying messages. In 1938 she married a prominent local party member— and then disaster struck. He was arrested a year later and carted away to prison. She would never see him again. Soon thereafter, Dinh was herself arrested and separated from her newborn child. She spent 1940 to 1943 in a French labor camp and then resumed her political activities. She participated in the Viet Minh seizure of power in her home province in 1945 and thereafter played a prominent political and military role in the southern resistance, first to the French and then to the Americans.[13]

A Vietnamese Revolution in the Chinese Pattern. Revolutionary developments in Vietnam strikingly paralleled those in China. In both cases foreign subjugation and humiliation during the nineteenth century had set the stage. Political elites found that the imperial political system, a proud past, and a strong cultural identity were not enough to beat back foreign demands and gunboats.

Galled by this abasement, Chinese and Vietnamese nationalist movements began to take shape early in the twentieth century. They aimed not just at eliminating foreign control but also at renovating their backward, "feudal" societies, developing their poor, peasant-based economies, and realizing visions of strong, unifying states. These aspirations were most warmly embraced by educated youth. Chinese students were active by the 1910s; their Vietnamese counterparts were in ferment by the following decade. The most radicalized would take the lead in forming revolutionary organizations, the CCP in the 1920s and Vietnam's Communist Party soon thereafter. Both sets of young activists were drawn by the appeal of Marxist-Leninist ideas; both would look to the Comintern in Moscow for funding, schooling, literature, and advisors; and both would produce a charismatic leader. Both Mao and Ho played a critical role in expanding the appeal of their parties. Both relied on united-front organizations to mobilize support. Both looked to peasants to sustain guerrilla warfare and thus wear down better armed foes.

The revolutionary struggle in both cases proved extraordinarily prolonged. The CCP gained political power in 1949, nearly three decades after its founding, and then under Mao's guidance launched a program of radical transformation that convulsed China well into the 1960s. Vietnam's revolution was aimed less at internal transformation than at foreign powers standing in the way of independence and unity. For a quarter century France was the prime enemy, followed by the United States for another two decades. (The story of these two intimately related revolutions resumes in Chapter 6.)

NEW STATES UNDER CONSERVATIVE ELITES

In contrast to China and Vietnam, where considerable revolutionary momentum developed, new regimes elsewhere in Asia followed a more gradual, less violent path toward more limited objectives, especially where colonial masters proved more accommodating to demands for independence. The United States had already before World War II pledged independence for the Philippines, and in 1946 Washington made good on that promise. A year later the British were on their way out of India. From once great imperial possessions emerged the new states of Burma (Myanmar), Ceylon (Sri Lanka), and Pakistan as well as India (see Map 3.1). In 1957 Britain also abandoned Malaya, though not before British forces put down a communist insurgency led by ethnic Chinese. In the East Indies the Dutch at first rebuffed calls for independence but finally in 1949 retreated in the face of an internal resistance movement and under U.S. pressure.

The colonial retreat by the Americans and the British left already entrenched elites in charge and ruling with the cooperation or acquiescence of their former foreign masters. Under these arrangements, the former colony became formally independent but perpetuated attitudes and practices that had taken root during the period of control. Some scholars call this pattern of continued influence from outside "neo-colonialism" and see it in operation not only in the cases to follow in this chapter but also in sub-Saharan Africa where the British and French ruled or even in Central America and the Caribbean where the United States replaced Spain as the dominant power. Under neo-colonialism, foreign influence usually derived from the local elite's identification with and education under the old regime and was sustained by political and economic clout still in foreign hands such as corporate operations or control of prestigious schools. These neo-colonial regimes were averse to fundamental social change. They did little to mobilize the peasantry; indeed, they regarded manifestations of peasant discontent as a threat to the postcolonial order. They also harbored reservations about strong, autonomous state power so important to Chinese and Vietnamese revolutionaries.

India's Status-Quo Independence

British control over India had its origins in the seventeenth and eighteenth centuries. So important did the British presence become that in 1858 the British crown and parliament assumed direct rule over two-thirds of the subcontinent. The actual exercise of control fell to a British viceroy on the ground, who in turn depended on a British bureaucracy extending down to the district level, a British-led army, and various consultative councils integrating Indian influentials such as landholders and businessmen. The remainder of India stayed in the hands of local princes subordinated to the British. The landmass of this major colonial possession was half the size of the United States with a population that would reach 250 million by 1920.

British India was a place of astonishing cultural diversity. It included four distinct language families each with its own subdivisions, over which was laid English as the language of colonial administration and modern education. Religion added to the complexity. Hinduism was the leading faith, but Islam claimed the adherence of a quarter of the population. Adding to this diversity were sharp regional differences based on ethnicity as well as language. Even after independence many Indians were still more attached to their region than to central authority wielded from the capital, New Delhi. Local movements demanded special standing for one or another of the some 1,500 indigenous tongues spoken in the country, and pressed for political autonomy and even in some cases territorial independence. Finally, at the local level, especially in the countryside, a variety of strong social patterns prevailed that sharply divided Indians into different status groups within a strong caste system. (Caste was a hereditary status that had carried down from precolonial society and ranged from Brahmins at the top to "untouchables" whose spiritual pollution placed them at the bottom.) These layers of different identities made central control and political change difficult not only for the British colonial administration but also for the post-independence leaders.

The British colonial regime planted the seeds of its own undoing. Although justifying its control as a civilizing influence, in practice it gave priority to more mundane and self-interested goals. Foremost were improvements in transport, communications, and administration essential to preserving political control and social stability, extracting taxes to help maintain British power around the world, and promoting trade (mainly the import of British manufactured goods in exchange for Indian raw materials). Only a small fraction of the colonial budget (around 4 percent) went toward such areas critical to human welfare and economic development as education and health. The adverse effects of foreign rule for most Indians could be measured in terms of a per capita income that did not increase in the two centuries preceding independence and a life expectancy that actually fell some 20 percent between 1872 and 1921. In 1885, less than three decades after London had brought the subcontinent together under the direct rule of the British crown, indigenous resistance took organized form with the creation of the Indian National Congress. The leaders of this loose political assemblage were English speakers, mostly university-trained professionals and mostly from the higher castes. They took up the ideas of their British educators on nationalism and self-determination—and turned those ideas against their teachers. They charged that a "civilized" country professing to have the best interests of its subjects at heart was in fact draining away India's wealth in the service of its own enterprise and empire and refusing to allow its subjects a significant voice in their own affairs.

Gandhi and the Quest for Self-Rule. Mohandas Gandhi emerged as the commanding figure at the forefront of the independence drive. Born in 1869, he was the son of a minister in one of the semi-autonomous princely states that survived under British rule. His devout mother saw to his careful training in the family's Hindu faith. He gained an English education in India and in 1888 (then at age nineteen) arrived in London to study law. After completing his degree, he went to work in British-controlled South Africa. Appalled by racial discrimination there, the young lawyer championed the rights of Indian residents.

In 1915, now a well-known and experienced political figure and an exponent of nonviolent protest, Gandhi returned to India. He stood for something as personally complex as India was culturally complex. Here was a British-trained lawyer able to deal comfortably with the colonial authorities, an astute political tactician committed out of deep principle to nonviolent methods, and a person of such spirituality and charisma that he would emerge as a venerated holy man widely known as Mahatma (or Great Soul). His simple, direct challenge to British rule and his mass appeal bore away at British confidence and ultimately determined if not the fact of independence at least the form in which it came.

Gandhi's special contribution to the independence struggle was his philosophy and strategy of nonviolent protest. He had worked out his ideas while leading the civil rights struggle in South Africa and began applying them to India in 1919 when he launched a campaign for self-rule. Drawing from his South African experience, he relied on such novel tactics as work stoppages, boycotts of British goods, massive demonstrations peacefully defying British authority, and prayers and fasts to advance the nationalist cause. Gandhi himself assumed an increasingly simple, even severe, lifestyle that commanded respect across a diverse population. He gave up Western clothes in favor of a loincloth and shawl, spun his own fabric, wrote and meditated in a spare cubicle, and refrained from sexual intercourse. By generally cultivating a spiritual outlook, he sought to signal his belief in an Indian way distinct from a degraded, materialistic Western way imposed by the British and to challenge the moral authority of the colonial regime. That regime had, he charged, exploited his country and lured Indians toward a "modern" civilization inferior to their own. He dreamed of an India emerging from the independence struggle that would be the antithesis of the West—just, harmonious, egalitarian, and tolerant. He hoped that these values

Gandhi with Jawaharlal Nehru
By the time of this photo in 1936, Nehru was emerging as Gandhi's heir within the Congress party and within the broader Indian nationalist movement. (© Bettmann/ Corbis)

would transcend the many differences of language, class, caste, region, and religion that divided the subcontinent and would lay the foundations for an enlightened and united country.

This public persona—politically assertive, populist, frail, and profoundly moral—drew a mass following to the Indian National Congress cause for the first time. Repeated rounds of arrests and imprisonment for Gandhi and other Congress leaders failed to still the protest. In 1930 an emboldened Gandhi began pressing for full independence. During World War II he redoubled the pressure, knowing that the British needed peace in India to repel Japanese forces threatening the eastern frontier. In August 1942 the Congress party passed a "quit India resolution" making a bold claim to "India's inalienable right to freedom and independence" and conditioning support for the war on the grant of immediate independence. The party proclaimed that it could no longer accept "an imperialist and authoritarian" rule holding back India's national development.[14] Confronted by this challenge, British authorities were unbending. They rode out the mass protest that followed, but their victory was transient.

World War II fatally weakened an already infirm British grip on the subcontinent. During the interwar period, rising nationalist feeling had forced the colonial regime to admit Indians into administration and to give them a growing role at the provincial and local level. They gained a say in economic affairs, a power quickly used to raise protective tariffs and promote an indigenous steel and textile industry. With the outbreak of war, colonial officials cracked down in the face of Congress party demands for a set date for independence. They jailed Gandhi and his associates. The war also brought fresh suffering and sacrifice to ordinary Indians as Britain's global war effort drained food and other goods from India, sparked inflation, and in places caused starvation. By the end of the war, colonial authority faced not just widespread unrest, including the first serious outbreaks of violence, but also the loss of the last shreds of legitimacy. At least in the eyes of Hindus, the Indian National Congress with Gandhi as its symbolic head had become the unquestioned leader of the nation. As sentiment shifted and independence became more likely, collaborators on whom British rule depended became more reluctant. These trends steadily raised the potential cost of maintaining control by force for a Britain exhausted financially and spiritually by war. The British Labour Party was already on record favoring independence, and the Americans, now Britain's senior partner on the world stage, worried that a prolonged, violent independence struggle would radicalize the colony to the embarrassment of the free world and to the benefit of international communism. In August 1947 Britain transferred power to British-educated moderates at the head of the Congress party.

Gandhi had emerged as India's founding father but also as a figure of international reputation and influence. The philosophy of nonviolence as a way of demonstrating unity and determination against a more powerful but morally compromised foe won converts around the world (as subsequent chapters will show). Gandhi's example would lead Kwame Nkrumah to peacefully confront the British in Ghana, and in South Africa nonviolence would become an important part of the anti-apartheid struggle. Even in the developed world nonviolent methods would gain adherents—for example, Martin Luther King Jr. at the head of the civil rights campaign in the United States in the late 1950s and early 1960s and Czechs facing a Soviet invasion in 1968 (see Chapter 4).

Gandhi's Dream Denied. But independence also brought Gandhi immediate disappointment. Even as the British laid down an independence timetable, splits appeared between the leaders of the Indian National Congress and the Muslim League, organized in 1906 by Muslims no longer willing to work within the Hindu-dominated Congress party. The League's declared purpose was to guarantee protection of India's diverse and scattered Muslim communities from majority Hindu prejudice, which was particularly virulent among an extremist minority committed to a religious definition of Indian national identity. As independence drew nearer and the actual distribution of communal power became a pressing, practical issue, communal violence erupted. Gandhi's dream of a united, secular, harmonious, tolerant India drowned in the blood of as many as a million dead and the sorrow of some fourteen million refugees. One high-level British official recalled watching appalled as "panic and a lust for revenge stalked the land."[15] In early 1948 Gandhi suffered assassination at the hands of a Hindu militant intent on punishing the frail old man for trying to stop the violence and hold the subcontinent together.

Partition seemed the only solution, and India's first prime minister, Jawaharlal Nehru, reluctantly agreed to the creation of a separate sovereign Muslim state—Pakistan—led by Mohammad Ali Jinnah of the Muslim League. This internal trauma would leave the subcontinent deeply and bitterly divided. On the one side was a Hindu-dominated but formally secular India inheriting the British-trained army, police, and civil service. It struggled to contain persistent currents of Hindu hostility toward Muslims, who even after partition constituted 10 per-

cent of the population and made India one of the largest Muslim countries in the
world. On the other side was a new Pakistan openly devoted to Islam and incor-
porating Muslim majority areas in two widely separated parts of the subcontinent, the larger in the northwest and another smaller but densely populated piece
in the east that in 1971 became the independent state of Bangladesh. The armies
of the two new states at once clashed over borders, especially in the Kashmir
region, a point of lasting tension (see Map 3.3).

In the years following his death, the goals that Gandhi had preached would
fail in a second, major way. In 1945 he had written of his old dream of a rural-
based, egalitarian society resistant to Western materialism. "My ideal village will
contain intelligent human beings. They will not live in dirt and darkness as animals. Men and women will be free and able to hold their own against any one in

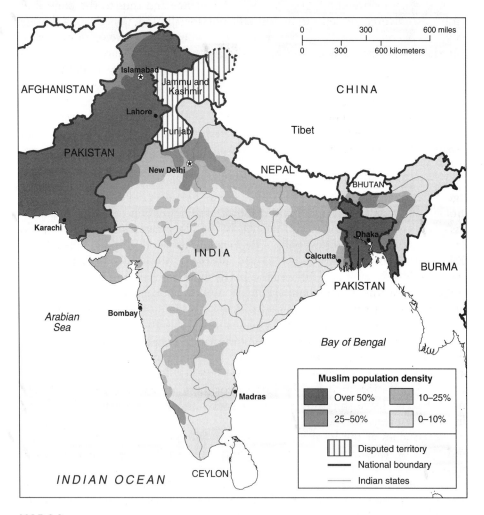

MAP 3.3
The Partition of British India, 1947

the world. There will be neither plague, nor cholera nor smallpox; no one will be idle, no one will wallow in luxury. Everyone will have to contribute his quota of manual labor."[16] Gandhi singled out for particular censure the severe discrimination suffered by untouchables and women.

The new government made merely half-hearted efforts to realize Gandhi's vision of social justice. As early as 1949 it outlawed "untouchable" as a category and thus sought to lift disabling stigma from some 14 percent of the population. But despite this and later attacks on caste-defined bars to educational and occupational opportunity, caste continued to determine social status and its rigidities still shaped fundamental aspects of life from marriage to residence to occupation. Women likewise got promises of government help that proved largely empty. Despite protective legislation, they remained subject to imposed marriage arrangements in late childhood or early adolescence and thus to the control of husbands. Divorce or separation was still not socially sanctioned even though each had become legal. Women were left largely illiterate, restricted in matters of inheritance and property ownership, and thus had few opportunities aside from the most menial of jobs. A poor peasant woman from northern India described her sense of this sorry state of affairs: "We women stay at home and do backbreaking work even if we are feeling ill or if we are pregnant. There is no sick leave for us. But we do not have any money of our own and when the men come home we have to cast our eyes down and bow our heads before them."[17] Abused, debased, and exploited, women committed suicide at rates unmatched anywhere else in the world.

Rural poverty persisted despite land reform legislation and a campaign of village development launched in the 1950s. These measures did little to change the shocking facts on the ground. In the 1950s a hundred million peasants were landless or homeless or both, and 80 percent of the electorate in the world's largest democracy was illiterate. Poverty and deprivation in the countryside where four-fifths of Indians still lived in the 1960s contrasted powerfully with the urban world of the educated and the wealthy. In the face of population increases of ten million a year, the government finally in 1959 endorsed family planning but failed to commit sufficient resources to slow this rapid increase. Between 1950 and 1975 population would grow by nearly a quarter of a billion.

The failure of Gandhi's populist commitment to equality and a better life had several sources. The Congress party lacked ideological coherence and discipline and thus proved in power more of an impediment than an instrument of deep-seated reform. Not only was the party a coalition of diverse interests and outlooks, but its leadership was averse to sweeping social programs. The party disproportionately served industrialists, well-educated party leaders, and their privileged allies at the local level. A business community that had taken shape under British protection and that had financially backed the Congress party's push for political independence reinforced resistance to social policies involving redistribution of wealth. The civil service was also conservative in its instincts and application of the law. Influential local interests, well entrenched economically and socially, constituted the Congress party's political base, and as such were able to block significant change. The failure of Congress-dominated national and provincial governments to invest in education, health care, and social welfare helped perpetuate the cycle of chronic ill health, infectious disease, and crippling illiteracy and despair. In the end, this failure doomed much of India's population to some of the worst poverty seen in the third world. A historian of India has provided a graphic reminder of what the abstract notion of poverty meant in this case: "almost perpetual hunger, a monotonous and unbalanced diet at the best of times, cramped and squalid housing, perhaps one change of meagre clothes, insufficient bedding to prevent deaths from cold in the northern Indian winter, children's absence from school for lack of clothes or books or the need to earn to feed the family, and no money for doctors or medicines."[18]

Nehru and India's Colonial Legacy. In a broad sense, India's colonial legacy also played a role in undermining Gandhi's vision of a just, egalitarian society. The top of India's political class hailed from privileged groups that had been trained in the best British schools, socialized in British ways, plugged into "old school" networks of influence, and co-opted into the colonial government. They shared with the British upper crust who had ruled India a belief in their right to lead. They also shared a commitment to preserving a strongly hierarchical, secular, class-conscious social system that favored them and their kind.

Jawaharlal Nehru was one of those well-born English speakers. His was a prominent Brahmin family, whose wealth came from his father's practice of English law and whose lifestyle was heavily Westernized. Between 1905 and 1912 the young Nehru lived in England, attending a prestigious private secondary school, going on to college at Cambridge, and finally getting a law degree in London. Along the way he acquired the dress, bearing, and outlook of an English gentleman. Once back home, he found purpose in the independence crusade and discovered in the course of his political organizing a side of his country that he had never seen before: a rural population that was "naked, starving, crushed and utterly miserable."[19] Thanks to a razor-sharp mind, a movie-star attractiveness that was balanced by a quiet reserve, and a deep well of energy, he emerged as Gandhi's chief lieutenant, assumed leadership of the Congress party, and took on the job of negotiating with the British the terms of independence. He would go on to serve as India's first prime minister, dominating the government and the national political scene until his death in 1964. Throughout he talked of ending poverty but never matched his high-sounding words with effective action.

Instead, his major legacy was to lay the basis for a political dynasty. Two years after his death, his daughter Indira Gandhi (not related to Mohandas) would take control of the government and remain the presiding political figure for almost twenty tumultuous years. Following her assassination in 1984, her son Rajiv Gandhi assumed leadership of the country and the Congress party. After Rajiv was also assassinated in 1991, his widow and a favorite of Indira, the Italian-born Sonia Gandhi, tried to sustain family influence as head of a now-faltering Congress party. (See Chapter 8.)

Both the institutions and values of the new Indian state drew heavily on a colonial legacy. The state's backbone was an army and bureaucracy trained under the British. Its economic policy was heavily influenced by the British Labour

INDIA'S PATH TO INDEPENDENCE

1858	British crown begins to assert direct control over territory later to become the independent states of India, Pakistan, and Burma (Myanmar)
1885	Hindu-dominated Indian National Congress organized
1906	Muslim League organized
1919	Gandhi launches nonviolent campaign for Indian self-rule
1942	Indian National Congress led by Gandhi demands immediate independence
1947	Britain grants independence; Indian subcontinent partitioned between India led by Nehru and Pakistan led by Jinnah; partition sets off communal violence and war between India and Pakistan
1948	Gandhi assassinated by a Hindu extremist
1964	Nehru's death; political power passes to his daughter Indira and later to her son Rajiv

Party's commitment to a mixed economy with a prominent role for public enterprise and bureaucratic regulation. State investments made through a series of five-year plans together with generous economic assistance from both sides in the Cold War made India's major cities look like British centers of heavy industry. Though Hindi was designated the official language, English remained the most widely accepted. The English-trained and English-speaking officials of the new India with their eyes set on industrial development took pride in their country's role as a leader of states refusing to take sides in the Cold War even while taking money from the Cold War rivals. Their neglect of the countryside left India what it had been under their colonial predecessors—a land of stark inequalities. With their social prestige, political influence, and economic advantages at stake, high-status Indians in government as well as outside had no sympathy for meaningful measures to promote equality or alleviate poverty.

New Delhi's modest domestic agenda and even more modest achievements make a striking contrast with the persistence and vigor with which the Chinese and Vietnamese states tackled the problems afflicting their societies. Economically, for example, India fell behind China. The two countries' per capita income were roughly on a par from the early nineteenth century to 1950. But India's development strategy had by 1973 left per capita income lagging significantly behind (see Figure 3.1). The gap would continue to widen as a result of a low Indian economic growth rate and Indian neglect of population control, whereas the Chinese began to effectively address the population problem in the 1970s. In contrast to China's revolution-minded Communists, India's conservative socialists moved cautiously to address gaps between rich and poor, raise literacy and longevity, and better the lives of women. Gandhi's and Nehru's dreams of

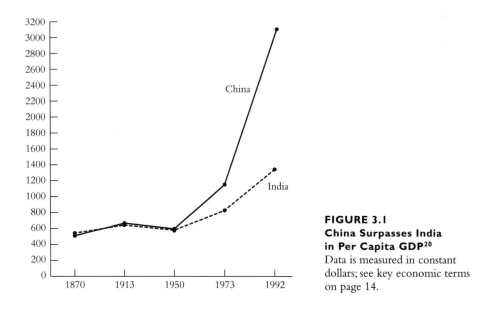

FIGURE 3.1
China Surpasses India in Per Capita GDP[20]
Data is measured in constant dollars; see key economic terms on page 14.

development had led to outcomes that in comparison to Mao's did not serve the interests of ordinary people well. On the other hand, an activist state in China could make mistakes with terrible consequences (as we will see in Chapter 6). The verdict on the Indian model—with its more modest programs and smaller risks—thus remains mixed.

The Collaborative Impulse in the Philippines

In the islands making up the Philippine archipelago (see Map 3.1), the colonial experience bore parallels with that of India. The Spanish had consolidated their control earlier than the British—in the course of the latter half of the sixteenth century. But as in India by the nineteenth century, subjects increasingly integrated into international commerce and exposed to notions of nationalism were becoming restive. By the mid-1890s Spain faced armed resistance led by urban, Western-educated Filipinos from a new middle class impatient under the restrictions of Spanish rule. The course of this incipient revolution took a sudden and surprising turn when American forces arrived in 1898 during the Spanish-American War. Though the cause of the war was Spain's control of Cuba, the Philippines became the main territorial prize claimed by the victorious Americans.

Filipinos responded to the new colonial master with more armed resistance beginning in 1899. Not to be thwarted, the administration of U.S. president William McKinley committed as many as 70,000 troops to pacify the islands. Those troops encountered a stealthy foe who operated with civilian support over familiar home terrain. The war led not only to atrocities by frustrated U.S. forces but also to a stunning loss of life. The number of Filipinos killed in action came to at least 20,000. More striking, war-related famine and disease during the period of resistance first to Spain and then to the United States around the turn of the century produced among the general population approximately three-quarters of a million deaths (out of a population of about 7.5 million in 1900). In other words, about a tenth of the archipelago's population perished.

The brutality of pacification combined with charges that Americans were betraying their own ideals resulted in a basic redirection of the American colonial project. U.S. proconsuls in the Philippines struck a compromise with what they described in 1902 as "Filipinos of education, intelligence, and property." From the American perspective, this elite could help bring the fighting to a close and then cooperate in breaking the "medieval-religious" obstacles to progress posed by the entrenched position of the Catholic Church and the legacies of Spanish misrule.[21] Those inclined toward collaboration were themselves unhappy with the costs and doubtful about the long-term viability of resistance. In exchange for their immediate acceptance of American rule, well-to-do, landed Filipino leaders got a promise of ultimate independence for their country, an increasing role for themselves in governance, and the promise of orderly social and economic modernization. In 1916 the United States made formal its pledge of independence, and in 1935 the islands gained self-governing status in preparation for an early end to American control. These arrangements laid the foundation for an enduring neo-colonial relationship between the Philippines and the United States.

During these pre-independence years the U.S. colonial administration compiled a mixed record. Public health improved significantly. Education became more widely available, and together with a better transport and communication system helped diminish regional identities in favor of a stronger sense of national unity. Though formally democratic, the country was run by prominent regional families. Their control of land and wealth gave them great power and prestige locally and provided the basis for competing for a share of national power in the capital, Manila, and with that power fresh opportunities for wealth and status. The Filipino model was also marked by economic stagnation and one of the world's widest gaps between the privileged and the poor. A peculiarly Filipino model of economic and political development had taken hold. Taxes favored the wealthy. Landlords resisted land redistribution programs. Desperate tenants were becoming politically active, and some among the urban educated exposed to social injustice were turning to radical politics.

The Rise of the Huks. Independence, long on the agenda, was delayed by the outbreak of war between the United States and Japan and the ensuing Japanese occupation of the islands in early 1942. Many leading political figures opted for collaboration with this latest set of foreign intruders, while guerrilla resistance sprang up in the countryside with popular support. The war years thus fed social tensions that would carry over into the postwar period. Finally, in 1946 the islands received their formal independence. But little changed. Alarmed by the advance of international communism, cold warriors in Washington kept U.S.

military bases on the islands and preserved close ties with the old elite. The elite too saw advantage in resuming collaboration with the Americans. This arrangement almost immediately encountered a revolutionary challenge. It erupted suddenly in the late 1940s and then subsided in the early 1950s, following a pattern that departed significantly from the Chinese and Vietnamese cases.

The challenge arose from peasant discontent that had become pronounced in the interwar period. A trend among landlords to turn their back on their local welfare obligations had left peasants without economic security. Landlords with whom peasants had once enjoyed a mutually supportive relationship increasingly embraced commercialized agriculture and "rationalized" their use of peasant labor so as to eliminate traditional but costly welfare practices. Where landlords might once have guaranteed tenants access to land and provided help in hard times, new-style landlords attuned to market forces viewed these kinds of welfare accommodations as unprofitable and thus unsuitable to a modern, rational economy. Landlords, explained one tenant reflecting on what he saw as the breakdown of the moral order, "no longer upheld their end of the relationship between the tenant and his landlord. They were being unfair to the peasants. It was unjust. Besides that, we had no protection anymore, and not enough to eat."[22]

Threatened by increasingly high rates of landlessness and tenant debt, peasants began in the 1920s resorting to sporadic, isolated acts of collective protest. The Socialist Party noticed this rising rural discontent and helped organize peasant unions. The Philippine Communist Party, established in 1930, had also by the end of the decade come around to endorsing calls for rural reform, though peasants were mystified why Communist speakers "went on...about how good things were in Russia. It wasn't relevant to our problems. It was also dangerous. The police could have thought we were a bunch of communists and arrested us."[23]

The Japanese occupation of the Philippines in 1941 set the stage for the creation of the People's Anti-Japanese Army, popularly known as the Huks. In March 1942 prominent Socialists and Communists met to organize a united-front, peasant-based force. They put at its head Luis Taruc, a leading Socialist. The son of a tenant farmer, he understood the discontents of his peasant followers and sympathizers. He also proved a charismatic leader, commanding the loyalty of his lightly armed but locally supported followers. The Huks resisted the invaders and punished Filipinos, many of them landlords, who collaborated with the Japanese. But unlike the CCP and the Viet Minh, Huk leaders failed to build a disciplined organization that would sustain their struggle over the long haul.

At the end of the war the Huks disbanded, but calls for improvements in rural conditions persisted. Peasant demands were, as earlier, modest and limited to assured subsistence. As one tenant explained, "We wanted the landlords or the government to guarantee us enough to eat and a roof over our heads." Local security forces sponsored by landlords quickly countered with repression. With the countryside in turmoil and wartime gains evaporating, armed Huk units began springing back to life in the latter part of 1946. One peasant recalled with pride his support for the Huks at this time. He and other peasants had shown that "we weren't slaves" of the landlords and the government. "We didn't lie down

Fighting for Land

The Huks pictured here were training for combat in central Luzon. These peasants, desperate and angry over loss of access to land to support their families, received only rudimentary equipment, and the Communists who seized the leadership of the insurgency were not attuned to their concerns and did not make effective use of them in waging guerrilla warfare. The Huks collapsed in the early 1950s. But the rural discontents that had drawn these men to the Huks in the first place would continue to simmer. (Edward Lansdale Collection, envelope B2, Hoover Institution Archives)

like whimpering dogs when they started to whip us. We stood up to them and fought for what was rightfully ours." The Huks reestablished themselves in their old stronghold in central Luzon and began expanding into the southern part of the island. The government responded with an "iron fist" strategy of dealing with restive rural areas. The brutality of army and irregular forces—arresting, torturing, raping, and looting peasants in contested areas—enhanced the Huks' popularity. By late 1949 Huk units had passed from the defensive to the offensive and were beginning to pose a threat to the government in Manila.[24]

In January 1950 the Huk leadership, now dominated by the Communist Party, decided to gamble on an all-out effort to seize power. That decision was prompted in part by the government's ineffectual response to the Huk challenge and in part by the Communist leaders' conviction that the United States was on the defensive in the Cold War and would not be able to save its Filipino allies. The expectation of an imminent economic crisis in the United States and the Communist triumph in China convinced party leaders that a favorable "revolutionary situation" was taking shape. The outbreak of the Korean War in June confirmed this optimistic reading of the international situation and sustained their determination to make a bold bid for power.

However, the general offensive failed and the Huks suffered a crushing defeat. Once the gravity of the Huk threat became clear during the first half of 1950, Washington had rushed assistance to its Filipino allies. Communist leaders for their part had lost popular support by neglecting rural grievances. Perhaps the most demoralizing blow was the capture of important Communist leaders in

October 1950. The survivors briefly persisted in the militant strategy and then retreated to a defensive approach intended to preserve remaining Huk resources. The resistance rapidly declined. At their peak the Huks had boasted 12,000 to 15,000 combatants and 1.5 to 2.0 million followers, but by the mid-1950s they had disappeared as an organized force.

The Establishment Prevails. In Ramon Magsaysay the United States found an effective Filipino partner in turning back the revolutionary challenge. Though he was known as "America's boy," he was also a product of the Filipino political establishment. He had married into a landed family. During World War II he had used his command of a U.S.-backed guerrilla unit to build his own patronage network. His close ties to Americans, his political skills, and his military background made him a natural choice for the government to place at the head of the anti-Huk effort. In September 1950 with the Huks threatening, Magsaysay became secretary of defense. He skillfully played on American fears of communism, with the result that Washington provided some $500 million in economic and military assistance between 1951 and 1956. He also got the CIA to promote his image as an effective leader. With these assets behind him, he transformed the army into a better-disciplined and more effective instrument of rural pacification, while himself promising land reform. These efforts, together with his success at capturing Huk leaders and at sowing dissension within the movement, further blunted the revolutionary thrust.

Magsaysay's election to the presidency in 1953 had strong U.S. backing and raised U.S. and peasant hopes for moderate reform. But those hopes would be disappointed by the time of his death in an airplane crash in 1957. True to his past, he cultivated landed interests, industrialists, the Catholic Church, and influential Chinese and U.S. businessmen, while supporting his own set of clients. Rather than dutifully following the U.S. lead, he backed nationalist demands during the renegotiation of U.S. base rights even while securing generous aid from Washington. In relation to his own people, this man of the establishment had no intention of launching a genuine, sustained challenge to the status quo, especially in the countryside. The pattern of a weak state under the sway of a strong elite was now

THE PHILIPPINES IN AMERICA'S SHADOW	
1896	Filipinos revolt against Spain
1898–1902	Spanish-American War leads to U.S. annexation of Philippines, provoking Filipino resistance
1942	Japan takes control of the Philippines; Huks organize anti-Japanese resistance with Luis Taruc as commander
1946	Philippines gains independence; Huks begin mobilizing against the government
1950	Huks reach peak strength and then weaken as a result of Magsaysay's U.S.-backed counterinsurgency policy

firmly in place. It would spell hardship for many ordinary Filipinos as well as poor overall economic performance for the islands in the decades to come.

Seen in comparative perspective, the case of the Philippines provides another illustration of how unusually strong was the preoccupation of Chinese and Vietnamese political intellectuals with reconstructing state power and exercising it to effect social change. After the ouster of the Spanish in 1898, the Filipino elite composed of prominent provincial families not only lacked a tradition or model of a strong state but also was compromised by a habit of collaboration with foreign masters on a scale unmatched in either China or Vietnam. After briefly resisting the American takeover, that elite settled into a collaborative relationship that safeguarded its domestic privileges while promising ultimate political independence. When the Japanese conquered the islands during World War II, that elite again accommodated to foreign rule. Finally, when the Americans returned, the Philippines resumed a dependent, neo-colonial relationship with the United States, which continued even after the attainment of formal independence in 1946. Rather than forcefully rejecting external domination, a dependent Filipino leadership developed a kind of submissive nationalism that from their perspective had the considerable virtue of protecting the domestic status quo.

CONCLUSION

The unrest already evident at war's end in Asia—in China, Korea, Vietnam, India, the Philippines, and Indonesia—provided a warning of what was to come in other third-world regions in the decades ahead. But more than that, the dramatic changes in the Asian political landscape defined two different paths that others seeking independence would follow.

One path, charted by India and the Philippines, led those demanding independence toward negotiations and compromise with the imperial power. In these cases, the transfer of control was relatively smooth and painless. Critical to this sort of outcome was the colonial power's ability to conclude with the indigenous elite a collaborative bargain that served the interests of both sides. Such a bargain usually set a timetable for independence and offered post-independence support from the former colonial power. Such a bargain spared that power a costly war in defense of formal control and provided a means of building a mutually advantageous neo-colonial relationship. That meant that the former colonial country could maintain considerable economic and cultural influence in the new nation. Indispensable to this arrangement was an indigenous elite inclined to cooperation. By affording Western education to a privileged few and then bringing them into colonial institutions, the colonial powers took a major step toward co-opting future independence leaders.

The other path to independence was marked by great powers doggedly hanging on to their colonies and dependencies. Under these circumstances, evident above all in China and Vietnam, the independence struggle turned into an extended internal conflict. The usual result was to radicalize the early challengers to the status quo, entangle local players in Cold War rivalry, and create bitterness and scars deeply dividing peoples within the same country. In these cases insur-

gent leaders had no commitment to preserving Japanese or French colonial institutions or accommodating powerful countrymen tied to the colonial order.
Moreover, faced with armed repression, these leaders often found themselves
seeking shelter in the countryside and support from peasants eager for land.
Finally, they often had little trust in the West and thus turned to the Soviet
Union as a source of outside support. These radical trends would (as Chapter 6
will show) become more pronounced as independence fever spread across the
entire third world.

RECOMMENDED RESOURCES

China's Revolution
The place to start for a **general treatment** is Jonathan Spence's *The Search for Modern China*
(2nd ed., 1999), a visually splendid, engagingly written text by a leading authority. See also
Spence, *The Gate of Heavenly Peace: The Chinese and Their Revolution* (1981), and *The Cambridge
History of China*, general editors Denis Twitchett and John K. Fairbank, vols. 12–15
(1983–1991). On **Mao Zedong,** see Philip Short, *Mao: A Life* (2000), for a fresh, full-scale
biography. Jonathan Spence, *Mao Zedong* (1999), brief and deftly drawn, emphasizes the personal qualities that made Mao the "lord of misrule." Mao's own recital of his early years is
recorded in Edgar Snow's classic *Red Star over China* (1938). The best short collection of
material on Mao is Timothy Cheek, *Mao Zedong and China's Revolutions: A Brief History with
Documents* (2002). Maurice Meisner, *Mao's China and After: A History of the People's Republic*
(3rd ed., 1999), offers a sympathetic appraisal of the state that Mao created in 1949. Michael
H. Hunt, *The Genesis of Chinese Communist Foreign Policy* (1996), traces the rise of the concerns that defined the early external relations of the People's Republic, while Odd Arne
Westad, *Decisive Encounters: The Chinese Civil War, 1946–1950* (2003), provides a fresh synthe-
sis of the conflict that put the CPP in power. Writings on **the Chinese peasantry** in an age
of revolution are rich. Peter Seybolt, *Throwing the Emperor from His Horse: Portrait of a Village
Leader in China, 1923–1995* (1996), and Huang Shu-min, *The Spiral Road: Change in a Chinese
Village through the Eyes of a Communist Party Leader* (2nd ed., 1998), are two especially engaging accounts—one by a historian and the other by an anthropologist. *Yellow Earth* (dir. Chen
Kaige; 1984; 89 min.) is a fascinating film by a leading director reflecting on village life in the
area near Yanan in the late 1930s.

Modern Southeast Asia
Milton Osborne, *Southeast Asia: An Introductory History* (7th ed., 1997), provides a good
overview of a complex region. David Joel Steinberg et al., *In Search of Southeast Asia: A Modern History* (rev. ed., 1987), is a pioneering text that still repays reading. Clive J. Christie's *Ideology and Revolution in Southeast Asia, 1900–1980: Political Ideas of the Anti-Colonial Era* (2001)
and his *A Modern History of Southeast Asia: Decolonization, Nationalism, and Separatism* (1996),
explore the antagonistic twin political impulses playing out in the region—the ideas animating state builders and the resistance issuing from a wide range of separatist movements.

Vietnam's Revolution
General perspectives emerge from William J. Duiker, *Sacred War: Nationalism and Revolution
in a Divided Vietnam* (1995), and Neil L. Jamieson, *Understanding Vietnam* (1993), with its
revealing use of literary material. Alexander Woodside, *Community and Revolution in Modern
Vietnam* (1976); Huynh Kim Khanh, *Vietnamese Communism, 1925–1945* (1982); and Hue-
Tam Ho Tai, *Radicalism and the Origins of the Vietnamese Revolution* (1992), have proven influential in shaping the views of scholars. Gareth Porter, ed., *Vietnam: A History in Documents*

(1981), brings together an excellent collection of primary sources from both the Vietnamese and American sides of the war. *Vietnam: A Television History* (prod. Richard Ellison; 1983; 13-part series), is a balanced treatment that offers excellent original footage. **Revolutionary leaders:** William J. Duiker's *Ho Chi Minh* (2000) provides a full and up-to-date treatment of a commanding personality. Nguyen Thi Dinh, *No Other Road to Take: Memoir of Mrs. Nguyen Thi Dinh*, trans. Mai V. Elliott (1976), develops the perspective of a peasant woman who emerged as one of the leaders of the southern resistance.

India's Independence

General treatments: Stanley A. Wolpert, *A New History of India* (5th ed., 1997), is an authoritative survey that gives substantial coverage to contemporary, mainly political developments. Judith M. Brown, *Modern India: The Origins of an Asian Democracy* (2nd ed., 1994), is important for its attention to the continuities running from colonial to post-independence times. On **Gandhi,** see Judith M. Brown, *Gandhi: Prisoner of Hope* (1989), the most up-to-date, single-volume biography; *Hind Swaraj and Other Writings*, ed. Anthony J. Parel (1997), which brings together seminal Gandhi material; and the movie version of the life, *Gandhi* (prod. and dir. Richard Attenborough; 1982; 188 min.), which wonderfully evokes the spirit and political acumen of the man. On **Nehru,** Brown's *Nehru* (1999) is a tight, accessible introduction to the life and times of Gandhi's chief lieutenant and successor. See also Nehru's own account, *Toward Freedom: The Autobiography of Jawaharlal Nehru* (rev. ed., 1941). **Ordinary life:** A sense of the hope and trauma that accompanied partition at the end of the colonial era emerges in the gripping fictional account *Train to Pakistan*, by Kushwant Singh (first published 1956; 1990). The novel *Nectar in a Sieve* (1954) by Kamala Markandaya uses the struggles of a poor peasant couple to bring rural conditions vividly to life.

The Philippines

For **overviews,** begin with Stanley Karnow, *In Our Image: America's Empire in the Philippines* (1989), and H. W. Brands, *Bound to Empire: The United States and the Philippines* (1992). For a more critical perspective, see Stephen R. Shalom, *The United States and the Philippines: A Study in Neocolonialism* (1981). Daniel B. Schirmer and Stephen R. Shalom, eds., *The Philippines Reader: A History of Colonialism, Neocolonialism, Dictatorship, and Resistance* (1987), gathers a handy collection of key documents. Details on the critical **early postwar years** can be found in Nick Cullather, *Illusions of Influence: The Political Economy of the United States–Philippines Relations, 1942–1960* (1994), and in Luis Taruc, *He Who Rides the Tiger: The Story of an Asian Guerrilla Leader* (1967), an influential participant's perspective on the Huk appeal and ultimate collapse. Good insights on **social divisions and conflict** emerge from Alfred W. McCoy, ed., *An Anarchy of Families: State and Family in the Philippines* (1993), and Benedict J. Kerkvliet, *The Huk Rebellion: A Study of Peasant Revolt in the Philippines* (1977), a classic on the economic pressures pushing peasants into politics.

PART TWO

THE COLD WAR SYSTEM UNDER STRESS
1953–1968

In late 1947 Kwame Nkrumah, confident and purposeful, returned to West Africa after twelve years away. In the years since his birth in 1909 he had traveled far. He had grown up in comfortable circumstances in the village of Nkroful on the southwest coast of Britain's Gold Coast colony (renamed Ghana after independence). His people, who belonged to the Akan group, had long been active in coastal commerce. His father was a goldsmith; his mother was a market trader. Nkrumah attended a mission school at a time when such opportunities for colonial subjects were sharply restricted, and then he secured a teaching post in 1930 that made him part of a privileged minority. In 1935, like other ambitious young Africans, he left to study abroad. During his ten years in the United States, he earned a bachelor's and a theological degree at Lincoln University, a major center for black education located near Philadelphia, and then a master's in education at the University of Pennsylvania. In May 1945, the thirty-six-year-old Nkrumah moved to London, where he continued his studies and served as general secretary of the Pan-African Congress, an alliance of pro-independence groups, before finally heading home.

Paralleling Nkrumah's literal journey was a figurative one—both intellectual and cultural. Growing up on the coast with its foreign trade connections had made him aware of the wider world. Missionary training followed by his long foreign sojourn had further expanded his horizons and sharpened his political commitment and personal sense of mission. In the United States he and other African students discussed how to combine the best of what they were learning in the West with their own traditions and then how to use that new, uniquely African synthesis to guide the region's political and social reconstruction during the coming era of independence. He read widely and was especially impressed by W. E. B. Du Bois, a black American intellectual who held that Africans and those of African descent scattered across the Atlantic world shared a common culture, a similar experience of racial oppression, and a need for political unity and cultural pride. Nkrumah spent summers working in a multi-ethnic Harlem that was electric with political discussions about the liberation of African peoples, whether in Africa itself or scattered by the slave trade across the western hemisphere. Later, in London, he continued his political education among the West African community there, also in the grip of independence fever.

Kwame Nkrumah on the Eve of Fame, 1947
Nkrumah appears here reunited with his mother immediately on his return home—a brief respite before plunging into national politics. (From *The Autobiography of Kwame Nkrumah,* Thomas Nelson and Sons)

Arriving home to West Africa, Nkrumah acted on three important convictions. First and most obvious was the need for the liberation of Africans from outside control. In a 1943 talk he had asserted his determination: "We must take the torch of liberty in our own hands. . . . We cannot get what we want by asking, pleading and arguing. . . . We are in a world of action, not talk. . . . We must rise and throw off the chains." He saw Africans following in the steps of the peoples of India and Vietnam who were already demanding an end to colonial control. Nkrumah's second article of faith was West African unity and the region's potential to serve as a base for an all-Africa liberation movement. As a 1946 resolution that Nkrumah co-authored put it: "The day when West Africa, as one united country, pulls itself from imperialist oppression and exploitation[,] it will pull the rest of Africa with her." Finally, Marxism attracted Nkrumah with its claims that a new, non-oppressive order was a historical inevitability within reach of those willing to organize and press forward. He was confident that socialist ideals and methods would occupy a central place in the new African synthesis, and by 1944 he had openly professed a socialist commitment.[1]

Nkrumah's homecoming would mark the end of one journey and the beginning of another. He immediately turned to political causes uppermost in his mind. Independence came first. He would lead the assault on British colonial control, take the first African colony to statehood, rally sub-Saharan Africa against colonialism, and both preach and practice a new path of development that he called African socialism. He looked to a planned, state-controlled economy devoted to promoting and protecting industry as the surest way to raise the standard of living and education and to end foreign economic control (what he and others in the third world came to denounce ever more insistently as neo-colonialism). But his program failed to bring the promised benefits. Overthrown by his own army in 1966 and driven into exile, Nkrumah still sustained his radical hopes. Writing in 1968, he glimpsed signs of a "world revolution against capitalism, imperialism and neo-colonialism which have enslaved, exploited and oppressed peoples everywhere."[2] At this moment when third-world radicalism reached its crest, he was confident that his beloved causes of pan-African unity and socialism were about to prevail.

Nkrumah was but one of a phalanx of third-world leaders whose hopes for decolonization accelerated in the 1950s and 1960s. Mao Zedong in China and Ho Chi Minh in Vietnam had helped to usher in this new age of liberation even as Nkrumah took his first steps on home soil in 1947. Behind them came leaders such as Jacobo Arbenz in Guatemala, Fidel Castro in Cuba, Mohammed Mossadeq in Iran, and Gamal Abdul Nasser in Egypt also intent on curbing foreign influence and embarking on ambitious plans for economic and social modernization. Like Nkrumah, many had traveled abroad the better to understand how to remake their own world, and they were drawn to Marxist ideas by the promise of rapid economic development and strong, centralized political authority. Also like Nkrumah, many saw their individual national projects as part of a larger global transformation. Their dedication to socialism and suspicion of the Western-dominated international market economy, coupled with their desire to avoid Cold War entanglements, gave rise to a strong third-world identity in the 1950s and 1960s.

This ferment within the third world was only one point of stress weakening the Cold War system and providing the first hints of its ultimate end. No less important was Stalin's death in 1953. It unleashed a reform impulse quickly harnessed by Nikita Khrushchev, who undertook a far-reaching reappraisal of Stalin's brutality and ushered in a less repressive and austere era in Soviet life. Closely connected with these domestic initiatives was the new, less threatening face that Khrushchev gave to Soviet foreign policy and his shift toward improved relations with the United States. A parallel lessening of Cold War ardor and suspicion was at work within a new administration in the United States. Truman's successor, Dwight Eisenhower, favored a less pugnacious and more cost-conscious approach to the superpower struggle. The first achievement of these new, more conciliatory Soviet and American outlooks came quickly: an end to the deadlocked war in Korea in mid-1953.

An overlapping set of pressures pushed both Cold War rivals toward their new position. A growing nuclear arsenal left Moscow and Washington equally petrified by the prospect of war. In addition, the post-Stalin and post-Truman leadership faced the first serious stirrings within their respective Cold War blocs. But the Cold War rivals were hardly ready to turn the page on their bitter and dangerous quarrel. However fearful nuclear weapons were, both sides continued to build more and better weapons, thereby feeding the anxieties of the other. At the same time, the restive third world proved an expanding area of competition that was even harder to manage. The resulting competition to win friends and defeat foes among the newly independent states complicated efforts by Soviet and American leaders to limit Cold War costs and risks.

Finally, between 1953 and the years immediately following 1968, the market-driven international economy over which the United States presided enjoyed a golden age—and by its very successes added yet another set of pressures on the Cold War system. At about the time of Stalin's death, the war-ravaged western European and Japanese economies regained their prewar levels of production and embarked on a prolonged period of strong, steady growth. These revived economies soon challenged U.S. economic supremacy and demanded a voice in international economic governance.

This era of prosperity effected subtle but profound changes in popular attitudes that added to the pressure on cold warriors on both sides. The stirrings were especially marked in the United States, where the politics of anti-communism had to compete with the politics of growth and an intensifying popular bias for a better material life. Calls for sacrifice in the name of Cold War crusading had little appeal as a new generation of Americans—born after World War II and raised in relative affluence in the 1950s—proved impatient with the social and political orthodoxies that had prevailed at the start of the postwar era. Their discontent would inspire a youth revolt in the 1960s and new attitudes toward race relations, foreign policy, gender roles, and the environment. Boom times in western Europe and Japan promoted these same popular expectations, and there too a new generation engaged in protests that would shake capitals throughout the developed world and beyond.

Times were good also in Soviet bloc economies as recovery from war and the growing availability of consumer goods raised living standards dramatically. But this socialist consumer revolution created pressure from below for more goods as well as for better food and housing. As elsewhere, young people were the most impatient with what they saw as social and political stagnation. Khrushchev and his colleagues labored to improve ordinary people's lives even if it took damping down the Cold War and providing more cultural freedoms. Thus in the Eastern bloc as elsewhere, the lure of material abundance increasingly defined national priorities and left many asking, "Why gamble the highest living standards in generations and the hopes for still more on a throw of the Cold War dice?"

By the late 1960s the strains on the Cold War system were becoming acute, creating new possibilities for the years to come. A surprise offensive in Vietnam in 1968 set in doubt the Cold War calculus behind the U.S. prosecution of that distant, now misbegotten war. That same year witnessed a weakening of the U.S. economy so serious that Americans would have to surrender their domination of international trade and finance. Finally, the confidence and fervor that animated Nkrumah and others in the third world climaxed only to rapidly collapse. It was becoming clear that the transformation of the third world was not the work of a historical moment but would take generations. The great achievement of the radicals—the end of colonialism—had by then been completed, and they were beginning to discover that their goal of fundamentally remaking their countries would be hard to realize. The years between 1953 and 1968 were, in short, a time of transition. The immediate postwar arrangements were on the defensive but not yet overturned; a new, more globally integrated world was only just coming into view.

CHAPTER 4

THE COLD WAR:
A TENUOUS ACCOMMODATION

No sooner had the Cold War begun to spread and to raise fears of a new, unprecedentedly costly world conflict than policymakers on both sides began to search for accommodation. During the 1950s and 1960s, the Cold War developed a dynamic that favored stability and imposed limits on the super-powers.

Looking back, it is possible to identify the pressures that began to put a brake on the U.S.-Soviet rivalry. Nuclear weapons helped make American and Soviet policymakers more prudent. The prospect of a nuclear catastrophe began to haunt leaders constantly attended by the "black box" that enabled them to authorize an attack. More subtle but no less important were domestic pressures that Cold War leaders could not easily ignore. In the democratic U.S. system, public opinion was always a potent force that elected officials might sway, but only within limits. The men in the Kremlin wrestled with the inescapable fact that their economy was too small to sustain superpower ambitions while also underwriting the better life that Soviet citizens were coming to expect.

Despite these constraints, the two wary international rivals moved only hesitantly toward accommodation. The arms race continued at a fast clip, while events in Cuba and then Vietnam demonstrated that Washington and Moscow could still maneuver themselves into dangerous and costly confrontations. The lack of progress toward ending the Cold War, but more generally the social and ideological rigidities associated with it, provoked increasing impatience, especially in the generation coming of political age in the 1960s. In 1968 that impatience erupted in city streets in the United States and western Europe as well as in Poland, Japan, and Mexico. All around the world young people demanded fundamental social and political transformations, challenging leaders from an older generation who seemed stuck in the past.

THE BEGINNINGS OF COEXISTENCE

During the 1950s, Premier Nikita Khrushchev and President Dwight D. Eisenhower began rethinking the dangerous rivalry in which their two countries had become locked. Both men found themselves in a nuclear world of enormous peril and increasing cost as strategic weapons proliferated. They found their publics wanting more than the risks and costs imposed by the Cold War rivalry. And both had to deal with Cold War allies with different priorities. However, neither the Soviet nor the American leader was prepared to fully repudiate the Cold War decisions made by his predecessors or step outside the worldview of his particular political culture. With one foot still solidly planted in the Cold War, each could only cautiously explore a new relationship.

Khrushchev under Pressure

The strongest impetus to dampen Cold War tensions came from Stalin's successor, Nikita Khrushchev. He was born in 1894 in a Russian village near the border with eastern Ukraine to a family of peasant origin. The family's poverty forced Nikita to work early and allowed him only minimal education. A schoolteacher with radical views first opened Khrushchev to the possibility of political change. His experience as a young man further politicized him. He watched revolutionary fever grip his village in 1905, and by age fifteen he had begun to train as a metalworker attached to mines that were a hotbed of labor radicalism. He attended lectures on political economy and read the Bolshevik newspaper, *Pravda,* and Marx's *The Communist Manifesto.*

Khrushchev's sharpening convictions led him into revolutionary politics. Between 1912 and 1914 he emerged as a labor activist leading strikes. By 1917 he was head of the local metal workers' union and had joined the Bolshevik party. He fought with Bolsheviks during the civil war in Russia following their revolutionary seizure of power. His dedication, energy, and ruthlessness, together with his working-class background, helped him move ahead in the party.

Khrushchev's political style and values reflected his peasant origins. He was not interested in abstruse theoretical debate. He wanted for the Soviet Union precisely what his own early years had denied him: a rapidly developing economy to provide for the popular welfare and a strong, stable political system to create respect and security from the outside world. His politics were generally Stalinist—he was impatient with the moderate economic policy of the 1920s and welcomed Stalin's shift to state planning in 1929. He voiced enthusiastic support for Stalin as the "genius-leader." As an administrator, he was hands-on—an activist who often acted impulsively. Convinced of the efficacy of administrative reforms in promoting economic development, he repeatedly resorted to such reforms despite his general lack of success with them. His outward appearance as a country bumpkin led many to underestimate his shrewdness and political skills and spared him suspicion during the purges of the 1930s.

In 1938 Khrushchev was put in charge of Ukraine. The next year he became a full member of the Politburo, though he seldom attended meetings in Moscow and enjoyed considerable latitude in running a region roughly the size of France. During his long stint there, Khrushchev built a political machine and recruited party allies such as Leonid Brezhnev, critical to his later rise to supremacy. In late 1949 Stalin called Khrushchev to Moscow to a place within Stalin's close entourage. Following Stalin's death in 1953, Khrushchev shared power with colleagues, but by 1955 the sixty-one-year-old Khrushchev was well on his way to consolidating his leadership. He had proved himself, as one party observer noted, "shrewder, more talented, energetic and decisive than the others."[1]

De-Stalinization. Khrushchev's decade in power was to produce a rush of reforms that became known as de-Stalinization. Most of those reforms Khrushchev and his rivals had begun exploring just after Stalin's death, and even those that Khrushchev had then opposed became his own after he secured his place at the top. The reforms were wide ranging, touching directly on political and cultural life, the economy, and foreign relations. Over each of these areas stood the ghost of Stalin. The fact that Khrushchev was a product of the Stalinist system made the break with the past all the more difficult.

Early in his tenure Khrushchev resolved to confront the ghost of his old master. To alter the Stalinist system required rethinking Stalin's significance to the development of the Soviet Union. The new leadership took the first step by downplaying the Stalin cult. In early 1954 Khrushchev issued instructions for gathering concrete data on Stalin-era repression, and two years later he stunned delegates to the Twentieth Party Congress by delivering an address laying out some of Stalin's crimes and the "conditions of insecurity, fear and even desperation" created by this "sickly suspicious" leader.[2] (The details of this supposedly secret speech traveled throughout the party like a whirlwind, and a copy of the speech itself quickly reached an amazed West.) In 1961 Khrushchev launched another, even more emphatic assault on Stalinism.

De-Stalinization brought into the open longstanding discontents within the party leadership. Khrushchev and his colleagues did not question the superiority of socialism over capitalism, the correctness of Marxism-Leninism as a guide to action, or the need for strong, one-party leadership. They acknowledged Stalin's important contributions to the revolution. But they did recognize that his mistakes had demoralized the party and the public and in turn damaged the party's pursuit of economic development and popular welfare, even while they took care to minimize their own complicity in Stalin's misdeeds. Khrushchev himself had begun to have doubts about Stalin in the 1940s. Watching his boss handle the crisis of war revealed to Khrushchev how out of touch and how distrustful of subordinates Stalin was. Possibly adding to the resentment was Stalin's supposed refusal to stop the execution of Khrushchev's son, a pilot shot down by the Germans and, like all returned Soviet POWs, suspected of treason. Seeing Stalin daily between 1949 and 1953 accentuated Khrushchev's awareness of the faults of the old man and of the system that he had built. Perhaps more broadly, Khrushchev realized that a half-century of traumas—the 1905 revolution, the German invasion during World War I, the 1917 revolutions followed by brutal civil war, Stalin's revolution from above, and the second German invasion during

World War II—had scarred his people. It was time for a respite from national mobilization, class struggle, and personal anxiety.

De-Stalinization had immediate consequences in the Soviet Union. Within the Communist Party, it gave party members and leaders greater security by curbing the terror apparatus that Stalin had wielded so ruthlessly. It affirmed the importance of collective leadership, so that Khrushchev had to pay at least pro forma respect to the opinions of his senior colleagues even as he grew more powerful. Khrushchev's bold attack on at least a part of the Stalinist past had a dramatic psychological impact as news of the event began to circulate ever more widely. Yevgeny Yevtushenko, a young poet often embroiled with the authorities in cultural disputes, remembered "how everybody read Khrushchev's so-called secret speech—in factories, at the Writers Union. Even non-party people like me read it. Many people cried and hung their heads. They were shocked."[3]

Reactions were distinctly mixed. Some party members and many intellectuals and artists who would come to refer to themselves as "Children of the Twentieth Party Congress" welcomed the critical scrutiny of Stalinism and hoped for the beginning of a more humane and open socialism. Some at the grassroots were confused. How could Stalin's associates not have known about his excesses, and why did they not stop his evil deeds? How could such excesses occur in a socialist country, and what was to prevent them from happening again? But the speech also gave rise to disbelief and resentment as Khrushchev's revelations collided with a Stalin cult propagated over two decades. At one university a student march to lay flowers on the local Stalin monument turned into a general protest against the unfair treatment of the "great leader." An angry soldier declared, "Stalin raised me from childhood in his ideas, and I will not reject these ideas now." A party loyalist recalled his distress. Even after finding out about Stalin's most serious flaws, he still found it "very difficult to extinguish in the heart that great love that was so strongly rooted in our whole organism."[4]

One of the most important effects of de-Stalinization was to open Soviet cultural life. Artists and intellectuals enjoyed more room for dissent and debate, and even those who defied the party faced a relatively mild response—a rebuke or exile, but not execution and punishment of family and friends. While Khrushchev's criticism of Stalin gave broad encouragement to this cultural thaw, his direct intervention resulted in the publication of new and more searching literature such as Alexander Solzhenitsyn's novel *One Day in the Life of Ivan Denisovich,* and Yevtushenko's poem "Stalin's Heirs." The latter was printed in the party paper, *Pravda,* after Khrushchev had moved Stalin's body from its place of honor in Red Square. It warned against the power of Stalin's ghost to shape the conduct even of those former colleagues now attacking him. Yevtushenko asked, "How can we remove Stalin from within the heirs of Stalin?"[5]

The rough-hewn and mercurial Khrushchev sometimes did not like what artists did with their new freedom. Jazz, he said, made him feel like he had "gas on the stomach." He detested abstract painting. To someone who worked in that genre, he offered his appraisal with characteristic bluntness: "It's a pity, of course, that your mother's dead, but maybe it's lucky for her that she can't see how her son is spending his time. What master are you serving anyway?... You've got to get out or paint differently. As you are, there is no future for you on our soil."[6]

Precisely because of these apparent excesses that came with greater freedom, Khrushchev felt the party had to keep a watchful eye on artists and intellectuals. Nevertheless, he allowed an unprecedented degree of openness to Western culture that ignited musical fads such as big band jazz, swing, and rock and roll. The foreign cultural influx stimulated the Soviet entertainment industry toward more adventuresome and popular work. Literature, for example, turned from tired political themes and spoke more often to readers' everyday lives and personal fantasies. Young people were especially quick to seize on new cultural trends, buying imported records and sporting Western-style clothes. Nightclubs filled with youthful crowds dancing one of a changing array of imported fads—from the jitterbug and boogie-woogie to the twist. One irritated state security officer watched lively young people in a nightclub in 1956 and grumbled, "All this energy could be invested in building a hydro-electric power station, rather than wasted here on a dance floor."[7] But however much the authorities might disapprove of some aspects of this budding consumer society, they did not question the need for a relaxation of the tensions and hardship that had so long marked Soviet life.

Presiding over cultural changes proved for the reformer in Khrushchev far less complicated than managing an economic system that was failing to deliver fully on its promise, especially to the Soviet people. Stalin had consistently favored developing defense and heavy industry, sectors that would sustain Soviet security and prestige. Khrushchev, by contrast, wanted to give more attention to light industry and agriculture in order to raise living standards. Khrushchev's "bread-and-butter" view of socialism left him sympathetic to pressure from consumers and convinced him that the ability of the system to respond to that pressure was a test of political legitimacy.[8] How could the Soviet Union, he wondered, make an impression abroad if it suffered shortages at home?

In May 1957 he dramatically promised to surpass the United States in per capita production of meat, milk, and butter within three years. In 1959 Khrushchev put into effect a seven-year plan meant to push the Soviet Union past the United States in per capita industrial and agricultural output by 1970 and to lay the basis for a fully communist society (one achieving a Western level of abundance, providing goods to its citizens on the basis of need rather than ability to produce, and in general following collectivist, egalitarian values). In 1960 he announced a decision to increase consumer goods production at the expense of the armed forces, and he cut the workweek from forty-eight to forty-two hours.

The achievements of the new, consumer-friendly leadership were considerable. The priority given to housing construction reduced the number of those trapped in the old, crowded communal living arrangements. Opportunities for schooling expanded. As a result of the shortened workweek, Soviet citizens enjoyed more time for leisure—for sports, movies, listening to the radio, reading, and visiting with family and friends. Vacations became more commonplace, and

Block after Block of Apartments under Construction in Moscow
From the Kremlin (pictured in the background here), Khrushchev directed
the drive to improve the general standard of living for Soviet citizens. (Stan
Wyman/TimePix)

people flocked to concerts, open-air poetry readings, clubs, and restaurants. Most
of the material and educational gains went to city dwellers. The countryside
lagged behind, but rural folk at least finally received an internal passport that gave
them greater freedom to travel within the Soviet Union.

Guns or Butter? Khrushchev had inherited an economy that strained to provide the resources required of a superpower. He thus faced a constant choice
between guns and butter—between spending on the military and foreign aid
critical to the Cold War competition, and diverting funds to meet popular needs.
His tilt toward the consumer involved him in a delicate balancing act. In the late
1950s he had bet on improved relations with the United States and cut spending
for conventional armed forces by one-third. To get the most out of his military
budget, he channeled funding to submarines, nuclear weapons, and the development of long-range missile systems. These kinds of advanced weapons would not
only insure Soviet security against U.S. attack but also demonstrate to the world
Soviet technological skills. The successful test of an intercontinental ballistic missile (ICBM) and the much-heralded launch of the first earth satellite (named
Sputnik), both in 1957, seemed to vindicate that strategy.

President John F. Kennedy's expansion of the U.S. military budget and the
Cuban missile crisis of 1962 dealt Khrushchev a blow, however, and demonstrated that gaining rough equality in strategic nuclear weapons would take a
major, long-term investment. Khrushchev began shifting funds from the consumer sector back to defense and heavy industry. That shift collided with rising

consumer discontent. Some complained, "What has become of consumer goods? We have to stand in line all day. Are we under blockade? The truth is that abroad they have everything, and here at home we have only rubbish."[9] In 1962 the southern Russian city of Novocherkassk became the scene of demonstrations protesting empty shop shelves, and scattered disturbances followed elsewhere. Responding to popular discontent, together with improved relations with the United States, Khrushchev by summer 1963 went back to advocating a better deal for consumers and cut defense spending.

While domestic economic pressures encouraged the post-Stalin leadership to consider a fresh approach to the Cold War, perhaps even more important was the fear of nuclear war. In the Soviet Union as in the United States, that fear had first taken hold among scientists. A few of those active in the Soviet bomb project anticipated the danger quite early. Reports of the enormous power of the first U.S. H-bomb test in 1952 alarmed the head of the Soviet nuclear program, Igor Kurchatov, and convinced him that nuclear war would end life on earth. He gained an ally in Andrei Sakharov, the designer of the first Soviet H-bomb. A 1953 tour of ground zero after a powerful test had shaken Sakharov. He found birds flapping helpless on the ground, their feathers scorched and their eyes burnt out. Buildings blown away like a house of cards, brick pulverized, and glass melted all conjured up terrible images of what nuclear war would do. Kurchatov, Sakharov, and others impelled by a sense of responsibility for their creation began a campaign to convince Stalin and his successors of the dangers of a growing nuclear arsenal. After a full briefing in 1953 shortly after Stalin's death, Khrushchev recalled being so shaken that "I became convinced that we could never possibly use these weapons." He made fresh disarmament proposals to the United States in 1955, and in his first summit with Eisenhower that year he made clear his realization that only a madman could contemplate nuclear war. He was reassured to learn that the Americans shared his understanding of the dangers of the new nuclear era. Now he realized, "Our enemies probably feared us as much as we feared them."[10]

Khrushchev and Soviet Foreign Policy. Khrushchev gave special prominence to the doctrine of "peaceful coexistence" in 1956 when the party elite gathered for the Twentieth Party Congress. He hinted at the way nuclear weapons had fundamentally transformed the nature of international relations. The future held only two choices—"either peaceful coexistence or the most destructive war in history. There is no third way." Arms control and better relations with the United States thus became important Soviet objectives. Embracing them did not mean abandoning hopes for the spread of socialism. In fact, Khrushchev argued that the rapid advance of socialism since the end of the war and the equally rapid disintegration of the colonial system foreshadowed the triumph of the Soviet camp. Precisely because the conditions were so favorable, he indicated that Communist parties might now gain power through parliamentary means, though he did not rule out revolutionary struggle in countries where elite resistance to change was particularly violent. By making this point Khrushchev was conceding, at least in theory, that Communist parties would follow paths appropriate to their particular national situations. In 1959 he extended his optimistic reading of the international situation by pronouncing "capitalist encirclement" of the Soviet Union at an end. By asserting that the country was secure against its external as well as internal foes, Khrushchev provided the basis for a policy of relaxation both at home and abroad.

Europe was a special target of Khrushchev's policy of peaceful coexistence. He promoted a settlement for Austria that ended its occupation by Soviet and Western forces and made it non-aligned within Cold War Europe. Although he responded to West Germany joining NATO in 1955 by forming the Warsaw Pact, a Moscow-led military alliance made up of Soviet eastern Europe clients, he also cultivated West German leader Konrad Adenauer in hopes of luring him away from the Americans. Khrushchev continued his peace offensive by proposing an end to both NATO and the Warsaw Pact, a comprehensive security treaty for Europe, and the withdrawal of U.S. troops from the continent. But the Eisenhower administration, still in the grip of Cold War suspicions, feared neutralization of Europe would be the prologue to Soviet domination.

The other major facet of Khrushchev's foreign policy involved managing his allies. He knew that he was at the head not of a mighty "communist monolith" (as Washington saw it) but of a brittle bloc that was inherently difficult to hold together. Allies and dependents wanted more aid than could be easily extracted from a Soviet economy straining to keep up with consumer demand. And they resented the Soviets' cultural insensitivity and often domineering attitude.

Every bit as much as Stalin, his successors were determined to maintain dutiful socialist regimes in eastern Europe. They needed forward bases to counter NATO, to keep "fraternal" parties in line, and if necessary to suppress popular demonstrations of anti-Soviet sentiment. But Stalin's heirs also wanted to handle the region with a lighter touch—to avoid his brutality but also to limit the costs of propping up unpopular clients.

Shortly after Stalin's death, the new leaders took steps to improve relations with Tito's Yugoslavia on the proposition that socialist regimes could legitimately pursue paths other than the Soviet one. Following his break with Stalin, Tito had denounced the Soviet system as a caricature of socialism. An entrenched bureaucracy in the USSR held the real power, not the working class, while internationally the Soviet state functioned as "an imperialist machine which is fighting for spheres of influence and the subjugation of other peoples."[11] Tito looked to the West for trade and aid, and he integrated the Yugoslav economy with a prospering western Europe. He also took an active role as one of the sponsors of non-alignment, popular among newly independent states wanting to avoid entanglement in the Cold War rivalry. He followed an independent line domestically as well and allowed a degree of intellectual freedom. The guiding economic idea in the industrial sector was self-management, a decentralized economic policy that put control in the hands of workers, not bureaucrats.

Once secure at the top, Khrushchev held to the more accommodating approach that had led to improved relations with Yugoslavia. His 1956 party congress speeches on Stalin and peaceful coexistence underlined his seriousness about the importance of reform and called for respecting national differences among socialist countries. To drive the point home he dissolved the Cominform, created by Stalin in 1947 as an instrument to control Communist parties throughout Europe. But Khrushchev's talk of pluralism and repudiation of Stalin's excesses stirred up unrest in eastern Europe, galvanizing reformers and angering hardliners who had climbed to power under Stalin and modeled themselves on his policy of tight control.

The first signs of discontent had appeared even before Khrushchev consolidated his position. In June 1953, soon after Stalin's death, workers in Berlin had made political as well as economic demands on the Soviet-backed East German Communist Party. Protests quickly spread to other cities. Alarmed over the possible loss of control, Moscow ordered the tanks of its occupying forces into action. Rapid repression saved the day.

Three years later Khrushchev suffered a close call in Poland. A strike began in June 1956 in Poznan, a major industrial center. When the protest spread, the authorities resorted to repression, resulting in over fifty deaths. In July a worried Soviet leadership decided to restore to power Władysław Gomułka, a former party leader who had fallen afoul of Stalin. With unrest continuing in October, Moscow prepared for intervention in the face of what it feared would be intense Polish resistance. Gomułka finally was able to scotch the invasion plans by promising Moscow to retain one-party control and membership in the Warsaw Pact. The crisis passed.

In Hungary the new light-rein policy suffered its most dramatic failure. In October 1956 news of protest in Poland and Khrushchev's denunciation of Stalin's crimes inspired public demonstrations honoring Hungarians who had fallen victim to Stalinist purges. As in Poland, workers took the lead, demanding "socialism but according to our own special Hungarian conditions, which reflect the interests of the Hungarian working class and the Hungarian nation." The reform party leader, Imre Nagy, heralded the mounting protests as "a great national and democratic movement, embracing and unifying all our people." He announced an end to one-party rule and withdrawal from the Warsaw Pact. With Hungary slipping into "counterrevolution," Khrushchev ordered military action in early November. As Soviet forces closed in, a Hungarian newspaper described over the wire to an impotent West scenes of freedom fighters "jumping up at the tanks, throwing hand-grenades inside and then slamming the drivers' windows. The Hungarian people are not afraid of death. It is only a pity that we can't stand for long." The Soviets crushed desperate resistance at the cost of several thousand lives, executed Nagy, and installed a more pliant János Kádár. Khrushchev's intervention made clear that pluralism had limits. Soviet-aligned regimes that failed to contain popular protest or themselves strayed from the socialist faith could expect Soviet military intervention and the installation of a more dutiful government.[12]

Moscow encountered even greater difficulties in dealing with China. Like the Yugoslavs, the Chinese Communist allies enjoyed considerable independence because they had come to power without the help of the Red Army. Khrushchev had tried to impress the Chinese with generous development support. But his

Stalin Brought to Ground
Hungarians handed down their judgment on the man who had imposed a system of internal
repression and foreign domination on their country. The head from a giant statue of Stalin lies
shattered in a Budapest street in the midst of the revolt against Soviet control in October 1956.
(Hulton/Archive by Getty Images)

speech on de-Stalinization as well as his policy of peaceful coexistence irritated
Mao, while Mao's predictions that China would surpass the Soviet Union in the
advance toward communism and his cavalier attitude toward nuclear war alienated Khrushchev. By 1959, less than a decade after the conclusion of the Sino-
Soviet alliance, cooperation between these two Communist giants was breaking
down. The Chinese began denouncing Soviet socialism as a sham and challenging
Moscow's claim to lead the socialist bloc. In mid-1960 Moscow abruptly ended its
aid program and recalled its advisors. By the early 1960s the split between the two
socialist giants was deep and headed toward military confrontation.

Other parties once tightly in the Soviet orbit also began drifting away. The
de-Stalinization policy gave a strong impetus to the rise of more independent
western European Communist parties in a trend that became known as Eurocommunism. For example, the head of the Italian party, Palmiro Togliatti, argued
that Stalin's excesses as well as his achievements in building socialism reflected the
peculiarities of the Russian context. Recognizing that parties would each follow
a national path, he declared, "Even in the Communist movement itself we cannot speak of a single guide."[13] These trends toward the breakup of the international communist movement were accentuated by the outbreak of the
Sino-Soviet dispute in 1959–1960. Albania followed China in condemning

THE KHRUSHCHEV THAW	
1953	Stalin's death; collective leadership is established with Khrushchev as party secretary; terror apparatus is dismantled as first step toward de-Stalinization; demonstrations occur in East Germany; Korean War armistice is concluded
1955	West Germany joins NATO; Warsaw Pact forms
1956	Khrushchev and Eisenhower recognize nuclear vulnerability; at the Twentieth Party Congress, Khrushchev denounces Stalin's excesses and advocates "peaceful coexistence"; protests erupt in Poland and Hungary (the latter crushed by Soviet troops)
1957	Soviet ICBM is tested and *Sputnik* is launched
1959–1960	Beginning of serious, public Sino-Soviet disagreements
1962	The publication of Alexander Solzhenitsyn's novel *One Day in the Life of Ivan Denisovich* marks cultural opening

Soviet "revisionism." Khrushchev retaliated by cutting off aid and encouraging a coup against the Albanian party leader, Enver Hoxha.

Khrushchev is a pivotal figure in Soviet history and the unfolding of the Cold War. Like Stalin, he hoped that in the long run capitalism's decline and the successes of socialism would put the Soviet Union in a position superior to the United States. Yet the crisis of capitalism did not materialize, and inefficiencies in the Soviet economic system persisted. The Soviet economy was not large enough to create the promised "workers' paradise" and at the same time fight the Cold War. Beset by contradictory pressures, Khrushchev recognized that some sort of reduction in tensions with the United States was the best all-around solution. The Soviet Union would become more secure, and economic resources could be shifted to the consumer sector. But were American leaders ready to support a decisive turn away from the costs and dangers of the Cold War?

Crosscurrents in American Policy

The preoccupations and pressures within the Soviet system—domestic reform, consumer demand, the nuclear danger, and problems with allies—had counterparts on the U.S. side of the Cold War line. Nowhere are the parallels more striking than in the way fear of nuclear war gradually gripped policymakers.

Although Harry Truman had come to rely heavily on nuclear weapons, Hiroshima and Nagasaki had schooled him in their potential for destruction. He began practicing restraint even before the Soviet Union broke the U.S. monopoly on nuclear weapons in 1949. He asserted civilian control over those weapons and their development and sidestepped military pressure to plan for a nuclear war. The Korean War confirmed his cautious attitude. Though once, in late November 1950 with American troops reeling in the wake of Chinese intervention, Truman did blunder into a public comment about the possible use of nuclear weapons to save the situation, he ultimately embraced the more prudent view: A nuclear campaign would probably not stop China's fighting force, might trigger Soviet retaliation, and would deeply agitate American allies in Europe. Just before leaving office in early 1953, Truman offered some chilling reflections on what living with the bomb had taught him. Nuclear war would bring "death and destruction" to civilians and result in nothing less than "the end of civilization."[14] The fears that had settled on Truman would haunt his successors.

Eisenhower and Cold War Commitments. The Korean War had helped to elect Truman's successor, Republican Dwight Eisenhower, president in 1952. Casualties inflicted by Chinese forces in Korea and war-induced inflation and shortages at home had eroded public support. By early February 1951, half of poll respondents judged this inconclusive limited war a mistake. Support continued to decline, to the considerable detriment of Truman's popularity but also to that of the Democratic Party. Eisenhower quickly arranged an end to the fighting, and the military swore "never again" to intervene with U.S. troops on the Asian mainland. Throughout his tenure in the White House, Eisenhower faced the question of military intervention with considerable caution. On the surface his enunciated policy of "massive retaliation" seemed a blatant denial of nuclear fear. That policy placed nuclear weapons at the center of his military strategy. The U.S. leader claimed that he was ready to meet any Soviet-bloc attempt to break through the containment line with an all-out nuclear attack on the USSR itself. He could thus dispense with costly conventional forces and rely on nuclear weapons, which would give him what the administration called "more bang for the buck." He accordingly authorized a steady expansion of strategic warheads (from 1,000 on entering the White House to 7,000 on his departure) as well as delivery systems (with bombers soon to be supplemented by ground and submarine-launched missiles).

But in private Eisenhower recognized nuclear weapons as both morally dubious and of limited utility. His first major security study acknowledged an emerging nuclear balance of terror. Three years later the president read a secret government report estimating that even under the most favorable conditions millions of Americans would die in a nuclear war with the Soviets. He sought to brake the expansion of the U.S. arsenal knowing full well from secret U-2 reconnaissance flights that Khrushchev's boasts of major advances in Soviet nuclear delivery systems were hollow. Eisenhower could not make this reassuring information public, but certain of the U.S. lead, he rejected calls for spending more on arms, even though his stand hurt his and the Republican Party's popularity.

Like Khrushchev, Eisenhower worried that Cold War commitments might make excessive claims on national resources and harm domestic welfare. Above all, the American president feared that a crusade for freedom abroad might mortally wound freedom at home. Initially, he thought about this danger in terms of sapping the vitality of the economic system on which long-term security depended. If heavy defense spending hurt economic productivity, the country would lose its ability to support containment over the long haul. But increasingly Eisenhower spied another danger—a threat to political freedom within the United States itself. He worried that the military budget would create concentrations of power beyond popular control and thus be harmful to American democracy. His farewell address of January 1961 warned that an emerging "military-industrial complex" represented just such a danger.

Public Nuclear Fears. Eisenhower was also, like Khrushchev, constrained by potent domestic pressures. By the late 1950s the public was feeling the nuclear fears that had first fastened on scientists and then gripped political leaders. In 1946 John Hersey's *Hiroshima,* a moving account of the devastation wrought by one atomic bomb, had driven home to a broad audience the nightmarish nature of this weapon of mass destruction.

The first overt manifestations of nuclear fear began to take shape in the 1950s as a result of growing awareness that radioactive fallout from atomic tests (some 423 by 1962) was a silent killer. Scientists had long known of radiation's damaging effects, but growing exposure in the laboratory and fallout that occasionally spread beyond the main U.S. test sites in Nevada and the Pacific intensified concern over this major public health problem. By 1954 a debate was warming up over the likelihood of fallout producing birth defects and leukemia and over the merits of halting tests in order to limit harm to humans.

Serious civil defense discussions also fed nuclear fear. Following the first Soviet atomic test in 1949, the Truman administration made plans for dispersing industry and population to make Soviet targeting more difficult, building bomb shelters, and planning emergency urban evacuations. But in general, Washington expected individuals to devise their own means of protection with the help of government advice. Much of the overall civil defense effort went into education and public drills. These had their most lasting effect by imprinting on a whole generation the memory of duck-and-cover exercises in classrooms and advice from Bert the Turtle on the importance of taking shelter at once after a nuclear flash. Although civil defense was intended in part to reassure the anxious public, it had the opposite effect, heightening nuclear anxieties.

Mainstream culture reflected the feeling of vulnerability. Already by the late 1940s popular fiction had picked up the theme of radiation-induced mutations. Movies followed suit. For example, *Them!* in 1954 projected before audiences giant mutant ants emerging from a New Mexico test site. Comic books developed their own heroes touched by radiation—Superman vulnerable to kryptonite and a scientist turned by radiation exposure into Spider-Man. Comedy routines and ballads (such as "What Have They Done to the Rain?" popularized by Joan Baez) also took up the theme of looming nuclear danger. Nevil Shute, an Australian, hit a chord in the United States with his 1957 novel *On the Beach,* made into a movie in 1959. It painted a bleak picture of a world doomed by fallout from nuclear war. The dangerous situation in which U.S. leaders had placed the country also was the subject of the influential Stanley Kubrick film *Dr. Strangelove, or: How I Learned to Stop Worrying and Love the Bomb,* depicting the arms race as an absurd competition conducted by lunatics and fools.

Anti-nuclear activists began to emerge as more and more of the public grasped the danger posed by atomic weapons. The first protest group, the National Committee for a Sane Nuclear Policy (SANE), took shape in mid-1957, quickly expanding to 25,000 members. In 1961 Dagmar Wilson, a housewife and illustrator for children's books, became impatient with the ineffectual all-male politicking on the issue and called for direct pressure by women. She launched Women Strike for Peace, a group devoted to staging public demonstrations and stressing the nuclear threat to children. Anti-nuclear groups in Britain, West Germany, and Japan—all allies and critical bases for the U.S. military—joined their U.S. counterparts in demanding an immediate end to nuclear testing and in developing effective publicity campaigns.

This mounting public concern ran up against deep-seated suspicions, especially among the president and his advisors, about negotiating with the enemy. The still vivid memories of World War II told this generation of leaders that appeasement always invited disaster. They had watched the democracies appease Hitler—an attempt that had not spared them war but seemed instead to encourage the ambitions of the German leader. The broad anti-communist consensus forged in the late 1940s and early 1950s was an additional constraint, coloring political debate and policy discussions within the United States and perpetuating a picture of the Soviet Union as a dangerous and implacable force in the world.

The result was a cautious U.S. response to Khrushchev's peace offensive. At first, headway on arms control was impeded by Eisenhower's insistence on an intrusive, on-the-ground, fool-proof inspection system. (The technology for remote monitoring of nuclear tests was not yet adequate.) The president did not trust Moscow to keep any bargain and so attached provisions that were unacceptable to a Kremlin determined to hide its inferior military technology. Eisenhower was also unable to control bureaucratic pressure for a nuclear buildup. He wanted to slow the expansion of the U.S. arsenal, but the air force successfully championed a strategy of matching every single additional Soviet weapon with several new American weapons. A breakthrough finally seemed possible when in March 1958 Khrushchev declared a unilateral suspension of nuclear testing and Eisenhower agreed in the fall to make it a joint moratorium. The American president now made a belated attempt to develop a personal relationship with Khrushchev. But any chance for progress collapsed in May 1960 when the Soviets shot down a U-2 spy plane, capturing its pilot. An angry Khrushchev publicly denounced the American leader and walked out of what had seemed a promising summit meeting.

CRISIS POINTS

Khrushchev continued to grope toward improved relations with Eisenhower's successor, John F. Kennedy. But with the Cold War still casting a long shadow, Moscow and Washington made only limited progress in containing their rivalry. Despite the horrible knowledge of what nuclear weapons could do, leaders were not prepared to check the arms race. And neither side was ready to endure the humiliation and political damage of abandoning overseas commitments. Indeed, despite the risks, both sides continued to probe for ways of gaining advantage. Khrushchev and Kennedy blundered into a nuclear crisis over Cuba, and then President Lyndon Johnson became ensnared in a second U.S.-Asian war. This time American forces fought against a Vietnamese foe backed by the Soviet Union as well as by China. Though arms control made a comeback after the Cuban crisis, the number of nuclear warheads on both sides continued to soar, further highlighting the firm hold the Cold War still exercised over the thinking and behavior of the superpower rivals.

To the Nuclear Brink in Cuba

The Cuban Missile Crisis of October 1962 transformed abstract talk of nuclear disaster into palpable, gut-wrenching fear. For nearly two weeks leaders, soon joined by their publics, lived with the prospect of imminent annihilation. But just as Kennedy and Khrushchev had helped maneuver their two countries to the brink of nuclear catastrophe, so too did they work together to avoid that last deadly step.

Kennedy campaigned for the presidency in 1960 charging that the Soviets had gained military superiority. Once in the White House he gained the data that refuted these claims but nonetheless dramatically increased American outlays as though the lag were real. This buildup added to an already impressive arsenal and gave the United States a marked superiority, perhaps even a first-strike capability (meaning possession of weaponry sufficient to destroy so much of an opponent's nuclear force so quickly that it would forestall a serious counterblow). The Soviets had about 500 strategic warheads, a paltry number compared with the U.S. force of about 7,200 warheads and some 300 long-range and submarine-launched missiles as well as a large fleet of long-range bombers.

Despite this nuclear advantage, Kennedy was prey to insecurity. This insecurity was pronounced in the Caribbean, where he faced a revolutionary regime in Cuba. Its leader, Fidel Castro, had overthrown the long-time U.S.-backed military strongman. Once in power, Castro had steadily moved domestic policy to the left and foreign policy toward the Soviet Union. (For more on the Castro revolution in Cuba, see Chapter 6.) Kennedy responded by endorsing a covert plan to overthrow Castro, but found himself deeply embarrassed when in April 1961 a CIA-orchestrated invasion by Cuban exiles failed dismally at the Bay of Pigs. Khrushchev had confronted the new U.S. president with tough talk at a summit meeting in Vienna in June and then endorsed the building of a wall through Berlin to stop East Germans from fleeing their country. Finally, Khrushchev shook Kennedy by predicting that wars of national liberation would sweep the third world into the Soviet camp. The Kennedy team felt beleaguered—and vulnerable to Republican critics. Kennedy had at least to demonstrate resolve in his own "backyard." He insisted that the CIA continue its covert operations aimed at Cuba, and in the summer of 1962 the U.S. military staged amphibious operations in the Caribbean against a nominally fictitious country ruled by the evil "Ortsac" (Castro spelled backwards).

Khrushchev responded to Kennedy's hard line by following a more aggressive nuclear policy. In September 1961 he resumed nuclear testing, culminating in a massive 60-megaton test. He resented U.S. placement of nuclear missiles in Turkey on the border with the Soviet Union—at a time when Washington was warning Moscow not to send any rocketry to points next to the United States. Perhaps most fateful was the Soviet leader's refusal to back away from supporting change and winning friends in the third world. In contrast to a cautious Stalin, Khrushchev actively cultivated the third world as an important field of peaceful Cold War competition. Early in his tenure, he had begun promoting Soviet influence in former colonial areas, visiting India, Burma, Afghanistan, and Indonesia and offering economic aid to newly independent countries, even if they insisted on non-alignment in the Cold War. This courtship won him friends in the Middle East (Egypt, Syria, and Iraq), in North Africa (Libya, Ethiopia, and Somalia), and in Asia (India and Indonesia). Khrushchev's sympathy extended from newly independent non-aligned countries to colonial peoples engaged in what he called "wars of national liberation." The Castro regime under U.S. siege was a test case. The Soviet Union would either have to provide help or lose its standing as the superpower genuinely supportive of new nations. Khrushchev began by sending economic and military assistance and then in spring 1962 decided to dispatch missiles secretly to Cuba to deter any American attack on the island.

Now it was Kennedy's turn for outrage when reconnaissance aircraft discovered the missile installations. He publicly demanded their removal. By late October 1962, the American and Soviet leaders were locked in a dangerous nuclear

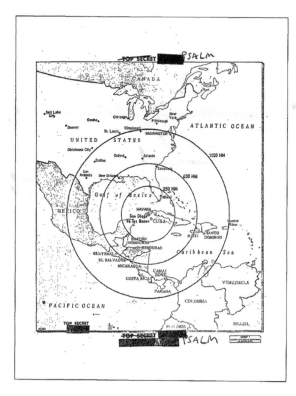

Cuba at the Epicenter of the U.S.-Soviet Nuclear Crisis

This CIA map, which circulated during the first days of the missile crisis in mid-October 1962, provided a sense of the range of Soviet weapons in Cuba. (Distance is expressed in nautical miles, slightly greater than a conventional mile.) The outer circle defined the farthest reach of medium-range missiles; the next circle marked the limits of light bombers. "Psalm" was the CIA designation for special handling of intelligence on Cuba. CIA mapmakers added Oxford, Mississippi, after Attorney General Robert Kennedy, the president's brother, asked in jest if Soviet missiles could reach that university town whose desegregation problems were agitating the administration. (C.I.A.)

confrontation. Khrushchev's daring gamble left both sides searching desperately for a way back from the brink of nuclear disaster and wondering if this day or minute might be the last for them and their loved ones. Deeply shaken, the antagonists moved to defuse the crisis. After exhausting deliberations with a special advisory group, Kennedy held out a pledge not to invade Cuba and privately promised to remove American missiles from Turkey. The Soviet leader also counseled caution. In a private letter to Kennedy, he described the Cuba issues before them as a knot that could become tied so tightly "that even he who tied it will not have the strength to untie it, and then it will be necessary to cut that knot, and what that would mean is not for me to explain to you, because you yourself understand perfectly of what terrible forces our countries dispose."[15] At the same time he pushed a belligerent Castro to the sidelines. The crisis ended when the Soviet leader accepted Kennedy's face-saving offer of a no-invasion pledge in exchange for removal of the missiles.

Khrushchev had previously pressed for arms control talks, and the Cuban Missile Crisis finally made Kennedy receptive. In a somber address at the American University in June 1963, the president conceded that the two nuclear powers had gotten caught in a costly cycle of competition and appealed to a sense of common humanity to overcome the distrust and to tame the nuclear danger. "We all inhabit this small planet. We all breathe the same air. We all cherish our children's future. And we are all mortal."[16] Kennedy and Khrushchev now agreed to some small but symbolically important steps. In June 1963 they arranged to install a hotline to facilitate rapid, direct communications between Washington and Moscow in future crises, and in August they signed the first arms control agreement, a ban on tests in the atmosphere.

But they would get no further. In November 1963, just a few months after concluding the test-ban treaty, Kennedy died from an assassin's bullet in Dallas, Texas. Khrushchev's days in office were also numbered. In October 1964 his colleagues, including his protégé Leonid Brezhnev, ousted him while he was out of Moscow on holiday. They had come to resent his increasingly autocratic leadership style and his rash initiatives at home and abroad. Khrushchev gave up power without a fight, remarking "Well, now I'm retired. Perhaps my most important accomplishment lies in the fact that they removed me from power by a simple vote, an act that would have caused their arrest under Stalin." Perhaps the fairest

TO THE NUCLEAR BRINK OVER CUBA	
1959	Castro's seizure of power alarms Washington
1961	Failure of Kennedy-approved invasion of Cuba by CIA-backed Cuban exiles at the Bay of Pigs
1962	Kennedy-Khrushchev confrontation over missiles in Cuba between October 16 and 28
1963	Kennedy and Khrushchev sign a treaty limiting nuclear testing
1964	Khrushchev is ousted in favor of Brezhnev

assessment of his leadership came from the poet Yevgeny Yevtushenko: "Khrushchev was a Stalinist and an anti-Stalinist. He was a rebel against himself."[17]

The problem of arms control was bigger than Khrushchev's flaws or a generally unresponsive U.S. policy. Neither side was prepared or able to break the seemingly relentless spiral of the arms race. Neither Russians nor Americans could control the technological imperative that had already produced the A-bomb and the much more powerful H-bomb as well as a succession of improved delivery systems such as ever better long-range bombers and intercontinental ballistic missiles of growing size and accuracy. They would be joined by still more impressive new weaponry, including submarine-launched ballistic missiles (SLBMs) and cruise missiles, new warheads, and finally, new defense systems, notably the anti-ballistic missile (ABM) defense. What policymaker could afford to refuse weapons development knowing that the other side might exploit the fresh technological possibilities constantly opening up before scientists?

The Cuban confrontation in particular convinced Soviet leaders that regardless of the difficulties and dangers of acquiring more and better weapons, they would have to plunge ahead if they wished to play the superpower game. In the aftermath of the Cuban crisis, one Russian diplomat supposedly observed: "You Americans will never be able to do this to us again."[18] As a result of this new urgency, Moscow would by 1970 raise its warheads to 2,400, five times what had been available during the Cuban crisis. A serious, sustained effort at arms control would from the Soviet perspective have to wait on the achievement of a rough nuclear equality with the Americans.

The Vietnam Quagmire

The deepening American involvement in Vietnam offers a second prime instance of the Cold War continuing to drive policymakers in spite of their considerable doubts. In mid-1965 President Lyndon B. Johnson made a decision to commit American combat troops on a major scale to that small country on the other side of the Pacific. Within two years half a million Americans would be fighting there, and ultimately some 58,000 would die. American taxpayers would have to pay $141 billion in military outlays between 1961 and the end of the war in 1975. In addition, the war would create bitter and lasting divisions within American society.

The Origins of U.S. Involvement. Johnson made his decision against the backdrop of a U.S. commitment to Vietnam going back fifteen years—and of a French struggle against a Communist-led resistance going back even farther (see Chapter 3). Washington's general anti-communist resolve first encompassed Vietnam in February 1950 when President Truman formally identified Vietnam and the rest of Indochina as an important front on the containment line. Neither he nor later presidents wanted to see their own forces bogged down in a peripheral area, but neither could they afford to lose Vietnam. Thus in that fateful February decision, Truman put aside the earlier U.S. reluctance to become implicated in a colonial struggle and threw his support behind the French military effort. At the same time Washington granted diplomatic recognition to a French puppet government headed by Vietnam's former emperor, Bao Dai. In May 1950 Washington made the first major grant of aid. As paymaster for French forces, the United States would cover three-fourths of the cost during the last years of their war. A long string of presidential decisions followed during the 1950s and early 1960s that repeatedly affirmed the need to block forces in that region allied with Moscow or Beijing.

Although containing communism was the dominant, formally articulated concern driving U.S. policy, American leaders were also guided by a sense of superiority over the politically "immature" Vietnamese. In addition, American observers generally regarded revolution in Vietnam as the product of the alien ideology of communism. In their view, its successes were the result of terror and other forms of coercion directed at a passive rural population. Finally, U.S. thinking on Vietnam was influenced by the memory of the democracies' appeasement of Hitler and the disastrous outcome of that course. To abandon Vietnam, so went the common refrain, was to plant the seeds of future trouble. None of the imagined consequences of abandoning Vietnam was more fearsome than the certainty of "falling dominoes," the collapse of nations throughout Southeast Asia and even in adjoining regions, were the Communists to triumph.

By 1954 French forces were in trouble. Communist troops had surrounded a major French base at Dien Bien Phu and were squeezing it into submission. By then the French electorate had turned against the war. President Eisenhower rejected direct U.S. military intervention to save the situation. An international conference in Geneva marked the end of French rule in Vietnam as well as in Cambodia and Laos, and it resolved on the temporary division of Vietnam at the seventeenth parallel. The Communists would take control north of that line, while those associated with the French were to evacuate to the south. All foreign forces were to withdraw from Vietnam. And within two years, the Geneva agreement stipulated, elections for a government for the entire country were to be held. The Eisenhower administration refused to sign the agreement even though it promised not to obstruct its implementation.

Reluctantly accepting the loss of northern Vietnam, the Eisenhower administration at once went to work on its defenses in the southern part of the country. The British novelist Graham Greene watched the Americans displace the French and anticipated the destruction those innocent newcomers might inflict on Indochina. Innocence, he warned prophetically, "is like a dumb leper who has lost his bell, wandering the world, meaning no harm." Heedless, the Eisenhower administration sent assistance to a new southern regime headed by Ngo Dinh Diem, a staunch anti-communist, a nationalist, and a Catholic, who would rule between 1954 and 1963. During the late 1950s the U.S. gamble on Diem seemed to pay off. He crushed his opposition (including the Communists) and consolidated his political position. But in the early 1960s Diem faltered. He neglected a resurgent Communist-backed insurgency in the countryside in favor of struggle against urban political foes, above all Buddhists resentful of the government's pro-Catholic policies. By then the Kennedy administration was reluctant to abandon a beleaguered South Vietnam, but the president was wary of a major U.S. troop commitment. "The troops will march in; the bands will play; the crowds will cheer." But then, he added, "It's like taking a drink. The effect wears off, and you have to take another." Finally, impatience with an increasingly isolated and ineffective Diem led Kennedy to give the nod to a coup by a group of Vietnamese generals. Despite military leadership in Saigon and rising levels of U.S. military and economic aid, the insurgents continued to gain ground. Washington had finally run out of options. Now the choices boiled down to either sending U.S. troops or reaching a negotiated settlement.[19]

"Johnson's War." In 1965, President Johnson made the critical Vietnam commitment. Born and raised in rural west Texas, Johnson had politics in his blood. He watched his father win state office. He served his own political apprenticeship as an assistant to a Texas congressman before launching his career, first in the House of Representatives and then in the Senate, where in the 1950s he emerged as the powerful Democratic majority leader. His bid for the presidency in 1960 fell short, and Johnson reluctantly agreed to become the younger, less experienced John Kennedy's running mate. Kennedy's assassination in November 1963 thrust Johnson into the position of leadership and power that he craved.

Vietnam was sitting on President Johnson's desk from the first day he took charge of the White House. Although he recognized that he had inherited a rapidly deteriorating situation in South Vietnam with little room for maneuver, he also believed the widely accepted arguments used to justify defending the South. Communist aggression had to be stopped. Retreat or appeasement in Vietnam would imperil lands far beyond as a result of the domino effect. Johnson himself explained to the public, "As long as there are men who hate and destroy, we must have the courage to resist, or we will see it all, all that we have built, all that we hope to build, all of our dreams for freedom—all, *all* will be swept away on the flood of conquest."[20] Johnson's other important inheritance was a Kennedy team of advisers committed to winning in Vietnam. None was more influential than Robert McNamara, the secretary of defense who brought to the conduct of the war a tough, can-do attitude.

Inexorably Johnson moved toward intervention. He took a major step in August 1964 following trouble involving two U.S. destroyers operating in the Tonkin Gulf off the North Vietnamese coast. On August 2, North Vietnamese patrol boats attacked the *Maddox*. Two days later, the *Turner Joy* mistakenly concluded that it also was under attack. Johnson responded by launching U.S. aircraft on a retaliatory raid against nearby enemy bases and then asked Congress for authorization to use U.S. military forces to defend the region. Congress complied with a nearly unanimous vote for what has become known as the Tonkin Gulf Resolution.

A landslide victory in the November 1964 election gave Johnson command of the powers of the presidency in his own right—and put him in a position to apply real pressure on Hanoi. In February 1965 he launched fresh bombing raids against the North in reprisal for attacks on American facilities in the South. He quickly turned the reprisals into a sustained bombing campaign—Operation

Rolling Thunder—intended to convince Ho Chi Minh and other leaders in the North to end the southern insurgency or face a barrage of punishing American blows. Hanoi did not flinch, and the war in the South continued badly for forces loyal to Saigon.

Sending in American combat troops was all that was left to avert a collapse of the Saigon government. In March 1965, Johnson ordered 3,500 marines to patrol around the U.S. air base at Da Nang. He soon gave permission for them to operate offensively. Fresh troops continued to arrive, and by early June 50,000 American soldiers were in Vietnam. By July, with a recommendation in hand from McNamara to make a major commitment of U.S. combat forces, Johnson had launched a troop buildup that would raise the number of American soldiers in Vietnam to half a million.

Johnson found that the Cold War's second "limited war" was no easier to prosecute than the first one in Korea. The Korean War experience had taught him and other U.S. leaders that China was likely to intervene directly if the United States threatened Hanoi's survival. The Soviet Union might respond by providing more supplies and equipment to raise the cost for U.S. forces. An all-out struggle would weaken U.S. defenses in Europe (the real Cold War prize) and

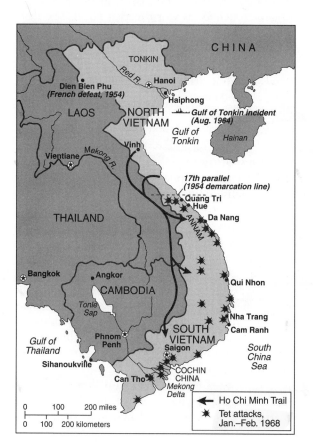

MAP 4.1
The Vietnam War,
1954–1975

might even trigger a nuclear confrontation. The degree to which Johnson grasped the risks of intervention is evident in a private telephone conversation with McNamara on June 21, 1965, barely a month before the definitive troop commitment. Johnson predicted, "It's going to be difficult for us to very long prosecute effectively a war that far away from home with the [popular] divisions that we have here and particularly the potential divisions." Not only did the president realize that the public was lukewarm on Vietnam, but he also accurately predicted that it was not likely to support him over the long haul. The enemy, on the other hand, was united and resolute—"I don't believe that they're ever goin' to quit." He felt his own bureaucracy had failed to come up with a "plan for victory militarily or diplomatically." He thoroughly understood that an American war could turn into a political nightmare. Johnson's advisers reinforced his fears. George Ball in the State Department is the best known of the dissenters. He warned of "a long-term catastrophe" in the making. Other insiders, including Vice President Hubert Humphrey, also candidly expressed their doubts.[21]

But despite their reservations and his own, Johnson could not break out of the Cold War framework. His predecessors had made commitments to South Vietnam that had to be honored. He had to preserve American credibility as a world leader. He had to respect the anti-communist consensus at home. As he grimly played out the limited war scenario, the president watched his worst fears realized. The daily headlines became routine: more troops and more casualties, more bombing of North Vietnam as well as Communist-controlled areas in the South, but no weakening of enemy resistance. China and the Soviet Union lined up behind the North, deterring an American invasion and providing critical support to Hanoi. The war became the target of ever-larger protests and began losing popular support.

The Vietnam War was soon threatening Johnson's ambitious Great Society programs. Launched in 1965–1966 with great fanfare and advanced skillfully through Congress by the president, those programs took aim at domestic poverty and racial injustice but also sought to improve education, urban conditions, the environment, and medical care. Opponents seized on soaring war costs to undermine this centerpiece of Johnson's domestic agenda, and even his supporters warned that he could not crusade both abroad and at home. Once more the choice between guns and butter confronted the leaders of the superpowers.

Privately, Johnson took a personal beating. He waited anxiously for news of air missions to reach the White House and agonized over daily reports of American losses. American allies in Europe shunned involvement, and the televised horrors of the war set off a global wave of anti-Americanism. In early 1968 on the Vietnamese new year known as Tet, the enemy launched a dramatically successful surprise attack. (See Map 4.1.) This Tet Offensive shook the Washington establishment, the public, and the president himself. In March 1968, Johnson told the nation that he was limiting the bombing of the North, opening negotiations with Hanoi, and would not seek another term in the White House.

What had gone wrong? Some critics have seen the Vietnam War as a failure to properly exercise American military power, with much of the blame resting on Lyndon Johnson for fighting the war with one hand tied behind his back. What they overlook but Johnson did not were the dangers of escalation.

U.S. ENTANGLEMENT IN INDOCHINA	
1950	The Truman administration commits substantial military aid to French forces fighting for control of Indochina
1954	French hopes are dealt a crushing blow by defeat at Dien Bien Phu; Eisenhower bows to Geneva conference division of Vietnam and supports an anti-communist state in the south
1961	Kennedy begins increasing U.S. military assistance to South Vietnam
1963	Diem is ousted by his generals with Kennedy's tacit approval
1964	Congress passes the Tonkin Gulf Resolution authorizing Johnson to retaliate for acts of aggression in Southeast Asia
1965	Johnson launches U.S. bombing campaign and sends first U.S. combat units to Vietnam
1968	Tet Offensive shocks American public opinion and strengthens protest against the war; Johnson opens peace talks and abandons his reelection bid

Other critics of this inconclusive war have shifted the blame from Johnson to the "liberal" media, which they argue was biased against resolute action. But in fact the collapse of political will at home was not the product of media betrayal. The policy establishment that decided on intervention in the first place was the first link to snap. By early 1966 key congressional figures had begun to defect, none more notable than Senator J. William Fulbright, who made his Senate Foreign Relations Committee a forum for criticism of the war. Privately, McNamara was losing faith in the war. The American people were the other weak link. As in Korea earlier, so too in Vietnam, the rising human and economic costs of the war drove more and more of the public to demand an end to the conflict. The Tet Offensive in early 1968 sealed public disaffection while throwing the American political elite into disarray. The Cold War establishment figures known collectively as the "Wise Men" whom Johnson had for several years been consulting on Vietnam reflected the new consensus when they told him to get out.

Still others have claimed to see in Vietnam above all the American failure to pursue political reform, economic development, and nation-building. This last position may be the most astute in its emphasis on the degree to which American leaders saw the communist threat essentially in military terms and missed the social and political dimensions of the Vietnam conflict. In other words, they failed to understand Vietnam itself, an insight that becomes clearer on examining the Vietnamese perspective (Chapters 3 and 6).

THE QUAKE OF '68

The Vietnam War was only one element in a confluence of developments that would shake American society during the 1960s and early 1970s. Behind opposition to the war, broad and corrosive doubts about the Cold War itself had been developing, which in turn were fed by a growing preoccupation with consumer goods. Nowhere were the doubts stronger than among the large youth population, conceived just after World War II and raised in the affluent 1950s. In the swelling ranks of college students, new attitudes challenged old ones with special force. The climax of this broad-based unrest came in 1968, a year in which hopes for change soared and then quickly crashed.

Americans passing through a social and ideological watershed in the post-1945 era were not alone. Indeed, a chain of global upheavals characterized the year 1968. In the industrially advanced market economies of Europe and Japan and even in some third-world countries, political authority came under sudden youth-led assaults. The disillusionment, anger, and violence playing out in Chicago also shook Paris, Berlin, Rome, Tokyo, and Mexico City. Not even the Soviet bloc was immune, though there students joined with restive Communist party leaders in tapping eastern Europeans' discontents with socialism and Soviet domination.

The American Epicenter

The U.S. government had demonstrated an impressive capacity to mobilize citizens in the Cold War struggle. But there were limits that first became apparent in resistance to higher military spending during the first years of the Cold War, in a war in Korea that quickly fell from popular favor, and in mounting anxiety over nuclear fallout. In the late 1950s civil rights protestors in the South posed a new challenge to policymakers fixated on foreign problems and comfortable with prevailing domestic race relations. But these signs of popular discontent would seem like twinges compared to the convulsions of the 1960s when the Vietnam War emerged as the dominant issue and in turn gave impetus to a striking range of fresh causes, including black power, women's liberation, and environmentalism. This succession of causes called into question not just Cold War policy but also the very society that policy was meant to preserve.

This challenge to the status quo, sustained over a decade and a half, was to a large degree the work of a passionate minority within a relatively large cohort of 45 million young Americans born between 1942 and 1954. Birth rates had stayed low during the Great Depression and World War II but then exploded after the war in what is known as the "baby boom." The most vocal, activist youth came not just from a dramatically expanded population of young people but from a rising proportion of that generation that was college-bound. (See Figure 4.1.) Most of the expansion occurred in public universities. Behind the burgeoning numbers of students was increased federal spending on higher education, the search for an alternative to military service, increasing enrollment by women and African Americans, and a boom in graduate programs. But above all it was postwar affluence that allowed youth the luxury of continued study, deferring adulthood with its constraining responsibilities of work and family.

Compared to a previous, quieter generation, the youth of the 1960s (at least the small but influential politically engaged subset) were less troubled by the communist threat but more anxious about the specter of nuclear war. Having

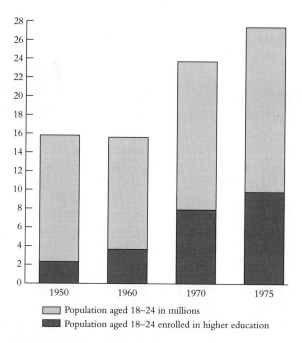

FIGURE 4.1
U.S. Higher Education Boom[22]

grown up in unprecedented affluence, not depression-era deprivation, they took for granted the postwar security and abundance that had allowed them to carve out their own cultural niche. It was defined by comic books such as *Mad* depicting raw violence and expressing bizarre humor, by rock-and-roll record collections and hi-fi sets, and by the freedom that came from owning a car. Sexual freedom would also become a prominent feature of the youth scene once the diaphragm and the birth-control pill became widely available. The ideals that the politically active youth espoused were much like those of their parents: They valued justice, equality, responsibility, decency, and honesty. But unlike their parents, they were determined to bring social practice into line with those values.

The Civil Rights Struggle. Young African Americans led the charge by drawing attention to the nation's flawed commitment to freedom at home. No one knew better than they the legal disabilities and the social, economic, and political discrimination that betrayed the promise of freedom and opportunity. They came of age just as these disabilities were coming under piecemeal challenge by the legal teams funded by the National Association for the Advancement of Colored People (NAACP) and the Southern Christian Leadership Conference headed by a young minister, Martin Luther King Jr. In 1954 in *Brown v. Board of Education,* the Supreme Court had declared that "separate but equal" schooling was "inherently unequal" and thus unconstitutional.[23] A bus boycott in Montgomery, Alabama, sparked the next year by a member of the local NAACP named Rosa Parks, struck another blow against the Southern system of racial segregation known as Jim Crow. King jumped into the fray, thus launching his meteoric rise to national prominence as a civil rights advocate of nonviolent social change inspired by India's Gandhi. At the grassroots, black communities in the South were in ferment with demands for legislation to protect African American voting rights, access to public accommodations, and implementation of the Supreme Court finding against school segregation.

The emerging civil rights movement finally captured the nation's sustained attention in February 1960 when four black students at North Carolina A&T University demanded service at the "whites-only" lunch counter of a Woolworth's department store in Greensboro. When the store refused, fellow students rallied behind them, defied angry whites, and finally forced the store to close. Other African American college students rapidly took up the civil rights cause across the South and became the backbone for annual summer campaigns for equality dubbed Freedom Summer Projects. Alongside white students rallying to the civil rights cause, they did the grassroots organizing and the public protesting and in the process ran the daily risks of beatings, bombings, and bullets from local and state police and mobs of enraged white supremacists.

From the start these young blacks sought organizational autonomy from their elders. In 1960, following the success of the Greensboro demonstration, they formed the Student Nonviolent Coordinating Committee (SNCC). It embodied their preference for a decentralized operation and for group participation. By 1966 the frustrations of the struggle had radicalized these young activists. They were especially impatient with the compromises favored by established civil rights organizations and with the go-slow attitude of white liberal Democrats in Washington, including Presidents Kennedy and Johnson. To be sure, Johnson had put through the 1964 Civil Rights Act, the 1965 Voting Rights Act, and the measures making up the War on Poverty (an important component of his Great Society program). But it had taken courageous efforts in the South and some 200,000 demonstrators in Washington in August 1963 to achieve these gains. Along the way the presidents had failed to use the federal government's power to protect civil rights organizers in the South, and the FBI was actively hostile. Young black campaigners for civil rights had watched Johnson make a costly commitment in Vietnam while he turned his back on the pressing needs of the poor and disenfranchised in the South and the mounting anger and frustration felt by inner-city black communities outside the South. It seemed as though defending freedom for foreigners had taken priority over winning freedom for American citizens.

SNCC as well as such urban groups as the Black Panthers became radicalized as they lost faith in white resolve to deal with the problems of race in America. The chair of SNCC, Stokeley Carmichael, denounced "the betrayal of black dreams by white America." Crowds roared as he proclaimed, "Black Power. It's time we stand up and take over; move on over [Whitey] or we'll move on over you." Demands for separatism came increasingly to the fore. Blacks would have to control their own organizations and agendas and move ahead on their own. Malcolm X, a spellbinding advocate of black nationalism, contended that if the ballot did not work, then it would have to be the bullet. Deepening conflict with whites at home and a war in Vietnam pitting whites against Asians suggested that solidarity among peoples of color should take precedence over national loyalty. Reflecting this alienation from their own country, the Black Panther platform in 1966 flatly stated, "We will not fight and kill other people of color." Even King conceded—belatedly, as far as the young radicals were concerned—the impossible moral problem posed by the Vietnam War, which made his own government "the greatest purveyor of violence in the world today."[24]

In declaring that time had run out on accommodation, the black radicals of the late 1960s helped to spur a revival of interest in the bonds uniting oppressed people of color all around the world, an internationalist outlook that had flourished during the 1930s and 1940s and that had inspired Kwame Nkrumah during his sojourn in the United States. Blacks had fought for freedom in two world wars and Korea and yet still lacked fundamental rights. They conformed to the Cold War orthodoxy but reaped meager political rewards. Setting aside anti-communism as a distraction to the critical task at hand, the radicals advocated a new strategy of demanding fundamental change at home as well as abroad. In their view it was not the grasping hand of Moscow but the dead hand of white colonialism and racism that threatened blacks and created common ground between a decolonizing world in ferment and African Americans. Blacks living outside Africa, like those still there, faced similar problems of oppression and wounded pride. SNCC, the Black Panthers, and Malcolm X could all argue that the success of revolutions abroad would hasten the revolution in race relations at home.

Anti-War Protests and Beyond.   This growing boldness of black protest galvanized young, well-to-do whites. Students from Ivy League colleges to state universities joined the civil rights movement, participating in Southern voter registration drives, Freedom Summer Projects, and protest marches throughout the early 1960s. One volunteer wrote home, "For the first time in my life, I am seeing what it is like to be poor, oppressed, and hated."[25] The civil rights movement was for many a kind of "boot camp" where they learned to challenge authority and came to savor the delights of working within a supportive community of shared values. Soon these students and others would be attacking the large public research universities for their competitive ethos, their impersonal and overbearing bureaucracy, and their restrictions on students' personal and political choices.

The deepening American involvement in Vietnam added to the discontent already loose in the land. Lyndon Johnson's decision in 1965 in favor of massive intervention would spark anti-war activism among a wide array of groups, including the Americans for Democratic Action, the Quaker-run American Friends Service Committee, SANE, and Women Strike for Peace. But from the start the heart of the resistance would be well-educated young people, mostly suburban whites from affluent or solidly middle-class homes, who tended to be excellent students—the "best and brightest" of a new generation.

The most influential group to speak for young anti-war activists was the Students for a Democratic Society (SDS). Organized in 1960 at the University of

Michigan, it operated through loosely coordinated branches on campuses across the country. The SDS set its agenda at a June 1962 meeting in Port Huron, Michigan. There one of its leaders, Tom Hayden, offered a sweeping critique of American democracy. This Port Huron statement expressed the concerns of activists that Americans' withdrawal from public life had weakened democratic institutions. The statement put the blame on large, impersonal bureaucracy that left workers and students feeling alienated and dissatisfied despite conditions of material abundance. The statement also blamed a foreign policy that had slipped out of popular control and increasingly reflected the interests of those with "economic and military investments in the Cold War status quo." SDS's manifesto gave priority to more participatory democracy, community building, and equality, and it argued that students, who were "breaking the crust of apathy," might build a coalition for change that included sympathetic faculty, labor and civil rights activists, and community organizers.[26]

The first protest took the form of a "teach-in" held at the University of Michigan in late March 1965 in response to Johnson's decision on bombing and the dispatch of the first U.S. combat troops to Vietnam. Three thousand students and faculty devoted an entire night to lectures, debates, and discussions. The teach-in model was at once taken up on thirty-five other campuses. The next month brought the first anti-war demonstrations in Washington attended by about 20,000 protesters. A second major demonstration followed in mid-October 1965, bringing together some 100,000 protesters in eighty cities and on a wide range of campuses. By year's end the protest against the war in Vietnam, though still relatively limited, had become a self-sustaining movement that would exploit a wide variety of techniques—from teach-ins and marches to letter-writing campaigns, civil disobedience, and draft-card burning.

In the course of 1967 the rivulet of protest turned into an increasingly turbulent river as public support for the war steadily fell. At the same time demonstrators turned to more provocative tactics, including harassing speakers who defended the war, burning flags, and occupying college administration buildings. The climax of this first phase of the anti-war protest came in the first half of 1968 with the "dump Johnson" effort. Unable to change the president's war policy, activists decided that they would try to deny him a second term and elect in his stead peace candidate, Minnesota senator Eugene McCarthy. Students flocked to his cause and delivered to McCarthy a stunning 42 percent of the vote in the first presidential primary. This triumph immediately drew a wavering Robert Kennedy, the younger brother and political heir of John Kennedy, into the race and helped force Johnson out.

But having dumped Johnson, the movement watched with dismay as the competing Kennedy and McCarthy candidacies produced a split among anti-war activists. Kennedy's assassination in June made Humphrey, Johnson's vice president, the odds-on favorite to win the nomination thanks to the backing of the party establishment. Humphrey had publicly defended the war, so "dump the Hump" became the new rallying cry as activists gathered for the Democratic convention in Chicago. Protesters and the police were soon clashing in a tear-gas haze hanging over that city's streets and parks, while a divided Democratic Party imploded within the convention center.

A diverse anti-war movement now fragmented in frustration. Moderates such as those from the clergy and established peace groups stressed coalition building and respectable forms of protest as the best way to win public support and get American troops out of Vietnam. Although the moderates constituted the majority of the anti-war movement, radicals with their outrageous views, public posturing, and demands for an immediate end to the war commanded disproportionate media attention. Some identified with the anti-U.S. Vietnamese struggle, and most were sharply critical of the national values and institutions that had created and sustained the war. Groups such as the Weathermen Underground carried out bombings, mostly on campuses but also against some banks and multinational corporations. Some young people gave up on politics altogether and instead cultivated a "hippie" lifestyle consistent with the call from one new-age guru to "tune in, turn on, drop out."[27]

The End of the Vietnam War. This growing radicalism, turn to violence, and shocking flamboyance alienated the public as much as it fascinated the media. Many Americans were angry over campus chaos and young people's disrespect for authority. That anger melded with resentment at African Americans over five successive summers of urban rioting beginning in New York's Harlem in 1964, continuing in the Watts district of Los Angeles, spreading more widely during the summers of 1966 and 1967, and climaxing in April 1968 when over one hundred cities exploded following the assassination of Martin Luther King Jr. in Memphis, Tennessee. Many concluded that President Johnson's civil rights and poverty program had helped spawn a disrespect for law and order. Racial tensions were heightened by the emergence of the black power movement. The seeming unraveling of the country helped put Richard Nixon in the White House, a political conservative who seemed ready to continue the war until he got an "honorable" peace.

By the late 1960s an anti-war movement increasingly irritating to many Americans was thriving on campuses nationwide, and the general public too, including many older people, expressed rising impatience to see an end to the fighting. Nixon's decision to send American troops across the Vietnamese border into Cambodia against enemy sanctuaries and supply lines (known as the Ho Chi Minh Trail; see Map 4.1) ignited demonstrations in May 1970 on hundreds of campuses. When the National Guard fired on students at Kent State University in Ohio on May 4, killing four, colleges across the country exploded in outrage. Once more protesters headed for the nation's capital, and Congress voted to revoke the Tonkin Gulf Resolution. April 1971 witnessed the last major demonstrations, including the dramatic scene of eight hundred disillusioned, angry Vietnam veterans gathering on the steps of the Capitol to throw away their medals won in a war they now repudiated.

The protest against the Vietnam commitment was arguably the most successful anti-war movement in U.S. history. Demonstrations had put Johnson on the defensive and kept pressure on Nixon to end the war. More broadly still, the 1960s was a turning point for postwar America. The anti-war and other protest movements popularized new social and political values that broke the rigidities of Cold War culture. Protesters unleashed a flood of new attitudes that Americans were to carry into the following decades: minority rights and pride (gay and lesbian, brown, black, and Native American), multiculturalism, feminism, environmentalism, and neighborhood activism. Each of these major offshoots of movement politics sustained its own criticisms of American life. Feminists scorned it as the sponsor of patriarchy and institutionalized violence. Advocates of the environment took aim at heedless consumption. Minorities saw hypocrisy in a land ostensibly dedicated to political freedom and human equality. Even among the broader population, the Vietnam years came to represent a major fall from national grace. Although Americans might differ on the precise nature of the fall, they tended to agree that the country's reputation had suffered serious, perhaps lasting, damage.

The Ground Shifts Abroad

The fissures opening in American society were also appearing in a surprisingly wide range of other countries. Student activism was the common denominator. All over the world, in places that were geographically and culturally disparate, students took to the streets in 1968 to demand social and political change.

The reasons for student prominence elsewhere bear some resemblance to the case of United States. Postwar birth rates had risen in much of the developed world (with the U.S. boom in the lead), and in most of the developing world those rates were even higher. A new postwar generation of young people grew up amid steadily improving living standards, and growing numbers were able to enroll in higher education thanks to generous state subsidies. Between 1960 and 1970 those enrolled in higher education in western Europe increased from 2 to 4.3 million.[28] Like their American counterparts, these students created a distinct, self-conscious culture with its own slang, music, clothes, and values. They compared the promise of social justice and political democracy championed by their elders with everyday practice in the world around them. The gap between promise and practice disturbed a generation that placed hypocrisy high on its list of sins and whose impulses were strongly individualistic, anti-institutional, and anti-bureaucratic.

Heightening youth discontent was an international news media that disseminated stories of student insurrections and revolutionary achievements in other countries. Mao's audacious young Red Guards taking on an ossified Chinese Communist Party, the courageous Vietnamese battling a formidable U.S. war machine, and Che Guevara championing a spontaneous revolutionary ethos in Latin America (see Chapter 6)—along with young Americans boldly demonstrating against the racism and imperialism gripping their own powerful country—all became transnational icons. These signs of rising discontent around the globe inspired student activists and others to challenge their own tired leaders and outmoded institutions in the name of popular liberation and popular politics.

Protest in Western Europe and Japan. Nowhere did student protest form with greater suddenness or break with greater force than in France. In a single week in early May 1968, students in Paris galvanized the nation. A minority of students in a branch campus just outside the city set the agitation in motion when they demanded fundamental reform of the university system. Their demands won the support among those attending the University of Paris located in the heart of the city. Police tried to quiet the agitation but succeeded instead in widening its appeal. What had begun as a dispute over university governance turned into a fight for individual emancipation from social and bureaucratic constraints and for greater democracy in what the students derided as a "monarchical republic" headed by President Charles de Gaulle. These themes struck a popular chord, first and most forcefully among other young people who flocked to the scene of the protest. The climax to a cycle of highly publicized confrontations between police and growing crowds of youth came on May 10–11, the "Night of the Barricades." Protesters sealed off the university quarter to back up their demands for the release of those arrested, a reopening of the school, and the withdrawal of the police. The voice of the protest, Daniel Cohn-Bendit, recalls

Student Demonstration in Paris, May 1968
One of the protestors, Caroline de Bendern, is waving the revolutionary flag in a setting that was placid compared to the violence to come. (Gamma)

crossing the police lines that night in a last-minute attempt to negotiate an acceptance of the demands and avoid another bloody confrontation. The police recognized him. "I've *never* seen such hatred on anyone's face. They were also frightened, I think. You could hear the sound of the crowd, the barricades being built up all around."[29] Early in the morning security forces started to clear the area, but their brutality created such public outrage that the prime minister, Georges Pompidou, had to bow to student demands.

The students had created a nationwide crisis that soon would paralyze the economy and shake the political establishment. Young workers, also impatient with the French power structure, saw a chance to act. If universities could be democratized, then why not industry? These mavericks demanded reform of authoritarian factory floor practices so that workers would have more of a voice in the workplace. Within a few days as many as nine million workers were on strike and marching with the students.

The crisis created by these young 68-ers (*soixante-huitards*) would evaporate by the end of June almost as rapidly as it had materialized. Old-line labor leaders were interested in long-standing demands for the redistribution of wealth rather than reform of workplace culture. They helped put the lid back on the bubbling discontent expressed by young hotheads among the rank and file. President de Gaulle also maneuvered to contain the agitation. Unhappy with his prime minister's concessions, he called a national referendum and played on popular fears of anarchy to win a major electoral victory. In the face of his challenge the political Left fragmented, while the students, many of whom were below the minimum voting age of twenty-one, turned their backs on conventional political activity.

Meanwhile, France's neighbors were passing through their own student-led assaults on the postwar system. In West Germany student activism reached its peak at Berlin's Free University between February and the fall of 1968. Protesters saw signs that fascism was still a vital force in their society. The general hostility that their protests engendered confirmed their pessimistic analysis even as it left them isolated and increasingly demoralized. A frustrated few turned to violence, organizing the terrorist organization the Red Army Faction (popularly known as the Baader-Meinhof gang). In Italy unrest began in the north in 1967 and spread to Rome. It continued sporadically into 1969, when the focal point of protest shifted from the university to industry, especially Fiat automobile plants. As in Germany, the protest movement left behind a terrorist residue, a Red Brigade that included among its victims prominent politicians and businessmen.

Youthful discontent also found an echo in an increasingly prosperous Japan. The country had been experiencing labor and political unrest since the late 1950s led by the Socialist and Communist opposition to the ruling Liberal Democratic Party. U.S. air attacks against North Vietnam sparked new protests in early 1965. Details of the bombing campaign and the mounting ground war, conveyed daily in newspapers and on television, called to mind Japan's own disastrous invasion of China in the 1930s and led to charges that Japan bore responsibility for helping to sustain the savage struggle. The Japanese economy profited richly from the war, while American forces in Vietnam depended on bases in Japan. As one of the protest leaders, Tsurumi Yoshiyuki, argued, "The Vietnam War is not a fire across a distant shore; it is a war that necessarily affects all Japanese in one way or another."[30] The first major demonstration occurred in July 1965, and by 1966 protesters had settled into a pattern of regular activity supplemented by letter-writing campaigns, teach-ins, civil disobedience, and distribution of anti-war leaflets at U.S. bases.

The resulting opposition movement was made up of a wide range of groups—from neo-nationalists to liberals to Socialists and Communists. It was decentralized and largely uncoordinated, indeed at times deeply divided. At its core was the Citizen's Federation for Peace in Vietnam, known for short as Beheiren. That key group's leadership was well educated and worldly. Some spoke English, had lived in the United States, and maintained close contacts with U.S. activists. Though sharply critical of the U.S. war in Vietnam and the U.S. effort to pull Japan into the Cold War, the Beheiren leaders admired what the U.S. occupation had done to bring democracy to Japan. They were also avid consumers of American goods. They could be seen at rallies wearing jeans and drinking Coke.

The outlook of Beheiren activists bore a striking similarity to that of their U.S. and European counterparts. They attacked large, impersonal organizations—big business, big universities, and big government—as threats to individual development and choice. Tsurumi, a major Beheiren voice, characterized the movement's goal as "a cultural revolution to create a new type of man determined to act, individually and voluntarily, on behalf of the cause of the antiwar struggle."[31]

While parting with Beheiren over the issue of nonviolent protest, new student groups embraced its emphasis on individualism and spontaneity. Students remarked how after entering college they were "experiencing freedom for the first time."[32] They scoffed at established authority and held out personal authenticity and participatory democracy as the highest goods. As elsewhere around the world, Japanese campuses became hotbeds of political activism as students focused on everything from the future of the Chinese revolution to university tuition increases. Hippies began to make their appearance, while others patterned themselves after the pure samurai warriors of an earlier era and clashed with the police in over 2,400 incidents in 1969 alone. Campuses also turned into battlegrounds as rival student factions battled each other.

Throughout 1968 and well into 1969, Japan experienced repeated waves of anti-war and anti-establishment dissent. But then the protests died back. The gradual American withdrawal from the Vietnam conflict helped to quiet the agitation, as did a rise in prosperity. With the tide of protest receding, frustrated dissidents, especially angry and radicalized students, reacted in a pattern familiar from other countries. They formed clandestine groups such as the United Red Army to intensify their campaign of violence not only inside Japan but abroad as well.

Turmoil in the Third World and Eastern Europe. While protests in the United States, western Europe, and Japan played out against a backdrop of prosperity that dampened the popular appeal of reform, the economic and political problems faced by third-world and socialist states in eastern Europe in the mid-1960s helped ignite discontent. In the major cities of such countries as Turkey, Egypt, Ethiopia, Senegal, and India, young people took to the streets in opposition to established authority. The most violent and traumatic confrontation played out in Mexico City. There student protests, intermittent since 1964, turned ugly. Infighting among student groups prompted the police to intervene on campus in late July 1968. But they did so with such brutality that students redirected their energy against the government. They charged that the ruling party habitually silenced dissent on the grounds that it was "subversive." By August and early September outraged students, now joined by city residents, were staging massive anti-government demonstrations. Rallies attended by as many as 400,000 protesters demanded government respect for democratic rights. On September 18 the government tried to break the protest movement by sending the army onto the campus of the country's major public university, the National Autonomous University of Mexico, but instead it set off street clashes and put in question Mexico's ability to host the upcoming Olympic games. On October 2 government forces with machine guns, helicopters, and tanks attacked a rally of nearly 5,000 students, leaving some 300 dead. Eyewitnesses vividly recalled the terror of flying bullets and accumulating blood—"lots of blood underfoot, lots of blood smeared on the walls."[33] The government had reclaimed the streets and silenced the protesters, but the massacre would remain an open wound in national politics for decades to come.

On the other side of the Iron Curtain, the quake of 1968 took a somewhat different form. Historically eastern Europe had been an economic backwater, so the demonstrably successful Soviet-socialist planned economy had had appeal after 1945 as a vehicle both for catching up with the economies to the west and for recovering from the extensive damage inflicted by World War II. Up to the mid-1960s these economies with their emphasis on heavy industry seemed to work in such Eastern-bloc countries as Poland, East Germany, and Czechoslovakia as the agent of modernization and prosperity. Social welfare gains for the bulk of the population were significant as the state provided jobs, housing, and basic health care and education. Growth in terms of GDP per capita was keeping pace with a prosperous western Europe in what was turning into the best economic run in over a century. But as Eastern-bloc economies ran into trouble in the mid and late 1960s, questions about the Soviet-defined postwar order took sharper form. Might giving more scope to the forces of supply and demand central to a market economy yield more abundance than the Soviet model of planning? The even more troubling question was whether more democracy and greater national autonomy from the Soviet Union was possible.

Czechoslovakia became the scene of the most dramatic of the explosions of 1968 on the eastern side of the Iron Curtain. Early in the year Alexander Dubček, an established political leader, took the helm of the Czech Communist Party and initiated a reform movement to create "communism with a human face." This effort would come to be known as the Prague Spring for the heady hopes that took hold in that season of renewal in the country's capital. Dubček quickly pressed for economic reforms and advanced supporters into high posts at the expense of hardliners at the top of the party as well as in sensitive security and military areas. These changes were wildly popular and in turn created momentum for more reform, including an end to censorship, the creation of new parties, and an increase in the power of the national legislature. An "Action Program" laid out by the Communist Party in April embraced all of these goals and more. Public discussion became ever more adventuresome, with journalists, intellectuals, and students especially vocal in their demands for opening the political system and bold in their criticism of the Czech Communist Party. A manifesto published in June coolly dismissed that "power organization" as a magnet for "power-hungry egotists, reproachful cowards, and people with bad consciences."[34]

Dubček quickly came under intense Soviet scrutiny and mounting pressure to pull back. He offered assurances to Leonid Brezhnev and other Soviet leaders of his country's adherence to the Warsaw Pact and his determination to preserve the Communist Party's leading role. He also urged his own media to curb their openly anti-Soviet sentiment. As enthusiasm for reform mounted and threatened to escape the control of the Czech Communist Party, Soviet leaders feared a repeat of events in Hungary twelve years earlier. In early August a half-million Warsaw Pact troops under Soviet command marched into the country in a bloodless coup and arrested Dubček and other reformers. The Soviets faced universal condemnation and peaceful resistance from the Czechs, but by 1969 they were finally able to organize "healthy elements" within the party and begin turning back the reforms. The "Prague Spring" had turned into a "Prague Winter" that would endure for twenty years.

Whereas the challenge to the Czech status quo came from the top, Poland proved truer to the broader European pattern of youth-led agitation. Young intellectuals in the Communist Party youth organization and in Warsaw University began as early as 1965 to criticize economic policy and challenge the party's claim to a monopoly on truth (derided by one writer as the "dictatorship of the dumb").[35] The main target of this discontent was the party leader, Władysław Gomułka. Since returning to power amid the unrest of 1956, he had maintained Moscow's trust by opposing domestic "revisionism" and supporting the Warsaw Pact as Poland's guarantee against the old German foe. But at the same time he had allowed limited political and economic reforms.

A slowing economy in the late 1960s upset Gomułka's balancing act. His government had to impose stiffer work norms and longer hours while reducing food and other subsidies. With popular discontent rising, security forces kept the critics under control until March 1968, when students at Warsaw University dramatically broke the peace, prompted by the reform push in neighboring Czechoslovakia. A student sign read, "Poland is awaiting its own Dubček."[36] Police repression failed to stop the rapid spread of strikes, riots, and demonstrations across the country. At the end of the month the students laid down a long list of demands, including a new youth organization, the end of censorship, economic reforms leading to self-governing enterprises and the introduction of a market mechanism, an independent workers' union, and an independent judiciary.

Brezhnev and his colleagues decided to sit tight, convinced that intervention would only make matters worse in this long-time hotbed of anti-Russian feeling. Gomułka was left to resolve the problem through the arrest of dissidents and a purge within the ranks of the party. By summer the political situation had stabilized, but it was only a reprieve. In August in the immediate aftermath of the invasion of Czechoslovakia, students organized protests once more, this time decrying Gomułka's involvement in the Warsaw Pact operation. Thereafter anti-party opposition passed to an increasingly restive labor movement that would eventually bring about the collapse of socialism in Poland.

Throughout the developed and the developing world, critics of the status quo led by young people had fallen short of their objectives. The national establishments that they had targeted had survived after an interval of embarrassment. But everywhere the critics had defined agendas for change that would remain prominent in the decades ahead. The old-line Communists and Socialists, who formerly had offered the only serious political and social alternatives, seemed to a new generation to be hopelessly doctrinaire and out of touch. Young activists championed instead a new set of values, above all sweeping individualism and broad freedom of personal expression. Stephen Spender, a British poet from the World War II generation, perceptively noted their strange new politics: "They equate revolution with spontaneity, participation, communication, imagination, love, youth."[37] Often denied in the short term, the values of the new generation would over time have almost revolutionary effects on their countries' social life and cultural values.

CONCLUSION

In the course of the 1950s and 1960s, the Cold War underwent an extraordinary transformation. Those middle decades of the superpower rivalry had opened with international lines of conflict sharply drawn. Both Moscow and Washington nervously marshaled their allies while lining up their own populations in support of the global struggle. By the late 1960s, the Cold War struggle looked strikingly different. The Soviet Union after Stalin's death had mellowed both domestically and internationally, while in the United States the Cold War consensus collapsed in the face of mounting self-doubts over the national commitment to freedom at home as well as abroad.

The forces that had achieved this transformation came from diverse directions. The shared trauma of the Cuban Missile Crisis brought nuclear fear to a critical pitch and gave the Cold War rivals the decisive push into an era of arms control. The long descent into the Vietnam War intensified disarray and disillusionment among Americans, while Soviet leaders could not escape the limits imposed by their modest economy and thus the tension between pursuing the international rivalry with the United States and responding to the material demands of their own people. The discontents of educated youth in the developed as well as the third world added to the assault on established habits of thought.

A once simple Cold War landscape was further scrambled in the 1960s by changes within the U.S. and Soviet alliances. Western Europeans and Japanese had lost their taste for Cold War confrontation well before the fever of 1968 reached their shores. Eastern Europe sought greater autonomy from Moscow, while the Chinese moved toward military confrontation. Even the repeated repression of eastern Europeans bent on charting their own path seems in retrospect less a Soviet triumph than a harbinger of greater troubles to come. As the region's socialist regimes relied increasingly on their own secret police and ultimately on Soviet tanks, they fed deep-seated discontents that would lead directly to the socialist collapse of 1989. Though few realized it at the time, the Cold War had taken a decisive turn that anticipated its dramatic conclusion two decades later (treated in Chapter 7).

RECOMMENDED RESOURCES

Leaders Struggling to Stabilize the Cold War

On **the Soviet side,** begin with William J. Tompson, *Khrushchev: A Political Life* (1995), which offers a thoughtful appraisal of a pivotal figure. *Khrushchev Remembers,* trans. and ed. Strobe Talbott and Jerrold L. Schecter with Vyacheslav B. Luchkov (3 vols.; 1970, 1974, 1990), lets the Soviet leader speak from his forced retirement. On **the American side,** see Robert Divine, *Eisenhower and the Cold War* (1981), a slim, sympathetic treatment of perhaps the shrewdest Cold War president; Lawrence Freedman, *Kennedy's Wars: Berlin, Cuba, Laos, and Vietnam* (2000), a full-scale reappraisal; and Paul K. Conkin, *Big Daddy from the Pedernales: Lyndon Baines Johnson* (1986), which is a good place to begin on a larger-than-life leader.

The Cuban Missile Crisis

Aleksandr Fursenko and Timothy Naftali, *"One Hell of a Gamble": Khrushchev, Castro, and Kennedy, 1958–1964* (1997), a fresh, full international history, provides the best overview of this complex event. Michael R. Beschloss, *The Crisis Years: Kennedy and Khrushchev, 1960–1963* (1991), is good on context. Laurence Chang and Peter Kornbluh, eds., *The Cuban Missile Crisis, 1962: A National Security Archive Documents Reader* (1992), pulls together a full collection of primary sources.

The American Commitment in Vietnam

From an enormous and constantly expanding literature, start with **standard historical treatments** to be found in George C. Herring, *The Longest War: The United States and Vietnam, 1950–1975* (4th ed., 2002), a long-standing favorite for its overview of U.S. policy; Marilyn B. Young, *The Vietnam Wars, 1945–1990* (1991), which opens a broad window on the war; and Michael H. Hunt, *Lyndon Johnson's War: America's Cold War Crusade in Vietnam, 1945–1968* (1996), a slim volume that weighs responsibility for the U.S. entanglement. **Works by journalists** stand out for their rich and engaging treatment. See David Halberstam, *The Best and the Brightest* (1972), an early indictment of American policymakers; Stanley Karnow, *Vietnam: A History* (rev. ed., 1991), which supplies a full survey of the war; and Neil Sheehan, *A Bright Shining Lie: John Paul Vann and America in Vietnam* (1988), which uses the life of an American adviser to construct a compelling overview of the American commitment. For **the perspective of American soldiers,** see Al Santoli, *Everything We Had: An Oral History of the Vietnam War by Thirty-Three American Soldiers Who Fought It* (1981). *The Anderson Platoon* (prod. and narr. Pierre Schoendorffer; 1966; 65 min.) is a revealing contemporary documentary capturing day-to-day combat operations.

The Global Social and Political Unrest of the Late 1960s

For **international overviews** of the tumultuous decade, see Arthur Marwick, *The Sixties: Cultural Revolution in Britain, France, Italy, and the United States, c. 1958–c. 1974* (1998), a big and broadly cast overview, as well as Robert V. Daniels, *Year of the Heroic Guerrilla: World Revolution and Counterrevolution in 1968* (1989). On student protest, the best place to start is Ronald Fraser et al., *1968: A Student Generation in Revolt* (1988), which gives the activists a chance to tell their own story. See also Ali Tariq and Susan Watkins, *1968: Marching in the Streets* (1998), which mixes illustrations with a month-by-month account. Thomas R. H. Havens, *Fire across the Sea: The Vietnam War and Japan, 1965–1975* (1987), and Elena Poniatowska, *Massacre in Mexico*, trans. Helen R. Lane (1975), highlight unrest outside the North Atlantic world. On **the upheaval within the United States,** Maurice Isserman and Michael Kazin, *America Divided: The Civil War of the 1960s* (2000), and Terry H. Anderson, *The Movement and the Sixties: Protest in America from Greensboro to Wounded Knee* (1995), are thoughtful guides. A good collection of primary sources can be found in Alexander Bloom and Wini Breines, *"Takin' it to the streets": A Sixties Reader* (2nd ed., 2003). The contention surrounding the Vietnam War is the subject of Rhodri Jeffreys-Jones, *Peace Now! American Society and the Ending of the Vietnam War* (1999). *Chicago 1968* (written and prod. Chana Gazit; 1995; 56 min.) graphically conveys the anger and violence marking the anti-war demonstrations during the Democratic convention. **American nuclear fears** that both anticipated and fed unrest in the 1960s is the subject of Allan M. Winkler's able synthesis, *Life under a Cloud: American Anxiety about the Atom* (1993). *The Atomic Café* (prod. and dir. Kevin Rafferty, Jayne Loader, and Pierce Rafferty; 1982; 88 min.) is an entertaining documentary treatment of the nuclear preoccupations of the 1940s and 1950s. *Dr. Strangelove, or: How I Learned to Stop Worrying and Love the Bomb* (dir. and prod. Stanley Kubrick; 1963; 93 min.), an irreverent film, marks a cultural watershed in attitudes toward nuclear war and more broadly the Cold War conflict.

CHAPTER 5

ABUNDANCE AND DISCONTENT
IN THE DEVELOPED WORLD

The American and British designers of the Bretton Woods agreement and its close cousin, the General Agreement on Tariffs and Trade (GATT), built well. Throughout the 1950s and 1960s, the structural reforms implemented at the end of World War II spurred international trade and investment. They helped incorporate western Europe and Japan into the global economy. And they carried at least some of the world's peoples toward unprecedented prosperity. Annual gross domestic product (GDP) growth for the entire globe between 1950 and 1973 was 4.9 percent, and world exports grew at a yearly 7 percent pace. These were rates far higher than anything experienced in any other period of recent history.

The economies of the developed world not only worked more closely and profitably together but also moved along slightly different if parallel paths. The consumer culture already flourishing in the United States became a force in the everyday life of other, increasingly affluent countries. Yet cultural differences remained across the developed world. While everywhere the state played a major role in making this freemarket system work to the benefit of its citizens, how precisely it played that role differed significantly from place to place. In Europe, states put in place an elaborate welfare system intended to cushion the shocks from the free market and at the same time moved toward greater integration to make the regional market work more efficiently. In Japan, the state played an equally prominent role but less as a direct guarantor of welfare and more as the coordinator of rapid economic growth. Despite the impressive economic record laid down in these years, the overall international economic system began to draw fire. Some observers began to worry about the impact of the developed world's steady growth on the environment, and others fretted over the disadvantaged position of women and the uneven distribution of the gains from growth between the developed and the developing. These worries would persist to the end of the twentieth century.

AMERICA AT THE APOGEE

The United States was the undisputed leader of the system of trade and investment that encompassed much of the globe in the 1950s and 1960s. Washington supplied aid to economies in distress, and the dollar served as the currency of reference, providing invaluable international monetary stability. U.S. allies on the whole quietly followed the American lead. Cold War fears kept them docile, but so too did the relatively benign role played by Washington, which not only talked about free trade but also opened its valuable domestic market to the products of its allies. What seemed to serve the world also served Americans, who enjoyed an unprecedented domestic prosperity and optimism about their model of abundance.

Triumphant at Home and Abroad

Though many Americans had entered the postwar period anxious over a repeat of the Great Depression, the economy quickly made the transition to peacetime and then marched steadily ahead. Between 1945 and 1960, GDP more than doubled and then nearly doubled again between 1960 and 1970. The fruits of this sustained growth fell into the laps of Americans in a seemingly endless stream. The tide of economic prosperity would continue to raise the income of most. As a result, a generation that had experienced the deprivation of the 1930s and the rationing of wartime would find themselves better nourished, better housed, better educated, and more productively employed than their parents or grandparents could have ever imagined.

However, Americans did not participate equally in the good times. For most, income rose sharply. By the end of the 1950s slightly more than half of all families were earning a comfortably middle-class income of $5,000 or more and the stock market, formerly a preserve of the wealthy, was attracting more and more investors (from 6.5 million in 1952 to almost 32 million in 1970). But at the same time, roughly a quarter of the population lived in poverty. The groups least likely to share in the good times were the elderly, households headed by women, rural and central city residents, and nonwhite workers. Along with general prosperity went steadily widening inequalities in wealth. The richest 5 percent of the population had controlled 19 percent of the country's wealth in 1949. A decade later, total wealth was even more concentrated at the top, with 1 percent controlling a third while the bottom 20 percent laid claim to less than half a percent.

The 1950s version of the American dream has come to be associated with the picture of a split-level house in the suburbs with a station wagon parked in front ready to take the family on vacation. There was considerable truth to this image. Home ownership expanded by 50 percent between 1945 and 1960. By that latter date, 60 percent of all families owned their own homes. Almost all the new homes that met this enormous demand sprang up in the suburbs, which were growing six times faster than cities. By 1960, one-quarter of the entire population lived in suburbia. With their incomes rising, Americans went on a spending spree on labor-saving appliances, home entertainment, and automobiles. By 1960, most families owned washing machines and televisions. To win customers

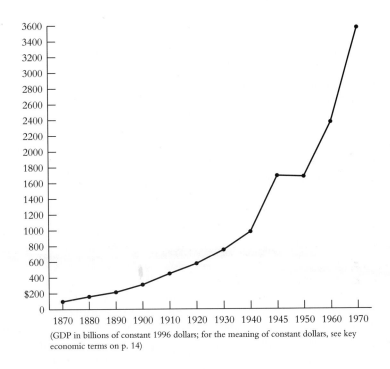

(GDP in billions of constant 1996 dollars; for the meaning of constant dollars, see key
economic terms on p. 14)

FIGURE 5.1
Extraordinary U.S. Economic Growth, 1870–1970[1]

in this era of high spending, companies quadrupled their outlays on advertising
between 1945 and 1960. The success of that effort—or perhaps the enthusiasm
of the public for its newfound abundance—is evident in the debt that families
piled up. By 1959, almost half of all families had borrowed so heavily that their
liquid assets averaged less than $200.

Passenger cars had perhaps the broadest impact of all the postwar consumer
goods. The number of cars rose dramatically—from 40 million in 1950 to 102
million in 1970. Cars made the rise of suburbia possible, encouraged the rise of
the mall as the prime shopping destination, kept city workplaces accessible to
scattered bedroom communities, and planted the seeds of national dependence
on imported oil. Cars boosted domestic tourism and promoted the rise of a new
automobile-friendly accommodation, the motel. Cars also facilitated population
shifts as one in four Americans moved each year, bidden by the expanded opportunities created by a flourishing economy. States and the federal government
responded to the car's popularity by improving and extending the road networks.
These efforts included the launching in the 1950s of the interstate highway system, a civil defense measure that quickly turned into one of the most popular
and costly features of the emergent car culture.

The 1950s and 1960s marked the beginning of the post-industrial, knowledge-
based economy that would loom large by the turn of the twentieth century. In

1940, roughly three million Americans worked in technical and professional occupations. By 1964, that figure had more than doubled. At the same time the number of industrial workers was beginning a decline, so that by 1956 white-collar employees outnumbered the blue collars for the first time. This shift was marked by the growing importance of large corporations whose billion-dollar budgets included a paycheck for hundreds of thousands. This shift was also marked by the growing importance of technology. For those providing services, innovations such as the computer were making possible the generation and control of enormous bodies of data. The computer developed rapidly from a costly general-purpose machine in 1944 whose five hundred miles of wire made it impossibly bulky. By the early 1950s, it had shrunk enough in size and price to appeal for the first time to businesses. Technological innovation was no less important on the shop floor, where it spurred productivity increases that enabled firms to raise output even while cutting back on their workforce. The rising importance of technology led an ever-increasing proportion of Americans to seek higher education. Publicly funded state universities, colleges, and community colleges multiplied beginning in the late 1950s.

Though it was a bastion of the free market, the United States of the 1950s and 1960s gave government considerable scope in the economy beyond funding infrastructure such as roads, airports, and education. It extended to science and technology. The first computer was built as part of government-sponsored wartime research that would expand in the context of Cold War competition with the Soviet Union. Government military contracts pushed the U.S. economy to the fore in such high-tech areas as electronics and aeronautics, and major research universities such as MIT and Stanford made the most of government largesse, conducting research in a wide range of scientific fields. By the mid-1950s the United States was in the midst of a revolution in government spending. By then it had climbed to 17 percent of total GNP, up from 1 percent in 1929. And the Johnson administration's Great Society programs would send the figure higher.

The economic advances of the 1950s and 1960s served to confirm Americans' self-conception as a special people destined for great things abroad as well as at home. The country could look forward to growing ever stronger and more prosperous, while realizing the dream of justice and abundance for all. In this context the performance of the American economy assumed nationalist significance in the Cold War contest with the Soviet Union.

During the 1960s the American disciples of John Maynard Keynes were confident that moderate, well-timed government intervention could keep the economy at full employment and thus ensure steady, substantial growth. Sustained by timely government action, the free market could churn out jobs and goods endlessly. This growth would in time promote social justice for the previously marginalized or excluded. Mobilization for World War II had already begun pulling women and African Americans into the urban, industrial sectors. Postwar prosperity would surely complete the job with funds left over to build a Great Society without rural poverty or urban blight while at the same time underwriting the costs of the Cold War.

Nikita Khrushchev and Richard Nixon Engage in the "Kitchen Debate," July 1959
The Soviet leader and the American vice president stand in front of the model kitchen at a U.S. exhibition in Moscow where they sparred over which system—socialist or capitalist—could produce the highest standard of living. This encounter dramatized the growing sense that political legitimacy and the outcome of the Cold War depended as much on generating consumer goods as on finding an effective political and military strategy. To counter Khrushchev's boasts of social- ist superiority, Nixon claimed that consumer abundance in the United States made it "closest to the ideal of prosperity for all in a classless society." He rehearsed the statistics: "44 million families in America own 56 million cars, 50 million television sets, 143 million radio sets, and 31 million of those families own their own homes." Khrushchev responded that the Soviet Union would soon surpass the U.S. economy and in any case the products Nixon touted were "fancy gadgets"—either useless or beyond the reach of ordinary Americans.[2] (AP Photo)

The United States continued in the 1950s and 1960s to use its considerable clout to shape the patterns of global trade and investment. The free trade agenda laid down at the end of World War II got a major boost in 1961 when President Kennedy secured congressional approval to bargain for trade expansion under GATT. By the late 1960s tariffs on industrial goods were falling significantly.

The removal of trade barriers was matched by the equally important first steps toward the removal of barriers to the flow of international capital. The Bretton Woods agreement had sought to facilitate international trade by making it easy to convert one currency into another and by making the dollar the linch- pin of the international currency market. But Bretton Woods had also conceded the right of states to intervene in currency markets in order to protect their recovering economies from outside pressures and reestablish a solid economic foundation for growth. Throughout the late 1940s and 1950s, U.S. leaders had followed an approach that reflected these contradictory impulses built into Bretton Woods, allowing both the dollar to flow freely around the world and U.S. allies to restrict the movement of capital across their borders. Private investors and speculators shifting their capital for maximum returns might undercut any one country's domestic economic strategies, create social turmoil, and (worst of all from the U.S. perspective) raise the popular appeal of the Communist party. However, with western Europe's and Japan's economies mended by the late 1950s, Washington began calling for an end to regulations limiting the international flow of capital. Cautiously these allies complied. By the 1960s, capital could move from one country to another with less hindrance than at any time in recent memory. A trend had begun that would in time fundamentally redefine the international economy and both constrain and at times convulse participants in that economy.

Finally, the United States sought to broaden the scope of international markets to include newly emergent nations. To integrate them into the U.S.-led alliance and trade system, Washington redirected the attention of the International Monetary Fund and the World Bank from an increasingly prospering western Europe to the third world. U.S. aid programs also refocused on the third world beginning in the latter part of the 1950s. Kennedy and Johnson continued the trend with well-publicized initiatives such as the Alliance for Progress in the Western Hemisphere.

Warning Signs of Economic Troubles

Most Americans were convinced that these glory days would last forever—thanks to the magic of the market, prudent government policy, and a long lead in science and technology. But by the 1960s a variety of threats to U.S. economic supremacy were taking shape, and those threats would combine in the 1970s and 1980s to deal a heavy blow both to the economy and to national self-confidence.

The first signs of trouble began to appear in the 1950s as a result of a growing accumulation of American dollars abroad. Some of that accumulation was the result of Cold War commitments. Maintaining American forces and a network of diplomatic and other government representatives overseas involved substantial outlays on the scene. In addition, valued military allies needed equipment and advisors, prompting more spending abroad. Generous economic aid directed first to Europe and then to the third world to secure political stability along the containment line added to the outflow of dollars. Further weakening the U.S. position was the slipping competitiveness of U.S. goods on international markets. Indeed, imports from Japan and western Europe were increasingly attractive to American buyers. The U.S. trade surplus (excess of exports over imports) began to shrink during the 1950s, and eventually (in 1971 for the first time since 1883) Americans imported more than they sold abroad. Adding to the outflow of dollars was a rising tide of tourism to Europe and the aggressive overseas expansion of American investments.

With more dollars going out of the country, foreigners held more and more U.S. currency. In the first decade of the postwar period, this overseas accumulation of dollars was welcome because it helped recovering economies. Dollars in foreign hands made possible purchases of U.S. goods critical to rebuilding, helped bolster weak currencies, and raised the standard of living in war-torn lands. Even after foreigners had a less pressing need for dollar reserves, they still gladly held them, so strong was international confidence in the dollar as a secure, liquid asset convertible on demand into gold.

During the 1950s that confidence began to erode as total U.S. payments overseas began regularly to exceed those coming in. By 1958 the accumulated foreign holdings of dollars had surpassed U.S. gold reserves, setting in question the U.S. government's commitment made at Bretton Woods to redeem dollars for gold at the rate of $35 an ounce. This doubt that the dollar was "as good as gold" was to deepen throughout the 1960s, and it foreshadowed an economic crisis that would dethrone the dollar from its special place and that would impose some wrenching changes for an American economy unable to bring its accounts with the outside world into balance.

Further eroding the U.S. economic position was a popular addiction to spending on consumer goods. The consequence was falling savings rates that diminished the domestically generated pool of capital and raised the costs for entrepreneurs wanting to make new investments. Moreover, those spending the consumer dollar had a penchant for foreign goods, and the resulting imports further decreased the U.S. trade surplus. Finally, good consumers resented taxes cutting into their disposable income but also did not like surrendering their own favorite government programs. The result was the beginning of a long-lasting federal budget deficit, the growing neglect of public investment in infrastructure, and the first inklings of what would turn into persistent inflationary pressure.

The most obvious solution to the mounting U.S. economic problem was the same one Nikita Khrushchev had confronted earlier—fewer guns or less butter or some combination of cuts. But cold warriors regarded blocking communist expansion as a top spending priority, and the public valued no less highly the good life that postwar prosperity had brought. Because devoted consumers also voted, their preferences registered clearly in Congress and the White House.

President Eisenhower tried to balance the tension between fighting the Cold War and keeping consumers happy. He ended the unpopular and costly war in Korea and worked to hold down military spending. Although this Republican's efforts merely contained rather than resolved the problem, his record compares favorably with that of his Democratic successors. John Kennedy set the pattern by sharply raising defense spending on coming into office. A brave Keynesian, he had no fear that increases in the budget would strain the economy and refused to worry about the resulting domestic budget deficit. Lyndon Johnson increased the budget deficit by immediately pressing ahead with his expensive Great Society programs. The rising costs of his Vietnam commitment worsened the budgetary imbalance. But Johnson refused to cut his domestic program to compensate.

The insistence on both guns and butter had by the end of the decade dealt two serious blows to the U.S. economic position. At home, high levels of government and private spending had combined to ignite inflation. Internationally, the balance of payments problem worsened with the annual gap at the $4 billion mark by 1967. In early 1968, Johnson reluctantly took action. "Our fiscal situation is abominable," the president conceded.[3] He proposed to Congress a special tax on individuals and corporations. Congress agreed but insisted on the president cutting government spending. At the same time, he capped the size of American forces in Vietnam as a way of containing military costs and imposed restrictions on overseas investment. Rather than restoring stability, these measures precipitated an unexpected combination of stagnant growth and continued inflation (labeled at the time "stagflation"). Here was a malaise that fit neither the Keynesians' experience nor their arsenal of policy tools. They wondered how a low or no growth economy producing well below its maximum capacity could generate inflation, which indicated a shortage of goods. Disoriented economists desperately searched for a cure while the electorate began to grumble.

Internationally, an aggravated balance of payments problem now combined with the onset of inflationary fever to further undermine the dollar's international standing. As the dollar debt abroad rose and inflation reduced the dollar's value, foreigners grew less willing to hold dollars. Foreign central banks, which kept most of their reserves in dollars, and those engaged in international transactions worried that Americans lacked the reserves to cover the debts they had incurred. Indeed, by the late 1960s the debt had climbed to $40 billion and the gold reserves at Ft. Knox had sunk to $10 billion. Foreign bankers began to sell their holdings, thus bringing closer the day of the dollar's devaluation and of significantly diminished American economic leadership.

Charles de Gaulle, the president of France, emerged in the 1960s as the leading critic of U.S. economic leadership. His government had obstructed U.S.–inspired trade expansion under GATT talks out of a determination to protect French agriculture from U.S. imports and complained of Washington's irresponsible policies. The Americans could not expect the world to continue to endlessly accumulate IOUs while U.S. consumers and cold warriors went their heedless way. Finally, in the mid-1960s the French government began presenting millions of dollars in debt for payment in gold, thus sending an unmistakable message to the Johnson administration that time was running out.

Even though Johnson understood that mounting financial difficulties hobbled the country in its exercise of world economic and political leadership,

CLOUDS BUILD OVER THE U.S. ECONOMY	
1950	First postwar balance-of-payments deficit
1958	Short-term financial obligations held abroad exceed U.S. monetary reserves; foreign governments soon begin turning in dollars for gold
1968	Fiscal crisis grips Johnson administration; the economy sinks into stagflation
1971	First trade deficit since 1883

he also understood that the postwar boom had helped elevate consumerism in the minds of the electorate into a basic American right. However beneficial to long-term national power and economic health, measures that impinged on consumer spending were sacrifices that the electorate was bound to resist.

Just as the Vietnam War did not create most of the divisions that marked 1960s American society, neither did that war alone direct the American economy onto the shoals of stagflation. Vietnam contributed in the latter case as in the former a critical impetus that compounded problems already developing. Americans had lived well, saved little, spent freely on foreign goods and travel, funneled aid to friends on the containment line, and in general claimed a dominant role that could not be sustained. By 1968 the pressures for change had become inescapable.

RECOVERY IN WESTERN EUROPE AND JAPAN

Whereas the 1950s and 1960s saw the gradual erosion of U.S. economic supremacy, western Europe and Japan were the star performers. The demand for new production facilities to replace those destroyed by war or outdated by rapid technological innovation prompted considerable investment and pushed their economies rapidly ahead. Guiding the investments was an experienced managerial class, and working the new machinery was an educated, skilled workforce. As economic vitality restored these old centers of international trade and investment to their former prominence, their citizens enjoyed an extraordinary run of prosperity.

As the main global economic centers moved into an era of shared prosperity, they still clung to patterns of doing business that reflected values and circumstances peculiar to each. The western Europeans looked to their individual states to create an economy that balanced social justice and efficiency and sought through regional integration enhanced prosperity and an institutionalized guarantee of cooperation among member states. In Japan the state was no less important in the promotion of prosperity and stability through collaborative arrangements at home and competitiveness in international markets. Looking at two different corporations—Italy's Fiat and Japan's Sony—provides a sense of those distinctions that would persist even as the forces of globalization were gaining headway, and reveals the strikingly diverse strategies for success that existed within the same broad international economic framework.

The Old World's New Course

In the fluid conditions that existed in the wake of World War II, the states of western Europe could have dutifully fallen in behind U.S. economic policy just as they had fallen in behind U.S. Cold War policy. The Marshall Plan had stabilized their economic situation, and in the process they had adopted some American advice and practices. To be sure, the American influence was real in stimulating recovery, providing a low-cost defense umbrella, sponsoring a trade-friendly international regime, and prodding Europeans to turn away from past colonial ambitions and toward cooperation. But this perspective should not obscure a critical shift in European political economy that has to be understood in terms not of U.S. influence but of the continent's recent history and political traditions.

The Rise of the Welfare State. In the aftermath of war, western Europeans embarked on a fundamental rethinking of the purposes that the nation-state was to serve. European states had not served popular welfare. Their policies had inflicted widespread loss of life and suffering during World War I and the Great Depression. The events of World War II only added to this disreputable record. Germany's wartime barbarities made a compelling case for the danger that the continued existence of the nation-state posed to humanity. Most of the rest of the twenty-six European countries existing at that time proved totally ineffectual in protecting their people or even preserving themselves as functioning states. Annexation, partition, occupation, and subordination became the common fate of the French, Dutch, Austrians, Poles, and Czechs, among others. Little wonder that many questioned the legitimacy of the nation-state and longed for some alternative international or regional basis for sovereignty.

But the European state system did not wither away. To the contrary, it enjoyed a post–World War II renaissance thanks to a basic reorientation of purpose. Acquisition of national and colonial territory gave way as the yardstick by which to measure state success, and in its place popular welfare and growth in national income emerged as new goals. Citizens would now judge their states on the basis of their performance in significantly improving the living conditions of all classes. This shift in attitudes was reflected in decisions in cities all across Europe to preserve untouched a patch of wartime destruction as a potent reminder of the dangers of state-driven political and military rivalry. Berlin's Kaiser Wilhelm Church, for example, was left a bombed-out skeleton standing amidst a rebuilt city.

Under the new dispensation, states thoroughly vindicated themselves and in the process won new legitimacy. Postwar governments guided their economies to their best performance of any time since the emergence of the global economy in the late nineteenth century. After regaining prewar levels of production in the early 1950s, western Europe moved on to enjoy a rapidly rising standard of living within a context of peace and social stability. This was made possible by a GDP growth rate for the major regional economies that ranged over the 1950–1973 period between 4 and 6 percent. By 1973 western Europeans had gone a long way toward catching up with U.S. living standards. With these high national growth rates went low unemployment, low inflation, expanding foreign trade, stable exchange rates, and rising public expenditures on welfare, education, and health. Times were extraordinarily good.

For ordinary Europeans, the most welcome feature of these good times was the availability of consumer goods. By the early 1960s western Europe was in the midst of an "auto-frigo" revolution. In fact, the rush to purchase automobiles, refrigerators, and other household appliances marked not the birth of a European consumer society but its maturation from a start in the interwar period. Now,

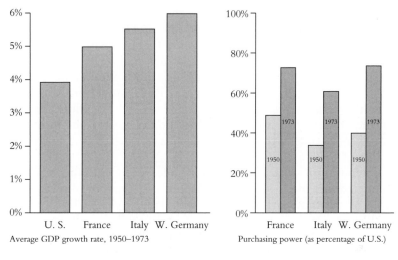

FIGURE 5.2
Good Times Come to Europe⁴

with more money in their pockets, consumers spent it on comfort and diversion. As in the United States, the emergence of a mass consumer market blurred European social divides. Tastes, distinguished by region and class, became more uniform. For example, no frills, self-service shopping, beginning often in small stores before reaching supermarket proportions, gradually spread as price took precedence over service. But western Europe was not becoming an American carbon copy. For example, social diversity persisted to a greater degree, and small family-run businesses survived, beloved by customers expecting expert and fine quality when purchasing clothes, hardware, bread, cheese, or meat. Government protection for small retailers and cooperative arrangements for bulk purchasing helped keep them viable.

Housing conditions in France provide a sense of the dramatic improvements in the lives of ordinary Europeans. In 1954, fewer than three in five French households had running water, only one in four an indoor toilet, and only one in ten a bathroom and central heating. By the mid-1970s, 75 percent of homes had indoor toilets, 70 percent indoor bathrooms, and 60 percent central heat. By then the labor-saving domestic appliances so familiar to American consumers had also made deep inroads. Sixty percent of homes had a washing machine, and almost 90 percent had a refrigerator. By 1990, these amenities were virtually universal. These years of growing consumerism also saw the beginning of the automobile revolution. By 1960, almost one-third of all French families owned a car, and the proportion would rise to three-quarters by 1990.

At the heart of western Europe's state-sponsored experiment in popular welfare is what one scholar has called the "politics of inclusion."⁵ The postwar parliamentary state had to succeed where the prewar state had failed in creating a broad working political consensus. That consensus depended on the state

catering to the interests of a wide range of groups but above all to labor, agriculture, and the lower and middle classes. John Maynard Keynes was the patron saint
of this approach. He had provided the rationale for an activist state addressing the
social and economic injustices that had spawned political upheaval during the
interwar period. The activist state in its Keynesian incarnation promised to
improve the human condition without the brutal impersonality of the free
market or the tyranny and inefficiency of Soviet-style socialism. This balance
between the efficiency of markets and the commitment to the inclusion of all
within a just social order were the two elements that defined the emergent European notion of welfare capitalism.

The consensus on welfare capitalism included western Europe's Socialist and
Communist parties, both long-time advocates of working-class interests and
champions of social justice. But concern with popular welfare became a staple of
the center-right as well, including Europe's Christian Democratic parties and the
politically influential Catholic Church. Pope John XXIII issued in 1961 an influential encyclical (a formal statement on the faith from the pope to his bishops)
that called for capitalism with a human face. This popular pope argued for softening the hard edges of the free market and condemned the cases in which "the
enormous wealth, the unbridled luxury, of the privileged few stands in violent,
offensive contrast to the utter poverty of the vast majority." The wealthy had a
moral obligation to use property "not only for one's own personal benefit but
also for the benefit of others." But John XXIII also argued that the state, too, had
an indispensable role to play in promoting social justice and political order.[6]

This emerging postwar consensus manifested itself in welfare initiatives and
employment guarantees that expanded steadily along with economic recovery.
For example, Italy began extending pension coverage and improving health
insurance from 1950 onward. Western Europe's overall welfare expenditures
(including those for education and housing) increased from 25 percent of GNP
in 1950 to about 45 percent in the mid-1970s. These measures did not burden
the economy. To the contrary, welfare policies promoted economic growth by
playing a counter-cyclical role, injecting into a lagging economy unemployment
funds calculated to stimulate spending and recovery and conversely taking
money out of people's pockets in the form of taxes when an economy showed
signs of overheating. Welfare policies also helped overall economic performance
by raising domestic demand. Money placed in the hands of the poor and spent
on such essentials as food, clothes, and housing spurred overall output.

In developing this welfare capitalism, European countries followed their distinct traditions. For example, Britain's Beveridge report, issued during World
War II, envisioned the promotion of popular welfare without the state getting
involved in micromanaging the economy. Germany was guided by Catholic and
patriarchal influences, so its welfare measures focused on the breadwinners and
left the welfare of women and children to the male head of the family. Sweden's
course was influenced by its tradition of state intervention to promote political
centralization and economic efficiency.

Of all European workers, farmers were perhaps the most favored under the
new dispensation. Their sector, once supreme in the European economy, had

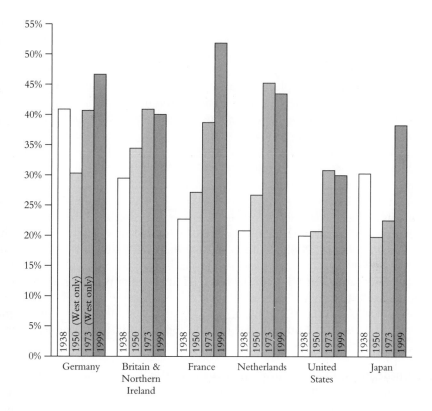

FIGURE 5.3
Government Spending in Western Europe Compared with the United States and Japan (as a percentage of GDP)[7]
The regional variations are notable, with the western European states at the high end over the last half-century. No less important, this data shows that the modern state has not withered away in the face of increasing globalization and, in some cases, has actually increased its share of the economic output during recent decades.

suffered a steady drop in the numbers employed and the share of national output that it accounted for. More serious, agricultural income had for over a hundred years lagged behind that of urban workers. The resulting rural discontent had fed the violent, authoritarian politics of the late nineteenth and early twentieth centuries, forcing governments to protect farmers against cheap foodstuffs from abroad and to try to raise prices by means of administrative controls lowering production. This growing intervention began to create close cooperative relations between the state and agricultural organizations.

After World War II, the number of farm workers continued to shrink due to labor migration to urban factories and the consolidation of land holdings into more efficient units. Those still engaged in agriculture nevertheless remained a disproportionately powerful interest group that continued to receive state assistance. Protectionist measures such as tariffs and import quotas remained in place. Governments still intervened in the market with price supports, subsidies, and official purchasing at set prices, while providing tax and loan assistance. All these measures helped to prevent rural citizens from falling further behind other groups between 1945 and 1960 and to share in postwar prosperity.

Despite their pursuit of inclusive and generous welfare policies, western European states did not neglect the basic issues of economic development and international competitiveness. Leaders all across the region recognized that popular welfare ultimately depended on economic modernization, and accordingly states had a responsibility to promote industry and invest heavily in advanced sectors of the economy. Governments resorted to intrusive and far-reaching measures, including nationalization of strategic businesses as well as guidance of private-sector firms and indirect management of the overall economy. By 1957 public enterprise accounted for 32 percent of total gross fixed investment in Britain and Northern Ireland; between 25 and 27 percent in Austria, France, and Italy; and between 13 and 15 percent in the Netherlands, Norway, and Sweden. Most prominently represented were steel, nuclear engineering, aircraft, and energy production.

Reflecting the growing importance of the state as the prime provider of immediate popular welfare and the sponsor of long-term modernization, by 1973 total government expenditures as a percentage of GDP had dramatically surpassed previous levels. Western European states were not only surviving but flourishing.

The Emergence of the European Community. Paradoxically, the very success enjoyed by individual states in western Europe made possible the creation of a new, overarching political, social, and economic framework for the region that would ultimately evolve into the European Community, or EC. Confident governments increasingly recognized that their individual interests were best advanced by cooperation on a widening range of issues. Only strong states could embrace a strategy of mutually beneficial interdependence and begin to shift some decision-making power to a common entity. As member states developed a symbiotic, mutually supportive relationship, Europeans would find themselves more regulated and better served than ever before.

The direction and pace of these developments were controlled by a new generation of national leaders best represented by Robert Schuman of France; Konrad Adenauer of Germany and his chief lieutenant and successor, Ludwig Erhard; and Alcide de Gasperi of Italy. All four were Roman Catholic politicians with deeply democratic impulses and a determination to meet their electorates' cry for a better, more stable life than their states had provided between 1914 and 1945. All agreed that interstate cooperation would facilitate their pursuit of popular welfare.

A western European community took form by gradual stages. The Organization of European Economic Cooperation, created in 1948 to coordinate Marshall Plan programs, sought to clear away some of the obstacles to regional trade. Two years later, the European Payments Union emerged to serve as a clearinghouse for financial claims among member states and to provide relief for members having financial problems. It remained in operation until 1958, by which time European economies had recovered sufficiently to insulate themselves against crisis.

In 1952 cooperation took more robust form with the formation of the European Coal and Steel Community. Jean Monnet of France, a leading architect of European unity, had in 1950 proposed a single market for coal and steel resources that would be supervised by a supranational European commission. Once implemented by the major western European economies (France, West Germany, Italy, Belgium, the Netherlands, and Luxembourg), it turned the continent's steel industry into a giant cartel regulating prices and production, and it gave governments a mechanism by which they could rationalize production and phase out inefficient plants and mines. Seen in long-term perspective, this cooperative body played a critical role in readying participating members to take the next step toward integration. Its creation forced states jealous of their autonomy—especially the larger states of Germany, France, Italy, and Britain—to formally endorse the idea of integration. Its members learned through the mechanism of negotiations how to reconcile conflicting national needs on specific issues within fixed deadlines. Finally, this critical experiment built trust between those two long-term rivals, France and Germany, without which further progress toward integration would have been impossible.

The crowning achievement of this steady trend toward regional cooperation was the EC. Created by a treaty signed in Rome in March 1957, it provided for expanded European free trade. Negotiations among the six governments already participating in the Coal and Steel Community culminated in the Rome treaty. Once in place, the EC moved steadily toward closer economic and financial integration. Success at dismantling tariffs and other obstacles to trade paved the way for more wide-ranging economic coordination. The Rome treaties also established the basis for closer political cooperation. The key institutions were the Council of Ministers (consisting of representatives from the governments of member states), the European Commission (a genuinely supranational body charged with implementing decisions reached by the member states), a European Court (increasingly influential in laying down precedents to be followed throughout the EC), and the European Parliament (an elected body eager to secure for itself a greater policy voice). To keep members happy, the offices of these institutions operated not in one EC capital but were parceled out to Brussels, Belgium, Luxembourg City, and Strasbourg, France. Attempts to carry cooperation further—into the areas of foreign policy and defense organization—foundered over fear of alienating the Americans and over disagreements between the British and French governments.

A collection of discrete considerations drove this trend toward regional integration. Foremost was a shared commitment to promoting intraregional trade as an engine in economic growth so important to political leaders throughout western Europe. Greater unity had the additional appeal of helping to solve the problem of Germany with its dubious past and rapidly reviving economic power. A Germany thoroughly integrated within the European community was less likely to return to its aggressively nationalist behavior. The desire for international influence also made unity attractive since only a united Europe could have a meaningful voice on the world stage. As the French minister of foreign affairs, Maurice Faure, put it in July 1957 when he appealed to the French parliament to approve the Rome treaties: "Well, there are not four Great Powers, there are two; America and Russia. There will be a third by the end of the century: China. It depends on you whether there will be a fourth: Europe."[8]

Agriculture did not drive the formation of the EC, but it was so important an element in the fundamental policies of its member states that it had to be incorporated in any regional agreement. A Common Agricultural Policy took shape in the 1960s, and by the end of the decade it was eating up 80 percent of the EC's administrative effort and 70 percent of its budget. This was so despite the fact that member states were among the most industrialized in the world and agriculture was an ever-dwindling part of their economies. The politics of inclusion that served farmers so well in individual states also got them favored treatment in a united Europe.

Whereas France, Germany, and Italy embraced greater integration, only Britain of the major western European economies hung back. London did not join the Coal and Steel Community, nor did it sign the Treaty of Rome launching the EC. The reason was not that British domestic policy differed so significantly from its neighbors. To the contrary, the postwar British commitment to full employment and welfare policies, integration of labor into the political establishment, and favoritism toward agriculture all mirrored trends across the English Channel.

The real source of British resistance to integration into Europe was the hold that a glorious imperial past exercised on policymakers' imagination. Clinging to dreams of global power and prestige, they turned their back on regional cooperation. Britain was "not just another European country," as the Labor government's foreign secretary, Ernest Bevin, insisted in mid-1947.[9] He and other postwar leaders sought to cultivate a relationship of close economic, diplomatic, and military cooperation with the United States. They also sought to preserve the position of the British pound as the premier European currency, and to that end they tried to maintain convertibility with the dollar despite the harm the effort did to British industry and consumers. Finally, the British government tried to hold the diverse parts of its rapidly dissolving empire together in a commonwealth. Though it was supposed to serve as a framework for close political and economic cooperation, by the 1960s divergences among its members had largely drained the association of its significance. For example, while London sought to protect traditional export markets, some former colonies such as Ghana and India followed import substitution policies (see p. 230) harmful to British exports.

London's preference for international prestige over closer ties to the continent proved a mistake. Glory imposed costs that Britain could no longer afford. It lacked the capital to invest in its colonies and maintain the troops abroad in defense of its dwindling empire. Manufactured exports, the basis for Britain's reputation as a great trading nation, slid dramatically. Accounting for one-quarter of the world's total in the early postwar period, by 1970 they were only a tenth. Britain's growth rate and productivity increases lagged behind those of the EC, and Britons enviously watched the rising living standard of their neighbors.

Already by the mid-1950s, competitive continental industry was driving British auto exports and other consumer goods from the European market. Germany's Volkswagen ousted Britain's Morris Minor from the low-cost car market. The country's weak economic performance was a source of national pessimism. Economic stagnation was putting consumer dreams beyond reach at the same time that it was undercutting dreams of international influence.

Fiat and Europe's Corporate Aristocracy

The strong trend toward western European economic integration helped preserve a distinct corporate style that dominated the region with some variations from country to country. Fiat, a large and powerful Italian conglomerate, reveals the characteristics associated with this postwar European way of doing business. Perhaps the most striking of these characteristics was family ownership. What also distinguished the European corporate culture was the class-consciousness of business leaders, their close ties to the state, and their sometimes contentious relationship with strong, independent labor unions.

Fiat began as an automobile company under Giovanni Agnelli. This astute entrepreneur came from a socially prominent land-owning family with roots in a small village near the northern Italian city of Turin. Convinced of the automobile's promise, he had created Fiat (short for Fabbrica Italiana Automobili Torino) in 1899. Demand during World War I made Fiat the third largest company in Italy and helped it diversify into new areas such as trucks, aircraft engines, and publishing. Agnelli was becoming a rich man.

Already Fiat had developed close ties to politicians in Rome who could guarantee the Turin-based company preferential treatment and government contracts. Agnelli's embrace of the young political upstart Benito Mussolini in 1914 paid rich dividends from the 1920s into the early 1940s when Mussolini presided over a fascist dictatorship. For example, when the U.S. auto company Ford tried to break into the Italian market by purchasing an Italian car maker, Fiat got Rome to block the deal, thereby preserving its dominance in the domestic market. When Mussolini fell from power as the war in Europe turned against him, Agnelli switched sides, welcomed the Allies, and formed a close relationship with the new postwar national government. American support in the form of Marshall Plan aid helped to rebuild production lines and to make Fiat a rival to Germany's Volkswagen in the race to become the largest European auto producer. Fiat also cultivated close ties to the ruling Christian Democrats, which in turn dealt sympathetically with powerful private business blocs, supported competitive exporters, and tolerated practices that in the United States would have fallen afoul of anti-trust or anti-monopoly laws.

Agnelli and the other well-born business leaders who ran Italy's major private firms from the economically dominant northern region felt a strong sense of social solidarity. This elite looked with suspicion on firms led by social upstarts. They coordinated their actions with the help of Italy's only commercial bank, the powerful Milan-based Mediobanca, which occupied a commanding place within the Italian economy.

Consistent with the strong class-consciousness of his circle, Giovanni Agnelli tended to deal with his workers paternalistically. He avoided layoffs and provided a range of benefits, including medical care, housing, nurseries for working mothers, and retirement homes. But these benefits did not satisfy workers looking for broader rights. Left-wing labor unions began to collide with Agnelli's paternalism during World War I. Labor unrest continued into the 1920s and would erupt once more after World War II.

When Giovanni Agnelli died in December 1945, Fiat remained firmly under family control. His grandson, the twenty-four-year-old Gianni Agnelli, was next in line to run Fiat, but he was more interested in leading a playboy lifestyle consorting with film stars, the titled, and the rich. Meanwhile the capable Vittorio Valletta, a veteran manager, directed the company. This loyal servitor had arranged for Fiat to receive a substantial portion of the Marshall Plan funds targeted for Italy. Valletta prepared the company to operate in a more open trading system that favored mass production for mass consumption. As part of moving Fiat in fresh directions, he introduced new technology and imposed greater labor discipline, quadrupling worker output between 1948 and 1955.

Finally in the early 1960s Gianni Agnelli began taking up the mantle of business leadership while remaining socially prominent and a devotee of the good life. Firmly in control by 1966, the new boss quickly accommodated to the prevailing corporate pattern. He worked with the long-ruling Christian Democrats, and this collaboration paid off in direct aid from Rome as well as from the EC headquarters in Brussels. The politicians helped with payments for laid-off workers, covering up to 90 percent of their lost pay. They restricted Japanese auto imports. They purchased struggling Fiat subsidiaries and sold off state-controlled firms to Fiat at below-market prices. Agnelli himself took a prominent place in the close-knit Italian corporate establishment, for example, serving in the mid-1970s as president of the premier industrial coordinating organization, Confindustria. Among the business elite, he made both a colleague and an adviser of the influential Enrico Cuccia, the head of the large state-owned IRI conglomerate as well as Mediobanca.

Agnelli took the company reins just as the Italian economy was entering a difficult period. Inflation was setting in, and the competitiveness of Italian goods was suffering on international markets. In addition, labor was restive. Fiat had hired large numbers of poor southerners to work in its Turin plants but did little to help the city deal with the economic and social stresses created by the newcomers. Fiat compounded local tensions by cracking down on high worker absentee rates and cutting payrolls in order to make the company more competitive. The fall of 1969 brought a climax to a decade of growing labor unrest. Strikes disrupted production, costs soared, and in the context of mounting political polarization executives faced intimidation and terrorism. Four were killed, and Agnelli himself carried a cyanide capsule against the possibility that terrorists might capture him. Fiat's problems persisted into the 1970s. An economic slowdown combined with high gas prices to hurt car sales, and labor-management relations remained volatile. Finally, to help restore industrial peace, Agnelli lent support to a nationwide scheme to regularly adjust worker pay to account for

Gianni Agnelli with His Wife, Marella Caracciolo di Castagneto
The couple's pose affirms their standing among "the beautiful people." The
Time magazine article accompanying this photo drove the point home,
describing them as "charter members of the international jet set." It could
have added that they were aristocrats with strong American ties: Marella was
a levelheaded Neapolitan princess who married Gianni in 1953 and put up
with his discreet extramarital affairs. Her mother was an American who had
married into the Italian aristocracy. Gianni's mother had been a blue blood
(Princess Virginia Bourbon del Monte), also with an American mother.
(Howell Conant/TimePix)

inflation. In 1975 the government put this indexed wage arrangement (*scala
mobile,* literally "moving stairs," or "escalator") into effect, thereby quieting some
of labor's discontents.

During the 1980s Fiat prospered. Renewed profitability enabled it to expand.
By mid-decade it employed 270,000 workers directly and several million indi-
rectly through suppliers, commanded an annual revenue of $30 billion, and
accounted for about 5 percent of Italy's total GNP. Auto production, Fiat's core
business, controlled 60 percent of the domestic car market. The empire had
grown to include 569 subsidiaries and 190 associated companies operating in
fifty countries. They covered the business gamut—from banks and insurance
groups to aerospace to textiles to publishing to cement and construction.

Their grip on this massive conglomerate made the Agnelli family Italy's
uncrowned royal house. With a 40 percent stake, Gianni Agnelli and his close relatives continued to keep a close eye on Fiat's affairs and worried that a merger in the
auto business with such auto giants as Ford or General Motors, prompted by purely
competitive concerns, would lose them the jewel in the family corporate crown.
The Agnellis struggled to maintain the tradition of family control even as they
began to face the competitive pressures of globalization. The end of an era came in
January 2003 with Gianni Agnelli's death. Thousands upon thousands—workers,

EUROPEAN REVIVAL AND CONSOLIDATION	
1945	Fiat begins rebuilding ultimately with the help of Marshall Plan funds
1952	European Coal and Steel Community marks first major advance toward greater integration
1957	Treaty of Rome lays basis for the European Community with France, West Germany, Italy, Belgium, the Netherlands, and Luxembourg as the founding members
1961	Pope John XXIII calls for a socially just capitalism
1966	Gianni Agnelli assumes full personal control of Fiat

soccer players, and government officials among a mass of mourners—paid their respects to the most important figure in Italian public life over the last half century. Sadly, Fiat was in deep economic trouble and family control in question.

The sort of close ties between Fiat and family were commonplace in postwar Europe. In Britain, France, and Germany too, families had founded and then as owners run or supervised major, internationally known corporations such as France's Peugeot, Renault, and Michelin. In Germany as late as 1969, 60 of the 150 largest firms were still family-dominated. In Italy almost half of the hundred most dominant businesses between 1950 and 1970 were under family control. This pattern persisted into the 1990s, when over three-quarters of Italy's top 150 companies were still family-owned (compared to only one in five in the United States). Even today no more striking example of this pattern can be found than Silvio Berlusconi, the head of a broadcasting empire who parlayed his power and visibility in the marketplace into political prominence and the post of prime minister. In all these cases, entrepreneurs have used strong family loyalties to mobilize resources, rejected autonomous management in favor of personal operational oversight, and resisted diffusing ownership through widely held stock holdings. Success has helped to shore up family wealth and social standing. At odds with the predominant pattern in the United States, business as the family domain has played a critical role in other regions of the world, nowhere more so than in the advanced economic sectors of Japan with its *keiretsu* and of South Korea with its family-owned diversified business groups known as *chaebol*.

The Second Japanese Miracle

The state, which figured centrally in the revival and reshaping of European economies, was no less critical to Japan's postwar development. The Japanese pattern of government involvement, sometimes described as "guided capitalism," had as its overriding goal the accumulation of national wealth through promoting exports and limiting imports. This approach produced the second Japanese economic miracle, surpassing the first one early in the century.

By the late 1950s Japan had demonstrated that it could grow at a rate that exceeded even the most optimistic expectations. By the 1960s the economy was booming. Its rate of GDP growth was stunning even by comparison with the robust European performance, averaging 9.2 percent between 1950 and 1973. The torrid pace helped lift the purchasing power of the Japanese people from less than one-fifth of the U.S. level in 1950 to two-thirds by 1973. Japanese goods were increasingly competitive within the U.S.-guaranteed international free trade regime. Its exports boomed, tripling their share of total world exports between 1955 and 1970. The overseas sales offensive combined with limited foreign sales within Japan swelled foreign exchange reserves from virtually nothing in 1955 to a respectable $18.3 billion in 1972. By 1968 Japan's economy was not just the leader in East Asia but also the third largest in the world. The loser of the Pacific War had become an economic superpower.

Prosperity through "Guided Capitalism." The improvement in the standard of living in less than a generation was extraordinary. In 1960 the cabinet of Prime Minister Ikeda Hayato committed to double the national income. By both expanding the country's wealth and ensuring an equitable division, Liberal Democratic Party leaders hoped to promote mass consumption that would calm the social tension and political conflict that had begun to roil the nation. Labor was unhappy and prone to strike. The Socialist and Communist parties enjoyed strong support. The alliance with the United States was controversial and had just ignited violence in the streets and in the legislature.

The Ikeda plan proved fantastically successful. Japan already had the most equal distribution of income among advanced industrial countries. With prosperity widely shared, Japanese could for the first time in large numbers indulge their taste for consumer goods, mainly appliances and entertainment. By 1970 virtually all urban households had a television, a refrigerator, and a washing machine, and one in five owned a car (rare a decade earlier). Members of this new middle class could buy their own homes and send their children to school in ever-larger percentages. High school graduates rose from half of the population in 1955 to 82 percent in 1970. Over the same period the percentage of college graduates more than doubled, reaching almost a quarter of the population by 1970.

Amazingly, Japanese families went on this spending spree while maintaining a savings rate so high that Japanese business did not need to turn to foreign capital to expand. Increasing prosperity seemed to reinforce rather than diminish this high propensity to save. The pattern persisted because the Japanese government, unlike those in western Europe, did not provide rich social security guarantees, so adults had good reason to save, especially to cover their retirement years. Fiscal policy offered tax breaks for savings and no breaks for consumer debt. Finally, consumer credit for major purchases such as home and car was not easily available. The byword among Japanese consumers was not "buy now, pay later" but "save now, buy later."

Central to Japan's success was a statist approach to economic development whereby bureaucrats would help firms gain an edge and maintain it by adjusting quickly to constantly changing market conditions overseas. To that end, government agencies encouraged cooperation among firms and exercised wide discretionary power. This "guided capitalism" became orthodoxy during the era of sustained high growth that began in the mid-1950s. In 1955 the government laid down the first of a long string of economic plans, this one geared to 5 percent annual growth. In implementing these plans, the Japanese state orchestrated industrial and export strategies. The Ministry of International Trade and Industry (MITI), created in 1949, worked along with the Ministry of Finance to construct a predictable framework for business growth, to promote efficiency, to ensure cheap capital to encourage investment, and to direct research and development projects toward promising new technologies.

Under this Japanese version of free market capitalism, the state had at its disposal a striking variety of mechanisms to promote its broad goals. The government might intervene to change the tax system, provide subsidies, or encourage new industries by reclaiming scarce land for factory sites or subsidizing the industrial use of water and electricity. To make sure that firms with the strongest growth prospects secured funding, bureaucrats could ration capital and limit foreign exchange, helping some and denying others. To shelter promising new industry from foreign competition, the state could impose trade restrictions and controls on currency exchange. What the government did not do, in contrast with European practice, was to acquire direct control of important segments of the economy. Nationalization was not in Tokyo's economic tool kit.

Perhaps the most peculiarly Japanese of these government economic tools was "administrative guidance," which involved laying down "guideposts" for business decision-makers. Bureaucrats, usually in MITI, consulted with business leaders on future levels of economic activity within an industry, proposing targets on the basis of their overall knowledge of economic conditions, and then persuading businesses to observe them. The business establishment had a strong bias toward cooperation, and in any case every firm knew that to defy the bureaucrats today would surely mean an unfriendly response to tomorrow's request for help with an export license or a low-interest loan. Government agencies stood ready to help should firms following the agreed-upon guidelines run into trouble. For example, in the case of unexpected over-capacity, MITI might step in to indicate how much each firm within an industry should cut back, in what product lines, and to what price levels for the remaining output.

Powerful and efficient career bureaucrats did not dictate to big business. Rather, they engaged in a steady dialogue with the leaders of "enterprise groups" made up of diverse industries linked in long-term relationships (*keiretsu*) permitted by occupation policy after the breakup of large family-controlled business conglomerates known as *zaibatsu*. (See Chapter 2.) It was up to business to decide how to maneuver on the free market domestically and internationally. Politicians from the Liberal Democratic Party constituted the third element in what some have called the "iron triangle" of the Japanese economy. This conservative, pro-business party first took control of the government in 1955 and ran the country almost continually to century's end. Its dominance guaranteed political stability and fostered continuity in this winning economic strategy. These three groups operated within a clubby, strongly pro-growth culture ("Japan

Incorporated," as some have called it) that made economic success the overriding national goal. Defenders of this tight, closed world argued that it got results and avoided the legal tie-ups and political wrangles common to the much-vaunted U.S. system.

The steel industry provides a good example of how Japan Incorporated worked. Between 1955 and 1974 MITI guided that industry in an orderly fashion from production of 9.4 million tons of crude steel to 117.1 million tons. By that latter date Japan's output was only slightly behind that of the leaders, the Soviet Union and the United States. At each step of the expansion process, MITI coordinated the plans of the nominally competing Japanese steel firms. In the 1960s it began to stress technological innovation as a response to a developing labor shortage. Faced with an increasingly competitive international market, MITI promoted consolidation of the two biggest firms. In 1970 the merger came to fruition, resulting in the world's largest steel company. Japan's steel industry might have gotten to this point on its own, but the path it took demonstrated that government-business collaboration worked very effectively.

In retrospect, it is clear that the Japanese economy had undergone a fundamental transformation during the 1950s and 1960s, made possible first by supplying U.S. forces fighting in Korea and then by exporting to an open U.S. market. U.S.-bound goods increased from $0.28 billion in 1954 to $1.12 billion in 1960. At the outset the main exports were low-quality, inexpensive goods such as toys and textiles. But increasingly production moved into high-technology goods such as cars and electronics that put Japan's manufacturers on the cutting edge of international competition. The introduction of new manufacturing technologies had steadily raised worker productivity and made export goods attractive to foreign buyers. As industry demonstrated that it could compete internationally, the government began in the early 1960s slowly to open the home market to foreign imports.

These critical economic developments had a profound effect on Japanese society. A country that by war's end had become a war machine lavishing its human and material resources on overseas ambitions was becoming an economic engine dedicated to supplying consumers abroad with quality goods and its own people with a richer life. The pieces of the economic juggernaut that would amaze and alarm the world in the 1970s and 1980s had largely fallen into place.

Capitalism Sony Style. The new direction of the Japanese economy and the energy and imagination of its business leaders in the high-growth export sector are exemplified by Sony, the world-famous consumer electronics firm. Sony's founders brought to their drive to capture foreign markets a long-term vision that stressed a paternalistic relationship to their employees, constantly upgrading technology to enhance competitiveness, and forgoing immediate profits to expand market share. Government backing helped them realize their vision.

The firm most often associated with the Japanese miracle had its origins in the months just after the end of war in the Pacific. The Tokyo Telecommunications Engineering Company had an unpromising name as well as limited start-up capital. But the founders had energy and good social connections as well as vision, and they recruited talented engineers. The senior partner, Ibuka Masaru, imagined a business whose employees "could become united with a firm spirit of teamwork and exercise to their hearts' desire their technological capacity." Morita Akio, thirteen years Ibuka's junior, was more interested in how to get new technology into customers' hands. His approach, he later explained, was "to lead the public with new products rather than ask them what kind of products they want. The public does not know what is possible, but we do."[10]

The Ibuka-Morita operation got its first big break in the early 1950s with the transistor. Bell Labs, the U.S. inventor of this solid-state electronic processor, imagined it as useful only in hearing aids, whereas Ibuka thought it might run a small radio. To arrange the $25,000 payment for a license to produce transistors, he had to convince MITI officials who doubted both the utility of the transistor and the ability of the small firm to bring a new product successfully to market. Ibuka's engineers proceeded to redesign the transistor, create parts for a small radio, and get it into mass production. Their first transistor radio appeared in 1955, and by 1957 they had it down to pocket size. An American firm beat the Japanese to market by a few months but then decided that pocket radios had no future and abandoned the field.

With its first major product doing well, the firm decided it needed a name that would travel internationally. The Latin word *sonus* ("sound") appealed, and after some playing with meanings in English and Japanese, "Sony" emerged. It meant nothing but was short and easy to remember and had a transnational look. In January 1958 it became the official name for a company that would become a

Morita Akio and Ibuka Masaru
Morita (left) and Ibuka were the cofounders of Sony and long-time colleagues whose conflicts were apparently limited to arm-wrestling. (Courtesy Sony Corporation)

symbol of the Japanese economic resurgence and a byword internationally for innovative consumer electronics.

Sony's overseas success was in large measure Morita's achievement. He was born in 1921 into a well-to-do, respectable sake-brewing family with roots in a village just outside the industrial city of Nagoya (southwest of Tokyo). The family had been making sake, Japan's national and ceremonial drink, for three hundred years. As the first son, Akio (meaning "enlightened") was slated to take over the business. While still attending elementary school, he began sitting in on board meetings.

The family atmosphere was distinctly Westernizing. Morita's parents gave him an elevated bed to replace the traditional on-the-floor *tatami*. The family imported a Ford car to take Sunday drives along narrow, bumpy cart roads and purchased a General Electric washing machine and a Westinghouse refrigerator. The father had a taste for foreign movies, including (so the son recalled) *King Kong*. His mother loved European classical music and attended concerts by touring artists. To help the young man develop a broader view of the world, the family sent him on tours of Japan, Korea, and Manchuria. Along with this interest in Western goods and practices went a sense of social obligation, especially toward the welfare of the family village, and a strong sense of family identity and social propriety.

Early on, Morita was gripped by a keen interest in science. He began to read about electronics, especially sound reproduction and radio, and to make electronic devices. His absorption in this hobby began to hurt his schoolwork, but he was still able to gain admission to Osaka Imperial University, where he studied in its outstanding physics department. During the latter stages of the war with the United States, he went into the navy to do research on heat-guided weapons and night-vision gun sights. He came out of the war with a keen awareness of how far Japan lagged behind the United States technologically. This awareness inspired a determination to catch up that gave Morita's business drive a nationalist impetus. Japan's postwar achievements, to which he would contribute, would be a source of special personal pride.

Already in the 1950s, even before the transistor deal put Sony on a solid foundation, Morita began looking for opportunities abroad. He made his first tour of the United States and Europe in 1953, studying their cultures, surveying their markets, and building business contacts. Even though the Japanese market began to grow handsomely around 1955, just as the transistor radio was appearing, Sony wanted to reach affluent foreigners. That meant overcoming their doubts about the quality of Japanese goods. Morita proved an energetic, outgoing, and confident leader in the export drive, able to work easily with Americans and Europeans. In 1960 Sony formalized its commitment to expanding into the U.S. market by creating Sony of America with Morita serving as president.

Within the world of Japan's self-effacing business leaders, Morita was a bit of a maverick. He was sharp-tongued and enjoyed the public spotlight whether promoting Sony's image or speaking out as Japan's business ambassador to the world. Determined to recognize good work at Sony, he took the revolutionary step of introducing a merit element in a salary scheme usually heavily weighted in favor of seniority. Rather than shelter his family, as was the norm, he brought them to New York for a year in the early 1960s to learn American ways. He himself took up skiing, wind surfing, and skin diving in his sixties. A stroke finally forced him to retire in 1994. His partner, Ibuka, died in 1997, and Morita two years later. Their successors came from within the company.

Under Ibuka and Morita, Sony made its reputation in the United States and overseas with a long string of innovative products. (See Table 5.1.) To achieve this extraordinary level of innovation, Sony put 6 to 10 percent of its sales into research and development. An integral part of product development was careful consideration of likely consumer response, and as a new product approached readiness for the market, Sony would carefully devise an advertising campaign to win buyers. Technology and advertising fueled explosive growth. By 1966 sales were thirty-three times higher than they had been a decade earlier. Over the following twenty years they increased another nineteen times. In 1991 Sony's sales hit $28 billion and its employees, a mere twenty at the outset in 1946, had climbed to almost twenty thousand.

The business philosophy at Sony reflected broader patterns that made Japan an economic powerhouse. Like the heads of other major firms, Morita thought of the company as a family and instituted measures that promoted loyalty to the firm. He recruited employees right out of college and expected them to stay for life and find satisfaction and support within the company. The task of management, Morita explained, was "to keep challenging each employee to do important work that he will find satisfying and to work within the family."[11] Superiors were supposed to stay in close touch with subordinates and cultivate bonds of loyalty. For example, all employees ate in the same dining room, shared work areas, and wore the same company jacket. Because the wage system rewarded seniority, the longer an employee stayed the higher the pay. Top-level executives were paid only about seven or eight times more than newly hired workers. Unions were organized within companies and promoted cooperation rather than confrontation. With management-labor harmony the watchword, companies functioned as teams and minimized the disruptive antagonisms and worker alien-

TABLE 5.1 The Innovations That Made Sony's Reputation	
pocket transistor radio	1957
transistor television	1959
home video tape recorder	1964
Trinitron color television picture tube	1968
Walkman audio tape player	1979
3.5-inch computer disk	1982
compact disk and player (developed jointly with Phillips of the Netherlands)	1982
8-millimeter video camcorder	1985

JAPAN BECOMES AN ECONOMIC POWERHOUSE

1946	Sony is created by Ibuka with Morita as junior partner
1955	Government prepares first economic plan; economy begins quarter-century of sustained high growth; Sony produces transistor radio
1960	Prime Minister Ikeda sets sights on income doubling; Sony launches U.S. operations, marking beginning of broad Japanese export drive
1968	Japanese economy enters ranks of top three

ation commonplace in economies where labor and management saw themselves as adversaries. The contrast between Sony, where unions were creatures of the company, and Fiat or Disney underlines the differences in national conditions shaping economic behavior.

Like other Japanese business leaders, Morita insisted on following a long-term strategy to gain market share rather than seek short-term profit that would make shareholders happy. To that end Sony sought to keep sales rising steadily, even in economic downturns and even if it meant cutting the profit margin. This strategy also helped to keep trained staff fully employed, avoid lay-offs, and thus honor the company's obligations to take care of employees. Japanese firms followed this course with the encouragement of their *keiretsu* partners, who in turn protected the company by working together to prevent hostile take-over bids and to keep foreign interlopers out of their home market. Because business leaders came from within the firms, they tended to give priority to the long-term growth of the firm and welfare of its workers. Moreover, high levels of corporate spending on research and development helped move Japan to the technological forefront, first in cars and consumer electronics and then in computers, engineering, communications, robotics, and instrumentation. Business happily supported heavy government investment in infrastructure and education that would make the overall economy more competitive and individual firms more productive.

Sony's success and that of other Japanese businesses is hard to imagine without government support. It promoted a broad social consensus in favor of economic growth, hard work, and limited consumption. The government also maintained a protectionist policy that guaranteed Sony a secure domestic market during its early years. Finally, the government not only tolerated but also encouraged the clubby atmosphere among leading corporations. Sony, for example, stockpiled economic and political influentials on its board of directors to ensure the company's strong ties with the major segments of the Japanese establishment. This sort of cooperation, all the partners agreed, was the key to economic stability and success. Morita himself described these arrangements with only slight exaggeration as not so much capitalism as "a socialistic and egalitarian free economic system."[12]

VOICES OF DISCONTENT

Just as the Cold War bred vocal critics (see Chapter 4), so too did a dynamic international economy generate discontents. Although the economic system produced an abundance of goods, it was also producing an abundance of pollutants. Social critics began to speak out on this issue. Within the developed economies, women began to call for equal opportunities to participate without discrimination in the system of production and consumption and thus to share fully in the new era of abundance. Finally, economists dissenting from free trade orthodoxy decried flaws in the international economy that disproportionately favored rich countries. These various critics of the international economy came into their own in the 1950s and 1960s and articulated a set of worries about the environment, the status of women, and the disparities in wealth that would increasingly grip the global community in the decades beyond.

The New Environmentalism

In 1969 the U.S. novelist Kurt Vonnegut looked at the pictures of the planet sent back from space and observed, "Earth is such a pretty blue and pink and white pearl.... It looks so *clean*. You can't see all the hungry, angry earthlings down there—and the smoke and the sewage and trash and sophisticated weaponry."[13] His remarks reflected a deepening concern that more and more people and goods were harming the environment. That concern would in time become international, but it took hold earliest in the United States, where the threat seemed most acute. In part Americans were sensitive because they were the first to confront sprawling suburbs, increasing numbers of autos, and consumer waste that boom times brought. But also stirring the unease was a chemical-dependent agriculture and fallout from nuclear tests on American soil. Once a similar constellation of concerns arose in Europe and Japan, environmentalism would gain momentum there as well.

Rachel Carson and *Silent Spring*.   The new environmentalism had its origins in 1962 when Rachel Carson, a popular nature writer and former government scientist, published *Silent Spring*. This landmark book—perhaps the most consequential work published in the United States in the twentieth century—identified the dangerous effects of the pesticide DDT, but Carson's broader message was the threat facing humans as part of the earth's complex and fragile ecosystem. This unlikely midwife to a new environmental consciousness and activism was born in 1907 just outside Pittsburgh. As a child, Carson was bookish and bright with a keen interest in nature. At college, she majored in biology, fascinated with the problems it posed. Her professor, a woman herself struggling in a man's world, played the role of mentor and urged Carson to go to graduate school. By the end of college Carson had become a feminist on the basis of seeing the limits imposed on other women. She had seen her mother defer to her father, himself an inept businessman, and had watched her college mentor, like other talented women, run up against closed doors to career opportunities.

Carson took her M.A. in marine biology at Johns Hopkins University in 1932. But there were no jobs for her in either industry or academe, especially with men given the preference during the Depression as family breadwinners. She was finally able to get a post as a writer for the federal government's Fish and Wildlife Service. It kept her up to date on the latest scientific findings while she made her name as a part-time popular writer adept at rendering those findings in clear, engaging terms. Unmarried, she particularly needed the income to care for her mother and extended family after her father's death.

Between 1937 and 1955 Carson established her reputation and financial independence as a popular writer. Her first book, *Under the Sea Wind* (1941), was overshadowed by Pearl Harbor as attention shifted suddenly to war, but her next two books, *The Sea Around Us* (1951) and *The Edge of the Sea* (1955), won wide critical recognition and many readers. Carson conveyed in this string of popular publications a sense of nature as a good in itself that deserved human wonder. Her prose could be sinuous, as for example in an *Atlantic Monthly* article in 1937 describing how in a marvelously intricate natural process

Rachel Carson
Carson is pictured at her summer home in Maine at about the time she was at work on *Silent Spring,* the landmark book that focused attention on the threat to the earth's complex ecosystem. (© Eric Hartmann/Magnum Photos)

the parts of the plan fall into place: the water receiving from earth and air the simple materials, storing them up until the gathering energy of the spring sun wakens the sleeping plants to a burst of dynamic activity, hungry swarms of planktonic animals growing and multiplying upon the abundant plants, and themselves falling prey to the shoals of fish; all, in the end, to be redissolved into their component substances when the inexorable laws of the sea demand it. Individual elements are lost to view, only to reappear again and again in different incarnations in a kind of material immortality. Kindred forces to those which, in some period inconceivably remote, gave birth to that primeval bit of protoplasm tossing on the ancient seas, continue their mighty and incomprehensible work.[14]

In 1958 Carson began work on her last and most important book. It would make a fresh argument: that nature deserved human protection. She was moved by her alarm over mounting environmental perils filling the news and the scientific literature—radioactive fallout, smog, food additives, and heedless pesticide use. She decided to focus on pesticides, galvanized by scientific studies showing the effects of DDT and other chemicals on wildlife and humans. She chose to treat DDT as a symptom of a broader problem, the absolute faith in science to improve life. DDT, for example, was touted as "the atomic bomb of the insect world."[15] Indeed, during this period American consumers, industry, and agriculture were embracing the quick, cheap chemical fix offered by a widening range of pesticides and herbicides. But Carson had another, more personal reason to write about carcinogenic pesticides. She knew that cancer was at work on her body. A radical mastectomy in 1960 failed to stop its progress, and in 1964, just two years after the publication of *Silent Spring*, cancer would kill her.

Silent Spring followed the model of Carson's earlier work. It was scientifically well grounded, beautifully written, and preoccupied with the natural balance. Its specific argument was that limits on pesticides were needed. Once released, they could not be contained but would cycle through the land, water, and air. Carson's call for limits rested in part on her concern for human safety. Pesticides could increase the risks for cancer, sterility, and birth defects. But she also argued that limits made economic sense, saving consumers and businesses from the costs of excessive spraying, protecting the health of employees, and forestalling the development of pesticide-resistant strains. She was not in favor of banning pesticides; she wanted them used more intelligently. In her view the long-term costs needed to be counted against immediate gain and more room left for the operation of nature's own system of insect control.

Carson's specific concerns with pesticides led her to see nature as fragile and technology as dangerous to the survival of humans as well as other species. She argued, "The question is whether any civilization can wage relentless war on life without destroying itself, and without losing the right to be called civilized." She warned: "The 'control of nature' is a phrase conceived in arrogance, born of the Neanderthal age of biology and philosophy, when it was supposed that nature exists for the convenience of man." From "so primitive a science" had come powerful compounds to be used against insects. But "in turning them against the insects [science] has also turned them against the earth." Carson's preoccupation with the threat that humans posed to the world around them established her standing as the herald of a new, anxious environmental out-look.[16]

The chemical industry, farm groups, and the U.S. Department of Agriculture launched a fierce counterattack. They attempted to block publication of *Silent Spring* and later threatened to withhold advertising from publications reviewing it favorably. When that did not work, they launched a public relations campaign to reassure the public and discredit Carson as a "hysterical woman" who lacked solid scientific credentials. Carson survived these attacks. Her dedication to the cause of the environment sustained her personally, while her scientific training and her deliberate and precise way of marshaling the evidence gave credence to her charges. Science could not conquer nature, she quietly but firmly insisted, only destroy it.

Environmentalism Takes Hold. Although Carson's talents help explain *Silent Spring*'s impact, timing was also important. Indeed, Carson spoke to an already worried U.S. public. The daily news was full of stories about contaminated milk and cranberries, birds killed by spraying against gypsy moths and mosquitoes, and the health dangers of nuclear fallout. A decade of prosperity had brought suburban sprawl, oil spills, and auto pollution. Technology and economic growth seemed to have run amuck, and government agencies such as the Department of Agriculture were so wedded to growth that they ignored environmental threats. Politicians began taking note of this incipient public environmental consciousness. In fact, President Kennedy publicly acknowledged Carson's charges and created a scientific panel to review them. The panel confirmed her findings and urged revising the guidelines for pesticide use.

More broadly, *Silent Spring* and the public response that it evoked need to be seen as an advance on earlier local and usually episodic responses to environmental problems accumulating over the course of the previous century. In the 1860s in Britain foul air in major cities produced by coal burning prompted clean air acts, the first notable environmental measures to become law. There as well as in Russia, Switzerland, Germany, and the United States in the late nineteenth and early twentieth centuries, nationalists joined the calls for action—to preserve rural life with its intimate connections to the country's past but also wilderness areas as another indispensable part of the national patrimony. Farmers in places as widely separated as Europe and Japan made their voices heard, organizing protests against new industries whose smoke stacks spewed pollutants into the air and poisoned the soil for miles around. But in industrial societies, whether under the control of capitalism or socialism, economic growth got the nod over environmental protection. National power took precedence over romantic notions about nature and the warnings about the effects of pollutants. The human costs could be terrible. In London in December 1952 a week of choking air produced by coal fires killed about four thousand people.

Carson's special contribution to environmentalism was to inaugurate an era of broad-based political and legal activism that built on these earlier localized concerns. In 1960 the major U.S. conservation organizations combined claimed a mere 300,000 members. Ten years later the largest of the environmental groups, the National Wildlife Federation, alone had 540,000 members. Burgeoning environmental organizations and public protest reflected deep-seated changes in attitudes and fed off the critical social movements that marked the 1960s, especially among young people. The ferment found expression in new approaches. For example, the Environmental Defense Fund, established in 1967, turned to the courts, using lawsuits and injunctions to champion "environmental rights." The media began popularizing environmental issues. The environmental boom came to a climax on the first Earth Day (April 22, 1970), when some twenty million Americans showed up to participate in teach-ins on college campuses and in major cities around the country. This celebration of the environment attended by calls for its protection would become an annual event observed around the world.

Mushrooming popular concerns with the environment quickly registered in Washington. Congress passed legislation such as the Wilderness Act of 1964 and the Water Quality Control Act of 1965, and in 1969 it created the Environmental Protection Agency. In 1972, in a development that would have given Carson special satisfaction, Congress finally banned the sale and use of DDT in the United States. However, the fact that it could still be manufactured in the United States for sale abroad and even brought back into the United States as residue on foreign agricultural products would have roused her ire and indicated just how much farther the environmental cause had to go.

The Feminist Upsurge

If modern environmentalism took shape in the United States, growing discontent among women about their social and economic status was distinctly more international, manifesting itself almost simultaneously in the United States, western Europe, and Japan. In maturing postwar economies marked by growing prosperity, consumerism, and job opportunities for women, gender relations rapidly emerged in the 1960s as an urgent issue. But the peculiarities of national traditions and social values made for a striking diversity among women from country to country. Not only was there no monolithic Western women's movement, but also Japan provided the first signs that trans-Atlantic societies would not define the terms for activism in the broader world. As we will see in Chapters 6 and 9, women in the third or developing world reinforced this pattern of diversity as they faced their own set of problems and articulated their own needs.

Women in the American Workplace. In the United States, women's steadily growing participation in the economy laid the groundwork for the rapid emergence of the women's movement in the late 1960s. The linkage was nothing new. The push for women's right to vote, finally successful at the national level in 1920, had coincided with the rise of the consumer culture, which gave women new economic clout and public prominence. The second wave of feminism in the 1960s was also tied to the pressures of an increasingly consumer-oriented economy. It was not only bringing Americans their golden age of material abundance; it was also attracting increasing numbers of women, no longer just as consumers but also as producers.

Mobilization during World War II had jumpstarted the process of drawing significant numbers of women into the labor force and opening visions of fresh possibilities. After Pearl Harbor, millions of women went to work, often in higher paying jobs previously closed to them. As the war ended, three out of four women wanted to continue working and were already questioning whether their only option was to give up their jobs to the returning soldiers and take their "proper place" within a male-dominated home. Many in fact managed to stay employed even if they had to step down to lesser jobs at lower pay. By the end of the 1940s women had actually increased their share of the workforce to 32 percent, up from 27 percent at the onset of the decade.

The trend continued during the supposedly conservative 1950s. Women entered the labor market at four times the rate of men. Nearly one-third of all wives were working by 1960, and by 1970, 60 percent of all families with an income over $10,000 had both husband and wife working. The paychecks that women brought home enabled their families to participate more fully in the consumer culture, making possible home purchases, European vacations, or special after-school activities or college for their children.

These advances highlighted for more and more working women the discrimination they suffered. They were still segregated into such "gender appropriate" occupational areas as clerical, retail sales, nursing, and teaching at the elementary level with few chances for advancement. The better-paid professions were largely closed, in part because of educational restrictions but also because of biases in hiring and promotion. Women seldom received pay comparable to men with similar qualifications and experience performing the same job.

Betty Friedan, *The Feminine Mystique*, and NOW. Betty Friedan's *The Feminine Mystique* (1963), published the year after *Silent Spring*, spotlighted the concerns of women and marked a no less seismic shift in popular attitudes. While Carson championed respect for nature and protection of the environment, Friedan made the case for American women participating more fully and freely in the workforce and thereby gaining the means to realize their full individual potential.

Friedan had come to confront this issue in the late 1950s. Married with three children and struggling to sustain a freelance writing career, she had discovered in surveying her fellow alumnae from the class of 1942 at Smith College that respondents who had played a role not just in the home but also in the broader world of work and professional advancement seemed more content with their lives. A more widely cast set of interviews soon confirmed her suspicion that women were ill served when they had to choose between the stark alternatives of home or work—between the popular notions of becoming either loveless, masculine, incomplete career women or nurturing, protected, and adored wives and mothers. When magazine editors shied away from the story, Friedan resolved to do a book on the "feminine mystique" that she saw constraining postwar women's options.

The energy that Friedan threw into the project—and that would thrust her forward as a leading voice for women in the United States and around the world—derived from the way the Smith survey results confirmed her own experience. A woman of remarkable energy and intelligence, she had been stifled by the expectations of her parents, teachers, and classmates growing up in Peoria, Illinois, in the interwar years. Once enrolled at Smith, Friedan blossomed among her bright and supportive classmates. But as graduation approached, social pressures and her own self-doubt ate away at her ambition and ultimately closed off a professional career in her chosen field of psychology. Turning to journalism, she found herself slighted by many of her male peers and was finally fired after becoming pregnant with her second child. Why couldn't a woman both have a family and work? Why were men so uneasy with—and dominant social values so hostile to—working women? Writing the book that would answer these questions was, Friedan later recalled, "mysterious, awesome." The book "took me over. It's as if my whole life, including the mistakes, the pains, the paths not taken, had prepared me for this."[17]

The success of *The Feminine Mystique* was a surprise. Friedan's publisher had planned on a printing of a mere three thousand. But 1970 the volume had sold some three million copies. It became something of a bible for feminists and a spur to political activism. Friedan went on tour, lecturing widely, appearing on radio and TV talk shows, and building networks of influential professional women determined to fight discrimination. Frustrated by state and federal officials' indifference to job discrimination, Friedan concluded that women needed an advocacy group to make the case for equal rights just as African Americans were doing through the NAACP.

NOW, the National Organization for Women, was formally organized in 1966 in a Washington, D.C., meeting of some thirty women from diverse professional backgrounds. Friedan herself helped draft the founding statement laying out the bread-and-butter issues on which she thought most women wanted to focus. According to that statement, NOW stood for "true equality for all women" and "full participation in the mainstream of American society." If women were to realize their potential and gain a prominent role in decision-making, they would have "to break through the silken curtain of prejudice and discrimination" blocking their way in every area of public life from government and industry to education and the churches. NOW demanded the removal of all barriers to "equal professional and economic advance."[18]

During the early 1960s, politicians began to recognize the frustrations that women were feeling and that Friedan was voicing. In 1961 President Kennedy, responding to pressure from professional women's organizations, appointed a commission to review the status of women. The commission's 1963 report highlighted workplace issues—discrimination in pay and the declining presence of women in the professions and executive positions. It recommended not just an end to inequities in government jobs but also paid maternity leaves, greater access to education, financial help for women seeking to enter the labor force, and childcare centers. Important legislative victories quickly followed. The Equal Pay Act of 1963 stipulated that women receive the same pay as men for the same work, and the Civil Rights Act of 1964 outlawed workplace discrimination on the basis of sex as well as race. But the federal and state governments were resistant to enforcing these protections. It was this very resistance to change that supplied the impetus for the organization of NOW in 1966, two years after the passage of landmark but initially empty civil rights legislation.

The 1960s and 1970s were marked by an upsurge in feminist activism. NOW took the lead, applying political pressure, litigating, and shaping public opinion. Other groups soon followed in what became a highly diverse, grassroots movement to redefine the social as well as economic role of women and remove rigid notions of gender relations and identities. For the white, middle-class mainstream that Friedan represented, the women's movement meant primarily equal access to jobs and education and individual control of reproduction. More radical groups called for a fundamental remake of social attitudes and practices. Radicals were dismayed by the reluctance of American society to embrace change and impatient with the macho, condescending attitude that they had encountered from the men leading the civil rights, anti-war, and student movements during the 1960s. They wanted an end to the objectification of women (for example, outlawing pornography). They wanted space apart from the repressive atmosphere of male-dominated institutions (for example, through women's health collectives, rape crisis centers, and women's studies programs at the college level). They sought recognition that the concerns and needs of minority women were often distinct from those of white women. They wanted acceptance for lesbianism and other forms of sexual freedom. And they reached out to third-world women on the basis of presumed common outlooks and interests.

Out of this multifaceted women's movement had come by the early 1970s a string of major achievements: the repeal of abortion laws, expanded career opportunities backed by legal enforcement, and soul-searching among men about their relationship with women as partners and as coworkers. Young women were the primary beneficiaries of the new dispensation. They began breaking into such male bastions as medicine and the law. By 1980 more than half of women with children under age six were employed, and only 15 percent of all families fit the old ideal of a working father and a stay-at-home mother (down dramatically from 70 percent in the 1950s). At the same time divorce rates climbed, and single-parent households, usually headed by women with limited income, rose from 11 percent in 1964 to 23 percent in 1980. Despite advances, women still held a disproportionate share of jobs in the low and dead-end part of the economy and accounted for most of the adults living in poverty.

Feminism in Europe. The burgeoning U.S. women's movement had a western European counterpart whose story diverges in important ways. The end of the war left European women facing notably greater social disorder. Some had lost husbands, and others found that men returning from war and prison camps were strangers. Food was in short supply, and the housing stock was reduced by bombing. Established notions of domesticity, epitomized for example in France by the term *femme au foyer* ("woman in the home"), placed on women the special responsibility for family care, especially during the difficult early postwar period.

With that challenge surmounted, women encountered a new emphasis on making housework efficient, even scientific, a trend encouraged by experts, classes, and how-to manuals. By the 1950s the appearance of domestic appliances associated with the emerging postwar consumer trends had begun to make housework easier. Leading the way were refrigerators, vacuum cleaners, and above all semi-automatic washing machines. So eager were women for mechanical relief from the drudgery of washing that working-class women who could not afford their own pooled their funds to purchase one for shared use.

In the context of rising postwar prosperity European women moved into the workplace, but on nothing like the scale seen in the United States. The rise in the proportion of women working outside the home was modest to nil on the continent and closer to U.S. percentages in Britain (see Table 5.2.). Women in the workplace ran up against the same barriers of lower pay, restricted opportunity, lack of job security, and discrimination as those faced by their American sisters.

Feminism in Europe exploded on the scene much as it had in the United States. By the late 1960s and early 1970s European feminists were espousing a diverse range of causes and ideologies. One strain had ties to the American movement for equal rights. It was influenced by *The Second Sex,* published in 1949 by the pioneer French feminist Simone de Beauvoir. She had argued that women's identity was a social construct that stood in the way of full equality with men. It was also influenced by Friedan's *Feminine Mystique.* Middle-class women read in their translations of Friedan about suburban U.S. women with a shock of recognition. "I saw them every day. They were my neighbors."[19] European feminists echoed the demands laid down by NOW in 1966 for greater equality as well as for control of reproductive rights. For example, women in France had not gotten the vote until 1944, and thereafter they made slow headway in expanding formal equality from politics to such matters of family law as control of property, contraception, and divorce. Everywhere abortion remained highly controversial. With abortion largely illegal, demands for access to contraceptive devices inten-

TABLE 5.2 Percentage of Women in the Developed-World Workforce, 1950–1980					
	1950	1960	1970	1980	Total Change
United States	37.2	42.6	48.9	59.1	21.9
Britain	40.7	46.1	50.5	58.2	17.5
West Germany	44.3	49.2	48.1	49.2	4.9
France	49.5	46.4	48.2	52.6	3.1
Italy	32.0	37.1	29.6	32.0	0.0
Japan	57.6	60.0	55.3	51.6	−6.0

This table reveals that the highest increases occurred in the Anglo-American economies and that changes on the European continent and in Japan were distinctly more modest. Definitions of "work" vary from one study to another and thus strikingly different data emerge. However, the general variation from country to country noted here is reflected in all the studies.[20]

sified throughout the late 1950s and 1960s. Opponents of the birth control pill responded that legalization would take from men "the proud consciousness of their virility" and make women "no more than objects of sterile voluptuousness."[21] Not until 1967 did the French Parliament accommodate women's demands, and even then legalization was qualified. West Germany adopted such a measure in 1961, but the Italian government did not act until 1971.

However, in broad terms, activist European women put less stress on equality and instead gave higher priority to transforming society in a way that was consistent with what they saw as the special concerns and role of women. This European "social feminism" reflected the conviction that women were not essentially the same as men and that it was a mistake to pursue demands for identical support and opportunities. To the contrary, women had interests to advance that were in critical respects different because women were fundamentally different from men in psychology and in physiology—and, by extension, in the indispensable reproductive role they played as the bearers and nurturers of children. A society cut to the measure of men ill served women and harmed the overall interests of society, they claimed. This social feminist stress on gender difference rather than simply equality was especially strong in Italy and France.

Social feminism appealed across a broad political spectrum. The Catholic center and right favored women staying at home and supported a family allowance to make this economically possible. The Left, on the other hand, took the view that women needed help in managing both work and home and thus embraced such programs as nationally funded daycare facilities, parental leave, reduced working days, and recasting of welfare programs to make them more responsive to the needs of mothers. Going a step further, to ensure that women had a voice in devising and implementing these programs, political parties and labor unions on the Left were strongly committed to getting women into elected and appointed public office. As a result, women's participation in political life in most European countries far exceeded the U.S. level. By the 1990s women in Scandinavia held legislative seats at rates six or seven times that in the United States, while in Austria, Germany, the Netherlands, Italy, and Spain it was anywhere from two to five times higher. From their position of influence within the political process, women activists worked for programs that supported mothers and children.

Feminism in Japan. If the American feminist movement bore some resemblance to that in Europe, it was largely irrelevant to developments in Japan. Postwar prosperity had seemed to set the stage for women moving into the workforce and then asserting a claim to greater opportunity and state support. As the economy recovered, consumer spending jumped. With household appliances to pay off, perhaps the first small car to buy, the children's college education to cover, and even a small apartment to purchase, Japanese women seemed bound toward new economic and social roles. But in fact changes came slowly and remained limited as Japanese women operated within rules that looked a lot like their own version of the "feminine mystique." The activism that did develop more resembled European social feminism than the individualistic and egalitarian concerns of Friedan and NOW.

Most Japanese understood the role of women in terms of "good wife, wise mother." This gender paradigm had emerged at the end of the nineteenth century and, with variations, survived the upheaval of early twentieth-century modernization and the Pacific War. In the postwar era it enjoyed the backing of politicians in the dominant Liberal Democratic Party, government bureaucrats, and employers. The "good wife, wise mother" ideology held that women had a role in the home that was separate but complementary with the working, public role of men. Women followed their own educational track. They usually attended junior colleges rather than the four-year institutions designed for men. There they took courses that prepared them for running the household (including managing the family budget) and raising children. Once out of school, single women might work fulltime; but once married—as all women were expected to do—family duties became a fulltime job. In the ideal "three-generation household," there were children to bear and raise and a husband to support, but also aging parents or in-laws to care for.

This governing gender ideology demonstrated its power by withstanding two challenges in the 1960s and 1970s. The first of these was a labor shortage that began in the early 1960s, creating a demand for married women to return to work. Whereas previously young, single women predominated in the workforce, older, married women now came to account for the majority of female employment. Wives were going back to work because they were having fewer children and living longer. In fact, women's life expectancy rose by nearly thirty-two years between 1950 and 1987.

Despite the changing presence of women in the workforce, they remained economically marginal. The older women came back to work as part-timers, making it possible for women to contribute to the national economy and raise family income while still attending to their domestic duties. State policies endorsed the return of older women to work on those terms, and employers welcomed the infusion of new labor into low-paying positions. Because they had no job security, older women provided employers with a welcome bit of labor force flexibility. They could be added to boost production and laid off during slack time. In contrast to fulltime male workers, firing female part-timers did not deprive the family of its main source of income, create social instability, or stir up labor unrest.

The governing gender ideology also demonstrated its power by withstanding the claims of rights-based feminism that dominated in the United States and was influential in Europe. Feminist organizations sprang to life in Japan as they had elsewhere during the 1960s and early 1970s. Activists most often came out of campus-based groups and the anti–Vietnam War protest, gathered for the first women's liberation conference in 1971, read Friedan's *Feminine Mystique* (translated in 1971), and followed developments in the United States. But the membership of these organizations remained small, and their initial focus on consciousness-raising had limited public appeal. Indeed, a sign carried in a 1970 march asking "Mother, is marriage really bliss?"[22] seemed to strike at the family as the bedrock of Japanese society and to commit the heresy of setting the rights of the individual above the needs of the group. By the mid-1970s women's groups had broadened their appeal by shifting attention to the reform of social institutions and government policy so that women would have more choices in schools, in the workplace, and in marriage.

Meanwhile, Japanese women remained politically reticent. The constitution drafted and imposed by the American occupiers had included sweeping guarantees of equal rights, including for the first time the right for women to vote. However, when interviewed on the subject of voting, women claimed that they cast their ballots not because they prized the right but because it was a new social expectation that they had to live up to. Few women ran for political office or held positions of authority within the influential state bureaucracy. Where women did protest, they acted not as advocates for their own interests but as defenders of the family and thus more in line with social feminist impulses. They demanded protection of consumers and the environment, and they sharply criticized the nuclear arms race, the presence of U.S. nuclear forces on Japanese soil, and steps toward remilitarization by their own country. Precisely because all these issues had a bearing on the health of their children and the safety of their families, women's organizations raised their voices and took to the streets.

Critics of Global Economic Inequalities

While some within the developed world began to fret over the pollution created by an economy of abundance and over constraints placed on women within that economy, critics in the developing world were posing their own challenges to the economic regime. These critics argued that the rules laid down by the United States and Britain at Bretton Woods benefited wealthy countries at the expense of the poor. In particular those rules, they complained, discouraged far-reaching state planning and economic intervention best suited to meeting the urgent development needs of the third world. Moreover, those rules prescribed a regimen of free foreign trade and free foreign investment calculated to help the developed world while in fact subjecting third-world economies to foreign control.

These views had their roots in Europe. There, countries—notably Germany and Italy during the interwar years—had built tariff walls around their economies. Behind this protective barrier the state had sought to coordinate domestic labor and capital and harness them to national goals. This pattern of development crossed the Atlantic to Latin American states headed by elites with close cultural and economic ties to Europe, dominated policy in key economies during the interwar years, and persisted well into the post-1945 period. This model and the charges its proponents lodged against free trade reverberated powerfully in third-world countries. But the influence of this Latin American development model was diffuse. By the time third-world countries began emerging in large numbers from colonialism in the 1960s, Latin Americans were reassessing their protectionist policies, while many leaders among the newly independent states in places as diverse as Ghana, Cuba, and Egypt (as we will see in Chapter 6) rejected the relative moderation of the Latin American model in favor of state socialism modeled on either the Chinese or the Soviet variant.

Structuralism and Import Substitution in Latin America. In the late 1940s, the critics of unbalanced development had formulated a coherent alternative to the Anglo-American model. Their base was the Economic Commission for Latin America created by the United Nations in 1948 and located in Santiago, Chile. The head of the Commission and the best known of these early critics was the Argentine economist Raúl Prebisch. He and his associates came to be known as "structuralist" for their argument that economic inequality and distorted development was an inherent, structural feature of the global system of exchange.

Experience running his country's central bank from the mid-1930s had led Prebisch to question the model of export-led growth long dominant within his own country. This talented, original thinker came to the conclusion that the participants in the free trade regime had unequal power. The central economies that manufactured industrial goods, notably Britain and the United States, were few in number and so could control the price of their exports. Moreover, as technology reduced production costs, they could sustain their old prices, thus increasing their profit. Agricultural producers on the periphery of the international economy such as farmers in his native Argentina were disadvantaged by this system. They were many, so competition among them drove down prices for their exports at the same time that industrial imports remained expensive. The growing postwar prominence of the United States was likely, Prebisch predicted, to accentuate this plight of the peripheral economies because the United States had its own highly developed agriculture and had little use for imported agricultural goods.

These unequal terms of trade were deeply damaging, the structuralists contended. They drained wealth from struggling third-world countries to already rich and developed economies. Thanks to accumulating capital, the central economies were able to invest in new, more advanced forms of production while maintaining their dominance over their third-world trading partners. Not only did peripheral economies remain poor and technologically laggard, but they also suffered an internal division between an outward-looking export sector and a large, backward, and stagnant subsistence agricultural sector. The latter was burdened by surplus labor that kept wages down, stifling the growth of the local economy. To increase international trade, as the United States and others wanted, would only intensify international economic inequalities and deepen the internal divisions within third-world economies.

To escape these fundamental structural constraints, Prebisch recommended that those economies embark on a program of "import substitution"—replacing the industrial imports coming from the advanced economies with homegrown industry. He assigned the state a prominent role as the promoter and protector of domestic industry. The state might impose tariffs on industrial imports to secure infant industries against foreign competition and create the domestic investment and demand for their products that would ensure their steady maturation. The state might also take over pivotal industrial enterprises as well as finance and communications and promote unionization to ensure a fair distribution of the benefits of industrial growth.

Import substitution would, in Prebisch's view, bring a long list of benefits. It would reduce dependence on high-priced imports and pressure to export low-value agricultural products to pay for those imports. It would raise domestic employment and income and thereby create a growing domestic market for continuing industrial development. It would end the stagnation that plagued much of the traditional economy, integrate the scattered pieces of the national economy, and improve popular welfare. In the long run, diversifying economic activity seemed the best way to ensure self-sustaining growth and a degree of insulation from the swings in international markets and from the pressures that major economies were sure to apply to advance their own interests.

Writing in the late 1940s, Prebisch and his colleagues provided the rationale for an approach that was already well established in practice. The Depression and World War II had in effect imposed an experiment in import substitution on such leading Latin American economies as Brazil, Mexico, Argentina, and Chile. (See Map 6.1.) The Depression had caused a drastic drop in international demand for their agricultural exports, and along with lower foreign earnings went difficulties in paying for industrial imports. The problem continued with the outbreak of World War II. As the economies of the belligerents turned to military production, they sharply curtailed the export of manufactured goods, creating shortages abroad. With international demand for Latin American raw materials high during the war and during the early stage of postwar reconstruction, late industrializers had a favorable environment for experimenting with new development strategies.

The major economies of Latin America responded to these developments in an ad hoc fashion. With finished goods now difficult to buy abroad, established domestic industries expanded and new industries started up. Then, in the early 1940s, authoritarian governments in Argentina, Chile, Brazil, and Mexico began intervening to further encourage the growth of the advanced industrial sector. These governments set up tariffs and other protections against foreign competition, invested in infrastructure, and nationalized key industrial sectors (steel in Brazil and Chile, and oil in Argentina and Mexico). These initiatives succeeded. Latin American economies began using more of their raw materials at home rather than exporting them. This strategy accelerated the pace of job creation and pushed annual growth rates higher.

With these successes to point to, by the 1950s structuralist thinking had become the new orthodoxy in Latin America and gained a wide following outside the region—in newly independent countries inclined to look to the state as the prime agent of rapid economic development. As early as 1947 during negotiations in Havana over the rules to govern international trade, delegations from Latin America as well as newly independent India sought to define national sovereignty to include such forms of state economic intervention as nationalization of foreign holdings and protection of nascent industries against imports. These mavericks also pressed developed countries to open their markets more fully to exports from poorer countries.

The third world's call for greater latitude in development policy and assistance from the developed world would remain a refrain throughout the Cold War. It would attract the non–aligned movement composed mainly of newly independent states in the 1950s and 1960s. In 1964 newly independent countries, known collectively as the Group of 77, organized to press for reforms of an international economic system tilted toward the interests of the developed countries and thus perpetuating the influence of the old colonial powers. They demanded nothing less than a redistribution of the world's wealth.

Modernization versus Dependency. Not surprisingly, neither Raúl Prebisch's views nor the state-sponsored programs of industrialization implemented in Latin America and elsewhere in the third world found favor in Washington. U.S. leaders complained that inward-looking economies burdened by state intervention ill served the interests of third-world peoples. President Harry S. Truman reflected the free market orthodoxy when he assigned private capital the leading role in creating prosperity. If Latin Americans wanted to attract investment from abroad, hold accumulated wealth at home, and maintain stability against leftist or populist agitation, they had to free their economies and respect the rights of private property. American-style capitalism was not just a way to a better life; its advance locked countries into the U.S. orbit amid the Cold War struggle.

American academics at Harvard and MIT reinforced this U.S. orthodoxy. These proponents of what would become known as modernization theory argued that the main task for developing countries was to make the transition from "traditional," subsistence economies to ones that were "modern" (meaning technologically intensive and industrial), and that to get there required a free market, supplemented by U.S. economic aid and advice. Together, free market policies and outside assistance would lead developing countries quickly along an economic path that the developed economies had already taken. As one of the leading writers on modernization explained, "What had happened in Europe and North America in the 19th and early 20th centuries was now, more or less, about to happen in Latin America, Asia, and Africa. The progress promised by the [West's] enlightenment...now beckoned the Third World newly freed from colonialism and exploitation, and straining against its own parochialisms."[23] The practical goal of modernization U.S.-style was to head off the appeal of communism by promoting material progress and political stability. Notions of proper economic development thus closely dovetailed with the U.S. policy of containment. Modernization theory helped legitimate a redirection of a growing proportion of U.S. development assistance away from a recovering Europe during the late 1950s. Soon virtually all of it was going to the third world.

By the early 1960s structuralism was facing criticism within Latin America as well. Import-substitution programs had faltered over the previous decade. Leading economies had been hurt by a decline in agricultural demand and by the onset of inflation. Latin American economists with a free market preference went on the attack, arguing that their countries should follow the U.S. advice and rejoin the international economy. Export-import was the best path to prosperity, in their view.

Economists with roots in the structuralist school resisted the swing back to free trade. They argued that the structural policies of the 1950s had gotten into trouble not because they were wrong but because the sources of unbalanced development in Latin America were more profound than previously appreciated. Prebisch noticed growing income disparities within Mexico, Brazil, and Argentina, where the wealthy spent their money on imported luxury goods rather than on productive investment, while popular demand for domestic products was weak. By 1963 he was calling for internal social reforms (including land and income redistribution to close the wealth gap), controls on non-essential imports, and measures to stimulate demand for domestically produced goods. Prebisch was also worried by the neglect of investment in education needed to train a skilled workforce and by the inefficiencies that had developed within Latin America's protected industries.

Latin American scholars elaborated on these insights, further shifting the focus from the structural inequalities inherent in free trade to the social and economic damage such trade inflicted on dependent countries. An increasingly hostile political environment in the region gave an edge to their analysis. Repressive military regimes took power in Brazil in 1964 and for the second time in Argentina in 1966. They both sought close ties with the United States. The U.S. government itself was less tolerant of diversity within the hemisphere, especially after the Cuban revolution (see Chapter 6). The Johnson administration shifted away from the reform-minded Alliance for Progress initiated by President Kennedy and in 1965 invaded the Dominican Republic to arrest perceived communist inroads. The Cuban revolution that was causing such alarm in Washington was one of the few bright spots from the perspective of those searching for independent paths to economic development.

These scholars who had moved beyond import substitution came to be known as the dependency school. In their view, the problem confronting the third world was the capacity of advanced economies to create a class of dependent collaborators within peripheral economies. These collaborators helped multinational corporations exploit the labor and resources of their country, and for that assistance they were richly rewarded and, where necessary, protected against any internal threat to their dominant economic position as landlords growing export crops and employing large numbers of low-paid workers in plantation agriculture. Dependency scholars were in effect charging that the landed elites functioned as instruments of the global economy. Though long a part of the local scene, they were indifferent to the plight of the people around them and were primarily oriented overseas, where they not only sent their children to school but also invested much of their wealth. By creating and defending inequalities in the social and political life of their countries, these capitalist collaborators sparked popular discontent as well as created rigidities that impeded long-term economic development. Conditions in Central American countries such as Guatemala corresponded closely to this dependency interpretation (see Chapter 6).

The dependency school took direct issue with U.S. economic orthodoxy. In their estimate North American ideas about modernization were ethnocentric.

Not all countries were like the United States and not all countries would travel the same development path. In fact, notions of modernization in the hands of American academics and policy pundits seemed suspiciously like a rationalization of U.S. dominance within the hemisphere. Latin American and other countries around the world that would not fall into line and allow favorable access to their raw materials and markets faced retaliation. Washington would block investment and aid, impose trade sanctions, and as a last resort overthrow offending regimes by subversion or outright invasion.

By the late 1960s and 1970s dependency ideas were gaining wide currency on the Left in Latin America and abroad. But they never won the official acceptance that structuralism had earlier enjoyed. Though Prebisch had had an affinity for dependency analysis, he never become a convert, and his import-substitution ideas still exercised considerable mainstream influence. Latin American governments during the 1960s and 1970s combined to various degrees import substitution with international integration financed by foreign investments and facilitated by multinational corporations.

Argentina offers the clearest and earliest example of this return to the international free market. The retreat from import substitution had begun in the mid-1950s. Juan Perón, the dominant political figure there during the mid-1940s, had at first favored state-sponsored industrialization and had catered to the working class mobilized politically in state-controlled unions. He had nationalized such key sectors as railroads, banks, insurance, and shipping. He had created a state agency to market the country's major exports and to direct domestic investments. But after the economy began slowing in 1952, Perón took a friendlier attitude toward foreign investors. After the military seized power in 1955, it continued the trend toward a more free market strategy, and following a second military coup in 1966 the government attacked unions, froze wages, privatized public companies, and courted foreign investors. Popular resentment in turn spawned growing resistance from the Left, including urban guerrilla movements. In response, the military resorted to a vicious campaign of repression. Violence at home combined with defeat at the hands of the British in 1982 in a struggle over the Falkland Islands finally discredited military rule. A new civilian government had to shoulder heavy debts that left no choice but to accept continued international integration as the price of financial rescue from the international banking community.

In Chile, the retreat from activist state involvement in the economy came later, but it came suddenly and violently. The socialist government of Salvador Allende Gossens, elected in 1970, had sought to push through long-stalled social and economic reforms. With divisions within the country deepening and the Nixon administration in the United States pressing for a coup, the military seized power in 1973. It quickly repudiated the course of heavy state intervention promoted by Allende and his predecessors, and it insisted on a rapid and thorough shift to free markets and integration into the international economy. That shift would define Chile's policy even after the military returned to the barracks in the late 1980s.

In Brazil, import substitution survived despite growing emphasis on international economic integration. The dictator Getúlio Vargas, who had dominated the political scene from the 1930s until his suicide in 1954, had sustained a strategy of heavy state involvement. Successor governments hewed to that popular course while trying to address the problem of concentrated landholdings in the rural sector. Resentful landed families resisted those reforms, and in 1964 the military sided with them, seized power, and dramatically altered economic policy. It cut state spending and encouraged an import-export economy. The strategy at first produced rapid growth. But in 1974, under pressure from a flagging global economy, the military made another dramatic shift—back to import substitution, higher government spending, and greater state involvement in the industrial sector. That policy would soon fall victim to a debt crisis similar to the one that constrained the Argentines. In Brazil as in Argentina, by the early 1980s the military was ready to give up power, and leave to civilians the burden of managing an economy now in crisis.

Mexico proved the most consistent practitioner of internal industrialization and protection against foreign goods and capital. This consistency was the product of the governing party's continued iron grip on political power and of the popularity of economic measures that produced a growth rate in the 6 to 8 percent range from the 1950s to the mid-1970s. During the latter part of this period, a major oil boom contributed significantly to Mexico's success, and industry and the service sector grew dramatically. But as with Argentina and Brazil, financial crisis would grip Mexico in the 1980s. The result was a long and at times painful retreat from the protectionism that had helped produce industrialization and prosperity. Mexico embraced a course that would lead to economic integration with its neighbors to the north.

CONCLUSION

The success of the international economy in the 1950s and 1960s had a paradoxical quality for Americans. That period marked the high point of their country's power and influence. Just as the United States led the anti-communist coalition of states that it had formed after World War II, so too did it preside over a global economy shaped to its preferences and lavish in its rewards to its citizens. Americans enjoyed a golden age of prosperity during which many came to see the promise of American life more in terms of an ever-rising level of material abundance than the prosecution of the global anti-communist struggle. The nuclear crisis over Cuba and the growing costs and disruption occasioned by the Vietnam War drove home the point that the fundamental American international and domestic preoccupations were not necessarily compatible. Basic economic weaknesses such as low savings rates, as well as the recovery of other developed economies, intensified the threat to American competitiveness and influence and began to diminish the relative power of the United States, whose financial resources and markets had contributed significantly to its allies' recovery in the first place. Increasingly, Washington had to take into account the views of its once junior partners across the Atlantic and Pacific. Americans were on the brink of a dispiriting period when both the promise of abundance at home and the proud role of freedom's defender abroad would fall into question.

Western Europeans and Japanese had acquired the power to alter the international landscape because each had crafted in the early postwar period an effective economic strategy suited to their particular political and cultural preferences. Their choices—welfare capitalism in one case and guided capitalism in the other—paid handsome dividends: a period of sustained prosperity and stability without equal in the history of either. Income levels rapidly rising toward that of the United States translated into a flourishing lifestyle, including elements that were becoming more familiar around the globe. In western Europe, with these economic successes came greater economic integration. The EC would prove a herald of more ambitious plans to come to fruition toward century's end. The Japanese economic miracle ratified another kind of integration—a powerful establishment consisting of corporate leaders, government bureaucrats, and prominent politicians working closely to ensure Japanese international competitiveness and domestic prosperity.

In some quarters, the very prosperity of the 1950s and 1960s encouraged critical reflections on the flaws of the dominant system of production. Critics decried its tendency to privilege men, wealthy countries, and short-term gain over long-term welfare. Those critics such as some Western feminists asking for a share of the growing economic pie were relatively easy to accommodate, but those such as environmentalists and advocates for the third world calling for deep-seated, structural changes posed an unsettling and less easily answered challenge. Those questioning a new world of abundance that damaged the environment, made half the population second-class citizens, and distributed its benefits unevenly so that the rich became richer and the poor poorer would continue to speak out, intensifying concerns about flaws in what was to become an increasingly globalized economic system.

RECOMMENDED RESOURCES

The U.S. Golden Age
For basic treatments encompassing the 1950s and 1960s, see the recommendations at the end of Chapter 2.

A Revitalized Western Europe
General works: Aside from the items cited in Chapter 2, see Alan S. Milward with the assistance of George Brennan and Federico Romero, *The European Rescue of the Nation-State* (2nd ed., 2000), and Philip H. Gordon and Sophie Meunier, *The French Challenge: Adapting to Globalization* (2001), both of which make an important argument about postwar state survival and economic culture. John McCormick, *Understanding the European Union: A Concise Introduction* (2nd ed., 2002), provides an overview of the origins of regional integration and the resulting institutions and policies. On **Fiat,** see Alan Friedman, *Agnelli and the Network of Italian Power* (1988).

The Japanese Revival

For **general insights,** see Shigeto Tsuru, *Japan's Capitalism: Creative Defeat and Beyond* (1993), which is especially good on the critical contributions of the Japanese government to economic growth, and Yutaka Kōsai, "The Postwar Japanese Economy, 1945–1973" (trans. Andrew Goble), in *The Cambridge History of Japan,* vol. 6: *The Twentieth Century,* ed. Peter Duus (1988). Laura K. Silverman, ed., *Bringing Home the Sushi: An Inside Look at Japanese Business through Japanese Comics* (1995), uses an extremely popular adult genre to convey a sense of the white-collar world of the "salary man." The personalities and innovation that defined **Sony** come across in John Nathan, *Sony: The Private Life* (1999), and Akio Morita with Edwin M. Reingold and Mitsuko Shimomura, *Made in Japan: Akio Morita and Sony* (1986).

The Emergence of Environmentalism

For **overviews,** see J. R. McNeill, *Something New under the Sun: An Environmental History of the Twentieth-Century World* (2000), especially strong in highlighting a period of unprecedented change, mostly for the worse; and John McCormick, *Reclaiming Paradise: The Global Environmental Movement* (1989). For **developments in the United States:** Kirkpatrick Sale, *The Green Revolution: The American Environmental Movement, 1962–1992* (1993), an overview written from the perspective of an environmental activist; and Benjamin Kline, *First along the River: A Brief History of the U.S. Environmental Movement* (2nd ed., 2000), a compact and clear treatment of the last half-century of environmental concerns in the context of thinking about nature going back to the first settlements. On **Rachel Carson,** see Mary A. McCay, *Rachel Carson* (1993), for a compact, informative biography, but also Linda Lear, *Rachel Carson: Witness for Nature* (1997). "Rachel Carson's Silent Spring" (written and prod. Neil Goodwin; 1993; 57 min.) brings to life an influential writer and her path-breaking book.

The Rise of Feminism

Betty Friedan, *Life So Far* (2000), recounts a colorful personal story. Joanne Meyerowitz, ed., *Not June Cleaver: Women and Gender in Postwar America, 1945–1960* (1994), and Amy Swerdlow, *Women Strike for Peace: Traditional Motherhood and Radical Politics in the 1960s* (1993), help set in context Friedan and the feminist revolution launched in the 1960s. For a revealing overview of developments in one key country, see Claire Duchen, *Women's Rights and Women's Lives in France, 1944–1968* (1994), and her *Feminism in France: From May '68 to Mitterand* (1986). Karen Offen, "Defining Feminism: A Comparative Historical Perspective," *Signs* 14 (Autumn 1988): 119–57, and responses in 15 (Autumn 1989): 195–209, consider the differences between the concerns of activist women in the United States and Europe. *Postwar Japan as History* (1993), edited by Andrew Gordon, contains excellent overviews on Japanese women by Kathleen S. Uno and by Sandra Buckley.

The Critics of Global Inequality

Cristóbal Kay, *Latin American Theories of Development and Underdevelopment* (1989), and Joseph L. Love, "Economic Ideas and Ideologies in Latin America since 1930," in *The Cambridge History of Latin America,* ed. Leslie Bethell, vol. 6, pt. 1 (1994), chap. 7, provide thoughtful introductions. The boldest and most accessible statement of the dependency position can be found in *Capitalism and Underdevelopment in Latin America* (1967) by the German-born and U.S.-educated André Gunder Frank. Ariel Dorfman and Armand Mattelert, *How to Read Donald Duck: Imperialist Ideology in the Disney Comic,* trans. David Kunzle (1975), first published in Chile in 1971, graphically develops the argument for thinking about dependency in cultural as well as economic terms.

CHAPTER 6

THIRD-WORLD HOPES AT HIGH TIDE

By the 1960s the third world had reached the flood tide of change. Demands for decolonization were overwhelming the old colonial powers. At the same time, nominally independent states had begun to assert their right to chart an autonomous course free of foreign interference. Those leading this assault on the old order shared a vision of national liberation and domestic renovation. They saw independence not just as a formal condition easily met once the offending foreigners decamped but rather as one step toward sweeping internal changes. They sought economic autonomy and development. They wanted to replace a national psychology of dependence with one of pride. They aimed to heal social divisions created by long-term foreign influence and to fashion programs with popular appeal. They even looked beyond their borders, where they hoped to join with like-minded states in constituting an international community friendly to a new order of things. In this heady time, it was easy to believe that more and more people around the world would embrace the Marxist critique of capitalism and take the socialist model of development as their own.

This radical impulse played out in four distinct regions. By looking at each in turn we can see how that general impulse varied in its origins and consequences and how it intersected in different ways with the Cold War while setting bounds on the U.S.-sponsored, market-oriented international economy. We begin by returning to the two countries whose revolutions foreshadowed the growing ferment of the 1950s and 1960s. Revolutions in East Asia—in China and in Vietnam—entered a new stage, and through their strength and persistence they became as much a source of inspiration to others in the third world as they were a cause for alarm in Washington. We then turn to the two regions that began to stir for the first time in the 1950s—the Caribbean and sub-Saharan Africa—and look closely at the cases of Guatemala, Cuba, and Ghana. Finally, we turn to the Middle East and North Africa, where radicals in Iran, Egypt, and Algeria committed to combating Western influence and renovating indigenous institutions made dramatic advances. Regardless of the differences among these cases, all reveal the sharp discontents with the old order taking shape in the third world and now translating into a simultaneous assault on the impediments to fundamental change both domestically and internationally. In each case calls for patience and moderation went out of season while bold plans flourished.

REVOLUTIONARY TRAJECTORIES IN EAST ASIA

China and Vietnam had both embarked on a revolutionary path guided by an attachment to centralized political power. (See Chapter 3.) However, during the 1950s their courses diverged. After taking power in 1949, Mao Zedong's Communists set to work consolidating political control, redefining China's relationship with the superpowers, restoring its hold over border regions, and reviving its economy. With this ambitious program largely completed, in the mid-1950s Mao began to indulge utopian notions of fundamentally transforming Chinese society. As a result an aging, stubborn leader would plunge China into chaos and precipitate a basic shift in China's development path. Ho Chi Minh was by contrast still mired in the struggle to rid Vietnam's "sacred soil" of the foreign presence. No sooner had his forces defeated the French than the Americans stepped in. After trying to limit U.S. involvement throughout the late 1950s and early 1960s, Vietnamese Communists finally took up the challenge of destroying U.S. resolve just as they had with the French between 1946 and 1954. Radical domestic programs had to take a backseat during this exhausting battle to reunite the country.

The Maoist Experiment in China

In the course of the 1950s the Communist leaders of the People's Republic of China (PRC) came increasingly to disagree over how to translate their general vision of building a "new socialist China" into concrete measures. The majority of Mao's senior colleagues favored strong central bureaucratic control and carefully planned economic development. A poor China desperately needed to build on its most advanced sectors—the cities and the more industrialized coastal provinces. Mao's colleagues' vision included using the talents of the bourgeoisie—the better-off and educated people living in cities—and foreign trade opportunities to restore the economy and stimulate growth. Mao's colleagues preferred to give more scope for incentives for productive workers and the work units to which all Chinese were assigned, and hence they were ready to tolerate greater inequalities among social groups as well as regions. In their estimate, mass rallies and revolutionary exhortations distracted from this main task of creating the economic base essential to realizing socialism.

   On the other side, Mao as the national leader and voice of the revolution argued for a strongly populist, revolutionary strategy. He wanted to maintain the equality, personal sacrifice, and popular mobilization that had marked the party's pre-1949 period of struggle. Mao was haunted by the fear that China's revolutionary spirit would die away and remnants of the old society would reappear. He saw the major danger coming from bureaucrats and technical experts and from the vestiges of the bourgeois class, which seemed to him to have almost magical powers of regeneration. In Mao's view, periodic campaigns against state and party officials and "the intellectuals" (by which Mao meant the educated and politically engaged among the middle class) were needed to prevent the rise of a new, privileged class. In thus setting his sights on continuously rejuvenating the party's and the people's revolutionary commitment, Mao looked to the rural poor and educated youth as his most reliable allies.

Tension at the top developed as Mao increasingly insisted on following his own insights and judgments and began to intervene in daily policymaking, thereby betraying the principle of collective decision-making. In 1950 he overruled his colleagues who questioned the wisdom of confronting a nuclear-armed United States in Korea. Mao again acted on his own in 1952 when he abandoned party plans to stress the multi-class alliance that had helped win the civil war and that the party leadership had deemed important to economic development. This shift removed the bourgeoisie from the revolutionary coalition. In May 1953 Mao wrested from his colleagues the right of ultimate approval of all documents sent out from the party center. At about the same time he resolved to push peasants toward fully collectivized agriculture. By 1955–1956 peasants had handed over their private land, tools, and farm animals to shared enterprises that paid them in relation to their labor contribution measured in work points. Only the land on which their houses stood remained private.

In pursuing this path Mao acted on his faith that tapping the spontaneous energy and socialist instincts of the peasantry would unleash new productive forces in the countryside. His skeptical colleagues objected to his insistence on haste and on a single policy applied to China's diverse agricultural conditions. This "adventurism," they warned, had China racing toward socialism faster than the country's still short economic legs could carry it. Mao dismissed these objections for their excessive caution. "Some of our comrades are tottering along like a woman with bound feet, always complaining that others are going too fast."[1]

The Great Leap Forward. By the late 1950s Mao's discontents had reached a boiling point. He blamed an ossifying and privileged party and state bureaucracy for favoring urban intellectuals and the experts, while the rural poor lagged ever farther behind. The 1956 upheavals in Poland and Hungary strengthened his fear that Communist parties could lose touch with the people. Mao was also turning against the Soviet model of economic development, formally copied in 1953 with the PRC's first five-year plan and backed with Soviet aid and advisors. Instead of slavishly copying the Soviets by nationalizing private enterprise, building up state-controlled heavy industry, and promoting technical expertise, Mao wanted a distinctly Chinese model of development.

Once aroused, Mao took the offensive. In 1957 he invited intellectuals to criticize Chinese Communist Party (CCP) errors in what he described as letting "a hundred schools of thought contend, a hundred flowers bloom." But rather than simply question CCP methods, some among the educated began to question the party's very legitimacy. This sharp response to the "Hundred Flowers" campaign convinced Mao that his revolution was in even greater danger than he had thought. He attacked intellectuals suspected of "rightist" views in what became a long, dark period for many educated Chinese.

In 1958 Mao took an even bolder step by launching the Great Leap Forward, a visionary economic plan for accelerating China's industrial production. He ordered a still higher, communal form of organization in the countryside with newly formed "people's communes" containing on the average 20–25,000 peasant families. Peasants now shifted to shared living, eating, and childcare arrangements as well as production responsibilities and resources. They were to start up small-scale steel making as a demonstration of an alternative to the Soviet model of centralized, large-scale industrial production. With the Great Leap Forward, Mao sought to launch the peasantry into a world of previously unimagined abundance. He argued that rapid socialist development could occur only if "the boundless creative powers" of the masses and their "inexhaustible enthusiasm for socialism" were brought into play.[2] Properly led and inspired, the "poor and blank" could become the main builders of his new society. Within fifteen years a mobilized people could catch up with the West, while the communes with their rigorously egalitarian rules would create a classless society and thus take China to communism even before the Soviet Union.

At first hailed as a magnificent success, Mao's experiment ended disastrously. The Great Leap disrupted planting and harvesting. Flood and drought compounded the crisis. Worst of all was distorted information reaching leaders at the top. Lower-level officials under heavy pressure to meet targets perpetrated various frauds on their superiors to convince them misguided policies were actually working. They passed off specially prepared model plots as typical, and they reported soaring production at a time when it in fact was in free fall. Belatedly Beijing realized that it faced a calamitous situation. Between 1959 and 1961 an estimated twenty million people died as a result of starvation or hunger-related disease. It was perhaps the greatest human disaster in Chinese history or in the annals of a century no stranger to disaster. When faced in 1959 with criticism of his costly economic experiment, Mao confessed, "I am a complete outsider when it comes to economic construction, and I understand nothing about industrial planning."[3] A chastened Mao retreated into a less active policy role between 1960 and 1962, leaving his chief lieutenants—Liu Shaoqi, Deng Xiaoping, and Zhou Enlai—to implement more flexible policies to restore production while preserving collectivization itself.

Mao was by this point deeply worried about the Soviet Union, and his doubts ultimately destroyed the unity of the socialist bloc. He saw the Soviets undergoing a kind of corruption at home as their Communist Party became a new privileged class. This corruption set in doubt Soviet credentials as leader of the bloc and the reliability of Soviet support for China. Mao had been unhappy with Khrushchev's unilateral denunciation of Stalin, a figure as important to the international communist movement as to the Soviet Union. Mao had resented the Soviet characterization of his Great Leap plans as hare-brained and Moscow's hesitation over supplying China with nuclear technology. He had profoundly disagreed with Khrushchev's call for peaceful coexistence with the United States and chided the Soviets for not keeping up with China's support for national liberation movements in Asia, Africa, and Latin America. In Mao's view, while the masses around the world were putting imperialism on the defensive, the leaders of the Soviet party were cuddling up to the Americans. Mounting Sino-Soviet tensions resulted in a sudden cutoff of Soviet aid in 1960, and by 1963 the split between the two heavyweights of the socialist bloc had become irreconcilable. China's test of its first atomic bomb in 1964 added to Beijing's confidence and Moscow's fears.

The Cultural Revolution. The 'Great Proletarian Cultural Revolution marked Mao's second major attempt to promote a distinct, Chinese revolutionary way. Mao still followed an egalitarian vision—of reducing the differences between manual and mental labor, between peasants and workers, between agriculture and industry. His party colleagues had for the most part stayed on the wrong side of these issues. The exceptions were Lin Biao (the minister of defense) and Jiang Qing, a former actress who had become Mao's wife in 1938. With them behind him, he began making a familiar set of charges: A bureaucratic, bourgeois, "revisionist" spirit infected his party just as it had the Soviet's; and the CCP cadre were cut off from the people and afraid of criticism. At the same time he worried that young people were not carrying forward China's revolutionary tradition. He complained in 1963 that they "don't understand the bitterness, the hardships of the Revolution, and what sacrifices it took to get where we are today."[4]

To help cleanse the party and revitalize youthful idealism, the army distributed millions of copies of the "little red book" containing the quotations of Chairman Mao. He used the new text, which acquired almost holy status, to mobilize youth known as Red Guards against party members whose lack of ideological fervor revealed their preference for "following the capitalist road." Mao claimed that these supposed capitalist-roaders were led by none other than his designated successor, Liu Shaoqi. The first Red Guard revolt erupted at Beijing University in 1966 and soon spread throughout the country, setting off ever more severe attacks on party leaders, educators, factory managers, newspaper editors—indeed, against almost every kind of authority. Mao believed that a little dose of anarchy was just the tonic that China's backsliding revolution needed.

But as authority declined, Mao got more anarchy than he wanted. Local conflicts and resentments led to torture, executions, damage to cultural monuments, and general insecurity. Many of Mao's old party comrades perished in this grim period of persecution. Mao himself did nothing to save Liu Shaoqi or any other party leaders from beatings, torture, and death. Finally, in 1967 he ordered Lin Biao's army to restore order, but this proved easier said than done. The Cultural Revolution had degenerated into virtual civil war, with loss of life estimated in the tens of thousands and with millions subjected to persecution. By 1969 the Cultural Revolution as an official mass movement had come to an end, and one by one those who had supported it lost power. Lin Biao was the first to go in 1971 under mysterious circumstances. (Supposedly after a bungled coup against Mao, Lin fled for the Soviet Union only to have his plane crash en route.) Lin's demise led to the gradual restoration of the functions of the state and party. In 1972 the

Cultural Revolution Poster
The poster attacks "revisionism" as identified (lower left corner) with the Soviet Union's Khrushchev and Liu Shaoqi. Liu, formerly Mao's heir apparent, is now branded a dangerous "capitalist roader" within the CCP. Dominating the poster are a young Red Guard, a worker, a peasant, and a soldier. Armed with the writings of Mao Zedong, they are about to erase revisionist influences "in politics, in thought, and in theory." (Collection International Institute of Social History, Amsterdam)

Red Guards that Mao had called to life were formally disbanded and sent into the countryside to be "re-educated through labor" alongside the peasants.

Mao's Legacy. Mao's last years were a time of political disappointment and bitterness. Mao had given his life to party- and nation-building, and he had seen those around him—both family and political associates—suffer for the cause. Yet his dreams of making China into a revolutionary utopia seemed no closer as his life drew to an end. Indeed, those dreams had twice—during the Great Leap and again during the Cultural Revolution—turned into nightmares. The Cultural Revolution in addition had ravaged the party that Mao had created and slain men with whom he had closely collaborated since the 1920s and 1930s.

By the early 1970s Mao was ill and isolated. He suffered most seriously from a disease that caused progressive degeneration of the nervous system. Lin Biao's betrayal had been a heavy psychological blow. Estranged from Jiang Qing, he found comfort in the devoted young women attending him. He kept at a distance his associates, now behaving like jealous courtiers, each seeking the chairman's favor and each anxious to secure power after his death. In July 1976 a massive earthquake shook northern China, killing a quarter of a million people and reviving an old popular conviction that disorder in the natural world mirrored disorder in human affairs. Six months later Mao was dead.

Mao's passing from the scene in September 1976 set the stage for an early, major assessment of his reputation as party leader and founding father of the PRC. Many had reason for a revising of accounts. Each turn of the political wheel by the elderly autocrat had ruined careers and disrupted lives throughout China. But many Chinese also credited Mao with great achievements. He had led the CCP to power and laid the enduring foundation for the PRC. He had regained much of the territory formerly controlled by imperial China. He had forced the major powers to deal with China as an equal and pushed his way into the prestigious club of nuclear-armed powers.

Mao also deserved credit for having overseen a period of generally successful economic development. Despite all his talk of helping the countryside, industry dominated the economy, rising from 30 percent of total output in 1949 to 72 percent by the time of Mao's death in 1976. By that time China had become one of the world's top six industrial powers. Reflecting general economic progress, per capita income quadrupled between 1949 and 1978. Improvements in health care and nutrition raised life expectancy from thirty-five years before 1949 to sixty-five years in the mid-1970s. Chinese people enjoyed expanded educational opportunities, higher levels of literacy, and in general greater social mobility. The CCP managed to avoid a bloated urban population characteristic of much of the third world. A strictly enforced pass system kept peasants working productively on the land rather than becoming marginalized city-dwellers living in poverty or straining the welfare system. These achievements provided a basis for the stunning material gains that China would score in the 1980s and 1990s.

For the majority of Chinese—those living in the countryside—the Mao years began hopefully with a decade of rapid improvement. Peasants had generally welcomed the early phase of land reform. Many had benefited at the expense of absentee landlords or abusive local bullies. The shift to cooperative arrangements appealed to the poorer peasant families, the overwhelming majority in most villages, who had the most to gain. Full collectivization proved a harder sell because it asked peasants to give up the one thing they prized above all else: control over their land. But peasants accommodated in hopes that the party would once more deliver improvements.

The Great Leap Forward ended the honeymoon. The party rewarded peasants' trust with a famine. Survivors vividly recalled "the torment of hunger" and "the chronic pain in the stomach, the dizziness and emptiness in the head, and the constant craving to chew on something that is solid and edible."[5] Although the famine passed, the time of trial continued well into the 1970s with peasants demoralized by central planning that constrained their initiative and judgment and by endless rounds of tiresome and unproductive political meetings. Peasants proved to be lackluster workers on the collectives because individual effort bore no relationship to reward and an increase in total output would simply boost government claims on that output. Perhaps most serious, neglect of population control during the Mao years left villages with more mouths to feed from only minimally higher levels of agricultural output. As a result, peasants were no better off at the end of the 1970s than they had been two decades earlier.

But the party-state was also able to provide real and wide-ranging benefits during the three decades (1949–1976) over which Mao presided. Peasants appreciated the party's success at bringing order to a violent and chaotic countryside. The PRC provided protection against calamity, shoring up dikes, spraying against locusts, and providing food and tax relief in lean years. Gradually, the CCP state brought the hallmarks of modernity to the countryside. It promoted better production by introducing chemical fertilizers and new seed strains and by providing technical advice and education. It brought public health campaigns and clinics to villages and extended electricity to power engines, radios, and eventually televisions. It built and upgraded roads, canals, and communications lines that further opened villages to the outside world. Thanks to CCP initiatives, peasants overall lived healthier, longer, and better lives than they had before 1949. Little wonder that many who had suffered during the old order and had benefited from CCP programs grieved over Mao's death in 1976. A long-time village leader gratefully recalled "Chairman Mao's" legacy: "land, an end to banditry, a happy life."[6]

Peasant women were special beneficiaries of the revolution. Mao described women as "holding up half the sky," and the CCP had a history of promoting equal rights for women. Once in power, the party abolished a wide range of oppressive practices, including forced marriage, marriage of infants and children, concubinage, infanticide, and foot binding. It legalized divorce and abortion. It made education open to all children. The shift to collective agriculture brought other benefits. Because women were able to earn work points, they helped raise overall household income. Their economic contribution previously taken for granted, received official recognition, and women's status in the family and in the community rose accordingly. But revolution hardly ended male dominance. Men still directed production units, and on the whole their work received greater rewards. Men were still the heads of families and village organizations. Sons remained important to continuing the family line, so giving birth to a son

THE MAOIST PROJECT IN CHINA	
1949	People's Republic of China is created and initially follows a moderate domestic program as well as an assertive foreign policy
1955	Mao implements collectivized agriculture
1957	Mao turns on intellectuals for "rightist" tendencies in the "Hundred Flowers" campaign
1958	Great Leap Forward is inaugurated, resulting in famine and death of an estimated 20 million and Mao's temporary retreat from leadership
1959–1960	Open split begins with the Soviet Union
1966	Mao launches the Cultural Revolution with help of Lin and Jiang, resulting in persecution and violence by Red Guards
1976	Mao's death

remained a major family preoccupation. Daughters, who traditionally joined their husband's families, were regarded as investments that brought no return, and this mindset would continue well into the twenty-first century.

Vietnam's Fight for the South

Whereas China's revolution could proceed apace after the victory of CCP forces in 1949, Vietnam's Communists had far to go. The triumph over the French in mid-1954 was a major step forward. The agreement reached at the Geneva conference in July of that year ended the colonial era. But the immediate goal of the revolution—independence for all of Vietnam—was still unfulfilled. The great powers had imposed a line of temporary political division at the seventeenth parallel (at the country's narrow waist). The United States had indicated that it would not be bound by the Geneva accords, including provisions for national elections by 1956 to unite the southern part of the country with the Communist-controlled Democratic Republic of Vietnam (DRV) with its capital in Hanoi. It would take two decades of struggle and sacrifice to achieve unification.

Hanoi's Southern Strategy and the NLF. Initially, between 1954 and 1959, Ho Chi Minh and his colleagues at the head of Vietnam's Communist party decided to delay the unification drive and thus avoid provocations that might draw the United States deeper into the contested South. They concentrated instead on their five-year plan to build socialism in the North, helped by about $1 billion in foreign aid from the Soviet Union and China. Predictably that meant industrialization and nationalization of commerce and industry. In the countryside, the party pushed land reform to destroy the landlord class, though it also led to executions and injustices that embarrassed the party and drove some peasants into open revolt. After recovering from this setback, the party returned to the task of collectivization, which was essentially completed by the early 1960s.

In 1959 Hanoi shifted its attention back to the South, setting the stage for renewed conflict. The catalyst for this shift was Ngo Dinh Diem, who had become head of the U.S.-backed regime in the main southern city of Saigon in 1954. As we saw in Chapter 4, the Eisenhower administration supported Diem's government with assistance that by 1961 totaled $7 billion. Relying heavily on members of his immediate family, Diem crushed his opposition, consolidated his political position, and ignored the countrywide elections agreed upon at Geneva.

Diem's very success put Ho in a difficult position. The cancellation of the elections seemed to rule out peaceful unification, while Saigon's ruthless campaign of repression threatened the survival of the former Viet Minh who had organized the anti-French resistance and had stayed behind after the 1954 partition. Isolated and vulnerable, they warned that Hanoi's lack of support would cost them their lives. It would also cost Hanoi organizational structure and experienced personnel that would in time be essential to winning the South.

The leaders of the DRV finally responded by embarking on an active southern strategy, first authorizing in early 1959 military force by southern cadres to protect themselves and their organization. Hanoi took another step on the road to full-scale civil war the next year when it created the National Liberation Front (NLF). The NLF would serve until 1968 as the main instrument of Hanoi's drive to win the South. Modeled on the Viet Minh, the NLF was a united-front organization meant to appeal broadly to South Vietnamese, including peasants, students, religious and labor leaders, and prominent nationalist politicians. By playing up the Ngo family's political oppression, dependence on the Americans, and regressive land policy, the NLF won broad southern support. Also like the Viet Minh, it operated under veiled Communist control, enabling Hanoi to work effectively behind the scenes. To sustain the southern resistance, Hanoi built up the Ho Chi Minh trail running through the eastern part of the country, and it used Cambodian territory along the South Vietnamese border as a sanctuary where NLF and later northern forces could rest and resupply. (See Map 4.1.)

The NLF fought during this period on three fronts as it attacked a politically vulnerable Diem and later an unstable Saigon military government. One front was in the cities, where the NLF underground promoted anti-government protest, won influential recruits, and infiltrated the Saigon bureaucracy and military command. The second front was on the battlefield, where the NLF had to learn to neutralize the new military technology such as helicopters and armored troop transports that the Kennedy administration provided to the South Vietnamese army. Villages scattered across the southern countryside constituted the NLF's third and most critical front. Here the NLF built on the earlier successes of the Viet Minh at land reform, appealing to peasants with the promise of an end to exploitation and opportunities for social mobility and peasant control.

From his first years in power Diem had made the Viet Minh look especially good by comparison. He allowed landlords to return to the countryside to reclaim fields previously distributed by the Viet Minh. Once the NLF-supported insurgency began, the Diem government resorted to police raids and military sweeps that further antagonized a rural population already inclined to support the NLF. This support was pivotal to the ability of Ho's southern forces to grow stronger and ultimately triumph. Saigon finally attempted land reform as a positive response to NLF inroads, but it came too late. The effort was in any case half-hearted because the Diem regime depended on the support of the landlord element that had the most to lose from genuine land reform. The battle in key southern provinces for the control of "hearts and minds" (a phrase much invoked by Americans preoccupied with winning Vietnamese support) was settled by the early 1960s. Many villagers did not see Saigon as a legitimate regime, and they viewed the American support for that regime as simply a continuation of the repugnant French colonial presence.

During the early 1960s, even while supporting the NLF, Ho remained hopeful of avoiding a costly collision with U.S. forces. He trusted, he remarked in the fall of 1963, in the good sense of an American ruling class that was "more practical and clear-sighted than [in] other capitalist nations." Surely, he argued, "they will not pour their resources into Vietnam endlessly. One day they will take pencil in hand and begin figuring. Once they really begin to analyze our ideas seriously, they will come to the conclusion that it is possible and even worthwhile to live in peace with us."[7] Ho's strong Marxist assumptions led him to these views and also to the conviction that the American "masses" would no more support a hard, distant war than the French had.

The Conflict Escalates. Between 1964 and 1968 Communist leaders in Hanoi stepped up their efforts in the South. Diem's overthrow in late 1963 and the unstable military governments that followed suggested that the South was vulnerable. Hanoi decided to gamble on a quick victory before U.S. military intervention could save the collapsing Saigon regime. The first North Vietnamese combat units reached the South in December 1964 following the Tonkin Gulf clash in August. (See Chapter 4.) The inauguration of the U.S. strategic bombing campaign against the North and the appearance of American forces in the South raised the stakes during the first half of 1965. Hanoi moved quickly to match the Americans on the ground, intensifying the conflict while denying Washington victory. The USSR and China both supported the DRV with substantial military aid. By mid-1965 the first of a quarter-million Chinese support troops began arriving in the DRV, and additional forces stood ready just across the border.

In July, at the very time that President Lyndon Johnson and his advisors were debating massive intervention, Le Duan (the general secretary of the Communist party) explained why the Vietnamese could expect victory. "The U.S. rear area is

Vietnamese Peasants Guarded by a U.S. Marine, 1965
Taken during a sweep by a marine unit through a village near the coast of central South Vietnam, this photo captures the gulf between the young American soldier as part of a massive, well-armed expeditionary force and the people that it sought to protect, operated among, and fought against. (© Bettman/Corbis)

very far away, and American soldiers are 'soldiers in chains', who cannot fight like the French, cannot stand the weather conditions, and don't know the battlefield.... To fight for a prolonged period is a weakness of U.S. imperialism." The United States might even attack the DRV, Duan predicted, but that course would trigger direct Chinese or even Soviet involvement.[8]

Between 1965 and 1968 this escalating conflict visited death and destruction throughout Vietnam. The North absorbed a pounding from the air while sending able-bodied young men south to fight until victory. ("Born in the North to die in the South" was these recruits' favorite, sardonic slogan.) The South suffered extensively from bombing, defoliation, free-fire zones, and search-and-destroy missions. The violence disrupted all aspects of society, imposed widespread economic hardship, and sent floods of refugees into the cities.

The decisive encounter of the Vietnam War came in 1968 with the Tet Offensive (so named for the new year holiday in Vietnam's lunar calendar). Hanoi had decided to employ virtually all the NLF forces in a general offensive intended to shake the Saigon government's hold on its urban strong points. The party appealed for a maximum effort by its rank-and-file in order "to avenge evil done to our families, to pay our debt to the Fatherland, to display our loyalty to the country, affection for the people and love for our families."[9] In early 1968 the NLF launched its surprise attack, seizing cities all over the South, including parts of Saigon. NLF forces were eventually beaten back with heavy losses, forcing northern troops to bear the brunt of the fighting during the balance of the war. But, as we have seen (Chapter 4), the Tet Offensive deeply shocked and unsettled both U.S. policymakers and the public and finally cracked Johnson's resolve.

Still the war raged on for another seven years, with the fighting in the South reaching its most destructive phase after Tet. Peace talks, begun in late 1968, deadlocked. As implacable as ever, Hanoi sustained its forces in the field despite high casualties and weathered President Richard Nixon's bombing campaigns

NORTH VIETNAM TAKES ON THE UNITED STATES	
1954	Geneva conference agreement leaves Ho in control north of the 17th parallel and U.S.-backed Diem takes charge to the south
1959	Diem's repressive policy prompts Hanoi to endorse military as well as political struggle in the South
1960	National Liberation Front (NLF) for South Vietnam is created
1963	Diem's overthrow and assassination; South Vietnamese army takes charge in Saigon
1964	Hanoi introduces combat units into South Vietnam and begins to line up Soviet and Chinese support
1968	Tet Offensive washes over cities all over the South, including Saigon; peace negotiations with United States begin; American policy of "Vietnamization" looks to turning the main war effort over to the South Vietnamese government
1973	Paris agreement on withdrawal of U.S. forces is concluded
1975	South Vietnam falls to the North

and expansion of the ground war against its sanctuaries and supply lines in Cambodia and Laos. Finally, in January 1973 the two sides reached a compromise in the Paris Agreement. Washington dropped its insistence on North Vietnamese troop withdrawal from the South, and Hanoi gave up its demand for the end of the South Vietnamese military government. Nixon had to force Saigon to submit to this compromise.

With the American troops out, the war ended sooner than anyone expected. The strategy of "Vietnamization" of the war, begun by Johnson after Tet and continued by Nixon, had sought to strengthen the South Vietnamese army and air force so that they could cope on their own. But the Saigon government's forces remained hobbled by corruption and inept leadership. The North Vietnamese spring offensive in 1975 revealed how fragile that force was—and how empty were Nixon's assurances of continuing support. South Vietnamese defenses collapsed rapidly, and Saigon fell in April. Hanoi had emerged victorious after a long and costly struggle.

Now, Vietnamese patriots celebrated the realization of a dream of independence and unity that was a century old. Ho Chi Minh did not live to see that victory. But his contributions, above all as a national symbol and party builder, helped make that triumph possible. His public image as a warm, conciliatory figure and his adherence to collegial decision-making helped win broad popular support and keep the party leadership together through a series of lopsided struggles and difficult choices. Ho thus left as his legacy a leadership style that differed considerably from that of his Chinese contemporary, Mao Zedong, whose later years were marked by erratic policies and the demise of collegial governance.

Shortly before his death in September 1969, Ho had appealed to compatriots in an almost lyrical celebration of the country that he had devoted virtually the whole of his life to liberating. "The American invaders defeated, we will rebuild our land ten times more beautiful."[10] But Ho had only to look around to see some of the costs, and others would become evident only at the end of the war. An estimated 1.7 million Vietnamese died during the last decade of the long Vietnamese struggle (1965–1975). The environment suffered lasting damage from bombing that tripled the total for World War II and from the extensive use of herbicides that destroyed not only plants holding down fragile tropical soil but also human genes, resulting in widespread birth defects. Over 10 million South Vietnamese became refugees between 1965 and 1973, and by the war's end Vietnam had some 1.4 million disabled and half a million orphans to care for. Substantial parts of the southern countryside were depopulated with the land lying idle, while urban industry and commercial activity had ground to a virtual halt. However sweet the victory, prolonged conflict had imposed a heavy price on Vietnam.

THE CARIBBEAN BASIN: BETWEEN
REACTION AND REVOLUTION

In the Caribbean and Central America as in East Asia, the postwar period opened with a rising challenge to the old order. Strong individual leaders had dominated national politics. The military played an active role, sometimes

MAP 6.1
Latin America and the Caribbean

directly ruling, sometimes operating behind the scenes. A small number of families held the ultimate power, running the economic as well as the political system, thanks to a close working relationship with a staunchly conservative Catholic Church as well as the military. This coalition of wealthy families, strongmen, the military, and the Church had crushed groups attempting to break its grip on national life.

At the close of World War II reformist regimes and populist movements sprouted everywhere, drawing sustenance from Allied propaganda that victory over fascism was only the prelude to building more prosperous and open societies. Reformers, committed to broader political participation, expanded the right to vote beyond the ranks of propertied males and legalized labor unions. They also concerned themselves with pressing questions of social justice and redistribution of wealth in societies marked by glaring inequalities. The urban middle class and the working class as well as students and intellectuals were the chief advocates of these changes. As dictators fell and repression lifted, parties on the Left, including Communist parties, began to play a prominent political role, and unions became more assertive and saw their membership increase.

Sharpening the demands for change was pervasive nationalist resentment against U.S. domination. By the early twentieth century the United States had established itself as the dominant regional presence that left states, most independent since the 1820s, only nominally free to chart their own course. At times, especially between 1898 and 1933, U.S. control took the form of direct rule— over Cuba, the Dominican Republic, Haiti, and Nicaragua. But this sort of direct control, justified by the Monroe Doctrine with its long-standing claim to U.S. dominion over the Americas and to the right to intervene, was costly and an embarrassing contradiction to national principles of self-determination. So in the 1930s the Roosevelt administration promoted a "good-neighbor" policy rejecting colonialism and even direct military intervention. Nevertheless, Washington continued to protect its sphere of influence by working through friendly local elites, supplying military and economic aid, and applying diplomatic pressure. The memory of past U.S. interference and the continuing reality of pervasive U.S. constraints created fertile ground for radical politics in postwar Central America and the Caribbean.

Nowhere in the broad Caribbean basin region did the radical impulse grow stronger than in Guatemala and Cuba in the course of the 1950s. In both cases demands for change sharpened long-standing internal divisions. Those demands also stimulated powerful U.S. fears of communist advances in the U.S. backyard. Washington's forceful opposition would doom fundamental social and economic change in Guatemala, while Cuba's revolution would survive but at a heavy cost.

Guatemala's "Ten Years of Spring"

Radicalism in Guatemala arose within a society that was, like others in the region, deeply divided. The Spanish conquest in the sixteenth century and the subsequent period of colonial rule had created the divide, and it had persisted beyond independence in 1821. On one side was a large underclass composed primarily of descendants of the Maya, a people living in Mexico and Honduras as well as Guatemala. They had numbered as many as fourteen million in the eighth century. The Mayan civilization, composed of strong city-states surrounded by farming communities, had reached its peak of power in the tenth century before being overwhelmed by invasion, civil war, and natural disasters. Spanish conquest, followed by three centuries of Spanish rule, completed the abasement of this once powerful people, while diseases introduced by the Spanish sharply reduced their numbers.

Some of the survivors were enslaved, and the rest took refuge in remote regions practicing subsistence agriculture. But even remote settlements were increasingly threatened in the late nineteenth and twentieth centuries as export-oriented agriculture expanded. An 1871 law expropriated Indian as well as Catholic Church land in order to make it available for well-to-do families building up the country's coffee plantations. Indians stripped of their land were forced to accept work tending and harvesting export crops. The steady encroachment of plantation agriculture at the end of the century further disrupted Indian communities and left rural labor ever more poorly paid. To protect themselves culturally and economically, some Indian communities sought to isolate themselves in remote highlands, especially in the western part of the country.

In recent times the Maya, still slightly over half of Guatemala's population in 1950, suffered from poverty, malnutrition, poor health, short life expectancy, and an illiteracy rate at over 70 percent. They lived in scattered groups, each with its own language. While identifying with their local communities, they continued to carry a keen sense of their Mayan heritage and of their oppression as a conquered people.

Ladinos occupied the other side of the Guatemalan social divide. Broadly understood, *Ladino* refers to people of European descent and anyone else (including descendants of Indians) who adopted European social standards and language. Many Ladinos felt contempt for the Indian, who seemed to them more animal than human. They also feared Indian uprisings that could disrupt production and endanger the agricultural system. When these uprisings occurred, the army brutally repressed them.

A Ladino minority—a small collection of powerful families—ran the country. Their ancestors had taken a leading role in the sixteenth-century Spanish conquest and in colonial governance, and they remained prominent after independence from Spain. Their ranks had been steadily reinforced by the arrival of Europeans and Spanish-descended peoples from other parts of Latin America. This elite controlled an economy dominated by plantation agriculture. Two percent of landholders from that class owned roughly three-quarters of agricultural land. They used their wealth derived from export agriculture to import finished products from industrial countries, to expand their holdings, or to make secure investments abroad. Those same families also controlled the government. In the twentieth century this elite expressed its fear of popular unrest by labeling as communist any challenge to its control, even moderate calls for social reform and labor unions. This privileged class with much to lose and much to fear gravitated to repressive, authoritarian rule as the best guarantee of order and stability. The vote was limited in the interwar period to literate males, and urban opposition parties then taking shape were crushed and their leaders exiled or killed.

This yawning gulf between the privileged and the poor—a minority of European descent and the largely indigenous majority—created a society marked by gross inequalities and ethnic domination. Those conditions in turn bred resentment and fear and political tension that often spilled over into armed conflict—altogether a poor climate for long-term economic development. Because Guatemala and other countries in the region were overwhelmingly agricultural, control of land usually figured prominently as the most sensitive political issue. Land represented patrimony and privilege for the upper class, whereas for peasants it was the stuff of survival and dreams for a better life.

Jacobo Arbenz and the Vision of a New Guatemala. In 1944 Guatemala entered what some have looked back on nostalgically as the "ten years of spring in the land of eternal tyranny." That decade witnessed the unfolding of a reform program intended to promote national unity and popular welfare. This era of promise began with the overthrow in 1944 of Jorge Ubico Castañeda, a military dictator in power since 1931. A revolt led by students, professionals, and military officers drove him into exile and opened the way for two elected reformers—first Juan José Arévalo Bermejo, and then Jacobo Arbenz Guzmán.

A prominent and eloquent intellectual untainted by the old regime, Arévalo was an attractive leader for the new era. He won the presidency in December 1944 with 85 percent of the vote and then legitimized political parties, opened up public debate, broadened the right to vote, and made it possible for workers to organize. Arévalo's successor as president, Jacobo Arbenz, broadened the reform agenda from 1951 to 1954, giving it a distinctly radical tinge. His father was a Swiss German who had settled in Guatemala in 1901. Jacobo was born in 1913. The bankruptcy of his father's pharmacy closed his avenue to university, so he turned to the military academy. He was an excellent cadet and officer. In 1939 he married an upper-class Salvadoran, María Vilanova. She had a gregarious personality (in contrast to her somewhat introverted husband), was U.S.-educated, and was interested in a broad range of social and cultural issues. In 1944 Arbenz joined other young officers pressing for Ubico's removal. Thereafter he served as minister of defense, keeping the army loyal to Arévalo and actively encouraging the reform program. In 1950 Arbenz won the presidency with 64 percent of the vote.

Both Arbenz and his wife had by then developed a sensitivity to social injustice that pulled them to the political left. Exploring the sources of Guatemala's underdevelopment and extreme poverty, they determined that deep social and ethnic divisions were to blame. They were also perturbed by their country's economic dependence on the United States. Indeed, the Boston-based United Fruit Company was Guatemala's largest private landowner and biggest employer. It occupied a privileged position that made it a state within a state. Backed by Washington, it defied postwar legislation that gave labor the right to organize and collect a minimum wage. Arbenz was not alone in resenting U.S. arrogance and attributing Guatemala's economic backwardness, at least in part, to the dominant influence of American capitalists and their alliance with the landed elite. In their quest to understand Guatemala's plight, the Arbenz couple turned to Marxist writings. Marxism offered hope that history was on the side of change—that in the end neither Guatemala's own reactionary classes nor the American imperialists could block progress. But if Arbenz was becoming a Marxist, he was a cautious one, for he wanted to avoid provoking Washington, and he knew that he would get no significant Soviet support.

Domestically Arbenz realized that socialism was a distant dream. Guatemala had first to develop capitalism and end the feudal conditions that defined the lives of so many of his compatriots. He thus wanted to promote education and private enterprise, improve working conditions, and bring the peasantry into touch with the broader world. He also sought to promote a shared national identity, and that meant drawing what he and other Ladinos saw as a superstitious and backward Mayan population out of what he viewed as its brutish isolation. He genuinely believed that helping Indians shed their indigenous values in favor of "modern" ones would improve their lives while promoting economic development and justice.

Arbenz's deepening convictions on domestic and foreign policy made the still outlawed Guatemalan Communist party his natural partner. While other political parties suffered from internal quarrels and corruption, the Communists commanded the only disciplined, honest political organization in the country. After they helped Arbenz in his 1950 election campaign, he legalized the party and made its leadership trusted presidential advisors.

Agrarian reform was the major tool by which Arbenz would try to push his country forward. His reform law passed Congress in June 1952. Its sponsors argued that peasants given their own land would work harder, boost agricultural production, lead better lives, and develop a more sophisticated, market-oriented mentality. The reform, which called for the expropriation and redistribution of land to peasants, largely exempted small and medium-sized holdings (estates of less than 224 acres). Large holdings with substantial idle land were subject to expropriation. Those losing land included Arbenz himself and some of his close advisors. Owners were to be compensated in bonds amounting to the declared tax value of the land taken. This provision punished those, including the United Fruit Company, who had always grossly understated their land value in order to avoid taxes.

By June 1954 the Arbenz program had transferred one-quarter of the arable land to the benefit of as many as half a million Guatemalan poor (out of a population of nearly three million). Reformers went beyond handing out land to politicizing peasants—involving them in the redistribution process in order to overcome their political passivity and fear. To make sure that peasants prospered, the government provided credit, technical assistance, education, and roads to get crops to market. At the same time it encouraged rural wage laborers to unionize in order to raise their pay and to support the new order in the countryside.

This rural reform program exacerbated long-standing tensions, especially between the Maya and Ladinos. Land had become ever scarcer because of two long-term trends—population growth and concentration of holdings in the hands of the wealthy. The scarcity had ignited feuds within and between villages that could last for decades and create bitter divisions. Postwar democratization provided a political arena for the expression of this struggle for land usually pitting the Maya (often landless laborers) against Ladinos (often the major local landowners). The injection of the land reform process in 1952 added oil to a long-smoldering fire. Officials arriving in a town to redistribute land had to sort out a complex tangle of local alliances and decades-old rivalries. The more affluent Ladinos increasingly feared that popular unrest, with the backing of the Arbenz government in Guatemala City, would undermine their social control. In their view, the reform was a disguise for an emerging revolutionary threat.

Opposition at Home and Abroad. By 1953 the Arbenz government was facing growing American opposition. The United Fruit Company resented government attempts to renegotiate contract terms and enforce newly passed labor measures. The agrarian reform was the crowning blow, depriving United Fruit of three-fourths of its holdings of about 600,000 acres. Washington soon joined the ranks of the opposition. As we saw in Chapter 5, U.S. leaders approached the region convinced that private capital was the key to creating prosperity. To attract investment from abroad and hold accumulated wealth at home, countries such as Guatemala had to maintain stability against leftist or populist agitation, limit state intervention in the economy, and in general respect the rights of private property. During Arévalo's tenure, United Fruit was warning the Truman administration of trouble in Guatemala. By the time Arbenz became president, Washington's fears were fueled primarily by U.S. diplomats. The U.S. ambassador applied what he called his "duck test" for determining if a country was undergoing a quiet communist takeover. Watch for the signs, he suggested. If the bird walks, swims, and quacks like a duck, then it's a duck "whether he's wearing a label or not."[11] His conclusion was that the Arbenz government met the test.

Internal opposition to reform was also mounting. Already under Arévalo landowners had begun plotting coups. The Arbenz land reform made them even more determined to find a military dictator to beat back the supposed communist threat. The leading members carried their vivid fears to a receptive U.S. embassy. Through the press and the radio stations it owned, this upper class gradually convinced the middle class of the danger of economic and social upheaval. This consolidation of opinion among the affluent urban classes left Arbenz heavily dependent on the support of peasant and labor organizations.

The other early, major source of internal opposition was the Catholic Church. It feared a rising tide of Marxism that threatened Christian values as well as the Church's privileged status. Guatemala's strongly authoritarian archbishop warned, "Sad experience shows that liberty left to the caprice of each individual only disorganizes [our people] into opposing bands, weakens them, and begins to destroy them."[12] The Church was not, however, monolithic. In contrast to the staunchly conservative native-born clergy, foreign priests, especially those working with the Guatemalan poor, supported reform out of a sense of social justice.

In Guatemalan politics the army cast the swing vote on the fate of the reform project. Arbenz had respected the army's autonomy, pampered its officers, and received its loyalty in return. What finally strained the relationship was the prospect of a collision with the United States that would bring certain defeat and possibly the loss of the army's privileged position. The only alternative was for officers to get rid of Arbenz.

At first the Truman administration sought to push Arbenz from the clutches of the communists by applying diplomatic pressure and denying his government economic aid and weapons sales. Truman's successor, Dwight Eisenhower, embraced more aggressive measures late in the summer of 1953, authorizing the CIA to engineer a coup. On June 17, 1954, a rebel force of only several hundred men, trained in Nicaragua and led by Carlos Castillo Armas, crossed into Guatemala. The CIA planners decided that the key to success was to shake the loyalty of the army and secondarily to demoralize the civilian population. So they backed up the invaders with radio broadcasts, a few aircraft that dropped leaflets and intermittently bombed and strafed the capital, and a U.S. navy blockade.

	GUATEMALA STILL DIVIDED
1821	Guatemala gains independence from Spain
1871	The government gives legal sanction to land consolidation to promote export agriculture
1944	Dictator Ubico is overthrown; Arévalo is elected president and presses for democratization
1950	Arbenz is elected president with help of the Guatemalan Communist party
1952	Arbenz launches a broad-based program of land redistribution
1954	CIA-sponsored exile force invades Guatemala; armed forces topple Arbenz government; new U.S.-backed military government restores land to elites

The Guatemalan army finally deserted the already shaken Arbenz government. On June 27 the exhausted president resigned. He explained in a public statement that "the sacrifice that I have asked for does not include the blood of Guatemalans." In private, American leaders exulted over the effectiveness of this low-cost covert operation. Publicly they were more circumspect. President Eisenhower proclaimed to the press, "The people of Guatemala in a magnificent effort have liberated themselves from the shackles of international communist direction and reclaimed their right of self-determination."[13] In Arbenz's place, Washington installed the reliably anti-communist Castillo Armas. His government severed diplomatic ties with the Soviet bloc. It banned the Communist party and persecuted its members. Rural activists either fled or faced violent repression. Little of the domestic reform program survived. Eventually, 1.03 million of the 1.30 million acres expropriated under the 1952 law would be restored to their owners.

This return to pre-1944 conditions had strong support from the well-to-do. They did not want to see repeated anything like the Arbenz land reform, described by a leading newspaper as "the most monstrous act of robbery ever perpetrated by any ruler in our history."[14] This class feared real democracy and it looked to the military and police to check any challenge to the system. Guatemala had returned to type—a country deeply divided along ethnic and class lines and unable to accommodate even peaceful change that might bridge that divide.

Arbenz survived as his dream of a new Guatemala collapsed. In exile, he at last joined the Guatemalan Communist party, but he remained haunted until his death in 1971 by his political failure. On the Latin American Left the Arbenz reform effort was mythologized. The Chilean Communist poet Pablo Neruda wrote "In Guatemala," an elegy for the dashed hopes.

I saw the rose bloom in Guatemala.
I saw the poor man's land defended,

and justice arrive to every mouth.

. . .

The North American arsonists
dropped dollars and bombs:
death built its finery,
the United Fruit uncoiled its rope.
And thus Guatemala was assassinated
in full flight, like a dove.[15]

Some on the Left lamented Arbenz's failure to arm his loyalists the better to protect his program from its powerful enemies. This lesson was drawn most consequentially by Cuban revolutionaries. When they came to power, they expected strong U.S. opposition and so prepared themselves militarily. Their reading of the past thus helped them survive. For Washington, on the other hand, Guatemala marked a turning point toward a more interventionist policy in Central America and the Caribbean. To forestall leftist inroads that might benefit Moscow, U.S. policymakers increased their support for right-wing regimes and created aid-programs (notably President John F. Kennedy's Alliance for Progress in the early 1960s) to ensure social stability. But where the communists did threaten, Washington was prepared to intervene, confident of success after the easy victory against Arbenz.

Cuba and the Revolution That Survived

Events in the island nation of Cuba took a dramatically different course from those in Guatemala in part because of differences between Arbenz and Fidel Alejandro Castro Ruz, the author of the Cuban revolution and its presiding presence throughout the last four decades of the twentieth century and beyond. He guaranteed at least a footnote for himself in Cuban history on July 26, 1953, when he staged an attack on a military barracks in Santiago de Cuba on the eastern end of the island. He hoped the attack would spark a nationwide revolt against the government of dictator Fulgencio Batista. The twenty-six-year-old Castro had no more than a hundred fifty young factory and farm workers behind him, and after more than an hour of fighting the outmanned rebel leader fled to the mountains with a band of sixty, only to fall into government hands within a week. This young upstart's political career seemed doomed, but it had only just begun. He would ultimately get the best of his foes and leave an enduring stamp on Cuban national life.

The other major distinction can be found in social differences. While Cuba suffered, like Guatemala, from deep inequalities that divided the countryside from the city and that favored those of Spanish descent, Cuba more resembled the rest of the Caribbean in the identity of its underclass: primarily descendants of the four million slaves brought from Africa to supply labor, usually on the sugar plantations that became the mainstay of the colonial economy. Slavery had persisted until 1886 in Cuba, one of the last places to embrace emancipation. Also unlike Guatemala, Cuba's bankers, business leaders, and prominent landowners did not constitute a cohesive, independent upper class resolute in defense of the status quo. Nor was there an isolated peasantry on the fringes of national politics. Large-scale cane sugar operations, which dominated the economy, had integrated the peasants as renters of company land, as landowners selling their limited production to the company, or as wage laborers.

In the U.S. Shadow. Castro's revolution developed under the shadow of its giant North American neighbor. U.S. expansionists had fantasized throughout the nineteenth century about making Cuba, then a colony within the decrepit Spanish empire, into a state of the union. The Spanish-American War in 1898, which made the United States the colonial master of the Philippines, also paved the way for lasting though informal control over Cuba. Before 1898, the island had been in a state of simmering revolt against Spanish rule from the 1860s on, but it had taken U.S. intervention in 1898 to finally break Spain's grip. U.S. troops occupied the island until 1902, when Cuba gained independence.

But that independence was highly qualified. Cuba had to accept the U.S. right to intervene militarily to maintain order and to hand over Guantanamo as a military base, and the U.S. embassy became the kingmaker in Cuban politics. In addition, Cuba's sugar economy had become tightly tied to the U.S. market and dominated by American investors. By the 1920s, two-thirds of all arable land belonged to U.S. companies, and U.S. firms controlled Cuba's mineral wealth as well as its public utilities and transport. Trade reinforced this subordination. Indeed, Cuba's sugar industry came to depend on privileged access to the U.S. market at prices above the world-market level, and (in a pattern that aroused advocates of import substitution) U.S. producers supplied Cuba with manufactured imports while a high U.S. tariff discouraged Cuban manufacturing.

Batista was the last in a string of U.S.-backed leaders. This anti-communist strongman used his control of government revenue to dispense patronage to political supporters and keep the army happy with generous funding. The middle class prospered, the North Americans were satisfied, and Batista successfully intimidated his critics—at least until the late 1950s.

Castro, like other Cuban nationalists, charged the Batista regime with making Cuba a "neo-colonial" dependency of the United States. He realized that so tight was the U.S. grip that he could not challenge Batista and seek internal reform without also ending that dependence. Complicating Castro's thinking was his intimate relationship to the United States that he shared with many well-to-do Cubans. He had taken his honeymoon there and later visited Cuban communities in New York and Florida to raise funds during his periods of exile. Castro was also a baseball player of considerable skill and a long-time devotee of the Yanqui sport much beloved on the island. So large did the United States loom in the imagination of Cubans that they tended to compare themselves not to other Latin American countries but to their rich northern neighbor. This complex entanglement with the United States had helped shape Cuban nationalism. Castro fully shared that nationalist spirit and publicly invoked it in his struggle to remake Cuba.

Castro and the July 26 Movement. In September 1953, Fidel Castro went on trial along with others implicated in his failed uprising and received a thirteen-year prison sentence. Before the court he delivered an address, "History Will Absolve Me." He attacked corrupt politicians and laid out a reform program to serve the interests of ordinary Cubans. He draped his appeal in the folds of Cuban patriotic mythology while omitting all reference to communism or socialism, making no attack on the United States, and raising no call for revolution. Secretly reprinted and widely circulated, this call for political democracy and social justice enhanced Castro's reputation as a moderate eager to create a broad-based opposition. In 1955 Batista issued a general amnesty that freed Fidel and his men, and Castro went into exile in Mexico. There he concentrated on building his political organization, named the July 26 Movement (after the date of his 1953 revolt). There he also met an Argentine doctor, Ernesto "Che" Guevara, who would become his chief advisor along with Castro's brother Raúl.

In December 1956 Castro and eighty-two associates slipped back to Cuba on a small, overcrowded boat. The landing miscarried, and Castro in one of his repeated strokes of good fortune made it to the Sierra Maestra mountains (in eastern Cuba) with eighteen of his men. He learned the terrain and enlisted the backing of local bandits. He also got *New York Times* journalist Herbert Matthews to report that the rebels were a major force, thereby scoring a propaganda coup in both Cuba and the United States. In fact, a wide range of Cubans was beginning to embrace the anti-Batista cause, and dozens of other opposition groups were springing up. By early 1958 the opposition movement numbered about twenty thousand active supporters and two thousand guerrillas in scattered bands. It was a force in cities, and in the countryside it had taken the military initiative against Batista's demoralized army. On January 1, 1959, the dispirited dictator fled the country. The next day opposition forces entered Havana. Castro himself began a long, triumphant pilgrimage across the island of seven million to the capital. He reveled in the popular adulation.

What had brought Castro so rapidly—within six years of his daring uprising—to this surprising victory? His origins give some clues. He was born in August 1927 on a farm in eastern Cuba. His father, a deeply religious but rough-hewn and illiterate man, had come from Spain and labored hard to acquire his own farm. He eventually accumulated a net worth of half a million dollars. Young Fidel was energetic, athletic, and independent with an outgoing personality. He attended a prominent Jesuit school in Havana for children of the upper crust. There he absorbed the Catholic ideas on social justice.

In 1945 Castro entered the University of Havana to study law. Attracted to rough-and-tumble campus politics, he demonstrated a talent for public speaking, and increasingly turned to national political issues. He focused on the failure of corrupt politicians to address popular welfare, especially the gap between privileged city dwellers and impoverished rural folk. He made his first run for elected office in 1952, only to have Batista seize power and close down the political process. The dictator came to represent in the eyes of this ambitious and impatient young man the two problems plaguing Cuba: its social ills and U.S. domination.

By the time of Batista's fall in 1959, Castro's political daring, charisma, and effectiveness as a guerrilla leader had established him as the dominant figure within a loose alliance of liberal-left opposition groups that included the Cuban Communist party as well as the July 26 Movement. Castro's striking capacity to tap popular sentiment made him the voice of the revolution and increasingly put his views beyond challenge. Castro himself appears to have had no revolutionary blueprint. Until 1961 he avoided any clear statement of long-term policy that might alienate his broad coalition of supporters, as critical to his anti-Batista struggle as it was to the Vietnamese in their anti-colonial cause.

Castro made his first important decision in May 1959 when, in response to popular demands for vengeance, he approved the dramatic public trial and execution of Batista loyalists charged with the deaths of some twenty thousand opposition figures. At the same time Castro failed to calm U.S. fears of communism gaining a foothold in the hemisphere. Worried that Washington would turn against any government that embraced meaningful social change, he plunged ahead anyway by nationalizing U.S.-owned oil refineries. When Eisenhower retaliated with an economic embargo, Castro responded by nationalizing additional U.S. property. In January 1961 the two sides broke diplomatic relations. As we saw in Chapter 4, John Kennedy endorsed CIA plans formulated under Eisenhower for an invasion by Cuban exiles modeled on the Guatemala operation. Che Guevara, who had personally witnessed Arbenz's overthrow, warned Castro that he must anticipate American intervention. Castro took the warning seriously, and when the U.S.-backed invasion force (made up of Cuban expatriates) came ashore at the Bay of Pigs in April 1961, Castro's forces easily prevailed. The Kennedy administration was shocked. Castro remained a problem not just for Kennedy but for all his successors in the White House.

American hostility gave Castro reason to further tighten his control. In the course of 1959 he banned liberal parties as enemies of the revolution, and liberals followed the old regime into prison or exile, mainly in Miami, Florida. Free elections were never held, and free speech was severely curtailed. With the political situation polarizing, exile-sponsored raids only added to the crisis. Castro saw that he needed a reliable political instrument to carry out his policies. The Cuban Communist party would be that instrument, even if Castro disliked its ideological rigidity and its subservience to Moscow. It had a well-organized mass base, and it shared his opposition to American imperialism and his vision of social justice.

In December 1961 Castro publicly embraced socialism as the best way to promote the popular welfare. But there is some doubt about when his conversion actually took place—indeed, even how thorough a conversion it was. Castro himself remarked in a 1964 interview, "It was a gradual process, a dynamic process, in which the pressure of events [after the revolution] forced me to accept Marxism as the answer I was seeking..., I can not tell you just when."[16] Like other third-world radicals, including Arbenz and Ho, his values were as much populist and nationalist as Marxist. His domestic program aimed to eliminate abject poverty, promote literacy, make medical care widely available, and reduce the birth rate and infant mortality. He expropriated wealthy property owners (both foreign and Cuban) and moved toward collective agriculture. As in China, the new regime limited migration from the countryside into the capital, Havana,

Fidel Castro, 1965

This photo of an impromptu public conversation captures the populist charm that made Castro beloved to many Cubans. An 87-year-old man asks for a pension so he'll have the money to start a small business growing cocoa trees. Castro at first expresses surprise that the old man has no pension and promises to check into the matter but jocularly dismisses the idea of going into business so late in life. "What sheer madness!" When the old man persists, Castro finally surrenders amidst much laughter from onlookers. "Help! No more, no more! You will have your pension, *viejo* [old man]. Ay, these *campesinos* [country folk], going into business when they are nearly ninety. They are never going to understand what socialism is all about, that's for sure!"[17] (Lee Lockwood/TimePix)

to head off out-of-control urban growth. And it expanded rights for women. The positive effects of Castro's policies quickly became evident. Economic redistribution raised ordinary Cubans' purchasing power and closed glaring gaps in welfare. But badly formulated economic policy and the flight of foreign capital plagued the revolution from the outset.

Expensive domestic policies and U.S. hostility turned Castro toward the Soviet Union. He became increasingly reliant on that country as a military and economic patron. In fact, Castro saw friendly relations with the USSR as a way of demonstrating his independence from the United States while also garnering the economic assistance not available elsewhere. Relations with the Soviet bloc developed rapidly beginning in February 1960 with trade and aid agreements with Moscow.

Despite his triumph at the Bay of Pigs, Castro remained fearful of a second invasion attempt, led this time by U.S. forces. The Kennedy administration's militant rhetoric underlined by U.S. naval maneuvers justified these fears. So Castro appealed to Khrushchev, who responded in the spring of 1962 by sending Soviet nuclear missiles to deter an invasion. During the ensuing crisis of October 1962 (treated in Chapter 4), Castro seemed eager to see a Soviet-American clash of arms. When Khrushchev went behind his back to strike a deal with Kennedy, the Cuban leader was outraged. But even if Castro had no say in the decision to remove the Soviet missiles, he could take comfort in the American pledge not to sponsor another invasion, although U.S. hostility (and covert operations) continued. A visit to the Soviet Union in May 1963 healed the breach with Khrushchev and signaled Cuba's full-fledged membership in the socialist bloc.

Exporting Revolution. During his first two decades in power, Castro thought of his revolution as the spearhead for third-world liberation. His victory at the Bay of Pigs had made him the hero of the Latin American Left. Castro enthusiastically embraced this new role, giving rebel groups from neighboring countries a secure base of operations on the island and supporting insurgencies in the Dominican Republic, Guatemala, Argentina, Bolivia, and Venezuela. None was successful, and Che Guevara, who served as his overseas agent, was caught and killed in the jungles of Bolivia in 1967. Chastened for a time, Castro's hopes for revolution in the hemisphere revived in the late 1970s with the dictator Anastasio Somoza's overthrow in Nicaragua and the appearance of left-leaning governments in Grenada and Jamaica.

Castro's interest in exporting revolution extended well beyond the Western hemisphere. He had given assistance to Algeria's independence struggle against France in 1960 and backed Kwame Nkrumah's call for black liberation by setting up guerrilla training camps in northern Ghana in 1961. In 1965 Guevara led the first small Cuban contingent to fight in the Congo, and soon thereafter Castro extended his support to other black African liberation movements. These commitments became a source of friction with Moscow following Khrushchev's overthrow. In 1966 Castro accused the new Soviet leadership of turning its back on third-world struggles, thus positioning himself as their foremost advocate. In 1975 Castro would renew his engagement in Africa—in Angola and Ethiopia—and, as a result, end any chance for normalization of relations with the new U.S. administration under Jimmy Carter.

Why did Castro survive the American onslaught whereas Arbenz suffered defeat and exile? One part of the answer can be found in the lessons that the Cubans drew from the Guatemalan failure. Another part of the explanation is Soviet support proffered to Castro but not to Arbenz. But perhaps above all we need to consider the role of Castro's personality. He combined self-confidence with a fatalistic sense of destiny in a way that gave him that intangible thing called charisma—the power to elicit hope and sacrifice from his followers. Those who came within his ambit found him irresistible. Someone who had known Castro during his Mexican exile recalled, "When he puts his hand on your shoulder... ten minutes later you are saying yes to everything."[18]

Castro's revolution offers the sobering reminder that even successful programs for radical change cannot easily solve the political and economic problems that provoked the effort in the first place. The Cuban revolution struggled to create a prosperous, just, and truly independent Cuba. On the plus side it made gains in social welfare matched by no other country in the region, dramatically improving life expectancy and literacy rates and significantly lowering infant mortality.

(See Table 6.1.) But these achievements in social welfare have to be seen in light of the relatively high standard of living and high literacy rates that Cuba already enjoyed before the revolution. Still, advances in social welfare under Castro were, by any standard, impressive. But Castro's revolution carried a cost. The continuing confrontation with the United States and the large Cuban exile community determined to bring Castro down forced him to spend heavily on his armed forces. In addition, an embattled Castro would not allow real democracy and had little tolerance for public expressions of political dissent. In this one-party state, activists demanding political rights were jailed or otherwise restricted.

Economic development was yet another area in which the revolution did not live up to its promise. Cuba remained tied to a single export crop—sugar. The only difference was that under Castro heavy dependence on the United States had given way to heavy dependence on the USSR. In 1972 Cuba joined the Socialist bloc's Council for Mutual Economic Assistance (COMECON) and became integrated into Eastern bloc economic planning. Relentless U.S. sanctions and Castro's shifting policies resulted in an economy defined by cycles of crisis and recovery from the early 1960s on. In the late 1960s Castro experimented (much as Mao Zedong had done in China's Great Leap Forward) with a shift in emphasis from industry to agriculture and reliance on mass mobilization to dramatically increase production. This strategy failed. Verging on economic collapse, Cuba became more dependent than ever on Soviet support. Castro retreated to a more moderate, market-oriented policy to revive the economy, but by 1985 he shifted again out of fear of emerging "capitalist" tendencies.

The collapse of the USSR in 1991 plunged the Castro regime into a crisis of unparalleled severity. Now without a powerful patron, Castro had to face alone the continuing U.S. policy of economic blockade, diplomatic isolation, and military threat. The Cuban leader sought new trading partners and sources of investment, but the attraction of a better life in the United States, made evident daily in television beamed from Miami, challenged the regime's legitimacy and worried Castro about how he would keep the spirit of revolution alive for the next generation.

TABLE 6.1 Castro's Revolution in 1990: A Comparative Balance Sheet[19]			
	Cuba	Latin America and Caribbean	Leading Industrialized Countries
Life expectancy (average years)	75	67	75
Infant mortality rate (deaths to age 5 per 1,000 live births)	14	70	18
Literacy (percentage of population)	94	84	99–100
Military spending (percentage of GNP)	11	2	5

CUBA'S REVOLUTION

1898	The United States goes to war to end Spanish control of Cuba
1902	Cuba gains independence as a U.S. protectorate
1953	July 26 attack on a military barracks propels Castro to prominence as an opponent of Batista
1956–1959	Castro builds an opposition movement that topples Batista
1960	Castro cements close ties to the Soviet bloc
1961	U.S.-sponsored invasion force is defeated at the Bay of Pigs; Castro declares himself a socialist
1962	Castro accepts Soviet missiles, setting off a nuclear confrontation between the superpowers
1991	Soviet collapse deprives Castro of his chief source of international political and economic support

DECOLONIZATION IN SUB-SAHARAN AFRICA

Africa south of the Saharan Desert—the bulk of the continent, excluding Morocco, Algeria, Tunisia, Libya, and Egypt—is a place of enormous diversity. Roughly five thousand miles from north to south and forty-six hundred miles from east to west, it accounts for one-fifth of the earth's surface. Its size—three times that of the United States—is matched by the variety of its landscape, the range of its climates, and the richness of its natural resources. Yet the region fits in its own distinct way into the broad patterns previously attributed to the third world. Like much of the rest of the third world, the sub-Saharan region experienced foreign conquest and exploitation. In the late nineteenth century the European powers completed Africa's subjugation, carving it into colonies (formalized at the conference of Berlin in 1884–1885). The only exceptions were Liberia (colonized by African Americans and independent since 1847) and the kingdom of Ethiopia. This subjugated region was the home of vital societies, sprawling empires, long-distance trade, warfare, and cultural interchange among a wide array of peoples. Europeans added new features. They diverted inland trade into imperial, maritime patterns; they shaped local economies to suit their short-term strategies of exploiting resource-rich land and cheap labor, especially in extractive industries and plantation agriculture; and they kept their costs low by minimizing investment in local economies.

Also like other third-world peoples, Africans began in the wake of World War II a sustained drive against European colonial control. By the late 1950s and early 1960s they had made enormous strides toward throwing off that control. (See Map 6.2.) In most cases colonial powers had worked out collaborative arrangements with indigenous elites. This was the favored British path. As in the case of India, London had consistently preferred a low-cost, light-rein approach to colo-

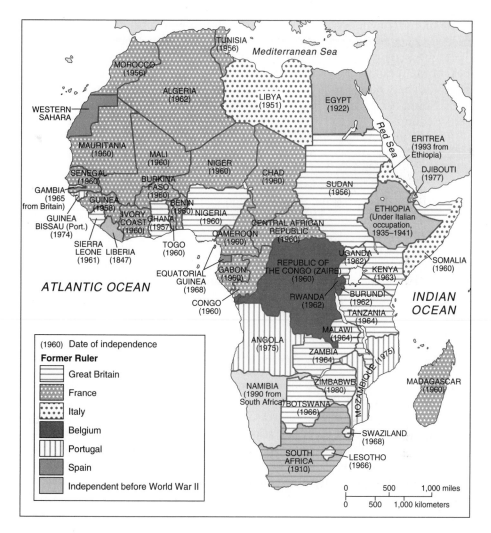

MAP 6.2
Africa: From Colonialism to Independence

nial administration that left substantial authority in the hands of local leaders and even anticipated conceding greater autonomy to the "natives." When the cry for independence went up after World War II, London usually accommodated rather than engage in a costly defense of colonial authority that would radicalize post-colonial leaders. Former British colonies such as Ghana, Nigeria, and Kenya began their national life with parliamentary governments and a place in the association of former colonies known as the British Commonwealth. The French had, by contrast, pursued policies of assimilation intended to create a close, permanent bond with their colonies. But France had to retreat in the face of indigenous pressures and after 1958 offered its remaining sub-Saharan colonies a choice between full independence or an association with France that would preserve some mutually beneficial ties. A third pattern involving prolonged conflict over independence and majority rule was evident in Zimbabwe, South Africa, and the Portuguese colonies of Mozambique and Angola. In these cases substantial numbers of European settlers supported the colonial status quo. Their tenacity set the stage for long, bitter struggles with African liberation movements. (Chapter 9 treats South Africa as the most extreme example of the persistence of European settler control.)

The ghost of Karl Marx hovered over Africa during the early phase of decolonization. Many independence leaders were to tilt left for familiar reasons. Capitalism was a system that had brought them few benefits in the colonial era and that the former colonial powers still championed. Socialism, by contrast, seemed most relevant to their aspirations for rapid economic and social development. The Soviet Union proved more supportive of true independence and autonomous development than the West, and Mao Zedong's peasant revolution offered a model suited to third-world social conditions. Leaders in diverse settings—from Patrice Lumumba in the Belgian Congo to Nelson Mandela in South Africa—drew ideological inspiration and political support from the Left. The most influential figure in the heyday of African decolonization was Kwame Nkrumah, Ghana's founding father.

Ghana and Nkrumah's African Socialism

The land to which Nkrumah returned in late 1947 after his long sojourn abroad (see p. 147) was under British control. Between 1874 and 1901 the British, with the help of local allies, had taken over Ghana's territory (then known as the Gold Coast). Just as the political consolidation was coming to a close, the colonial economic transformation began as cocoa production for export took off. By 1910 Ghana controlled almost half the global market. At the same time the small colonial administration was cultivating and educating an elite of teachers, bureaucrats, and entrepreneurs.

Nkrumah as the Spearhead of Independence. On arrival home, Nkrumah found the road to full independence blocked by a cozy alliance between the British and local elites consisting of tribal chiefs, merchants, crop brokers, and urban professionals (teachers, doctors, lawyers, and civil servants). This minority of political notables—roughly a thousand in total—had worked closely with the British, traded with the British, and received education under British rule. They strongly favored a gradual transition to independence that would enable them to take control without inviting dangerous social upheaval. As the first formal step in that direction, this elite organized the United Gold Coast Convention (UGCC) in 1947. By embracing this "responsible" established class of influentials, London hoped to guide the Gold Coast toward independence in a way that would maintain Britain's political and economic influence. Already in 1946 Britain had given the colony a constitution as a first step toward what was supposed to be a long, peaceful evolution toward independence.

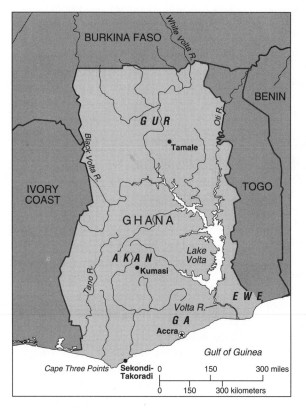

MAP 6.3
Ghana with Its Main Ethnic Divisions
Akans, located in the southern half of the country west of the Volta River, made up roughly half the population. They were not one group but a variety of groups, including Ashanti and Fante, with a common language and cultural patterns (including a generally matrilineal system). The Gur-speaking peoples of northern Ghana constituted about a third. Isolated from the rest of the country, they felt some resentment toward coastal peoples who benefited from British rule. The Ewe group accounted for 13 percent. They had become part of Ghana when, after World War I, London took possession of German-held Togoland and made it a part of the Gold Coast. As a result of this decision made by distant foreigners, Ghana gained a substantial body of Ewe people living in the resource-poor corner of the country east of the Volta River, but the majority was left just across the border in what became the independent state of Togo. The fourth broad group, those speaking Ga, made up 9 percent. They lived along the coast around the capital, Accra.

Nkrumah disrupted this comfortable arrangement. Working within the "establishment" UGCC, he set up a newspaper, schools, and a youth organization to create a base of popular support. Nkrumah's energy and success unnerved the UGCC leaders and the colonial administration. Sensing in increasing popular agitation a "communist" plot, worried colonial authorities had Nkrumah and the other prominent UGCC figures arrested in 1948. When they were released from jail, the UGCC leaders attacked Nkrumah as a "rabble-rouser." Now resolved to chart his own path, Nkrumah created his own Convention People's Party (CPP) to advocate immediate independence and a popular role in national politics. Though Nkrumah and others at the CPP forefront lacked wealth and close working ties with the British, they still had important assets—a familiarity with the West, political experience, and popular support.

Nkrumah pressed ahead with a nonviolent program to force concessions from the British much as Gandhi had done in India earlier. The response was at first repression, including his second arrest early in 1950. Now more popular than ever, Nkrumah ran for the legislature from prison and won a resounding victory in 1951 along with others of his party. London realized that like it or not, it had to deal with Nkrumah and accelerate decolonization if it wanted to keep peace and protect commerce. Further facilitating the decision was the absence of a substantial European community tenaciously clinging to the colonial order. The British government released Nkrumah, asked him to form a government, and promised to move the colony rapidly to self-rule. In 1957 the colony with its almost seven million people became a fully independent state within the British Commonwealth. It took the name of Ghana after an interior West African trading empire that had flourished a thousand years earlier.

As Ghana's first president, Nkrumah was an articulate, internationally recognized figure bent on exploring an African road to socialism. This impatient modernizer envisioned a country quickly and drastically made over. He wanted universal, free education and health care, safe water and good sanitation, affordable housing, and wide access to electricity. But he could not advance popular welfare without addressing the injurious economic impact of the colonial era and the continuing subordination in trade and finance to the former colonial masters. As Nkrumah saw it, Ghana was poor because of foreign exploitation. The British had profited from his country's wealth; Ghanaians had gained little as their natural resources and the fruit of their labor flowed abroad.

Nkrumah, like other leaders of the independence era, made neo-colonialism (see Chapter 3) a major issue. This system of influence by former colonial powers over newly independent countries was reinforced by the Cold War superpower, the United States, which for the first time took an interest in Africa as a region of instability that the Soviet Union might exploit. Washington pressed Ghana and other newly independent states to align with the West politically as well as economically and to eschew socialist policies. Nkrumah argued that these neo-colonial pressures created a formidable obstacle to charting a path that would best serve his people.

Nkrumah devised a two-pronged prescription for achieving genuine independence and meaningful economic development. First, he opted for a domestic development strategy intended to alter the pattern of foreign trade. As long as the country exported cheap raw materials and imported expensive finished goods, it would remain underdeveloped and exploited. To break this pattern Nkrumah implemented a policy of import substitution, promoting rapid industrialization so that Ghanaians could produce their own finished goods as a substitute for imports, while also raising production of raw materials for processing within Ghana, thereby increasing their export value. (See Chapter 5 on the emergence of this strategy of import substitution.) Impatient with private enterprise, Nkrumah created state-owned corporations to take over gold mines, plantations, processing industries, transport, and marketing. The government improved the road and rail network, built port facilities, established a national airline and shipping line, and constructed a major hydroelectric project. As a result of this effort Ghana went deeply into debt, but the long-term benefits were expected to be large. In March 1964 Nkrumah inaugurated an ambitious seven-year development plan that would gradually restrict private enterprise in favor of a state-controlled economy.

The second part of Nkrumah's prescription was pan-Africanism with its dream of uniting black Africa politically, economically, and militarily. As Africans emerged from colonial rule, he hoped that they would recognize their common bonds, work closely together, and thus undo the divisions among them created when the Europeans had imposed arbitrary lines of partition. A great African union would transcend boundary issues and submerge ethnic differences that weakened individual African states. It would permit the creation of a unified armed force to fend off U.S. or European interference and to secure decolonization from European powers struggling to hold on to their African possessions. It would help create an African market with the capital to finance its own development and the buying power to absorb its own production. This pan-African idea may have been the sturdiest of Nkrumah's dreams, going back to the early 1940s. In a speech to a meeting of African leaders in Addis Ababa, Ethiopia, in May 1963 he urged them to "unite in order to achieve the full liberation of our continent."[20] This speech heralded the creation of the Organization of African Unity (OAU). Nkrumah made good on his verbal commitment, serving personally as patron of independence movements and making training bases available for their use.

The End of the Nkrumah Era. By 1966 Nkrumah was in deep trouble. His pan-African dreams were not shared by other heads of state, who shied away from creating a single continental economy and polity. They wanted the OAU only as a consultative body. At the same time socialism was not bringing prosperity to Ghana. Population growth was outpacing food output, forcing Ghana to import food for the first time. At the same time, the price of the prime export, cocoa, fell on the world market, and Ghana experienced a foreign-currency shortage. Consumer products disappeared from shop shelves, and inflation soared. With an empty treasury, a heavy national debt, and a struggling economy, Nkrumah's promise of a better life and his calls for patience and sacrifice rang hollow.

Finally, the CPP was failing Nkrumah as a political tool in part because of Ghana's overlapping regional and ethnic divisions. The broad northern territories kept a distance from the CPP, and the central sections dominated by the Ashanti nobility with its own proud tradition of kingship and system of chiefs fought for autonomy against the CPP's centralizing tendencies. Cocoa producers in the Ashanti region, the source of nearly half of Ghana's output, added to the clamor against the CPP for its policy of setting crop prices. In the southeastern region, the Ewe turned their back on the CPP, eager to unite instead with kinfolk in neighboring Togo. (See Map 6.3.)

Adding to these ethnic difficulties, the CPP had become faction-ridden and self-serving with its members happily enriching themselves as party and government bureaucrats. A disillusioned Ghanaian novelist wrote of the corruption associated with CPP rule. "Men who know nothing about politics have grown hot with ideology, thinking of the money that will come. The civil servant who hates socialism is there, singing hosanna. The poet is there, serving power and waiting to fill his coming paunch with crumbs."[21] When Nkrumah's attempt to crack down on official corruption, nepotism, and ethnic rivalry, and bureaucratic inertia failed, he began silencing an increasingly vocal opposition and moving in 1964 to a one-party state. By then Nkrumah had become a "big man" who dominated the political system with a style that became increasingly autocratic. A personality cult promoted by sycophants insulated him from criticism.

With internal tension building, powerful outsiders looked to hasten Nkrumah's exit. France was troubled by Nkrumah's help to its former colony, Guinea, then struggling to survive independence, while his support for liberation struggles in Portuguese colonies, in Rhodesia, and in South Africa caused more general irritation in the West. He struck bilateral economic deals with eastern European regimes, the Soviet Union, and China, and he publicly attacked exploitation of the third world by multinational corporations.

The ranks of Nkrumah's enemies were reaching formidable proportions by the mid-1960s. He had survived three attempts on his life. Finally in February 1966 his years in power ended with a coup carried out by disaffected police and senior army officers (largely of Ewe origin) while Nkrumah was visiting Vietnam. From exile in Guinea he watched excitedly the growing militancy of blacks in the United States and imagined a global alliance of peoples of African descent advancing alongside other liberation movements toward the overthrow of capitalism, imperialism, and neo-colonialism. While his old pan-African dream flowered for the last time, his plots to regain power in Ghana failed, and he died of cancer in 1972.

Whatever his failures, Nkrumah does not deserve our condescension. He ventured abroad and into another culture from one that was politically subjugated and branded inferior by the West. He explored a world of new ideas, seeking the ones suitable for his country. He maneuvered Britain into giving up colonial control without serious bloodshed, and his quest for a brighter future for Ghana and Africa commanded world attention and inspired enthusiasm in the region. His economic plans failed, perhaps largely because the CPP did not

GHANA'S NKRUMAH	
1909	Nkrumah is born on the coast of Britain's Gold Coast colony
1935–1947	Nkrumah studies in the United States and Britain
1948	Nkrumah plunges into the independence movement, splits with United Gold Coast Convention, and forms his own Convention People's Party
1957–1960	Ghana moves to full independence, signaling the rapid end to colonial order in sub-Saharan Africa
1963	Nkrumah presses for pan-African unity
1964	Nkrumah launches his seven-year economic plan and imposes one-party rule
1966	Nkrumah is ousted (dies in exile in 1972)

become the sort of tight, disciplined Leninist party-state that was critical to imposing change in the USSR, China, Vietnam, and Castro's Cuba. Although Nkrumah's pan-Africanism never took hold, the OAU still exists as the African Union, and his idea of a continent with a common interest in cooperation also survives.

Colonial Legacies in Ghana and Beyond

Nkrumah and other independence leaders faced serious limits on their freedom of action. Perhaps the most important of those limits were the legacies of the colonial past. The practices and decisions imposed by Europeans had consequences that carried over powerfully into the post-1945 period and help explain the difficulties that new states encountered in the postcolonial period. To be sure, Africa south of the Sahara is marked by a diversity that rules out simple, rigid generalizations. Ghana is only one country of the fifty-one in the region, and more than most its early post-independence experience reflected radical currents flowing through the third world generally. Even so, Ghana can tell us a good deal about the way the past weighed heavily on African countries regardless of their political orientation.

Economic and Social Transformation of the Countryside. One of the prime colonial legacies was a transformed rural economy. Commercializing agriculture altered the lives of rural people (the majority of the population) and created a gap between the city and the countryside. To understand this transformation, we need to look back at least a century. Throughout much of Africa before the first Europeans reached the coast, peasants engaged either in subsistence agriculture or in trade along interior lines. The arrival of the Europeans, beginning with the Portuguese and the Spanish in the late fifteenth century, marked a gradual reorientation of commerce toward the coast. Agricultural products, timber, minerals, and slaves were gathered in the interior and then shipped to the coast for export to Europe or the Americas. The slave trade alone had a deeply disruptive effect over a long period extending from the fifteenth to the nineteenth century. During that time not only were 15 million Africans forced into slavery, but also two to five times that number may have died in the fighting that attended slaving.

By the time of the colonial carving up in the late nineteenth century, a clear economic pattern had emerged that would shape contemporary Africa. Powerful chiefs and merchants formed strong and profitable commercial networks with European business firms. These arrangements saw African peasants more and more involved in producing for the global market. Goods passed through growing port cities that connected internal commercial networks with the international trading system. Those same cities were also becoming the center of colonial administration and the home of a small but influential African elite that had accommodated to European dominance.

Ghana was a microcosm of this process of economic transformation. For example, the shift to cocoa production in the early twentieth century had enormous social effects. As it became central to the economy, cocoa production displaced the formerly dominant crops of palm oil and rubber. The new crop drew migrants from far in the interior into the central region where growing conditions were good. The newcomers either cleared their own land to farm or worked for others. This rush of activity gave rise to a more complex and fluid society. At the top were the larger farmers with command of capital, brokers who purchased cocoa for sale to exporters (usually European) in the major ports, and the colonial bureaucrats who regulated and taxed the cocoa trade. Below them were smaller independent farmers. Still lower were sharecroppers and contract and wage laborers.

Within villages in Ghana but also elsewhere in Africa and other parts of the third world, the rise of export crops grown for cash initiated a profound shift in values. The new commercial ethos associated with this export crop encouraged more individualistic behavior and eroded the sense of moral community. Those growing up before colonial commerce took hold would have learned the virtues of cooperation, kindness, and concern for others. As the sense of reciprocal responsibility declined under the pressures of the new trade, the tight village system with its strong welfare elements gave way to families and individuals pursuing their own interests and to the wealthy turning their backs on their poorer neighbors.

Family and village lands earlier held in common passed into private control. The loss of communal land and the tendency toward concentration of land in the hands of those with the resources to grow and market the export crop in turn increased the number of landless who at one time could have made a claim on a portion of the communal holdings. As public land disappeared and the revenue from that land dried up, village chiefs lost control of resources that could be used for the common good. Thus their power declined relative to the new class of entrepreneurs.

These changes were especially detrimental to women. Before Western economic networks began penetrating into the rural interior, women had had an important voice in village affairs while also bearing a special responsibility for family well-being and community harmony. Commercialization undermined the power and status of women at the same time that it expanded opportunities for men. Encroaching cash crops ate up land previously dedicated to communal subsistence and deprived women of their say in the disposal of the crop even as they continued with their old chores of planting, weeding, and harvesting. As village society fragmented, separation and divorce became more common. Abandoned women could no longer depend to the extent they once had on communal resources for help in caring for children.

Colonial administrators who promoted the growth and sale of export crops as well as missionaries who spread new values accentuated the crisis for women. They applied European gender codes that gave formal authority to men. Convinced that women had no place in politics or the mainstream economy, British governors reserved for men alone the opportunity for education, professional advancement, employment in the modern sector of mining and industry, participation in long-distance trade, and decisions about lucrative cash crops. Colonial policies ignored flourishing women's associations and discouraged women from continuing to play their long-established role in marketing food and fabrics.

The elaboration of trade and the growth of port cities combined with the strains felt by villages to set in motion a major rural exodus typical of most of the third world. Migrants (primarily men) set off to carve out a better life in the privileged urban sector. The human exodus depopulated villages and left behind mainly women, the very young, and the very old. Village women who carried a mounting burden of responsibilities depended on funds sent home by migrants. Some also found serving as a bridge between city and countryside a rewarding niche that built on their traditional role in petty trading. Market women in Ghana, for example, developed distribution networks and general trading savvy. Operating in associations defined by type of goods, they served as commercial intermediaries. They purchased local produce, often perishable, in the country-side and sold it at the markets that they ran in nearby cities. Thanks to this independent source of income, these women were able to support themselves and their children when husbands proved unreliable.

The Urban-Rural Divide. The second colonial legacy, closely related to the first, was a generally parasitic relationship of the city to the countryside. Functioning within an urban environment, colonial governments from Mali to Mozambique made scant economic contribution to the life of rural people. Indeed, they drained resources from the countryside in the form of taxes and labor in order to pay for administration and whatever projects were essential to external trade such as roads, rail lines, and port facilities. Otherwise, colonial administrators were inclined to leave rural people to fend for themselves.

In Ghana the chief instrument for the exploitation of the countryside was the cocoa marketing board, established by the British during World War II. The board guaranteed producers a minimum price and pocketed the difference when world prices were higher, thereby accumulating substantial reserves. Resentment against this blatant form of economic exploitation had helped to feed independence fever. Although the board and its reserves fell into Nkrumah's hands at independence, he did not abolish this unfair fiscal system, nor did he use the savings to help the rural producers who had been its source. Instead, like other African leaders, he pursued large-scale development projects such as dams and heavy industry designed to showcase the country's claim to being modern. While the reserves went into those projects, he intensified the effort to squeeze money from the countryside. Because Nkrumah's projects did more to help the city than the countryside, cocoa farmers felt exploited.

Behind this pervasive pattern of favoring the city over the countryside was condescension toward the rural population felt by the Western-trained, urban-ized elites who led the national independence movements. Like the Ladino elites in Guatemala and the Congress party leaders in India, many were educated abroad, thus strengthening their attachment to Western ways. Exposure to the comforts of modern urban life and the power of the modern Western state during sojourns overseas engendered a stinging sensitivity to the backwardness of their own societies and a deep-seated impatience with the adherence of peasants to old ways of doing things. Overwhelmingly, the rank and file that joined in the independence drive were also city dwellers, whereas rural Africa remained politically peripheral.

Nkrumah strikingly illustrates these post-independence, pro-urban biases. Growing up on the coast among a commercial rather than an agricultural people, then studying with missionaries, and finally experiencing life in the United States and Britain had shaped his view of what Ghana should become. He wanted to transform the countryside, replacing small-scale, "backward" peasant production with "modern," mechanized, state-controlled agriculture. He repeatedly expressed his faith in science and technology wielded by rational people operating in a framework of socialist principles to create a new Ghana. It was the grand march of progress, not the daily struggles of rural folk, that excited him.

In according cities a privileged status, these indigenous leaders were following, perhaps unconsciously, the colonial lead. Cities throughout the colonial world had arisen as the site of European residence, political administration, and sometimes trade. The very independence leaders who denounced economic control by outsiders proceeded to practice a kind of internal cultural colonialism by favoring the city over the countryside. New African leaders focused their concerns on the modern urban sector where their political supporters and political institutions along with industry and other major projects were located. They invested in urban infrastructure and education and lavished food subsidies as well as housing and health care on the urban population. This favoritism placated urban elites and forestalled political discontent. The neglect of the countryside combined with an improving urban living standard not surprisingly acted as a powerful magnet for peasants. Rather than working productively in the countryside, they piled up in enormous shantytowns but added little to economic output.

This imbalanced development created long-term economic problems. To be sure, immediately after independence economic prospects seemed generally favorable. Though initial per capita income in most countries of sub-Saharan Africa was less than $100 per year, school enrollments still climbed, life expectancy rose from thirty-nine years to forty-nine years, and major construction projects moved ahead. But the first flush of optimism quickly passed, and as we have seen, the large, urban-based state sector got the lion's share of resources while burdening agriculture.

The Impact of Ethnic Diversity. The final major colonial legacy can be found in the ethnic patchworks that came to characterize sub-Saharan states. Though Africans account for only 13 percent of the world's population (832 million in 2002), they were fragmented into at least a thousand ethnic and linguistic groups. When European colonizers came to this world, they paid no attention to ethnic homogeneity and in some cases preferred a diverse population within one colony so administrators could exercise divide-and-rule tactics. Colonial officials created their own ethnic map, deepening old social divisions or fostering new ones. As a result of arbitrary decisions by nineteenth-century Europeans, newly independent states were not real nations. Each held a considerable variety of groups within its borders, with some of those groups spilling over into adjacent states. This ethnic pluralism made post-independence governance difficult.

Ghana's divisions were minor compared to some other African countries. For example, Zambia contained within its borders seventy-three ethno-linguistic groups, and Kenya had about forty. Nigeria, the most populous of sub-Saharan states was divided into 250 ethnic groups overlaid by major religious differences (with roughly half of the population Muslim and a third Christian).

States riven ethnically had to find ways to contain rivalry, though this effort has often failed and led to violence. Nigeria provided early and bloody testimony to the dangers of these divisions. Growing ethnic and religious tension evident immediately after independence in 1963 erupted in open conflict three years later. Not until 1970 was a secessionist movement in the eastern, Ibo portion of the country finally crushed with the loss of more than a million lives. More recently, Rwanda has revealed the terrible potential for internal conflict created by colonial division of the continent without regard for ethnic homogeneity of individual states. In the colonial period, Belgian authorities not only combined diverse people but also accentuated differences by promoting the Tutsi (people with favored physical features) over the Hutu. Independence in 1964 found the majority Hutu in control, which in turn generated armed Tutsi resistance and finally in 1994 a genocidal campaign by militant Hutus opposed to any compromise power-sharing deal. At least 800,000, perhaps a million, mostly Tutsi, died in the course of several months of organized slaughter at the hands of their compatriots. Ghana has been spared ethnic warfare, but it has nonetheless faced interregional tensions. The Ewe, split by the border with Togo, have entertained the idea of secession. The political assertiveness of the Ashanti has worried other groups, while the Ashanti felt discriminated against when Nkrumah made them bear the burden of his development policy. His characterization of their mentality as "primitive" in some youthful writing suggests the deep-seated ethnic stereotypes that made political cohabitation difficult.

We should not think of sub-Saharan Africa as somehow peculiar in having to cope with internal divisions of this sort. Europe five hundred years ago (not to mention modern-day Yugoslavia and Indonesia) offers parallels. State boundaries, drawn then at the pleasure of monarchs, contained multiple and overlapping language groups. The resulting disputes helped plunge European states into nationalist wars that tore apart empires and created new, more homogenous political units. By contrast, African states during their first decades took as a first principle the legitimacy of the inherited colonial administrative boundaries. Post-colonial elites worked to protect those boundaries by containing centrifugal and secessionist forces within them. They feared national disintegration both for the frightening warfare it would unleash among ethnic groups and for the predatory opportunities it would create for neighbors.

This commitment to holding divided states together helped give rise to an autocratic (often despotic) and parasitic political system—what some observers have called the "big-man" syndrome. Typically, a leader in power would proceed to enrich himself, his family, and the ethnic group that was his base of political support. But if he were to survive, he also had to use his access to the country's wealth to appease other ethnic groups. By widely distributing state largesse, the "big man" ensured even those on the fringe of political power a share in the system and a stake in his continued rule. In that sense the state functioned as a prized resource to smooth over ethnic tensions; this was in contrast to Central America, where it served to bolster the position of a few wealthy families, or East Asia, where it functioned as the agent of either economic or revolutionary mobilization.

Nkrumah had big-man counterparts in most of the post-independence African states—figures who dominated the political landscape for years. Kenneth Kuanda controlled Zambia for its first quarter-century, relinquishing power only in 1991. Jomo Kenyatta not only led Kenya to independence in 1963 but also dominated until his death in 1978 and handpicked a successor, Daniel arap Moi (in power until 2003). Félix Houphouët-Boigny ruled Ivory Coast for thirty-four years until he died in 1993. The infamously corrupt and brutal Mobuto Sese Seko took power in the Belgian Congo (later renamed Zaire) in 1965, became president in 1970, and exploited his poor, mineral-rich country until he was driven into exile in 1997. In Nigeria, a string of military leaders occupied the big-man role through the bulk of the period following independence in 1960. Julius Nyerere, who led Tanzania to independence from Britain in 1961, ruled for twenty-seven years.

Of all these legacies, the European creation of multi-ethnic states seems to have given rise to the most fundamental constraints to political and economic development in sub-Saharan Africa. Divergent loyalties and competing values not only made a common national vision impossible but also proved a constant source of political tension and armed conflict within newly independent countries. The persistence of ethnic division and jealousy in turn made the "big man" an attractive solution to the problems of integration, while the improvisation and shifts in policy to accommodate ethnic pressures and interethnic alliances virtually ruled out a coherent development policy. Nkrumah grasped from the outset of his career the promise of African integration as a solution to the burdens deeply divided countries would face. His own attempt to act on a transnational vision and move Africa as a whole toward liberation and greater cooperation only partially succeeded. But among his last words was a familiar message: "When Africa is a united, strong power, everyone will respect Africans, and Africans will respect themselves."[22] The insight seems even more profound today than in Nkrumah's time.

REMAKING THE MIDDLE EAST AND NORTH AFRICA

The countries stretching from North Africa to the edge of the Indian subcontinent gave expression in the 1950s and 1960s to the deep discontents that were evident in other areas of the third world. Those discontents were rooted in the experience of foreign domination and came to the fore as peoples in the region sought full independence and explored new paths to prosperity and unity. However, bold dreams for recasting individual societies and even the entire region fell short of realization. For the most part, popular welfare improved only marginally. At the same time, Europeans fought a rear-guard defense of their interests while the superpower rivals intruded on the scene, making it one more part of the global Cold War battleground.

The European powers had begun incursions into the region in the fifteenth century and continued with even deeper inroads during the nineteenth century. The climax came in a burst of colonization early in the twentieth century. The Ottoman Empire, which had controlled much of the region for four hundred years, lost one territory after another. Algeria became a French colony in 1848 and Tunisia a French protectorate in 1881. By the turn of the century, Iran as well as Afghanistan had fallen under the joint sway of Britain and Russia. Egypt came under British influence during the 1880s and became a formal protectorate in 1914. Italy colonized Libya in 1911, and the next year France and Spain divided Morocco. After World War I the victors took additional Ottoman lands as mandates, nominally under the supervision of the League of Nations. As in Africa, Britain and France imposed borders on the new states of Syria, Lebanon, Iraq, Transjordan (later Jordan), and the mandate of Palestine without regard to ethnic and religious makeup. (See Map 6.4.) Handpicked rulers served imperial interests, and when they did not, Paris and London were ready to intervene, militarily if necessary, to set matters right.

As elsewhere in the third world, this imposition of foreign control gave rise to nationalist demands for independence and reform. The modern states that would define the region in the postwar years began emerging in the interwar period. Britain ended its Iraqi mandate in 1932 and gave Egypt limited independence in 1922 (though keeping bases in both countries). In Iran a feeble dynasty collapsed under international pressures and domestic demands for reform. World War II intensified the colonial crisis in the Middle East. Weakened by conflict, the Europeans were less able to maintain their position in the region. At the same time, the Allied commitment to self-determination inspired nationalists with hopes for a new postwar order. A defeated Italy surrendered Libya, which became independent in 1951. France granted Syria its independence in 1944, and the next year Lebanon won its freedom. Morocco finally gained full independence in 1956. In Tunisia, France resisted independence demands in the late 1940s but then gave way in 1956 to prevent radical elements from taking power. Algeria, which witnessed the last stand of the old European order, finally forced France out in 1962.

These developments unleashed a complex set of political and ideological currents. Although monarchies survived—some longer than others—in Morocco, Libya, Egypt, Jordan, Saudi Arabia, Iraq, and Iran, military regimes were on the rise as officers began to step forward as authoritarian national leaders. Communist parties and socialist critiques of the domestic and international order commanded an unprecedented appeal among politically active urbanites. Secular nationalism was in the ascendance, but conservative notions of a restored Muslim polity also won followers, especially among those alienated by the effects of long-term Westernization. Talk of pan-Arab solidarity was widespread, spurred by

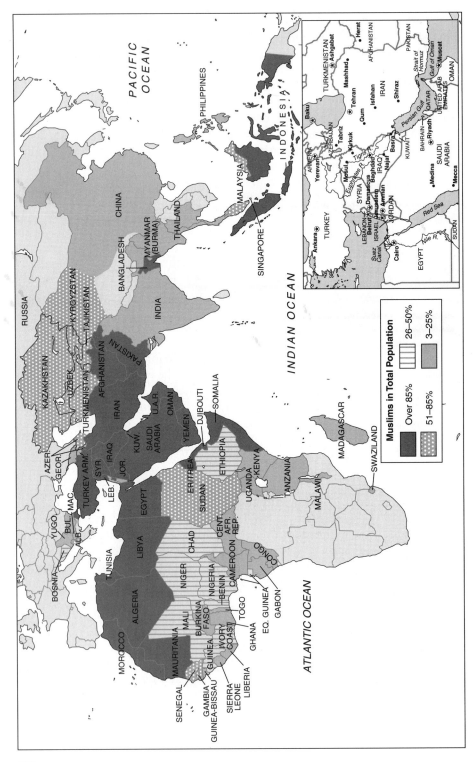

Muslims in Total Population

Over 85%	26–50%
51–85%	3–25%

PACIFIC OCEAN

RUSSIA

KAZAKHSTAN

KYRGYZSTAN

UZBEK.

TURKMENISTAN

TAJIKISTAN

CHINA

MYANMAR (BURMA)

BANGLADESH

THAILAND

PHILIPPINES

MALAYSIA

SINGAPORE

INDONESIA

INDIA

PAKISTAN

AFGHANISTAN

IRAN

INDIAN OCEAN

BOSNIA

YUGO.

BUL.

MAC.

ALB.

TURKEY

ARM.

AZER.

GEOR.

SYR.

LEB.

IRAQ

JOR.

KUW.

SAUDI ARABIA

U.A.R.

OMAN

YEMEN

DJIBOUTI

SOMALIA

ETHIOPIA

ERITREA

EGYPT

SUDAN

LIBYA

TUNISIA

ALGERIA

MOROCCO

MAURITANIA

MALI

NIGER

CHAD

CENT. AFR. REP.

UGANDA

KENYA

TANZANIA

MALAWI

MADAGASCAR

SWAZILAND

CONGO

GABON

EQ. GUINEA

CAMEROON

NIGERIA

BENIN

TOGO

GHANA

IVORY COAST

BURKINA FASO

GUINEA

GUINEA-BISSAU

GAMBIA

SENEGAL

SIERRA LEONE

LIBERIA

ATLANTIC OCEAN

TURKMENISTAN

Ashgabat

AFGHANISTAN

Herat

Mashhad

PAKISTAN

Tehran

IRAN

Isfahan

Qum

Shiraz

Tabriz

Strait of Hormuz

Gulf of Oman

Muscat

OMAN

ARMENIA

Yerevan

Baku

AZERBAIJAN

Persian Gulf

BAHRAIN

QATAR

UNITED ARAB EMIRATES

Mosul

Kirkuk

Tigris R.

Euphrates R.

IRAQ

Baghdad

Basra

KUWAIT

Najaf

SYRIA

Damascus

LEBANON

Beirut

Jerusalem

ISRAEL

Amman

JORDAN

Riyadh

SAUDI ARABIA

Medina

Mecca

TURKEY

Ankara

Red Sea

SUDAN

Suez Canal

Cairo

EGYPT

Nile R.

European imperialism and the creation of the state of Israel in 1948 at the expense of the Palestinians living in the area.

Politically explosive questions of national or regional identity had to be answered in the context of intense Cold War pressures. The United States wanted to promote containment and to protect oil resources critical to the economies of its allies. The Soviet Union feared American influence on its southern border. Both powers thus recruited regional clients. The most important for the United States were Israel and Iran; for the USSR it was Syria and Iraq. Egypt shifted sides in an attempt to play the Cold War rivals against each other.

Economic Nationalism in Iran

Iran, one of the two most populous states in the Middle East, nicely illustrates the interplay between domestic differences over development and superpower pressures. Known until 1935 as Persia, Iran was a vast country that was largely arid and mountainous, with the exception of a lush and fertile strip along the Caspian Sea in the north. During the nineteenth century, this non-Arab people had increasingly fallen under European domination. Its agricultural system shifted to cash crops—chiefly cotton, silk, and wheat—for sale on international markets. Landlords consolidated their holdings to exploit this opportunity, rendering many peasants landless. A parallel political process of subordination had been completed by the turn of the century as Britain and Russia each asserted their sphere of influence. Britain enjoyed a privileged position in the south, with its chief prize an oil concession held by the Anglo-Iranian Oil Company (AIOC; later British Petroleum). Russia was predominant in the north. A weak and unpopular native dynasty, the Qajars, ruled from the capital in Tehran. Its critics demanded modernizing reforms, above all the creation of a constitutional monarchy.

In 1921 Reza Khan, a tough officer who had risen through the ranks, marched his forces into Tehran. The old dynasty was failing, and the country had descended into social disorder, which the British exploited to extend their influence. Reza Khan began by restoring calm in the countryside and building up his military force. Then in 1926 he replaced the Qajars with his own Pahlevi dynasty. This autocrat, now known as Reza Shah (or king), strengthened the state bureaucracy, replaced Islamic courts with those following European legal principles, promoted industry and communications, and encouraged a strong sense of national identity. At the same time he ruthlessly repressed dissent and aggressively lined his own pocket. Only the British resisted his reach; their southern stronghold functioned as a virtual independent state within Iran, with the oil operation, the country's largest employer, remaining firmly in AIOC hands. The rule of this strong but unpopular autocrat came to a sudden end in 1941. Early that

◄**MAP 6.4**
The Islamic World and the Middle East

year Britain and the USSR had sent troops into Iran to safeguard a supply route into the Soviet Union that was critical to the war effort. Once those two powers decided that Reza Khan was too pro-German, he abdicated in order to save the monarchy.

Reza Shah's successor was his son, Mohammed Reza, the man who came to be known—at least in the West—simply as "the shah." The son ascended the throne in his early twenties just as World War II began to reshuffle the pattern of foreign influence over his country. U.S. troops joined in the Anglo-Soviet occupation and the United States established itself as the dominant power, pushing out the Soviets and marginalizing the war-weakened British. In 1946 the Truman administration confronted the Soviets over their troops still in Iran and over their support for a secessionist movement in the northwest corner of the country. Stalin withdrew his forces, the Iranian army crushed the secessionists, and Washington began to integrate Iran into the containment line stretching around the Soviet Union. Mohammed Reza Shah began to seem to Washington like the very man to keep Iran firmly aligned with the United States.

Mossadeq as a Nationalist Champion. Allied promises of a new postwar order had in the meantime revived nationalist unrest within the country at the same time that the tentativeness of the young shah created a political vacuum. A wide range of political groups—from Communists to middle-class professionals to religious conservatives—now demanded change. The common denominator among them was a desire to end Iran's dependence on foreign powers and to avoid entanglement in the Cold War. They especially resented the young shah's willingness to leave Iran's oil, its major economic resource, under the control of foreigners. Like other Middle Eastern oil companies at the time, the AIOC decided on the rate of extraction of oil, set oil prices, and thus controlled the level of revenues from royalties that Iran would receive. Nationalists also resented British interference in the country's political life, especially its collusion with landed elites and its support for tribal peoples resisting central government control.

The widely respected Mohammed Mossadeq emerged as the most prominent champion of a nationalist program. He was born in 1882 into an influential family. His father was a major landowner, and his mother came from the Persian royal line. He had gone to universities in Switzerland and France, earned a doctorate in law, and brought home Western notions of state building and economic development. Consistent with that background, Mossadeq argued during his political career for shifting power from the royal court to the national legislature and for asserting greater control over the British-controlled oil industry. These positions had led him to lock horns with the shah's father and suffer imprisonment and internal exile between 1928 and 1941. His views put him on a collision course with the young shah as well.

In 1951 this reform nationalist rode to power on a wave of anger over the shah's acceptance of a new, one-sided contract with the AIOC. The legislature responded by defiantly passing a bill nationalizing the oil industry and forcing the shah to accept Mossadeq as the new prime minister. Mossadeq's supporters were organized into a loose coalition known as the National Front. They came largely from the urban middle and lower classes and included nationalist and often radical groups but not the popular and well-organized Iranian Communist party (known as the Tudeh or "Masses" Party). Mossadeq at once put the oil nationalization into effect and then began to chip away at the shah's powers, hoping thereby to move the country toward a constitutional monarchy. These initiatives ignited a crisis that would grip Iran for two full years. The consequences would reverberate for decades.

The decision to nationalize the oil industry outraged the British government, which had a 50 percent stake in the AIOC. Anthony Eden, then the British foreign minister, characterized Mossadeq, the leading proponent of nationalization, as a "fractious child" and a "megalomaniac."[23] London retaliated at once. It organized an international boycott of Iranian oil that sent the economy into a tailspin. It threatened military reprisals. And it enlisted long-time Iranian allies, notably large landowners and powerful tribal leaders, in a covert campaign to overthrow Mossadeq and turn back the clock on oil policy.

In the standoff over Iran's oil, the U.S. government cast the deciding vote. The Truman administration joined the economic boycott but restrained London from taking military action. When Eisenhower came to office in 1953, he moved closer to the British out of fear that Iran's Communists might exploit this crisis to take power. With British secret operations in trouble, Eisenhower ordered the CIA to step into the breach. In August 1953 the CIA's agent in Tehran went to work promoting street demonstrations and sabotage that weakened an already strained pro-Mossadeq coalition. It had been hurt by the economic downturn, and Mossadeq's advocacy of secular reforms had alarmed conservative and religious allies. As clashes grew more violent, army units loyal to the shah took control. Placed under arrest, Mossadeq defiantly defended himself during his trial. "My only crime . . . is that I nationalized the Iranian oil industry, and removed the network of colonialism, and the political and economic influence of the greatest empire on earth from this land."[24] After several years of imprisonment Mossadeq was confined to his home, where he died in 1967, then in his mid-eighties and still defiant.

The Return of the Shah. The shah, who had fled abroad during the coup attempt, was its major beneficiary. With Mossadeq gone, he proceeded to consolidate his family's hold on Iran with the long-range goal of restoring his country's imperial greatness. To buttress his own political authority, he purged dissidents from the army, built up the police force, including the feared secret police, and brought the legislature under tight control. At the same time, the shah cultivated close relationships with the U.S. government and oil companies, breaking the British monopoly control of Iran's oil. The turn toward Washington brought security against pressure from his Soviet neighbor as well as a large influx of American advisors and American economic and military aid.

Confident that the shah was a reliable client and Iran a solid base for defending the Middle East, U.S. policymakers in the late 1950s and early 1960s turned toward a policy of modernization in Iran. The State Department and the CIA

IRAN AND THE POLITICS OF OIL

1926	Reza Khan establishes the Pahlevi dynasty in place of the Qajars
1941	Mohammed Reza Pahlevi becomes shah after the ouster of his father by British and Soviets
1951	Mossadeq champions a nationalized Anglo-Iranian Oil Company and a limited monarchy
1953	CIA-backed coup overthrows Mossadeq; the shah regains control with U.S. support
1963	Shah launches "White Revolution" reforms
1970s	Soaring oil prices enable the shah to spend lavishly on industry, the military, and public works

were convinced that the long-term prospects for internal stability depended on Tehran undertaking a program of social and economic reform. Bowing to U.S. pressure, the shah embarked on what became known as the White Revolution. Formally launched in 1963, it was a top-down effort to transform Iran into a modern, secular country. Its major goals were to build up industry, liberate women, promote advanced education as well as basic literacy, carry out land reform, and establish civil law in place of Islamic law. These changes pointed to a transformation in Iran every bit as radical as the program Mossadeq had championed, and in time they would generate a backlash as potent as the one that had toppled Mossadeq.

The funding for this multifaceted program came from oil. On his return to power in 1953, the shah had given the AIOC its property back in exchange for an increase in royalties on oil production. As international oil prices rose in the 1970s, so too did government revenue. This oil money paid for urban and industrial development, military power, and courtly pomp. It also raised per capita gross domestic product (GDP) almost three-fold between 1963 and 1977.

The 1970s seemed to prove the Tehran-Washington collaboration a great success. Iran's growing wealth encouraged the shah to dream of exercising more than regional power. He told a confidant in 1974, "To be first in the Middle East is not enough. We must raise ourselves to the level of a great world power." But rapid and unbalanced economic development together with autocratic rule was breeding increasingly serious internal discontents. The shah denounced critics as wild radicals and pawns of the superpowers plotting to block Iran's rise to power. Though he sensed that something was amiss in his relationship to his people, he could not conceive of a revolutionary outbreak. "Our farmers and workers are far too happy," he asserted in private in 1973. Washington welcomed this ever-stronger Iran as a bulwark of stability in the oil-rich Persian Gulf, and beginning with the Nixon administration it gave the shah carte blanche to buy whatever arms he wanted. The shah spent lavishly to the benefit of the American arms industry and the U.S. balance of trade. Little did either the shah or Washington realize that they had planted the seeds for an Islamic revolution (treated in Chapter 9) that would shake the country, the region, and even the two superpowers.[25]

A New Order for Egypt and the Region

The radical impulse animating the Mossadeq program in Iran also took hold in Egypt. The stakes were equally high. Like Iran, Egypt was one of the most populous and influential countries in the region. But unlike Iran, the new order realized in Egypt demonstrated greater staying power. During the 1950s and 1960s, Gamal Abdul Nasser was the leading voice for regional unity and struggle against Israel while also championing Cold War non-alignment. At home he promoted a secular and socialist course that left a deep imprint.

Egypt reached its radical moment by a familiar route. Like others in the region, it had been pulled tightly into the European orbit in the course of the nineteenth century. Commercial agriculture, above all cotton, reshaped life in the countryside by consolidating land holdings. More and more of the population were left with little or no land. At the same time, Britain was establishing its position as the dominant power in Egypt, first economically after its textile industry came to rely on Egyptian cotton. The Suez Canal, completed in 1869, gave Egypt strategic significance to Britain. Connecting the Mediterranean to the Indian Ocean, the canal provided an indispensable link to India, the jewel in the British imperial crown. (See Map 6.4.) Economic and strategic interests combined to put Egypt firmly under British sway in 1882, though it remained at least formally an autonomous province of the Ottoman Empire. The outbreak of World War I gave London an opportunity to end the ambiguity surrounding Egypt's status after the country's nominal rulers, the Ottomans, aligned with Germany. The country became a formal protectorate.

Simmering Egyptian discontent with these arrangements burst into the open in the interwar years. The cry directed at British overlords was "Egypt for the Egyptians." London responded by granting limited independence in 1922. But continuing restrictions on Egypt's foreign relations and a major British military presence angered nationalists. As in other parts of the colonial world, World War II inspired Egyptian hopes for securing full independence.

Nasser and a Resurgent Egypt. The decade between 1942 and 1952 set the stage for the fall of the old regime and the rise of the new one. In February 1942 Britain fatally compromised the nationalist credentials of the monarchy and the leading elite-dominated political party by demanding the appointment of a pro-British prime minister. Faced by British tanks, the reigning monarch, Farouk, and his political supporters acquiesced. The king made a bad situation worse after the war by cavorting on the French Riviera while corruption flourished at court and the country stagnated politically and economically. Groups across a wide political spectrum—from educated, liberal middle-class elements, to conservative Muslims, to a small number of Marxist intellectuals—protested their country's impotence and humiliation. European exploitation had left Egypt backward. Britain kept a major military presence in the country and continued to wield substantial influence. Egyptian and other Arab armies had failed to prevent the establishment of a Jewish state in Palestine, a fresh European intrusion into the Arab world. The culmination of these developments came in January 1952 when British forces, now skirmishing frequently with nationalist guerrillas linked to the Egyptian military, attacked a police station and left over fifty people dead. Cairo exploded in anti-British violence.

The January riots underlined the growing divisions and disorder within Egyptian society and set the stage for the emergence of the Free Officer movement. Consisting of about a thousand middle-level officers from modest backgrounds, the Free Officers had secretly organized in opposition to King Farouk, whom they blamed for continuing British domination and festering domestic problems. During the January 1952 riots, these officers seized their chance to take action when the king had to call on the army to restore order. They overthrew Farouk and the next year declared Egypt a republic.

One of those officers, Colonel Gamal Abdul Nasser, emerged as the leading figure. He was born in 1918 into a family with rural roots. His father moved to the city of Alexandria to work as a clerk in the postal service. As a high school student, Nasser participated in the interwar anti-British demonstrations. In 1936 he enrolled in the military academy. A career in the army offered an avenue to social mobility otherwise closed to someone of his limited means. He served in the war to prevent the creation of the Jewish state of Israel in 1948, and in the wake of that defeat he helped organize the Free Officer movement. After the king's overthrow, Nasser quickly established his preeminence. He restrained other nationalist groups, repressed those who challenged him, and gave charge of the state apparatus to his close military associates. Nasser firmly established his own charismatic personality as the lodestar of Egyptian politics following an assassination attempt in October 1954. Surviving nine bullets, he proclaimed to a crowd on the spot his readiness for patriotic martyrdom: "My life is yours, my blood a sacrifice to Egypt.... I have lived for you, and will do so until I die, striving for your sake."[26]

At the start of his rule, Nasser recognized how widespread was the "dream of a strong[,] liberated Egypt." But making that dream reality was, he conceded, "the most complicated of our problems."[27] From the start Nasser took an assertive, independent international position. He provided support for anti-French independence movements in North Africa and leadership in the Arab campaign to drive out the Israelis. He resisted pressure to take sides in the Cold War, sought economic assistance from both superpowers, and joined India and Yugoslavia in championing non-alignment. At home his main concern was to relieve suffering in the countryside. About 5 percent of landowners held 65 percent of cultivated land, whereas the remaining 95 percent of the population had 35 percent (usually miniscule plots). By 1952 more than half of all rural families were landless. Shortly after seizing power, the Free Officers took a dramatic step toward addressing these inequities by redistributing the royal estates as well as large land holdings controlled by mainly absentee owners.

Of all his policies, non-alignment would embroil Nasser in the most trouble, setting off a major international crisis in 1956 and pushing him sharply to the Left. He tried to dissuade fellow Arab rulers from signing up as Cold War allies of the United States while at the same time himself looking for help from both the Soviets and the Americans. In 1955 he worked out an arms deal with the Soviet bloc to bring the Egyptian army up to the level of Israel while securing a World Bank loan of at least $1 billion for his showcase domestic project, the Aswan High Dam. Nasser envisioned building a major project that would harness the Nile, control floods, expand arable land, provide electricity, and thus dramatically lift Egypt into the modern age. He boasted, "In antiquity we built pyramids for the dead. Now we build pyramids for the living."[28] The dam would also raise Nasser's prestige and Egypt's influence in the Arab world.

The Eisenhower administration, provoked by Nasser's "neutralism" (that is, non-alignment in the Cold War), suddenly withdrew its support and thus undercut the World Bank loan for his grand project. The Egyptian leader struck back by nationalizing the one major asset available to him, the Suez Canal Company owned by British and French interests. With control of the canal went control of the flow of oil to Europe. Nasser's assertive nationalism added to the danger from the perspective of London and Paris. The British, French, and Israeli governments now conspired to cut Nasser down to size. In late October 1956, Israeli forces struck the first blow, followed by their European allies on the excuse of "restoring order." Outraged by this aggression, Eisenhower demanded that the invaders pull back. Nasser's prestige in the region soared.

Where Mossadeq had failed, Nasser had succeeded. But in the process he had become heavily reliant on Khrushchev's Soviet Union for economic and military aid. Khrushchev helped the first Soviet client in the Middle East complete the Aswan project, built up Egypt's army and air force, and provided access to technical training. Nasser insisted that he still favored a position of non-alignment and wanted help from the United States as well as the Soviet Union. He justified his pro-Soviet tilt on the grounds that Moscow did not insist on drawing Egypt into the Cold War and did not support Israel.

Arab Unity and Arab Socialism. In the wake of the Suez crisis, Nasser became a vocal exponent of Arab unity. He embraced the general view that Egyptians were bound to other Arabs by a shared religion and language, the experience of Western domination, similar domestic problems, and a common opposition to Israel's presence in the region. But Nasser's nationalist commitment to Egypt came first and led him toward a utilitarian conception of regional unity. Solidarity among Arab peoples had the best chance of eliminating the last vestiges of colonial influence, blocking unwanted intrusions of the superpowers in the region, and ousting the Israeli presence. Progress on all these fronts would make Egypt more secure and more independent. His views carried far and convincingly because he had stood up to the West at Suez. In 1958 Nasser turned vague talk of unity into a dramatic political experiment linking Egypt to Syria to form the United Arab Republic. Nasser served as the union's president, and Egypt occupied the dominant position within the union.

Nasser's post-1956 domestic policies combined nationalism and social justice in what became known as "Arab socialism." Like Nkrumah and other third-world radicals, Nasser regarded socialism as a scientific, efficient way to provide a better life for his people. He did not prize it as a doctrine of class conflict. The Suez crisis gave him an excuse to nationalize foreign businesses with French and British connections. In 1960 he shifted to a planned economy, launching his first five-year plan with a heavy stress on industrialization. During the 1960s he further expanded state economic control to include all major industry and commerce, even foreign trade. Only small-scale trading and agricultural operations remained in private hands. Mindful of rural poverty, he implemented further rounds of land redistribution in 1961 and 1969.

Nasser could boast major achievements. His government ran the Suez Canal efficiently, turning it into an important source of national income. Economic growth during his tenure stood in marked contrast to the virtual economic stagnation during the first half of the twentieth century, and living standards improved. Per capita income doubled by 1973, although gains would have been greater had it not been for a large population increase. Unrelenting tension with Israel also held the economy back by diverting scarce resources from the civilian sector while the state-run part of the economy spawned a large, inefficient bureaucracy. Women gained expanded work and educational opportunities, but restrictive family law remained unchanged because Nasser did not want to challenge the Islamic values underlying that law. And while women and men both made headway in gaining literacy during the Nasser years, the gap between the two remained substantial. The much-touted Aswan High Dam proved disappointing. It began silting up while at the same time producing a variety of adverse environmental effects, including loss of fertile lands along the Mediterranean and poisoning of once productive fields. The limits of Nasser's socialism were most evident in the countryside. Land reform had created greater equality and especially benefited a small group of middle peasants rather than the large numbers of rural poor still without land. But a high birth rate perpetuated poverty and landlessness and bred peasant discontent. As the agricultural system failed to support the rural population, migration to the cities and abroad accelerated.

Nasser's attempts to promote unity within the region and destroy Israel were the least successful parts of his program. He intervened fruitlessly on behalf of allies in Jordan, Yemen, and Iraq, and in the process he wasted Egypt's resources and made enemies within the Arab world. The experiment in building a United Arab Republic collapsed in 1961, and the idea of Arab cooperation was further discredited in 1967 when Egypt, along with Syria and Jordan, went to war against Israel and suffered defeat. Preoccupied with protecting his prestige at home and in the region, Nasser had blundered into the Six-Day War (discussed in Chapter 9) and lost the Sinai Peninsula and the Gaza Strip. (See Map 6.4.) With Egypt and Israel still locked in a sullen confrontation punctuated by frequent armed exchanges, Umm Kulthun, a singer of enormous popularity in Egypt and elsewhere in the Arab world, gave concerts to raise funds and rally support. Her song, "The Ruins," expressed a widely felt sadness and grim deter-

The Funeral of Gamal Abdul Nasser
Six million people are supposed to have jammed the streets of Cairo in an emotional outpouring
following the Egyptian leader's death in 1970. (© Bruno Barbey/Magnum Photos)

mination in the face of victorious Israel with its links to that old enemy, imperialism. "Give me my freedom. / Untie my hands. / I gave, I held back nothing. /
Ah, your bonds have made my wrists bleed."[29]

Despite the shocking setback of 1967, Nasser retained his extraordinary popular appeal at home. His offer to resign evoked a groundswell of public support,
just as three years later his death from a heart attack occasioned deep mourning.
Nasser's passing marked the end of an era of radicalism for Egypt in both domestic and foreign policy. The high hopes for Egypt and the region that had flowered
in the postwar years began to dim. What was said by a colleague of Nasser during his eighteen years in power applied equally to Egypt during that time: "He
was a strong starter, but a lousy finisher."[30]

Although Nasser's successors shared his views and background, they revised
important elements of his policies. Anwar Sadat, a long-time Nasser associate,
launched one last military challenge against Israel with Soviet support in 1973.
When initial success turned into a military stalemate, he was able to argue more
convincingly for a shift to a pro-U.S. international position. He pulled Egypt out
of the anti-Israel coalition and moved toward a peace agreement that restored the
Sinai to Egyptian control. At home he privatized parts of the economy. Sadat's
assassination in 1981 foreshadowed growing religious discontent with the government's long-standing secular orientation and its increasing accommodation
with the United States and Israel. Sadat's successor, Hosni Mubarak, maintained

THE NASSER ERA IN EGYPT

1882	Britain asserts control over Egypt
1922	Britain concedes limited independence
1928	Muslim Brothers is founded
1952	Free Officer movement overthrows Egyptian monarch
1956	Crisis over the Suez Canal radicalizes Nasser
1958	Egypt and Syria join in a short-lived United Arab Republic
1960	Nasser embraces a socialist economic program
1967	Egypt suffers stunning territorial losses to Israel in the Six-Day War
1970	Aswan High Dam is completed; Nasser's death
1981	Nasser's successor, Anwar Sadat, is assassinated and replaced by Hosni Mubarak

nonconfrontational relations with Israel while working to curb Islamic critics at home who objected, like many in the region, to a future conceived primarily in Western, secular terms.

Of Sadat's and Mubarak's Islamic critics, the organization known as the Muslim Brothers was the oldest, most popular, and best organized. Founded in 1928, it espoused a nationalism that held Islam critical to Egypt's future but also to the future of the region. It pursued a populist, reformist strategy, promoting land redistribution, workers' rights, broad access to education and medical care, and provision of emergency food aid. But it also had a violent side, directed from time to time against its enemies. Nasser repressed the Brothers in 1954 and then in 1966 hanged its leading thinker, Sayyid Qutb. The Brothers in general and Qutb in particular exercised a strong influence throughout the region, with off-shoots springing up in Syria, Jordan, Palestine, and Sudan. In the 1970s, following Sadat's shift to a more tolerant policy, the Brothers regained their prominence within Egypt. Frustration with government corruption, economic inequality, and lack of democracy led some members to reject the organization's emphasis on gradually building Islamic institutions. The militants launched a campaign of violence, including the assassination of Sadat and other government officials as well as attacks on tourists, Christians, and prominent secularists. State repression followed, setting off a costly cycle of conflict dividing the country and hobbling the tourist-dependent economy.

Colonial Crisis in Algeria

Algeria had the misfortune of becoming a battleground in the most violent process of decolonization that the North Africa–Middle East region would witness. Demands for independence ran up against a wall of French resistance. Geographical proximity does much to explain the French tenacity. Located just across the Mediterranean from France, Algeria was by 1945 home to one million set-tlers, and Paris claimed the colony as an integral part of France itself. Talk of inte-gration, however, ran up against a settler community resistant to any concessions to Algerians that might threaten its political dominance and economic privilege.

Amidst this paralysis of colonial policy, an Algerian nationalist movement took shape between World War I and World War II. Growing numbers of the poor and landless moved to the cities, where exposure to colonial practices and proximity to the settler community sharpened their anti-French sentiments. At the same time, French education made the Algerian elite sensitive to the gap between Europe's professed liberal and nationalist ideas and the colonial reality. World War II added impetus to burgeoning independence sentiment, encour-aged by the Atlantic Charter's commitment to self-determination. Wartime eco-nomic deprivation and clashes with police heightened the sense of grievance. The more vociferous the calls for independence, the more stubborn settlers became in defense of the status quo and the more repressive the measures the French military took. In putting down one round of demonstrations at the end of the war, colonial authorities killed some 20,000 to 40,000 Algerians.

Tensions building for several decades came to a boiling point in mid-1954 with the formation of the National Liberation Front (Front de Libération National, or FLN). The Vietnamese victory at Dien Bien Phu that year demon-strated that armed resistance to French forces was a viable liberation strategy. The FLN encouraged Algerians to believe that they too could break away from France. The Front leadership was highly diverse, including military men operat-ing inside the country and those forming FLN armies in neighboring Tunisia and Morocco after those two countries gained independence from France in 1956. It included leaders such as Ahmed Ben Bella, who spent most of the strug-gle in French prisons, and others who guided the FLN from a sanctuary in Cairo provided by the Nasser government. Some among the leadership wanted nothing less than unconditional independence, whereas others were ready to settle for a compromise. Some viewed the world through the prism of European leftist and liberal ideas; others championed indigenous Arab and Islamic values.

Popular support came from an equally diverse range of groups—from migrant workers in France and French intellectuals to Algerian peasants, some newly arrived in the city. Women participated no less than men. The strategies of resistance employed in this at first seemingly impossible challenge to a formidable colonial presence were no less diverse. An underground organization challenged French administration. Guerrilla operations and cross-border raids by FLN forces threatened French control in the countryside. Urban terrorists struck at the settler population, against Algerians collaborating with the French, and within France itself. Street demonstrations and general strikes underlined the breadth of revolutionary support.

Paris responded to this bold defiance by deploying 400,000 troops. Increas-ingly frustrated and demoralized senior French military officers conducted the war with grim determination. They had surrendered to the Germans during World War II and more recently to the Vietnamese, had abandoned control of Morocco and Tunisia without a fight, and had suffered humiliation in the Suez crisis. They were now eager to prove their mettle, vowing that they would not be deprived of this victory. The army's strategy of mass arrests, sweeps in the countryside, resettlement and destruction of villages, sealing off the border, and meeting FLN terror with counter-terror and torture successfully contained the FLN threat. These actions would in the end result in deaths on the Algerian side estimated as high as 300,000 out of a population of about eight million. Some 10,000 of the French forces would die.

However, the French could not turn the stalemate into victory. Repression deepened Algerian alienation from French rule, brought new recruits to the FLN, and provoked international condemnation of French policy. Within France itself, by the late 1950s the brutality of the highly publicized urban struggle and the costs of the war in terms of life and property had polarized the public and paralyzed the political system. Some regarded Algeria as a lost cause; others felt an obligation to defend the imperiled settlers and the last shreds of imperial glory.

Resolving this domestic political crisis in France ultimately proved critical to resolving the war in Algeria. Charles de Gaulle came to power in 1958 occupying a constitutionally strengthened presidency. With his base at home assured by 1961, de Gaulle moved to negotiate an end to the war over the violent objections of rebellious officers serving in Algeria and their allies within the settler community. Their acts of terrorism and threats of a military takeover in Paris gave special urgency and peril to de Gaulle's peacemaking. Finally in March 1962 de Gaulle and the FLN reached an agreement to bring this long, bloody war to an end. France yielded on independence but got in return continued access to military bases and preservation of economic ties. The agreement included safeguards for European settlers, but by the end of the year virtually all but the poor and elderly had fled.

Independence found the new Algerian government facing high public expectations but daunting circumstances. The educational system was rudimentary and the illiteracy rate high. Colonial policy had created an imbalanced economy. Agriculture, which provided employment for the majority of the population, had stagnated for half a century, whereas gas and oil production had developed rapidly beginning in the 1950s. Some three million rural people displaced by the war needed attention. The loss of capital and technical skills, resulting from the flight of the settlers, plunged the economy into crisis.

During the first years following independence, the FLN-controlled government was preoccupied with establishing its authority and formulating a coherent policy direction. Ben Bella led this process until 1965, when Colonel Houari Boumediene took power in a military coup. By 1967 Boumediene's position was secure enough for him to launch a state-directed economic development program. Determined to end economic subordination to France and other major powers, the Boumediene government nationalized foreign-controlled sectors of the economy such as gas, oil, and banking. It directed government investments into petroleum and heavy industry, leaving almost nothing for the consumer and agricultural sectors. The implementation of fresh land reform measures failed to lift agriculture out of its long-term stagnation. During the Boumediene years

(1965–1978) technical specialists, bureaucrats, and the military ran the country. GDP growth rates averaging 7.2 percent between 1967 and 1978 provided some insulation against critics of the FLN's authoritarian rule and secular policies.

The similarities of Boumediene to Nasser, apparent in intensifying domestic reform, extended to international affairs. Like Nasser, the Algerian government insisted on a position of non-alignment in the Cold War and joined India, Egypt, and Yugoslavia in championing that position in the UN and at international conferences. It also expressed its commitment to third-world causes by strongly opposing imperialism in the Middle East and throughout Africa. It sharply criticized Israel and supported the claims of displaced Palestinians. And it was an outspoken foe of white-minority rule in South Africa and of surviving colonial regimes elsewhere in sub-Saharan Africa.

During the 1980s Algeria's post-independence order began to unravel. International oil prices declined late in the decade, thereby shrinking the country's prime source of revenue. Even before this setback, economic growth had barely kept up with population increase. The long-term FLN failure to raise living standards, followed by new economic difficulties and an austerity program imposed by the International Monetary Fund (IMF), led to student and worker protests between 1986 and 1988. The FLN had lost its political legitimacy in the eyes of many. An even more potent expression of popular discontent arose in the form of an Islamist party, the Islamic Salvation Front. Its leader, Abbassi Madani, called for completing the Algerian revolution. The previous generation had expelled France *"physically";* now the time had come "to banish it *intellectually and ideologically,* to break with its supporters who have sucked its venomous milk."[31] The Front swept to victory in 1990 and 1991 in the country's first free elections since independence. Its demands for restricting rights given to women and more generally for instituting an Islamic state frightened the more secular and Europeanized part of the population and prompted the military to intervene to nullify the election results and repress protest. As Algerian turned violently on Algerian, the country entered the 1990s needing more urgently than ever a consensus to ensure national cohesion but now realizing that democratic politics might accentuate internal differences rather than help transcend them.

DECOLONIZATION IN ALGERIA	
1848	Algeria becomes a French colony
1954	The National Liberation Front takes up the independence struggle against France
1961	De Gaulle presses for a resolution of the bitter conflict
1962	Algeria gains independence, with Ben Bella as leader
1967	Boumediene moves Algeria toward state-directed economic development
1990–1991	Electoral gains by Islamic forces prompt a military crackdown

CONCLUSION

Looking back on the third world in the middle years of the Cold War, what is striking is the strong appeal of Marxism to many of its leaders. To understand that appeal we need to put ourselves in their place. Marxism helped them explain, as no other ideology could, how a few foreigners had come to subjugate their peoples and demean their old and proud cultures. "Imperialism" had driven economically advanced countries to dominate and exploit, just as "feudal" conditions had rendered the third world weak, divided, and thus easy prey. As third-world leaders began to think about the practical problems of ousting entrenched foreign influences and neutralizing native collaborators, they came to prize the single-party model often patterned on the tight Leninist party organization. It would enable them, as no open political system or democratic process could, to mobilize popular support and direct it through the often long, arduous liberation struggle. To be sure, the prominence of peasants in the third world ill accorded with the preoccupations of western Marxism, and the impatience of leaders to effect change collided with the ponderous planning ethos associated with development Soviet-style. But Marxism and Soviet leaders eager for influence were to prove flexible enough to accommodate diverse societies and ambitious timetables.

The Soviet Union—and then, by the 1950s, China as well—reinforced this radical trend. Even if Stalin had been cautious in offering help to anti-colonial struggles, at least the Soviet Union in his time had been bold in denouncing Western domination. Under Khrushchev, the third world found Moscow more inclined to back its rhetoric with offers of aid and protection. Mao's China also stepped forward with support even if on a more limited scale than the Soviets. In addition, both socialist powers followed a course of dramatic domestic development that inspired confidence in the capacity of a centralized system of state economic planning to transform a backward economy into a modern one.

The disappointing American record further accentuated the leftward drift in the third world toward socialist principles, state-directed economic development, and one-party politics. For a time elites had taken seriously public American professions of support for national self-determination. Woodrow Wilson had loudly proclaimed the principle during World War I. The Atlantic Charter in August 1941 had at Roosevelt's insistence included a sweeping commitment to "respect the right of all peoples to choose the form of government under which they will live."[32] But by mid-1945 British and U.S. leaders were expressing reservations about colonial peoples rushing toward freedom without a suitable period of European tutelage.

Perhaps worst of all, as the independence fever spread throughout the third world, American officials privately expressed a sense of superiority that was hard to conceal. And their actions during the Cold War were consistent with their paternalistic and racist attitudes, sharpening the sense within the third world that the United States had betrayed its much-touted commitment to freedom. The United States either aligned with Britain and France on colonial issues or asserted its own restraining influence out of fear of instability and communist encroachment. Washington increasingly backed military dictatorships, launched covert operations against non-aligned or left-leaning governments (as in Iran, Guatemala, and Cuba), and occasionally dispatched U.S. forces (as in Lebanon, the Dominican Republic, and Vietnam). Repeated U.S. interventions to preserve the status quo created widespread disappointment and anger that further enhanced the appeal of radicalism that was so alarming to American leaders.

The sweeping ambitions associated with the radicalism of the 1950s and 1960s were proving difficult to realize, while U.S. hostility imposed costs that new and relatively poor countries could ill afford. East Asian success at integrating into the international market economy suggested an attractive alternative to development through import substitution and state planning. This combination of domestically inspired second thoughts, potent international pressures, and a booming international economy would break the spell of radicalism and push third-world countries in so many different directions that it would become increasingly difficult to find anything in common among them (see Chapter 9).

RECOMMENDED RESOURCES

Third-World Radicalism
Frantz Fanon, *The Wretched of the Earth,* trans. Constance Farrington (1965), an extended reflection on the traumatic psychological effects of colonial domination, is a classic statement from the radical high tide. Forrest Colburn, *The Vogue of Revolution in Poor Countries* (1994), looks back disapprovingly on the radical notions that gripped the imagination of leaders in the third world.

East Asia
For **general treatments** of China and Vietnam, see the sources cited in Chapter 3. On **the second phase of China's revolution:** Stuart R. Schram, ed., *Chairman Mao Talks to the People: Talks and Letters, 1956–1971,* trans. John Chinnery and Tieyun (1975), offers a window into the elderly Mao's hopes and frustrations. Liang Heng and Judith Shapiro, *Son of the Revolution* (1983), is an engaging first-person account by a foot soldier in the Cultural Revolution. Michael Schoenhals, ed., *China's Cultural Revolution, 1966–1969: Not a Dinner Party* (1996), makes available a wonderful range of documents. Jung Chang, *Wild Swans: Three Daughters of China* (1991), details the life of a well-placed urban family during Mao's years in power. On **the struggle for South Vietnam,** see Truong Nhu Tang with David Chanoff and Doan Van Toai, *A Viet Cong Memoir* (1985), which recounts the revolutionary awakening of a young, well-to-do southerner and his subsequent disillusionment. For local studies that are critical to understanding Vietnam's rural politics and rural conflict during the period of deepening American involvement, see Jeffrey Race, *War Comes to Long An: Revolutionary Conflict in a Vietnamese Province* (1972), and Pierre Brocheux, *The Mekong Delta: Ecology, Economy, and Revolution, 1860–1960* (1995). The Saigon government perspective can be found in Bui Diem with David Chanoff, *In the Jaws of History* (1987); and Larry Engelmann, *Tears before the Rain: An Oral History of the Fall of South Vietnam* (1990).

The Caribbean Basin
For **general approaches to a region in ferment,** start with John C. Chasteen, *Born in Blood and Fire: A Concise History of Latin America* (2001), a lively, balanced, up-to-date treatment that allots three of eleven chapters to the post-1945 period. On **U.S. regional dominance,** see the fine survey by Lars Schoultz, *Beneath the United States: A History of U.S. Policy toward Latin America* (1998), as well as Walter LaFeber, *Inevitable Revolutions: The United States in*

Central America (rev. ed., 1993). The best treatment of **Guatemala in upheaval** is Piero Glei-jeses, *Shattered Hope: The Guatemalan Revolution and the United States, 1944–1954* (1991), though it should be supplemented by Jim Handy, *Revolution in the Countryside: Rural Conflict and Agrarian Reform in Guatemala, 1944–1954* (1994). **Insights on Cuba's revolution** in long-term perspective emerge from Louis A. Pérez Jr., *Cuba: Between Reform and Empire* (1988), and Pérez, *Cuba and the United States: Ties of Singular Intimacy* (1990). *Memories of Underdevelopment* (dir. Tomas Gutierrez Alea; 1968; 97 min.), a classic of Cuban cinema, med-itates on the aimless and melancholic life of a middle-class, middle-aged writer displaced by the revolution. **On Castro,** turn to Tad Szulc, *Fidel: A Critical Portrait* (1987), and Peter G. Bourne, *Fidel: A Biography of Fidel Castro* (1986), both thoughtful treatments of a fascinating life. Martin Kenner and James Petras, eds., *Fidel Castro Speaks* (1969), draws together important early work of the Cuban revolutionary. "Castro Speech Databases," a website based at the University of Texas and found at <http://www.lanic.utexas.edu/la/cb/cuba/castro.html>, offers an easily searched collection of later Castro materials.

Sub-Saharan Africa

To set the subcontinent's **decolonization in context,** turn to Basil Davidson, *Modern Africa: A Social and Political History* (3rd ed., 1994), a short, clear introduction by a long-time author-ity. See also D. K. Fieldhouse, *Black Africa, 1945–80: Economic Decolonization and Arrested Devel-opment* (1986), and Roland Oliver and Anthony Atmore, *Africa since 1800* (rev. ed., 1994). On **Kwame Nkrumah's early years,** see Basil Davidson, *Black Star: A View of the Life and Times of Kwame Nkrumah* (1974), a sympathetic account written from first-hand knowledge of the subject but in need of revision in light of the findings in Marika Sherwood, *Kwame Nkrumah: The Years Abroad, 1935–1947* (1996). Nkrumah speaks for himself in *Revolu-tionary Path* (1973), a substantial collection of his writings, and in *The Autobiography of Kwame Nkrumah* (1957). The novel by Ayi Kwei Armah, *The Beautyful Ones Are Not Yet Born* (1969), captures the corruption and general political demoralization afflicting Ghana by the time of Nkrumah's overthrow. Parallel developments in **Nigeria** emerge in two fine novels: Buchi Emecheta, *The Joys of Motherhood* (1979), which brings into focus the role of family and gender in a society in transformation at the close of the colonial era; and Chinua Achebe, *A Man of the People* (1966), which expresses deep political disillusionment over postcolonial developments.

The Middle East

Context on the heyday of secular and radical nationalism is available in William L. Cleveland, *A History of the Modern Middle East* (1994), an accessible and sound textbook. Albert Hourani, *A History of the Arab Peoples* (1991), traces the roots of modern developments going back to the seventh century while also providing a substantial section on the post-1939 era of the nation-state. Roger Owen, *State, Power and Politics in the Making of the Middle East* (2nd ed., 2000), develops the fruitful theme of state building. For a broad approach to the **nationalist impulse in Iran,** turn to Ervand Abrahamian, *Iran between Two Revolutions* (1982), which follows critical political and social developments from the late nineteenth cen-tury to the revolution of 1979. James A. Bill, *The Eagle and the Lion: The Tragedy of American-Iranian Relations* (1988), provides a first-rate overview of the interplay between the Cold War and Iranian politics from the 1940s onward. On **Egypt,** P. J. Vatikiotis, *Nasser and His Genera-tion* (1978), does a splendid job of placing Nasser's life in the context of intense political and social change. Peter Woodward, *Nasser* (1992), offers a tight, fluent, measured assessment. "Umm Kulthun: A Voice Like Egypt" (dir. Michal Goldman; 1996; 67 min.), is an engaging film documentary of an immensely popular cultural figure whose career offers a window on the collective imagination of the Nasser era. For **Algeria,** the place to start is John Ruedy, *Modern Algeria: The Origins and Development of a Nation* (1992), a careful, illuminating overview. Alistair Horne, *A Savage War of Peace: Algeria, 1954–1962* (rev. ed., 1987), is the standard account of the prolonged and violent conflict leading to the end of French control. *The Battle of Algiers* (dir. Gillo Pontecorvo; 1966; 123 min.), provides a taut, nerve-wracking reenactment of the brutal struggle in 1956–1957 to control Algeria's main city.

PART THREE

FROM COLD WAR TO GLOBALIZATION
1968–1991

The fabled moment in the history of the McDonald's Corporation came in 1954 when an innovative idea met its messiah. Ray Kroc, a fifty-two-year-old salesman, walked into a Los Angeles area restaurant run by the McDonald brothers—Richard and Maurice. What Kroc saw that so impressed him was the "McDonald's Speedee Service System." A carefully coordinated kitchen team quickly produced good fifteen-cent hamburgers and quality fries for drive-up customers in a clean, friendly environment. In Kroc's version of this tale, he at once envisioned restaurants serving up cheap, fast food just like this one "dotting crossroads all over the country."[1] He quickly secured from the brothers the rights to franchise the concept, and in 1961 he borrowed $2.7 million to buy them out. The gamble paid off handsomely. By the time of his death in 1984, Kroc was a millionaire many times over.

Kroc had the pluck and energy associated with the American myth that everyone has a shot at riches. Born in 1902 just outside Chicago, he dropped out of high school to work as a traveling salesman for everything from Florida real estate and paper cups to milk-shake mixers and folding furniture. Following his 1954 encounter with the McDonald's operation, Kroc became a fervent advocate of the fast-food concept, championing it with dogged optimism, energy, and ingenuity. After pouring the rest of his career into the effort, this ambitious perfectionist would look back and observe, "Work is the meat in the hamburger of life."[2]

But Kroc also owed his success to the special postwar ethos that first took shape in southern California. Wartime defense plants had brought jobs and rising incomes to the area. The Cold War kept defense industries humming and the local economy booming in the 1950s. At the same time, with the initiation in 1956 of a network of interstate highways, federal dollars were helping to create a thriving car culture. Southern Californians exploited the mobility made possible by car ownership, moving to the suburbs and shopping at stores relocated from downtowns to outlying malls with ample parking and easy road access. Customers were ready for restaurants that were easily reached by car and that offered inexpensive, tasty, and dependable food produced using the very industrial, production-line techniques familiar from defense plants. Kroc banked on this wave of social change to realize his vision of a McDonald's at thousands of major intersections.

But would this system of food production and consumption, so peculiarly American, ever catch on overseas? In 1968 Fred Turner, a Kroc protégé, took over the company and began giving overseas expansion close attention. The first efforts to set up operations in Canada, the Caribbean, and the Netherlands misfired. Turner learned to stick closely to the approach that had succeeded in the U.S. market: Select managers willing to embrace the company's philosophy and direction, insist on adherence to the McDonald's formula for food preparation and service, and maintain strict oversight of each franchise. The first breakthrough came in 1971 when Japanese businessmen proved enthusiastic converts to the fast food formula. McDonald's scored similar successes in Germany and Australia. By the late 1970s the Chicago-based corporation had established a solid beachhead outside the United States—it could claim almost four hundred outlets operating in twenty countries (sixty-six in Tokyo alone) and had begun negotiating access to Eastern–bloc countries. The outlets that soon opened across eastern Europe represented breaches in the old Cold War lines. In 1990, in a telling sign of the times, McDonald's planted itself in downtown Moscow, where the "Beeg Mek" attracted crowds larger than at the Kremlin or Lenin's tomb—fifteen million customers during the first year.[3] The opening in Beijing two years later broke the company record for the most transactions in one day.

By the 1990s McDonald's had become an economic powerhouse and a global icon. It had over twenty-five thousand stores worldwide, with as many outside the United States as within. It held the largest collection of real estate in the world. And by spending more money on advertising and marketing internation-

TABLE III.1 McDonald's Feeds the World	
	(number of restaurants as of December 2002)[4]
United States	13,491
Canada	1,304
Brazil	584
Mexico	261
All other Latin America	760
Britain and Northern Ireland	1,231
Germany	1,211
France	973
All other Europe	2,655
Japan	3,891
Australia	726
China	546
All other Asia Pacific, Middle East, Africa	2,392
Total	30,025

ally than any other brand, it had displaced Coca-Cola as the best-known commercial product. The corporate mascot, the clown Ronald McDonald, had eclipsed Mickey Mouse in fame.

McDonald's was also emerging as a lightning rod for debate over the complex and contentious issues raised by globalization. Its critics saw numerous sins. Industrially produced food inflicted cruelty on animals while imposing restrictions on farmers and ranchers that robbed them of their independence. An insatiable demand for disposable paper products and large-scale, intensive assembly-line agriculture damaged the environment. McDonald's imperiled local culinary traditions by substituting synthetic materials and flavors for natural ones. It endangered good health. High in calories and saturated fat, the McDonald's staple of burgers, fries, and shakes promoted obesity. Problems of weight and health, first evident in the United States, were soon showing up abroad, even in developing countries such as China, as fast food became a part of a younger generation's daily diet. Finally, McDonald's exploited its largely inexperienced, unskilled, part-time workforce, paying low wages and offering no benefits. When union organizers appeared, McDonald's headquarters joined with its restaurant managers in stubbornly fighting back. On occasion McDonald's subjected its critics to long, costly libel suits and even monitored and disrupted their activities. Siding with the critics, French president Jacques Chirac declared, "I detest McDonald's." Israel's president, Ezer Weizman, wrote of the need to be "wary" of this threat to the country's culture and religion.[5]

Some observers were more sympathetic. They saw McDonald's as responding to the needs of overseas consumers, who were in important ways becoming like their U.S. counterparts: Rising incomes made possible spending on non-essentials; working parents had limited time for food shopping and preparation; and children on their own after school had allowances to spend on diversions. In this sense, McDonald's was not an intruder forcing its tastes on customers but a pioneer, meeting a demand for fast, friendly service and cheap, dependable food in a sanitary setting. Having blazed the way, McDonald's time and again found itself facing serious competition from locals who had borrowed one or more elements of the McDonald's model. Imitation was an admission that the foreign interloper had correctly read changing customer tastes.

Social trends alone did not guarantee success. McDonald's had to make adjustments that varied from country to country. The most obvious was some tinkering with the standard McDonald's menu. When Hindus balked at eating meat from the sacred cow, McDonald's in India substituted lamb patties. If Germans wanted beer, then McDonald's went along. If Norwegians hankered for familiar fish, then they got a salmon burger. No less important was the latitude owner-operators overseas had to select store sites, to work out arrangements with local suppliers, and to select locally appealing advertising themes. More subtle but no less significant, McDonald's sometimes had to compromise the fast-food model, which expected customers to eat quickly and leave. For example, in East Asia, young people used McDonald's as a safe, comfortable setting in which to study or socialize. The elderly and women used McDonald's as a meeting place. Families came to celebrate birthdays and other family occasions. The curious

McDonald's on Paris's Champs-Elysées
No gaudy drive-in, this restaurant was discrete and pedestrian friendly. By looking like a café from the outside and obscuring the four hundred seats within, McDonald's remade itself to fit in. Parisian customers came to refer affectionately to the restaurant with the golden arches that appeared in neighborhoods around the city as "McDo," even as French cultural nationalists denounced this foreign interloper. (AP Photo/Remy de la Mauvinière)

went to savor a modern lifestyle just coming into reach and acquire a cosmopolitan veneer. These various kinds of accommodations to local needs and tastes made McDonald's seem less like an American firm and more like an indigenous one. Little wonder that young people overseas growing up with McDonald's reportedly exclaimed with surprise and delight when they visited the United States, "Look, Americans have McDonald's too!"

For good or ill, the overseas expansion of McDonald's was part of a relentlessly rising tide of global economic activity from the 1970s onward. International trade accelerated as tariffs worldwide came down, and capital moved more freely as states removed controls. Increasingly integrated and powerful, the world economy exerted its influence over the domestic affairs of countries—whether developed or developing, whether free market or socialist—and shaped both public agendas and private taste. It hastened the rise of the consumer ethic that was so beneficial to McDonald's. Consumers enthusiastically embraced a wide range of mass-market products. Many were American in origin, ranging from casual clothes and fast food to TV programming and popular music. But Bombay movie producers and Qatar television news programming demonstrated that others could also exploit the possibilities of broader cultural markets. At the same time, the global economy intensified competition and placed pressures on producers in all countries to become more efficient. These pressures in turn were socially disruptive as industrial jobs migrated to low-wage areas, employment in the service sector (including fast food) expanded dramatically, and the earnings of the poor lagged behind. Government spending fell under assault as the source of deficits that would scare away international investors and as an affront to the free market principles that were becoming orthodoxy. These developments created their own backlash, leading to charges that uncontrolled economic growth harmed the environment, smothered local cultures, and accentuated inequalities. The resulting controversies over the impact of globalization would not only envelop McDonald's but also outlast the Cold War.

At the same time, efforts by McDonald's to adjust to local conditions reflected the persistence of diversity within the market-oriented international economy. Indeed, intensifying economic integration had as its counterpoint intensifying economic differentiation. The leading economies of Europe, East Asia, and North America continued the postwar trend toward consolidating into major blocs, each with its own understanding of how the market ought to operate. Global governance would increasingly if informally pass into the hands of the major economies of these three blocs. No longer able alone to orchestrate the flow of global goods and investments, Washington came to accept its relative decline and with it the need for collaboration with other bloc leaders.

Seen in broad terms, the success of McDonald's paralleled the last act of the Cold War and foreshadowed its conclusion—a resounding victory for consumer culture. The spread of franchises overseas developed apace with interest in calming superpower tensions. The negotiations for McDonald's franchises in eastern Europe and the USSR were as much the herald of the Cold War's end as arms control agreements. McDonald's would survive; the Soviet empire would not. On both sides of an increasingly porous Iron Curtain, popular preoccupations with the good life constrained superpower policy as much as it enriched McDonald's. In the United States, western Europe, and Japan affluence from the 1960s onward was taken as a fact of life—a right to be protected and enjoyed, especially by a new generation raised in relative affluence, wearing blue jeans, drinking Coke, and listening to rock music. In the Soviet bloc where state-run ("command") economies were falling behind popular expectations, the good life was only partially realized, stirring not only dreams of better housing, more appliances, and a car but also alienation from a socialist system that had failed to deliver the goods as promised.

Soviet and American leaders during the final two decades of the Cold War took careful note of this popular aversion to sacrifice or to run the risk of nuclear war. Acting on these concerns, President Richard Nixon initiated the era of détente, which then faltered and seemingly collapsed under presidents Jimmy Carter and Ronald Reagan only to suddenly revive in the late 1980s under Mikhail Gorbachev. Seeking to resolve the tension between guns and butter already evident in the Khrushchev years, Gorbachev launched a daring experiment meant to invigorate the Soviet economy and thus catch up with the abundance and technological innovation of a capitalist West. Ending the costly Cold

War was an essential part of Gorbachev's plan. That policy part succeeded just as the overall economic plan failed, with unpleasant consequences for Soviet leaders and people alike.

Finally, McDonald's was an indicator of strong economic currents fundamentally transforming the third world. The revolutionary phase there had peaked in the 1960s, and increasingly thereafter the demonstrable success of countries integrated into the international economy began to make the socialist model look passé. Only a few such as Cuba and North Korea stoutly hewed to that model. And Marxist-inspired revolutions went out of fashion, with the notable exception of Cambodia. Indeed the most significant revolutionary upheaval of the late twentieth century—that in Iran—looked to Mohammed, not Marx. To most in the developing world, the global economy held out the greatest promise—access to capital and technology and the transfer of manufacturing to low-wage countries suffering from falling commodity prices. The countries of maritime East Asia such as South Korea and Taiwan demonstrated that international economic integration was more than a promise; it was an effective development strategy.

The cumulative result of these changes was to undermine not only the appeal of radical programs in the third world but also the very idea of a third world as a coherent concept. Countries that had followed a similar trajectory from colonial control to anti-colonial resistance to independence with its promise of rapid, socialist-inspired transformation now began moving in strikingly different directions with strikingly different results. Some, especially in East and Southeast Asia, successfully came to terms with the global economy. Others in sub-Saharan Africa and Latin America were less successful. Population growth and the neglect of women as a critical resource made progress difficult, but more burdensome still were the long-standing internal conflicts that consumed such places as South Africa, Guatemala, and Israeli-occupied Palestine. Those whose economy floundered found themselves having to turn for relief to international bankers every bit as ideological as the old socialist planners. The bankers' prescription was giving more scope to the market and less to state welfare, which spelled for the short term at least more social pain and political tension for states already in trouble. A rough gauge of the winners and the losers in an increasingly diverse postcolonial world was which ones had a McDonald's and which ones still lacked the purchasing power, good economic prospects, and political stability to make a franchise a safe bet.

CHAPTER 7

THE COLD WAR
COMES TO A CLOSE

O nce begun, the Cold War was not easily ended. After warily circling each other for a decade, Moscow and Washington had taken the first tentative steps toward putting their dispute on the negotiating table in the mid-1950s. Bolder action was needed if they were to break out of Cold War suspicions. The Cuban Missile Crisis and the deepening U.S. role in Vietnam had testified to the continuing power of those suspicions into the 1960s, and they persisted not only over Soviet-backed Cuba and North Vietnam but also over the Soviet invasion of Afghanistan in 1979 as well as insurgencies at multiple points in Central America and Africa. Nevertheless, a string of initiatives took shape beginning in 1969 that finally brought the rivalry to an end in the late 1980s. The forward motion was, however, slow and uneven, obstructed on both sides by deep doubts and strong institutionalized interests in preserving the Cold War status quo. And the two leaders who took the greatest political risks to push the process forward, Richard Nixon and Mikhail Gorbachev, would be thoroughly discredited at home. But their efforts would be rewarded with success—a surprisingly sudden superpower peace in 1989.

The Cold War world then quickly turned upside down. Beyond the wildest imaginings of Western specialists and even of socialist-bloc leaders themselves, the USSR surrendered its grip on its client regimes in eastern Europe, and one after another they toppled in the face of domestic protest. At the same time a reform program introduced within the USSR itself veered out of control. The empire created by the czars and restored by Stalin fragmented in 1991, and the Communist Party of the Soviet Union was discredited. These events not only transformed the scene in the old Soviet bloc but also dramatically recast the international landscape.

THE RISE AND FALL OF DÉTENTE

The 1970s witnessed a distinct lessening of Cold War tensions known as détente. It built on earlier efforts to avoid a superpower collision with accompanying nuclear risks. To diminish tensions policymakers sought from 1969 onward to promote greater dialogue, hold regular summit meetings, and negotiate arms control and other bilateral agreements. By the late 1970s, however, détente was under assault within the United States even as it retained support among American allies and from the Kremlin. The Cold War seemed to have acquired a life of its own, and most observers assumed that the Soviet-American rivalry had become a permanent feature of the postwar world.

The Nixon Policy Turnaround

President Richard Nixon was the unlikely author of détente. Anti-communism had carried him to political prominence. Elected to the House of Representatives in 1946, he made his name pursuing a former State Department official, Alger Hiss, suspected of espionage. In 1950 he won a seat in the Senate after charging that his liberal opponent, Helen G. Douglas, was "pink right down to her underwear."[1] Once established in Washington he had helped lead the Republican charge against the Truman administration. He accused Democrats of appeasement in China and in Korea, and he urged strong U.S. backing for the French during their last stand in Vietnam in 1954. But extensive exposure to foreign policy schooled him in the ways of the world. His education began as Eisenhower's vice president between 1953 and 1960 and continued for an additional decade in two runs for the presidency and wide foreign travel. He became convinced of the truth of a syllogism that Franklin Roosevelt would have accepted: Great powers have legitimate interests; the USSR and China as well as the United States were great powers; the task of diplomacy was to locate the areas of essential national interest (where mutual tolerance should prevail) and to concentrate negotiations on the areas of mutual interest (where compromise was possible).

The Cold War was thus not a moral crusade to annihilate evil. Nixon saw dialogue with the Soviet Union and China as a necessity. As he told his staff in 1971, "the world will not be worth living in if we can't get the great potential explosive forces under control." In any case, he pointed out, the relative decline of U.S. economic power meant that a world dominated by "just two superpowers" had given way to one under the sway of "five great power centers"— the Soviet Union, China, western Europe, and Japan as well as the United States—engaged economically in both cooperation and competition. In keeping with this shift away from Cold War thinking, Nixon limited the growth of U.S. nuclear weapons and made deep cuts in the military budget.[2]

Nixon's personality made him an unlikely policy innovator. He was closed off emotionally, his words often rehearsed, and his smile forced. He was prey to inner conflicts that occasionally burst through to the surface, often as part of the mood swings to which he was prone. He would then lash out at liberals, Jews, African

Americans, the media, the Northeast establishment—any group that had offended him over the course of his political career. In one of his vengeful fits he told his staff how to handle critics: "Get them on the floor and step on them, crush them, show no mercy."[3] He worked hard and contrasted his own personal struggle with the privileges that came by birth to others such as John Kennedy. He had had to turn down admission to Harvard for want of funds, and instead he attended Whittier College close to home. After earning a law degree at Duke University, he did not get an offer from the Wall Street firms that he hankered to work for, and he had to settle for a position with a hometown law firm. After service in the Pacific during World War II, he embarked on the political career that would bring him the recognition that had thus far eluded him. Nixon took pride in his capacity as a man of humble origins to gain public eminence. This pride, together with his determination to prove to the public, future historians, and perhaps even himself that he was an accomplished leader, drove him forward and made risk-taking and even flexibility possible.

When he became president in 1969, conditions in the United States posed challenges to the old policies and gave an advantage to a political leader willing to adjust. The controversy over the deepening conflict in Vietnam had seriously eroded the Cold War consensus, the bedrock for the policies pursued by Nixon's predecessors. The shift in attitudes became evident in a Congress less and less inclined to defer to presidential leadership. (See Chapter 4.) No less serious,

Richard Nixon, 1969
The president is captured here in a reflective mood, talking with senior aide John Ehrlichman in the Oval Office of the White House. Nixon loved long conversations in which he could ruminate about whatever was on his mind. Those meandering sessions drove his busy aides crazy. (Nixon Presidential Materials, National Archives #2665–08)

Nixon governed a country suffering from deep divisions. Even as he campaigned for the presidency in 1968, Americans seemed about to descend into civil war over Vietnam, race relations, and other issues. To round off the challenge, from the start of his presidency Nixon faced economic difficulties. The dollar was under attack internationally, and at home the economy was entering a period of stagnation and inflation dubbed "stagflation." The time was ripe to trim American ambitions.

Nixon entered the White House with three basic foreign policy goals that he pursued with the assistance of his chief foreign policy advisor, Henry Kissinger. The first was to end the unpopular Vietnam War as quickly as was consistent with American honor. Nixon publicly suggested that he had a secret plan to bring "a peace with honor," an objective that he held to grimly. As we saw in Chapter 4, Nixon calculated that a new campaign of bombing and an expansion of the ground war into North Vietnamese sanctuaries in Cambodia and Laos would give the U.S.-supported government in the South a reasonable chance of survival. And he continued the peace talks in Paris begun by President Johnson in 1968. Those talks would ultimately yield a compromise agreement in January 1973, in which Washington dropped its insistence on North Vietnamese troop withdrawal from the South, and Hanoi gave up its demand for the end of the Saigon government. By spring 1975, when the North Vietnamese launched their final offensive, scandal had already forced Nixon from office and neither his successor, Gerald Ford, nor the American public nor Congress showed any taste for investing more money or troops to block Hanoi's impending victory.

Nixon's second goal was to open up relations with China. Proponents of diplomatic recognition for the People's Republic of China had become more vocal during the 1960s, and Nixon himself had gingerly endorsed that position in public in 1967. After his 1968 election, Nixon secretly pushed ahead with diplomatic contacts. His China initiative arose from long-term considerations. Nixon had concluded that the United States would have to learn to live with rather than convert or destroy Communist China. He explained to his cabinet, "In 25 years you can't have a quarter of the people of the world isolated and have any chance of peace."[4] The president also hoped that his closer ties to Beijing would worry Moscow and Hanoi—and nudge them toward concessions on arms control and in the Paris peace talks.

In early 1972 Nixon made a triumphal visit to Beijing to meet with Mao Zedong and lay the foundation for a new relationship. A joint statement issued at the end of the visit confirmed the new commitment to normalized Sino-American relations and set Taiwan aside as an unresolved bone of contention—as a part of China (as Beijing claimed) but not to be regained by force (as Washington insisted). This compromise agreement provided the basis for the new relationship, but it also left that relationship hostage to sudden crises in the Taiwan Strait. Nixon had already lowered expectations about U.S. defense commitments on the other side of the Pacific by declaring in 1969 that Asian rather than American boys would henceforth have to bear the primary burden of defending noncommunist regimes, backed by preexisting U.S. defense arrangements, notably for South Korea, Taiwan, and Japan. These decisions to step away from the containment line in East Asia established by Truman was consistent with the experience of a president who twice in his political career had seen the electorate recoil at Americans fighting and dying on the Asian mainland.

For his part, Mao at age seventy-eight (more than twenty years Nixon's senior) was a disappointed and increasingly frail revolutionary, anxious to protect his political achievements at home. Whom was he to trust with his legacy? He was also increasingly concerned with China's enemies. His confrontational policy had antagonized both superpowers so that their forces now lodged right up against China's southern, eastern, and northern frontiers. Sino-Soviet tensions had been deepening throughout the 1960s, climaxing in armed clashes in 1969 along the inner Asian border. Particularly troubling to Mao was the threat posed by over one million Soviet troops and nuclear weapons deployed against China. At the same time, he had provoked Washington by endorsing revolution in Asia and resuming aid to Vietnam in 1964. Korea was still divided and tense, with the South serving as a base for U.S. forces, and Taiwan was no closer to liberation thanks to an American blanket of protection. The Chinese leader decided to pre-empt a dangerous strategic encirclement by his two formidable enemies by improving relations with one. He would thaw relations with the United States after twenty years in the deep freeze.

Nixon's third and most important foreign policy goal was to reduce tension in U.S.-Soviet relations and minimize the dangers of nuclear war. To achieve this, he worked with Soviet leader Leonid Brezhnev. They built on the two earlier steps toward bringing the strategic nuclear arms race under control: a 1963 ban on tests in the atmosphere, and a 1968 agreement against proliferation of nuclear weapons. Their major achievement was the Strategic Arms Limitations Treaty (SALT I) concluded in 1972. It aimed for the first time at creating stability and capping the competition. It froze the number of launchers each side could have (2,568 for the USSR and 1,764 for the United States) and limited each side to two anti-missile defense systems. It did not, however, limit the number of war-heads on each launcher, thus opening the arms race on a new front. Nixon and Brezhnev also developed economic and cultural exchanges to promote under-standing and improve relations. In Nixon's view, an understanding with Moscow was meant to create stability and minimize the nuclear danger but not rule out competition. He thus felt free, for example, to heavily bomb the Soviets' Viet-namese allies, undermine the Soviet position in the Middle East, and topple the socialist regime of Salvador Allende in Chile.

The Brezhnev Era

Nixon's Soviet partner in détente, Leonid Brezhnev, embodied conservative impulses within the Soviet Communist Party. Like Khrushchev, he was a product of the Soviet system. He was one of many of working-class background who had advanced rapidly and gained privileges under Stalin. But much more than Khrushchev, Brezhnev was wedded to the status quo. He thought Khrushchev's reformist, anti-Stalinist tendencies misguided if not dangerous. This conservatism would define an era—from Brezhnev's accession to power in 1964 until his death in 1982. Brezhnev dropped the attacks on Stalin, pulled back on reform in key areas, and protected the position of party cadres.

Stifling Dissent. Perhaps the most striking expression of this domestic conservatism was Brezhnev's intolerance for critical voices, many left over from the Khrushchev cultural thaw. Outspoken and sometimes harsh, these voices reveal how much intellectuals had recovered their position of moral authority and confidence after Stalin's attempt to crush them. A look at two of the most prominent provides a sense of the political hopes and moral passions that sought to break through the crust of official conservatism.

The novelist Alexander Solzhenitsyn was deeply antagonistic to the Soviet regime. Profoundly attached to prerevolutionary Russian society and values, he provocatively called for the party to admit that it had taken the country down a blind alley lured by false Western notions of constant material progress and faith in technology and reason. In the process the party had cut Russia off from its cultural and moral roots, despoiled the land, and created a brutal urban society. Marxism seemed to him nothing more than "this grim jest of the twentieth century." Solzhenitsyn favored a restoration of the Russian Orthodox faith, "the only living spiritual force capable of undertaking the spiritual healing of Russia." He also favored an enlightened authoritarian political system until the people were ready to govern themselves. At the very least he wanted the party to open the system to free expression. In 1973 he admonished the leaders in the Kremlin, "Let the people breathe, let them think and develop!"[5]

The physicist Andrei Sakharov, the father of the Soviet hydrogen bomb, followed a much more cosmopolitan agenda. This star in the Soviet scientific establishment was driven to dissent initially by alarm over the dangers posed by the hydrogen bomb that he had helped develop. In 1968 he called for applying scientific norms of open discussion broadly to public life. He said what many in the scientific community had long thought—that science was a model of rationality and democracy that should shape the Soviet system. The publication of his views abroad led to the loss of his security clearance. His human rights campaign in the 1970s got him into still deeper trouble. By then he had concluded that a closed, authoritarian Soviet system could not address the nuclear danger and, more broadly, the problem of international insecurity. He began demanding greater intellectual freedom, thus striking directly at the party's control over political and cultural life. "As long as a country has no civil liberty, no freedom of information, and no independent press, then there exists no effective body of public opinion to control the conduct of the government and its functionaries."[6]

By the end of the 1970s the Brezhnev leadership had managed largely to silence these and other troublesome dissident intellectuals. Solzhenitsyn was deported in 1974 after circulating copies of his classic account of the Stalinist prison system, *The Gulag Archipelago*. (He settled in rural Vermont.) The leadership decided to get rid of Sakharov after he openly criticized Soviet military intervention in Afghanistan (treated later in this chapter). To isolate him from the international press, the Kremlin exiled Sakharov to the city of Gorky in 1980. Others promoting human rights, such as the Russian section of Amnesty International, were charged with "antisocial" and "anti-Soviet" activities and accused of being in league with the American enemy.

Social and Economic Doldrums. Despite the Soviet Union's problems, Brezhnev favored letting the system plod ahead. He sidestepped the main challenge that Khrushchev had wrestled with—the inability of an inefficient state-controlled, command economy to meet rising consumer expectations while also supporting a military with superpower aspirations. Far from catching up with and then surpassing capitalism, the socialist system was lagging, especially in science and technology. Industry as well as agricultural and service sectors suffered from low productivity.

There was a long and familiar list of reasons for the poor state of the economy. The state's intrusive, all-inclusive system of planning inculcated passivity. Malingering on the job was commonplace, the subject of such popular sayings as "It doesn't matter where I work, it only matters that I don't work." Management and workers alike became implicated in corruption and graft. The gap between the countryside and the city in terms of living standards and educational opportunities remained substantial and encouraged those who could to flee rural hardship for a richer life in the city. The resulting failure of the "official" economy to provide consumers with adequate goods and services gave rise to activity outside the control of the state planners—a "second economy" that was part "gray" (officially tolerated if not condoned) and part "black" (illegal).

Alcoholism offers an especially good barometer of the social stress that accompanied these economic troubles. Excessive alcohol consumption had been a problem in the late imperial and early Soviet periods, but the problem took on new, worrisome proportions in the post-Stalin years. Between 1955 and 1979, per capita consumption of both legal and home-brewed alcohol, mainly vodka, rose steadily and dramatically—more than doubling by conservative estimates. With working adults in cities drinking as much as a bottle a day of heavily alcoholic drinks, an unusually large share of family budgets went to alcohol—by one estimate 15 to 20 percent of disposable income. A growing proportion of young people and women began to drink regularly and heavily. University students were, according to a secret police report, drinking "every day . . . before lectures, after lectures, and now in the breaks as well."[7]

Alcohol provided an appealing substitute for the shortfall in other kinds of consumer goods, a temporary escape from rural poverty and general boredom, and an accessible way of coping with the stresses of urban life. But excessive drinking produced an appalling range of social problems, including illness, premature births and birth defects, divorce, domestic violence, accidents on the road and at work, and crime. Rampant alcoholism took a heavy economic toll in the form of absenteeism, theft, and shoddy work. "If vodka interferes with your work, quit working," counseled a cavalier piece of folk wisdom. Drunkenness may have cut overall productivity by 10 to 20 percent. All these manifestations of alcoholism threw into embarrassing doubt Soviet claims for progress toward "developed socialism." Indeed, critics called the Brezhnev years the time of

— Может, лучше яблочка, Адам?   Рисунок Е. ГУРОВА.

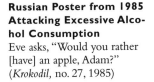

**Russian Poster from 1985
Attacking Excessive Alco-
hol Consumption**
Eve asks, "Would you rather
[have] an apple, Adam?"
(*Krokodil*, no. 27, 1985)

"developed alcoholism." It and other social maladies were interpreted as signs of a moral crisis.[8]

Brezhnev's conservatism hindered his capacity to deal with this tangle of social and economic problems even though this immobility constrained the Soviet Union in its competition with the United States. He would not repeat what he regarded as Khrushchev's "harebrained" attempts at economic reforms, and he insisted on honoring the claims of the military and the military-related heavy industry. But consumers would not let him off the hook. Workers engaged in sporadic protests over shortages and pay, while the secret police reported widespread popular discontent over the leadership's long-deferred promises for a better life. Images of Western lifestyles carried by media and observed by travelers underlined Soviet backwardness and whetted the taste for consumer goods. In a bow to public demands, Brezhnev presented a program to the party congress in 1971 for raising living standards.

That program helped carry the Soviet population further along the road toward a consumer culture that was already well rooted in the United States, western Europe, and Japan. The most pressing need was housing, because 40 percent of the urban population still lived in communal apartments in the late 1960s. Brezhnev devoted resources to increase substantially the number of single-family apartments. Citizens were quick to fill those private apartments with consumer goods such as refrigerators, telephones, radios, and televisions. TVs, for example, had been available to only 5 percent of the population in 1960. By the late 1970s TVs could be found in almost every home. Leisure time increased as well. Despite the lure of television, a public that was virtually universally literate still loved to read, especially nostalgic writings about a rural way of life that was disappearing, historical novels set in imperial times, and detective fiction. Movie-going remained popular, and Western musical genres found their way into the country with official approval (except for rock and roll). Jazz, folk, and "disco" mixed with indigenous musical forms to create a hybrid popular music heard on radio, television, and recordings as well as in restaurants and clubs. Sports and drinking were major leisure-time activities for males.

Escapist popular entertainment combined with party authoritarianism to alienate the public and push individuals into their own private worlds. Cynicism flourished in a political system in which officials no longer commanded respect. Jokes abounded about the slow, dogma-bound Brezhnev. One of those jokes began with the announcement that the Soviet Union was going to top the American achievement of getting a man on the moon by sending a space team to the sun. When a Soviet cosmonaut protested that the team would be "burned alive," Brezhnev was quick to reassure him, "Don't worry. We have planned every detail. We have arranged for you to land at night."[9]

The political estrangement of youth was especially worrisome to party leaders. The Soviet Union had developed its own youth culture in stages roughly paralleling that in the West. It had begun to take hold in the 1950s and 1960s with the relaxation of international tensions, and it flourished in the 1970s and early 1980s. Its hallmark was a fascination with Western musical styles and from the late 1960s onward, especially rock and roll. The first homegrown rock group, The Slavs, had appeared in imitation of the Beatles. By late in the 1960s there were 263 informal bands in Moscow alone, including Soft Suede Corners, Young Comanches, and Little Red Imps. The best-known Soviet rock group, Time Machine headed by Andrei Makarevitch, attacked social conformism, political hypocrisy, and the endless government appeals for popular sacrifice. Despite official disapproval and even police harassment, hippie culture—jeans, bell-bottoms, peace signs, miniskirts, and bare feet—spread through an underground of communes, hangouts, and clubs.

Holding the Line on Foreign Policy. Brezhnev's foreign policy was as conservative as his domestic course. Within the East bloc, he crushed the 1968 Czech reform movement (described in Chapter 4), sending a clear signal that Moscow would defend the status quo there. The Czech attempt to forge an independent path threatened not only bloc unity but also the Soviet Union itself. It inspired separatists in western Ukraine as well as Moldavia, Georgia, and the Baltic region. Dissidents within the USSR expressed sympathy with the Czech experiment and began to circulate translations of key Czech documents. The outspoken Sakharov hailed the Prague Spring, and many Soviet college students also expressed sympathy for what the Czechs were attempting. Brezhnev's fears for the survival of the Czech Communist Party, reinforced by those expressed by hard-line party leaders in Poland, East Germany, and Bulgaria, finally resulted in a Soviet-led Warsaw Pact intervention in August 1968. Brezhnev took the occasion to formally articulate the doctrine that the USSR had in fact been acting on

since 1945: "when internal and external forces hostile to socialism are threatening to turn a socialist country back to capitalism, this becomes a common problem and a concern of all socialist countries."[10] This public declaration of the
Soviet right to intervene to preserve socialist regimes would become known as
the Brezhnev Doctrine.

The international costs of intervention proved high. It completed China's
alienation, while Albania, already pursuing an independent course, responded by
severing all ties with the Warsaw Pact and making China its chief patron. The
intervention provoked vehement opposition from the Communist parties of
Spain and Italy where sympathy for the Prague Spring was especially strong, and
in general it gave a fresh boost to Eurocommunism. The crushing of the Czech
reform movement also revealed serious morale problems among the Soviet-led
Warsaw Pact forces, including Polish, Hungarian, and East German units. Eastern
Europeans were cowed by Moscow's show of force, but they were also more anti-
Soviet than ever. Among Moscow's friends and clients in the third world, the
Czech intervention dealt a damaging blow to Soviet prestige.

Brezhnev's partnership with Nixon fit within this larger pattern of a conservative but problem-plagued Soviet Union. The Soviet leader wanted to establish
the USSR as an equal to the United States. To that end, he wanted Washington
to accept as legitimate the Cold War lines separating the superpower spheres in
Europe and cooperate in limiting the dangers and costs of the nuclear arms race.
He remarked at a May 1972 party meeting that even though the United States
remained the "main force of imperialism," the danger of nuclear war made good
relations critical. Thus he, like Khrushchev, sought a relationship of "peaceful
coexistence." Brezhnev could embark on this policy because he felt more secure
against U.S. nuclear blackmail thanks to the post–Cuban Missile Crisis buildup of
Soviet strategic forces. In this new situation of rough nuclear parity, both sides
had to recognize, Brezhnev publicly observed in 1975, "the senselessness and
extreme danger of further increasing tension." He underlined the impact that
Soviet parity had had on the thinking of its adversaries. "Now the leaders of the
bourgeois world can no longer seriously count on resolving the historic conflict
between capitalism and socialism by force of arms."[11]

Western Europe and Détente

Western European leaders joined Mao and Brezhnev in the overseas contingent
of détentists. Washington's NATO partners were tiring of Cold War tensions;
influential segments of their publics demanded East-West measures to promote
peaceful relations. Driving this demand was the knowledge that a superpower
misstep could set in motion the troops of the two powerful alliances facing each
other across the German border. War might come without even a word from
Europeans whose lands would serve as the battlegrounds, perhaps even be
reduced to nuclear cinders.

The first official European critiques of the Cold War confrontation came
from the formidable Charles de Gaulle, the dominant figure on the French political scene from his election as president in 1958 until his retirement in 1969. His

foreign policy was driven by an abiding concern with establishing French leadership in a western Europe that could act as an independent force in world affairs. This goal entailed a rejection of any bipolar notion of how the postwar world should operate; it particularly meant resisting American attempts to work with Britain to determine the fate of Europe; and it led him to a close working relationship with West Germany's Konrad Adenauer.

De Gaulle thus became for a decade the bane of U.S. policymakers, ready to frustrate the Americans at every turn. In 1959 he began distancing France from NATO and developed an independent nuclear force to set his country on a symbolic par with the superpowers and Britain, the only other states with nuclear weapons at that time. In 1963 he blocked Britain's admission to the European Community in part because London would be a rival for European leadership but also because he believed that Britain would represent U.S. views in European councils. He rebuffed U.S. free traders intent on opening the European market to American farm products. He criticized U.S. intervention in Vietnam. And he accelerated the descent of the dollar into crisis by demanding gold in exchange for the large dollar reserves that a prosperous France had been piling up. (See Chapter 5.)

The stirrings within the NATO alliance took fresh form just as de Gaulle retired from the political scene in 1969. The West German elections of that year ended two decades of control by Adenauer's Christian Democratic Party. That party had given priority to integration of West Germany into NATO to achieve security from attack and to gain international acceptance from neighbors still mindful of past German aggression. In keeping with early Cold War rigidities, Adenauer and his associates had refused to formally accept Germany's division or the broader pattern of Soviet domination in eastern Europe. The 1969 election produced a center-left coalition led by Willy Brandt—and with it a major shift in West German Cold War policy.

In what became known as *Ostpolitik* (literally, a policy oriented toward the east), Brandt sought to reduce tensions by accepting the division of Germany and the dominant Soviet role on its side of the European Cold War line. But his goal was not to freeze the status quo. To the contrary, he argued that the prospects for internal economic and social changes in socialist societies were dim as long as fear and repression prevailed. He sought to promote conditions that would lower political and military tensions and thus set in motion significant changes in the Eastern bloc. The measures that Brandt promoted in pursuit of this goal included high-level exchanges with Soviet leaders, reduced military tensions between the armed forces facing off across the Iron Curtain, and the promotion of cultural, economic, and technological exchanges. Brandt calculated that as contacts multiplied and tensions diminished, the prospects would increase for a loosened Soviet grip on its European allies and for closer links between East and West Germany.

Brandt's fresh approach bore fruit. He signed formal agreements with East Germany, Poland, and the USSR accepting postwar boundaries as legitimate, and he gained an agreement for the free movement of peoples between the two German states. Thanks to this warming trend, West Germany became the Soviets' largest trading partner in the West. Brandt's agenda got a major boost from the Helsinki Accords signed by the superpowers and the Europeans in 1975. The Accords legalized the European borders that prevailed at the end of World War II, encouraged trade between the two sides of the Iron Curtain, and promoted the free movement of peoples and ideas. Perhaps most important, they stipulated respect for the full range of human rights. Brezhnev and leaders in the Soviet bloc accepted the agreement as a harmless piece of paper, but they soon had reason to regret making this international commitment. Just as Brandt anticipated, Helsinki gave legitimacy to the activities of human rights groups within eastern Europe and the Soviet Union and inspired external pressure and monitoring that Communist regimes resented and resisted but could not outright rebuff.

The Brandt policy initiatives reflected changes going on within Germany itself and Europe more broadly. The physical division of Berlin, created by the construction of the Wall in 1961 while Brandt himself had been mayor of West Berlin, had become a symbol of the human costs of the Cold War, cutting off contact between German families on the two sides. At the same time the West German state was riding high. It had won the gratitude of its citizens by engineering an economic miracle in a land devastated at war's end. It had also neutralized much of the international hostility left over from the war, and it had won acceptance as a full-fledged alliance partner in NATO. Other European governments favored the Brandt policy as a welcome step toward relaxing Cold War tensions and reducing the chance of war. Polls revealed deep public anxieties about the arms race. For example, a survey conducted in early 1963 already registered lopsided support in Italy, France, West Germany, and Britain for completely eliminating nuclear weapons.

The détente-minded Nixon administration found *Ostpolitik* troubling despite Brandt's insistence that he would maintain close ties to NATO and consult regularly with the Americans. While publicly supportive, Nixon and Kissinger worried in private that the Brandt government in Bonn might be exploring an independent and more nationalistic course or even that West German–Soviet contacts might upstage Washington's talks with Moscow. In mid-1970 an irritated Kissinger told a West German emissary, "Let me tell you something! If anyone is going to pursue détente with the Soviet Union, it will be us."[12] This growing European independence would continue to trouble Washington, especially after U.S. leaders shifted back to a more militant Cold War stance during the late 1970s and early 1980s.

The U.S. Retreat from Détente

A policy shift as fundamental as Nixon's was bound to come under fire within a U.S. political culture still deeply anti-communist and viscerally afraid of seeming weak in the eyes of the world. Thus even before Nixon's resignation in 1974, détente had come under assault, and the domestic opposition would continue to grow during the presidencies of Gerald Ford (1974–1977) and Jimmy Carter (1977–1981).

Of all Nixon's domestic enemies, he was himself perhaps the worst. He made his policy vulnerable in part because he failed to build a public consensus or create support within the foreign policy bureaucracy. Secretive and impatient, Nixon preferred to keep policy out of sight of what he saw as an ignorant public, a jealous bureaucracy, an opportunistic Congress, and irritating special interests. He extended his telling comment on the public—"You don't take the people where they want to go, you take the people where they ought to go."[13]—to include the other potential participants in the policy process. Nixon was also limited by an inability to break completely with Cold War thinking. He remained obsessed with the maintenance of American prestige and worried that his country might seem "a pitiful, helpless giant." His stunted ethical sense proved most directly his undoing during the Watergate affair. By authorizing "dirty tricks" against his political enemies, including the attempted burglary of the Democratic National headquarters, he committed crimes that he tried in turn to cover up. As he dug himself in deeper in the face of a relentless congressional investigation, Nixon began to discredit his entire presidency. Threatened with removal through impeachment, the embattled Nixon resigned in August 1974. Henry Kissinger, now serving as secretary of state, sought under President Gerald Ford to preserve the gains of détente. But by then even that term had fallen into disrepute.

Carter's Flip-Flop. Nixon's policy initiative finally lost all momentum during the presidency of Jimmy Carter. That genial Southern Baptist, U.S. navy nuclear engineer, and Georgia governor had no foreign policy experience. He was, moreover, gripped by conflicting impulses on broad foreign policy goals. He shared Nixon's dissatisfaction with the earlier, over-militarized containment policy. He pursued a new round of arms negotiations, capped in 1979 by an agreement (SALT II) with Brezhnev to limit each side to 2,400 launchers and reduce each side to one defensive anti-ballistic missile system. (There were still no limits on the number of warheads that a single missile might carry.) But Carter also sought to make the United States the guardian of human rights everywhere, even in the Soviet Union. He eyed Soviet involvement in the third world with concern. Brezhnev supported Cuba; drew close to North Vietnam from 1965 onward; cultivated Mozambique, Angola, and Ethiopia as footholds in Africa; and drew neighboring Afghanistan into a dependent relationship. These decisions, following along the same activist track pursued by Khrushchev, disturbed the American president. To make matters worse, Carter's chief advisors, Secretary of State Cyrus Vance and White House aide Zbigniew Brzezinski, were themselves at odds on how to deal with the Soviet Union. The result was what the Soviet ambassador in Washington perceptively described in a report for his bosses in mid-1978 as "a selective, half-hearted conception of détente."[14]

Increasingly the anti-Soviet Brzezinski prevailed in White House councils. He pushed normalization of diplomatic relations with China as a way to put the Kremlin on the defensive, and he gave higher priority to standing up to the Soviets than reaching agreements with them. His ascendancy was complete by 1979 as a new Cold War chill set in. The Soviet invasion of Afghanistan did the most to make the temperature plunge. The actions of two Soviet allies—the Vietnamese invasion of Cambodia and the dispatch of Cuban troops to Africa—combined with the Iran hostage crisis (see Chapter 9) and the Afghanistan invasion to leave Carter shaken by late 1979. Both Brzezinski and a new, more militant Carter saw a dangerous "arc of crisis" running from Afghanistan, through the Middle East, and into the heart of sub-Saharan Africa. Pro-Soviet regimes and insurgent groups were making headway in all these areas as well as in the Central American countries of Nicaragua and El Salvador.

The president toughened his tone, began a dramatic increase in defense spending, and shelved the SALT II agreement awaiting ratification in the Senate. In August 1980 the administration announced a major shift in nuclear war strategy—making the enemy's nuclear weapons and communications systems rather than cities and industries the main target. The threat of massive loss of life and economic disruption under the old policy was supposed to deter an attack on the United States. Because the number of urban and industrial targets was fairly stable, the number of warheads did not need to grow beyond a certain point. The new policy, by contrast, was less stable and more costly. It required a constantly increasing number of nuclear weapons, first to match the many warheads on the other side and then to keep up as the Soviets increased their arsenal to avoid getting wiped out by an American strike and losing their retaliatory capability. Advocates of the new policy seemed to regard nuclear war as a game, which a skillful player might win.

What Carter and Brzezinski could not grasp were the problems besetting the Soviet Union. Sino-Soviet enmity had been a terrible blow to Soviet security, forcing the military to stand watch on two widely separated fronts. Poland was drifting from Soviet control, defying the Brezhnev Doctrine, and the rest of eastern Europe was also in ferment. The Communist parties of western Europe were publicly challenging Moscow's claim to lead the international socialist movement. And as we have seen, disaffection was no less a problem within the Soviet Union among intellectuals, youth, and national minorities. Economic difficulties were deepening. The Kremlin watched Afghanistan anxiously because the Brezhnev team feared it might serve as a point of entry for subversive Islamic influences into the southern and heavily Muslim Soviet republics. But the costs of decisive intervention, it was equally clear, would be high. As Foreign Minister Andrei Gromyko summed it up at a meeting early in 1979, "The army there is unreliable. Thus our army, when it arrives in Afghanistan, will be the aggressor. . . . Afghanistan is not ripe for a revolution. And all that we have done in recent years with such effort in terms of détente, arms reduction, and much more—all that would be thrown back. China, of course, would be given a nice present. All the nonaligned countries will be against us."[15] Even so, with the situation deteriorating, Moscow finally resolved late in the year to send Soviet troops to prop up a failing and ineffective ally in a war that would, like the one in Vietnam, prove unpopular at home and demoralizing to the troops in the field. Over a million Afghanis and fifty thousand Soviets would fall as casualties by the time the conflict ended in 1989. (See Chapter 9 for additional details.)

Carter's shift toward a hard-line stance seemed to vindicate long-standing criticisms of détente as politically naïve and morally misguided. The Committee on the Present Danger was at the forefront of that criticism. It had been organized in 1975 in reaction against Nixon's "sell-out" to the USSR and China, and it kept up the fire on what it saw as Carter's fuzzy-minded, ineffectual policy. Its prominent members included Paul Nitze (drafter of NSC-68, the alarmist 1950 articulation of the containment policy), Norman Podhoretz (editor of the organization's mouthpiece, *Commentary*), and Jeane Kirkpatrick (Georgetown political scientist). They believed in a strong military establishment, a boldly interventionist foreign policy, and presidential leadership unimpeded by congressional restrictions or the public. They suspected that the Democrats had lost their nerve, and so they turned to the Republican Party to close the strategic "window of vulnerability" and defeat Moscow's strategy of expansion.

Reagan and the "Evil Empire." Ronald Reagan embraced the Committee's arguments and made them central to his 1980 presidential campaign. This actor and Hollywood labor leader turned two-term California governor promised that he would stand up to the communists and make the tide of history flow again in favor of freedom. This promise of restored national pride and power, along with a commitment to smaller government, helped Reagan defeat Carter in 1980. Once in the White House, the new president launched initiatives that smashed Nixon's plans for détente, and his landslide reelection victory in 1984 in a campaign that proclaimed "Morning Again in America" left scant hope for reassembling the pieces anytime in the foreseeable future. Reagan was not strong on policy details. (He long believed that missiles once fired could be recalled.) He did not make good use of his staff. (The intense battles at the highest levels to influence Reagan's thinking damaged his presidency.) And he husbanded his energy. (Reagan liked to joke that hard work never killed anyone, but then why take a risk.) But despite all these deficiencies, the president had a strong and simple vision of America's place in the world, and he could articulate it with charm and conviction that played on nationalist themes popular with the public. America was, in a phrase he frequently invoked, "the last best hope of man on earth."[16]

The new president sustained Carter's military buildup. His public pronouncements suggested a depth of enmity toward what the president called "the evil empire" not seen since the darkest days of the Cold War in the late 1940s and early 1950s. He gave members of the Committee on the Present Danger prominent places in his administration. He continued Carter's counter-targeting strategy, expanded the nuclear weapons arsenal, talked about a "winnable" nuclear war, and in 1983 committed the country to forging a high-tech shield against missile attack (the Strategic Defense Initiative, popularly known as Star Wars). He denied critics' claims that missile defense would prove unworkable and costly, would provoke Soviet countermeasures, and (most serious of all) would create a dangerously unstable relationship between Soviet and American nuclear forces. Only on China did Reagan promise pressure and then retreat, keeping the lines to Beijing open.

Reagan's third-world policy was as confrontational as his approach to the Soviet Union. His administration funded "freedom fighters" in Central America,

Afghanistan, sub-Saharan Africa, and Cambodia. Especially alarming for the Reagan administration was the communist onslaught in the Americas. In Nicaragua the Sandinista revolutionary movement (named for Augusto Sandino, who had opposed U.S. occupation between 1912 and 1933) had taken power in 1979 after overthrowing the long-time U.S.-backed dictator. Reagan authorized a CIA campaign of pressure, armed anti-communist exiles known as the "Contras," and imposed a trade embargo. These measures, controversial at home and internationally, slowly ground down Nicaragua's government as well as its economy, and in elections in 1990 U.S.-backed candidates ousted the Sandinistas. In El Salvador, where an insurgency was gathering strength when he entered the White House, Reagan supplied money, weapons, and advisors. With the assistance of death squads and U.S. aid, the conservative government was able to stalemate the opposition in a bitter, brutal civil war costing the lives of 75,000. In 1983 U.S. forces invaded the island nation of Grenada, making quick work of its Marxist regime aligned with Cuba.

In these and other third-world cases, the Reagan team made no pretense of supporting economic development or nation building. Kirkpatrick, now Reagan's representative at the UN, had explained why stopping radical revolutions was so important even if it meant backing dictators on the Right. In a swipe at Carter's failure to protect long-time U.S. allies in Nicaragua and Iran, Kirkpatrick observed in late 1979 "that traditional authoritarian governments are less repressive than revolutionary autocracies, that they are more susceptible of liberalization, and that they are more compatible with U.S. interests."[17]

THE SHORT CAREER OF DÉTENTE	
1968	Soviet-led forces intervene in Czechoslovakia (justified by the Brezhnev Doctrine)
1969	Sino-Soviet border clashes break out; Nixon initiates "détente" with the Soviet Union, opening to China, and "peace with honor" in Vietnam; Brandt presses *Ostpolitik*
1972	Nixon and Brezhnev sign SALT I; Nixon makes groundbreaking visit to China
1973	Paris peace accords end involvement of U.S. forces in Vietnam
1975	Helsinki Accords are concluded; Committee on the Present Danger is organized
1979	Carter and Brezhnev conclude new strategic weapons treaty (SALT II); Soviet forces invade Afghanistan, resulting in Carter boosting U.S. military budget and shelving SALT II treaty
1980	Reagan is elected president as foe of "the evil empire"
1983	Reagan announces plans to build a high-tech shield against missile attack

True to its conservative instincts, the Brezhnev leadership clung to its earlier preference for détente. By the late 1970s Brezhnev himself was showing signs of failing health, and senility would become increasingly evident. But whether speaking his own words or those of his colleagues, Brezhnev reiterated his earlier argument about the dangers of nuclear war. In 1981 with Reagan on the ideological offensive, Brezhnev bluntly told a party congress, "To count on victory in a nuclear war is dangerous madness." The next year, he pledged that the Soviet Union would not be the first to use nuclear weapons and thus risk destroying "world civilization" and even "life itself on earth." His successors would stick with what had now become virtually an article of faith in Soviet policy.[18]

THE GORBACHEV INITIATIVES

The 1980s witnessed a revival of the reform spirit in the Kremlin—and soon a campaign to breathe life into détente. Brezhnev's death in 1982 brought a pair of transitional figures to power—first Yuri Andropov for two years, and then Konstantin Chernenko for barely more than a year. They wanted to invigorate an economy suffering from a slowing growth rate and to address social problems such as workplace indiscipline and alcoholism. But both men were cautious reformers. Their successor, Mikhail Gorbachev, began with a similarly cautious approach but then gradually developed a more intense and wide-ranging program for change, one that would lead not only to the end of the Cold War but also to the collapse of the Soviet bloc and then the Soviet state itself.

Glasnost, Perestroika, and a New Foreign Policy

The last Soviet leader was born in 1931 into a peasant family in southern Russia. The family had carried black political marks as "enemies of the people": one grandfather was sent into exile in 1933 and another suffered arrest, imprisonment, and torture in 1937. Gorbachev's father, on the other hand, had won honor during World War II at the front, where he was twice wounded. In the immediate postwar years young Mikhail compiled an outstanding record as a student and worker in collective agriculture. He went on to study law at Moscow University between 1950 and 1955, a time of transition from the lean, repressive Stalinist era. In 1952 he joined the Soviet Communist Party. In 1953 he married Raisa Titorenko, a gifted classmate.

From 1955 to 1978 Gorbachev rose through the party ranks. His first official posts were in his home region, but his appointment in 1978 as Central Committee secretary with responsibility for overseeing agriculture brought him fulltime to Moscow. By then Gorbachev had prudently veiled but nonetheless clear views on the need for reform going back at least to the Twentieth Party Congress in 1956. Khrushchev's speech on Stalin had made a strong impression on him, as it did on others of his age. "I was shocked, bewildered and lost. It wasn't an analysis, just facts, deadly facts."[19]

In 1980 he became a full Politburo member with growing support and experience within the upper reaches of the party. Andropov's succession to party leadership in 1982 thrust Gorbachev into greater prominence. Worried by lagging technological standards and slowing economic growth, Andropov enlisted Gorbachev's help in shaking up the system and extended his authority from agriculture to the entire economy. Gorbachev pushed for decentralization, with greater autonomy to be given to lower-level managers. After Andropov's death, Gorbachev served as the frail Chernenko's vigorous second-in-command and made an impressive international debut, traveling to Canada, Italy, and Britain. At the same time he positioned himself as an advocate of reform in carefully worded public statements. He offered a franker assessment to his wife: "We cannot go on living like this, we must change."[20] Upon Chernenko's death in March 1985, the Politburo voted Gorbachev the party's new General Secretary.

As party head, Gorbachev set off on what his biographer has described as a "revolution from within."[21] He began slowly but soon enough was calling for a major transformation of the system. Within six years he had converted virtually without violence a communist dictatorship into a system that mixed authoritarian and democratic elements. The turning point came in January 1987 at a meeting of the entire Central Committee. Putting aside narrow economic goals, Gorbachev made the case for an ambitious makeover of the system as the only way to stimulate technological innovation, improve consistently poor agricultural performance, and end official corruption. He got Politburo backing for these and other reform goals by bringing in like-minded leaders and removing doubters. By summer 1988, Gorbachev had completed his shift away from piecemeal reform to sweeping domestic change. By then he had espoused democratic socialism closely akin to a western European model of political pluralism and mixed economy.

One part of his emerging program was *glasnost* (openness), reflecting a commitment to getting Soviet citizens to discuss publicly the problems of their system and seek solutions. Gorbachev wanted to promote a freer flow of information between the USSR and the outside world in science, technology, and culture. It was important to make leaders accountable, so he encouraged popular scrutiny and criticism, even the airing in the mass media of social, economic, and environmental problems that those responsible might otherwise seek to sweep under the rug.

As the champion of *glasnost*, Gorbachev ended the persecution of dissidents, even lent them his backing. He paved the way for publication of Solzhenitsyn's works for the first time in the Soviet Union, and he arranged Sakharov's return to Moscow. The physicist would quickly convince Gorbachev that the U.S. Star Wars program was vulnerable to cheap countermeasures and thus no reason to hold up arms control agreements. Sakharov went on to win a seat in the 1989 election for the Congress of People's Deputies shortly before suffering heart failure. Gorbachev even reached out to young people with admiring remarks on John Lennon and recollections of how much during his college days he had preferred Tarzan movies over dreary documentaries idealizing Soviet life.

The other part of Gorbachev's domestic program was *perestroika*, the restructuring of the economy and the closely linked state bureaucracy that planned and controlled production. *Perestroika* had as its general goal a gradual reduction in the size of the state-administered (or command) economy and the creation of more scope for market forces. Industry would become more accountable and self-supporting. In agriculture, Gorbachev wanted to give more responsibility to farmers but stopped short of privatizing the land. He proposed the removal of subsidies for food, housing, farm machinery, and other goods that ate up nearly a fifth of the state budget. *Perestroika* would make prices reflect the real cost of production, thus bringing more efficiency to the economy. It anticipated cutting the central planning bureaucracy in half. And it sought to give wide scope for private property and privately owned enterprise, especially for the supply of consumer goods and services.

Determined to make his foreign policy serve his domestic program, Gorbachev launched the crowning initiative to end the Cold War. To some extent he acted on the old logic of Khrushchev and Brezhnev—that the rough nuclear balance with the United States and the unthinkable destructiveness of nuclear war made arms control negotiations imperative. He also acted on the premise that domestic reform required a more relaxed international environment as well as reform in eastern Europe to make regimes there more popular and less dependent on Soviet aid for survival. He regarded greater trade, loans, technology transfers, and reduction of his defense budget as important to advancing his domestic agenda.

In short order, Gorbachev moved to create the international conditions conducive to reform. One key step was to liquidate the costly and unpopular conflict in Afghanistan. Soviet forces would complete their evacuation in 1989. On the European front, Gorbachev launched a dual effort. He cultivated western Europeans and especially West Germans, entrancing them with his urbane style and vision of Russia as part of the European family. At the same time he prodded eastern European clients toward liberalization. He warned that if they did not begin their own programs of *glasnost* and *perestroika,* the Soviet Union would not block the rise of popular leaders who would. He thus in effect repealed the Brezhnev Doctrine's threat of military intervention to preserve the status quo. Enthusiastic receptions during his tours of eastern Europe suggested that the peoples there shared his commitment to revitalized socialism.

Perhaps the most important part of the Gorbachev international initiative was winning Reagan to arms control. In meetings beginning in 1985 Gorbachev quickly convinced the American president to renew the policy of détente. Faced with this new kind of Soviet leader, Reagan found irresistible the chance to make his own mark in history. His impulse was reinforced by an American public whose nuclear anxiety had been revived by talk in Washington about strategies for fighting and winning nuclear war. Reagan stopped referring to the "evil empire," and got down to work with Gorbachev in five summit meetings between 1985 and 1988. In 1987 the two leaders completed an agreement to eliminate 1,836 intermediate-range Soviet and 867 U.S. missiles in Europe. They pushed ahead on Strategic Arms Reduction Talks (START) that would sharply cut back strategic nuclear weapons.

As Reagan's successor, George H. W. Bush continued to work with the Soviet leader to relax tensions, though he remained suspicious of Moscow's intentions, and the phrase "the Cold War is over" seemed to stick in his throat. That momentous point finally came at the first summit meeting between Gorbachev and Bush, held in December 1989 on a Soviet cruise liner docked in Malta harbor and buffeted by gale force winds and high seas. Gorbachev had no difficulty saying simply to the U.S. delegation, "We don't consider you an enemy anymore." He was equally definitive in the closing press conference: "The world leaves one epoch of Cold War and enters another epoch." Bush, still cautious, pronounced the two powers at "the threshold of a brand new era."[22] Deeds counted more than words. Two years later they signed the START agreement. That July 1991 accord committed the United States and the USSR to significant reductions in warheads on long-range missiles. Both sides were soon talking about substantial additional cuts.

The Demise of the Soviet System

By 1989, with foreign policy successes piling up, Gorbachev was beginning to discover how destructive were the forces that liberalization had unleashed. First, they destroyed not just the Warsaw Pact but also the Soviet grip over its neighbors to the west. Winds of change that he had encouraged began blowing down rickety socialist regimes. His calls for reform had shaken the confidence of ruling old-line Communists. Their critics, often tapping a deep anti-Russian and anti-socialist sentiment, realized that Moscow would no longer intervene. When those critics took power and began to move out of the Soviet camp, Gorbachev could only watch.

The Collapse of the Clients.   The grip of those leaders had been slipping for at least two decades largely as a result of economic problems. After strong growth in the 1950s, eastern Europe encountered in the 1960s the first hints of trouble ahead. The labor supply ran short and productivity failed to increase. At the same time the Soviet economy, to which the region was tied by the Council for Mutual Economic Assistance (COMECON), started to slow, and Soviet subsidies fell. Eastern European economists began to question the rigid, ponderous Soviet model. They urged instead seeking efficiencies through the market mechanism, introducing new technologies, and becoming more involved in the capitalist economies through foreign trade. Some governments followed this advice and concluded loans to create an export industry. This strategy backfired. After piling up international debt, their foreign trade did not grow because their products were of poor quality, and in any case the economies in the West happened to be slowing at this time and thus were importing less. From the mid-1970s growth rates in Soviet satellite states slumped, and in some years Poland, Hungary, and Czechoslovakia suffered an absolute decline in national output.

Eastern Europeans could see that their standard of living was stagnating. Worse, visits abroad and exposure to foreign media made clear that those standards compared poorly with levels in the West. As vaunted "social rights" seemed increasingly hollow, popular resentment was directed against the *nomenklatura,* that is, party officials who enjoyed special access to goods and services while talking of shared sacrifice and worker sovereignty. The governments in the region kept calling for popular patience and sacrifice as officials sought to get their economies moving. By the 1980s they had little to show for their efforts, while critics began to question workplace safety, technological stagnation, poor quality control, and accumulating environmental damage. Pollution from outdated heavy industry created acid rain that killed forests, contaminated waterways, fouled urban air, and gave rise to an epidemic of cancer and respiratory diseases. The catastrophic reactor failure of a nuclear power plant at Chernobyl in neighboring Soviet Ukraine in 1986 dramatized the mounting environmental danger as it released radiation greater than the bombing of Hiroshima and Nagasaki.

At this moment of vulnerability for European socialist governments, Gorbachev's intervention opened the floodgates of change. Poland and Hungary were the first to feel the effects. A labor organization (Solidarity) had taken form in Poland in 1980, propelled by worker discontent. One striking worker muttered in 1988, "Forty years of socialism and there's still no toilet paper!"[23] Gorbachev's thaw created favorable conditions for Solidarity under the leadership of an electrician in Gdańsk's Lenin Shipyard, Lech Wałeşa, to press for fundamental economic and political reform. The beleaguered Communist party headed by Wojciech Jaruzelski finally agreed to hold parliamentary elections in June 1989. Solidarity won handily, signaling the beginning of the end for Communist control in Poland. In Hungary memorial demonstrations for Imre Nagy, executed by the Soviets after the 1956 revolt (see Chapter 4), shook the government. By October 1989 Hungary had a new constitution, and elections in March-April 1990 brought non-Communists to power.

In East Germany, tremors in the neighborhood together with strong signals from Gorbachev set off a wave of demonstrations that shattered the nerves of already demoralized Communist leaders. Despite police violence, peaceful protestors rapidly grew from hundreds in the epicenter of open discontent in Leipzig in September to half a million marching in East Berlin on November 4, 1989. The crowds sang the U.S. civil rights favorite, "We shall overcome," as well as the "Internationale," the anthem of the political left that now served as an expression of longing by many for a reformed socialism. They chanted "Gorbi, Gorbi," "We are the people," and "We are one people," while carrying signs that ranged from "Stop privilege" to "I want to visit my girlfriend in Holland."[24] The climax came on November 9 when, amidst official confusion, citizens broke through a border checkpoint to West Germany and then in the most dramatic event of that year began hammering the hated Berlin Wall into pieces. During the next four days more than a quarter of the population traveled west, most to return with bags filled with consumer goods.

The death throes of the East German party-state intensified popular pressure in Czechoslovakia. The catalyst was the arrest of dissidents, including playwright Václav Havel, the leader of an organization of independent intellectuals known as Civic Forum. In late October 1989 student protestors publicly challenged the old regime. The government responded with police repression but then in November conceded the need for reform. Its retreat almost at once turned into a rout. The turnaround was so smooth and fast that it was called the "velvet revolution." At the end of November a rehabilitated Alexander Dubček, the hero of the Prague Spring (see Chapter 4), appeared alongside Havel before an exultant crowd of hundreds of thousands chanting his name, a sure sign that with the Soviet brakes off the political wheel was finally turning. In December Havel was elected president, and six months later candidates from Civic Forum and its Slovak counterpart organization won the first free elections and with it control of the government.

In Romania and Bulgaria the events of 1989 did not mark so dramatic a break with the past. In both countries officials prominent in the old socialist regime clung to power under the banner of reform Marxism. Romania witnessed the most violent repression. Challenged by demonstrations against Nicolae Ceauşescu, the despot in power since the mid-1960s, the military fired into crowds in two cities, setting off protests elsewhere. The crisis abated when a palace coup ousted Ceauşescu and his powerful wife, Elena. They were executed on Christmas Day. The new government was led by high-ranking officials from the old one. Though it faced continued protests well into 1990, this old guard preserved its power. Communists in Bulgaria made a smoother transition to the new order, perhaps in part because they had not been compromised by popular anti-Soviet feeling so prominent elsewhere in the Eastern bloc. By late 1989, the government had lost control to demonstrators and opted for talks with the opposition. In January 1990 the Communist Party agreed to surrender its monopoly of political power. Elections in mid-1990 brought strong support for reform Marxists leading a now renamed Communist party.

The USSR Unravels. By 1989 the destabilizing effects of liberalization were also becoming apparent in the Soviet Union itself. By that spring so much had changed that the USSR had lost the main structural and ideological features defining a Communist country. The leading role of the party was gone. So too was democratic centralism, the ultimate goal or legitimizing myth of building a communist society, and a sense of membership in (if not leadership over) an international socialist community. State ownership of the economy was still largely intact, but Gorbachev had begun the process of creating a mixed economy, thus stimulating fresh popular economic demands.

The parliamentary elections in March 1989 began the unraveling of the Soviet Union. Those elections unleashed centrifugal forces, especially ethnocultural sentiments, that firm (even brutal) central control had for decades held in check. The USSR contained twenty-two different ethnic or national groups with two million or more members. When each gained a voice, political disintegration and economic confusion soon followed. Already Armenia-Azerbaijan and the Baltic region had begun to slip beyond Moscow's control. Cities, republics, and regions used the March elections to assert their interests and in some cases even claim autonomy or independence. Following Boris Yeltsin's election as president of the Russian Republic in June 1991, Russia declared itself independent. Gorbachev had fought to preserve the union but now faced a total rout as others of the USSR's fifteen republics also opted out.

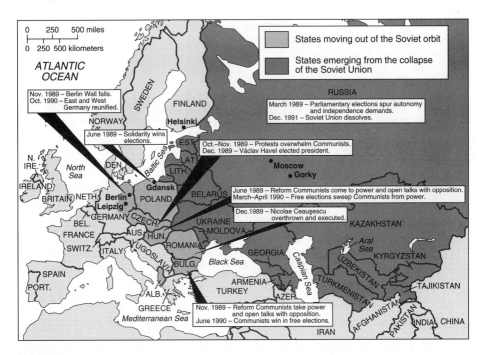

MAP 7.1
The Soviet Collapse, 1989–1991
The unraveling of the Soviet empire began in eastern Europe in 1989 and had by 1991 worked its way home.

Paralleling the political disintegration of the USSR went a failure on Gorbachev's part to push hard on the economic restructuring envisioned by *perestroika*. As the old centralized system of state planning fell apart, Gorbachev was not able to put a new system in its place that could even equal old production levels. After growing at a rate of 3.2 percent in 1989, Soviet gross national product (GNP) began a relentless decline, falling to negative 7.6 percent by 1991. Despite the incentives of the market, agricultural production also fell, as did energy production. Inflation soared. With supplies disrupted, hoarding of goods became commonplace, and cities and regions had to implement rationing. Workers became militant in their demands for higher wages and resorted to crippling strikes. For example, during the summer of 1989 coal miners walked out in what was the first major public protest since 1962. Gorbachev bowed to their demands, the first retreat ever by the Soviet state in the face of working-class protest. The economic slide resulting from bungled economic reform would prove prolonged and deeply painful to many throughout the 1990s. The hard times were reflected in a sardonic tale that went the rounds in Moscow about a Russian boy. Asked by his mother what he wanted to be when he grew up, he replied: "I want to be a foreigner."

Growing political upheaval and economic deprivation now propelled Gorbachev toward the end of his career and the Soviet Union to collapse.

Mikhail Gorbachev (left) with Boris Yeltsin
Gorbachev and Yeltsin appear here together in a meeting in the immediate aftermath of the failed August 1991 coup. Many Russians ultimately judged Gorbachev a terrible failure. Yeltsin, a leading challenger to continued Communist Party control, went on to head the post-Soviet Russian government. (© Peter Turnley/ CORBIS)

Consumers standing in long lines looking at empty shelves were unhappy. So too were party leaders who stood to lose their power and privileges, bureaucrats doomed to unemployment, and the military facing deep cuts. A desperate Gorbachev tried to salvage a deteriorating situation in 1990 by bringing hardliners into his inner circle, retreating on economic reform, and acquiescing in a military crackdown in the Baltics. He thus stumbled into still greater danger. In August 1991 elements of the Soviet Communist Party, including some of his own associates, staged a coup with hopes of strengthening the center and preserving the union. Gorbachev, confined to his vacation house, furiously denounced them as "adventurers and criminals" and refused to cooperate. In downtown Moscow, Yeltsin rallied popular opposition to the coup. Facing resistance at home and criticism abroad, the plotters' nerves cracked, the coup collapsed, and several committed suicide. The chief of staff of the Soviet armed forces, a fifty-year veteran who had collaborated closely with Gorbachev in arms control negotiations with the United States, left a note: "I cannot live when my motherland is dying and everything that I ever believed in is being destroyed."[25]

This bungled effort to turn back the clock destroyed Gorbachev's fading authority, administered a serious blow to the legitimacy of the Communist Party itself, and gave full vent to autonomist and independence movements already tearing the Soviet Union apart. On December 25, Gorbachev resigned. In his parting words, he defended his record on domestic reform and détente but conceded, "The old system collapsed before a new one had time to start working."[26]

This impersonal verdict clouded Gorbachev's own responsibility for the failure of reform and, even more important, for the destruction of the state and party that might have survived sometime longer without his ministrations. An experiment intended to make the Soviet Union stronger instead extinguished it. Of all the stunning events of 1989–1991, none was more incredible than the sight of

THE GORBACHEV EXPERIMENT	
1982	Brezhnev's death brings briefly to power Andropov and then Chernenko
1985	Gorbachev emerges as reform-minded Soviet leader, championing *glasnost* and *perestroika*
1986	Reagan and Gorbachev revive arms control talks
1987	Gorbachev and Reagan agree on reducing nuclear forces in Europe
1989	Soviet elections release regional and nationalist impulses, fragmenting the Soviet Union; socialist regimes collapse in Europe; Gorbachev and Bush declare the Cold War over
1990	Germany is reunited
1991	Bush and Gorbachev sign the START agreement on reducing warheads on long-range missiles; coup against Gorbachev fails, discrediting Communist Party; Yeltsin emerges as the leader of Russia as the Soviet Union collapses

Mikhail Gorbachev leading the Soviet Communist Party into the dustbin of history (where the capitalists were supposed to end up) and pushing the state created by his hero Lenin into extinction less than seventy-five years after its creation. There was a real irony in Gorbachev's role. He failed disastrously as a reformer at home but was lionized abroad for his success as an international peacemaker. Indeed, the collapse of the Soviet Union, the result of his failed reforms, was the definitive signal that the Cold War was over.

EXPLAINING THE COLD WAR OUTCOME

The sudden end to the long, costly, and dangerous U.S.-Soviet contest soon followed by the demise of the Soviet Union is so bizarre that it begs for an explanation. One can be found in a popular Russian joke at the time: A KGB agent asks a CIA agent, "You were responsible for the meltdown of the nuclear reactor at Chernobyl, right?" "No." "For the war in Afghanistan?" "No." "For what, then?" "Gorbachev!" But because the CIA was as surprised as everyone else by Gorbachev, we have to put aside conspiracies and consider some other explanations. We are still quite close to this complex set of events, so it is necessary to keep any conclusions tentative.

The Role of Leaders

Gorbachev was not a CIA plant, but his role in the events of 1989–1991 was of central importance. He represented a generational shift among the ranks of the Soviet leadership. The Khrushchev and Brezhnev generation preceding him had grown up amidst the traumatic social upheaval of 1905–1921 and embraced the Bolshevik cause around the time of the revolution of 1917 and the civil war that followed. They came from working-class or lower middle-class backgrounds. And they had little formal schooling, usually limited to some technical education. Although party members were by the early 1980s distinctly better educated than most Soviet citizens, at the time of Brezhnev's death none of the Politburo members (aside from the relatively youthful Gorbachev) had a full college-level education. This aging leadership was exhausted intellectually as well as physically.

Those of the Gorbachev generation had grown up entirely within the Stalinist system. It had structured their lives and given them education and privilege. The seminal political event for them was Khrushchev's secret 1956 speech. It encouraged them to believe in the possibility of a more humane, open socialism. For that reason this generation of political activists and intellectuals were known as the "Children of the Twentieth Congress." Some of the prominent figures from this generation operated within the system. Others, such as Solzhenitsyn and Sakharov, operated outside it. Even during the dark Brezhnev years, foreign travel and foreign contacts fed the reformist impulse among the young influentials in the state and party bureaucracy. They could see the discrepancy between Soviet propaganda and the capitalist reality, and they watched with interest the experiments in reform socialism in eastern Europe. This well-informed comparative perspective on the state of their country deepened this generation's impulse to embrace change.

Even though the Gorbachev generation was predisposed to reform, Gorbachev himself stands out for the increasing boldness of his program and also for his ineptitude in implementing it. He decided simply to reject the old rules of the game and call the Cold War over. He was determined to concentrate on domestic renewal, so he simply walked away from the rivalry with Washington. Reagan seized the chance to shift from confrontation to cooperation. The Soviet leader's charm as well as his concessions made it difficult to say no, whereas Reagan's own easy optimism and unimpeachable anti-communist credentials facilitated the switch even while his more ideologically rigid associates fumed.

The irony is that it was Gorbachev's domestic reforms that doomed the Soviet economy. It is here—in his shortcomings as a leader—that the personal and contingent element in this particular bit of history may be most important. Arguably, reform went haywire because Gorbachev tried too much, too fast, with vague slogans but no coherent plan. His speeches consisted of mushy generalizations, and his policy relied on improvisation. There is much merit in the notion that Gorbachev was not driven by some popular groundswell and that Soviet collapse was accidental, not inevitable. Gorbachev may thus represent, as one of his aides put it in retrospect, "a genetic error of the system."[27] Could a more skilled reformer have saved the system? The case of China (treated in Chapter 8) suggests yes. There, cautious Communist leaders focused on moving from a command to a market economy, put political liberalization on hold, and successfully managed sweeping reform. Or was there such resistance to change within the Soviet system that any reform effort had no chance? Perhaps Gorbachev had only two choices as a reformer—admit defeat or press forward on a front so broad that it was bound to put the entire Soviet system in peril.

Impersonal Forces

However important his choices may have been, Gorbachev as well as Reagan acted within a web of constraints and pressures that also deserve examination if we are to understand the end of the Cold War and Soviet collapse. Perhaps the most important was broad popular disaffection with the costs and risks of the Cold War. Nuclear anxieties and the longing for a better life ate away at Cold War orthodoxies in both camps, but nowhere more consequentially than in the thinking of the U.S. electorate. Western European and Japanese opinion had only a marginal effect on American leaders; Gorbachev was well ahead of his own still ill-articulated public opinion; but Reagan had to heed popular preferences if he and his party wanted to retain power.

Nuclear Fear. Throughout the Cold War, even in times of détente, the destructive nuclear arsenals of the superpowers continued to grow. The nuclear buildup fed suspicions on both sides, drained away national resources, and inflicted widespread, lasting environmental damage. By the end of the Cold War the USSR and the United States had together over fifty thousand warheads of all types in their arsenals when five hundred of the large, strategic warheads were enough for either power to destroy the other. Soviet and American leaders accompanied by black boxes that could instantly initiate nuclear war were understandably worried and sought a way to control if not eliminate the danger.

Even as the multiplication of destructive power drove leaders to arms control, crafting meaningful and lasting agreement was fraught with difficulties. The habits of worst-case thinking and the relentless development of new technologies

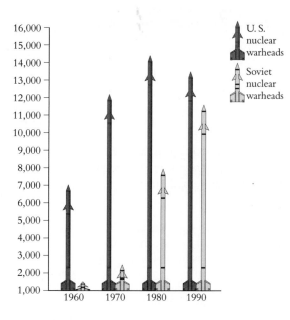

FIGURE 7.1
Superpower Nuclear Arsenals, 1960–1990[28]
Adding smaller, "tactical" nuclear warheads would raise the count substantially. For example, in 1990 the United States had 7,800 tactical warheads and the Soviet Union 21,600.

of destruction continually hindered cooperation. With national survival at stake, policymakers were wary of taking risks on questionable arms control deals. Moreover, they and their technical experts had to cope with ever more complex strategic systems on both sides that made it difficult to strike a balance and to deal with problems of verification. Even the most carefully worked out agreement was soon undercut by new technologies. It was also difficult, at least in the United States, to bring the public into debates over nuclear weapons policy or to build a public consensus.

Even so, nuclear fear had twice built to politically significant dimensions and given impetus to arms control negotiations. The first bout of fear, evident by the late 1950s (Chapter 4), had been quieted by cooperative measures beginning in the wake of the Cuban Missile Crisis. The second bout came in the early 1980s when Ronald Reagan entered the White House casually invoking the prospects of fighting a nuclear war.

Loose talk in Washington accompanied by the deployment of American missiles sparked an intense reaction overseas. Europeans on both sides of the Iron Curtain knew full well that in even the most limited war the ever more numerous nuclear-armed missiles in the region would devastate them. By late spring 1981 northern Europe was the scene of large demonstrations and intense political polemics. The Japanese were even more averse to nuclear weapons and the superpower arms race. A national consensus had existed on these matters since the mid-1950s, sustained by memories of Hiroshima and Nagasaki. Even in the Soviet Union dissidents such as Sakharov openly voiced concern.

In the United States the awakening anti-nuclear movement in spring 1982 followed the pattern of the late 1950s. Scientists played a leading role in warning the public that (as one put it) "we are not free to doom generations yet unborn." Carl Sagan, a Cornell astrophysicist, made "nuclear winter" a household term. A nuclear war, he predicted, would shroud the earth in debris. With sunlight cut off and the planet plunged into unending winter, human life would flicker out. George Kennan, influential in shaping the containment policy in the late 1940s, decried in 1981 the mindless course that the arms race had taken: "We have gone on piling weapon upon weapon, missile upon missile, new levels of destructiveness upon old ones. We have done this helplessly, almost involuntarily: like the victims of some sort of hypnosis, like men in a dream, like lemmings headed for the sea."[29]

Nuclear war was soon at the forefront of public discussion, and nuclear fear began to influence popular culture. Jonathan Schell's *Fate of the Earth*, a bestseller in 1982, drove home to millions of readers the horrible effects of even limited nuclear war in powerful, personal terms:

> Now we are sitting at the breakfast table drinking our coffee and reading the newspaper, but in a moment we may be inside a fireball whose temperature is tens of thousands of degrees. Now we are on our way to work, walking through the city streets, but in a moment we may be standing on an empty plain under a darkened sky looking for the charred remnants of our children. Now we are alive, but in a moment we may be dead. Now there is human life on earth, but in a moment it may be gone.[30]

In 1984 Dr. Seuss, the author of popular children's books, published the *Butter Battle Book* about an escalating arms race between the Yooks and the Zooks, who deployed ever more impressive weapons such as the Triple Sling Jigger and the Bitsy Big Boy Boomeroo. The work with perhaps the widest impact was a 1983 made-for-television docudrama, *The Day After,* which depicted the death and suffering inflicted on Lawrence, Kansas, by a nuclear attack. It gave a hundred million viewers a two-hour taste of what nuclear war might mean for them, and it forced Reagan's secretary of state, George Shultz, to appear on television to reassure the public. The idea of a "nuclear freeze" caught on at the grassroots. Virtually all Americans favored bringing a halt to the arms race through hard-nosed negotiations rather than engaging in a military buildup that would bring not security but a Soviet response that would raise the stakes even higher.

Popular Longing for a Better Life. The hopeful twin to this corrosive nuclear fear was consumerism. The siren call of the good life increasingly gripped the public in both the East and the West and inspired an aversion to ideological crusades and nuclear adventurism. Everywhere leaders could hear popular demands that they address problems of livelihood and environment. In western Europe, Green parties sprang up to press a pro-environment as well as anti-nuclear agenda. In eastern Europe, a brave band of dissidents pointed to the need for action on pervasive environmental damage. Workers in the East no less than electorates in the West wanted vacations, health care, and better pay—not international tensions and possibly war.

The constraints were especially marked in the United States after the Vietnam War. The call for "no more Vietnams" reflected the widespread realization that the public's priorities were at home, not abroad. A nervous public, an assertive Congress, and senior military officers helped tie the hands of even Ronald Reagan, the most militantly anti-communist of the late Cold War presidents. When he discovered that American forces in Beirut were vulnerable to attack, he quickly pulled them out. In Central America he had to fight communists by proxy (the right-wing Contras) or through the CIA because the public would not support direct U.S. military intervention. So strong was public skepticism that the Reagan administration had to fund its operations by secretly selling weapons to Iran, resulting in the Iran-Contra scandal that shook Reagan's presidency.

In the Soviet Union, leaders also faced consumer expectations and at the same time tried to wage a Cold War—all while drawing on an economy that was smaller and far less efficient than that of the United States, produced goods of lower quality, and was slow to innovate. These disparities left the USSR at a constant disadvantage and straining to catch up. Current data indicate that the Soviet economy grew at a low but fairly steady rate in the Brezhnev and Gorbachev years (in the 2 to 3 percent range). But that rate was trending downward, and between 1979 and 1981 the economy probably shrank before resuming its expansion until 1989, when it was overwhelmed by the disruptions brought on by the Gorbachev reforms. The sardonic jibe often attributed to Soviet

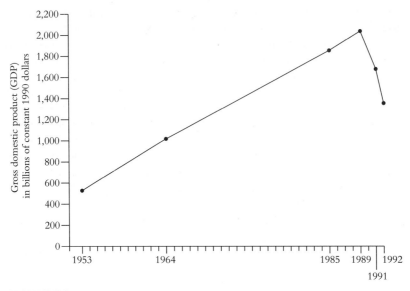

FIGURE 7.2
The Rise and Fall of the Soviet Economy[31]

workers—"We pretend to work and you pretend to pay us"—captured the fundamental alienation and inefficiency holding back the economy.

It is tempting in this connection to consider the argument that the accelerating U.S. arms expenditures in the 1980s won the Cold War. Some have contended that Carter and Reagan had shrewdly challenged the Russians to keep up. The Kremlin proceeded to spend the USSR into the ground. This appealingly simple cause-and-effect explanation has yet to be documented. Indeed, current evidence indicates that Moscow did not respond to the U.S. buildup in kind but rather held military spending fairly steady (measured as a proportion of GNP). But on the other hand, it is true that Moscow had long strained to make the smaller, less dynamic Soviet economy carry the weight of global aspirations, whereas Washington had the luxury of being able to draw on a larger, more dynamic economy. Even after the Carter-Reagan buildup, military outlays accounted for at most a modest 6.5 percent of U.S. GNP.

Flaws in the Soviet Regime. Finally, we need to consider the argument that the Soviet Union was so flawed in principle that it was bound to fail, both in its competition with the United States and as a working political and economic model. Of the several forms this argument takes, the most common and obviously ideological is that Gorbachev collided with the irresistible tide of freedom. Like his Bolshevik predecessors, he was tied to a morally bankrupt and thus doomed system. But this interpretation seems more a leap of metaphysical faith than a historically grounded explanation. The case is certainly easier to make after the Soviet collapse; beforehand, virtually no Western observers saw the Soviet Union as tottering. To most it looked impressively sturdy. In any case, no groundswell of popular pressure drove Gorbachev to take his democratizing initiatives, and it is not yet clear even today how democracy will fare in Russia. Large parts of the former Soviet Union remain distinctly authoritarian in their politics.

This argument about the deficiencies of the Soviet system takes a second form: Gorbachev was overwhelmed by the global capitalist economy. He needed new technology and access to the international market, but to get that access he had to open the country and ultimately to transform the economy and with it the entire system. Though the Soviet Union made only limited headway during the Gorbachev years in building links to the outside world, the domestic opening weakened the hold of the central government, threw out of kilter an already faltering and inefficient planned economy, and gave a boost to the internal forces that tore the Soviet state apart. There was no halfway position, so this argument goes, between involvement in the international economy and staying out. Although there may be some truth in this point of view, it is important to recall once more the case of China. During the 1980s and 1990s, it demonstrated that deepening international economic involvement need not lead to domestic political instability. The Chinese leaders preserved party power while integrating China with global markets.

The most sophisticated of the arguments about the flaws in the Soviet system contends that Gorbachev was doomed to fail because he was shackled to a monolithic and rigid party. The Communist Party had served as an effective instrument for Lenin's revolution and Stalin's economic development drive. But, as Khrushchev first discovered and then Gorbachev after him, it was a poor instrument of reform because its leading members, the *nomenklatura,* had become a self-interested, privileged class. One of the most discerning of Communists, the Yugoslav Milovan Djilas, had already in the mid-1950s identified the rise of this powerful new class. He had noticed that wherever Communist parties had come to power—whether in the Soviet Union or eastern Europe—its members came to command all the resources even while claiming to promote equality and an end to class distinctions. He had predicted that they, like capitalists, would tenaciously defend their privileges.

By one rough estimate *nomenklatura* in the mid-1980s enjoyed a standard of living nearly four times as high as the Soviet average (with their low salaries offset by a rich array of benefits). The gap between the top 1.5 percent of the population who were *nomenklatura* and the Soviet average was probably about the same as between the top 1.6 percent of the wealthiest in the United States and the average American. Caught between popular criticism and resentment on the one side and fear of losing its privileged control over the economy on the other, the party elite became paralyzed. It could neither accommodate change nor effectively defy the reform-minded leader of what was still in the mid-1980s a centralized, authoritarian party.

CONCLUSION

The Cold War's final phase provides a fine illustration of history's unpredictability. Anyone who might in early 1969 have imagined locking Nixon, Mao, and Brezhnev in the same room would have justifiably predicted general mayhem, not some kind of rough accord, among these three toughened cold warriors. The threesome was divided not just by political beliefs but also by personal background and age. But as it turned out, the American, Soviet, and Chinese leaders shared a recognition that the time was ripe for fundamental changes in the Cold War. They proceeded to do the completely unexpected, diminishing confrontation and promoting détente. Similarly, observers in 1985 did not imagine that Gorbachev and Reagan might form a partnership that would end the Cold War just before the Soviet Union itself disappeared. These major surprises serve as a salutary reminder of how history seldom sticks for long to the same course and how difficult predicting the future can be.

The vision of leaders, especially Nixon and Gorbachev, played a large role in shaping this outcome. So too did pressures within the societies of the superpowers and within their alliance systems. But to the list of reasons for the end of the Cold War should be added the international economy, which in the 1970s and 1980s began to show signs of greater international integration and at the same time increasing consolidation of the major developed economic regions. In contrast to the bipolar Cold War, the international market economy was becoming, as Nixon recognized, multipolar and less subject to U.S. control. It was also becoming, as Gorbachev came to see, a striking contrast in its productivity to the old Stalinist command economy. Important in its own right, the international economy that had once been subject to Cold War pressures was making itself felt as a force pushing the United States and the Soviet Union away from the Cold War.

RECOMMENDED RESOURCES

The Final Phase of the Cold War
The best overview is to be found in the authoritative and suitably critical two-volume account by a U.S. policy insider and Soviet specialist, Raymond L. Garthoff, *Détente and Confrontation: American-Soviet Relations from Nixon to Reagan* (rev. ed., 1994), and *The Great Transition: American-Soviet Relations at the End of the Cold War* (1994). H. W. Brands, *Since Vietnam: The United States in World Affairs, 1973–1995* (1996), provides a readable account emphasizing the U.S. point of view.

On Shifting U.S. policy
For the beginnings of détente, see Stephen E. Ambrose's *Nixon*, Vol. 2: *The Triumph of a Politician, 1962–1972* (1989), a fair assessment of a difficult subject; H. R. Haldeman's *The Haldeman Diary: Inside the Nixon White House* (1994), which makes available intimate insights captured by a presidential assistant; and Walter Isaacson's lively *Kissinger: A Biography* (1992). On **the struggle over U.S. policy following Nixon,** begin with John Ehrman, *The Rise of Neoconservatism: Intellectuals and Foreign Affairs, 1945–1994* (1995), on the early U.S. critics of détente. On **Carter policy,** see David S. McLellan, *Cyrus Vance* (1985), and Gaddis Smith, *Morality, Reason, and Power: American Diplomacy in the Carter Years* (1986), both of which build on memoirs and interviews. *Power and Principle: Memoirs of the National Security Adviser, 1977–1981* (1983) is an engaging insider account by an important Carter advisor, Zbigniew Brzezinski.

The Gorbachev Era
On **Gorbachev and his impact,** see Archie Brown's judicious assessment, *The Gorbachev Factor* (1996). Early attempts to make sense of the reform era can be found in Moshe Lewin, *The Gorbachev Phenomenon: A Historical Interpretation* (rev. ed., 1991), and Stephen F. Cohen and

Katrina vanden Heuvel, *Voices of Glasnost: Interviews with Gorbachev's Reformers* (1989), which offers a sense of the reform impulse in the words of some of its most influential advocates. On the **ferment below the surface of Soviet bloc life** from the 1950s into the 1980s, see Timothy W. Ryback, *Rock around the Bloc: A History of Rock Music in Eastern Europe and the Soviet Union* (1990), which traces cultural trends from the 1950s into the 1980s, and Richard Stites, *Russian Popular Culture: Entertainment and Society since 1900* (1992), especially the chapters covering the post-1953 period. Stephen White, *Russia Goes Dry: Alcohol, State, and Society* (1996), opens a fascinating window onto social strains and limits of official control. *Repentance* (dir. Tengiz Abulaze; 1986; 152 min.), an unsettling film fable about a Stalin-like dictator in a Georgian town, expresses late Soviet intellectuals' preoccupation with the Stalinist past.

The Last Phase of the Cold War

The richest interpretation of **U.S. policy** at Cold War's end can be found in Frances Fitzgerald, *Way Out There in the Blue: Reagan, Star Wars and the End of the Cold War* (2000), a pungent examination of the Reagan foreign policy. Other accounts that stick closer to the events: Michael R. Beschloss and Strobe Talbott, *At the Highest Levels: The Inside Story of the End of the Cold War* (1993), especially rich in oral history, and Don Oberdorfer, *From the Cold War to a New Era: The United States and the Soviet Union, 1983–1991* (rev. ed., 1998). George P. Shultz, *Turmoil and Triumph: My Years as Secretary of State* (1993), lays out the perspective of an influential moderate within the Reagan administration. Michael J. Hogan, ed., *The End of the Cold War: Its Meaning and Implications* (1992), brings together reflections by diplomatic historians. For a good sense of the explosion of political activity that led to **the collapse of socialist regimes in eastern Europe,** see Gale Stokes, *The Walls Came Tumbling Down: The Collapse of Communism in Eastern Europe* (1993); Gale Stokes, ed., *From Stalinism to Pluralism: A Documentary History of Eastern Europe since 1945* (2nd ed., 1996); Vladimir Tismaneau, *Reinventing Politics: Eastern Europe from Stalin to Havel* (1992); Timothy Garton Ash, *The Magic Lantern: The Revolution of '89 Witnessed in Warsaw, Budapest, Berlin and Prague* (rev. ed., 1993), a vivid and historically sensitive piece of reporting; and *People Power, 1989* (prod. and dir. Angus Mcqueen; 1998; 56 min.), part of the *People's Century* video series.

CHAPTER 8

GLOBAL MARKETS:
ONE SYSTEM, THREE CENTERS

T he market-driven international economy tightened its grip on the globe in the 1970s and 1980s, penetrating into almost every place on the planet. In the process it blurred state boundaries, overwhelmed the competing socialist model, and imposed on national economies a sometimes painful discipline enforced by bankers and other masters of international finance. Leaders in the third world and even in the socialist states had to recognize the market's capacity for wealth creation—$4.5 trillion added to the world's economy in the 1980s alone.

At the same time that the world economy was moving toward greater integration, the differences among its foremost centers of production and investment stood out in increasingly sharp relief. The international economy could be three as well as one. The relative decline of the U.S. economy was at the heart of this growing regional differentiation. Further altering the landscape was the ascent of the Japanese and the Europeans thanks to a long stretch of growth within the Anglo-American designed international economy. These three distinct regional blocs defined a new configuration of power. The United States occupied a preponderant place in North America. Close trade and investment ties and a shared approach to economic policy created a loose community of interests between Japan and its partners in maritime East and Southeast Asia. Europe was launched on a far-reaching process of integration. While the trade among these three blocs flourished, trade within them rose even more rapidly, suggesting that the trend toward inward integration was at least as strong as the outward global integration. In fact, globalization in this case was having the paradoxical effect of creating more distinct regional economic groupings.

Each of the three blocs had its own distinct, closely linked economic and cultural style. What people within each region considered appropriate economic behavior had a lot to do with prevailing social values—a faith on the part of individualistic Americans in the free market, a constellation of Confucian values prevailing in eastern Asia, and a European belief in tempering the free market with

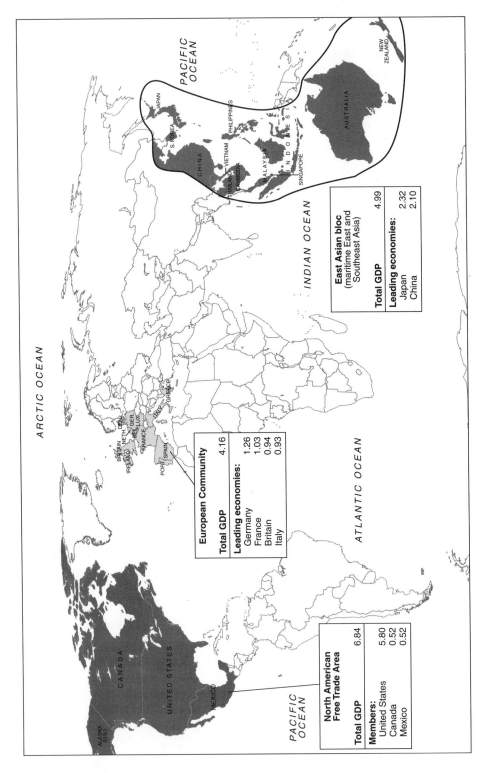

ARCTIC OCEAN

PACIFIC OCEAN

PACIFIC OCEAN

ATLANTIC OCEAN

INDIAN OCEAN

North American Free Trade Area

Total GDP	6.84
Members:	
United States	5.80
Canada	0.52
Mexico	0.52

European Community

Total GDP	4.16
Leading economies:	
Germany	1.26
France	1.03
Britain	0.94
Italy	0.93

East Asian bloc (maritime East and Southeast Asia)

Total GDP	4.99
Leading economies:	
Japan	2.32
China	2.10

ALASKA (U.S.)

CANADA

UNITED STATES

MEXICO

DEN.
NETH.
BRITAIN GER.
IRELAND BEL. LUX.
FRANCE
PORT. SPAIN
ITALY GREECE

JAPAN

S. KOREA

CHINA

THAILAND
CAMBODIA
VIETNAM

PHILIPPINES

MALAYSIA

SINGAPORE

INDONESIA

AUSTRALIA

NEW ZEALAND

strong welfare programs. These attitudes reflected preferences about which was better: production or consumption, individualism or community, equality or hierarchy, small government or big.

THE UNITED STATES AND THE NORTH AMERICAN BLOC

For roughly a quarter century—from the late 1960s to the early 1990s—Americans traveled a bumpy economic road. Inflation, slow growth, loss of international competitiveness in a range of key industries, and mounting trade and government deficits suggested deep-seated problems and cast a dark shadow over the dream of a better life for a generation then coming of age. Some observers saw a relative decline that was inevitable as other powers grew economically stronger; other observers saw disaster ahead. But no sooner had pessimists staked out their positions than prosperity returned. Indeed, the rallying of the U.S. economy during the 1990s ensured it a place as first among equals internationally and the dominant presence within an integrating North American bloc that also included Canada and Mexico.

The Erosion of U.S. Dominance

The Organization of Petroleum Exporting Countries (OPEC) provided a sharp push to an American economy already staggering by the late 1960s. Middle Eastern leaders had organized this oil cartel in order to diminish the control that the major multinational corporations such as Standard Oil of New Jersey, Royal Dutch-Shell, and British Petroleum had exercised in the Persian Gulf oil fields throughout the 1950s. The governments of the United States and western Europe, preoccupied with access to a strategic commodity, lent their backing to these corporations. A unilateral decision in 1959 by these companies to cut prices angered the shah of Iran (see Chapter 6 for discussion of the CIA-backed coup that restored him to power) and the king of Saudi Arabia (whose country held at least one-quarter of the world's oil reserves), and in 1960 they sponsored a meeting to organize oil-producing countries. The goal of OPEC was to coordinate policies with the long-term objective of fixing production and price levels. The steady climb in demand for oil in the industrial countries throughout the 1960s strengthened OPEC's position, and prices began slowly to rise. For the United States and the rest of an energy-hungry world, the stage was set for a major crisis.

The U.S. economy, along with the European and Japanese, absorbed two major oil shocks in the course of the 1970s. The first came in 1973 when Arab

◄**MAP 8.1**

The Three-Bloc International Economy in the Early 1990s[1]
The gross domestic product (GDP) data (expressed in trillions of dollars) show that the blocs were of roughly equal size in 1990 and that the United States, Japan, and China, and Germany, Italy, France, and Britain were the leading economies within their blocs.

producers in OPEC shut off exports to the United States, Israel's major backer, in response to the outbreak of fighting between Arab states and Israel. Simultaneously they dropped oil production, sending prices soaring to four times the prewar level and precipitating a recession in the industrial economies. Though the boycott ended in 1974, rising demand and strict production limits held prices up. Turmoil in Iran in 1979 (see Chapter 9) gave another major boost to oil prices by disrupting supply. The price spikes of 1973 and 1979 combined to send prices to a level painful for developed countries and devastating for developing countries. By late fall 1980 oil was selling at $32 a barrel, compared to below $2 at the highest point in the late 1960s.

From Stagflation to Soaring Deficits. Higher basic energy costs further fueled the inflationary fires already smoldering in the United States in the 1960s. Inflation became self-perpetuating as shaken producers and consumers got used to rising prices and rushed to make purchases, thereby accelerating the very trend they feared. Between 1968 and 1975 the price of consumer goods rose by 62 percent. This inflation-driven shopping spree accentuated a decline in savings with damaging effects on overall economic performance. (The decline was especially marked in comparison to other major economies, such as Japan and West Germany.) This low savings rate drove up the cost of borrowing capital and in turn discouraged investment in infrastructure, research and development, plants, and machinery. By 1989 the United States was running well behind the competition.

The difficulty of obtaining capital on attractive terms slowed productivity gains to an annual rate of 1 percent per year between 1973 and 1995, down from 2.7 percent in the immediate postwar period. This drop in percentage may seem small, but it had major consequences over the long term. At the 1 percent rate, it takes seventy years for living standards to double, whereas at 2 percent they double every thirty-five years. U.S. productivity gains were also low compared to the improvements experienced by competitors, most dramatically Japan. For the United States, small gains in productivity together with inflation and low savings created an economic malaise evident in the slowing of economic growth and a dramatic decline of per capita income relative to other advanced economies. By 1990 U.S. per capita income still exceeded that of its major competitors, but the gap had closed dramatically.

At the same time, a sluggish U.S. economy yielded the government lower revenues. Federal budget deficits in the 1970s and 1980s became a persistent, worrisome feature of the economic scene. Americans were faced with a choice of either raising taxes or paring back government spending. The electorate and its representatives in Washington refused to do either. Indeed, the deficit soared during the Reagan-era experiment with supply-side economic theory. Reagan cut taxes certain that the additional money in the hands of Americans would boost investment and stimulate the economy. However, the lower tax rates did not result in the higher government revenue that supply-siders had predicted. Reagan compounded the fiscal woes by doubling military spending between 1981 and 1986 even as Congress refused to make offsetting cuts in domestic

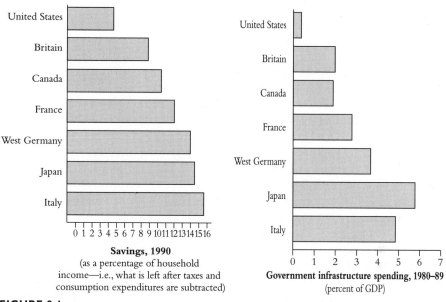

FIGURE 8.1
The U.S. Economy Falls Behind[2]
These two graphs measure U.S. performance against its competitors in two key areas commonly used by economists.

programs. Combined, these budget decisions opened a yawning gap between the federal government's income and expenditures. One young supply-sider charged with implementing Reagan's economic revolution emerged from the experience convinced that it had been "radical, imprudent, and arrogant."[3]

Each year's deficit added to the federal debt with cumulative effects that were dramatic. When Reagan became president, the total deficit was $1 trillion. By 1986 it had risen to $2 trillion, then in 1989 when Bush senior entered the White House to almost $3 trillion, and by the time he handed the presidency over to Clinton to $4 trillion (with interest payments on the deficit claiming about 15 percent of the federal budget). Alarmists liked to point out that the accumulated debt apportioned on a per person basis amounted to about $16,000. Combined with corporate and consumer debt, it approached $10 trillion—or twice the nation's gross national product (GNP). In fact, third-party candidate Ross Perot complained in his 1992 presidential campaign that the persistent debt problem was "like a crazy aunt we keep down in the basement. All the neighbors know she's there, but nobody wants to talk about her."[4]

Popular expectations about consumption made these interlocking problems difficult to resolve. Americans already burdened with personal debt and hard pressed to maintain their lifestyle in the face of stagnating personal income resisted higher taxes to pay for the government programs that they continued to demand. While the average worker failed to gain significant ground during the 1970s and 1980s, blue-collar workers experienced a fall in real wages. These trends stood in sharp contrast to the first twenty-five years of the postwar period when real wages for the average worker had more than doubled. The economy was failing to deliver on the promise of abundance that postwar Americans had come to take for granted, and many felt cheated. Disillusionment was particularly strong among young adults denied the opportunities available to their parents. Bruce Springsteen, a rock star with a pronounced populist streak, expressed the pessimism in "Born in the U.S.A.," his popular anthem from 1984. "Down in the shadows of the penitentiary/Out by the gas fires of the refinery/I'm ten years burning down the road/Nowhere to run ain't got nowhere to go."[5]

The accumulation of intractable internal problems in turn left domestic producers exposed to competitive global pressures greater than at any moment in recent memory. As these pressures increased, U.S. industry declined. For example, American steel, which had accounted for 39 percent of the world's production in 1955, had fallen to 15 percent by 1981, while automobile production had plummeted from 68 percent to 21 percent of world output. By 1980 Japan was not only outstripping the United States in quantity but also in quality and fuel efficiency of its Toyotas and Hondas; and one major American manufacturer, Chrysler, was teetering on the edge of bankruptcy. The U.S. television industry, a giant with ninety manufacturers making seven million sets in 1951, had disappeared by 1995 with the sale of the last company (Zenith) to a South Korean firm. Older, heavily labor-intensive industries such as textiles moved production abroad to stay competitive. As international competition ate away at U.S. manufacturing, well-paid workers lost their jobs by the thousands, and the entire northern tier of industrial states turned into a "rustbelt" of closed factories, declining neighborhoods, and high unemployment. Chicago steelworkers, like blue-collar laborers all around the country, saw opportunity closing for them that had been open to their parents' generation. "I'm workin' harder, makin' less money, got less of a future," lamented one. Another confessed, "It's the fear about maybe takin' a step down in society. Everyone's got that fear."[6]

The growing American taste for foreign goods and the difficulty American products were having winning foreign customers led to mounting trade deficits, which tripled between the late 1970s and the late 1980s ($153 billion by 1987). Those recurring annual deficits put ever more American debt in foreign hands, with the result that the country suffered a dramatic shift from creditor to debtor standing. By 1982 the United States had lost its surplus as foreign investments in the United States came to exceed U.S. investments abroad. By 1987 in a stunning reversal the United States had earned the dubious distinction of becoming the world's leading debtor nation.

Japan-Bashing. This national fall from economic grace put strains on the consensus that had developed around free trade since the 1950s. Influential supporters including journalists, economists, exporters, policymakers, and some labor leaders could point to the fact that the General Agreement on Tariffs and Trade (see Chapter 2 on GATT) had made possible new jobs and a wider range of consumer goods at lower prices. But by the 1980s with the country entering its second decade of economic difficulties, more Americans were questioning whether global trade was indeed good for the country.

Japan became the lightning rod for chagrin and anger over this rapid national decline. At the height of the Cold War, Americans had welcomed Japan's recovery. It seemed to affirm the U.S. model of economic development, vindicate U.S. international leadership, and strengthen the free world in its struggle against communism. However, American attitudes shifted dramatically in the 1980s as Japan made claim to the status of "number one" in the economic sphere where Americans had long prided themselves on primacy. At the same time that Japanese automobiles and electronics were flooding the U.S. market, American industry was having difficulty penetrating the Japanese market. The cumulative effect of this persistent trade imbalance was to put more and more American IOU's in the hands of Japanese businesses and banks. They in turn poured money into the American stock market and real estate, including such national icons as New York City's Rockefeller Center. Pointing to Sony's purchase of CBS Records in 1988 and Columbia Pictures the next year, a *Newsweek* magazine cover announced: "Japan Invades Hollywood."

By the early 1990s the tensions in U.S.-Japan relations had reached a postwar peak, and some alarmists claimed to see in Japan a successor to the now-defunct communist menace. Business and labor led the call for protectionist measures, and some disgruntled Americans charged that the Japanese had become an economic juggernaut because they did not play fair: They imposed informal obstacles to foreign goods and services or unnaturally suppressed consumer demand. Some even claimed that Japanese economic success was the result of a sinister conspiracy or a deformed society at odds with the "natural" desire for individualism and consumer debt. Japan-bashing became politically popular. For example, conservative presidential hopeful Pat Buchanan targeted the Japanese as he championed a more isolationist economic policy. The American public seemed to share some of this resentment. A 1992 poll revealed that 40 percent of respondents regarded Japan as an unfair competitor, and 55 percent suspected that the Japanese secretly looked down on Americans.

Nevertheless, mutual self-interest limited the gathering tensions. By 1984 U.S. trade across the Pacific had surpassed U.S. trade across the Atlantic, making Asia the largest U.S. foreign market. Japanese investors buoyed Wall Street and property values. And when Washington asked Tokyo to remove barriers to trade, including tariffs and other obstacles to foreign business, and to offer inducements for higher spending on U.S.-made imports, Tokyo gave enough ground to calm U.S. ire although not to eliminate the trade gap.

Whatever its causes, economic battering in the 1970s and 1980s had seriously eroded U.S. economic dominance and weakened the dollar's pivotal role in international finance. Poor economic performance had gradually undercut the value of the dollar, which was accumulating in foreign hands, and caused a flight into other currencies, chiefly the German mark and the Japanese yen. Unable to sustain the fixed dollar-gold price ratio at $35 per ounce, Nixon took the dramatic step in 1971 of breaking the dollar's fixed link to gold that had made the U.S. currency the single point of reference for international trade and investment since the end of World War II. The dollar now "floated" ingloriously, subject like any other currency to the tides of the market.

The United States now had to engage in greater coordination with the other economic powerhouses, known collectively as the Group of Seven (G-7 for short). This small club consisting of Japan, the United States, Canada, Britain, France, West Germany, and Italy began to meet on a regular basis to coordinate industrial, trade, and financial policies. Under its auspices, important elements of the Bretton Woods system survived the relative American decline. The leading powers still espoused the goals of free trade and currency stability, and they continued to control its chief institutions—GATT (transformed into the World Trade Organization—WTO—in 1995), the IMF, and the World Bank. With over one hundred signatories, GATT served as the vehicle for repeated rounds of multilateral trade talks. By 1995 it had reduced world tariffs to an average of 5 percent, one-eighth of what they had been right after World War II.

U.S. policymakers also found that hard times denied them the deep economic pockets to which they had become accustomed during the early phase of the Cold War. No longer was it possible to deal unilaterally or generously with global problems. Washington wanted to smooth the transition to democracy and free markets in post-socialist eastern Europe and Russia but lacked the resources for generous grants of the sort given to western Europe after World War II. Similarly, Iraq's invasion of Kuwait in 1990 (see Chapter 10) found the United States constrained economically. Like a poor but muscle-bound cousin, Washington had to ask its affluent relatives to subsidize the American military effort to free Kuwait. The Japanese, Kuwaitis, and Saudis obliged.

The Free Market Faith

Two decades of economic stress helped bring about an important shift in fundamental economic philosophy in the United States. The free market faith came into vogue. Its gurus were the Austrian economist Friedrich Hayek and the American Milton Friedman. They might be best described as neo-liberal because they wanted to revive what they regarded as the true liberalism of the nineteenth century with its robust faith in free markets. They argued that the free market was not only the most efficient way of arranging economic activity but also an essential feature of a democratic society. They saw themselves in sharp opposition to the "false" liberalism that John Maynard Keynes had promoted (see Chapter 2). They concluded that much of the economic malaise of the time was due to excessive government intervention in the international no less than the domestic economy. Hayek had formed his ideas in reaction against the pre-1945 German and Italian fascist experiments as well as the Soviet model. He and like-minded economists had hoped that a war fought for freedom would bring an end to the statist model. To them it was clear that governmental control over the economy, however laudable its objectives, was neither politically wise nor economically effective. They watched with dismay as Soviet-backed regimes imposed state planning in eastern Europe, radical third world regimes pursued state-sponsored industrialization, and Keynesian ideas prevailed in the West. Even the United States in the 1960s seemed to be going down a dangerous collectivist road as welfare spending dramatically increased. In calling for shifting power from the state back to the market, the neo-liberals laid the intellectual groundwork for a conservative political resurgence in the United States as well as Britain.

Friedman and the Neo-Liberal Consensus. The most influential neo-liberal was Milton Friedman. Born in 1912 in Brooklyn, New York, he taught economics at the University of Chicago from 1946 to 1977. Throughout much of his early career, Friedman criticized Keynes and advocated the virtues of the free market. The economy was doing fine, however, enabling the Keynesians to take credit. But by 1978 when Friedman received the Nobel Prize in economics, the Keynesians were on the defensive, and Friedman was enjoying wide intellectual influence among economists looking for fresh solutions to U.S. economic malaise. His own students spread the gospel, and some became influential in policy circles in the United States and abroad. (For example, Chile's post-Allende military government was heavily staffed with Friedman's disciples.) Conservative politicians increasingly drew on Friedman's ideas in their drive to dismantle the welfare state and political obstructions to free enterprise.

Friedman's *Capitalism and Freedom,* written in close collaboration with his economist wife, Rose D. Friedman, was the best known of his works. Published in 1962, it made a special point of rescuing the term *liberal* from the corruption that Friedman believed it had undergone in the twentieth century. That the Roosevelt administration and its Democratic successors down to Lyndon Johnson had used state intervention to promote welfare and equality made them (as Friedman phrased it) "men of good intentions and good will" yet still dangerous. In his estimate, they had surrendered freedom as the ultimate good and developed a faith in the state to achieve social change that aligned them with the coercive tendencies of totalitarian systems. This recast liberalism was thus a corruption, even a betrayal, of an older and better strain going back to the end of the eighteenth century. Classical liberals whom Friedman saw as his intellectual antecedents had had the wisdom to recognize "freedom as the ultimate goal and the individual as the ultimate entity in the society." Starting from that premise, they had "supported laissez faire at home as a means of reducing the role of the state in economic affairs and thereby enlarging the role of the individual." They had seen "free trade abroad as a means of linking the nations of the world together peacefully and democratically." Politically they had espoused "the development of representative government and of parliamentary institutions, reduction in the arbitrary power of the state, and protection of the civil freedoms of individuals."[7]

Friedman called on postwar Americans to return to this older tradition that recognized the close relationship between economic and political freedom. A free economy "gives people what they want instead of what a particular group thinks they ought to want." It thus encouraged social and political diversity. It reduced "greatly the range of issues that must be decided through political means," thereby minimizing the range of government intervention. Finally, "if economic power is kept in separate hands from political power, it can serve as a check and a counter to political power."[8]

Mounting difficulties in the U.S. economy throughout the 1960s brought these neo-liberal ideas into fashion. Keynsian fiscal policy had failed to end stagflation. Proponents of neo-liberal programs pressed the case for taking the problem out of the hands of the president and Congress, where political concerns prevailed, and handing it over to the Federal Reserve Board that served as the U.S. central bank. There economists could make decisions about the size of the money supply on technical grounds and thus provide a more stable, less politically influenced context for the functioning of the economy. With the bias toward inflation removed, markets would work better to achieve real growth.

Neo-liberals looked beyond monetary policy to a broader restructuring of the American economy. They believed that the state imposed a heavy burden on businesses by taxing too much to fund wasteful programs such as welfare and siphoning off capital otherwise available for productive investment. Bureaucratic red tape got in the way of market transactions, often raising costs with no appreciable gain. Downsizing the government was the neo-liberal mantra—and it became the mantra of every president after Richard Nixon, Democratic as well as Republican. Like other forms of magical incantations, its effects are hard to prove. In any case, the federal budget continued to climb (to one-fifth of GDP by 2000), although perhaps not at the rate that it otherwise would have.

These neo-liberal economists also advocated greater reliance on markets to keep the international economy healthy and growing. The most general change that they championed was the liberation of international currency and capital movements. This represented a major departure from the attitudes promoted by the Bretton Woods architects, who had regarded currency speculation as dangerously disruptive and linked the sustained downturn of the 1930s to its destabilizing effects. By putting the dollar in a pivotal role and by allowing states to keep currency controls, they raised a significant barrier to speculation and instability. Nixon's decision to unhitch the dollar from gold meant that the U.S. currency would now float in value relative to other currencies. With both the fixed dollar and state restrictions gone, fluidity on currency markets could turn almost instantly to panic.

Nixon's decision on convertibility of the dollar and cuts in government spending carried him only partway toward the neo-liberal position. As part of his attack on the country's economic woes, he imposed a 15 percent import surcharge as well as wage and price controls. These measures did not produce a turnaround, as the neo-liberals were quick to point out, so Nixon soon removed them. Inflation surged, consumer spending fell, and the Federal Reserve raised interest rates in a failed attempt to control inflation. In 1974 real GNP declined by 2 percent, and unemployment reached 7.2 percent. The country was in the grip of the most severe economic downturn since 1945.

The failure of Nixon's heavy-handed intervention emboldened neo-liberals. Now was the time to try a new regimen on the sick economy: Get the government out of the economy except for controlling the money supply, and let the markets find a cure for the national economic ills. Major banks hoping for greater freedom from government regulations supported these views, and U.S. industry shifted in this direction as its growing multinational operations aligned its interests closer to those of banks. Only labor expressed sustained, serious opposition.

During the Reagan and Bush administrations, the neo-liberals got their way on domestic policy. The Federal Reserve tightly controlled credit in order to check inflation. This bitter medicine produced a deep recession in 1981–1982 and another brief bout of recession in the early 1990s, but it also achieved its goal of squeezing inflation out of the system. At the same time these Republican administrations, true to supply-side principles, lowered taxes, expecting Americans to spend and invest more and thus to stimulate the economy and ultimately raise revenue sufficient to offset the cuts. Those cuts did in fact strongly stimulate the economy, but the federal deficit continued to balloon. During the same period American corporations made themselves more competitive internationally, going on a frenzy of consolidation, holding down wages, and investing significantly to upgrade plant and equipment and thereby raise productivity.

The neo-liberals scored a second success when they convinced the U.S. government to press for a general opening in the international financial markets. Already in the early 1970s, Washington was not only blocking calls for capital controls coming from western Europe and Japan but also lifting the last of its own capital controls. Britain soon got into step, eliminating in 1979 its forty-year-old restrictions on capital movement. Australia and New Zealand soon followed. Both western Europe and Japan were now under pressure to embrace the new orthodoxy. Resistance seemed unwise. The creation of national financial markets to handle large, unregulated capital flows could be profitable, as the American and British bankers had already shown. Moreover, states that did not embrace the principle of free capital movement would not be able to compete effectively for international investments. As a result, both western Europe and Japan initiated financial liberalization measures beginning in the 1980s. By 1990 the advanced sector of the global economy was marked by a degree of freedom not known since the 1920s.

Freed from restrictions, capital began to move in quantities previously unimagined. By the early 1990s the *daily* volume had climbed to $1 trillion. Much of the exchange was unconnected to real goods or direct investment in overseas production. It was, rather, prompted by dealers speculating on the rise or fall of one national currency or another. Capital movements had become large enough to capsize small developing economies and threaten major ones. Predictably, financial crises became more commonplace. Mexico set off an international debt crisis in 1982. France experienced speculative currency pressure in 1982–1983. The global stock market crash of October 1987 raised far-reaching fears. In the late 1990s the economies of East and Southeast Asia, Russia, and Latin America became the latest victims of the vagaries of the financial markets.

The Prosperous 1990s. Americans enjoyed an economic boom in the 1990s as a result of a convergence of developments. One that appeared earliest was the moderating of oil prices that in turn slowed inflation. Energy conservation measures and greater efficiency gradually lowered oil demand at the same time that the opening of new oil fields increased supply. Prices also moderated because the very success of the OPEC cartel had given the wealthier producers a direct stake in the prosperity of the major oil-consuming countries. Kuwait and Saudi Arabia, which had accumulated an enormous pool of capital, had billions invested in the real estate and stock markets of the advanced economies. The OPEC moguls now set oil prices with care so as not to hurt the very economies in which they had so substantial a stake.

Perhaps more important to the return of U.S. prosperity was the role of technology, both in making old industries more competitive and in creating new industries. Thanks to the infusion of new technology, the productivity growth rate moved higher—to a 2 percent level—after 1995. The star of the new class of technology was the computer, which could handle massive amounts of data, facilitate communications (including the Internet), and bring more automation to the production line. The computer and other innovations were the product of a postwar system of collaboration among government agencies, university research teams, and corporations. In the Cold War era Washington wanted to keep on the cutting edge of science and technology for reasons of national prestige as well as advantage against the Soviet foe. But rather than impose a centrally run program, Cold War leaders opted for a diverse and decentralized approach better suited to American values. Out of this security-driven collaboration emerged breakthroughs in such areas as nuclear weapons, jet aircraft, and antibiotics. The government also created agencies such as the National Science Foundation to channel funding into pure research and the National Aeronautics and Space Administration (NASA) to keep the United States ahead in the space race. As the available R&D funding expanded, so too did the ambition of university scientists. They competed for big grants and carried out large-scale research in a team effort. Corporations watched closely for promising discoveries to come out of this government-university collaboration while at the same time underwriting their own research. Industries that benefited heavily included electronics, telecommunications, aeronautics, and biopharmaceuticals.

The Internet illustrates how collaboration produced major technological breakthroughs. Conceived by an MIT engineer closely tied to government projects, the Internet first took rudimentary form in October 1969 when a computer at UCLA "talked" to another computer located some three hundred miles away at the Stanford Research Institute. This simple system developed under the aegis of the Defense Department into Arpanet, which was meant to serve as a means for university-based researchers working on military projects to share computer resources. But as early as 1973 Arpanet users had turned it instead into primarily a tool for communications. Other features of what is today associated with the Internet fell into place gradually. The addressing system using the @ symbol appeared in 1972. The systems of domain names (those ending in ".com," ".org," and so forth) took root in 1984. Mosaic, a graphical interface or "browser," proved itself in 1991, providing the basis for the development of widely used Netscape and Microsoft products.

Thanks to lower inflation and higher productivity, a formerly ailing American giant turned in the 1990s into the most robust of the world economies. Growth held steady, and inflation and unemployment dipped to levels previously thought unsustainable for a prolonged period. Wages for most Americans began to grow once more and the stock market boomed, dramatically enriching the already affluent. Dotcom businesses exploiting the Internet became the darling of the investors, and some such as Amazon, Napster, and eBay became household names. Though most dotcoms lost money on a stunning scale, they appealed to the peculiarly American optimism that new technology offered individualistic, can-do people more abundance and greater freedom.

Alan Greenspan was the economic wizard presiding over what would turn into the longest era of sustained growth in U.S. history. Greenspan had abandoned a musical career playing the clarinet and saxophone in favor of economic consulting. Reagan had appointed him chair of the Federal Reserve in 1987. From that post, he stood guard against the slightest hint of returning inflation, warned against the "irrational exuberance" of the stock market, and helped contain financial crises at home and abroad. So great was Greeenspan's prestige that market analysts carefully studied his poker face during public testimony and pondered every nuance in his speeches, supposedly written in his bathtub.

American goods were more competitive internationally. Even though U.S. firms no longer dominated such industries as automobiles and consumer electronics, they were strong in such high-tech fields as aircraft, entertainment, biotechnology, computers, and telecommunications. Even the venerable steel industry, victimized by competition, slimmed down, upgraded, and staged a comeback. More competitive goods helped to narrow but not close the trade gap and to dampen frictions with trading partners. By 1994 U.S. trade was still running a deficit of $154 billion, one-third of it with Asian countries, mainly Japan and China.

The U.S. economic revival helped shore up the country's position as the premier player on the global stage. It still accounted for one-quarter of world output

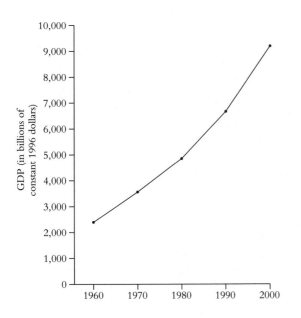

FIGURE 8.2
U.S. Economic Performance, 1960–2000[9]
The steady rise in GDP shown here contrasts with the slowing and then plummeting Soviet economy in Figure 7.2 (see p. 332).

and almost one-fifth of world trade at mid-decade. The dollar retained its world-wide appeal as the currency of choice. In the mid-1990s nearly 60 percent of the foreign exchange holdings of central banks and governments was in dollars, and over 80 percent of foreign exchange transactions involved the purchase or sale of dollars.

No less reflective of U.S. economic power was the gravitational pull it exercised over Canada and Mexico, partners in the emergent North American bloc. This partnership gave the United States social and political as well as economic influence that its neighbors had long resented. But the U.S. market was simply too large to ignore and too powerful to resist. In 1989 Canada had consolidated its ties to the American economy by signing a free trade agreement. A similar agreement, negotiated by the first President Bush, extended the arrangements to Mexico in 1994 under what was now formally known as the North American Free Trade Agreement (NAFTA). And some began to talk of a free trade zone encompassing all the Americas. This North American free trade bloc was the largest in the world ($6.84 trillion in GDP in 1990). Reflecting the values of its dominant economy, the NAFTA bloc shared neither the social policies that were integral to the development of the European Community (EC) nor the mechanisms of state guidance commonplace in East Asia.

For Mexico more than Canada, a formal link to the American economic giant involved profound changes. Canada, already heavily export oriented, embraced NAFTA as a guarantee of access to a large, rich, important market. As a developing country, Mexico entered the pact with its authoritarian political system intact, with wide disparities of income and considerable poverty, and with a legacy of state intervention dating back to the days of import substitution policies. In 1994, even as Mexico embraced NAFTA, reminders of its underdeveloped status came in the form of a peasant, predominantly poor Indian rebellion in the southern state of Chiapas and a severe financial crisis that required a $20 billion U.S. bailout. NAFTA accelerated the trend toward neo-liberal economic policies set in motion by a major debt crisis in 1982 and promoted by a string of U.S.-trained Mexican government officials. NAFTA also ignited a Mexican export boom while workers hungry for jobs crossed an increasingly porous U.S.-Mexican border. With free trade, heavy U.S. investment, and sizable migration went a marked shift toward democratization. Just as the import substitution era had transformed Mexico, so too now was neo-liberalism reshaping the country.

The Hidden Costs of the Free Market Model. By the 1990s the U.S. economy better than any other exemplified the neo-liberal faith in market mechanisms, strong individual property rights, low taxes, and limited state interference. But the U.S. case also made clear that the neo-liberal model with its high per capita GDP and low unemployment had worrisome side effects. Some were environmental. The relentless, headlong rush to exploit the seemingly endless resources of the North American continent despoiled land, air, and water (see Chapter 10). Other effects were economic and of a sort to worry observers of a neo-liberal persuasion. As firms aggressively consolidated by buying up their competition in sectors as diverse as agriculture, airlines, energy, telecommunications, and print media, competition within the marketplace became constrained. At the same time, the political clout of individual firms grew as they made large campaign contributions and financed major lobbying operations in Washington to secure special tax, regulatory, copyright, and other breaks.

Beyond purely environmental and economic effects, the prevailing neoliberal exaltation of individual choice diminished support for public investment and inculcated a deep-seated popular skepticism about the existence of a common good. This skepticism found expression in widespread political cynicism and alienation reflected in public opinion polls and in low voter turnout even in presidential elections. "Don't vote—it only encourages them" expressed a widespread view not only about politicians but also about the democratic process.

Although this personal disengagement was dangerous to democracy, it also contributed to mounting social problems. American society was marked by the widest economic disparities between the richest and the poorest parts of the population found anywhere in the developed world. Homelessness had become commonplace, and levels of infant mortality and poverty among children compared poorly with those of other developed and even some developing countries. Though Americans spent on health care a share of GDP almost twice as much as France or Germany and almost three times that of Britain and Japan, they were virtually alone among citizens of developed countries in not having a comprehensive national health care system. Left to cope largely on their own, individuals could find economic hard times especially trying. A West Virginia pastor described his dying steel mill community outside Pittsburgh: "The suicide rate is phenomenal here. Unemployment is just so devastating. Fifty-five percent of the heads of households in these towns are unemployed. They lose their house, they lose their car, their marriage, they're snappin' at each other, they turn to drink, abuse of children, run out of food, abandon their families, they lose hope."[10]

Americans also experienced unusually high levels of social violence. Some 2.1 million Americans died from gunfire between 1968 and 2000, more than the loss of American military personnel in both world wars, Korea, and Vietnam combined. Murder rates were nine times higher than in Japan and four times higher than in Britain. The Minneapolis police chief, interviewed in the 1980s, bemoaned the appearance of "an underclass" where this violence was concentrated: "We are screwing the poor people. The family is disintegrating. The divorce rate has tripled. The drug culture among the young is growing. Television is . . . making us more violent and druggy."[11] Not surprisingly, social breakdown produced record-high levels of incarceration, with African American neighborhoods hit especially hard. With 1.86 million under lock and key in 1999, the United States shared with Russia the dubious distinction of having the highest percentage of its population in prison.

Americans did not fare well educationally. Measurements of literacy and numeracy put the United States at the bottom among the industrial countries. According to a 1993 study, nearly half (or 88 million) of American adults were in functional terms barely literate and could not handle such basic tasks as writing a letter about a billing error, making sense of a newspaper article, or filling out a

THE FALL AND RISE OF U.S. ECONOMIC INFLUENCE

1959	Iran's shah and the Saudis take the lead in creation of OPEC
1962	Friedman publishes *Capitalism and Freedom*
1971	Nixon ends the fixed gold-dollar exchange rate, allowing the dollar to float
1973	Boycott by Arab members of OPEC deals oil shock to U.S. and other industrial economies
1979	Iran's revolution disrupts oil supplies and creates second oil shock
1981	Reagan administration initiates supply-side economic policy
1987	U.S. overseas debt becomes highest in the world; Reagan appoints Greenspan to head the Federal Reserve
1989	United States and Canada sign free trade agreement
1990	U.S. federal debt hits $3 trillion
1994	NAFTA integrates Mexico into the regional bloc
2000	U.S. economy reaches end of the longest run of prosperity in its history

form. On worldwide surveys of literacy Americans had steadily fallen, with women forty-ninth and men fifty-seventh by the 1990s. This widespread failure in basic education raised worrisome questions about the skills most Americans would bring to the workplace in a time of increasing global economic competitiveness.

THE RISE OF AN EAST ASIAN BLOC

While Americans struggled in the 1970s and 1980s, the Japanese continued to enjoy their economic miracle. Nearly four decades of high growth rates had made Japan one of the top three world economies and its people among the most prosperous. Japan's neighbors closely watched this unfolding success story. Taiwan, Singapore, and South Korea applied aspects of the Japanese strategy to their own situations. As smaller craft traveling toward prosperity in the 1970s and 1980s in the wake of the great Japanese vessel, they too would experience high growth rates. With Japan as the model, the region would come to constitute a loose regional bloc united less by formal institutional arrangements than by economic interdependence and a shared economic outlook.

State-led economic growth strategies would begin to transform the broad sweep of countries running from the Korean peninsula to Indonesia and Thailand and produce an extraordinary shift in the percentage of the world's GNP claimed by all of Asia. Only 4 percent in 1960, it would rise to 25 percent by 1990. At the same time the region was becoming a pivotal part of world trade. By 1992 the total exports of countries from the western Pacific Rim exceeded those of the United States or the European Community, and in both cases the trade surplus in favor of Asia was substantial. These vibrant Asian economies made dramatic improvements in the lives of their peoples. In the mid-1970s six of ten households were marked by absolute poverty. By the mid-1990s only two of ten fell into that category.

Japan Stays on Course

Despite heavy energy dependence, the Japanese economy showed considerable resilience in weathering the OPEC oil shocks of the 1970s. Even though the jump in prices early in the decade ignited inflation and squeezed profit margins, it also encouraged investment in energy efficiency that stimulated the economy and made Japanese products more cost competitive. By the late 1970s the Japanese were embarked on a prolonged period of stable growth, Japanese goods were as competitive as ever, and the home market was difficult for foreigners to penetrate. The trade surplus and investment holdings abroad soared. Between 1955 and 1985 Japan's share of world exports had quadrupled (to 10.1 percent). Its GNP had grown over the quarter century ending in 1984 at three and a half times the U.S. rate. By the late 1980s per capita income had climbed to U.S. and West German levels and far outstripped the British. This gathering economic momentum eventually fed a speculative fever. Land prices boomed along with the Tokyo stock market.

The Japanese were proud of their success in reaching the position of the leading economic performer, and they bristled over American attacks on the Japanese model in the 1980s and early 1990s. The strongest reaction came from the economy's "iron triangle" of powerful government bureaucrats, Liberal Democratic Party politicians, and leaders of *keiretsu* (the enterprise groups that united large corporations). They cautioned against reforms that would not only hurt economically but also undermine Japan's social cohesion and throw into chaos a stable, ethically attuned society rooted in a thousand years of tradition. They worried particularly that an American-style open economy would lead to crime and social breakdown. A prominent Finance Ministry official warned against unleashing "naked market forces." "It would be the end of Japanese-style capitalism if we pushed this kind of change too far. Japan would be split, as America is split."[12]

A widely read response to American criticisms appeared in the 1989 book *The Japan That Can Say No* co-authored by Sony's Morita Akio and Ishihara Shintaro, a popular and outspoken politician. They conceded that "whites, including Americans, have built the modern era." But the authors insisted that the "pride [of whites] is too strong" and their ignorance of the cultural achievements of Japanese and other Asians over the last five centuries was appalling. The authors wondered "if the historical pride has gone to the length of inerasable arrogance. Right now, the modern civilization built by whites is coming close to a period of practical end."[13] Behind this confident and defiant Japanese reaction was a widely shared feeling of vulnerability. As they saw it, their small, resource-poor island-nation had struggled since the late nineteenth century to catch up with the West and win international respect as an equal. Despite stunning economic success, other countries and above all the United States continued to treat Japan as a second-rate power.

Japanese Nurse a Sense of Grievance
This cartoon appeared in a leading Japanese newspaper in 1990. It shows a
small, vulnerable Mount Fuji (symbol of Japan and its purity) facing an overbearing, militaristic United States demanding reform. Mount Fuji is labeled
"The Japan that cannot say no," playing off the popular critique of Japanese
subservience to the United States titled *The Japan That Can Say No.* The
caption reads: "Isn't 'postwar' over?" suggesting that it was time to end the
dependent relationship established during the U.S. occupation after World
War II. (© Yokoyama Taizo, *Asahi Shimbun*)

Japanese commentators, business people, and government officials countered
American demands on Japan with an agenda of changes for the United States to
implement. They wanted an end to U.S. free trade hypocrisy; it was time to give
Japanese steel and autos full access to the U.S. market. They suggested that Washington address its own economic problems rather than telling the Japanese what
to do. Americans might learn from the Japanese model such fundamental economic virtues as personal sacrifice and social cooperation. The Japanese public,
proud of their country's success, agreed, and many resented the United States for
making Japan a scapegoat for its own economic problems.

The Rise of the "Little Dragons"

By the 1990s a distinct economic bloc was taking shape in East Asia. Japan's success had been followed first by the "little dragons"—South Korea, Taiwan, and
Singapore—in the 1960s and 1970s. (Hong Kong is often included among the

little dragons, but its unusual niche role as a free trade center handling goods moving between China and the outside world distinguished it from the others.) Their development of vibrant economies with vital export industries was not just an imitation of Japan's guided capitalism. Taiwan and South Korea both built on infrastructure and an educational foundation laid by Japanese colonial administrations. Both, along with Singapore, had benefited significantly from Japanese investments drawn by low labor costs and the prospect of getting around host country and U.S. import restrictions. Finally, they had benefited from U.S. Cold War policies favorable to foreign trade, U.S. cold warriors' preference for strong leaders who could maintain political stability, and the economic stimulation from U.S. military spending (the equivalent to the role the Marshall Plan had played in Europe). Thanks to this set of favorable conditions, the little dragons had moved successfully into the production of household electronics such as radios and televisions and then on to semiconductors. The addition of the big dragon (China) in the course of the 1980s, followed by Vietnam, broadened the zone of Asian prosperity.

All these successful economies relied on strong state direction. They started from the premise that the international free trade regime offered significant opportunities for growth but that success required more than outdated technology and low wages. The state had to provide promising industries incentives in the form of subsidies and capital available on easy terms. The state also had to buffer these industries against outside competition by raising tariffs and other barriers to imports. At the very time that neo-liberals in the West were mounting their attack against state intervention, these economies were demonstrating that state capitalism and import substitution did in fact work.

The cultural-economic characteristics of this East Asian bloc might best be summed up by the term "Confucian capitalism." The values underlying bloc success arose from long dominant social and political patterns often described as Confucian. Political legitimacy rested not on abstract laws or constitutional arrangements but rather on the virtue evident in the ruler's character. A well-ruled state was marked not by ideological diversity and debate but rather by broad acceptance of a state-sponsored sociopolitical orthodoxy. Finally, society was in Confucian terms not a collection of competing, self-interested individuals. Members of society were mutually dependent, with common goals that transcended individual interests and that required a modicum of group cooperation and sacrifice. This strong and widely shared set of values helped sustain the very conditions that made East Asian economies work so well, including notably authoritarian politics, a stress on public order, loyalty to family and organization, an ethic of hard work, and a faith in the importance of education. The Japanese and their neighbors operated on the principle that a market mechanism driven primarily by self-interest would not create a decent, moral society and might not even make for an efficient economy. Individualism, with its rejection of group obligations, seemed from the Asian vantage point a dysfunctional trait.

Countries on the periphery of this East Asian core came strikingly alive in the 1990s despite not having strong state direction or residual Confucian values. What they all did have linking them to the Asian economic core was a small but wealthy and highly entrepreneurial Chinese community. The most dramatic gains occurred in Thailand, Indonesia, Singapore, and Malaysia, where an influx of foreign investment (mainly from Japan, South Korea, and Taiwan) stimulated export-led growth. They—together with the Philippines—formed the regional pact, the Association of Southeast Asian Nations (ASEAN), in 1967 to provide a loose consultative framework. The addition of Brunei, Vietnam, Laos, Myanmar (Burma), and Cambodia had by 1999 raised ASEAN's population to 500 million, its combined GDP to $737 billion, and its total trade to $720 billion.

Taken together, the entire region's economies put on a display of productivity, technical innovation, and enterprise that rivaled that of the United States and Europe. Trade figures offer one measure of the growing importance of the bloc: By the early 1990s both the United States and the EC were beginning to do more business with East and Southeast Asia than either did across the Atlantic, previously the major avenue for international trade and investment. GDP figures offer another measure: The four leading economies alone had a total GDP in 1990 of $4.99 trillion.

Some outside observers saw in Japan at the head of this Asian bloc a new imperial presence in the world about to subordinate the formerly dominant West. What such fears overlooked were the diversity of political systems in the region and old regional animosities that drained any political will for the tight economic integration of the sort that Europe had embraced. Some in the region such as the Chinese and Koreans vividly recalled Japan's wartime brutality and its attempt in the late 1930s to impose its economic as well as political control (see the Introduction), and others feared China's growing power.

The 1990s turned into a testing time for economies that in most cases had enjoyed a long run of success. Japan was the first to stumble when speculative trends in the late 1980s and early 1990s led to a stock market crash. The economy went into recession, real estate values collapsed, and banks found themselves carrying as much as a trillion dollars in bad debts. Large firms had to break their pledge of lifetime employment and fire workers, and unemployment rose to levels that were high by Japanese standards although low for western Europe and the United States. Plagued by scandals, the Liberal Democrats in 1993 lost their long-time, vise-like grip on the government, but the iron triangle survived as the Liberal Democratic Party's political competitors quickly created their own close ties to business. Japan-bashers abroad at first took pleasure at this blow to Japanese pride but then watched with growing frustration as reforms failed to materialize and business proceeded as usual.

Fears that Japan's troubles might drag the region and even the world down were partially realized in 1997. The downward pressure exerted by the Japanese economy on its neighbors set the stage for a full-blown crisis. When international investors began pulling some of their investments out of regional economies that seemed shaky, others followed suit to avoid being stuck with bad debt. Panic toppled one economy after another, with South Korea, Thailand, and Indonesia falling especially hard. Indonesia rapidly lost over half of its GDP. As foreigners sold off their stakes, regional stock markets and currencies lost 30 to 70 percent of their value within a year, and unemployment doubled or tripled in Indonesia, Thailand, South Korea, Malaysia, Hong Kong, and Singapore.

TOWARD TURBULENT TIMES IN EAST ASIAN MARKETS

1967	ASEAN is formed
1970s	Japanese economy rebounds from OPEC oil shock; South Korea, Taiwan, and Singapore enter second decade of rapid growth
1988	Japanese per capita income overtakes that of United States and West Germany
1990	U.S.-Japan economic friction peaks, and then Japanese stock and real estate markets collapse and economy sputters
1997	Financial crisis engulfs South Korea, Indonesia, and Thailand

The IMF and other international agencies with the support of private international bankers and the political leaders in the G-7 rushed to stem the spread of the panic and chart a course for the recovery of the hardest hit of the regional economies. Here, as in other instances of IMF rescue, the price was invariably neo-liberal reforms, including cuts in government economic regulation and spending often at the cost of social programs, privatization of state-owned industry, and greater openness to foreign trade and investment. While foreign investors and firms benefited along with indigenous elites who had the skills and resources to exploit new market opportunities, women and poor families absorbed the hardest blow. They lost education, health care, food, and housing. Perhaps most significant, developing countries lost control of even the shadow of sovereignty.

Tempers ran high among those in the region against the IMF's tough terms. South Koreans groused that the price of their $60 billion rescue package concluded in December 1997 was a humiliating makeover of their economy. After the IMF bailout of Thailand, one newspaper there grumbled that the terms were "a subtle triumph of U.S. financial imperialism," while another warned against "economic colonialism" developing as a result of this outside intervention.[14] For those saved on IMF terms, immediate economic pain often failed to lead to the promised economic gains. While South Korea quickly regained its footing, Indonesia was slow to recover.

Capitalism with Chinese Characteristics

While the successes of the little dragons added to the margins of the East Asian bloc, China's turn to capitalism and the international market revolutionized the region's economic landscape, dramatically expanding the scope of the bloc and creating a potential competitor for bloc leadership. Gradually, beginning in the late 1970s, China abandoned central planning in favor of state-guided growth while preserving the dominant role of the Chinese Communist Party (CCP). The result might be described as capitalism with Chinese characteristics. The resulting economic transformation of China, the world's most populous country and once the region's most prominent revolutionary standard-bearer, stands in importance on a par with Japan's "miracle" of the 1950s and 1960s.

Deng Takes the Helm. Deng Xiaoping was the party leader who sharply reoriented the direction of China's development path. Deng was born in 1904 in the interior province of Sichuan as the son of a landlord. In 1920, after schooling in Confucian classics as well as Western studies, the sixteen-year-old set off for France to participate in a work-study program. As with other future leaders such as Ho Chi Minh and Kwame Nkrumah, the sojourn would prove critical to his cultural as well as his political outlook. In France, Deng made a commitment to the CCP that would endure for a lifetime, and for his labors at publishing party material he earned the nickname "Doctor of Duplication." (Those years also created an abiding passion for soccer and croissants.) In January 1927, after training in Moscow, he returned to China.

Over the following decades—as the CCP fought its way to power (see Chapter 3)—Deng played an increasingly prominent role. He participated in the fabled Long March that carried Mao to leadership, built one of the CCP's armed base areas, won critical battlefield victories during the civil war, and administered China's southwest after the CCP came to power in 1949. In 1956, now one of Mao's chief lieutenants, Deng assumed the prominent position of general secretary of the CCP. He brought to the post not just experience in political and military affairs but also a broad familiarity with economic issues. By the early 1960s, with Mao less active following the Great Leap Forward disaster, Deng shared leadership with Liu Shaoqi and Zhou Enlai.

Years of loyal service no more saved Deng from attack during the Cultural Revolution than it did others close to Mao. But unlike many at the top accused of "taking the capitalist road," Deng survived denunciation and imprisonment and won rehabilitation in 1973. Purged again in 1976, Deng this time sought protection of military leaders in the south. Mao's death in September 1976 marked the end of an era. A month later the "gang of four," the radical Maoist group led by Mao's wife, Jiang Qing, were arrested and sentenced to long prison terms for persecuting some 730,000 and causing the death of 34,800. Deng's standing as a senior party leader and his extensive political and military relationships built up over half a century of party service now paid off. Colleagues rallied to his support, and he quickly established himself as China's new leader, elbowing aside Mao's own choice as successor, Hua Guofeng. Even as his health failed, Deng would remain China's "paramount leader" until his death in 1997.

The man holding the destiny of China in his hands had abilities long recognized within the CCP. Mao is supposed to have pointed Deng out to Khrushchev during a 1957 meeting in Moscow: "See that little man there? He's highly intelligent and has a great future ahead of him." Round-faced and standing barely five feet tall, Deng was neither a deep thinker nor a charismatic public figure. He was rather a skilled, no-nonsense administrator, a pragmatic problem-solver, a fierce party loyalist, and a thorough patriot committed to making China strong and its people prosperous. He was a man of few and simple words. (Asked by his daughter to describe his experience during the epic Long March, Deng responded laconically that he "went along.") He was, finally, a devoted family man. Deng's 1939 marriage—his third—created a tight-knit family that provided a sanctuary from the pressures of an up-and-down political career. [15]

Deng decided that he could not lead the party forward without first confronting its past. He and his colleagues needed above all else to examine Mao's record for the lessons it might yield, for the mistakes to be avoided or corrected, and for the legitimacy Mao's genuine achievements might confer. In June 1981 party leaders offered a public reassessment that praised Mao's early leadership but condemned his later errors, notably the Great Leap Forward and the Cultural Revolution, and his imperial style of governance with its frequent and ill-considered policy shifts. The CCP's efforts at coming to terms with its past invites comparison with Khrushchev's own attempt earlier to deal honestly with the legacy of Stalin.

Deng's highest priority was reinvigorating the CCP, above all restoring the early commitment to internal democracy and firm but moderate party discipline that Mao had undermined beginning in the 1950s as he started turning viciously on his comrades. Deng wanted a return to open, frank discussions among the leadership. Out of negotiations and compromise among the top leaders would emerge consensus decisions. Deng expected loyal party members to abide by these decisions and maintain party discipline (just as Deng himself had stoically done throughout his career). For party members who strayed, Deng preferred to apply education and rehabilitation. The chief task of a restored party was in Deng's estimate to implement a practical, careful program of economic development. Here too Deng looked to the strategy during the CCP's first years in power of promoting production, building up the intellectual and organizational infrastructure critical to economic development, and minimizing class conflict in favor of enlisting the talents and resources of rich peasants as well as the capitalist class. (See Chapter 3.)

The "Four Modernizations." Deng committed the CCP to a rapid, market-driven economic strategy linked to greater openness to the outside world. He described his approach as "building socialism with Chinese characteristics," but "four modernizations" is the term that finally stuck. Although it might sound like the name of a Chinese rock group, the term was in fact one Zhou Enlai had coined in 1975. To develop, so the proponents of this course argued, China had to advance on four major fronts—by promoting advanced technology and science, a modernized military, competitive industry, and productive agriculture.

In the greatest surprise of all, the new policy lent support to the emergence of a market economy. Dissolving communes and returning individual plots to peasants was the first striking step, taken in 1978. Although peasants did not own their land under the new policy, they exercised formal control as long as they sold a contracted portion of their crops to the government. The rest was for them to sell on their own account at market prices. Responding to the new incentives, peasants raised production by 25 percent between 1975 and 1985, and China exported grain for the first time in recent memory. The liberation of rural entrepreneurs set a precedent for privatizing other parts of the economy. At the same time businesses still part of the government-controlled public sector gained greater autonomy in decision-making. The result of these changes was a mixed economy in which market forces played a generally broader role and in which the state-controlled sector accounted for an ever-smaller portion of national economic activity. Some have described the practical result as a "negotiated economy" because the official role remained substantial; others have preferred the term "market socialism" with its suggestion that the old ideological orthodoxy remained at least partially alive.

These reforms were accompanied by a deepening involvement in the international economy. Foreign investors first began testing the water and then plunging in with greater enthusiasm as the 1980s wore on. The effects of this new global orientation could be seen in the vogue of copying foreign management

Consumerism Reaches the Chinese Countryside, 1981
This peasant girl from a village in southeastern China is showing off a prize of the new rural prosperity. The bicycle as well as the radio and electric fan (in the background) were just the first of a series of new products that eager rural consumers would bring home thanks to higher income made possible by agricultural reform and opportunities to work in the cities. (© Pok Chi Lau)

techniques and in Chinese exports carving out a place in foreign markets. Intellectuals, above all those in technology and the sciences, won expanded opportunities to speak out and to travel abroad. Under the new dispensation CCP leaders held that cultivating China's best minds and giving them some latitude was more likely to hasten economic development than persecuting them as in the past.

Though Deng was able step by step to gain acceptance of his economic policy within the CCP's Politburo, his initiatives did encounter resistance from some of his closest and oldest associates. During the 1980s and early 1990s they expressed fears that he was going too far too fast. They worried that privatization would create social inequalities, weaken the party's control, and negate the achievements of the revolution. Critics also worried that the erosion of the state sector and loss of subsidies would rob workers of their job security and leave them prey to impersonal market forces. Finally, critics feared that the promotion of foreign trade and investment and access to foreign education would give rise to "spiritual pollution," evident in Western bourgeois values and practices such as individualism, conspicuous consumption, and immoral behavior such as prostitution and drug addiction. In articulating these fears, Chinese were echoing concerns felt earlier by Japanese and other East Asians reluctant to sacrifice core social principles in the name of the unrestrained free market.

Deng and his allies in the leadership responded that the new economic initiatives represented the creative application of Marxism, not its abandonment. The reforms were in one view the necessary updating of the insights of Karl Marx to a world much changed since his death over a hundred years earlier. Deng's approach, his supporters explained, represented a blending of Marxism with elements from capitalism, especially the market principle, to make Chinese-style socialism work better. Reformers argued that building socialism required a developed modern economy and that the long-term hope for socialism was thus best advanced by tapping whatever techniques worked to create that economy. Deng himself seemed to take this tack when he observed that whether the cat is black or white is not important as long it catches mice. So too with the economy. Whatever produced growth was good.

Assessing Deng's "Revolution." Whatever the justification, the reform program was on the whole a success, in marked contrast to the other major socialist reform program initiated by Gorbachev in the Soviet Union, which was already foundering by the late 1980s (see Chapter 7). China's economy began to boom in the early 1980s, although it had a tendency to overheat, forcing the government to implement a slowdown, quickly followed by recovery, a new round of inflation, and re-imposition of government restraints in what became a familiar cycle. China's overall growth rates—the highest in the world—averaged over 9 percent from the initiation of the Deng reforms down to 1993. This impressive performance pushed GDP (adjusted for inflation) from $1 trillion in 1979 (the year after Deng launched his reforms), to $2 trillion in 1988, then to $3 trillion in 1994, and finally to over $4 trillion in 1999. By then China had become the world's second largest economy.

Chinese leaders took special pride in their achievements. Their focused, incremental, party-directed economic reforms were in marked contrast to Gorbachev's broad assault on both the political and economic system of the Soviet Union. They had proven that a CCP-led China could succeed in an increasingly competitive, technologically driven international economy. They could look ahead to having, after another two decades of comparable growth, an economy larger than that of the United States. They could even boast that infant mortality and literacy data already looked better for children born in Shanghai than for those in New York City.

In Deng's China there was room for only four modernizations, not a fifth—democratization. Political dissidents and some urban intellectuals argued that democracy was essential to China's development. In their view, China could not modernize economically and socially if it did not modernize politically or at least take a step toward political liberalization by loosening party control. They pointed out that centralized power, especially when exercised by one leader, had repeatedly led the CCP to arbitrary and costly decisions. They called for more government autonomy from the CCP in the implementation if not the formulation of overall policy. They also asked how relevant party ideology was to a rapidly changing Chinese society.

Deng responded to these critics by linking his program of economic modernization to a stand-pat political program. He insisted that the CCP retain its monopoly of political and military power and that the CCP's interpretation of socialism remain the country's official orthodoxy. Deng's adamantly authoritarian stance reflected worry that chaos might erupt if political restrictions were removed. It may also have reflected the fear that a more open system would stimulate independence movements in the inner-Asian border territories occupied by majorities of people who were not of the dominant ethnic Chinese group, especially in Xinjiang and Tibet.

Although Deng's tolerance for dissent was greater than Mao's, any direct attack on the commanding position of the CCP was sure to rouse him. In 1979 he closed down Beijing's Democracy Wall, where dissidents were posting their criticisms of the CCP and their calls for political pluralism. The most outspoken were subject to harassment, arrest, and imprisonment. Wei Jingsheng, a former Red Guard working at the Beijing zoo, went to jail when he refused to moderate his public statements. Clashes with students and intellectuals testing the limits of the new system carried over into the 1980s as Deng launched campaigns against dissent in the name of checking "spiritual pollution" and "bourgeois liberalization."

The spring 1989 "democracy" demonstrations brought to a climax tensions building over a decade both between the party and its critics and within the party leadership itself. The demonstrations began innocently. The mourning surrounding the death in mid-April of the former CCP general secretary and reformer Hu Yaobang gave students in Beijing an opportunity to vent their dissatisfaction with party corruption and with the effects of inflation on students and others trying to live on fixed incomes. Demonstrations on campuses quickly snowballed into major marches to the city center demanding greater party

THE DENG ERA

1978	Deng secures primacy in CCP, offers a mixed verdict on Mao's legacy, and launches the policy of "four modernizations"
1979	Deng represses democracy activists
1989	Deng again crushes protests but holds to course of economic reform
1997	Deng dies, but his economic and political policies survive

accountability to the public. By early May the government and the students were locked in a standoff. Emboldened by a stream of replacements arriving from schools in other cities, by rising worker activism, and by the vocal support of ordinary Beijing residents, the student leadership took a distinctly more confrontational approach toward government officials. When the official response to student demands proved insufficient, the students made the fateful decision to occupy Tiananmen Square in a direct challenge to a party headed (as one of their declarations phrased it) by "an emperor without a crown, an aged, fatuous dictator."[16] Alarmed by this "chaos" in central Beijing and by the demonstrations breaking out in other cities, party elders resolved in late May to crack down. Troops struck on the night of June 3–4, killing at least several hundred protestors, appalling party reformers, and outraging foreign observers. Though seen at the time as an Asian analogue to the popular revolt against socialist regimes then gaining headway in eastern Europe (see Chapter 7), this upheaval played out differently. China's government enjoyed considerably more legitimacy and proved considerably more effective in holding its ground against protest.

The 1989 crackdown should not obscure the achievements of the Deng era. Whether viewed as nation builders or as the architects of a development strategy, CCP leaders could claim remarkable success. They had managed to move dramatically closer to realizing the nationalist dream of making China "prosperous and powerful," in effect lifting it to a position of parity with the modern West and Japan fervently embraced by Mao's generation and a generation of leaders before that. The CCP's eclectic approach to economic development had produced results with few equals in the third world. It is hard to imagine another third-world case where national weakness was so dramatically turned around, and certainly the scale of the enterprise—whether measured in territory or population—puts China's experiment in development in a class by itself.

But the success of the Deng "revolution" came at a price of which the repression of 1989 was only a small part. Rapid development created marked regional inequalities and tensions. While China's coastal areas were beginning to behave like and integrate with its prosperous neighbors such as Hong Kong, Taiwan, South Korea, and Japan, peasants in interior regions deprived of the opportunities to ride the recent wave of economic growth seethed under agricultural stagnation and exploitation by local party bosses. Many set out to look for employment in the cities, swelling a great floating workforce mounting into the tens of millions that slipped out of state control and set urban order in peril.

Employees in the struggling, debt-ridden state sector of the economy faced a future of mass unemployment and an unraveling of the social compact that formerly had given them security. Dissidents kept their heads down and continued to organize, sustained by a burgeoning free enterprise system and by hopes that the next political spasm would find the Communists more vulnerable.

China's "growth-at-any-cost" philosophy was, moreover, incurring a hidden but steep and pervasive cost in environmental degradation. The manifestations, to be found virtually everywhere, included severe water pollution, water shortages in the north, and pollution from heavy use of high-sulfur coal for energy production. China's cities were wrapped in smog, and China's contribution to global atmospheric pollution was growing larger.

A final specter that hung over the economic miracle was population growth so high that it eroded material gains. In the Mao years birth control had been neglected and at times even denigrated. As a result, population (at half a billion in 1949) soared and gathered a momentum that would persist well into the new century, reaching 1.3 billion by 2001. Deng gave birth control high priority. He instituted a one-child policy that offered incentives such as health and educational benefits for those who complied and criticism, harassment, and fines for those who did not. But the countryside proved resistant to these limits. Peasants still valued large families and insisted on having children until they got a male heir.

As societal problems accumulated, the party seemed to lose both its grip and its vision. The CCP suffered from plummeting morale as socialism went into eclipse abroad, while at home party members plunged into business and traded on their insider connections. Popular resentments over the brutal repression in 1989 still festered. Thus the question of the fifth modernization still hung over China.

Vietnam in China's Footsteps

Vietnam was no stranger to emulating the larger, culturally related land to the north. As China moved toward a more market- and export-driven economy, Vietnam followed close behind and thus further extended the grip of the global economy in this extraordinarily vital economic region. Hanoi's decision to shift in a dramatically new direction was made under intense internal pressure. A Vietnamese Communist party good at organizing a popular revolution and waging war against strong powers had proven inept at economic reconstruction and development, at political reconciliation, and at the realization of old dreams of peace and prosperity.

To be sure, the 1975 victory had left the party facing inherently difficult problems. The northern economy, on a war footing since 1965 and battered by a decade of bombing, had to make the transition to peacetime production. With war's end, demobilized soldiers flooded labor markets. At the same time, China cut off aid, the Soviet Union reduced its support, and the southern economy suffered from the total loss of U.S. assistance.

Northern leaders compounded these unavoidable problems by mishandling the integration of the heavily French- and American-influenced South. Early in 1978 Hanoi ordered the South to fit the northern economic mold. Agriculture was collectivized, industry was nationalized, and central planning was put in place. The reaction was intense. Southerners, remembering the National Liberation Front's (NLF's) promise of gradual integration, felt betrayed. Peasants who had supported the NLF to win, not surrender land, balked at the new policies. Some resorted to sabotage to express their opposition, and newly formed agricultural collectives collapsed. By 1979 the economy was in a tailspin. Mismanagement by the planners, as well as the lack of incentives and a fair market price for produce, led to a fall in rice production. Shortages of food and other products necessitated rationing and the import of foodstuffs. Per capita income declined. Unemployment and inflation were both high. The flight of merchants and entrepreneurs of Chinese descent—some 700,000 between 1978 and 1982—further disrupted the economy while swelling the ranks of the "boat people" (those fleeing the country in small and often unseaworthy crafts).

These problems were compounded by corruption in the ruling party that gave the lie to its continuing claim to serve the common good. The old wartime solidarity began to dissolve into a scramble for advantage, with party cadre now grabbing at the spoils of victory. Vietnam was experiencing a familiar phenomenon. Much like the Soviet *nomenklatura,* a party elite benefited from its privileged access to scarce consumer products, quality medical care, personal transportation, and subsidized materials that could be sold on the black market at a handsome mark-up.

Driven by economic crisis, the Vietnamese Communist Party made a fundamental decision in favor of a new domestic program in December 1986 when Nguyen Van Linh emerged as the party leader. Linh instituted a far-reaching policy of "renovation" (*doi moi*) that closely resembled the program already under way in China. Linh's long service in the South during the war had taught him the importance of tapping its considerable economic potential, both its entrepreneurial spirit and its rich natural resources. More broadly, Linh's experience had left him doubtful that a centrally planned economy would provide adequate incentives for production. He looked instead to private enterprise to spur agricultural output, increase the production of consumer goods, and help Vietnam move as a competitive player into international markets. Linh implemented economic reforms on several fronts. They included a liberal foreign investment code, put in place in 1988 to overcome Vietnam's lack of capital and poor infrastructure. In the late 1980s Linh also cut back support for state enterprises, abandoned central administrative direction in favor of indirect control exercised through tax and fiscal measures, let the currency trade at international market values, and gave peasants virtual ownership of the land that they worked. He moderated policies toward ethnic Chinese in hopes that they would resume their important middleman role in the economy.

The reforms began to brighten the prospects for Vietnam's 71 million people. Stores began to fill with consumer goods. By 1990 light industry and agriculture

VIETNAM SHIFTS COURSE	
1976	Hanoi unifies the North and South politically
1978	Hanoi imposes a socialist economy (including collectivized agriculture) on the South; flight of the "boat people" begins
1986	Linh adopts a market-oriented economic strategy
1990	Reforms begin to spur strong, steady economic growth

were growing at a good pace, and Vietnam reemerged as a significant rice exporter for the first time in decades. New oil production covered the country's energy needs. Tourism began to develop as an industry. Foreign trade expanded, with Japan being the major trading partner, and more foreign investors (with Taiwan and Hong Kong capital in the lead) were finding their way to Vietnam. Inflation was brought under control, and living standards were on the rise. Although still one of the poorest countries in the world measured by annual per capita income (about $200), Vietnam was on track to taking a place in the vibrant East Asian economic zone. Even though party leaders continued to insist that their ultimate goal was socialism, they did not pretend that they would get there anytime soon.

Like Deng's reform program, Linh's was largely economic and only marginally political. Although the national assembly gained more power to shape policy and journalists and intellectuals gained more scope to expose political corruption and abuse of power, few critics dared openly advocate the overthrow of the ruling party or the creation of a multiparty system. Even the most enthusiastic proponents of markets among the leadership worried that too much economic freedom might compromise political stability and national security. Linh himself was increasingly explicit in his attacks on sweeping political liberalization. Party leadership was critical to rapid, stable economic development; Western-style democracy would only lead to chaos, he argued. Unrest in 1989 in eastern Europe, the USSR, and China reinforced these fears about the destabilizing effects of an open political system.

In Nguyen Van Linh's Vietnam, as in Deng Xiaoping's China, Communist leaders had effected a dramatic shift. They had long taken as an article of faith the decline and inevitable collapse of capitalism, and they had behind them a lifetime of practical schooling in the hostility of capitalist powers to their national independence and socialist development. Despite all this, they had come to embrace the rules of an international system defined by a seemingly still vital capitalism. Economic growth came at a price. They had to accept some considerable loss of control of the economy and an openness to the outside world that threatened to change the political and cultural environment at home. "Spiritual pollution" from abroad was proving a formidable challenge to party orthodoxy and socialist values.

REVIVED BLOC BUILDING IN EUROPE

Like Americans, the Europeans in the 1970s and 1980s suffered an economic slowdown. Inflation had taken hold in the late 1960s, and the escalation of oil prices compounded the problem of rising prices. Thus, for example, between 1968 and 1975 consumer costs in France and Italy climbed about 90 percent. These rising costs in the major western European economies between 1973 and 1989 contributed to lower per capita GNP growth—roughly half of what the region had experienced between 1950 and 1973, but still significantly better than in any other prolonged period since 1870. In this regard the leading western European countries (Britain, France, West Germany, and Italy) lagged during the 1970s and 1980s behind the Japanese but stayed ahead of the Americans.

Where Europeans could count unmatched progress was in pushing forward with regional economic integration. By the 1990s they had gone considerably farther than either the North Americans or the East Asians. Geographically coherent but without a single dominant power, this emergent community of rough equals struggled to chart its own course in the face of sometimes antagonistic global currents and internal divisions. The socialist collapse of 1989 promised to expand the search for a distinctive European way.

Renewed Integration and the EU

The road toward integration and growth on which the Treaty of Rome creating the EC had set western Europe turned for a time distinctly bumpy. As we saw in Chapter 7, throughout much of the 1960s French leader Charles de Gaulle had obstructed British membership and stymied attempts to breathe some independent life into EC institutions. He could not bear the thought of a proud France ruled "by some sort of technocratic body of elders, stateless and irresponsible."[17] The first of the oil shocks in 1973 posed a new kind of challenge to the Community. The rapid price increases hurt a region heavily dependent on oil imports. Quickening competition from high-tech, low-cost competitors, especially in East Asia, compounded the problem of weakening international demand for important European exports such as automobiles and steel. These economic blows were exacerbated by political inertia. Rather than retrench, most European governments sought to maintain their full array of social programs. The result included ballooning budget deficits and rising inflation, as revenues from slowing

TABLE 8.1 Comparing Per Capita GNP Growth, 1970s–1980s	
	(average percentage annual increase)[18]
United States	1.6
Britain and Northern Ireland	1.8
Continental European leaders	2.1
Japan	3.1

economies faltered at the very time that the economic downturn created a demand for more, not less, government welfare. Like their American counterparts, politicians were not prepared to risk imposing fundamental reforms needed to restore international competitiveness. Economic investment declined dramatically, leaving European firms even worse off.

By the late 1970s and early 1980s with voters registering their discontent, political leaders began to put forward austerity programs. These included notably higher taxes and curbs on government spending in order to close the budget deficit and bring down inflation. Even left-leaning governments had to tighten their belts, and more conservative governments launched campaigns to privatize inefficient state-owned companies.

Nowhere was the shift in political tone as well as policy more dramatic than in Britain during Margaret Thatcher's years as conservative prime minister (1979–1990). "There is no such thing as society, only individual men and women and their families," observed the "iron lady" in an assertion of her strong neoliberal philosophy.[19] Consistent with that view, she tamed the unions, cut welfare programs, and denounced dependency on the "nanny state." And in the bargain she demonstrated that the British imperial impulse was not dead by defeating the Argentines in a war for control of the Falkland Islands (a remnant of empire in the South Atlantic near the southern tip of Argentina).

West Germany typified the continent's continued preference for an activist state to manage the economy. To soften the oil shocks, the government in Bonn promoted energy efficiency. Oil consumption quickly fell by 20 percent. At the same time Bonn encouraged an export drive that especially targeted the now cash-rich OPEC countries. This combination of initiatives soon turned a trade deficit into a surplus. At the same time the West German central bank took vigorous steps to contain inflation, with the result that West Germany's inflation rate between 1968 and 1975 was the lowest of Europe's major economies. But the prices for keeping inflation in check were slower growth and rising unemployment.

Concerned over the persistent sluggishness of western Europe's economy, EC members embarked on a series of discussions out of which emerged a consensus in favor of intensifying integration. The new course rested in part on hopes of stimulating economic expansion just as the creation of the Coal and Steel Community and the EC itself had in the 1950s. European leaders were also aware of their region's slipping competitiveness in areas such as computers and military technologies. Concerted research programs and shared production might improve Europe's international position in the increasingly important high-tech sector. In 1986 EC members resolved to take steps to create a single market by the end of 1992. German unification in 1990 accelerated the timetable by convincing neighbors that further integration would offset augmented German influence. These trends culminated in a decision in December 1991, formalized by a treaty signed in Maastricht in the Netherlands, to create from the EC a new, tighter European Union (EU). Its principal sponsors were France's François Mitterand and the leader of the new Germany, Helmut Kohl—once more highlighting the importance of Franco-German cooperation to European integration. The Maastricht Treaty called for the creation of a common currency and a European central bank. It also looked ahead to a political union that would build on EC institutions and expand their responsibilities. Finally, the treaty, which went into effect in 1993, provided for a common citizenship for all members of EU countries, free movement within the EU, and the creation of a common currency, the "Euro," in 1999 (in full circulation by early 2002).

While intensifying integration among its core economies, the European bloc was also steadily expanding in scope. In 1973 Britain, Ireland, and Denmark joined. Subsequently, the EC brought in Greece (1981) and Spain and Portugal (1986) after those three embarked on a course of democratization following the fall of right-wing dictatorships in the 1970s. In 1995 Austria, Sweden, and Finland joined the EU, bringing total membership to fifteen (with thirteen applicants eager to join and further extend the EU's scope).

Throughout this process of intensifying integration, British leaders as well as the public hesitated to fully embrace a continental destiny. When Britain finally did join the EC in 1973 it was a move prompted largely by economic problems, including the highest rate of inflation of any of the major European economies and lagging growth. EC membership did not prove a panacea. Britain's per capita income growth over the ensuing sixteen years (1973–1989) fell at the low end for the major European economies while doing marginally better than the United States (see Table 8.1). Hesitation about a closer relationship to the continent again came to the fore during the talks leading to the Maastricht Treaty. British leaders repeatedly voiced objections and finally opted out of the plans to create a single currency.

Within the EU, no single national economy occupied a role comparable to that of either Japan or the United States in size of output or magnitude of influence. Though West Germany was often regarded as dominant, in fact three of its neighbors—Italy, France, and Britain—were quite close in output, even after East and West Germany merged. The four contributed almost equally to a combined output of $4.16 trillion in 1990. And although German conservative fiscal policy and the attractions of the mark have given Germany prominence and power, the shadows of the Nazi past have inhibited the vigorous exercise of that influence.

Social and Cultural Developments

The emergent European community experienced significant social and cultural changes that left it quite different in the 1990s from what it had been at the beginning of the postwar boom when integration had begun to gain headway. In general the trends were strikingly similar in the core economies across the region.

The most obvious of these was the deepening grip of consumer culture. Rising income levels caught up with the United States, permitting families increased discretionary spending. Perhaps even more than Americans, Europeans prized the leisure that affluence made possible. They enjoyed shorter workweeks and took longer vacations (roughly a month for most industrial workers, compared to eleven to twelve days for their American and Japanese counterparts). In a 1994 poll, workers ranked family, leisure time, and friends ahead of their jobs. Still, the long-term effects of consumerism were evident in greater materialism and secularism within European culture. The inroads were strikingly registered in Italy, where the once powerful Catholic Church suffered repeated defeats—the legalization of divorce in 1972 and abortion in 1980, and the end of Catholicism as the state religion in 1985.

Consumerism also promoted homogenization, eroded class distinctions formerly evident in speech and dress, and dampened class conflict. Children of the industrial working class moved into white-collar service jobs. A youth culture promoted tastes in entertainment, language, and dress that cut across class lines. Previously militant and powerful unions in France, Italy, and Britain shifted from demands for sweeping political and economic change to a stress on bread-and-butter issues. German unions took the lead in making the case for moderation. They avoided inflammatory rhetoric, worked with management to make their industries competitive instead of going on strike, gained a voice on actual production procedures, and provided retraining for workers in declining industries. Thanks to this strategy, German workers led the continent in wages.

This consumer society witnessed basic shifts in the workforce. Agriculture and industry declined in overall importance, while white-collar employment in the service sector moved the western Europeans toward what has been tagged a post-industrial economy. Agriculture suffered the steepest drop, as labor left the countryside for work in the city. For example, in Italy the portion of the workers in agriculture fell from 40 percent in 1954 to 8 percent in 1992. With these changes went a dwindling of small-town life and a formerly influential class of small shopkeepers.

But class differences persisted despite the surface tendency toward cultural homogenization, working-class moderation, and changes in areas of employment. Even though education became increasingly the ticket to employment and advancement in an ever more technologically based economy, family prominence and wealth were the best predictors of who would get the best schooling and hence the most important jobs. In Britain those who attended prestigious and expensive private schools and then went on to university at Oxford or Cambridge tended overwhelmingly to come from privileged backgrounds. This educational track created influential networks of classmates and smoothed their way to the top in government and business. Similarly, in France exclusive *lycée* schooling comparable to the British private schools and then highly selective professional schools (known as *les grandes écoles*) produced high-level government and business leaders. In the somewhat less confined Italian and German systems, law degrees tended to be the ticket to high status and high pay. In general, at the end of the twentieth century the top rungs of government and corporations were as much dominated by elites as they had been early in the postwar period. The major exception was Scandinavia and above all Sweden, where democratization of schooling led to major strides toward democratization of the elites.

Societies marked by a high degree of ethnic homogeneity at the outset of the postwar period had become strikingly more diverse by century's end. Immigrants, largely unskilled labor from Turkey as well as North Africa and other areas earlier colonized by Europe, flocked to Britain and the continent to fill the many open service and industrial positions created by the early postwar boom. Friction between foreigners and natives remained low until the economic downturn of the 1970s. As unemployment soared, so too did resentment over the burden associated with this foreign workforce. German and French nationalist politicians responded with calls for immigration controls. For example, in Germany a strong backlash developed against "guest laborers" (*gastarbeiter*), especially Turks, who had flocked to the country during more prosperous times. Some demanded the departure of these longtime foreign residents, and a fringe element occasionally turned to violence. But a return to prosperity in the 1980s and 1990s blunted nativist sentiment. Jobs went unfilled because birth rates among the native-born were falling and workers were shifting to the white-collar service sector. Workers from outside the EC continued to arrive, increasingly from an economically troubled eastern Europe. By 1986 foreigners had come to account for 7 percent of the German and French populations and 15 percent of the Swiss.

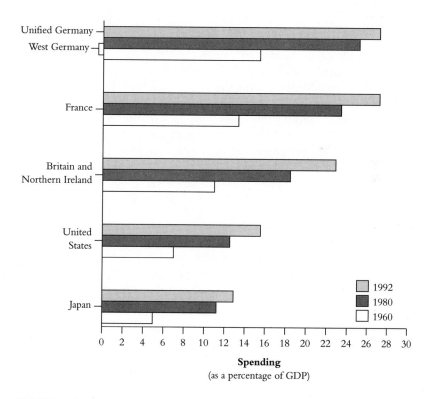

FIGURE 8.3
Social Security Spending in the Three Blocs[20]
In the three major European countries social security expenditures have steadily grown over the last half century and outpaced the United States and Japan usually by a factor of two. Here, as in other matters of political economy, Britain was betwixt and between—below the continental states but ahead of the United States and Japan.

Despite the economic austerity and rapid social change of the 1980s and 1990s, the western European bloc retained a distinct economic culture biased in favor of a mixed economy with a strong state role and a strong commitment to social welfare. While governments began to retreat from the high water mark of state control in banking, communications, and transport as well as some industries, those governments continued to provide citizens with social welfare benefits that remained far ahead of those in the United States and Japan. As a result, taxes remained relatively high. For example, in 1990 tax receipts as a percentage of GDP in Germany, France, and Italy hovered around the 40 percent mark compared to about 30 percent for the United States and Japan. Britain was in the middle—above the figure for the United States and at the low end for this sample of EU countries.

"Welfare capitalism" is the term that best captures the regional expectation—within the EU as well as along its periphery—that the state would soften the hard edge of capitalist competition and defend vulnerable groups in the name of social justice. Traditional laissez-faire parties that had resisted welfare capitalism had virtually disappeared, and conservative parties either converted (as in Britain) or had actually taken the lead in developing a rich array of social programs (as in the case of the Christian Democrats in Germany and Italy). A 1990 poll revealed continuing, widespread European support for the state playing an important, multifaceted economic role. In West Germany, Italy, France, Spain, and Hungary as well as the former Soviet Union, the system that won the highest support was "democratic socialism" or "social democracy." Predictably those same polls registered reservations about unbridled "capitalism" (or an unconstrained free market). Only in Poland and Britain were reactions to "capitalism" more positive than negative.[21] This persistent regional concern with the commonweal was reflected in steadily rising levels of welfare spending among major western European countries after 1945. The upward trend persisted even into the 1990s when the strong winds of global competition were supposedly sweeping away all before them.

Post-'89 and the Opening to the East

Already the most integrated of the blocs, western Europe found itself facing fresh opportunities for expansion and consolidation with the sudden collapse in 1989 of socialist states with close, dependent ties to the Soviet Union. Though usually regarded as the last act in the Cold War drama, the political upheavals in the old Soviet-controlled bloc paved the way for significantly expanded EU influence, a healing of the political divisions imposed by the superpowers after World War II, and perhaps even the rise of a greater Europe. Americans may have won the Cold War, but the western Europeans were the major beneficiaries. The one significant exception to this trend came from a surprising quarter—not one of the collapsing Soviet clients, but an independent socialist Yugoslavia, which dissolved in open ethnic conflict just as its neighbors were following a peaceful path toward collaboration with the EU. American intervention finally calmed the situation, again to the EU's benefit.

Toward One Europe. The post–Communist states of eastern Europe looked to their neighbors to the west for a variety of reasons. The most economically advanced, including Poland, Hungary, and the Czech Republic (a product of the peaceful 1992 breakup of Czechoslovakia), had developed under the cultural and economic shadow of the German and Austrian empires and France. Further inclining the new states westward were shared political aspirations. The dissidents that toppled socialist regimes had demanded free elections, genuine parliamentary government, and civic pluralism in place of Soviet-style political repression and economic constraints.

Among ordinary citizens freedom implied something no less important—the promise of shopping in well-stocked stores with full pockets, owning a home, buying a car, and traveling abroad on vacation. This freedom to consume was one of the most attractive features of Western societies that East-bloc citizens had gotten to know through travel, trade, television, and pop music long before 1989. In East Germany the lure of a better standard of living—closer to that of their German cousins on the other side of the Berlin Wall—may have been the most important factor motivating the protests of 1989. For example, the banana—commonplace in the grocery stores of West Germany but scarce and costly in East Germany—became a symbol used by protestors of the socialist failure to deliver what its leaders had promised and what western Europeans took for granted.

Finally, the two halves of Europe were united by a shared commitment to welfare capitalism. The cries for freedom during 1989 did not signal the victory of neo-liberal values. Nor did the end of socialism bring a smooth economic transition and the rapid realization of a western standard of living. It instead brought eastern Europeans face to face with something new—the rigors of the free market and the wrenching adjustments of economic reorientation. The removal of price controls set off inflation, which in turn necessitated government austerity measures to bring the inflation under control. Despite rising prices, wages did not increase, while food and other subsidies on which many depended disappeared. At the same time unemployment rose as a result of closing the almost invariably inefficient, debt-ridden state-run industry. The economy contracted for the first several post-socialist years. Businesses had to refashion themselves in order to win western European markets, including attracting investment capital, integrating new technology, and instituting new management techniques. The rapid erosion of the old socialist welfare system and the strong IMF-administered free market medicine prompted a new appreciation for the role of the state and a consensus in favor of something like western Europe's welfare capitalism.

The most important development during this time of transition was the rapid reunification of East and West Germany. Once demonstrators had shaken the resolve of East German Communist leaders, no broad-based, well-organized opposition was ready to fill the political vacuum. With elections looming in March 1990, West Germany's Christian Democrats promised that rapid unification was the key to prosperity. This appeal brought them victory and enabled Bonn to control events. The sixteen million East Germans became citizens of the

West German state; overnight East Germany ceased to exist. The promise to rehabilitate the East's economy—to upgrade infrastructure and production facilities—would prove costly to the West. With more than 36 percent of all workers in the endangered public sector, unemployment soared in the East. By mid-1991 industrial production there had fallen by 70 percent, and 3.5 million workers out of a total workforce of 8.5 million were unemployed. Though the move toward unity imposed a heavy social and economic burden in the short run, it promised to establish Germany as first among equals within the EU and as an influential intermediary between the EU and formerly socialist countries to the east.

Of those countries, Poland, the Czech Republic, and Hungary made the most rapid turn westward and were soon on track to joining the EU. Part of the reason for this northern tier's quick adjustment was its close geographic proximity to the magnet market of the EU and its ability to attract substantial foreign investment. Poland led the way, achieving an economic recovery in 1992. By then roughly three-quarters of Poland's trade was tied to western Europe. These

Prosperity Comes to Budapest in the 1990s
Old East-bloc cities acquired a new glow after the fall of socialist regimes, as this scene from 1994 makes clear with its cell phone, well-dressed pedestrians, inviting sidewalk cafés (featuring EU brands), and appealing storefronts (one with an English-language sign). But even in Hungary, where the transition was relatively smooth, there was a price to be paid: widening income inequalities and painful social dislocation for those ill-suited to the new market-oriented economy. (Copyright Miklos Szabo)

countries were also helped by a smooth transition to post-socialist politics, in which former Communists played a major role. Nothing was more surprising than the durability of seemingly discredited Communist politicians. Their parties had been at first in disarray after 1989, stunned by public repudiation expressed through the ballot box in Poland and Hungary, and through massive demonstrations in Czechoslovakia. But in both Poland and Hungary Communists could take credit for having contributed even before 1989 to the gradual rise of multi-party democratic politics. In those two countries as well as the Czech Republic, they had by the 1994 round of elections made a striking comeback, presenting themselves as social democrats and promising a mix of market reform and social welfare. They had managed to retain a base of support that other parties, led by dissident-era intellectuals, lacked. There was irony in old-line Communists having failed at creating "socialism with a human face" now helping to build a kinder, gentler capitalism.

Romania and Bulgaria followed a different pattern, moving so haltingly into the post-socialist era that their ultimate relationship to the EU was uncertain. In Romania holdovers from the old Ceauşescu regime formed a cautiously reform-oriented National Salvation Front. In Bulgaria Communist leadership was only briefly interrupted; party leaders made a quick comeback in the 1990 elections. Despite taking the "shock" therapy prescribed by the IMF, the economies of both countries struggled. Bulgaria was the last of those in the region attempting economic reform and showed no signs of economic recovery until 1995. Romania's transition to a market economy, launched in 1990, attracted little of the foreign assistance that reformers had hoped for, and as a result already difficult economic conditions did not improve significantly.

Yugoslavia and the Ethnic Peril. A third, nightmarish pattern asserted itself in the post-1989 period in the form of reawakened ethnic nationalism. The crisis and collapse suffered by Yugoslavia reminded Europeans of the virulent nationalism that they had repudiated in favor of a peaceful, economically integrated postwar order in western Europe. Yugoslavia's collapse gave rise to fears of a general resurgence of ethnic enmities, a continent awash in refugees, and an explosion of separatist and nationalist claims threatening to the integrity of virtually all European states. This prospect was especially worrisome in eastern Europe with its patchwork of discontented minorities no longer under the thumb of repressive socialist government. The demise of a federated Czechoslovakia contributed to the alarmist view. The post-socialist era brought to the surface strains between the more economically developed Czech region with about two-thirds of the population and the Slovak region. However, the two were able to reach an amicable decision in 1992 to divide the old state into two new ones, the Czech Republic and Slovakia. In the end all the potential hotspots in the EU borderlands stayed cool except Yugoslavia, which imploded in the most virulent display of violence that Europe had seen since the end of World War II.

The state of Yugoslavia was marked by unusual cultural diversity befitting a zone of constant imperial competition. The pattern began with the Roman empire and continued with invasions by the Ottoman, Austro-Hungarian, and

Russian empires, Hitler's Third Reich, and Mussolini's Italy. Conquerors brought new faiths to the area, resulting in a patchwork of groups—Catholic Croats, Orthodox Serbs (subdivided into those living in Serbia, Montenegro, and Macedonia), and Muslims in Bosnia and Kosovo. These diverse communities had a long history of both harmony and strife.

The first half of the twentieth century was marked by communal conflict interrupted only briefly when a fragile peace followed the creation of Yugoslavia (meaning Land of the South Slavs) in 1918 out of the ruins of the Austro-Hungarian empire. Following World War II, Yugoslav leader Tito made a heroic effort to contain ethnic rivalry within a federal Yugoslavia composed of the republics of Serbia, Montenegro, Croatia, Slovenia, Bosnia, and Macedonia as well as the autonomous republics of Kosovo and Vojvodina. He suppressed historical controversies that might fuel old bitterness and leaders that seemed bent on promoting nationalist agendas. Tito's death in 1980 was a turning point. As in Gorbachev's Soviet Union, so too in post-Tito Yugoslavia, weakening central authority unleashed separatist sentiment. With Tito's considerable prestige and authority no longer there to hold them back, Serbs expressed mounting resentment over the gains made by other ethnic groups and fear over the possible loss of their fabled Kosovo homeland, where the Serb population had dwindled to about 10 percent of the total and the ethnic Albanian majority were asserting their political rights.

With the nationalist tinder piled high, a Communist leader with strong Serbian attachments, Slobodan Milošević, tossed in the match. Born in 1941, Milošević was raised by his mother, a strait-laced Communist activist and a teacher. The son was socially aloof and bit old-fashioned in dress and outlook. His marriage to Mirjana Markovic opened political doors through her family's connections within the Yugoslav Communist Party. A professor of Marxism at Belgrade University, she served as advisor to her husband as he advanced in the party. Although generally dismissed as a dull, unpromising figure, Milošević saw by the late 1980s the potential for tapping a strong Serbian nationalism devoted to uniting Serbs scattered across the region. In 1987 he stepped forward as the champion of Serbian control of Kosovo and committed himself to the protection of Serbian residents in that autonomous region. Taking this popular position energized this normally reserved party functionary, making him (one friend observed) "like a heated stove."[22] On the basis of this blatant nationalist appeal, Milošević shouldered his way to power. Having established control of the party, the government, and the media, he launched his campaign to create a Greater Serbia within an increasingly unstable Yugoslavia.

In March 1989 Milošević abolished autonomy for Kosovo and put Serbs in control of the police, the university, and local government, which raised the specter of Serbs attempting to dominate other parts of Yugoslavia. When Croatia and Slovenia responded by declaring their independence in 1991, he in turn asserted a claim to a substantial Serbian population in part of Croatia. The fighting quickly spread across Croatia, and initially the Serb-controlled army and Serb-armed militias drove out Croatians in what amounted to the first round of "ethnic cleansing." This removal of one ethnic group by another usually but not

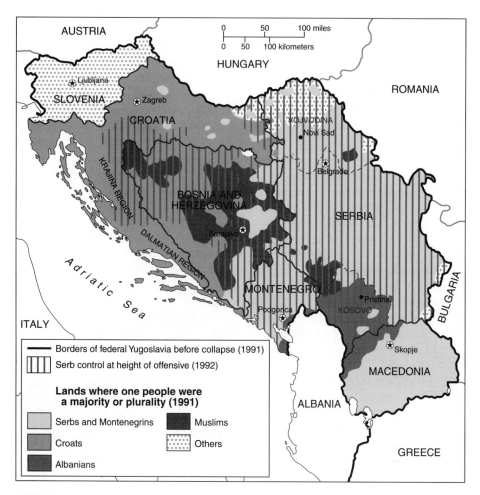

MAP 8.2
Yugoslavia Implodes, 1989–1999

exclusively began with intimidation of the local population (for example, murder of its leaders and mass rape) followed by seizure of property, internment, the deportation of some, and the execution of others. With this success in Croatia, Serb forces in 1992 took the offensive in the ethnically mixed Bosnian region, setting off a three-way battle among Muslims, Serbs, and Croats. All practiced ethnic cleansing, but none on wider a scale than the Serbs. The focal point of the conflict was Bosnia's besieged capital, Sarajevo, long a harmoniously multi-ethnic city.

By 1995 it was clear that Milošević had overplayed his hand. The Croatian army rallied and drove out the enemy, putting to flight some 170,000 Serbs, who had inhabited the area for several centuries. As Yugoslavia spun apart politically,

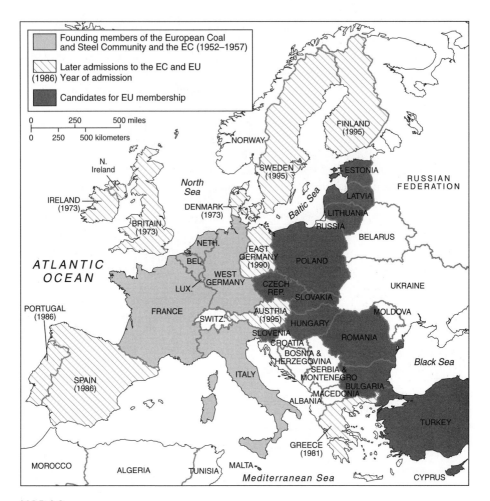

MAP 8.3
Advancing European Integration

The territorial advance received a major boost as a result of the collapse of socialist regimes in eastern Europe in 1989 and the consequent reorientation of their economies westward. Poland, Hungary, the Czech Republic, Slovakia, the Baltic states (Lithuania, Latvia, and Estonia), and Slovenia, along with Malta and Cyprus, are slated for admission in 2004. The process of integration, especially in finance and currency, took a leap forward in 1993 when the European Community became the European Union. The introduction of the single EU currency ("Euro") in 1999 was widely celebrated as a landmark event, though one taken without the British. While registering these gains during the 1990s, the EU proved ineffectual in dealing with an unraveling of Yugoslavia, thus highlighting the limits of European integration in foreign and military policy and by default continuing dependence on the United States.

ethnic violence displaced some three and a half million people (at least one million of them Serbs) between 1991 and 1995 alone.

Although western European leaders had claimed from the start that the Yugoslav conflict was a European problem, they could not formulate a coherent response to this unfolding human disaster. Despite economic integration, they were still not sufficiently united politically to respond to the crisis in their backyard. Germany backed independence for Slovenia and Croatia, whereas others argued that it was irresponsible to hasten Yugoslavia's unraveling without devising an overall solution to the crisis. Germany prevailed, and in December 1991 a European summit decided to grant recognition but failed to agree on any other concerted action. The European economic giant now looked to the United States for a solution. By 1995 reports of ethnic cleansing had created international outrage and intensified calls for intervention. After considerable indecision, the Clinton administration stepped in to save the situation. Bombing by U.S. aircraft of Serb positions in Bosnia paved the way for a peace agreement that preserved Bosnia as a state of three federated ethnic groups and provided for sixty thousand NATO-led troops to keep the peace.

Ethnic conflict, now contained on one front, broke out on another. The tension in Kosovo that had served as Milošević's vehicle to power in the late 1980s finally exploded in 1999. Guerrillas demanding independence openly battled Serbian forces, with civilians caught in the crossfire and subject to Serb abuse. Once more the United States had to take the lead with its European allies close behind. A NATO ultimatum failed to stop the mass expulsion of Albanians by Serbian forces, so U.S.-led NATO forces went into combat for the first time since the creation of the alliance half a century earlier. NATO bombing of Serbia finally forced Milošević, who had once more overplayed his hand, to capitulate and allow another NATO force into that strife-torn province to ensure peace and the safe return of refugees.

By decade's end Milošević's campaign for a greater Serbia would look like one of the most misguided expansionist drives in recent history. At its peak in 1992 Serbia controlled one-quarter of Croatia, two-thirds of Bosnia, and all of Kosovo. But after nearly a decade of campaigning Milošević had lost most of this land, and Serbia itself had suffered international economic sanctions and bombing. The economy was devastated, the country isolated internationally, and its leaders wanted for trial as war criminals. An opposition movement finally ousted Milošević in 2001 and turned him over for trial before an international tribunal for his part in Serbian atrocities during his deadly decade in power. The postwar European order was, for the moment at least, safe.

CONCLUSION

By the late twentieth century the three centers of the global economy were locked in a relationship marked by both cooperation and conflict. They shared a stake in a smoothly functioning, expanding system that could absorb their increasing output of goods and services. They thus had good reason to work together in formulating a widely accepted set of economic rules, overseeing their implementation, and resolving problems and containing disputes. But the U.S., the East Asian, and the EU economies could collide over how the one-world market should operate. They differed significantly among themselves over such issues as the proper role of the government in economic policy and regulation and over control of strategic sectors such as banking, telecommunications, and such heavy industries as steel and oil. When one party tried to universalize rules at odds with another's fundamental assumptions about the nature of the good life and social justice, the resulting tensions could slow or threaten the trend toward global integration.

These three major economic blocs provide a useful reminder that the international system remained pluralistic. We should not assume that the American economic model has prevailed in the unfolding global order, nor that it will anytime soon. The solutions to the challenges facing both former socialist regimes now in transition to the market and less developed economies still searching for an appropriate path are as likely to come from European or East Asian practices as from American. Asian growth rates make a powerful argument for giving the state ample power to promote and sustain economic competitiveness. At the same time, the European example argues for the virtues of state-promoted economic inclusion of all citizens and generous welfare provisions.

The American, European, and East Asian models do not constitute fixed, stark alternatives. Rather, they offer a range of choices that can be combined in almost endless ways. Each has evolved over time and contains significant internal tensions. For example, the United States may be the paragon of the free market. But the portion of GDP claimed by the government has been steadily growing, and government regulation, unemployment insurance, monetary and tax incentives, and bailouts of troubled corporations have played an important role in policing, directing, and at times even suspending the operation of the market. The advanced economies taken collectively offer a great buffet of goals and strategies among which peoples around the world are likely to choose according to their traditions and values.

RECOMMENDED RESOURCES

The Evolving International Economic Framework
Overview: Eric Helleiner, *States and the Reemergence of Global Finance: From Bretton Woods to the 1990s* (1994), highlights how the freeing of international finance from the 1960s onward transformed the Bretton Woods system, while Jeffrey Hart, *Rival Capitalists: International Competitiveness in the United States, Japan and Western Europe* (1992), makes the case that states continue to play an important economic role in spite of the neo-liberal tide. For **the neo-liberal faith** that has exercised considerable influence not just in the United States but also over the global economy, see the classics by Friedrich Hayek, *The Road to Serfdom* (1944), and by Milton Friedman with the assistance of Rose D. Friedman, *Capitalism and Freedom* (1962). Robert Solomon, *The Transformation of the World Economy* (2nd ed., 1999), a compact insider account, follows the neo-liberal policy trend around the world during the 1980s and 1990s, while Kevin Phillips, *Wealth and Democracy: A Political History of the American Rich* (2002), and Studs Terkel, *The Great Divide: Second Thoughts on the American Dream* (1988), contemplate the consequences of neo-liberalism for U.S. society.

The Asian Bloc and Japan

The recent rise of Asia is placed in historical perspective in Eric Jones et al., *Coming Full Circle: An Economic History of the Pacific Rim* (1993), and Andre Gunder Frank, *ReOrient: Global Economy in the Asian Age* (1998). On **U.S.-Japanese trade frictions** during the 1980s, see the enormously popular *The Japan That Can Say No: Why Japan Will Be First among Equals* (1991). Morita Akio joined Ishihara Shintaro as the author of the Japanese edition but refused to associate his name with this translation despite its more restrained tone. John Dower, "Graphic Others/Graphic Selves: Cartoons in War and Peace," in Dower, *Japan in War and Peace: Selected Essays* (1993), 287–300, is an entertaining look at the tensions in U.S.-Japan relations. On **the foreign impact on Japan's consumer society,** Joseph J. Tobin, ed., *Re-Made in Japan: Everyday Life and Consumer Taste in a Changing Society* (1992), offers revealing examples of how foreign goods and practices became "domesticated." Mark Schilling, *The Encyclopedia of Japanese Pop Culture* (1997), drives home the point that such cultural products as movies, films, television programs, and toys need to be understood in terms of a complex interplay of international and domestic influences whose outcome is distinctly Japanese.

China under Deng Xiaoping

Standard overviews include David S. G. Goodman, *Deng Xiaoping and the Chinese Revolution: A Political Biography* (1994), and Richard Baum, *Burying Mao: Chinese Politics in the Age of Deng Xiaoping* (1994). Geremie R. Barmé, *Shades of Mao: The Posthumous Cult of the Great Leader* (1996), graphically demonstrates Mao's continuing grip on the popular imagination even in the reform era. Insights on **the upheaval of spring 1989** emerge from Han Minzhu, ed. and trans., *Cries for Democracy: Writings and Speeches from the 1989 Chinese Democracy Movement* (1990), a valuable documentary record; and *The Gate of Heavenly Peace* (prod. and dir. Richard Gordon and Carman Hinton; 1995; 189 min.), a penetrating, full-length documentary on that controversial event. For a sense of **daily life** during the Deng era and earlier, see Zhang Xinxin and Sang Ye, *Chinese Lives: An Oral History of Contemporary China,* trans. and ed. W. J. F. Jenner and Delia Davin (1987), and B. Michael Frolic, *Mao's People: Sixteen Portraits of Life in Revolutionary China* (1980).

Postwar Developments in Vietnam

Authoritative **scholarly assessments** can be found in Gareth Porter, *Vietnam: The Politics of Bureaucratic Socialism* (1993), and William J. Duiker, *Vietnam: Revolution in Transition* (2nd ed., 1995). On **the integration of the South,** see Doan Van Toai and David Chanoff, *The Vietnamese Gulag* (1986), good on the difficulties northerners faced in asserting control over a diverse and resistant southern society. For a moving reflection on **the costs of Vietnam's decades of struggle,** turn to Bao Ninh, *The Sorrow of War: A Novel,* trans. Frank Palmos and Phan Tranh Hao (1994), a best-seller by a veteran.

European Integration

On the **course of European integration,** see the recommendations at the end of Chapter 5. On **the Yugoslavia crisis,** Robert D. Kaplan, *Balkan Ghosts: A Journey through History* (1993), stresses ethnic hatred as a hardy source of regional conflict. Noel Malcolm, *Bosnia: A Short History* (rev. ed., 1996), points to the key role of Serbian nationalist leaders in precipitating a prolonged and bloody crisis. Tim Judah, *The Serbs: History, Myth and the Destruction of Yugoslavia* (1997), tries to strike a balance between popular passions and elite decisions in explaining the rise of an aggressive nationalism. Julie Mertus et al., eds., *The Suitcase: Refugee Voices from Bosnia and Croatia,* trans. Jelica Todosijevic et al. (1997), captures the views of ordinary people whose lives were disrupted and dreams destroyed by the violence of the 1990s.

CHAPTER 9

DIVERGENT PATHS
IN THE THIRD WORLD

The third world was never a monolith. The colonial impact, the course of the liberation struggle, and the choice of development models began to distinguish one place from another quite early in the postwar era. The distinctions among former colonial regions and even within regions were to grow steadily greater. By the 1970s and 1980s, those distinctions—whether measured by per capita income, life expectancy, infant mortality, or levels of literacy—had grown so large that they strained beyond credibility the idea of a single postcolonial condition or identity.

One major source of this growing diversity was the decline of a radical vision within the postcolonial world. The hope for national liberation and for a more equitable international system that had served to bring much of the third world together in the 1960s faded in the following decades. The Stalinist and Maoist development model lost favor. The leading disciples of Marx and Lenin in Asia, the Communist parties of China and Vietnam, moved to embrace the capitalist free market. (See Chapter 8.) The collapse of the eastern European socialist regimes amidst economic crisis confirmed for third-world observers that command economies and five-year plans were not a panacea for poverty. Finally, the Cold War record demonstrated to third-world leaders that any leftist upstarts were likely to encounter strong, even potentially deadly American opposition. In East Asia alone, conflict in which the superpowers were implicated in the thirty years following the end of World War II had already cost the lives of 10.4 million people.

In the developing world from the 1970s onward, authoritarian regimes committed to stability and order were far more common and long-lived than those devoted to fundamental social change. The revolutionary outbreaks that did appear at century's end took forms that would have surprised Marx and Lenin. They arose in reaction against regimes of ethnic or religious oppression (for example, in Guatemala, South Africa, and Palestine) or gave expression to long-smoldering ethnic or religious impulses toward social purification (as in Cambodia and Iran). The most common trend was a turn from inward-looking models of state-dominated economic development to approaches allowing greater room for market forces. This experiment worked for some, especially in East Asia, but for most the outcome was problematic. Markets often promised more than they could deliver. Population growth nullified much of whatever gains the shift to markets yielded. And women in countries making the transition to the market frequently found their status and welfare diminished, thus shackling half of the workforce and undermining the prospects for long-term economic gains.

THE CHANGING FACE OF REVOLUTION

Left-leaning revolutionary regimes continued to appear toward century's end in places as diverse as Ethiopia, Grenada, Cambodia, and Nicaragua. Few had any staying power, and most amply confirmed the hardnosed observations of the Italian political philosopher Niccolò Machiavelli over four centuries earlier: "There is nothing more difficult to carry out, nor more doubtful of success, nor more dangerous to handle, than to initiate a new order of things."[1] Cambodia serves as an example of the rocky terrain that late-arriving revolutionaries had to cross. The racial hatreds that informed that revolution provoked Vietnamese counter-measures that proved fatal to its survival. Astonishingly, the most revolutionary regimes of the era would emerge not from a Marxist tradition but from a potent strain of Islamic political thinking. In Iran a clergy committed to a faith much older than Marxism led a revolution that secured its firm grip on power. Iran's revolution would transform that country, send powerful reverberations throughout the Islamic world stretching from North Africa to Southeast Asia, and leave the superpowers stunned and on the defensive.

Cambodia's Genocidal Revolution

A seemingly quiet political backwater, Cambodia became the improbable scene for the most radical and destructive revolution of the late twentieth century. Prince Norodom Sihanouk's long rule created the illusion of calm and set the stage for the upheaval that would ultimately engulf him and his people. Sihanouk led his country to independence from France in 1953, riding on the coattails of the Vietnamese struggle. Until the mid-1960s he held power virtually unchallenged, thanks in large measure to the popular deference to the monarchy that was especially strong among the peasantry, some four-fifths of the population.

Sihanouk pursued a nonaligned course in the Cold War in hopes of securing development assistance but also of insulating a weak country with a proud past from outside pressures. Cambodia had once been a power in the region—a great Buddhist kingdom that flourished between the tenth and fourteenth centuries and that is best known for the architectural marvels of Angkor. But then it declined rapidly. Early in the nineteenth century, Thailand and Vietnam had squeezed Cambodia territorially from either side. Then in 1863 the French imposed a protectorate, making Cambodia a part of their Indochina holdings. Many Cambodians blamed their national decline on foreign meddling.

Escalating conflict in neighboring Vietnam soon made neutrality impossible. Cambodia had become a critical part of Hanoi's war strategy as both supply route and troop sanctuary. (See Map 4.1.) Washington responded by trying as early as 1963 to get Sihanouk to live up to his claims to nonalignment or to replace him with a leader more responsive to U.S. direction. In March 1969 a frustrated President Richard Nixon launched a secret campaign of B-52 carpet-bombing in Cambodia, at first along the border and then deeper into the interior. Over half a million tons of bombs would fall over the following four years.

Pol Pot and the Khmer Rouge. As Sihanouk's rule began to unravel during the late 1960s, Pol Pot seized the opportunity as head of the Cambodian Communist Party (generally referred to as the Khmer Rouge—literally red Khmers, or Cambodians). He was born in 1928, the offspring of a peasant family in a town north of the country's capital, Phnom Penh. Drawing on family connections with the royal palace he won a scholarship to study in France, where he arrived in 1949. Like other prominent third-world figures such as Nkrumah, Ho, and Deng, and like other youths later influential in Cambodian revolutionary politics, he was radicalized by communist and anti-colonial ideas. Those who knew Pol Pot then remembered him as charming and self-effacing. "He would not have killed a chicken," noted a fellow Cambodian.[2]

In 1953 Pol Pot returned home to join the Khmer Rouge. When Sihanouk's secret service drove senior party leaders to take refuge in North Vietnam, their younger comrades, including Pol Pot, were left in Phnom Penh to run a struggling party. By the early 1960s he had advanced to the top of this internal wing of the Khmer Rouge. He shifted operations from the capital to the safety of rural base areas in eastern Cambodia under the protection of Hanoi.

In January 1968 Pol Pot called for armed struggle against Sihanouk, setting off an intricate and deadly political dance between the two men. Representing an old elite tradition and a populist and egalitarian approach, the rivals would alternately fight and ally over the next thirty years. In starting this first civil war, Pol Pot defied Hanoi's pressure on the Khmer Rouge to do nothing to undermine Sihanouk, who was acquiescent to the North Vietnamese presence in his country. In any case, Pol Pot's prospects seemed poor. He had behind him only some five thousand ill-equipped and poorly led guerrillas whose appeal to peasants was limited.

In March 1970 a pro-U.S. military junta led by Sihanouk's defense minister, Lon Nol, seized power in Phnom Penh. This coup reshuffled political relationships and set in motion a new, fiercer round of fighting. The Nixon administration at once threw substantial military backing to the new, anti-communist regime and authorized a military "incursion" into Cambodia by eighty thousand U.S. and South Vietnamese troops. The operation was meant to destroy the North Vietnamese command center, but it mainly served to push North Vietnamese forces deeper into Cambodia and into a one-sided collision with Lon Nol's poorly trained army. Sihanouk himself, now in exile in Beijing, threw his support to the Khmer Rouge against Lon Nol and the Americans. So too did China and North Vietnam.

Pol Pot's position was further strengthened by the effects of the U.S. carpet-bombing and the intensifying conflict on the ground. Together they disrupted rural life, reduced agricultural production, and flooded the cities with refugees. Khmer Rouge propaganda blamed the Lon Nol government for Cambodia's misery, while young, poor peasants blazing with anger flocked to its guerrilla forces.

Attacking from its rural bases, the Khmer Rouge defeated Lon Nol and took Phnom Penh in April 1975, just as the war in Vietnam came to a close. Now in power, Pol Pot launched Cambodia (renamed Democratic Kampuchea) on a draconian and destructive revolutionary course. Its strong utopian and violent qualities made it quite different from the revolutionary path followed by the neighboring Vietnamese. The new regime summarily emptied the cities. Pol Pot would crush not just the wealthy and influential tied to the old regime but the entire bourgeois class by destroying their urban strongholds. He also initiated a ruthless persecution of ethnic minorities (including Vietnamese), some 20 percent of Cambodia's population. Any signs of resistance doomed to death entire families and communities. Finally, Pol Pot initiated a hunt for suspect elements within the Khmer Rouge itself. The prison in Phnom Penh took in thousands of these "tainted" party members; virtually none survived.

Most extraordinary of all, Pol Pot set in motion an experiment in social mobilization unmatched in twentieth-century revolutions. The Khmer Rouge pressed the entire Cambodian population into mobile work teams laboring under party direction. The brutal labor regime, the exercise of terror to secure compliance, repeated bouts of starvation diet, forced resettlement, and the collectivization of land and living arrangements alienated even the most supportive of peasants. The party that many had embraced took from them what they most prized—land, family, and religion. One mocked the government's promises of a better life to be achieved through heavy labor on water control projects. "Before, we cultivated the fields with the heavens and the stars, and ate rice. / Now, we cultivate the fields with dams and canals, and eat gruel." Cambodian society had become what survivors of the revolution would describe as "the prison without walls."[3]

Finally, Pol Pot pushed his revolution in an anti-Vietnamese direction that would prove its undoing. Long resentful of Vietnamese paternalism toward the Khmer Rouge, he now became suspicious that moderates within his own party were traitors working for the Vietnamese. Trained and aided by Hanoi, was it also possible they were acting as agents of Vietnamese ambitions? In late 1971 Pol Pot had struck at the Vietnamese patron by conducting the first of a string of party purges and by soliciting China to serve as the Khmer Rouge's new patron. Once in power, he injected into revolutionary policy his bitterness toward Vietnam, which he described as "a black dragon" spitting poison at Cambodia.[4] With China already by 1976 committed as his protector and major source of aid, he turned on his old enemy with fury, demanding the immediate withdrawal of all Vietnamese troops from Cambodia. He drove over 150,000 ethnic Vietnamese living in Cambodia across the border, and he sent troops to reclaim from the Vietnamese disputed borderlands and islands in the Gulf of Thailand. By June 1978 his cross-border attacks had forced three-quarters of a million people on the Vietnamese side to flee their homes.

A Revolution Unravels. By 1978 with tensions high, Vietnam's leaders moved toward a decision to overthrow Pol Pot. That prospect in turn forced the major powers interested in the region to take sides. Beijing issued stern warnings to Hanoi, and Washington aligned with China against Vietnam. These developments deepened Vietnam's dependence on the USSR as a counterweight to a hostile China and as a source of aid as Hanoi rebuilt its army and organized units made up of the survivors of Pol Pot's successive purges.

In December some one hundred and fifty thousand Vietnamese and fifteen thousand Cambodian troops crossed the border. In January they set up a new government in Phnom Penh, headed by Heng Samrin, a former Khmer Rouge military commander. Pol Pot retreated to the countryside, where he resumed the kind of guerrilla warfare that had won him power in the first place. He found support from Thailand, and China continued to back him because it did not want Vietnam to dominate Cambodia and to ally with the Soviet Union. Deng Xiaoping launched an invasion into northern Vietnam to underline his unhappiness. The Carter administration also retaliated by withholding diplomatic recognition, embargoing trade and investment, and vetoing assistance by the World Bank and the International Monetary Fund. Despite revelations of the horrors of Pol Pot's rule, the Khmer Rouge won support from Prince Sihanouk and from the Association of Southeast Asian Nations (ASEAN) as well as from China and the United States. The Vietnamese and their Cambodian allies retained the upper hand militarily, but Hanoi found Cambodia a quagmire requiring a costly ten-year occupation (1979–1989) that in turn perpetuated tensions with Beijing and Washington.

Talks on ending the fighting began in late 1987 among the exhausted contenders for power, and in September 1989 the Vietnamese withdrew their troops, leaving behind the government of Hun Sen (another of the former Khmer Rouge who had returned with the Vietnamese in 1979). In 1991 the rival groups arranged a cease-fire. To help secure the peace, the UN dispatched a multinational force of over twenty thousand to disarm the warring factions and arranged for refugee resettlement. An election held under UN auspices in 1993 resulted in a coalition government dominated by Hun Sen's party of former Communists and the royalist party run by Sihanouk's son. Sihanouk remained on the political scene, a symbol of national reconciliation. The peace process left the Khmer Rouge politically isolated and crippled by splits among its leadership. Before the last bit of Khmer Rouge strength dwindled away, Pol Pot died in 1998, supposedly peacefully in his sleep and never to be held to account for his crimes.

The Cambodia that emerged from this era of revolution, foreign occupation, and three civil wars was devastated. During the bombing and fighting between 1970 and 1975, up to half a million died and some two million became refugees. Once set in motion, Cambodia's revolution became genocidal with an unprece-

CAMBODIA CONVULSED

1951	Cambodian Communist Party (Khmer Rouge) is organized
1953	Cambodia gains independence from France under Sihanouk
1964– 1965	Escalation of war in Vietnam raises importance of Cambodia as a supply route and troop sanctuary
1969	Nixon launches massive bombing campaign in Cambodia
1970	Lon Nol overthrows Sihanouk
1975	Khmer Rouge led by Pol Pot takes power
1979	Vietnamese forces oust Pol Pot regime and put in power former Khmer Rouge aligned with Hanoi
1989	Vietnamese forces withdraw, leaving Hun Sen in control

dented speed and impact as the new regime turned on Vietnamese and other minorities, descended into deadly political in-fighting, and (most significant of all) embarked on a ruthless social mobilization with no care for human consequences. The spasm of violence and inhumanity between 1975 and 1979 resulted in at least another 1.5 million deaths. In other words, about a fifth of the population of eight million had perished from overwork, starvation, or execution. The survivors faced grim economic conditions, demolished educational and health care systems (only three hundred doctors for the entire country), and a reduced life expectancy of forty-eight years (one of the lowest in the world). It is easy to look back and feel sympathy for Sihanouk's failed attempt to prevent regional and superpower conflicts from engulfing his country with destructive consequences even he could not have imagined.

For Vietnam, the end of its Cambodian intervention gave a welcome boost to hopes for prosperity and regional peace. In 1990 Beijing and Hanoi began the process of normalization. To improve relations with the United States, key to gaining access to advanced technology and loans for infrastructure development, Hanoi began in 1985 cooperating in the search for the several thousand Americans missing in action from the Vietnam War. This cooperation, together with the end of the Cambodian occupation and the shift toward a free market strategy, led President Bill Clinton to normalize trade relations in 1994, and the next year he restored full diplomatic relations. To round out the new regional diplomacy of peace, Vietnam began improving ties with Thailand and Indonesia and moving toward membership in ASEAN.

Religious Challenge in Iran

In contrast to the relatively short-lived Cambodian revolution, the Iranian revolution of 1978–1979 had considerable staying power. The story began with British and Russian penetration in the nineteenth century and continued with the arrival of the United States during World War II. In short order the Americans managed to evict the Russians, overshadow the British, and remove the government led by Mohammed Mossadeq bent on nationalizing Iran's oil resources. Those steps paved the way for the dominance of Mohammed Reza Shah Pahlevi over three decades beginning in 1953. The shah's policies dovetailed with U.S. Cold War interests in containing Soviet influence in the Middle East and securing control of oil as a critical resource. (See Chapter 6.)

The Shi'i Clergy and Popular Grievances. The consolidation of the shah's power left the Shi'i clergy (*'ulama*) as the proponents of the only alternative vision of Iran's future. The clergy built on a tradition going back to the seventh century when Arab conquerors had introduced the Shi'i branch of Islam to the country. Shi'a meant literally "faction," referring to those devoted to Ali, the prophet Mohammed's son-in-law and successor. From the Shi'i perspective, Ali's murder broke the legitimate line of descent within Islam. The opposing Sunni branch won a position of dominance in the Muslim world that it retains today. (Nine out of ten of the world's 1.2 billion Muslims are Sunni.)

While the shah and Washington sought to break the grip of feudal, traditional ideas and institutions, Iran's Shi'i clergy clung to a faith that represented to many stability in a time of rapid social change and continuity in the face of challenges to indigenous cultural values from Western ideologies—mainly capitalism but also Marxism. The clergy's popular appeal arose from a long tradition of wielding moral and political authority at the local level. They had, for example, collected and spent taxes, maintained large landholdings, dispensed justice, managed basic education, and attended to social welfare.

Not all the clergy was politically engaged, but one segment became increasingly activist in opposition to the tide of Western influence and the shah's anti-clerical policies. These disaffected activists began to argue that the only legitimate state was one that strictly followed Shi'i religious ideals as interpreted by religious authorities (the ayatollahs). This politicized clergy came to constitute a revolutionary party. They had used their long-established theological schools to develop and popularize their doctrine of resistance to unjust civil authority, in effect creating a revolutionary ideology—populist and xenophobic. In those schools were some three to four thousand students who could serve as organizers. The activists and their students would prove a potent political combination.

Alone, the clergy would have been a troublesome but not formidable opposition. However, the clergy won many followers as a result of the political alienation produced by the far-reaching impact of the shah's modernization program. Land reform, begun in 1962, initially improved the lot of some peasants, but increasingly it served to consolidate land into large mechanized farms that displaced peasants or subordinated them to government direction. Many projects associated with the shah's modernization program were dramatic and visible but did little for economic development or popular welfare. Large dams, airports, grand avenues, modern military equipment, and new government buildings absorbed much of the government spending. At the same time, corruption and patronage were widespread throughout the government and business. Unsettling

Western influences, promoted by the shah's program and symbolized by some fifty thousand American residents by 1978, provoked a backlash. For many outside the charmed circle of the royal court and the expanding middle class, modernization seemed to bring hardship, waste, and moral decline.

Even though Iran became wealthy on oil, the actual distribution of that wealth was marked by extremely wide disparities. These were especially glaring in the capital, Tehran, and other large cities where by 1979 half of the population resided, including an alienated and unemployed underclass driven from their rural homes by the consolidation of land holdings. Peasant loss of land had begun in the nineteenth century when commercialization of agriculture had seen landlords assemble large estates in order to grow cotton and opium for the international market more efficiently and profitably. By the mid-1930s land consolidation had by one estimate left 96 percent of the rural population landless. Desperate peasants sought a new life in the cities, a trend that accelerated as the shah's modernization program and the oil boom rained riches on the urban sector. But the newcomers suffered from inflation, poor housing, government neglect, and the cultural shock of city ways at odds with values carried from the countryside.

Growing resentment among Iranians over cultural defilement and economic exploitation was reinforced by memories of the 1953 coup (widely attributed to the Americans). Many viewed the shah as the political tool of American and Israeli interests. Although the shah did not try to hide his U.S. ties, he preferred to conceal his trade, military, and intelligence links to Israel, not wanting openly to defy the Arab policy of no contact. But his critics were not fooled. By the 1970s political discontent had spread to a wide range of social groups. They included dispossessed landowners and peasants, urban poor, students and educated professionals committed to greater democracy and more balanced economic development, and an influential merchant class (the *bazaari*).

The Ayatollah's Road to Revolution. Ruhollah Al-Musavi Al-Khomeini was the inspirational figure who combined these varied discontents into a successful revolutionary movement. He articulated the Islamic values of the clergy and echoed the reformist and nationalist complaints of the other alienated groups. One of his admirers described that charismatic cleric as a person of "spirituality and erudition, asceticism and self-discipline, sobriety and determination, political genius and leadership, compassion for the poor and deprived, and relentless hatred of oppression and imperialism."[5] That assessment came to be widely accepted in Iran.

Khomeini was born in September 1902 into a well-to-do, respected family in a town about sixty miles from Tehran. Both his father and grandfather had been religious scholars. At age nineteen he left home to study religion. Later at the religious center of Qum he gained distinction as a teacher of ethics and philosophy. In 1943 he authored a tract that openly criticized Reza Shah for his secularizing politics, but he otherwise remained silent on politics, playing no role in the Mossadeq crisis of the early 1950s. In the early 1960s he recovered his political voice and emerged as an opponent of Reza Shah's son at a time when few dared to speak out. In 1963 he denounced the secular, U.S.-backed White Revolution that reflected the shah's commitment to Westernizing Iran. He charged the shah with tolerating corruption, immorality, and materialism and undermining the religious values at the heart of Iranian life. He also censured the shah for his humiliating ties to the United States and Israel. "The government has sold our independence, reduced us to the level of a colony, and made the Muslim nation of Iran appear more backward than savages in the eyes of the world!"[6] To this point he demanded reform, not the regime's overthrow.

This attack had a nationwide impact and marked the beginning of a prolonged and bitter struggle. The shah immediately countered, raiding religious centers and imprisoning Khomeini in 1963 but then soon releasing him as a concession to popular pressure. The cleric continued to speak out on political issues, so the shah exiled him in 1964. For the next fourteen years Khomeini maintained contact with the opposition, offering encouragement and guidance in a cause he came to define as the overthrow of "the tyrannical regime imperialism has imposed on us" and its replacement by "an Islamic government."[7] His clear, direct pronouncements circulated widely in Iran and established him as the leading clerical opponent of the shah.

By 1970 the conflict in Iran was turning violent as terrorist activities, directed against Americans as well as the shah's regime, became common. As earlier, the shah responded to protest with police repression and the exile of opponents. But now spreading disaffection left him with a shrinking base of political support, even within the urban middle class and within the royal court and its clients, the primary beneficiaries of Iran's new wealth.

In January 1978 Iran entered a period of sustained political conflict, culminating late that year with nationwide urban rioting led by militant youths serving as anti-shah shock troops. Bloody government repression fed the outrage and led to more massive protests until the police and army were powerless to defend the regime. From Paris Khomeini declared the anti-shah protest a holy cause and lauded those killed as martyrs. In January 1979 the shah fled, and on February 1 Khomeini, the central figure in the loose coalition of opposition groups, returned to Tehran in triumph. The Pahlevi dynasty was at an end, as was the U.S. strategy of using the shah as a regional surrogate. An American position built up over a quarter-century collapsed almost instantly, and Washington no better understood the situation on the ground than it had in its earlier defeat in Vietnam.

The Islamic Republic. Once back in Iran, Khomeini held adamantly to his vision of an Islamic Iran and soon began to translate that vision into an Islamic republic. Initially he depended on moderates within the anti-shah coalition to lead the government. But increasingly clerics took charge. In effect, autocratic rule by the clergy replaced the shah's autocracy.

Under clerical rule Iran experienced a real social and political revolution. Revolutionary courts, a revolutionary council, and revolutionary guards exercised power and enforced the will of the clergy. Parliament was restricted in its membership, and its laws were subject to review by a veto-wielding Council of Guardians, consisting of six clerics and six lay persons. The government set out to make public behavior conform to religious ideals. Alcohol and coeducational classes were banned, and the media was purged of Western cultural influences

Poster Depicting the Ayatollah Khomeini Triumphant
Khomeini appears in the role of Moses towering over the shah. The desperate monarch, his crown cracked and his sword broken, reaches for support from a composite figure of other enemies of Iran and Islam: Britain (the flag on the shirt front), the United States (the flag to which the shah is clinging), and Israel (the star of David on the hat). The small figures in the upper lefthand corner undergo tortures in hell awaiting those such as the shah who have been unjust. This poster combines the style of traditional Persian miniature painting with passages from the Koran. "There is a Moses for every Pharaoh"—a line not from the Koran, just to the right of Khomeini's head—was frequently invoked by the anti-shah opposition. The iconography here is dense but would have communicated even to the illiterate who might have seen this poster along a Tehran street.[8] (Franz Brunner)

spread by imported movies, music, and literature. Women were enjoined to return to the veil in public and to abandon business and public affairs. The new government extended social services to the urban poor, carried out some land reform, and nationalized major financial and industrial enterprises.

These changes were effected in the face of considerable domestic turmoil. Members of the old regime as well as left-wing Islamic militants earlier allied with Khomeini fought the drift toward clerical rule. They assassinated leading clerics and bombed the headquarters of the Islamic Republican Party. The clerics struck back and began to purge moderate allies. Some were exiled; others were executed. Between 1979 and 1981 perhaps ten thousand died amidst the violence and half a million (mostly middle-class professionals) fled abroad. At the same time Iran became locked in a long war with Iraq (treated below).

Following Khomeini's death in 1989, two of his clerical colleagues shared power. Hashemi Rafsanjani, the elected president, and Ali Khamenei, the new supreme religious leader, put the brakes on the revolution. The economy was suffering from inflation, a slump in production and foreign trade, and low oil prices. The war with Iraq, the most destructive conflict since the end of World War II, had martyred a generation and inflicted significant material destruction.

The ruling religious elite now moved away from the social justice and sharply anti-imperialist messages of the revolutionary years. Khamenei and Rafsanjani promoted more market-oriented policies at home, called for respect for private property, and loosened cultural restrictions (for example, allowing more latitude in women's dress and a greater variety of music). Concerned with rapid population growth, they instituted a highly effective program of family planning. In an increasingly pluralistic system, the parliament became the scene of real debate among diverse points of view. The new regime followed an equally moderate international policy, seeking to restore diplomatic relations with the outside world and encourage foreign investment.

The election in 1997 of Mohammed Khatami as president drew a new line of division within the clerical ranks: How much political liberalization was possible without endangering the republic's Islamic ideals? Those most committed to clerical control faced an explosion of fresh ideas coming out of Iranian literature and film, an active women's movement, and a strong electoral reaction against the regime's restrictions. The revolution's successes in education—from raising basic literacy among the young to dramatically expanding college enrollment— brought more Iranians into political life and added to the pressure for change. The revolution that Khomeini had made was now secure enough to try to find an amalgam between Islamic values on the one hand and on the other some form of democracy, greater parity in gender roles, and integration into the world economy. Nothing better captured that emerging amalgam than the twentieth anniversary celebration of the overthrow of the U.S.-backed shah featuring such cartoon figures as Mickey Mouse and Bugs Bunny.

Revolutionary Aftershocks in the Middle East

The revolution that convulsed Iran also created international shock waves. The United States and the Soviet Union were both alarmed by the specter of "Islamic fundamentalism," and both were drawn into regional conflicts as a result. Superpower intervention would prove costly for all concerned.

The administration of President Jimmy Carter was the first to feel the impact. Initially in 1978–1979, the president and his top aides tried to find a middle way between what they saw as strident and hostile "religious fanaticism" and the collapsing regime of an old ally, the shah. That approach failed when the shah lost control and fled the country in early 1979. Carter then faced a Khomeini-dominated government demanding that the shah be brought to justice and that the United States end its interference in Iranian politics. In October the Carter administration, acting on the pleas of American supporters of the deposed ruler, admitted him to the United States for cancer treatment. Early the next month Revolutionary Guards in Iran retaliated by taking hostage sixty U.S. diplomats in the Tehran embassy. The condition for their release was the return of the shah for trial along with the riches that he had accumulated.

Carter's humiliation had only just begun. The American media began to count the days of captivity (ultimately 444), and the hostages became a virtual obsession for the public and Carter himself. Increasingly desperate, the president launched a secret rescue mission in April 1980, but the attempt failed. The resulting frustration among the electorate helped doom Carter's bid for a second term as president. In a final twist of the knife, Iran ended the hostage ordeal in January 1981, just hours after Carter had vacated the White House for Ronald Reagan.

Moscow too felt the effects of Iran's revolution. In December 1979 a Soviet leadership headed by the ailing Brezhnev sent Soviet combat forces into Afghanistan. This first step in a ten-year entanglement was widely taken by U.S. cold warriors as a revival of Soviet expansionist ambitions. But in fact Moscow in 1979 acted, like Washington, out of fear of the new Islamic upsurge. The leaders in the Kremlin saw a friendly Afghani government as a firewall against the spread of a disruptive "fundamentalism" from Iran into the Muslim populations of Soviet central Asia.

The Soviet effort to prop up its Afghan allies strikingly parallels the American effort in Vietnam. Moscow inherited a situation of political instability following the murder in April 1978 of long-time strongman Mohammed Daud, who had charted a nonaligned course while accepting Soviet aid. In a story familiar to U.S. officials in Saigon, Moscow then began a search for a group within the local Communist party who could take Daud's place while pushing forward a modernizing, anti-feudal revolution. But despite Soviet aid and advice, the Afghan Communist party faltered in its control of the countryside, and party leaders soon fell to battling among themselves. Facing a stark choice of military intervention or the potential collapse of its client regime, Moscow marched its forces into Afghanistan. The Soviet intervention galvanized a broad-based Afghan resistance whose center of gravity was Islamic and whose support was international, including strong backing from Pakistan and Iran as well as Saudi Arabia, China, and the United States. The Carter administration provided almost $2 billion in covert support while also imposing economic sanctions on the USSR and boycotting the 1980 summer Olympics in Moscow.

Over one hundred thousand Soviet forces and one-third that many Afghan government troops failed to defeat the resistance. Again parallels to Vietnam are striking. Soviet forces occupied the cities—assumed to be strategically decisive. But when Soviet units sallied forth to search for the enemy in the countryside, the guerrillas simply dispersed into the mountains, attacked the Soviet flanks and communications lines, and then returned to their base areas after the Soviet sweeps. By 1987 the Soviets had assumed a passive posture to reduce casualties. In 1988 Gorbachev resolved to cut his losses, and in 1989 he completed troop withdrawals. As Soviet troops disengaged, the conflict became once again an internal struggle. A semblance of order would come to the war-torn land only in the late 1990s with the rise of the Taliban, a Pakistan-backed political movement that instituted an Islamic code exceeding in severity the practices during Iran's first revolutionary years.

Iran's revolution also helped spawn the Iran-Iraq war of 1980–1988. It had its origins in Tehran's appeal to the Shi'i faithful in Iraq to overthrow the secular Saddam Hussein regime dominated by Sunni Muslims. Baghdad struck back in September 1980 when Iran was still distracted by revolutionary conflict, seizing disputed oil-producing territory near the Iran-Iraq border. Zealous Iranian forces

THE IRANIAN REVOLUTION	
1963	Shah jails Khomeini for public opposition and then exiles him in 1964
1978	Khomeini backs mounting anti-shah protests
1979	Shah flees abroad; Khomeini returns and consolidates power of the Islamic Republic; Shah is admitted to United States for medical treatment; U.S. diplomats are taken hostage (held until January 1981); Soviet forces intervene in Afghanistan
1980	Iran-Iraq war begins (ends in 1988)
1989	Khomeini dies; revolution enters a more moderate phase; Soviet forces retreat from Afghanistan

rallied, thus setting the stage for a prolonged bloodletting. Adding to the horrors was the Iraqi use of poison gas for the first time on a wide scale since World War I. This stark violation of long-standing international law evoked no outcry from the world community. Indeed, Iran was all but isolated internationally with support coming only from Syria, while Iraq received arms, intelligence, and economic aid from the United States, the Soviet Union, and France as well as neighboring Kuwait, Saudi Arabia, and the United Arab Emirates. A mix of nationalism and faith in Islam sustained popular support in Iran throughout this long, costly struggle. A father whose sons had died fighting Iraq revealed that faith when he observed, "In the markets of martyrdom they sell their souls very cheaply."[9]

Finally in 1988 Iran agreed to peace, driven by economic exhaustion and heavy losses that had climbed to four hundred thousand. Iraq had also paid dearly. Some three hundred thousand troops had died, and the country's debt had soared to $100 billion. But Iraq was also strengthened militarily. This second war in the wake of the Iranian revolution had planted the seeds for the third, the U.S.-Iraq war of 1991 (treated in the Conclusion).

OPPOSITION TO SETTLER COLONIALISM

Toward century's end a phenomenon known as "settler colonialism" had tied some complicated knots in parts of the third world and had given rise to resistance that marked a further diversification of conditions in post-colonial states. These new battlegrounds looked different from communist-inspired revolutions in Cambodia or China, from the culturally defensive impulses that animated the Iranian revolution, and from the liberation movements that broke the fragile colonial grip in India and Ghana.

The problem originated in substantial numbers of European settlers carving out a place for themselves in third-world lands at the expense of indigenous peoples. These transplanted Europeans came to constitute a privileged class who dominated the economy and politics. A high living standard and social status gave them a strong vested interest in preserving the status quo. Settler regimes blocked opportunities for subject peoples, in particular by denying them advanced education, administrative office, and access to land. This domination by outsiders created deep, lasting social divisions. It could be quite old as in Guatemala (first treated in Chapter 6) or South Africa, or newly minted as in Israeli-occupied Palestine. The ever-present threat from the majority indigenous people tended to stimulate among the European minorities a bunker mentality, strong racial or religious justifications for inequality, and a heavy reliance on armed force to sustain their position. The results were societies marked by fear and enmity that made political compromise and social cooperation difficult.

The settler problem had been at the heart of some of the most tangled cases of decolonization early in the postwar period. French settlers in Vietnam were a potent voice for maintaining colonial control just after World War II, while French residents in Algeria provided influential support for a bitter war in the late 1950s and early 1960s to preserve their way of life (see Chapter 6). In parts of sub-Saharan Africa where the settler presence was strong, the decolonization battle continued into the 1970s and 1980s. Mozambique and Angola, each home to about a quarter-million Portuguese residents, witnessed prolonged conflicts. In Rhodesia (now Zimbabwe), English settlers declared independence in 1965 and held out against majority rule until 1980.

No less difficult were the three cases that moved to prominence in the last decades of the twentieth century—that of the Dutch settlers in South Africa, Zionist state builders in Palestine, and the elites of Spanish descent in Central America. Each fought tenaciously against indigenous opposition forces, resulting in conflicts that were cruel, exhausting, and intractable.

South African Apartheid under Siege

South Africa stands as perhaps the starkest example of settler colonialism. In what became a carefully regulated racial hierarchy, a minority of whites (16 percent of South Africa's 29 million people in 1980) stood on top. A majority of blacks (72 percent) were on the bottom. "Coloureds" (people of mixed race) and "Asians" (primarily Indians), totaling together about 12 percent, fell in between. The mythology of white supremacy masked the diversity of the population. Whites were not monolithic but broke into Anglos and Afrikaners, with the latter accounting for more than half of all whites. Blacks were also diverse, with most belonging to one of five groups. The Zulu was the largest, followed by the Xhosa.

Afrikaner Control. European settlers, primarily Dutch but also French Protestants and Germans, came to southern Africa's Cape of Good Hope beginning in the mid-seventeenth century under the auspices of the Dutch East India Company, which sought a way station to its colonies in South and Southeast Asia. In the course of the eighteenth century, these settlers developed a distinct national identity and their own Afrikaans language. As these settlers moved into the countryside to produce goods for local consumption, they set off a brutal frontier struggle with indigenous peoples, whom they drove from their land and coerced into farm labor on terms quite close to slavery. Just as in the European coloniza-tion of the Americas, diseases introduced by the foreigners ravaged the indige-nous populations. During the nineteenth century the British, drawn by diamond and gold deposits, constituted a new and aggressive presence, crushing resistance from the Zulu kingdom along the east coast and then engaging the Afrikaners in an armed conflict known as the Boer War (1899–1902). This struggle ended with the British prevailing militarily but resolved to move toward a political accommodation. The Union of South Africa, set up in 1910, was the first step toward the creation of an Afrikaner-controlled state in which British residents would run mining and industry and enjoy the privileges Afrikaners demanded for all whites.

Afrikaners resisted the post–World War II trend toward decolonization. They had made South Africa their home and so had everything to lose by conceding majority rule. The 1948 election victory of the Afrikaners' National Party estab-lished *apartheid* (literally, "apartness") as the guiding principle in South Africa's domestic affairs, rationalizing and regulating a regime of white supremacy. The party promoted the view, sanctioned by the Dutch Reformed Church, that Afrikaners were a chosen people working out their destiny in a God-given land: The pious early settlers had justly swept away a scattering of "heathen natives," preserved their way of life, and made the land blossom into the most economi-cally developed country in Africa.

Apartheid was a rigid and intricate system whose chief goal was to isolate whites from nonwhites insofar as modern industrial life and white comfort made it possible. Blacks were to live in government-designated tribal homelands (*bantu-stans*) scattered across South Africa. This scheme assigned blacks (nearly three-quarters of the population) their own states occupying a bit more than one-tenth of South Africa's land, most of it poor. Though in fact only half of all South African blacks ever lived in their assigned homeland, they nonetheless legally ceased to be citizens of South Africa. Afrikaners could now claim that there was no black majority, only collections of black "tribes," each of which had its own land. These pseudo-states operated under the close supervision of the South African government in Pretoria, and none was recognized internationally.

With a developed, industrial economy heavily reliant on black labor, apartheid had to tolerate black settlements near all the major cities, but an intri-cate system of pass laws strictly controlled blacks' movement and kept them from settling too close to whites. The pass laws required that blacks carry written per-mission to travel from homelands, to live in makeshift townships, and to travel from those townships to work. Apartheid also made interracial contact—whether public or private—illegal. On the job blacks were restricted to menial work. They had limited opportunity to advance to more skilled positions or to acquire education. Pay was dramatically lower for blacks than for whites doing the same work. Blacks could not participate in national political institutions. State repression and censorship protected the system from critics, and a vigilant, ruth-less security force silenced dissidents and responded violently to demonstrations.

As a system of control, apartheid rested ultimately on violence. Black children quickly learned this basic fact. One youth later recalled an early morning raid in

1966 when a pair of black policemen enforcing the pass law had burst into his family's shack in a black township just outside Johannesburg.

> Before I knew what was happening one of them had kicked me savagely on the side, sending me crashing into a crate in the far corner.... [M]y knees had turned to Jell-O, my eyes were cloudy and my head pounded as if it were being split with an axe. As I tried to gather my senses, another kick sent me back to the floor, flat on my face.... My head burned with pain. Blood began oozing from my nostrils and lips. Several of my teeth were loose. I started screaming, . . . begging for forgiveness from my assailant for whatever wrong I had done.[10]

A six-year-old had learned a hard lesson about the power of apartheid to effect social control through terror.

Apartheid also left its mark on South Africa's external policy. South Africa was first roused to action by the rise of independent, black-ruled states sharply critical of apartheid. Growing international criticism further increased Pretoria's sense of isolation and its grim determination to protect its way of life. To ensure that it could defend itself in the face of an international arms embargo, South Africa developed its own arms industry and an advanced nuclear weapons program, both in cooperation with Israel. To maintain a security buffer, South Africa sought to intimidate its neighbors. It retained control of Namibia (a German colony before World War I), defying UN calls for independence and fighting a Namibian resistance movement (SWAPO) operating out of Angola. Elsewhere it intervened to overthrow or destabilize governments that provided refuge for anti-apartheid activists.

Mandela and the ANC. The African National Congress (ANC) emerged as the chief foe of apartheid. Established in 1912, it sought democratic freedoms and an end to segregation in all forms. It was guided at first by middle-class blacks committed to nonviolent struggle. In their approach they had been influenced by the direct example of Mohandas K. Gandhi, who had during his time in South Africa fought for civil rights in this way and later employed nonviolent tactics in the movement for India's independence (see Chapter 3). Following the victory of the National Party in 1948, the ANC became ever more militant. The Sharpeville massacre in March 1960 marked a turning point. The killing of sixty-seven unarmed blacks protesting the pass laws made clear that the white-controlled state would not bow to peaceful demands for change. Moreover, the incident was followed by the banning of the ANC and the arrest of eighteen thousand people. The ANC, now operating underground and in exile, shifted to a strategy of armed struggle. An ANC flyer explained, "The choice is not ours; it has been made by the National government which has rejected every peaceable demand by the people for rights and freedom and answered every such demand with force and yet more force!"[11] ANC leaders conducted the struggle in a way that would limit loss of life. They discarded terror tactics as too likely to produce bitterness that would make it difficult for whites and nonwhites to live together in a post-apartheid society. The ANC also rejected open rebellion as too costly in terms of black lives.

The ANC program contained three main elements. It looked to a united South Africa in which the artificial homelands would be eliminated. It sought black representation in the national parliament on a one-person, one-vote basis. And it anticipated a continued white presence in a society accepting of all races. What was not clear was how far the ANC would go in redistributing wealth and how far in general it might want to take control of the economy. The leadership did not agree on these delicate issues, and in any case it did not want to take a stand that might alienate white allies and overseas supporters and investors.

Nelson Mandela emerged as the leader of the ANC. Born in 1918, he was the son of a minor chief. After attending a mission school, he enrolled in 1938 in a black university but in 1940 was expelled after heading a protest with another future ANC leader, Oliver Tambo. In 1942 Mandela got his law degree, and in 1952 he and Tambo formed the first black law partnership in Johannesburg. In 1957 his first marriage ended in divorce; his second wife was Nomzamo Madikizela (better known as "Winnie"), who would in time play her own independent role in ANC politics.

Over a twenty-year period Mandela rose to political prominence. In 1944 he joined with Tambo and others to organize the ANC's Youth League, and in 1949 this new generation of leaders took over the whole organization. They insisted on the vision of a multiracial South Africa. (Blacks opposed to this multiracial vision left the ANC in 1959 to create the Pan-Africanist Congress.) The new leadership also insisted on moving beyond talk and petitioning to public protest and civil disobedience. After the Sharpeville massacre, Mandela joined in the decision to abandon nonviolence and was arrested in 1962. He used his trial as a platform for ANC goals, telling the court, "I have cherished the ideal of a democratic and free society in which all persons live together in harmony and with equal opportunities. It is an ideal which I hope to live for and to achieve. But if needs be, it is an ideal for which I am prepared to die."[12]

Convicted and given a life sentence, Mandela spent the first eighteen years in a harsh maximum-security prison, and then from 1981 he enjoyed more comfortable confinement with increasingly free access to visitors and information. During his long imprisonment Mandela served as the symbol of the ANC's steadfast resistance, while Tambo headed the organization in exile. A defiant Mandela turned down offers by the government to release him if he promised to abstain from involvement in politics. He warned that demands for an end to apartheid and power sharing would eventually prevail—if possible through negotiations but if necessary through violence. Looking to a post-apartheid future, he sought to reassure whites: "Unlike white people anywhere else in Africa, whites in South Africa belong here—this is their home." On this point he was emphatic. "We want them to live here with us and to share power with us."[13]

Despite vigorous government efforts to crush it, the anti-apartheid movement continued. The ANC enjoyed strong support from a younger generation, apparent in the 1976 Soweto riots in which 575 people were killed and again in the riots throughout the summer of 1985, in which unrest reached for the first time from black townships into white residential areas. Other groups joined the ANC in pressing the anti-apartheid cause. The Black Consciousness Movement, devoted to the idea of separate black development, flourished in the late 1960s, part of a broader trend in the African diaspora. At first the National Party approved, but in the early 1970s Pretoria repressed the movement, and its leader, Steve Biko, was murdered in police detention in 1973. Peaceful opposition to apartheid then fell to the United Democratic Front (a moderate, multiracial organization created in 1983), churches, and religious leaders such as Anglican bishop Desmond Tutu. But they too ran afoul of government restrictions and were banned from political activities. Finally, labor organizations became more influential as they incorporated an increasingly politically aware black industrial working class. Black unions, legalized in 1979, had leverage because white owners recognized their heavy dependence on black labor and their vulnerability to disruptive protests and strikes.

This mounting domestic pressure on the white government was reinforced by outside pressures. Neighboring territories were moving during the 1970s toward independence and open support of the anti-apartheid movement. Portugal was ready after 1974 to give up control of Mozambique and Angola, while the white settler government in Rhodesia began to crumble in 1979. Criticism from the United States and other Western countries culminated in the 1980s in an international sanctions and divestment movement to isolate the apartheid regime and get corporations to sell off ("divest") their holdings in South Africa. As international pressure mounted, the Reagan administration promoted "constructive engagement," arguing that persuasion was more likely to secure concessions and least likely to tear South Africa apart. But American leaders were also looking after their own interests, for they feared instability in the region that communists might exploit, worried about loss of access to strategic minerals, and wanted to protect the significant U.S. investments in South Africa.

The combination of internal protest, international pressure, hostile neighbors, and capital flight created intense pressures on the South African government and sent the economy into an alarming decline during the 1980s. P. W. Botha, the leader of the National Party and prime minister between 1978 and 1984, responded by offering the first limited concessions—what he called the "modernization" of apartheid. He was prepared to allow limited power-sharing with some nonwhites but not blacks. He wanted to revise the rules on segregation in order to accommodate the need for a black workforce near the site of industry, and he was ready to cut back on "petty apartheid" dividing the races at movie houses, beaches, and other public gathering places. Botha warned his white countrymen that South Africa had to "adapt or die."

These reforms spelled the beginning of the end for apartheid. They created divisions among Afrikaners and opportunities for greater organized resistance under the umbrella of the United Democratic Front. In 1985 in the face of rising protest, Botha (now president of the republic) began to crack down. While still promising reforms, he unleashed his security forces, which carried out mass arrests, engaged in torture, and conducted assassinations. In 1986 Pretoria declared martial law, and an uneasy truce descended on the country. But the ANC remained popular; it became increasingly well organized, and it retained a headquarters in nearby Zambia. Influential whites more and more recognized

Nelson Mandela on His Release from Prison in 1990
Mandela appears here with his wife, Winnie. They had married in 1958 just as the ANC was entering prolonged, fierce struggle against apartheid. Winnie valiantly supported Mandela and the ANC during his twenty-eight years of imprisonment and developed her own political following. Her more militant views, controversy over violence by her loyalists, and a gulf created by the long separation ultimately destroyed the marriage. (© Gideon Mendel/Magnum Photos)

that repression had failed and that the government would have to talk with the ANC if the transition to a new order was to be achieved without destroying the economy and their privileged lifestyle with it.

Botha's carrot-and-stick strategy having failed, his successor, F. W. de Klerk, moved more boldly to work out an accommodation. In 1989 de Klerk began dismantling major elements in the apartheid system, disengaging from costly interventions in neighboring states, and accepting independence for Namibia. He was even prepared to legalize the ANC and begin negotiations with it. But initially he was not willing to give blacks the vote. In 1990 de Klerk took the dramatic step of releasing Mandela from prison and discussing terms for a transition to full democracy. Under a one-person, one-vote system, blacks would be the overwhelming majority, so the minority whites sought safeguards. In February 1993 the ANC reached an agreement with de Klerk on a five-year transitional period of power-sharing. During that time minority parties would have a guaranteed voice in the government. White monopoly of political power was to end with elections in April 1994 for a 400-seat assembly that would in turn elect the president. The gradual approach was justified within the ANC as essential to avoiding a backlash among whites, who still controlled the state bureaucracy, the security forces, and the economy.

SOUTH AFRICA EMBATTLED

1652	First European settlers arrive
1899–1902	Boer War pits British against Afrikaners
1912	ANC is created
1948	National Party representing Afrikaners begins constructing a formal apartheid system
1960	Sharpeville massacre is followed by the banning of the ANC and the arrest or exile of its leaders; ANC abandons nonviolence
1962	Mandela is sentenced to life imprisonment
1976	Soweto riots set off broad protest in South Africa
1978	Botha begins limited reform of apartheid
1984	Protest becomes endemic in black townships, forcing Botha to resort to repression and declare state of emergency (1986)
1989	De Klerk begins dialogue with ANC; South Africa withdraws forces from Namibia
1990	Mandela's release from prison speeds move to power-sharing
1994	First post-apartheid elections put the ANC in power and Mandela in the presidency

These dramatic changes encountered some resistance. Alarmed Afrikaners organized in the Conservative and neo-Nazi parties made up one pocket of opposition, while within the ANC, Communists and some regional branches protested Mandela's go-slow course. Outside the ANC the Zulu-based Inkatha Freedom Party led by Mangosuthu Buthelezi wanted to protect regional Zulu interests and was willing to work with the white government to achieve that goal. From the other end of the political spectrum, the militant Pan-Africanist Congress attacked ANC moderation.

The April 1994 national elections successfully inaugurated the new democratic system while yielding, as expected, a victory for the ANC and the election of Mandela as president. But a South Africa in which blacks had finally won freedom now had to confront issues long familiar to sub-Saharan states that had gained their independence some three decades earlier: how to reconcile imposed Western economic and cultural forms with the values and institutions of the majority population. Like Ghana (see Chapter 6) and other states in the region, South Africa's course was complicated by the diversity of its population.

Yet, whatever the commonalities, the effects of a developed and diverse economy as well as prolonged political repression set South Africa on a course that distinguished it from the rest of the region. The movement of blacks into mining and industry had eroded local loyalties, so influential in other sub-Saharan states.

As migrants left homelands for jobs in the modern sector, black urban residents increased from 4.9 million in 1960 to 9.2 million in 1980. Black labor had grown over those years from 0.5 million to 1.1 million, or three-quarters of the work-force. Political struggle against apartheid had further blurred ethnic lines. ANC membership from the start had transcended "tribal" identity, and the long exile and imprisonment of ANC leaders intensified their tendency to see the future in nonsectarian terms. Finally, Mandela's successor, Tabo Mbeki, would not attempt a socialist quick fix in response to the profound frustration of blacks over their living standards. Mbeki, himself a devotee of the free market, agreed with Mandela that a significant redistribution of wealth would alienate skilled whites, scare off foreign investment, and thus undermine the advanced sectors of the economy. South Africa would have to live with the divisive and potentially dangerous legacy of sharp inequalities bequeathed by apartheid.

Conflict over Palestine

Palestine, a land hugging the eastern coast of the Mediterranean, has multiple claims to historical fame. Three of the world's major religions—Judaism, Christianity, and Islam—have venerated its chief city, Jerusalem, as a holy place. Palestine has also been the crossroads of empires for several thousand years—from the ancient Jewish kingdom three thousand years ago, to Roman overlordship dating back two thousand years, to Islamic conquest during the seventh century, and finally to European dominance in the nineteenth and early twentieth centuries. The last half-century has brought another chapter in Palestine's history with striking similarities to the case of South Africa. Here too settler colonialism took the form of a European-inspired and -promoted nationalism bearing strong religious overtones. In Palestine as in South Africa, European success came at the expense of indigenous people, and it gave rise to fierce and determined opposition. In this case the creation and expansion of the Jewish-dominated state of Israel, itself an expression of nationalism, provoked Arabs, for the most part Muslim and long settled in the region, to develop their own distinct Palestinian nationalism.

The Zionist Drive for a Jewish Homeland. The contest for the land occupied by the state of Israel began well before its creation in 1948. On the Jewish side, a Zionist faith sprang up in the late nineteenth century that inspired dreams of winning a homeland. Jews scattered throughout the Mediterranean world and across Europe had lived as second-class citizens, often discriminated against and sometimes brutally persecuted. Theodore Herzl and other leaders of the early Zionist movement argued that only when Jews had their own state would they be free from discrimination and violence. The nationalist movements taking shape in nineteenth-century Europe provided an even more important spur; Jews had either to embrace the identities decreed by these movements or construct their own distinct national identity. The appeal of Zionism was strongest among Jews in western Russia and Poland, where both anti-Semitic violence and combat among nationalist groups were most intense. The first Zionist congress, held in 1897, focused its search for national territory on Palestine (the site of the king-dom of David three thousand years earlier and of the twice-destroyed Temple of Jerusalem) and supported a campaign to convince the Ottoman Empire to allow Jewish immigrants into this part of its domain. One early settlement proponent, a Russian Jew who reached Palestine in 1882, made clear Jewish determination to become "masters of their ancient homeland." The task, he explained, was clear: "We must establish agricultural settlements, factories and industry. We must develop industry and put it in Jewish hands. And above all, we must give young people military training and provide them with weapons."[14]

During World War I, Britain took Palestine from the Ottomans. This appar-ent imperial asset quickly turned into a liability as British authorities became caught between two conflicting populations. On the one side were some eighty thousand Jewish settlers by 1914 representing Zionist aspirations. On the other side was an Arab majority, in excess of half a million, resentful of the foreigners pressing in on them. In 1917 Britain put itself squarely in the middle of this emerging ethnic conflict by issuing what was known as the Balfour Declaration. That document raised Zionist hopes by endorsing the idea of "a national home for the Jewish people" in Palestine, but at the same time it promised not to "prej-udice the civil and religious rights of existing non-Jewish communities" there. Indeed, Britain indicated in the course of the war that it favored the creation of an Arab state.[15]

After World War I, tensions grew as Zionist organizations in Europe contin-ued to finance a growing Jewish presence in Palestine. Persecution of Jews in Germany and elsewhere in Europe in the late 1930s gave a special urgency to immigration. By 1939 some four hundred and fifty thousand Jews were in Pales-tine, constituting 30 percent of the population. The newcomers steadily encroached on Arab land and threatened majority rights. Zionist leaders expected Arab resistance and saw no choice but to overcome it. As one put it candidly, "I don't know of a single example in history where a country was col-onized with the courteous consent of the population."[16] By the mid-1930s Palestine was the scene of growing social unrest, which Britain tried to calm by limiting Jewish immigration and instituting strict control of land sales to Jews. London also announced plans to end its control within a decade, adding that it did not support the creation of a Jewish state.

Arab-Jewish relations in Palestine, already under severe strain, collapsed under the pressure of World War II. The accumulated costs of war undercut Britain's capacity as a colonial power to control the situation in Palestine. At the same time the Zionist drive intensified as a result of the Holocaust. The death of six million European Jews gave fresh international moral force to long-standing Zionist aspirations. Sympathy in the United States was particularly strong, and American Jews became vocal and generous supporters of the homeland drive. At the same time many Holocaust survivors were struggling amidst the chaos of the early postwar period to reach Palestine. Anticipating British retreat and eager to receive these desperate refugees, armed Zionist groups began to assert territorial claims in 1944. Jewish political leaders such as David Ben-Gurion, the leading figure in the independence struggle, were determined to make Palestinian Arabs accept Zionist predominance: If they refused, then the Jews had to persuade them by force. The logic of military force, already central in Zionist thinking, would come to define Israel's relations to its Arab neighbors.

With tensions mounting and the British on their way out, the newly established United Nations tried in 1947 to devise a compromise solution. The proposal was to split Palestine into an Arab and a Jewish state with Jerusalem designated an international city. The United States and the USSR both supported this proposed partition, as did the Jews of Palestine. But Arabs facing loss of their homeland adamantly refused to accept any Zionist political entity, and their irregular forces began attacking Jewish settlements. When in May 1948 Jewish leaders formally proclaimed the founding of the state of Israel, a league of Arab states (Egypt, Syria, Transjordan, Lebanon, and Iraq) attacked. Though outnumbered, Israeli forces were well armed and well led, and they managed to defeat the Arab coalition. The fighting finally ended in 1949 under UN auspices with Israel gaining more territory than originally envisioned in the partition plan (including half of Jerusalem). The conflict had driven seven hundred thousand Palestinians to take refuge in neighboring countries. Many were driven from their homes by Israeli forces; some fled in fear. About one hundred fifty thousand were still left in Israel. But they were now a minority in a state dominated by a Jewish majority of nearly seven hundred thousand.

Israel and the Occupied Territories. The strong Zionist vision of a new homeland and the generosity of the Jewish community abroad, key ingredients to the birth of the new state, were also key to the state's survival and expansion amidst hostile neighbors. This state born in war faced almost constant border conflicts with its neighbors and repeated wars. The next war erupted in 1956 with Ben-Gurion's government plotting with Britain and France to attack Gamal Abdul Nasser's Egypt. In June 1967 Israel passed through its third major test of arms known as the Six-Day War. With tensions building on both the Egyptian and Syrian frontiers, the Israeli military launched a surprise attack, confident of its superiority. In six days of fighting it scored a stunning victory, taking the Sinai and the Gaza Strip from Egypt, the West Bank (including East Jerusalem) from Jordan, and the Golan Heights from Syria. (See Chapter 6.)

The 1967 conquests not only deepened the hostility throughout the Middle East but also cast Israel into the role of an occupying power exercising control over a substantial and resentful Palestinian population in the West Bank and Gaza. On the West Bank, Israel would make strenuous efforts to encourage Jewish settlements, seize Palestinian lands, and destroy Palestinian homes. But despite new settlements and military and bureaucratic repression, Israelis could not keep up with the natural Palestinian population increase. By 2002 Jewish settlers accounted for only 10 percent of the total West Bank and Gaza populations, while within all Israeli-controlled territory (Israel proper along with occupied lands), Jews dropped from 65 percent of the population just after the 1967 war to 51 percent by the year 2002.

MAP 9.1
Israeli Expansion, 1947–2000

The future of these occupied lands became the most divisive issue in Israel's fragmented democracy. The Labor Party, the creation of Israel's founders, was the most influential advocate of a deal trading occupied land for peace. Without resolving the Palestinian problem, so Labor leaders argued, Israel would remain a garrison state that could not focus its resources on domestic development, cultivate cooperative relationships with neighbors, and end the cycle of violent protest and brutal repression. In the 1970s an alternative, more religious and expansionist position articulated by the Likud Party gained popular support, and Likud remained into the 1990s the most influential party. Likud governments dreaming of a "Greater Israel" pushed Jewish settlements on the West Bank (calling them by the Biblical names of Judea and Samaria) and resisted concessions that might compromise control of the occupied lands.

The 1967 war and the rise of Likud completed Israel's transformation into a type of settler colonialism that denigrated the locals as backward and terrorists and denied their claims to a distinct political identity and state. As Israel's prime minister, Golda Meir, famously observed in 1969, "It was not as though there was a Palestinian people . . . and we came and threw them out and took their country away from them. They did not exist."[17] Predictably in Israel, as in South

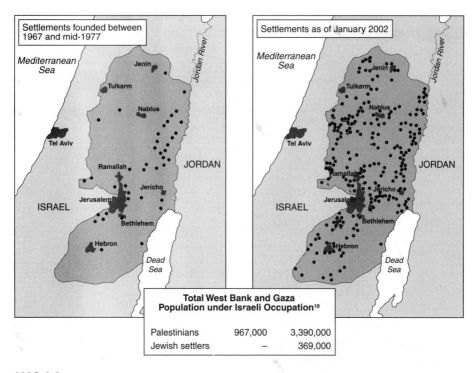

MAP 9.2
Israeli Settlements in the West Bank, 1967–2002
Jewish settlers moved almost exclusively into East Jerusalem and the West Bank. In 2002 settlers in the Gaza Strip totaled only five thousand (about 1 percent of all settlers).

Africa, an externally inspired process of settlement and state building would eventually provoke from the overwhelmed indigenous people their own counter-response.

The Rise of Palestinian Nationalism. At the very time in the 1960s and 1970s that the colonial tide was receding elsewhere and Zionism was scoring major victories, desperate Palestinians began to consolidate their own sense of identity and find ways to give that identity political and cultural expression. The chief vehicle for this gathering nationalist movement was the Palestine Liberation Organization (PLO), created in 1964 by Palestinians living in exile in the Persian Gulf oil states. The PLO charter, issued in the aftermath of the Six-Day War, called for armed struggle by the "Arab nation" to liberate all of Palestine from a "racist and fanatic" Zionist presence backed by "international imperialism."[19] In 1969 Yasir Arafat, head of the PLO's Al Fatah faction, took the helm of this coalition of guerrilla organizations.

But Arafat's PLO encountered setback after setback. The PLO resorted to a campaign of terror within Israel and attacks along its border. At first it operated out of Jordan, but a political crisis in that country forced the PLO in 1970 to make Lebanon its base. Israel responded in 1982 by launching an invasion aimed at eliminating the PLO from Lebanon and creating a security zone in the southernmost part of that country bordering Israel. (The intervention intensified a civil conflict that had since 1975 divided Lebanese along religious and politics lines and would claim the lives of 144,000 until finally in 1990 Syrian forces imposed peace.) Under Syrian pressure in 1983, Arafat and his PLO associates had to abandon Lebanon for Tunisia.

At the same time, Egypt and other Arab states were deserting the Palestinian cause. Egypt's defection from the anti-Israel united front was an especially serious blow. Egypt's leader, Anwar Sadat, had confronted Israel militarily in October 1973 with the hopes of drawing the United States, Israel's main source of international support, into a more balanced, mediating role in regional disputes. In the talks that followed the war, Sadat conceded the right of Israel to exist, and in return Israel agreed to return the Sinai. Sadat's dramatic visit to Israel in 1977 marked his country's public abandonment of the anti-Israeli united front. Muslim militants gunned Sadat down in 1981, while Israel still firmly held the other fruits of the 1967 war.

These blows to the externally based PLO during the 1970s and 1980s created an opening for a campaign of resistance by Palestinians in the West Bank and Gaza. Their uprising (or *intifada,* literally, "shaking off") began in the Gaza Strip in December 1987 after an Israeli truck hit and killed a group of Palestinians, and it quickly spread to the West Bank. It was inspired by a desperate realization that neither the Arab states nor the PLO had made any headway against an increasingly oppressive Israeli occupation. Those who daily bore the indignities and losses at the hands of that occupation resolved to act. Rock-throwing and other public acts of violence against Israeli forces as well as campaigns of civil disobedience such as withholding of taxes and general strikes became the main expression of this new strategy of resistance. With the *intifada* came new leaders who included prominent local figures loyal to but not formally a part of the PLO but also those linked to the Islamic Resistance Movement (or Hamas). Hamas called for open, violent resistance as the only language the Israelis would understand. Leading the Palestinian protest were students and youth groups. A leaflet circulated by the resistance one month into the *intifada* breathed defiance: "We will burn the ground under the feet of the occupiers. Let the whole world know that the eruption . . . by the Palestinian people will not be extinguished until the achievement of independence in a Palestinian state with Jerusalem as its capital."[20]

Hanan Mikhail-Ashrawi was one of this new generation of Palestinian nationalists. She and others like her combined higher education (sometimes in foreign universities) and a keen identification with their imperiled homeland. They made their mission finding a voice for their people in art, literature, and education as well as politics. Ashrawi was born in October 1946 in Nablus at the end of the British mandate. Her father was a medical officer in the Palestinian army. Both parents were Christians. After attending Quaker school, she went on to college at the American University in Beirut. The Six-Day War was the enduring trauma in Ashrawi's life. Israel's refusal to accept the existence of Palestinians as a separate people with their own roots in the land became less tenable as that identity became ever sharper in the minds of those sent into exile or those such as Ashrawi still living under occupation, many in grim refugee camps.

One of her poems captures the importance of place—of land that had belonged to her family and fields, streams, rocks, and paths that she had known as a child, now subject to aggressive Israeli expropriation and to bulldozers that demolished home after home.

> Have you seen a stone house die?
> It sighs, then wraps itself
> Around its gutted heart and lays
> Itself to rest to become
> One with the earth who's in
> The process of giving birth to
> Yet more stones.[21]

Loss of the land—or perhaps worse, exile from it—was a nightmare that she shared with others now radicalized by prolonged occupation.

Ashrawi's keen sense of Palestinian identity carried her into political activism, following in the footsteps of her father who had played a role in setting up the PLO. Galvanized by the Six-Day War, she worked in Palestinian refugee camps in Lebanon and learned to deal with the foreign press. After getting a doctorate in literature at the University of Virginia, Ashrawi returned home in 1973 to build an English department in the Palestinian Birzeit University, tutoring students in the language of Palestinian nationalism. The *intifada* made her a public figure—the voice of the protest movement to the international media and a member of a political committee to speak for the *intifada*. Ashrawi proved a blunt, spirited, and articulate spokesperson. She made it difficult for foreigners, especially Americans, to dismiss her people as "terrorists." They suffered, she made clear, real injustices that cried out for resolution.

Pressures were now building in favor of compromise. The *intifada* was proving costly to both sides. Within the first two years alone, 615 Palestinians had been killed, over fifteen thousand wounded, and fifty thousand arrested and imprisoned. Israelis also paid a price—45 killed, the expense of maintaining an occupation force of some ten thousand troops, and growing popular divisions among Israelis over the repression. In 1988 Arafat extended an olive branch by recognizing Israel's right to exist. He now became a more eligible negotiating partner. Washington remained Israel's chief supporter, providing $3 billion a year in aid and using its UN Security Council veto to protect Israel against international sanctions. However, the fading of Soviet influence gave Washington new freedom to maneuver. The first Bush administration was soon making diplomatic contacts with Palestinians, pressing successfully for Middle East peace talks, and withholding loan guarantees to stop the creation of new Jewish settlements on the West Bank. Israel also felt the end of the Cold War indirectly in the growing exodus of Soviet Jews. As a result of the liberalization of Soviet immigration pol-

Hanan Ashrawi in May 1999
Israeli police push Ashrawi from a site in traditionally Arab East Jerusalem
where Palestinians were protesting the building of apartments for Jewish
settlers. Ashrawi emerged as a forceful international voice during the first
intifada. She remained prominent as a member of the legislature and minister
of education in Arafat's Palestinian Authority. (AP Photo/ZOOM 77)

icy, about three hundred and fifty thousand Soviet Jews reached Israel between
mid-1989 and early 1992. As long as Israel stayed on a war footing, the housing,
social services, and jobs needed by the newcomers would be in short supply.

In 1993 representatives from the PLO and Israel's Labor government headed
by Yitzhak Rabin (the commander of Israeli forces during the Six-Day War)
finally met in secret. In what became known as the Oslo Accords, each agreed to
formally recognize the existence of the other and attempt to reach a mutually
acceptable resolution of the status of the West Bank, Gaza, and occupied East
Jerusalem. Thanks to these contacts, Arafat was able to return home in July 1994
and organize a de facto government known as the Palestinian Authority. His initial area of control was limited to Gaza and the city of Jericho on the West Bank.
He did not get Jewish settlements stopped, nor did he secure any clear timetable
for the creation of a Palestinian state. The administrative and military initiative
was still in the hands of the Israelis. Some who had led the *intifada* resented the
terms Arafat negotiated but also the corruption and backstage factional dealing
that characterized PLO control.

The lack of progress toward ending the occupation opened the way to polarization on both sides and rising levels of recrimination and violence. Frustrated
Palestinians embraced the Hamas hard line in what became known as the second

THE STRUGGLE FOR PALESTINE

1897	First Zionist congress calls for a Jewish homeland in Palestine
1917	British forces take Palestine after promising support to Arabs and Jews
1948–1949	Britain abandons Palestine; Israel declares independence, turns back attack by Arab neighbors, and expels Palestinians to neighboring countries
1956	Israel joins Britain and France in an abortive attack on Egypt
1964	PLO is formed
1967	Six-Day War ends with Israel's defeat of Egypt, Jordan, and Syria; Israel gains the Sinai Peninsula, the West Bank, the Gaza Strip, and the Golan Heights
1969	Arafat assumes leadership of the PLO
1970	PLO is ousted from Jordan
1973	Israel defeats Egypt in the October War
1977–1979	Egypt's Sadat defects from the Arab united front, makes peace with Israel, and gains return of the Sinai Peninsula
1982	Israeli forces invade Lebanon, create security zone in the south, and put the PLO on the defensive
1983	PLO is forced by Syria to abandon Lebanon; relocates in Tunisia
1987	*Intifada* begins in Gaza and the West Bank
1993	Israel and the PLO initiate direct contacts, paving the way for the creation of a Palestinian Authority for the West Bank and Gaza
2000	*Intifada* resumes

intifada inaugurated in September 2000. Many Israelis still saw Arafat as a terrorist. Jewish settlers regarded any move to surrender their West Bank land as a historic betrayal, and they regarded even Jews as illustrious as Rabin ready to trade land for peace as traitors deserving of death. (A Jewish extremist did in fact assassinate Rabin in 1995 for precisely this reason.) Israeli forces withdrawn early in the reconciliation process returned to retaliate against bombings and attacks on settlements. Palestinians killed by air strikes, ground forces, and assassination automatically became "terrorists" in the pronouncements of Israeli authorities and martyrs in Palestinian eyes. Israeli public opinion hardened, and the Likud Party and its hard-line religious allies resolved to meet resistance with military retaliation and renewed occupation. The tide had turned against peace; the future seemed to promise the kind of prolonged bloodletting all too familiar from other cases of settler colonialism.

Repression and Resistance in Guatemala

Stubborn systems of internal oppression drawn along racial lines in South Africa and along national lines in Palestine assumed yet a third form in Guatemala. In this third case of settler colonialism, the European conquest came in the form of the Spanish conquest of the Mayan people, thus deeply dividing the country into two groups (Ladino and Maya) astoundingly unequal in power and wealth and creating an enduring fault line. The Maya had intermittently resisted but not effectively until the latter third of the twentieth century, when they gained Ladino allies driven by a sense of class injustice and determined to work with the Maya to change the system. This trans-ethnic coalition found Ladinos accustomed to privilege and deference as determined and brutal in defense of their position as Afrikaners and Zionists.

Mobilizing the Maya. During Guatemala's era of reform and even after the 1954 coup against Arbenz (see Chapter 6), the majority Mayan population had sat on the sidelines of national politics. But beginning in the 1970s they began to enlist in a smoldering rural insurgency launched by dissident Ladinos. During what proved to be one of the longest of Central America's civil wars—lasting into the early 1990s—the insurgents with their base of Indian support never came close to toppling the government, but sabotage and armed clashes left Guatemala disrupted and tense.

The first signs of open internal conflict appeared in 1962. Junior military officers, angry over the government's rollback of the Arbenz reforms and inspired by the Cuban example, launched an insurgency. They failed to build a base of popular support, so when the army finally in 1966–1967 moved decisively against them, the insurrection collapsed, and the leaders fled to Mexico to regroup. After a brief period of calm, the insurrection resumed on a broader, more popular base. In 1972 the Guerrilla Army of the Poor inaugurated operations just across from the Mexican border under the leadership of Ricardo Ramírez. The son of an army officer, he had as a teenager supported the Arbenz reforms. The 1954 coup and the ensuing repression drove him to join the insurgency in the early 1960s. The failure of that effort convinced him that the ethnic struggle of the Indians was as important as class struggle. Thus concerns about working and living conditions for peasants and workers going back to the reform period joined with issues of cultural autonomy and respect that appealed to Mayan communities. The Guerrilla Army's focus on the cultural as well as the economic would draw the Indian population into the insurgency for the first time and ensure it a broad base.

The Guerrilla Army was joined in 1982 by other, smaller resistance groups under the umbrella organization known as the Guatemalan National Revolutionary Unity (GNRU) headquartered in Mexico with Ramírez the leading figure. Also participating were newly militant labor unions and dissident Catholic priests and nuns espousing a "liberation theology" of helping the poor through social action. It was not enough to save souls, they insisted; the Church should attack the sources of oppression and poverty. Long-festering social discontent sharpened by an economic crisis that began in 1973 and by the destruction wrought by a massive earthquake in 1976 created a sympathetic audience for groups calling for a new order in Guatemala.

This time Indians were ready to embrace the opposition. Indian political activism arose initially within peasant associations organized by the Committee of Peasant Unity, known by its Spanish acronym CUC. It had emerged in 1978 to stem the steady loss of Mayan land holdings. For the first time Indians made contact with each other across language divides, began to engage in sustained political organizing and education, and even developed ties with poor Ladinos. Government repression finally pushed newly politicized Indians into the arms of the guerrillas.

Faced with growing rural as well as urban unrest, the regular army emerged as the guarantor of the status quo and eventually became the dominant institution exercising control over the country. The army was assisted by civil defense patrols and vigilante groups and by the Johnson and Nixon administrations, which supplied military aid and advisors. Officers were becoming privileged, isolated from society, and above the law. When U.S. officials counseled restraint, army leaders responded defiantly. "If we want to kill each other off it's our business. The United States has no right to interfere."[22]

The army-controlled government conducted a campaign of violence against both guerrillas and labor activists that became most ferocious under General Romeo Lucas García, president between 1978 and 1982. He was alarmed by the leftist surge in neighboring countries that threatened to leave Guatemala more exposed to subversion. Sandinistas were about to overthrow the Nicaraguan dictator Somoza, while in El Salvador insurrection battered the government. The first rural repression occurred in the village of Panzós, where in May 1978 the army used indiscriminate killing of civilians as a counterinsurgent tool. If sufficiently intimidated, the army leaders argued, peasants would turn their backs on the rebels. Thus isolated, the rural resistance would surely collapse. Two years later the security forces began systematically "disappearing" labor organizers. Seized on the street or at home, these organizers were usually tortured and executed, their bodies left on remote roadsides as a warning to others with subversive ideas.

A Country in Deadlock.   By the early 1980s the army had blunted this second round of insurgency but at the price of alarming international investors and stirring up widespread international condemnation. In 1977 President Carter had cut off aid because of human rights abuses. In 1982 a military coup replaced Lucas García with General Efraín Ríos Montt, who tried to soften the counterinsurgency policy with the slogan "beans and bullets" and professed concern with popular needs. But the military remained deeply suspicious of popular organizations such as the CUC. Army units continued to attack entire villages suspected of sympathizing with the guerrillas, while the security forces and civil defense patrols abducted, tortured, and murdered suspected opponents. Ríos Montt noted candidly, "We have no scorched-earth policy. We have a policy of scorched Communists."[23]

Woman in Mayan Garb Protesting "Disappearances" The sign says, "Enough trampling on the dignity of our brothers! Immediate release of students detained yesterday!" The woman belongs to GAM, one of two major activist groups organized by women. (© Jenny Matthews)

In the face of this repression, many fled deep into the mountains or to Mexico. But the insurgents were able to maintain a force of several thousand in the field, while women's organizations sprang up (first GAM—Grupo de Apoyo Mutuo or, Mutual Support Group—in 1984 and then Conavigua in 1988) and sponsored demonstrations that boldly challenged the government. They demanded an accounting for "disappeared" husbands, sons, and other male relatives. They also pursued a program familiar to social feminists (see Chapter 5) of demanding help in their daily effort to make a living and raise their children. They wanted food, medical care, housing, and clothing; government assistance in meeting education costs; and legislation to protect the interests of widows and poor women. In a society deeply divided along ethnic lines, widows and other women came together on the basis of common experiences of gender oppression and common grievances against the government. As one activist observed, "Our suffering has helped us to understand our social situation and it encourages us to be more active in changing it. We know that if women don't do something, this killing is never going to end."[24]

THE PRESSURE BUILDS IN GUATEMALA	
1962	Junior officers launch an insurrection
1972	Guerrilla Army of the Poor restarts resistance with appeal to Indian population
1978	CUC emerges; government of Romeo Lucas García intensifies repression against guerrillas and labor unions
1982	GNRU is formed to coordinate resistance groups
1984	First of women's organizations (GAM) takes to the streets
1986	Army leaders step aside in favor of an elected civilian president
1991	Government opens talks with GNRU
1996	Peace accords are concluded

Changes in the upper class also held some promise of ameliorating Guatemala's crisis. Up to World War II the elite had consisted of only two hundred families. In the postwar period it expanded its ranks while also extending its holdings from land into banking, industry, and commerce. By the 1990s it was in a quandary. It feared that concessions to the poor—higher wages, improved sanitary conditions, better education, and help for agricultural cooperatives—would only lead to demands for more far-reaching change, especially land redistribution. But to reject change was to lock Guatemala in underdevelopment and leave the upper class to face a resentful and militant underclass on the one side and an out-of-control army on the other. By 1986 the civil war had intensified the country's social crisis, with two-thirds of the population in poverty and illiterate and at least one-half unemployed or underemployed. Finally, the receding radical tide in neighboring states left elites feeling less exposed. In 1990 the Sandinistas were voted out of power in Nicaragua, and two years later peace talks in El Salvador brought an end to the civil conflict there.

The ballot box began to hold some appeal in the mid-1980s as a way of breaking Guatemala's costly deadlock. After a series of military coups, the army decided in 1986 to hand the government over to the first elected civilian leader in twenty years. The new president had run on a social reform platform, but once in office he found his hands tied by an army that still regarded itself as the ultimate arbiter of the nation's destiny. His successor, elected in 1991, was Jorge Serrano Elías, an evangelical Protestant. Serrano believed that economic development depended on peace, which in turn meant negotiating a cease-fire and drawing guerrillas into the electoral process. By then Ramírez, speaking for the resistance coalition, had also recognized that peace negotiations were the only way out of the country's destructive deadlock. Talks between the government and the resistance began in April 1991 and finally produced an accord in 1996 that promised social reforms, free elections, and respect for Mayan languages and traditions. The return of Arbenz's remains for burial with honors in 1995 and the creation of a truth commission to bring to light past abuses were significant albeit symbolic steps toward reconciliation. Guatemala had gained relief from violence that had caused the death or disappearance of two hundred thousand people, which investigators attributed almost entirely to government forces. But the country still faced the formidable challenge of creating a shared sense of nationhood and a working consensus on economic development. As in Palestine, so too in Guatemala, settler colonialism had generated a conflict by entangling two very different peoples yet leaving little grounds for compromise.

DREAMS OF DEVELOPMENT IN DISARRAY

While revolution of one sort or another continued to convulse some parts of the developing world and bitter internal conflict engulfed others, the siren call of integration into the international economy gripped a third substantial segment. In the early postwar period a wide sweep of the third world had embraced extensive state control and promotion and protection for industry and then found that it yielded disappointing economic growth rates. In most cases transition to the market was attended by frustration related in some measure to external conditions such as whether demand was weak or strong for the commodities available for export. But internal problems—notably the adverse effects of rapid population growth, the neglect of women as an important human resource, and deepening environmental degradation—also put a drag on economic growth and offset gains that struggling economies in transition were able to eke out. This plunge into the market left many developing countries adrift, without a galvanizing vision to put in the place of the formerly appealing socialist and revolutionary models.

Stalemated Economies

The widespread shift during the last decades of the twentieth century from inward-looking, usually socialist policies to outward-oriented market principles had several sources. The Soviet economic model was losing its appeal, and then Soviet assistance declined and finally disappeared along with the Soviet Union itself. The palpable success of the "little dragons," those capitalist outposts on Asia's maritime periphery, strengthened the case for the free market. China underwent a gradual economic transformation that left it socialist in name but increasingly market driven in fact, and Vietnam was close behind (see Chapter 8). Chile's economy thrived after the military seized power and technocrats forced market reforms on the country with bayonets backing them up. These profitable adaptations undermined the notion that capitalism was an inherently exploitative dead-end for the third world.

But it soon became apparent that the turn to international markets worked for some but not all. Countries heavily dependent on one or two crops or minerals for export (such as Kenya with its coffee and tea, Nigeria with its oil, and Honduras with its coffee and bananas) remained vulnerable. Developed countries continued to protect their own agricultural sector from developing world exports, and in any case a sudden drop in prices on international markets could quickly turn prosperity into hard times for producers of raw materials. Moreover, international investors could decide overnight to pull out, paralyzing production and undoing years of progress. Finally, the transition to the market required domestic sacrifices that fell heavily on the poor, generated pressure on elected leaders to pull back from painful market reforms, and imperiled the investment in infrastructure on which long-term competitiveness depended. The cases of Ghana, Brazil, and India illustrate the different ways in different regions that hopes for salvation through the global market gave way to sober reflection. Even countries that did all the right things measured progress in painfully small increments.

Ghana under Rawlings. A leader in the era of independence for sub-Saharan Africa, Ghana suffered through two decades of troubled economic policy. The difficulties had begun with Nkrumah's socialist project, which had fed ethnic suspicions and exhausted the country's financial reserves without generating sustainable growth. (See Chapter 6.) However, Nkrumah's successors between 1966 and 1981 through eight changes of government and five military coups followed an erratic and ineffective course that was even more harmful to the economy. Average annual gross domestic product (GDP) growth dropped from 2.8 percent in the 1960s to a negative 5.2 percent in the early 1980s. With the economy falling and the population rising from 6.2 million in 1957 to 12.2 million in 1984, Ghanaians watched their standard of living drop by about one-third. High infant mortality and low life expectancy indicated that development no less than democracy was in crisis.

Finally, a junior air force officer, Jerry Rawlings, came to the rescue. The man who would dominate Ghanaian politics over the next two decades was born in 1947 to a Scottish father and a Ghanaian mother (of Ewe background), earning him during his childhood the derisive description "a rusty white man."[25] His marriage to an Ashanti woman would further blur his ethnic identity. He joined the air force in 1967, just after Nkrumah's fall. Ghana's accumulating problems increasingly worried him. Those problems were in his view rooted not in economic exploitation by the West but rather in the misbehavior of Ghana's own elites—in-fighting among political parties, corruption among top military leaders, and mismanagement of the economy. He felt the need for a government that would focus on improving economic welfare and increasing mass political participation (including a greater role for women in the political process). In 1979 Rawlings joined other low-ranking soldiers in a bid for power. By late 1981 a Rawlings-led military government had taken firm control.

Although first attracted to Nkrumah's socialist vision, Rawlings dramatically shifted to free market principles championed by the World Bank, the International Monetary Fund (IMF), and other international lenders. His first step was to impose an austerity budget favored by Western financial advisors, slashing subsidies and producing hardship in both the city and the countryside. In 1985 Rawlings pushed his policy further forward by privatizing parts of the state-controlled

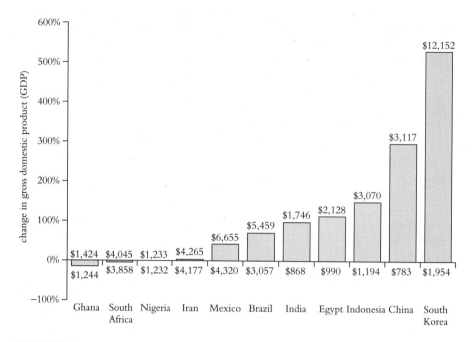

FIGURE 9.1

A Scorecard on Economic Performance in the Developing World, 1970–1998[26]

This graph shows the strikingly different rates of growth of selected developing countries over a quarter century. Those at the far left failed to make headway in increasing the size of their economies sufficient to improve the lives of their rising populations. The performance of individual countries listed here mirrors the overall performance within the main regions of the developing world. East Asia and parts of Southeast Asia did far and away the best. South Asia and Latin America followed with moderately strong growth. The economies of the Middle East and Africa were flat, showing either negligible increases or small declines. Some relatively well-to-do developing countries such as South Africa stagnated, while others that began this period poor, such as China, made dramatic headway. Actual per capita GDP (in constant 1990 dollars) is shown with 1970 figures at the baseline and 1998 figures at the far end of the bars.

economy, relaxing government regulations standing in the way of production, and cutting government budgets and bureaucracies. He tempered these measures by promoting rural development and reforming education to focus on skills. His reward was better economic performance. Agricultural production rose and food imports fell. Duly impressed, international investors made new loans available, and Ghana was able to import goods to develop industry and infrastructure. Economic growth turned strong, averaging 5 percent annually for six years running. To effect his economic reforms, Rawlings resorted to the devices of the strongman. In 1982 he banned all political parties and used detention to silence his critics. Finally in the early 1990s with the reforms securely in place, he called for a transition to democracy. In 1992 Rawlings won the presidency in a five-way race. Charges of fraud blemished that election but not the one in 1996 when he was reelected in a strong multiparty campaign overseen by a vigilant press.

GHANA AFTER NKRUMAH

1966–1981	Government merry-go-round following Nkrumah's overthrow leaves Ghana adrift
1981	Rawlings consolidates political control
1985	Rawlings imposes market disciplines
1992	Rawlings is elected president in a questionable election
1996	Rawlings is re-elected in an open election despite uneven economic progress

However, prosperity still eluded Ghana. Production continued to lose its race with population increase. Even with the improved economic performance, by 1992 per capita income was still slightly lower than it had been some forty years earlier. The steady drop in cocoa prices on the world market compounded Ghana's economic problems. By 1989 the commodity sold for only one-fifth of its 1977 value. At the same time the price of imported goods was rising, and Ghana was still burdened by heavy external debt. Clearly, embracing the international economy was not a cure-all.

Trends Elsewhere in Sub-Saharan Africa. What little Ghana had achieved with good luck and strong leadership was far from the grasp of much of the rest of the continent. Indeed, nowhere in the developing world was the transition to the market less fruitful than in sub-Saharan Africa. Grinding poverty was more than ever a problem. With its population of 559 million in 1987, Africa had a total GDP about the size of Belgium's (a country of 10 million people). By the 1980s, 29 of the world's 34 poorest countries were in Africa. One-quarter of its population (over 100 million people) faced chronic hunger. Prolonged civil war or several years of drought could leave many starving. The highest population growth rate in the world guaranteed that the situation would get worse and inspired troubling forecasts of a doubling of the continent's population to about 1 billion by 2010. Compounding the poverty were endemic health problems. Malaria and dysentery were common. Two-thirds of Africa's population lacked safe drinking water. An HIV/AIDS epidemic had killed 14 million people by 2000 and accounted for over 29 million cases by 2002, 70 percent of the world total. With almost one-third of the adult population testing positive in some countries, the epidemic was putting severe strains on families, economic productivity, and health systems. Africa's fragile ecology was also under stress, thus threatening food production. For example, the need for firewood caused the loss of millions of acres of forest each year. Much of the continent's dry lands and rangelands were gradually becoming more desert-like.

This grim state of affairs was intensified by integration into the international economic system in the course of the 1980s. Long-term neglect of the countryside was compounded by a downward slide in the international market price for raw materials. This spelled serious trouble for already stagnant sub-Saharan economies, hurt rural producers, and meant that countries with already high levels of international debt would either face defaulting on those debts or have to limit domestic programs, creating in turn public protests and military mutinies. As a result of this combination of adverse developments, living standards across sub-Saharan Africa fell by 15 percent between 1979 and 1985. The decline was serious for countries already close to the margin, and in places it wiped out the middle class.

The World Bank and major creditors began intervening in the course of the 1980s, setting limits on loans and demanding austerity. Debtors had to accept an export-driven development strategy. The elements in the new program included implementing price incentives to promote agricultural production, improving distribution systems, making investments in the rural sector, privatizing the economy, and cutting subsidies to public enterprises. In return for these reforms, African countries got funds to help them through the crisis. International loans were supplemented by foreign assistance amounting to $13 billion per year between 1980 and 1987.

Economies remained in trouble even after acting on World Bank advice. The prescribed cutbacks in government spending hurt health and education. Austerity also increased unemployment, sharpened inequalities, and created popular unrest among the privileged city residents (particularly over rising food prices). And the pain did not bring economic gain. Between 1980 and 1987 per capita income fell by 10 percent, thus deepening poverty. Foreign investors did not come in as anticipated. International commodity prices remained low. And Africa's share of the world market declined to 1.5 percent. Indeed, Africa became the most heavily indebted region of the world, with external obligations equal to total GNP and with payments on the debt eating up half of export earnings. With the end of the Cold War and of the superpower competition for clients, aid programs declined sharply.

Prospects for democratization on the African subcontinent were equally poor. While Rawlings was promoting democracy in Ghana, much of the region remained in the grip of strongmen and the military. Moreover, political sentiment was not solidly behind Western-style democracy. To be sure, some argued that free elections would bring stability, more accountable government, and less corruption. Authoritarian politics and military-dominated governments were, according to these pro-democracy advocates, at the root of Africa's economic woes. But some skeptics wondered if democracy might stir up ethnic or religious rivalries better contained under a strongman, and they noted a regional preference for "traditional" forms of decision-making by elders though consensus building and an antipathy to dissent and permanent opposition parties. Finally, doubters argued that democracy was a product of economic development, not its source. From this point of view, Africa was better off following the example of Japan, Taiwan, China, and South Korea whereby authoritarian politics and state-guided economies geared to international trade had put economic growth first and let democracy follow behind.

Abandoning Import Substitution in Brazil. Every bit as much as sub-Saharan Africa, Latin America joined the trend toward integration into the global economy. Whereas Chile under military rule illustrates one current within Latin America, Brazil exemplifies the other—the perils that making peace with global capitalism could create. Here volatile foreign investments, widening social divisions, and environmental stress combined to limit real overall progress.

The return of an elected civilian government in 1985 after twenty years of military rule marked the beginning of a shift from import substitution toward neo-liberal economic policy. (See Chapters 5 and 8.) The military had borrowed heavily to carry out its domestic programs. Rising interest rates and shrinking markets in the developed world quickly saddled Brazil with the world's largest foreign debt and a payment crisis that threatened to bankrupt the country. Like many African and other Latin American countries in debt difficulties at this time such as Argentina and Mexico, Brazil had to turn to international banks and the IMF for help with debt repayment. The price for help was a move to the market. That meant limiting state intervention in the economy, lowering tariffs that protected domestic industry, privatizing state-owned companies, cutting welfare programs, and in general creating conditions favorable to foreign capital and corporations. By the 1990s neo-liberalism seemed triumphant. In a sign of the pro-market times, Brazil joined Argentina, Uruguay, and Paraguay in 1991 in creating a regional free trade zone known as MERCOSUR (Southern Cone Common Market). The 1994 presidential election was also telling: The victor, Fernando Enrique Cardosa, had been a leading advocate of import substitution, but he now championed neo-liberal measures to control inflation and to attract overseas investment.

But the economy was still vulnerable. In early 1998 it fell victim to panic on financial markets sparked by problems in Russia. Only a short time earlier Cardosa had made the point that "the market ought to reward effort, work, technical innovation, and the entrepreneurial spirit, and not speculation."[27] In this case he was wrong, and Brazil's economy stalled. At the same time both winners and losers in the new market economy—those seeking big profits and those seeking survival—overran the Amazon frontier. Unchecked exploitation swept aside vast tracts of ecologically priceless tropical rainforest, destroyed fragile soils, and made the land useful only for cattle ranches owned by the wealthy. The distribution of income under the new regime favored the already well-to-do. Brazil had the dubious distinction of having one of the widest gaps between the rich and poor in a region that itself led the world in inequality. By 1995 the poorer half of the population claimed only a bit more than one-fifth of national income while the richest 10 percent took almost two-thirds. Government programs for the poor dwindled, and unemployment soared as privatization eliminated jobs faster than foreign investments could create new ones.

The resulting popular discontent left the neo-liberal policy vulnerable at the polls. Critics pointed out that Brazil's economic problems remained the very ones that Cardosa and other structuralists had pointed out decades earlier: a heavy dependence on the export of commodities and the import of foreign capital. Brazil was thus still hostage to outside economic forces indifferent if not hostile to social justice and environmental sustainability. In the name of the market, Brazil was neglecting its human resources and spending down its nonrenewable natural resources. The 2003 election of Luiz Inácio Lula da Silva—a former shoe-shine boy, factory worker, and labor leader popularly know as "Lula"—suggested that free markets and economic efficiency had been oversold, at least in the eyes of the electorate.

India's Cautious Move to the Market. For India, the turn to the market was considerably more cautious than either Ghana's or Brazil's, though it proved equally problematic. Change came slowly because the leaders of the dominant Congress party had long been strong proponents of a mixed economy in which the government exercised a major, multifaceted role. This dominant view on economic policy reflected the experience of Gandhi, Nehru, and the party's other early leaders, who associated capitalism and international trade with colonialism. The British socialist critique of capitalism to which they had been exposed during their school days reinforced this connection, while the perceived Soviet economic success confirmed the wisdom of development that combined the market with state planning and regulation.

India's mixed economy could claim some notable gains. A series of five-year plans had boosted the country into the ranks of the top ten industrial countries, and the large nationalized sector provided good jobs for twenty million people. But despite state intervention and a large influx of foreign aid, India's overall economic record down to the mid-1980s was unimpressive. For example, by 1985 about 55 percent of the population was still below the poverty line (most were extremely poor), compared to 20 percent for China.

The largely passive social policy of the Nehru dynasty (Jawaharlal Nehru, who was the first prime minister, followed by his daughter, Indira Gandhi, and then her son Rajiv) and the Congress party undermined the benefits of what limited growth there was. The government failed to check population increase, which soared from 350 million in 1947 to an estimated 850 million by 1991 and which in turn depressed per capita income. Whereas China by 1992 enjoyed a per capita income level five times that of 1950 ($2,098), India's had only doubled ($1,332). In the face of more and more people to feed, India was saved from disaster by the "green revolution," the introduction of high-yield varieties of wheat and rice in the mid-1960s. By the 1970s India could feed itself. But the challenge was hardly over, with the population projected to reach 1.5 billion by 2025.

India lagged in other areas critical to economic growth. The government had failed to control the massive exodus of the landless from the countryside. The result was an accumulation of great pools of unproductive urban poor in the slums of such major cities as Calcutta, Bombay, and Delhi. Government neglect of primary education resulted in a literacy rate of only 36 percent in 1980 (compared to 77 percent for China by that date). For rural women the levels of literacy were even lower—20 percent. Health care initiatives had raised life expectancy to 51 years by 1980 (up from 32 years in 1947) but paled by comparison with China's record (already at 65 years by the mid-1970s). While focusing on heavy industry and the cities, the government had neglected rural development even though 70 percent of the workforce was still in agriculture and 75 to 80 percent of all people still lived in the countryside. What rural programs there were overwhelmingly benefited the wealthiest, not the poorest.

The first hints of an interest in giving more play to the market mechanism came from within the Nehru dynasty despite its close association with the mixed-economy tradition. Indira Gandhi before her assassination in 1984, and then her son and successor, Rajiv Gandhi, gingerly explored deregulation. Growth rose to a respectable 3.5 to 5.0 percent range, but it was attended by serious problems including rising inflation and a large external debt. Despite criticism, the move toward the market accelerated following Rajiv's death in a bomb blast in 1991. The new prime minister, a lackluster Congress party loyalist, P. V. Narasimha Rao, moved with surprising speed and determination. He trimmed

The Face of Rural India
This family photo taken in a northern Indian village in 1994 captures Bachau Yadev sitting on one of the family's two beds, while Mashre Yadev stands holding one of their four children. The possessions spread out in front of their home for the camera's inspection consist of basic kitchenware, simple furniture, three blankets, and three bags of rice. There are no electronic goods of the sort finding their way into many homes around the world, and the only mechanical item, a bicycle, is broken. The most prized possession in the eyes of the adults is their representations of Hindu deities (in front of the father, hanging on the bicycle, and attached to the house behind the youngest child). These villagers are not only the largest part of India's population but also the most neglected. Among them is found the highest illiteracy, the steepest rates of mortality, and the greatest poverty. This family has no savings and has to endure two-week stretches with limited food. (© Peter Ginter)

the considerable influence wielded by state bureaucrats over the economy and forced formerly sheltered Indian producers to compete with foreign imports.

This strong dose of neo-liberalism invigorated the economy but had serious side effects. As in Brazil, mainly the educated and affluent benefited, thus widening the gap between the rich and poor. Also as in Brazil, deregulation brought greater pollution by sanctioning a rush to exploit resources and by limiting government oversight. Finally, the new economy intensified long-standing social, religious, and political tensions. The Hindu majority (82 percent of the total population) resented what they saw as government favoritism toward the large Muslim minority (only 12 percent but still some 120 million). This rising resentment, punctuated by outbreaks of violence, propelled the Bharatiya Janata Party with its Hindu nationalist platform to power in 1997, displacing the venerable Congress party as India's dominant political force. Cutting across the Hindu-Muslim division were class and regional tensions. Privileged Hindu upper castes faced increasingly outspoken lower castes demanding a better life, stirring upper caste resentment and setting off riots, while disputes over water and land were the source of endemic violence among the castes at the village level. At the national level, economic inequalities separated wealthy states such as Punjab from poor backwaters such as Bihar. More threatening to India's unity were states and regions such as Kashmir and Punjab seeking autonomy or independence. (See Map 3.3.) These developments raised the question of whether India could face the risk of social upheaval that thoroughgoing market reforms might create.

The Population Explosion

In countries such as Ghana, Brazil, and India, rapid population growth seriously burdened attempts to create a better life by substantially offsetting and even canceling out economic growth. Viewed globally, three-quarters of the additional population at the end of the twentieth century belonged to the developing world, especially in sub-Saharan Africa, South Asia, and Latin America. Overpopulation added to the pressure on limited land in densely settled rural areas, degrading the environment and feeding civil unrest, itself harmful to production and investment and the provision of government services such as health care and education. The African state of Rwanda offers a chilling example of the potential consequences. Growing population pressure had over three decades reduced farm size by one-third—from 5 acres for the average family to 1.8 acres. The struggle for land contributed to interethnic tensions climaxing in the slaughter of as many as one million Tutsi and their supporters by their Hutu neighbors. But even as population growth surged in much of the developing world, some areas were showing the first signs of a slowing in the birth rate. This trend promises to make economic development easier because there will be fewer mouths to feed and fewer demands on natural resources.

Explaining the Rapid Increase. The population boom of recent decades is part of a long-term trend curving dramatically upward. By about 1804 world population had reached 1 billion. By 1927 (123 years later) it had doubled. Then in rapid succession it jumped to 3 billion (1960), 4 billion (1974), 5 billion (1987), and 6 billion (1999).

Why did population, particularly in the third world, increase with such speed? Western medicine had a major impact by raising the chances for infant survival and by extending lifespans. Much of this advance came during the late nineteenth and early twentieth centuries through the imperial enterprise. Colonial officials promoted public health projects to safeguard foreign residents with benefits that ultimately trickled down to local populations. The officials put in proper sewage disposal that helped check cholera outbreaks. They attacked insects that carried malaria and typhus. They built hospitals in major administrative centers while working with missionary groups to introduce modern medicine to remote, rural areas. Colonial schools and Western universities diffused medical techniques among the indigenous population. Progress continued into the post-1945 period. New UN agencies were especially helpful in maintaining the momentum in public health improvements. Major achievements in this postwar period included the eradication of polio and smallpox and the control of malaria.

As a result of these favorable developments, infant mortality declined dramatically over the course of the twentieth century. In India, for example, infant deaths per one-thousand live births fell from 237 in 1900 to 65 in 2000. At the same time, life expectancy in developing countries such as Mexico and India was rising dramatically—and catching up with the developed world. (See Figure 9.2.)

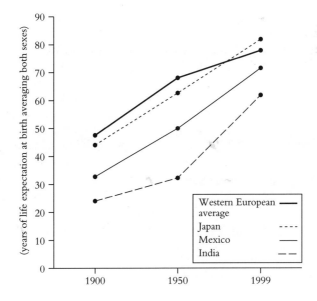

FIGURE 9.2
The Days of Our Lives Grow Longer[28]

Even though much of the developed world also experienced significant increases (usually somewhat short of doubling across the twentieth century), the developing world scored the most spectacular gains.

The other explanation for a soaring population was to be found in birth rates that remained high throughout the developing world well into the postwar period. Even as the conquest of such long-time killers as malaria saved infant lives and extended life expectancy, peasants and poor city dwellers continued to have babies at the former high rate as though mortality levels had not changed.

Peasants were especially cautious about limiting family size, for in an economy of scarcity and adversity where infant mortality was high, a large number of births were needed to ensure survivors. Moreover, large families had traditionally been an asset rather than a liability in the countryside. Children were valued as laborers in the field, as caretakers of younger siblings and aging parents, and as a new link in the chain of family and village life. The wisdom of the past thus taught that the more births and hence the more survivors, the better off the family and the community would be. The value placed on producing at least one male heir gave an additional impetus to child-bearing.

Catholic and Islamic areas displayed an especially strong bias toward large families. In Latin America, South Asia, the Middle East, and northern Africa, religious leaders warned that birth control would encourage promiscuous sexuality. Political fears in the developing world further strengthened doubts about birth control. The Mexican government in the 1950s, China under Mao, and the heads of some sub-Saharan Africa states denounced family planning as a Western plot to weaken their countries.

A Demographic Transition. During the 1960s and 1970s the population tide began to turn as the idea of restricting family size gradually took hold. Worldwide fertility fell from five children per woman in 1960–1965 to three in 1990–1995. Reproduction rates began to fall in the developed world in the 1960s. At about the same time the runaway population growth in Asia and Latin America began a steady, long-term decline. The demographic turnaround was slowest in Africa, but even there in the 1980s and 1990s a drop became evident for the first time.

Driving this demographic transition everywhere were new medical technologies and changes in attitudes. A widening choice of contraception—including rubber condoms, diaphragms, contraceptive pills, and surgical sterilization—gave couples more power to limit family size and to space children. Peasants were beginning to learn, especially as they moved to the city, that education was the key to opportunity. Now that each child required more of an investment from scarce family resources, poor people saw an incentive to have fewer children. The declining demand for agricultural labor and the unmistakable evidence that more children were surviving reinforced this trend toward smaller families.

Political leaders once doubtful about birth control began to appreciate the burden that a growing population put on the economy and the environment. The new view in the developing world held that economic progress was impossible without reducing the birth rate and that government action—usually in the form of clinics and educational campaigns—could make a major difference. Not surprisingly, socialist states had the tools to impose the most far-reaching and effective population controls. For example, in China by 1987 three-quarters of all couples used some form of contraception. Nonsocialist states were slower to embrace birth control measures and more tentative in their implementation.

Mexico provides a good example of the latter, slower reaction to rising birth rates. State policy was influenced by a conviction that a larger population was a guarantee of Mexico's territory against the grasping neighbor to the north. Catholic hostility to most methods of birth control also stood in the way of action. But the economy could not grow fast enough to ensure employment for all those seeking work. The specter of rising unemployment prompted the government in the mid-1970s to launch a vigorous population control effort, including a media campaign and a network of family planning clinics. Women proved receptive. Throughout the 1960s and early 1970s, their growing interest in birth control had already led to a black market in contraceptives despite government and Church opposition. The conjuncture of this shift by the state and women produced a significant rise in the use of contraceptives by couples—from only 13 percent on the eve of the campaign in 1973 to 53 percent by 1987. Birth rates fell dramatically—from 7 children per woman in 1965 to 2.5 in 1999.

The story was repeated in other countries. Indonesia's moderate program of family planning, for example, pushed contraceptive use up from 19 percent in 1976 to 48 percent in 1987. Where states put neither education nor financial resources behind birth control, the incidence of family planning practice was low and the progress on curbing growth was slow. Guatemala at a 23 percent contraception rate in 1987 was one of these laggards, as were parts of Africa that registered below 15 percent.

The new consensus on population growth inspired international initiatives. Beginning in 1975, the United Nations sponsored international conferences and funded programs that highlighted the important link between population control and provision of education and autonomy for women so that they could play a more active role in reproductive decisions. To that end, the UN as well as nongovernmental organizations set up health clinics and schools and arranged small business loans for women breaking into the market.

Even as birth rates continued to fall, people continue to have babies, giving population growth a momentum of its own. Projections indicate that it will take several generations before a rapidly rising population will stabilize. UN projections in 2001 estimated that the planet's human inhabitants would level off in 2050 at almost nine billion. This would represent an extraordinary threefold increase in less than a century. The three billion additional people over the next half-century will pose a challenge to political stability, economic growth, and social welfare at many points in the developing world.

Women and Development

If sputtering economies and growing populations were the most obvious problems hobbling developing countries making the transition to the market, glaringly inequitable gender relations hurt in ways less frequently noticed. Those celebrating the market have tended to see it as a liberating force creating opportunities for human development at the same time that it stimulated material abundance. But in fact its contributions to the welfare of women in the developing world were distinctly limited and in some cases actually regressive. Despite encroaching global trade and finance, male social and economic domination persisted. Even where female literacy and life expectancy rates rose, they were still generally lower than those for men. Half the population was limited, often severely, in the contributions it could make to economic production or social order and continuity in an increasingly competitive world economy that rewarded education and technological innovation.

Patterns of Discrimination. The reasons that the broad pattern of "life chances" had long been stacked against women are multiple and daunting. Most third-world cultures valued male over female offspring because men usually carried the family line forward, whereas women married out of the family and thus did not count as long-term family assets. A son would remain at home to work in the fields and care for elderly parents, whereas a daughter in most cases became part of her husband's family. Immediately after birth, female infanticide was an illegal but nonetheless real option in some rural areas (notably in India and China). Once modern medical tests became available that could reveal the sex of the fetus, gender-based abortion took the place of infanticide. The discrimination against women persisted into childhood. Under conditions of scarcity, poor parents had to decide how to allocate limited resources. Almost invariably they gave their sons better health care and more food. These forms of discrimination translated into a cumulative loss of female life reflected in skewed gender ratios within the general population. For example, in India in 1995 there were 927 women for every 1,000 men—a 7.3 percent gap.

As girls matured, their families further disadvantaged them by cutting them off from public activities on the grounds of protecting their daughters' virtue as well as the family's reputation and resources. As a result daughters received less education than sons and thus suffered from low literacy rates. In most of sub-Saharan Africa, for example, those rates were 20 percent below those for men, even though women predominated in agriculture and even though more education would have made them more productive cultivators.

Restrictions carried over into marriage, where control of the woman and whatever property she brought with her passed from her father to her husband or her husband's family (often a mother-in-law exercised direct daily supervision within the enclosed family domain). The bitterness that discrimination and dispossession could bring is captured in a song from northern India:

> To my brother belong your green fields
> O father, while I am banished afar . . .
> This year when the monsoon arrives, dear father,
> send my brother to fetch me home.
> When my childhood companions return O my father
> send me a message, O.[29]

The wife had no independent standing; her status derived from her husband and his family. The husband made the decisions that defined her life, including how many children to have and whether birth control was appropriate. A woman's failure to have at least one child (ideally a son) often reduced her to a pitiable failure in the eyes of the entire community. Barrenness could serve as legitimate grounds for abandonment or divorce. A pronounced double standard applied to relationships outside marriage. The woman was bound by strict standards of fidelity, and any breach was severely punished. Husbands, by contrast, enjoyed more latitude for liaisons outside the home (with the attendant risk of contracting and spreading HIV/AIDS) and greater impunity if found out. Given the considerable power that husbands possessed, they often exercised it violently against women as well as children.

Women who sought to break out of this iron cage of social restrictions found their way blocked by rank upon rank of males—within the family, the village, the courts, and the political system. Most men were tied by custom or self-interest to the status quo. Women attempting to become economically self-supporting were told to attend to household tasks. Those working outside the home did so on the condition that they were to supplement the husband's earnings, not supplant it or establish personal independence from him. Moreover, women's work was limited to peripheral economic activities such as small-scale agriculture or petty trades in the informal sector of the economy. (We have seen the example of Ghana's market women in Chapter 6.) Access to the capital and credit needed to run a business was limited, if not entirely closed off. Formal restrictions often reinforced informal ones. For example, the law often constrained women wanting to enter into contracts, a major commercial hindrance.

What explains this pervasive pattern of male dominance in rural societies in the face of considerable social and economic flux over the last half-century or more? Whatever the upheavals, males have managed to preserve their dominant position within the family, political system, and the economy, and in some cases they have strengthened their dominance. Their success can be explained by the imposing package of assets that men brought to changing conditions. These included greater literacy, a near monopoly of decision-making power, far superior political connections, and economic experience. In many cases men's traditional position of dominance had been enhanced by Western influence. Colonial administrators and missionaries introduced Victorian notions of domesticity that restricted women's access to the public sphere. Combined, these substantial advantages put men in a better position to make the most of periods of change, while women who took on new economic responsibilities assumed them on top of their traditional domestic duties of birth and childcare. The resulting double burden accentuated already substantial gender disadvantages.

Women and the Free Market. Commercialized agriculture, the leading catalyst for rural change, altered village life sometimes rapidly and usually beyond recognition—and in the process significantly widened the gender gap. For the reasons noted above, men were better situated to seize the opportunity for profit presented by encroaching market forces. Men would make the decisions on how family resources including the labor of women would be used and what crops would be grown.

The pattern was surprisingly similar around the globe. For example, we saw in Chapter 6 the impact that the arrival of cocoa as a commercial crop in Ghana had on women's lives. Whereas this cash crop opened doors for men, it diminished the socially sanctioned rights of women and left them scrambling for sources of income to care for their families, whether in petty trades or small-scale cocoa growing using their own and their children's labor. In rural Iran women found that closer ties to the city and the broader economy had the effect of narrowing their life to the domestic sphere and of adding to an already staggering burden of work carried by those whose husbands had gone away to find jobs. As private space for women narrowed, public space was more than ever male dominated. One woman in a village in central Iran lamented, "Only a dead woman is a free woman."[30]

Where men gambled on cash crops and won, they controlled the additional resources. If the gamble failed, women were left to cope with the consequences. A Kenyan village that converted from corn to sugar cane offers an example of how commercialization could hurt women. Under the contract concluded by the men, women were to tend the cane, outside crews with mechanical harvesters were to take it for processing, and the men were to collect a cash payment. After one growing cycle, the women protested that they still worked in the field but now without ultimate control of the crop and that cane had squeezed out corn so that there was no available food once the men had spent the cash. In a village meeting, men and women congregated separately before the village chief and presented their two cases. The chief acceded to the women's call to hold back some land for corn and to give them some say in the disposal of the cash. The sugar contract, it soon turned out, prevented reallocation of land use, and men disgruntled by this challenge to their authority were unwilling to make any substantive concessions. The women had lost out.

Women suffered disproportionately when free market economies went into crisis. Debt-ridden countries such as Guatemala and Nicaragua in the 1980s and 1990s got financial relief from the international banking community at the price of programs of fiscal austerity that added significantly to burdens already carried by women and their families. Food and education subsidies disappeared. Health care and child care became more expensive. Living costs rose while income stagnated or fell.

Paradoxically, it was precisely under the discredited socialist regimes that women had made the most progress. Socialist revolutions took equality as a fundamental goal and promised to end gender oppression no less than class oppression, both evils attributed to the old feudal and capitalist orders. Those revolutionary parties on the Left that won power did address women's welfare. The results were evident, for example, in Cuba, where women enjoyed a literacy rate of 95 percent by the 1990s (46 points ahead of women in free market Guatemala). Chinese women, to take another revolutionary case, were significantly ahead of Indian women in terms of literacy (by 35 percentage points).

But even in these more favorable circumstances, men dominated. During the period of revolutionary struggle, the Chinese and Vietnamese Communists were reluctant to press issues of gender equality for fear of alienating males who did most of the grassroots fighting and organizing. In the post-liberation period the political system remained male dominated, and rural males were still better off. If any group of women fared especially well in the aftermath of revolution, it was urban women. This was true in China and Vietnam but also in Iran, where revolutionary leaders were not comparably friendly to the cause of equality. In all these cases, better-educated urban women had valuable skills to apply to the post-liberation process of economic development and state-building and thus had a better chance of overcoming at least some of the well-rooted prejudices standing in their way.

This tendency for patriarchy to perpetuate itself became the subject of international debate in the 1980s and 1990s. Although feminists agreed that removing the extensive disabilities placed on third-world women was important to human welfare and economic development, they disagreed on the best solution. Some, especially in the developed world, argued for an agenda of equal rights informed by a faith in unfettered personal opportunity. This individualistic feminism, particularly influential in the United States and Britain, had little appeal for many third-world feminists. They favored the social feminism popular on the European continent (see Chapter 5) that honored women's unique role in procreating and nurturing children. Thus securing individual rights and opportunity was less important than promoting the interests of the family and the ability of women to contribute to societal well-being. Social feminists in the developing world, like those similarly minded women in Europe, gave high priority to government programs critical to women's lives such as family planning, health care, education, and social security.

Social feminists in the developing world often got caught in a cross-fire between men in their own societies and equal-rights feminists in the developed world. Their countrymen, defensive and often angry, told them to steer clear of public affairs, ignore meddling foreign women, and attend instead to their "natural" domestic realm of family, reproduction, household management, and marriage arrangements. At the same time those Western feminists who were convinced that gender was constructed and not fixed urged their sisters in the developing world to shape a fresh identity guided by ideas of individual autonomy and rights. Women in the developing world thus found the counsel of their men at odds with their own pressing bread-and-butter family preoccupations, while the foreign advice collided with their collectivist concerns. This debate raised a question of primary importance for all countries embracing the market-based international economy: How important were matters of family livelihood and social welfare to successful and sustainable development?

CONCLUSION

By the 1990s the pressures of a vibrant but unforgiving international economy were dissolving the commonalities of outlook and interests that had given the third world its unity and meaning. Revolutionary impulses, formerly anti-colonial and Marxist in origin, were now more likely to take shape as a reaction against the cultural baggage that came with integration into the global economy. The most important of the late twentieth-century revolutions fits this pattern. Iran's Islamic clerics successfully followed a course designed to win national autonomy from Western preferences and values. Regimes built on the foundation of settler colonialism—as in South Africa, Israel, and Guatemala—found themselves in the grip of internal crises that were likely to scare away investors, provoke boycotts in important markets, and in the end diminish the prospects for development. Elites with cultural roots in Europe clung with determination to their positions of power and privilege, but their response to the challenge of politically disenfranchised and economically marginalized indigenous peoples was constrained by the pressures of the international economy and by suasion exercised by the leaders of that economy. Finally, as the third world increasingly tried to make foreign trade and investment into an engine of significant, sustained growth, the results registered winners and losers. Autocratic Communist parties were as likely to succeed as right-wing military regimes. The deeper the countries of the old third world got into the postcolonial era, the more varied the problems they faced and the directions they took.

RECOMMENDED RESOURCES

Cambodia Convulsed
David P. Chandler, *The Tragedy of Cambodian History: Politics, War and Revolution since 1945* (1991), offers a helpful survey of events leading to Khmer Rouge revolution. Ben Kiernan, *The Pol Pot Regime: Race, Power, and Genocide in Cambodia under the Khmer Rouge, 1975–1979* (1996), brings a puzzling revolutionary movement into focus.

Iran's Revolutionary Discontents
On **the revolution and its main protagonists,** Shaul Bakhash, *The Reign of the Ayatollahs: Iran and the Islamic Revolution* (1984), is the place to begin. Roy P. Mottahedeh, *The Mantle of the Prophet: Religion and Politics in Iran* (1985), is an artful introduction to the world of the clerics. For a learned appraisal of Khomeini's powerful political ideas, see Ervand Abrahamian, *Khomeinism: Essays on the Islamic Republic* (1993). Abbas Milani, *Tales of Two Cities: A Persian Memoir* (1996), provides the perspective of a U.S.-trained intellectual who turned against the shah and ultimately against the clerics. *Iran: Adrift in a Sea of Blood* (writ. and dir. Ron Hallis; 1986; 27 min.) provides a self-portrait of those supporting the Islamic Republic. On **Iranian women,** see Erika Friedl, *Women of Deh Koh: Lives in an Iranian Village* (1991), an anthropologist's fascinating exploration of village life; and Haleh Esfandiari, *Reconstructed Lives: Women and the Iranian Revolution* (1997), featuring the accounts of well-to-do women in Tehran. *The Day I Became a Woman* (dir. Marzieh Meshkini; 2001; 78 min.), part of an outpouring of movies from Iran, is a poignant meditation on the straitened hopes and diminished lives of Iranian women in the wake of the revolution. On **the regional consequences of the Iranian revolution,** see David W. Lesch, *1979: The Year That Shaped the Modern Middle East* (2001).

The Anti-Apartheid Struggle in South Africa
Leonard Thompson, *A History of South Africa* (rev. ed., 1995), and William Beinhart, *Twentieth-Century South Africa* (2nd ed., 2001), are balanced surveys. Heidi Holland's accessible account,

The Struggle: A History of the African National Congress (1990), lays down the basic plot for the anti-apartheid movement up to the eve of victory. It should be supplemented by Patti Wald-meir, *Anatomy of a Miracle: The End of Apartheid and the Birth of the New South Africa* (1997), which captures the perspectives of the participants in the struggle. Nelson Mandela, *Long Walk to Freedom: The Autobiography of Nelson Mandela* (1994), allows the ANC leader to tell his extraordinary story. *The Long Walk of Nelson Mandela* (dir. Clifford Bestall; 1999; 120 min.) fol-lows the career of this extraordinary figure. For the impact of apartheid on everyday life for blacks, see Mark Mathabane's personal account, *Kaffir Boy* (1986).

The Struggle between Israel and the Palestinians

For **an overview** of a complex and controversial topic, start with Charles D. Smith's clear and balanced *Palestine and the Arab-Israeli Conflict: A History with Documents* (4th ed., 2001). Good collections of primary sources can be found in Walter Laqueur and Barry Rubin, eds., *The Israel-Arab Reader: A Documentary History of the Middle East Conflict* (5th ed., 1995); and Yehuda Lukacs, ed., *The Israeli-Palestinian Conflict: A Documentary Record, 1967–1990* (1992). David K. Shipler, *Arab and Jew: Wounded Spirits in a Promised Land* (1986), provides a journalist's evoca-tion of the mutual perceptions of two people locked in struggle. On **Zionism and the Jew-ish state:** Shlomo Avineri, *The Making of Modern Zionism: The Intellectual Origins of the Jewish State* (1981), offers an accessible biographical approach to the nineteenth- and twentieth-century ideological cross-currents that gave rise to Jewish nationalism. Zeev Sternhell, *The Founding Myths of Israel: Nationalism, Socialism, and the Making of the Jewish State,* trans. David Maisel (1998), is a more analytic study that conveys some of the ferment now surrounding the study of Zionism. For the recollections of a leader whose early years and rise to prominence offer a window on the Zionist movement, see Golda Meir, *My Life* (1975). On **Palestinians and the PLO,** see Baruch Kimmerling and Joel S. Migdal, *Palestinians: The Making of a People* (1993), for its attention to social as well as political developments; and Barry Rubin, *Revolution until Victory: The Politics and History of the PLO* (1994), a synthesis with a critical edge. Hanan Ashrawi, *This Side of Peace: A Personal Account* (1995), provides insight into the first *intifada* from an academic who became its international voice.

The Guatemalan Civil War

For helpful collections of readings, see Jonathan L. Fried et al., eds., *Guatemala in Rebellion: Unfinished History* (1983); and Margaret Hooks, *Guatemalan Women Speak* (1991), which brings together a collection of oral histories highlighting gender perspectives as well as social divi-sions. *I, Rigoberta Menchú: An Indian Woman in Guatemala,* ed. Elisabeth Burgos-Debray and trans. Ann Wright (1984), is an engaging memoir that set off controversy by stretching the truth to make its point about ethnic oppression. *Guatemala: The Dream of Land* (writ., prod., and dir. Lauren Drewery, David Hestad, and Randy Stringer; 1991; 28 min.) gives a sense of the importance of land as a source of livelihood and as a cultural symbol.

Development Patterns toward Century's End

Nigel Harris, *The End of the Third World: Newly Industrializing Countries and the End of an Ideol-ogy* (1986), makes the case for the importance of the state in economic development. *Africa: Dispatches from a Fragile Continent* (1989) by Blaine Harden, an American journalist, tackles the region with the most serious post-independence crisis in political and economic affairs. On **the role of women,** Janet H. Momsen, *Women and Development in the Third World* (1991), sur-veys the major issues in brief compass. Sonia Kruks et al., eds., *Promissory Notes: Women in the Transition to Socialism* (1989), chides socialist regimes for their shortcomings while indicating areas of progress. Leila Ahmed, *Women and Gender in Islam: Historical Roots of a Modern Debate* (1992), traces changing gender discourses over millennia and finds no "true tradition" of sub-ordinating women. See also Geraldine Brooks, *Nine Parts of Desire: The Hidden World of Islamic Women* (1994), whose vignettes reveal the diversity of contemporary women's lives and the surprising turns negotiations over gender norms are taking; and Margot Badran and Miriam

Cooke, eds., *Opening the Gates: A Century of Arab Feminism* (1990), a wide-ranging collection. Bina Agrawal, *A Field of One's Own: Gender and Land Rights in South Asia* (1994), and *With These Hands: How Women Feed Africa* (prod. and dir. Chris Shepherd and Claude Sauvageot; 1987; 33 min.) both provide insights on the interlocking themes of commercialization of agriculture and gender relations. The documentary *Asante Market Women* (dir. Claudia Milne; 1982; 52 min.), focuses on the Ghanaian women who link rural producers to urban markets.

CONCLUSION:
GLOBALIZATION ASCENDANT,
THE 1990s AND BEYOND

By the 1990s the world looked much different from that of the 1960s, and an observer comparing it with 1945 would find it unrecognizable. The Cold War contest, perhaps the most prominent feature of the postwar world, had faded from the scene and then disappeared between 1989 and 1991 along with one of the two main rivals. The separate national economies that emerged from the war began a slow but steady march toward regional integration, with western Europe in the lead. Finally, the third world that emerged in the wake of World War II had begun to move along diverse paths by the 1970s and 1980s. Some developing countries were benefiting from international markets; others who had tried were not faring well. Some had succeeded at controlling population growth; others had neglected it and were paying the price. Some had a strong, centrally administered state, whereas others were divided and fell prey to civil war and foreign intervention. Democracy had taken root in some places, but many remained autocratic.

Although these developments contributed to a fundamental global transformation over a half-century, they paled in comparison with the force and sweep of global economic integration. Its potential evident in the early postwar years, it accelerated beginning in the 1970s. While bringing economies together, the global system of trade and finance also unleashed an astonishing range of consequences. It widened gaps in wealth and welfare among the world's peoples, raised to prominence a neo-liberal political ideology, created an unparalleled environmental crisis, and stimulated efforts to create new rules and institutions to bring order to proliferating international contacts. Perhaps no development was as problematic and puzzling as the role that the United States would play in this new era. Following the collapse of the Soviet Union and the socialist bloc, the United States stood without serious rival, wielding unmatched military force, unsurpassed economic strength, and pervasive cultural influence while advocating the universal relevance of its form of democracy and free markets.

Throughout the 1990s popular commentators, the daily news, and advertisements trumpeted the notion that globalization had arrived. Despite the pervasive talk of the dawning of a "global age," the concept of globalization is seldom clearly defined. At its core, it is about the international network of goods, services, and finance and the global patterns of production and consumption tied to them. The intricate web of trade, investment, and settlement knit by global capitalism has had far-reaching cultural and social effects. It has meant the widespread diffusion of technology and business practices and the spread of values associated with mass consumption. Foreign trade, foreign labor, and foreign investment have increasingly figured as important issues in debates within countries over welfare and identity and thus have become significant in national and even local politics. Globalization has shaped the daily lives of people all around the world, influencing not just the goods they produce and purchase and the jobs they hold but also the way they live and think. In sum, for good or ill, this highly dynamic, worldwide system has had broad and powerful ramifications.

THE PERILS AND POSSIBILITIES OF GLOBALIZATION

Many recent observers of world affairs have embraced the view that globalizing trends are effecting changes that are unprecedented in scope and depth. This view is not entirely wrong, but it is so ahistorical that it distorts our picture of current developments. Globalization, which burst to the forefront of public consciousness in the 1990s, deserves to be seen as only the most recent act in a long-running drama that began in the nineteenth century, paused in the era of war and depression between 1914 and 1945, and then resumed in the post–World War II years. (See Introduction.)

Like the earlier phases of globalization, the one developing after World War II and especially since the 1970s did much to promote trade, capital movement, and labor migration with substantial benefits to people all around the world. Between the 1970s and 1997, global trade in goods and services nearly tripled; foreign direct investments in productive assets overseas (as opposed to shares in firms) jumped seven times (to $400 billion); and sustaining this increased level of international economic activity, the daily turnover in the markets for foreign exchange catapulted (from about $15 billion to $1.5 trillion). These global currents accompanied by a cascade of new technologies made the world's economy astonishingly productive, pushing total gross domestic product (GDP) during the second half of the twentieth century up dramatically (from $3 trillion to $30 trillion) and tripling average per capita income around the world. These additional material resources created new jobs and raised living standards to levels unprecedented in human history at a pace that was also unprecedented. This material wealth opened amazing possibilities for people to work, travel, and think freely, without the social and political restrictions long considered a normal feature of daily life.

On the other hand, this spectacular growth carried costs that those in the developed world were the least willing to recognize because they as consumers, producers, and investors benefited disproportionately from the system. Ever-higher levels of production and consumption created conditions of deepening environmental danger. No less serious was globalization's tendency to accentuate disparities in wealth, between but also within the developing and the developed worlds. In response to looming economic, environmental, and other problems, the world community, usually working through the United Nations, has sought to construct a set of understandings that would raise the level of global governance and bring some control over the chaos inherent in the highly dynamic international economy. That effort and its difficulties have been most notable in the search to define and apply global standards of human rights.

Environmental Stresses

Nothing better illustrates the negative effects of globalizing forces than mounting environmental dangers. Those dangers have increased in direct relation to both the rising standards of living promoted by global commerce and finance and the almost universal appeal of a consumer lifestyle. For the first time in history, those eager for development have combined with the already affluent in the developed world to push earth's resources to the limits, with consequences that are not clear. As one environmental historian has put it, "Humankind has begun to play dice with the planet without knowing all the rules of the game."[1]

Between the 1962 appearance of Rachel Carson's *Silent Spring* (see Chapter 5) and the present, thinking about the environment underwent a revolutionary transformation. Within a single generation, environmental values became an integral part of popular attitudes in the developed world. Within three decades those values gained such wide acceptance that they had come to constitute (in the words of the *New York Times* in 1990) "a modern secular religion."[2] As environmentalism gained ground, it became the subject of domestic politics and administrative regulations as well as frequent and often contentious international negotiations.

Fresh blows to complacency kept alive the popular and political concerns expressed on the first Earth Day in April 1970. OPEC's 1973 embargo drove home to consumers the notion of finite resources. In 1974 newspapers began to report the danger posed by chlorofluorocarbons (CFC's) to the ozone layer. The meltdown of a U.S. nuclear plant at Three Mile Island in 1978 stirred alarm, as did repeated oil spills, the worst of which was the 70 million gallons that leaked from the *Amoco Cadiz* off the French coast in 1978. In 1979 the U.S. government's Environmental Protection Agency reported the existence of as many as fifty thousand major hazardous waste sites across the country. And throughout the 1980s and 1990s, environmental activists expressed a new anxiety over rapidly rising population pressures in the developing world and high consumption levels in the developed world.

The Scope of the Crisis. Some of the end-of-century environmental problems were essentially regional in nature. In the more developed economies one of the most serious was the accumulation of contaminants. For example, the production of toxic chemicals in 2000, according to industry reports, rose to

38 billion pounds (up more than 25 percent from the year before), of which 7.1 billion was reportedly released directly into the environment. New pollution thus added steadily to old. Some was quite significant, such as the byproducts from nuclear weapons programs (whose cleanup would cost an astounding $212 billion, according to 2000 U.S. government estimates). The threat from contaminants in the United States, however, paled by comparison with the situation in the former Soviet Union and in its former European allies. There, heedless economic planners had wreaked far greater havoc on ground, air, and water.

In developing countries, as we saw in Chapter 9, population pressure was the chief environmental threat, severely straining local resources. To sustain themselves, land- and fuel-hungry peasants cleared mountainsides and species-rich rainforests. According to one conservative calculation, the encroachment of peasants together with ranchers and loggers resulted in the loss between 1980 and 1995 of at least a half-billion acres, more than the total area of Mexico or Indonesia. Over three devastating decades (1960–1990), about half of the tropical forest in Africa disappeared and nearly a third in Latin America. Once native vegetation was gone, the light, thin topsoil was prone to wash away, and the land then lost its fertility. According to one study, by the mid-1990s soil degradation had affected 65 percent of agricultural land in Africa, 45 percent in South America, and 38 percent in Asia.

Environmental stress was also beginning to manifest itself in global terms. Some informed observers pointed to a dismaying range of dangers. One was declining biodiversity, as species disappeared at a rate (as many as 150 daily) far higher than at any time in the recent past. Farming and logging were destroying rich forest habitats, and unregulated harvesting was driving economically valuable wild plants and animals to the brink of extinction. The introduction of genetically altered crops raised the specter of catastrophic food shortages if one dominant strain were to fail. A new threat, climate change, put in peril habitats on which particular species depended. Proponents of diversity warned that the extinction of a wide range of plants and animals would create imbalances in nature with consequences that were hard to predict for the web of life of which humans are a part. They also lamented the loss of species whose value to humans could not be foreseen. For example, a yet undiscovered wild plant might have life-saving pharmacological properties. Finally, these proponents regarded species loss as evidence of an arrogant human assertion of dominance over the natural world. They asked if all species did not have a right to survival and if humans did not have an obligation to leave the earth no poorer for their descendants.

Ozone depletion commanded even wider attention. CFC's used in refrigerators, air conditioning, aerosol sprays, and industrial cleaning agents rose into the upper atmosphere, where they broke down ozone molecules and allowed ultraviolet radiation harmful to plants as well as animals to more easily penetrate to the surface of the earth. Developed in the 1930s by General Motors and Du Pont, these ozone-destroying compounds had been heralded as some of the most useful ever invented. Scientists now proclaimed them a deadly threat to life on the planet's surface.

Finally, the earth was suffering from global warming (also known as the greenhouse effect) caused by burning coal, oil, and natural gas to meet rising energy demands. These fossil fuels yielded carbon dioxide (CO_2) and sulfur along with various metals, which accumulated in the air and trapped heat created by the play of infrared radiation from the sun on the earth's surface. Methane (the gas produced by raising domestic livestock and by growing rice in flooded paddies) and CFC's were additional sources of greenhouse gas. Computer models of global warming trends yielded a nightmare scenario. As the average temperature inched toward the highest point in ten thousand years, glaciers would melt, raising the sea level, inundating coastal areas inhabited by an estimated one billion people, and altering ocean currents. Rising temperatures would also introduce greater variations in climate patterns and increase rainfall, especially in temperate latitudes. The risk was thus high for serious disruption of agricultural production with catastrophic results for global food supply. These dire predictions provoked skeptics to question the scientific evidence and its interpretation. Was global warming the result of human activity or fluctuations within a normal temperature range? How was it possible to predict with any accuracy the impact of rising temperatures on a climate system as complex as the earth's?

The cumulative picture of developments in the century following 1890 was alarming. World population had quadrupled, and urban population had increased thirteen-fold. Industrial output was forty times higher, energy use had increased by a factor of sixteen, carbon dioxide emissions by a factor of seventeen. Overall water use was nine times greater, driven in part by a quadrupling of irrigated area. Thirty-five times more fish were being caught at the same time that bird and mammal species fell by 1 percent and forest area by 20 percent. Worrisome in their own right, these trends were in most cases accelerating, suggesting grim prospects for the health of the planet.

Rising Public Concerns. These accumulating environmental dangers pushed higher popular environmental consciousness, social activism, and political conflict. "Green" parties impatient for a bolder environmental agenda sprang up in western Europe and elsewhere in the developed world. New Zealand's was the first; Germany's, founded in 1980, proved the most politically influential, winning a place in the national parliament and in the late 1990s a role in the government. While in western Europe environmentalists fought to be heard alongside other major organized groups such as labor and business, in eastern Europe environmental concerns spurred by the Chernobyl meltdown and industrial pollution were helping to undermine socialist governments. (See Chapter 7.)

In the United States, the largest and most wasteful of the world's economies, environmental issues became a matter of growing public concern and debate during the 1970s. Congress passed major environmental bills, and the environmental movement became more deeply involved in the legislative and regulatory process. New national environmental groups sprang to life such as Greenpeace (1971), established groups expanded, and local activism increased. But this groundswell of activism provoked a counterattack in the 1980s led by

Republican neo-liberals in Congress and by the Reagan and first Bush administrations. Reagan's secretary of the interior compared environmentalists to Nazis and Bolsheviks, and a high-level Bush appointee huffed, "Americans did not fight and win the wars of the twentieth century to make the world safe for green vegetables."[3] Conservative think tanks such as the Heritage Foundation joined corporations in mounting a well-funded assault on environmental "hysteria." Even so, by 1990 three out of four Americans professed support for the highest possible environmental standards, though it was not clear what sacrifices they were prepared to make to realize those standards.

Governments in the developing world had their eyes on national economic growth and regarded environmentalism as a potential threat to their management of the economy. In authoritarian Singapore, for example, activists had to tread carefully to avoid government retaliation, couching protests in respectful terms and keeping some distance from outside organizations. Nigeria offers another example of this tendency. Oil production in the Niger delta had despoiled the landscape while also draining the region's wealth without local benefit. The local Ogoni people organized protests in the early 1990s. A corrupt military government heavily dependent on oil revenues from this prime area of production responded with displays of armed force, arrests, show trials, and executions. But these measures failed to silence the protest, and the hanging in 1995 of one of the protest leaders, playwright Ken Saro-Wiwa, brought international condemnation on both the government and the oil company.

The Search for Global Solutions. Paralleling the development of a local environmental consciousness and activism around the world was growing attention at the international level as it became clear that environmental problems showed no more respect for borders than global commerce did. International treaties and conventions on the environment multiplied, totaling 151 between 1971 and 2000. In this age of growing environmental concern, the United Nations emerged as the leading sponsor of fresh initiatives. The first major UN-sponsored conference on the environment in Stockholm, Sweden, in 1972 created a forum in which an expanding network of nongovernmental organizations could lobby for their favored causes.

By the time of the next major UN conference—the "Earth Summit" in Rio de Janeiro, Brazil, held in 1992—not only had anxiety over environmental deterioration intensified but also the conviction had grown that the problem had passed well beyond the power of a single country to resolve. Norwegian prime minister Gro Harlem Brundtland put the case for international cooperation succinctly: "Our Earth is one, our world is not."[4] It had also become clear that the environmental agenda had to go well beyond attacking physical pollution and protecting a few highly visible species such as whales. Now it seemed that the whole biosphere and entire ecosystems were in peril. Finally and perhaps most important, in the twenty years between Stockholm and Rio a consensus took shape that environmental protection on a worldwide basis was closely tied to economic development in poorer countries. If developing countries went into crisis, the developed world would lose markets and feel the pressure of refugee populations. If the developing world destroyed its forests, the effects would be felt globally in the contribution to the greenhouse effect. The new notion was "sustainable development." It emphasized striking a balance between the current material needs of all the world's people and the preservation of the vital resources on which future generations would depend.

The delegations from 178 countries as well as some twenty-five hundred nongovernmental organizations attending the Rio conference were ready for formal agreements on protecting biodiversity, cutting back gases linked to global warming and loss of upper-atmosphere ozone, and regulating the exploitation of undersea resources. But the ensuing negotiations revealed serious obstacles to sweeping action or meaningful regulation that a maturing environmental movement now faced. "We see the train coming," President Clinton observed on the problems of the environment, "but most ordinary Americans in their day-to-day lives can't hear the whistle blowing."[5] Clinton's comment on the U.S. situation captured the universal environmental challenge of trying to square the circle—of reconciling unbridled consumer desires in both the developed and the developing worlds with the preservation of environmental values.

Sharp differences had developed between the rich and poor. Those speaking for the developing countries resisted across-the-board cuts in pollution favored by the most developed, concerned that such an approach would impede economic progress in poorer areas. They pointed out that the advanced economies got to where they were at a time when regulations were few or none, and they asked why those who came late to the industrialization process had to accept burdensome limits. Not only had the advanced countries brought the environment to a critical point, but in addition their current high levels of consumption contributed disproportionately to the crisis. For example, carbon emissions associated with the greenhouse effect came overwhelmingly from the developed world (more than four-fifths of the output in 1992) despite the far larger population in the developing world. Thus poorer countries argued that the developed world had a responsibility to apply its ample financial and technological resources to the solution of a problem largely of its own making. A critical part of that solution was generous development aid. India's prime minister Indira Gandhi put the proposition provocatively at the 1972 Stockholm conference: "Are not poverty and need the greatest polluters?"[6] If the developed world did not help, desperate people all around the world would take from the earth what they could heedlessly—to the detriment of all.

A hunger in poor countries for economic development found its match in a reluctance among the developed to make sacrifices even though they used resources on a profligate scale and fouled the environment on an equally large scale. The United States as the world's third most populous country, its largest economy, and the land with the most avid consumers was arguably the most serious offender. Yet Americans were averse to a frontal assault on environmental degradation. Washington rejected the main Rio agreements regarding biodiversity, sea resources, and climate change endorsed by virtually all other countries. Behind this U.S. stance was an unusually powerful and well-funded coalition with a material or ideological stake in unrestricted marketplace activity. Publicists and lobbyists for major industries, free trade advocates, and libertarians all opposed international initiatives that might impinge on national and consumer sovereignty.

One World or Two?

Enthusiasts of globalization see powerful economic and cultural forces overriding national differences, creating lives and outlooks everywhere along similar lines, and thus knitting the peoples of the world together. The photo of "planet earth" as a small blue ball as seen from space captures the new sense of "oneness," and cell phones and cable modems reaching rapidly around the world seem to confirm the promise. But, in fact, a good case can be made that globalization has drawn a deep line of division around the world. On one side are those who have a commanding voice in international governance, maintain substantial control over their internal affairs, and have some hope of realizing certain cherished goals particular to their societies. On the other side are those who have no meaningful role in global governance, are captive to a sometimes disastrously fickle international economic system run by outsiders, and despair of realizing the dreams associated with the early postwar years of decolonization. This last spiritual loss is as serious as the material setbacks. Genuine independence and prosperity, a domestic regime of social justice, and an end to great-power dominance had once seemed achievable. But by the end of the twentieth century these goals were beyond the reach of much of the world's population.

Falling Behind, Not Catching Up. Perhaps the most worrisome feature of the global economy was the widening gap between rich and poor. By 1999, the richest fifth of the world's population received eighty-six times the income of the poorest fifth. This gap had grown at an accelerating pace from the early nineteenth century. In 1820 (on the eve of the first phase of globalization) the ratio between the income of the top and bottom 20 percent was 3:1, by 1913 it had grown to 11:1, in 1970 to 30:1, and in 1990 to 60:1. In absolute terms, latecomers to economic development generally managed to improve their conditions, so that each generation lived better than the previous one. But in relative terms, low or uneven economic growth left those in the developed world ever farther behind. Overall the wealthy free market economies between 1900 and 1987 achieved an annual average growth rate of 2.1 percent, well ahead of the pace for such parts of the developing world as Latin America (1.7 percent) and Asia excluding Japan (1.3 percent). The striking result was wealth so concentrated in the developed world by the late 1990s that the total assets of the top 225 billionaires equaled the combined annual income of the 2.5 billion people that make up the world's poorest 45 percent. In other words, the Euro-American world centered on the North Atlantic together with Japan had come to constitute an increasingly privileged club. (See Figure C.1.)

The growing global divide between rich and poor was part of a pervasive trend also evident within countries. Developed countries with a few exceptions such as Italy and Germany watched internal class divisions widen significantly. The United States offers an important case in point. The ratio between the

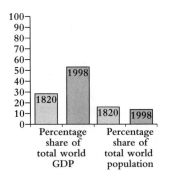

FIGURE C.1
The Growing Concentration of Wealth in the Developed World, 1820 and 1998[7]
The data given here is for western Europe, the western European offshoots (the United States, Canada, Australia, and New Zealand), and Japan. Over a 178-year stretch the wealthiest countries got wealthier, creating a striking concentration of economic power in the hands of a relatively small proportion of the world's population.

income received by the top fifth and the bottom fifth climbed from 4:1 in 1970 to 13:1 in 1993. Within developing countries, the domestic inequalities were even greater. For example, in Latin America, which had the widest income gaps of any region in the world, the ratio worsened, especially in the 1980s. For Brazil it was 32:1 and for Guatemala 30:1.

A group of major cities stretching around the world formed the backbone of global privilege. Linking these cities was a dense network of cheap transport and rapid electronic communications over which have moved during the last several decades the products of leading multinational corporations. Such products were less and less manufactured goods for mass consumption and more and more innovative financial services such as accounting, advertising, legal support, telecommunications, insurance, and securities. These cities boasted a highly specialized, skilled, mobile, and well-paid workforce with a cosmopolitan outlook and the transcultural skills (notably a command of English along with other languages) critical to navigating the rapid and diverse interurban flow. These features indicating a high degree of globalization were most evident in a handful of first-tier cities: New York, Chicago, and Los Angeles in North America; London and Paris within the European Union (EU); and Tokyo and Osaka within Japan. (Only Los Angeles was new to this role; all the others had occupied a dominant place during the first phase of globalization around the end of the nineteenth century.) These long-time leaders were linked to a second tier of cities such as Singapore, Hong Kong, Shanghai, and Seoul in East Asia; Mexico City, Buenos Aires, São Paulo, and Rio de Janeiro in Latin America; Calcutta and Bombay in South Asia; and Cairo in the Middle East. From these sites, modern culture spread—as it had for several centuries—from Europe and North America into the maritime periphery of the developing world. The elites within these outposts of modernity had the disposable income and free time to see a Disney film, to travel abroad, and to use the Internet. As they assumed the lifestyle of their overseas counterparts, they became increasingly divorced from the sentiments of their less privileged countrymen.

The sources of this growing income and wealth gap were much the same both within countries and among them. In general, the more highly educated the country or the group within a country, the more disproportionately rewarded they were, whereas the less skilled were excluded from the most productive and highest paying sectors of the national and global economy. For developed countries, technology played an increasingly important part in raising productivity and maintaining international competitiveness, making scientific research critical and general basic education essential for the workforce. To sustain technical progress, developed countries constantly built up their physical capital including plants, schools, and communications systems, and workers regularly upgraded their skills. When the elements critical to success came together in a stable, sustained way, developed countries enjoyed a reinforcing cycle of productivity and plenty.

Too often, developing countries found themselves trapped in a vicious cycle that doomed any drive to catch up with the developed world. Illiteracy was commonplace, thus rendering the workforce better suited to the export of raw materials or agricultural products than to technologically driven production. As we saw in Chapter 9, women were often not able to fulfill their economic potential, and swelling population put pressure on existing resources. Ethnic or class divisions like those in Guatemala, Nigeria, and India fed a sense of economic and social injustice and prevented the emergence of any kind of national consensus for promoting economic competitiveness and hence national welfare. Often these divided countries suffered from weak governments unable to guide economic development or create critical economic infrastructure. As a result of these problems, the developing world generally stood outside the circle of scientific and technological innovation so important to long-term economic welfare.

Young Famine Victim in Sudan in 1993
This image brings into sharp focus the grim toll hunger took among those under age five—approximately six million deaths around the world every year. Similar numbers of young children died from preventable diseases, often with malnutrition as a major contributing cause. (© Kevin Carter/Sygma/ Corbis)

Those with the greatest needs had the fewest resources to work with and thus the dimmest prospects for building a better life.

The human consequences of this global economic gap were evident in pervasive suffering in the developing world. By the 1990s some 800 million (more than 10 percent of the world's population) were chronically hungry. The death toll among malnourished children was especially high, often exacerbated by a lack of safe drinking water and crucial vaccinations.

To reduce cruel inequalities in the developing world, humanitarian organizations advocated a long list of measures that would be considerably simpler than putting a man on the moon. Land redistribution and better credit and extension services would help small-scale enterprises run by the urban and rural poor seldom served by commercial banks. Debt reduction for the poorest states could get them out from under almost impossible payment conditions and enable them to concentrate on serving urgent human needs. Safeguarding individual and community rights against pressures applied by powerful state bureaucracies and multinational businesses would help people most affected set the conditions for private investment so that it served environmental and social needs as well as economic ones. The reduction of state military spending would free resources for addressing soil erosion, water pollution, malnourishment, and inadequate shelter. Steps such as these were likely to reduce social tensions and minimize armed conflict while also improving economic prospects.

But in the 1990s and beyond, the developed world seemed less and less concerned with the fate of the developing world. Levels of official development assistance that were not large to begin with in terms of total gross national product (GNP) actually fell between the late 1980s and the late 1990s even as the inequalities grew. In 1986–1987, of the top five donor countries (France, Germany, Britain, the United States, and Japan), only France gave more than half of 1 percent of GNP (0.58). The United States was at the low end with 0.21 percent. By 2001, giving by the same top five had declined significantly. Apparently the world was one in terms of trade and finance but not of human compassion.

Economic Subordination, Not Real Independence. In the era of decolonization, peoples around the world had imagined an end to outside control and exploitation. By the end of the twentieth century those goals still seemed distant. Throughout the Cold War, the United States and stubborn colonial powers such as France had shown that they could impose heavy economic costs on countries such as Vietnam, Algeria, Cuba, or Iran who were bold—or foolhardy—enough to defy them. The end of the Cold War did not end the determination of the powerful to apply pressure against the most wayward. Iraq joined Cuba and Iran as a target of U.S.-sponsored international economic pressure. The developing world's shift to the market, already pronounced in the 1970s and 1980s, further enhanced the leverage in the hands of the United States and the other leading economies vis-à-vis smaller economies dependent on the import of finished goods, capital, and technology. Increasingly, developing countries were subject not just to overt, calculated sanctions but also to the rapid, severe, and impersonal discipline of capital that moved on the command of major banks and investment houses.

Instability had been part of globalization from its modern inception, but in its latest phase developing countries were much more vulnerable to financial panics than their more affluent cousins, cushioned by their larger economies and by the capacity of their central banks to coordinate a collective response to crisis. As a result of the rapid and unhindered transfer of funds, recent decades have seen a tendency for regional economies in particular to suffer sharp downturns. Developing countries were in most cases too dependent on foreign investments and too small to insulate themselves from sharp swings in financial markets. In the 1970s and 1980s Latin America and Africa were afflicted by a debt crisis brought on by higher OPEC prices. In the 1990s bouts of financial panic devastated the economies of South Korea, Thailand, Indonesia, Malaysia, Mexico, Brazil, and Russia. In 2002 Argentina became the latest victim as neo-liberal policies backfired, resulting in International Monetary Fund (IMF) demands for austerity, popular resistance, and political deadlock.

Critics of this volatile system of international finance have become increasingly outspoken. One group, the International Forum on Globalization, issued a declaration in November 1998 that illustrates the sharply critical views espoused by a broad coalition of advocates for the developing world as well as for the environment, human rights, and indigenous peoples. The declaration attacked the destructive system of globalized finance under the management of the IMF, the World Bank, the World Trade Organization (WTO), and other powerful but aloof international bureaucracies wedded to the fatally flawed assumption of "a never-ending expansion of markets, resources and consumers." The wild swings in the financial market produced by that system were yielding disastrous social, economic, and ecological results. These included "massive economic breakdown in some nations, insecurity in all nations, unprecedented hardships for millions of people, growing unemployment and dislocation in all regions, direct assaults on environmental and labor conditions, loss of wilderness and biodiversity, massive population shifts, [and] increased ethnic and racial tensions." In general, the declaration argued, not only states but also communities needed to reclaim power accumulating in the hands of distant and unaccountable "corporate led global trade bureaucracies."[8]

Leaders in the developing world echoed these themes. In April 2000, Cuba's Fidel Castro, hosting a meeting of leaders of poorer countries representing some 80 percent of the world's population, compared rule by the rich states and the financial institutions that they controlled to the Nazi Holocaust; Malaysia's equally outspoken prime minister, Mahathir Mohamad, attacked "rogue currency traders" that had brought disorder to East Asian economies and the IMF that had then offered neo-liberal rescue packages facilitating "the takeover of the country's economy and even politics." Nigeria's leader, Olusengun Obasanjo, warned that the great and widening wealth gap between the rich and the poor posed "a major threat to international peace and security."[9]

A Better Life Abroad, Not at Home. For many in poor countries suffering from slow economic growth and shaken by bouts of financial austerity, migration has become the road to survival. Abandoning home for a life elsewhere usually meant the failure of a rural dream: access to adequate land and sufficient stability to raise a family within a familiar circle of kin and compatriots. The intensifying pressure on the land created by larger populations put that dream farther from reach and forced on peasants everywhere a painful assessment of their survival strategies. Some tried to eke out a livelihood from marginal land and limited resources. Others converted some land from cash crops into food crops for subsistence, thereby partially insulating their families from the vagaries of the market. Still others started up part-time handicrafts or small-scale local industry to supplement their farm income. As we have seen in Vietnam and Guatemala, peasants under extreme pressure turned to political protest or even revolutionary activity.

The most common response of a growing but hard-pressed rural population was migration. So widespread did it become that it not only reshaped the face of the countryside in the developing world but also had major national and international ramifications. Peasants abandoning agriculture moved to nearby cities in hopes of finding work. For example, Guatemalan Indian women flocked to urban areas hoping to support themselves and their families by working as peddlers or domestics. China's poor rural interior sent a stream of its excess workforce to prosperous coastal cities, creating a migratory army of workers numbering in the tens of millions by the 1990s. Iranian villagers, facing narrowing opportunities in the countryside, swelled the shantytowns of major cities where they enlisted in the anti-shah crusade. This flight from the countryside to the cities of the developing world dramatically altered the rural-urban balance between 1975, when 60 percent of the world's population lived in the countryside, and 2000, when the number fell to just over 40 percent (although in absolute numbers those living off the land are greater now than ever).

Marching migrants hungry for work and security did not respect borders. An increasingly open and integrated global economy abetted their search for employment overseas. Booming economies in the developed world needed labor to take on the hard, poorly paid jobs that well-trained, well-paid local workers would no longer do. Without the foreigners, who would take care of domestic chores, clean streets, serve food, drive taxis, or do construction work? The migration response to these labor opportunities created a dense pattern of connections between developed and developing countries. The poor, for example, established a circuit connecting the Philippines to the oil-rich states of the Persian Gulf and to prosperous Hong Kong and Taiwan. They linked North Africa and Turkey to the more affluent economies of Italy, France, and Germany. They beat a path from Haiti, Mexico, and Central America to the United States. Over half the population of Los Angeles, New York, and Miami were by 1997 foreign born or the children of parents who had immigrated.

So large was the scale of migration that it transformed the human landscape in both the developing and the developed worlds. Those who migrated were

Santa Marta, above Rio de Janeiro, Brazil, 1997
The houses of this squatter settlement *(favela)* tumble down the mountainside toward the city below, providing precarious shelter for precarious lives. Roughly a third of Rio's population of nearly 6 million live in one of several hundred such *favelas*. The inhabitants, who migrate from the countryside seeking economic opportunities, find that city life, with its marked disparities between the rich and poor, is hard. They have to survive on neglected land, so steep and eroded that it is subject to landslides that annually kill hundreds. The government neglects basic services (running water, sewage, waste disposal, electricity, education, and public health). Unemployment is high. Those with work have low-paying jobs as day laborers, domestics, or street vendors, or operate in the lucrative but dangerous drug trade. (© Ricardo Azoury/Corbis)

mostly healthy young men and young, unmarried women. Their departure tore the social fabric of villages, leaving wives, young children, and the elderly to struggle to preserve the tattered threads of economic and social life. The migrants helped create within their own country cities swollen with the desperate poor with few if any marketable skills to ensure their survival. Mexico City—one of the most dramatic examples of urban explosion—experienced a sixty-fold growth: from a third of a million in 1900 to twenty million in 1997. Urban centers were swamped by the poor and the unskilled in need of education and services and living in squalor and insecurity. Even the lucky who found employment might remain on the economic margins with dim prospects. They would struggle to earn enough for remittances to serve as a lifeline for the families and communities they had left behind.

Adding to their troubles, migrants often found themselves despised outsiders with a precarious future. Local sentiment, inflamed by a large influx of foreigners, could turn on them for taking low-paying jobs from the poorest citizens or depressing wages, for burdening social welfare services, and for spreading crime and disease. Perhaps most volatile was the nationalist charge that newcomers introduced new cultural values threatening to the host country's identity and social cohesion. France offers a good example of this backlash. Openings in low skill–low pay jobs drew millions of North Africans to France, beginning in the 1970s. These newcomers began to change the ethnic composition of some cities such as Marseilles, and their high birth rate meant they would be a growing presence well into the future. Along with the large numbers came new cultural values. The number of practicing Muslims began to catch up with those who were practicing Catholics, and controversy arose over schoolgirls' headscarves and female circumcision. Right-wing nationalists such as French politician Jean Marie Le Pen charged that these outsiders threatened France's national identity.

Civil wars, often triggered or exacerbated by outside powers, added to the flow of migrants from the countryside. The destructiveness of these conflicts can be gauged by the estimated losses: some twenty million killed since the end of World War II. Debilitated by hunger and traumatized by violence, streams of refugees sought safety, sometimes in cities within their own country but often crossing national borders to refugee camps and, with luck, a new life in the developed world even if that life was at the bottom of the economic ladder. The most easily counted of the refugees were those crossing borders such as the Vietnamese "boat people" (see Chapter 8). The totals climbed dramatically during the late twentieth century—from slightly more than 1 million in the early 1960s, to about 3 million in the mid-1970s, to about 27 million in the mid-1990s. Hardest hit were the peoples of Afghanistan, Palestine, the Kurdish-inhabited region of the Middle East, the Horn of Africa, Angola, Mozambique, Liberia, Central America, and Indochina. The number of those displaced within their own countries is hard to determine. In some countries such as Liberia, Rwanda, and Bosnia, the internal displacement affected half or more of the entire population. Even under the best of conditions, refugees were a melancholic lot. One of the lucky ones who had fled the violence of Bosnia to safety and educational opportunity in the United States spoke for many when she lamented, "I don't have to be afraid anymore. But my soul is empty and cold. What is left is a 40-year-old woman in a 20-year-old body. I cannot even see the graves of my friends, the grave of my native village."[10]

The growing refugee problem gave rise to a range of international organizations specializing in relief and relocation. Of the UN agencies, the most important was the UN High Commission for Refugees, which evolved from a temporary operation in 1951 to a permanent bureaucracy with a budget at almost $1 billion in 2001. Joining the relief effort were a wide variety of private, nonprofit organizations such as Doctors Without Borders (Médecins sans Frontières), the British-based Oxfam, and CARE. With humanitarian needs great and resources limited, these organizations and their sponsors in the developed world fought an uphill battle to save lives in those parts of the developing world where postwar hopes for peace and development had turned into the worst nightmares of violence and privation.

An Emerging International Regime

As international environmental treaties and organizations such as the UN High Commission for Refugees have shown, the global community's shared aspirations and interests have sometimes produced precedent-breaking efforts to write rules of conduct and to address problems outside the scope of any one country or even region. This process of rule making and problem solving had it roots in the first phase of globalization in the late nineteenth and early twentieth centuries when conferences and treaties addressed such concerns as the law of the sea, rules for the conduct of civilized warfare, and the protection of minorities. The process gained increased attention and legitimacy after World War II. But only in the last several decades has management of international life gathered significant force and breadth. This growing realization that universal principles are needed to govern an ever more tightly integrated world gave rise to a sustained and complex international conversation involving states, international institutions, nongovernmental organizations, and domestic political forces. Out of these conversations came growing consensus on universal principles and the emergence of institutions to defend and promote those principles.

The United Nations and Human Rights. By virtue of its comprehensive international character, the UN played the most prominent role in regime building over the postwar period. It supplied a strong initial impetus after World War II inspired by the Allied wartime commitment to build a better world after the barbarism of two world wars, the collapse of economies everywhere, and the brutalities of fascist regimes in Germany and Japan. The UN charter in 1945, approved by the fifty-five signatory countries, formally articulated those hopes. Acting on this sense of a single emergent world community, the UN quickly turned to pressing problems of refugee assistance, economic development in the third world, and aid to war-shattered China and Europe, while also vindicating the principle of nonaggression after North Korea attacked the South in 1950. Subsequently, the UN remained important in promoting a global discourse concerning the nature of a just and equitable international society and in institutionalizing widely accepted values conducive to security, peace, and prosperity.

The most ambitious effort by the UN was a declaration in 1948 that enumerated a long list of human rights that should receive worldwide respect. The main impetus came from the horrors of World War II—what the declaration itself described as the "barbarous acts which have outraged the conscience of mankind." Like virtually all of the major postwar agreements contributing to the international regime, the 1948 declaration was the product of a sustained effort involving considerable negotiation and compromise. Eleanor Roosevelt, earlier an activist as First Lady during the presidency of Franklin Roosevelt, played a critical role over two years, chairing the commission that crafted the declaration and adroitly transcending the ethical, cultural, philosophical, and political differences to create a consensus. The declaration built on a fundamental assumption: "The world of man is at a critical stage in its political, social, and economic evolution. If it is to proceed further on the path towards unity, it must develop a common set of ideas and principles." In late December 1948 the UN General Assembly gave its approval by a lopsided margin (48 in favor, none opposing, and 8 abstentions coming from South Africa, Saudi Arabia, the Soviet Union, and its European allies).[11]

The final document took a stand on a striking range of issues. Political rights figured prominently: freedom of speech, conscience, thought, and assembly as well as the right to vote, to receive fair legal treatment, and to enjoy privacy. But the declaration also spoke to economic issues such as the right to basic education, to work, to earn a living wage, and to have opportunities for rest and leisure. It looked ahead to gender rights by stipulating not only nondiscriminatory employment and universal suffrage and education but also marriage with consent and the right to initiate divorce. Finally, it cast protection over dissidents by asserting the right of those persecuted to seek asylum in other countries.

The declaration asserted a point that was revolutionary in its long-term significance: In a world society in transition, states could no longer claim to make up its defining constituent parts. Increasingly the needs and interests of individuals, coherent groups such as ethnic and racial minorities, and even categories of people such as women, children, and migrants were also to be considered. Though the declaration was non-binding, it nonetheless asserted sweeping principles that were to apply to all states. Further, the declaration laid the foundation for over twenty major human rights agreements in the following decades, dealing with such varied subjects as genocide, torture, racial discrimination, forced labor, migrant workers, stateless persons, the rights of children and women, and the right to economic development.

Each step in the human rights campaign has provoked controversy. Perhaps the most universal issue has involved an essentially Anglo-American view of human rights as universal and absolute and defined primarily if not exclusively in civil and political terms. According to this perspective, the major human rights concerns should be free speech, voting, and such constraints on political activity and individual expression as arbitrary arrest and censorship. Critics of this human rights tradition have argued that rights are broader, including economic and social provisions that are equal to if not more important than the civil and political ones. Others have asked if the understanding of rights did not vary from region to region. Still others have resisted the notion that individual rights should take precedence over such collective interests as the family, clan, village, or state. Finally, critics have wondered if rights should not take into account socially defined roles (for example, the different interests of women devoted more than men to physical and social reproduction).

The Ambivalent U.S. Role. More than any single state, the United States contributed to regime building beginning in the early postwar period. American leaders brought to that effort a strong preoccupation with free trade and financial stability, which they linked to global prosperity, political democracy, and anti-communism. As we have seen, Washington moved quickly at Bretton Woods to design a new international economic system, and in subsequent decades promoted and protected it. By the 1990s institutions embodying the new outlook such as the IMF, the World Bank, and the WTO had come to constitute a powerful presence with ample means to enforce their neo-liberal policies. An international community of understanding had emerged even if the developed world seemed to be setting the rules, dominating the institutions, and reaping the chief benefits.

The 1970s and 1980s marked a renewal in regime building outside the area of economics. One front was the emergence of initiatives toward cooperation on global problems of the environment. Human rights was a second major front in which initiatives, building in this case on the 1948 declaration, took place. Western European and American leaders promoted human rights as a way of stimulating political change in many countries. The Helsinki Accords of 1975 (treated in Chapter 7) is the best example of this growing preoccupation. As a basic consensus on human rights took hold, those states blatantly violating international standards faced censure and economic restrictions.

The 1990s brought fresh progress—the widespread acceptance of norms holding state leaders responsible for criminal conduct. The basis for this development had been laid at Nuremberg and Tokyo immediately after World War II. There the leaders of defeated Germany and Japan faced charges never lodged before, for having committed war crimes and crimes against humanity. A half-century later, revelations from the genocidal revolution in Cambodia, news coverage of brutal ethnic warfare waged by regimes in Yugoslavia and Rwanda, and investigations into state terror created pressure to bring to account those responsible. The boldest response was the creation of an International Criminal Court to handle charges of war crimes, crimes against humanity, and genocide. At the same time, special courts emerged to deal with cases in the former Yugoslavia and in Rwanda. Elsewhere—in Guatemala, Chile, Argentina, and South Africa—truth commissions took the place of formal courts. In these cases trials would more likely have polarized societies than promoted national reconciliation. These truth commissions could vindicate new internationally recognized standards of civilized conduct by bringing past wrongdoing to public light while also creating a shared civic sense likely to forestall a recurrence of abuse. This trend toward holding leaders accountable took a new turn in 1998 when a British court at the request of a Spanish magistrate arraigned former Chilean president Augusto Pinochet for involvement in kidnapping, torture, and assassination. (Pinochet was saved from deportation and trial in Spain only by his failing health.) Three years later Slobodan Milošević, the leading figure behind Serbian atrocities during the 1990s, was brought before a special UN tribunal created to try crimes against humanity in the former Yugoslavia.

In general the chief obstacle to the development of an international regime—whether in economics, the environment, or human rights—has been state sovereignty. At the outset of the postwar period, proponents of state power secured wording in the UN charter stipulating that the organization had no authority "to intervene in matters which are essentially within the domestic jurisdiction of any state or shall require Members to submit such matters to settlement."[12] As the regime-building efforts proceeded, advocates for state sovereignty insisted on limits to outside interference and a respect for domestic standards. They saw dangers to giving outsiders, even benignly intentioned ones, control over national destiny.

No country was more jealous of its sovereignty than the United States, and none was more effective in obstructing progress toward agreement and enforcement of international rules, at least outside the economic area. By the end of the twentieth century Washington had rejected a long list of significant agreements, including the International Criminal Court along with conventions against use of anti-personnel mines, on the rights of children, and on exploitation of undersea resources. In addition, Washington resisted binding environmental regulations and a comprehensive nuclear test ban treaty. U.S. leaders argued that these agreements might set unreasonable limits on the exercise of U.S. military power. To a large degree the future of regime building had come to depend on the degree of support the leading global power was willing to give.

GLOBALIZATION AS U.S. HEGEMONY?

The ancient Greeks had a name—*hegemon*—for a state that occupied a position of overwhelming dominance over all other states. This term fits the United States of the late twentieth and early twenty-first centuries. Americans could claim political leadership on the world stage, an unmatched military prowess that underwrote their leadership, and unequaled economic and cultural influence. As a result, Americans have come to occupy a complex position, exercising power across wide stretches of the globe (including notably the Persian Gulf), facing attacks from elusive stateless groups, and grappling with skeptical questions about its motives and wisdom from old allies and even from critics at home.

U.S. hegemony carries forward a pattern of dominance by the North Atlantic world reaching back over several centuries. As earlier, so too at the end of the twentieth century, a community of states in western Europe and North America led by the United States wielded predominant power globally. At the beginning of a new millennium, they controlled the major international economic institutions, the only major working military alliance (NATO), and the resources of two of the three major centers of production, finance, and technological innovation. Moreover, this North Atlantic community took the lead in defining the terms for the emergent international regime on such key issues as free trade, human rights, environmental regulations, international police-keeping, the status of women, nonproliferation of weapons of mass destruction, and economic models for developing countries to follow.

"The American Century"

In February 1941, on the eve of the U.S. debut as the undisputed trans-Atlantic leader, Henry R. Luce published an influential essay titled "The American Century." Luce, an intellectually and emotionally intense media mogul, called on Americans to assert themselves in world affairs. The expansively nationalist credo that Luce promoted would become close to an official creed for postwar Americans. As a vision of the world modeled on U.S. values, Luce's views echoed in the decades ahead in the pronouncements of presidents and pundits, informed the ways newspapers made sense of the daily news, and defined the fundamental assumptions of public discourse. This powerful vision of a world order under American leadership gave every promise of persisting into the new century. "Because previous generations of Americans stood up for freedom and because we continue to do so, . . . all around the world more people than ever before live in freedom. More people than ever before are treated with dignity. More people than ever before can hope to build a better life." This declaration by President William Jefferson Clinton—himself a product of the iconoclastic 1960s—testifies to the endurance of the underlying faith in political and economic freedom articulated by Woodrow Wilson in reaction to World War I and brought up to date by Luce confronting World War II. Predictably, Clinton's predecessor, President George H. W. Bush, had associated the 1991 Gulf War with the dawn of an American-led "new world order," while George W. Bush, his son and Clinton's successor, rallied the country in yet another war (now against terror) invoking this same familiar nationalist refrain: "The advance of human freedom—the great achievement of our time, and the great hope of every time—now depends on us."[13]

Luce perceptively forecast the dimensions of American dominance. In the economic sphere, his prediction was vindicated at Bretton Woods and then throughout four decades of global economic growth. The United States itself boasted the largest and most vital of the national economies and the most attractive of the international currencies. It exercised veto power within major international economic institutions such as the IMF and World Bank. It set the agenda for the WTO. The sustained prosperity of the 1990s guaranteed continued U.S. economic preeminence into the twenty-first century.

No less important to Luce was the rising American cultural influence. Even as he wrote, he could see the deep impact of American popular music, movies, slang, products, and inventions, and he could imagine the international appeal of a vital and prosperous society, already "the intellectual, scientific, and artistic capital of the world."[14] With some reason he saw the United States as the first modern nation—the exemplar and vanguard of a way of life. The features from mass production and consumption to an assertive individualism that developed first and most fully in the United States (see Chapter 2) were soon emerging in other developed countries and even in the cities of the developing world. Not everyone liked the "American way," but virtually no one could deny the appeal of at least some of the features associated with it.

By the twentieth century's end the United States offered the oldest and most widely broadcast model of modernity. The U.S. model had prevailed over one set of European ideological rivals—nazism and fascism—and then overwhelmed the socialist variant on modernity. From this position of cultural hegemony, the United States would press for an international regime congruent with its values. Individualism figured as an unalloyed good. Political rights took precedence over economic rights. Democracy American-style represented the ideal political system with a claim to moral superiority over authoritarian regimes that favored the state over the individual. Determined to lay down the terms for how the world should work, Washington imposed with increasing frequency sanctions on states that deviated significantly from the norm and followed an independent course when collaboration with international organizations such as the UN threatened to interfere with U.S. goals.

To be sure, American values were spreading worldwide along with American goods. But as the countries treated in earlier chapters suggest, Americanization was neither uniform nor simple. For example, even as national economies became part of a single international system, economic and corporate culture still differed significantly from region to region. Just because the French adopted the term *le weekend* and the Japanese loved Mickey Mouse did not mean that their outlooks had become American. Sony, Fiat, and Disney were all deeply embedded in global capitalism, yet their histories reveal important differences in the way each related to the state, applied the market model, and embodied distinctive social values. The triumph of the American way was at best partial, and it represented only one form of modernity. The postwar trajectories of western Europe and East Asia defined by welfare capitalism and the strong state model (described in Chapters 2, 5, and 8) suggest that globalization allows for variations on the theme of what it is to be modern. Nor for that matter were Americans shaping others' lives without feeling countertrends. The taste for sushi, croissants and espresso, reggae and karaoke, Nintendo and Pokemon all reflect just some of the cultural imports that partially offset the heavy volume of American exports.

Playing the Global Policeman

Defeat of the Axis during World War II and then the Soviet Union during the Cold War were impressive demonstrations of American leadership. The U.S. experience in Vietnam raised fears of getting drawn into another long and inconclusive war. But the actual pattern of U.S. military intervention in the final decade of the Cold War and the opening decade of the post–Cold War period reveals a country ready to claim the world as its sphere of influence. Consistent with its prominent constabulary role, the United States kept its military budget during the 1990s at Cold War levels, so that of the top military spenders at the beginning of the twenty-first century annual U.S. outlays exceeded the total laid out by the next twenty-five countries. (See Figure C.2.) The president exercised formidable military authority with few formal restraints. Congress remained as deferential as it had been during the Cold War, and each successive president expected NATO and the United Nations to follow his leadership and accept responsibility for problems too peripheral or knotty for him to bother with.

Troubled Neighborhoods. The Caribbean basin—long a U.S. sphere of influence—was the scene of the most frequent, invariably unilateral interventions of the late twentieth century. Ronald Reagan had made communist influence in the region a prime concern and so focused on El Salvador, Nicaragua, and Grenada (see Chapter 7). His successor, George H. W. Bush, struck in 1989 at Panama, toppling the government of General Manuel Antonio Noriega and carting him off to an American prison. Bill Clinton carried forward the interventionist impulse by sending forces to Haiti in 1994 to remove a military government in the name of democracy.

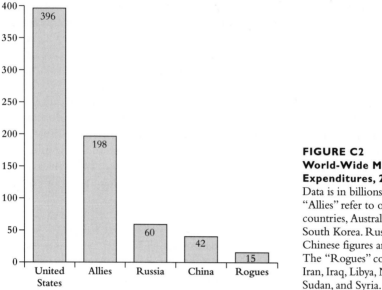

FIGURE C2
World-Wide Military Expenditures, 2001[15]
Data is in billions of dollars. "Allies" refer to other NATO countries, Australia, Japan, and South Korea. Russian and Chinese figures are from 2000. The "Rogues" consist of Cuba, Iran, Iraq, Libya, North Korea, Sudan, and Syria.

The Middle East had figured prominently throughout the postwar period as an important source of oil, as a link in the anti-Soviet containment line, and as battleground between U.S.-supported Israel and its neighbors. But it assumed an enduring place at the forefront of U.S. strategic concerns only after the Iranian revolution of 1979. Stunned by the Iranian revolution and then by the Soviet invasion of Afghanistan, Jimmy Carter proclaimed in 1980 that the United States would counter by military means if necessary any attempt to control the oil-rich Persian Gulf. Reagan aligned with Saddam Hussein's Iraq in its long war with Iran. He sent American marines into Lebanon in 1982 as part of an international force to calm violence involving Syrian, Israeli, and PLO forces as well as Lebanese factions. In 1986 he launched an air attack on Libya after mounting tensions with that country's strongman, Muammar al-Qaddafi. In early 1991 in a short and decisive war, a U.S.-led international coalition made Iraq's leader, Saddam Hussein, withdraw from Kuwait. In his last months in office the elder Bush committed U.S. forces to a humanitarian mission in Somalia sitting on the flank of an oil-rich region. In 1999 bombings of two U.S. embassies in Africa prompted retaliatory air attacks by the Clinton administration on Afghanistan and Sudan. A direct attack on the United States in 2001 prompted an even more sustained, intense bombing of Afghanistan and the dispatch of a military force to bring to justice those responsible.

In 2003 the younger Bush led the United States into its second war with Iraq. The effort dramatically underlined as well as deepened U.S. entanglements in the region. This decision was surrounded by controversy and confusion. Bush had proceeded despite domestic public opinion that had grave reservations about a unilateral course, despite criticism from a wide range of U.S. pundits and former policymakers, despite overwhelming popular opposition around the world, and despite criticism from the governments of all the other major powers save Britain's. Moreover, the goals of the Bush team were clouded by its own shifting rhetoric: liberating Iraq and the entire region, putting in place a new doctrine of regime change, blocking the development of weapons of mass destruction, and shutting down support for terrorism. Many suspected that the real though unstated American goal was control of Iraq's oil. Even as the fighting raged, the wisdom and consequences of the invasion remained the subject of heated debate, with critics claiming that the war was a needless and costly military adventure, a political quagmire, a boost to anti-American political movements inspired by Islam, a blow to the United Nations and international law, the beginnings of serious split with the two leading EU powers (France and Germany) as well as Russia, and a diversion from the more urgent problems of prosecuting the war on terror and addressing nuclear programs in India, Pakistan, and North Korea.

East Asia, by contrast, proved a relatively quiet part of the American policeman's beat following the end of the Vietnam War. U.S. troops still patrolled the 38th parallel, protecting South Korea against the surviving Communist regime to the north. And the Pacific fleet remained on call to protect Taiwan from invasion by China. As earlier, the security alliance with Japan was the keystone for U.S. strategy in the western Pacific. It provided invaluable bases for American land, sea, and air forces while also ensuring the cooperation of a significant Japanese military establishment. A gathering crisis between the administration of the second Bush and North Korea over the latter's revived nuclear program had by early 2003 left in doubt how much longer this neighborhood would remain quiet.

Although the American policeman kept busy, he did not answer all emergency calls. Some situations were extremely dangerous. India's longstanding and bitter quarrel with Pakistan, dating back to partition along religious lines (see Chapter 3), set off alarms after India's Hindu-nationalist Bharatiya Janata Party assumed power in 1997 and made good on its promise to make India a nuclear power. Pakistan quickly followed suit. A resumption of the quarrel over Kashmir, a majority Muslim area retained by India at independence in 1947, brought the two nuclear powers toward a showdown in 2002. The administration of George W. Bush did no more than counsel caution. Equally dangerous was the conflict over Palestine (treated in Chapter 9), which increasingly inflamed opinion throughout the Muslim world. Nonetheless, pro-Israeli influence in U.S. domestic politics tied Washington's hands and impeded any attempt to impose a territorial settlement that would honor the principle of self-determination or to participate in a peacekeeping force that would separate two peoples who were descending into daily mayhem.

Other situations cried out for action on moral and humanitarian grounds. Faced with unfolding genocide costing the lives of at least eight hundred thousand in Rwanda, the Clinton administration studiously avoided meaningful action for fear of a repeat of the Somalia fiasco and for want of any public outcry for intervention. Similarly, both the Bush and Clinton teams hesitated to deal with ethnic cleansing in Yugoslavia. With European leaders waiting for Washington to devise a response and the public upset by graphic media coverage, Clinton waffled, while his lieutenants kept characterizing Bosnia as a "problem from hell."[16] But by 1995 the Clinton administration, driven by outrage over Serb conduct, was ready to take forceful action. Four years later with the precedent set, Clinton acted with greater dispatch when Serbian forces went on the rampage in Kosovo. (See Chapter 8.)

Encountering Limits in the Persian Gulf. Of all these police actions toward century's end, the one prompted by Iraq's invasion of Kuwait in 1990 best captures the post–Cold War limits of U.S. resolve. Though Washington moved quickly to mobilize overwhelming force and liberate Kuwait, this operation was marked by significant constraints imposed by members of the coalition who helped fight and pay for the effort, by fear of U.S. casualties, and by the unknown consequences of overthrowing Saddam Hussein.

The Iraqi surprised the administration of the senior Bush. Preoccupied by the dramatic unraveling of socialist regimes in eastern Europe and the Soviet Union, the administration had failed to grasp the seriousness of the conflict unfolding between Saddam and neighboring Kuwait. The devastating Iran-Iraq war of 1980–1988 had left Iraq's economy reeling, and Kuwait compounded the problem by pushing oil production up and thus oil prices down and resisting settlement of a dispute over an oil-rich border area. Iraq's oil revenue was crucial to maintaining prosperity that contained domestic tensions and that underwrote the power and largesse of a state dominated since 1968 by Saddam and his extended family.

When Iraqi troops seized Kuwait in early August, President George H. W. Bush quickly swore before television cameras that the aggression against Kuwait "will not stand." He ordered two hundred thousand U.S. troops to Saudi Arabia to block any further Iraqi advance and quickly forged a broad, thirty-nation coalition, including Gorbachev's Soviet Union as well as two Arab states, Syria and Egypt. In November the UN Security Council authorized the use of force by this U.S.-led coalition to compel an Iraqi withdrawal. Saddam refused to surrender his trophy even in the face of a superior multinational force. To warnings of certain defeat, he calmly responded, "Only we are willing to accept casualties; the Americans are not. The American people are weak." So on January 16, 1991, U.S. forces went into action, beginning with a forty-one-day campaign of heavy bombing followed by a U.S.-led ground attack. A hundred hours of combat brought Kuwait's liberation and a cease-fire at a cost of 240 coalition deaths (including 148 Americans killed in combat). Estimates of Iraqis lost on the battlefield range from 10,000 to 150,000.[17]

This easy victory ignited celebrations among Americans anxious over the decline of U.S. power and eager to dispel the specter of Vietnam. Bush exulted, "By God, we've kicked the Vietnam Syndrome once and for all."[18] But the Gulf crisis also revealed the limits of U.S. hegemony. U.S. partners in the Middle East had drawn the line at American troops invading an Arab state, fearful of further inflaming popular passions in the region. Though defeated and his country subjected to UN arms inspections and severe economic sanctions, Saddam remained in power, a thorn in the American side. Whether the second U.S. war in the

THE UNITED STATES AS WORLD POLICEMAN

1981	Beginning of covert operations against the ruling Sandinista party in Nicaragua and support for the government in El Salvador fighting leftist guerrillas
1982–1984	Marines in Beirut, Lebanon, as part of a multinational peacekeeping force
1983	Invasion of Grenada to oust a Marxist government
1986	Air strikes against Libya in retaliation for sponsoring terrorist actions
1989	Intervention in Panama against a recalcitrant Noriega
1991	U.S.-led international coalition to end Iraq's occupation of Kuwait
1993	Military-humanitarian mission in strife-torn Somalia
1994	Intervention in Haiti to remove a military government
1995	Bombing of Serb positions in Bosnia and participation in a NATO-led peacekeeping force
1999	Air attacks on Afghanistan and Sudan in retaliation for bombing of U.S. embassies; U.S.-led NATO bombing of Serbia and participation in a NATO peacekeeping force for Kosovo
2001	Air and ground operations in Afghanistan in response to attacks on New York and Washington
2003	A second war with Iraq to topple the Saddam regime

Persian Gulf, waged in 2003, would remove the thorn and demonstrate unlimited power to shape events remained to be seen.

Doubts at Home. In general the U.S. public accepted the policeman role while also entertaining familiar doubts. We have already seen the public during the Cold War grow unruly in the face of higher taxes, constraints on consumption, and significant loss of American lives. The conflict in Vietnam followed by the economic slowdown of the 1970s and 1980s damaged the Cold War social compact linking plenty at home with crusading abroad. Americans showed scant patience for overseas commitments that might require sacrifice, inducing in civilian and military leaders an aversion to putting U.S. troops at risk except under the most favorable conditions. Military service ceased to be an obligation of citizenship. With the hugely unpopular draft gone, the armed forces were left to fill their ranks by active recruiting with offers of good pay and benefits. This new and pervasive caution was evident in resistance to intervention in Central America, the hasty evacuation of forces from Beirut, opposition to the 1991 war in the Persian Gulf, the cry to get troops out of Somalia, the indifference to a campaign of genocide in Rwanda, and the fear of a Balkan quagmire. At the same time Americans continued to take pride in their country's international leadership. The result was an approach to foreign relations that was incoherent, even schizoid.

The collapse of the Soviet Union compounded the doubts surrounding U.S. policy. It destroyed the clear and familiar Cold War focus on combating communism. Policymakers and pundits lost not only a widely shared sense of direction but also a specter to arouse the public. Globalization emerged during the 1990s as the new master theme that some believed would make sense of the post–Cold War world and command public support.

But those embracing it were in sharp disagreement on what it meant. Thomas Friedman, a *New York Times* journalist and author of *The Lexus and the Olive Tree,* took up the popular proposition that the free market capitalism behind globalization was a largely benign and in any case irresistible force. Samuel Huntington articulated a strong dissent. A widely read 1993 essay by this senior Harvard professor of government identified a "clash of civilizations," not economic integration, as the defining feature of the post–Cold War world. Others accepted Friedman's emphasis on the power of globalization but cautioned against its harmful effects. The most obvious were potentially catastrophic environmental degradation, lax labor standards, the transfer of jobs to low-wage areas, and surging capital flows able to capsize national economies. Globalization was also and less obviously undemocratic. Technocrats laid down sweeping rules that

Anti-Global Demonstration in Seattle
Perhaps appropriately, Seattle—the home of Microsoft, Boeing, and Starbucks—found itself the scene of the first major anti-global protest in November 1999, during a meeting of the WTO. Angered by its position on environmental protection, industrial agriculture, and labor standards, critics flocked to the city in numbers that surprised the police and paralyzed the WTO proceedings. Proponents of full-throttle globalization understood that they faced a broad-based, international opposition. Henceforth they would meet behind massive police protection or in remote enclaves, thus underlining the critics' charge that globalization was at heart anti-democratic. (© Al Crespo)

were not subject to review or recall by any electorate even though those rules might have a greater impact than any piece of national legislation. As one critic put it, American democracy was yielding to "a supergovernment of unelected trade bureaucrats."[19] Finally, globalization threatened to create a world emptied of spiritual and collective meaning in which market forces and market metaphors shaped society and individual consciousness. These critical points came from a diverse set of critics, including labor unions, protest organizations that first commanded wide attention during the major meeting of world economic leaders in Seattle in 1999, and a range of public figures from conservative politician Pat Buchanan to consumer advocate Ralph Nader.

Resistance Abroad

Increasingly, the U.S. critics of globalization found allies in Europe. The protestors that showed up in Genoa and at other meetings of the elite globalizers echoed the Seattle protests. Politicians on both the Left and Right looked more and more skeptically at the supposed benefits of globalization, and some denounced it (in the words of the conservative French politician Charles Pasqua) as "this new totalitarianism of our time." It represented in his view "the subjugation of people, languages, and nations to the commercial interests of multinational groups and the hegemonic will of the United States."[20] José Bové, a sheep farmer catapulted to fame in August 1999 by dismantling a new McDonald's franchise in a southwestern French town, underscored the international connections of the anti-globalization movement. He showed up a few months later in Seattle to join the attack on the WTO. How serious a threat these doubts growing within the heart of the globalization enterprise would pose, only time would tell.

The globe-girdling exercise of U.S. police power proved even more unsettling abroad, arousing diffuse resentment in some places and active resistance in others. Anti-American sentiment had flourished during the Cold War, usually under the sponsorship of socialist states and Marxist liberation movements. As the Cold War wound down, sources of opposition to the United States became more diffuse. A revealing poll conducted among opinion leaders in media, politics, business, and culture around the world after the September 11, 2001, terrorist attacks on the United States found widespread agreement that the United States was a self-interested power acting on its own without accomplishing a lot of good. This set of influential and well-informed respondents expressed sympathy for American suffering but also welcomed the fact that Americans had gained a sense of vulnerability all too familiar to other peoples.

Russia in Decline. In the ascendancy of its power, the United States loomed over Russia—an old foe whose post–Cold War decline was precipitous. Though the largest of the Soviet successor states, Russia had in the 1990s been weakened domestically and humiliated internationally. Boris Yeltsin had failed in the first years of his presidency to reassemble a shadow of the Soviet empire in the form of a Commonwealth of Independent States, while also facing ethnic unrest along the Russian border in such places as Tajikistan and the Caucasus region and even within Russia itself. A secessionist movement in the republic of Chechnya precipitated fighting during the period 1994–1996 (with some forty thousand deaths), and a second, more destructive round of fighting began in 1999. Twenty-five million Russians who had settled in non-Russian parts of the Soviet Union suddenly found themselves stranded, now strangers facing an uncertain future in one of the post-Soviet states.

Economic difficulties accentuated Russia's decline. Inheriting a Soviet economy in deepening crisis, the new Russian state attempted a rapid transition to a market economy, abetted by loans and advice from the IMF. After a long and painful decline, the economy began a recovery late in the decade only to absorb a heavy blow from the global financial crisis of 1998. Throughout these difficult years, living standards for most Russians plummeted. Inflation ate away at purchasing power. State workers were either laid off or not paid, and pensions disappeared. Longevity plunged, infant mortality soared, and total population declined. By century's end 40 percent of the Russian population fell below the poverty line. A formidable set of obstacles stood in the way of a return to the relative security and prosperity of Soviet times: corruption by insiders, often well-connected former Communists; an outdated industrial plant; an inefficient agricultural sector; flight of capital as well as talent abroad; and heavy dependence on the export of primary products such as oil, metals, and timber, whose international market prices were volatile. Russia was hardly alone in its ordeal; by 1998 the fifteen states formerly constituting the Soviet Union had seen GDP fall on average to half of what it had been in 1989.

Russian leaders fumed at the fact that the United States and its NATO allies counted their country of marginal importance even in matters most relevant to its long-term security. Over strong Russian protests, NATO admitted Poland, the Czech Republic, and Hungary to full membership in 1997. With other states in the former Soviet sphere of influence already in line to join, NATO was poised to advance right up to Russia's doorstep, while U.S. forces quickly established bases in former Soviet Central Asia as a part of the "war on terrorism." Only Moscow's control of the bulk of Soviet strategic nuclear weapons gave substance to its claim to great-power status. The U.S. determination to move ahead with a high-tech shield against missile attack left the significance of even that force in doubt, while the second Bush administration's decision to keep the old Cold War foe on its list of possible strategic targets gave rise to angry as well as ironic comment. One newspaper headlined: "AMERICA PREPARES FRIENDLY NUCLEAR STRIKE FOR RUSSIA." With their country diminished as an empire, as a regional influence, and as a world power, many Russian nationalists fell prey to nostalgia for what seemed like a golden age under Stalin, fondly recalled as a time of domestic stability, national unity, continental security, and international prestige. One nationalist politician with a substantial following promised to "bring Russia off its knees," while polls revealed the widespread longing for the old system of collective industry and agriculture. Signs of sustained economic growth in the last several years suggest that Russia will recover its international standing if not the old collectivist mentality, that Russia's eclipse will prove only temporary, and that Washington may have to give the old foe fresh respect.[21]

China on the Rise. While the basis for Russian resistance to the United States declined during the 1990s, China's capacity and resolve grew so that it had by then established itself as a regional power with credible aspirations to global standing. The dream of becoming a world power had animated Chinese nationalists well before the Communist victory in 1949 just as it had guided Mao's policy thereafter. Though Deng Xiaoping was best known for his program of modernization at home (see Chapter 8), he was no less wedded to elevating China's international power and prestige.

Deng jealously guarded China's multinational empire that Mao had reassembled. Borderlands such as Inner Mongolia, Xinjiang, and Tibet were in the view of most Chinese important national patrimony. Those regions were also important for their natural resources and strategic position along the long and vulnerable inner-Asian frontier. China thus retained the world's last great territorial empire even in the face of discontented minorities and international disapproval. Deng also built on Mao's achievement in making China a regional power with increasingly professional and well-equipped armed forces. As we saw in Chapter 9, Deng backed the Cambodian revolutionaries, the Khmer Rouge, as a counterweight to the Vietnamese-backed government in Phnom Penh and "punished" Vietnam in 1979 for its invasion of Cambodia. Deng maintained ties to North Korea while also cultivating an economically dynamic South Korea.

Deng's dealings with the United States picked up where Mao had left off. But whereas Mao had approached Nixon with strategic concerns uppermost in mind, Deng sought from the relationship trade, investment, technological transfer, and scientific education. He calculated in good Leninist terms that the lure of the China market would overwhelm Washington's political scruples about dealing with communists. Americans responded to Deng's brutal repression of the 1989 demonstrations with the sharpest and most enduring outrage of any country and with calls for sanctions. But then the first Bush administration proved Deng right, stressing China's international importance, the difficulty of imposing political change, the wisdom of supporting a development policy bringing prosperity and in time greater freedom to China, and the harm sanctions would inflict on American business. The Clinton administration followed suit. Communist rulers proved frustratingly durable.

At century's end, Chinese nationalists could look with pride on the achievements of their country, formerly denigrated as the "sick man of Asia." It was rapidly developing economically, redeeming long-lost territory such as Hong Kong, and solidifying its claim as a major power. But the United States seemed to stand in China's way, continuing to give Taiwan strong support and complaining periodically about China's record on human rights, its trade surplus with the United States, and its export of advanced weaponry to regimes Washington deemed unfriendly. Yet interdependence, marked by growing trade and investment, helped contain the tensions and moderate the policies on both sides. Fully one-fifth of China's burgeoning exports in 2000 (worth $48 billion) went to the United States, and corporations that accounted for the $20 billion in American goods that China imported lobbied for a stable relationship. As the twenty-first century began, China had sufficiently demonstrated its good standing as an economic partner that even congressional critics were not able to stand in the way of granting it full WTO membership.

Good trade and cultural relations notwithstanding, the accumulation of U.S. slights and provocations occasionally aroused nationalist resentments among a new generation of well-educated and worldly Chinese, who condemned the United States as a bully continuing its Cold War effort to undermine and intimidate China. They warned their fellow citizens and the government to wake up and see U.S. policy for what it was—an attempt to subordinate their country politically and culturally. Thus popular nationalism was an important feature of the Chinese political landscape. That young people were among the most vociferous in their expressions of patriotism was a sign that China's will to gain international prominence was not likely to fade.

Weapons of the Weak. Although Russia and China represented familiar sources of resistance to U.S. global influence, within the developing world some states and political movements turned to more furtive, desperate measures that might be described as "weapons of the weak." The most sinister of those weapons took nuclear, chemical, or biological form. For those bent on creating their own arsenal of mass destruction, the world of free trade with its porous borders made it easier than ever for clandestine operatives to obtain sensitive information, technology, and materials. Thanks to a trend toward nuclear proliferation going back to the 1960s, the twenty-first century opened with India, Pakistan, Israel, Iran, Iraq, Taiwan, China, and North Korea all having the capability to build and deliver an atomic bomb. Chemical and biological programs were generally run more secretively, and thus the number was harder to estimate. Though fear of neighbors was an important motive for acquiring these terribly destructive weapons, so too was the desire for a deterrent against U.S. pressure.

A more dramatic weapon for the weak was the small-scale "terror" operation designed to sow fear among Americans while removing some of the bitter taste of impotence in the face of seemingly overwhelming U.S. power. Nowhere did the tactics of terror find greater play than in a Middle East resentful of U.S. meddling. In league with Shi'i groups in Lebanon, Iran targeted Americans—both troops and private citizens—during the 1980s. The hijacking and bombing of passenger airliners, kidnappings, attacks on American embassies in Africa and troop billets in Saudi Arabia, and a failed plot to bomb New York's World Trade Center provided regular reminders that the disgruntled in foreign lands had ways to respond to what they perceived as profoundly unjust situations created and sustained by the United States.

That reminder hit home with devastating force on September 11, 2001, when suicide teams took over four U.S. passenger aircraft almost simultaneously and crashed three of them into symbols of American financial and military power: the World Trade Center towers and the Pentagon. Three thousand died in the resulting infernos. Americans who had not seen their territory attacked since Pearl Harbor were at first stunned and then united in an angry determination to bring the forces behind this outrage to justice. President George W. Bush quickly launched a U.S. intervention in Afghanistan. The prime target was Osama bin Laden, the Saudi businessman who had used the family fortune to fund and organize resistance first against Soviet intervention in Afghanistan during the 1980s and then against the U.S. military presence in Saudi Arabia from 1990 onward. In 1996 he had moved to Afghanistan, where under the protection of the Taliban government he could continue to prosecute his war against the United States. In 1998 he proclaimed, "To kill Americans and their allies, both civil and military, is an individual duty of every Muslim who is able, in any country where this is possible."[22] His instrument was an international network known as Al Qaeda (literally, "The Base") that had its origins in the 1980s as a way station in Pakistan for Egyptian and Saudi volunteers on their way to fight the Soviets in Afghanistan.

Americans briefly puzzled over the motives for the attack before settling into the complacent conviction that evil was at the root of the problem. What most Americans could not understand or accept was a hostility in the Islamic world toward U.S. policy that mixed confusingly with admiration and envy for U.S. wealth. Osama bin Laden, although exceptional in his resort to indiscriminate violence, gave clear voice to widespread antipathy toward U.S. support for Israel, U.S.–spearheaded sanctions against Iraq, and the U.S. military presence in Saudi Arabia. Perhaps more significant, his cause attracted a new generation within the Middle East suspicious of their own secular, Westernizing regimes. The backlash had first appeared in Iran's revolution (see Chapter 9). Bitter, sometimes violent opposition to regimes guided by such secular ideologies as socialism, nationalism, and neo–liberalism also emerged across a wide swath of the region and into South and Central Asia—in Algeria, Egypt, Palestine, Lebanon, Turkey, Syria, Iraq, Saudi Arabia, Pakistan, and Afghanistan. Those wanting to anchor national life instead in indigenous religious values not only attacked the moral bankruptcy of a secular path but also condemned the United States and, more generally, the West as the fount of a soulless materialism that had infiltrated and damaged the Middle East. According to this critique, Western influence had created cultural disarray, propped up hated secular leaders, and guaranteed the survival of the no less hated state of Israel. Oust the Western presence and expunge Western values, so some argued, and the region's problems would soon mend. Terrorist activities might not have elicited much sympathy, but their radical critique of present conditions in the region and their potent amalgam of religion and politics were widely shared in the Middle East. A war on terrorists would thus play out on a broader and more complicated terrain than just the plains and mountains of Afghanistan. Talk of "good versus evil" missed the point.

The inhabitants of the world today are better off in fundamental terms than they were a half-century ago. The Cold War with its regional conflicts and threat of nuclear annihilation had ceased to spread fear and dissension. Subjugated peoples had thrown off rule by distant powers that viewed them as markets to be exploited, plastic societies to be remolded, and cannon fodder to be expended. The international economy brought great material abundance to already privileged countries and opened up a markedly better future to some poorer countries. Even those in the most economically troubled states lived longer lives under improved conditions. In this much-transformed world, few people living in 2000 would want to trade places with the generation that came of age in 1945.

But significant advances came at a high, perhaps unavoidable, price. Rising population levels combined with rising levels of production to spawn new problems such as environmental degradation and to intensify old ones such as major gaps in wealth and welfare, especially along regional and gender lines. Instability remained a prime feature of the international economy. With the busts that seemed inevitably to follow the booms came economic hardship, social stress, and sometimes political unrest. These problems have stirred up an increasingly serious backlash that itself has assumed global dimensions. Critics ask if the benefits spawned by the system outweigh the costs and whether the corporate interests controlling the system and profiting from it have slipped beyond public control and accountability. Their demonstrations began to mar international economic meetings, forcing delegates to seek protection behind police phalanxes well away from the public eye. It remains to be seen whether these negative features could singly or in some combination threaten the global economy or whether they are merely incidental or temporary growing pains in what will be seen someday as an essentially benign process of worldwide growth and integration.

Yogi Berra, the legendary baseball player and master of the fractured aphorism, reportedly declared, "It's tough to make predictions, especially about the future." Those inclined to worry can dwell on a long list of potential disasters in addition to the perils and problems associated with the international economy itself. Drug-resistant diseases may proliferate, transported by migration, trade, and tourists (some 700 million on the move annually in 2000), and set off epidemics that could cut wide swaths throughout the human population. Mutant genes made possible by modern scientific wizardry could create havoc in an almost infinite variety of ways. One of a several thousand asteroids estimated to have a diameter of two-thirds of a mile or greater could strike the earth, sending enough debris skyward to block sunlight and lower the surface temperature, devastating agriculture and killing a billion or more people. Nuclear war—a more familiar human-made disaster—remains a specter, albeit less prominent than in earlier decades.

All these possibilities, however frightening, are not ones history can help us come to terms with. From our current perspective certain features of our world do loom large *and* provide good points of departure for speculating about the decades ahead as well as the most useful benchmarks for measuring change. Will the North Atlantic region consisting of the United States and its European partners still dominate culturally, militarily, and economically at the close of the twenty-first century? Will the transformations of this century prove as dramatic and far-reaching as those of the previous one? Will globalization continue its inroads on countries and cultures around the world and vindicate those convinced of its capacity to make the world not only better but also more uniform? Will inequalities between regions and within countries increase, setting off military conflict and social upheavals?

Anyone with a sense of history will realize the perils of prediction involved in answering these questions. The twentieth century more than amply demonstrated the capacity of events to evade expectation. The last five decades provide some striking examples of surprises. The decolonization process came with a sweep and suddenness that often outpaced the anticipation of colonized and colonizer alike. Although the ghost of the Great Depression haunted people in the developed world at the end of World War II, their economies experienced sustained growth with a tendency toward inflation rather than the falling prices and high unemployment accompanying serious downturns. Into the 1980s, Cold War commentators on both sides judged the Soviet bloc a sturdy structure only to watch in amazement as it came rapidly tumbling down. Even the recent passage to the new millennium brought a reminder of how predictions can go awry. The portentous Y2K computer threat turned into an embarrassing fizzle for Americans and the British, who had sunk substantial resources into heading it off while others had shrugged the threat off without serious consequences. Terrorism, a low-level preoccupation around the world before September 2001, suddenly jumped to the top of the list of major menaces in what seemed to many a world scene turned upside down.

A sense of the past offers a warning that today's predictions stand a good chance of proving grossly ill founded and of being overtaken or overshadowed by developments entirely beyond current imagining. It also offers an anchor against the daily rush of information and a tool to test the sweeping claims made by "authorities." In this sense history serves as a cautionary tale about the limits of understanding and the dangers of jumping to bold or seemingly self-evident conclusions. Surface impressions, we learn, sometimes hide deeper meaning that we need to have the patience to look for; and wishful thinking can, if we are not on guard, lead us into false positions that subsequent events will expose. Historically grounded skepticism is a weapon that arms us against the overwhelming impact of apparently momentous events and against the absolute confidence of punditry. It reminds us to look for perspective and patterns in what otherwise may seem a blur of events. With history we cannot know the future. But without history we have no frame of reference for understanding the present, no tool for intelligent anticipation of what lies ahead, and no resource for coping with the surprises that we are bound to encounter along life's way.

RECOMMENDED RESOURCES

Current Global Trends and Developments

For good sources of **up-to-date information,** see Dan Smith, *The State of the World Atlas* (6th ed., 1999), with its striking graphic format; *The World Factbook* (online at <http://www.odci.gov/cia/publications/factbook>), an excellent collection of country profiles and maps compiled and regularly updated by the CIA; and George T. Kurian, *Fitzroy Dearborn Book of World Rankings* (1998). The most **helpful periodicals** include *Foreign Affairs,* the venerable quarterly put out by the Council on Foreign Relations; *Foreign Policy,* a livelier bimonthly sponsored by the Carnegie Endowment for International Peace that has recently focused on issues of globalization; *The Economist,* an informed, British weekly that views the world through a free market lens; *Far Eastern Economic Review,* a weekly out of Hong Kong (online at <http://www.feer.com>) that is indispensable for keeping up with a diverse and dynamic region; and *Current History,* a monthly (except during the summer) that puts present issues in the perspective of the past.

Globalization
Popular works on the subject proliferated during the 1990s. Thomas Friedman, *The Lexus and the Olive Tree* (rev. ed., 2000), is an enthusiastic treatment of the new economy. Benjamin R. Barber, *Jihad vs. McWorld* (1995), offers a pessimistic appraisal of globalization as spiritually hollow, conflict prone, and undemocratic. Robert D. Kaplan, *The Ends of the Earth: A Journey at the Dawn of the 21st Century* (1996), paints a dark picture of a world fragmenting under mounting social, demographic, and environmental pressures. William Greider, *One World, Ready or Not: The Manic Logic of Global Capitalism* (1997), warns that the dynamic international economy harbors contradictions that could bring it down. Samuel Huntington, "The Clash of Civilizations?" *Foreign Affairs* 72 (Summer 1993): 22–49, challenges the assumption that globalization has fundamentally changed the international order. **The scholarly outpouring** is equally large. David Held and Anthony McGrew, eds., *The Global Transformations Reader: An Introduction to the Globalization Debate* (2000), captures the extraordinary range of controversy in an exploding literature. Paul Hirst and Grahame Thompson, *Globalization in Question: The International Economy and the Possibilities of Governance* (2nd ed., 1999), makes a skeptical examination of the sweeping claims associated with the debate over globalization. Fred Halliday, *The World at 2000* (2001), offers a clearheaded overview that looks at major issues through the prism of "modernity."

Special Issues
The environment is treated in Norman Myers, *Ultimate Security: The Environmental Basis of Political Stability* (1993), an influential broad argument for international cooperation, and *State of the World,* a regularly updated Worldwatch Institute report. On **human rights,** begin with Paul Gordon Lauren, *The Evolution of International Human Rights: Visions Seen* (1998), and the divergent assessments of democratic prospects for Asia in Daniel A. Bell et al., *Towards Illiberal Democracy in Pacific Asia* (1995), and David Kelly and Anthony Reid, eds., *Asian Freedoms: The Idea of Freedom in East and Southeast Asia* (1998). Amnesty International, the leading international nongovernmental organization advocating human rights, has an informative website at <http://www.amnesty.org>. **Human inequalities** are captured in concrete, human terms in Peter Menzel, *Material World: A Global Family Portrait* (1994), also good on the deepening incursion of consumer goods. Paul Collier and David Dollar, *Globalization, Growth, and Poverty: Building an Inclusive World Economy* (2002), is a World Bank volume that confronts worries about uneven global development. United Nations Development Programme, *Human Development Report,* issued annually, provides a rich statistical collection.

American Hegemony
On **guiding ideas,** see W. A. Swanberg, *Luce and His Empire* (New York, 1972), a full-scale, sharply critical study of a visionary American nationalist; and Tony Smith, *America's Mission: The United States and the Worldwide Struggle for Democracy in the Twentieth Century* (1994), which celebrates the American liberal mission. **The exercise of power** is the subject of Lawrence Freedman and Efraim Karsh, *The Gulf Conflict, 1990–1991: Diplomacy and War in the New World Order* (1993); Chalmers A. Johnson, *Blowback: The Costs and Consequences of American Empire* (2000); and Michael Ignatieff, *Virtual War: Kosovo and Beyond* (2000). On **McDonald's** as a symbol of spreading U.S. economic and cultural influence, see John F. Love, *McDonald's: Behind the Arches* (rev. ed., 1995), written with the company's cooperation; James L. Watson, ed., *Golden Arches East: McDonald's in East Asia* (1997), which is suggestive on how an American export has accommodated to Asian consumer preferences and which is summarized in Watson, "China's Big Mac Attack," *Foreign Affairs* 79 (May–June 2000): 120–34; and the website run by critics of McDonald's, <http://www.mcspotlight.org>. Eric Schlosser, *Fast Food*

Nation: The Dark Side of the All-American Meal (2001), offers an indictment of the American way of eating that has found growing appeal abroad.

Russia Declining, China Rising, and Terrorists Stirring

On Russia's traumatic transition to a post-communist era, see Rose Brady, *Kapitalizm: Russia's Struggle to Free Its Economy* (1999), strong on the wheeling and dealing involved with the shift to a market economy; and Stephen Kotkin, *Armageddon Averted: The Soviet Collapse, 1970–2000* (2001), a historian's account of how the Soviet elite destroyed its own system. On China, see *The Legacy of Tiananmen: China in Disarray* (1996), in which James Miles, a BBC journalist, makes an unsettling case for China as a crisis waiting to happen, and Samuel S. Kim, ed., *China and the World: Chinese Foreign Policy Faces the New Millennium* (4th rev. ed., 1998). On terrorism in the Middle East, see Fred Halliday's *Two Hours That Shook the World, September 11, 2001: Causes and Consequences* (2002), a clear analysis by a long-time student of Middle East politics.

NOTES

The notes for this volume serve to identify sources for quotes appearing in the text and for data used in the graphs and tables.

Preface

[1] Quoted in *The New World History: A Teacher's Companion,* ed. Ross E. Dunn (Boston: Bedford/St. Martin's, 2000), 360.

[2] Vera Zamagni, *The Economic History of Italy, 1860–1990,* trans. Patrick Barr (New York: Oxford University Press, 1993), vi.

Introduction   The 1945 Watershed

[1] John W. Dower, *Embracing Defeat: Japan in the Wake of World War II* (New York: Norton, 1999), 21.

[2] Michael H. Hunt, *Ideology and U.S. Foreign Policy* (New Haven: Yale University Press, 1987), 134; Michael H. Hunt, *Crises in U.S. Foreign Policy: An International History Reader* (New Haven: Yale University Press, 1996), 47–48.

[3] Karl Marx and Friedrich Engels, *Basic Writings on Politics and Philosophy*, ed. Lewis S. Feuer (Garden City, N.Y.: Doubleday, 1959), 43.

[4] Karl Marx and Friedrich Engels, *The Communist Manifesto*, ed. John E. Toews (Boston: Bedford Books, 1999), 164.

[5] Ibid., 69.

[6] R. H. Tawney, *Land and Labour in China* (reprint of original 1932 ed.; Boston: Beacon Press, 1966), 77.

[7] James C. Scott, *Domination and the Arts of Resistance: Hidden Transcripts* (New Haven: Yale University Press, 1990), v.

[8] Voltaire to M. Bertin de Rocheret, April 14, 1732, available at <http://humanities.uchicago .edu/homes/VSA/letters/14.4.1732.html>.

Part One   Hopes and Fears Contend, 1945–1953

[1] Michihiko Hachiya, *Hiroshima Diary: The Journal of a Japanese Physician, August 6–September 30, 1945*, trans. and ed. Warner Lee Wells (originally published 1955; reprint Chapel Hill: University of North Carolina Press, 1995), 16; Martin Harwit, *An Exhibit Denied: Lobbying the History of Enola Gay* (New York: Copernicus, 1996), 6.

[2] Hachiya, *Hiroshima Diary*, 17; *Widows of Hiroshima: The Life Stories of Nineteen Peasant Wives*, ed. Mikio Kanda and trans. Taeko Midorikawa (New York: St. Martin's Press, 1989), 42, 45.

[3] Haruko Taya Cook and Theodore Cook, *Japan at War: An Oral History* (New York: The New Press, 1992), 403.

[4] Allan M. Winkler, *Life under a Cloud: American Anxiety about the Atom* (New York: Oxford University Press, 1993), 36; Michael B. Stoff et al., eds., *The Manhattan Project: A Documentary Introduction to the Atomic Age* (Philadelphia: Temple University Press, 1991), 5.

[5] *Public Papers of the Presidents of the United States: Harry S. Truman, 1945* (Washington, D.C.: Government Printing Office, 1961), 199; Paul S. Boyer, *By the Bomb's Early Light: American Thought and Culture at the Dawn of the Atomic Age* (New York: Pantheon, 1985), 85.

[6] Michael H. Hunt, *The Genesis of Chinese Communist Foreign Policy* (New York: Columbia University Press, 1996), 150; Paul Gordon Lauren, *The Evolution of International Human Rights: Visions Seen* (Philadelphia: University of Pennsylvania Press, 1998), 213.

[7] David W. Ellwood, *Rebuilding Europe: Western Europe, America, and Postwar Reconstruction* (London: Longman, 1992), 4; Elena Zubkova, *Russia after the War: Hopes, Illusions, and Disappointments, 1945–1957,* trans. and ed. Hugh Ragsdale (Armonk, N.Y.: M. E. Sharpe, 1998), 34; Alan Brinkley, "World War II and American Liberalism," in *The War in American Culture: Society and Consciousness during World War II,* ed. Lewis Erenberg and Susan E. Hirsch (Chicago: University of Chicago Press, 1996), 314.

Chapter 1   The Cold War: Toward Soviet-American Confrontation

[1] Michael H. Hunt, *Crises in U.S. Foreign Policy: An International History Reader* (New Haven: Yale University Press, 1996), 132.

[2] Harry S. Truman, *Memoirs,* vol. 1 (Garden City, N.J.: Doubleday, 1955), 5, 19.

[3] Hunt, *Crises in U.S. Foreign Policy,* 136, 137.

[4] Ibid., 136.

[5] *Off the Record: The Private Papers of Harry S Truman,* ed. Robert H. Ferrell (New York: Harper and Row, 1980), 80.

[6] Hunt, *Crises in U.S. Foreign Policy,* 147.

[7] Ibid., 148, 156.

[8] David Holloway, *Stalin and the Bomb: The Soviet Union and Atomic Energy, 1939–1956* (New Haven: Yale University Press, 1994), 292; *Khrushchev Remembers,* trans. and ed. Strobe Talbott (Boston: Little, Brown, 1970), 307.

[9] *Khrushchev Remembers: Glasnost Tapes,* trans. and ed. Jerrold L. Schecter with Vyacheslav B. Luchkov (Boston: Little, Brown, 1990), 101.

[10] Joseph Stalin, *The Great Patriotic War of the Soviet Union* (New York: International Publishers, 1945), 67.

[11] Milovan, Djilas, *Wartime,* trans. Michael B. Petrovich (New York: Harcourt Brace Jovanovich, 1977), 477.

[12] Holloway, *Stalin and the Bomb,* 132.

[13] Hunt, *Crises in U.S. Foreign Policy,* 145–46.

[14] Ibid., 159.

[15] Russian Institute, Columbia University, ed., *The Anti-Stalin Campaign and International Communism: A Selection of Documents* (New York: Columbia University Press, 1956), 62.

[16] Holloway, *Stalin and the Bomb,* 204, 217.

[17] Michael H. Hunt, *Ideology and U.S. Foreign Policy* (New Haven: Yale University Press, 1987), 163; Scott Lucas, "The Limits of Ideology: U.S. Foreign Policy and Arab Nationalism in the Early Cold War," in *The United States and Decolonization: Power and Freedom,* ed. David Ryan and Victor Pungong (Houndmills, Basingstoke, Hampshire, Eng.: Macmillan, 2000), 141.

[18] Steven Hugh Lee, *The Korean War* (Harlow, Eng.: Pearson Education, 2001), 34.

[19] Ibid., 45, 131.

[20] R. W. Davis, "Economic Aspects of Stalinism," in *The Stalin Phenomenon,* ed. Alec Nove (New York: St. Martin's Press, 1993), 41.

[21] Elena Zubkova, *Russia after the War: Hopes, Illusions, and Disappointments, 1945–1957,* trans. and ed. Hugh Ragsdale (Armonk, N.Y.: M. E. Sharpe, 1998), 82.

[22] Ibid., 152.

[23] Ibid., 60.

[24] Ibid., 48.

[25] Ibid., 142.

[26] Sarah Davies, "The Leader Cult: Propaganda and Its Reception in Stalin's Russia," in *Politics, Society, and Stalinism in the USSR*, ed. John Channon (New York: St. Martin's Press, 1998), 121.

[27] Solomon Volkov, *Testimony: The Memoirs of Dmitri Shostakovich*, trans. Antonina W. Bouis (New York: Harper and Row, 1979), 156.

[28] Ellen Schrecker, *The Age of McCarthyism: A Brief History with Documents* (Boston: Bedford Books, 1994), 211–12, 214.

[29] Ibid., 64.

[30] Geoffrey S. Smith, "National Security and Personal Isolation: Sex, Gender, and Disease in the Cold-War United States," *International History Review* 14 (May 1992): 312; Schrecker, *The Age of McCarthyism*, 119–20.

[31] Schrecker, *The Age of McCarthyism*, 144.

[32] Smith, "National Security and Personal Isolation," 321; *Crises in U.S. Foreign Policy*, 159.

[33] This is Ellen Schrecker's summing up in *Many Are the Crimes: McCarthyism in America* (Boston: Little, Brown, 1998).

Chapter 2   The International Economy: Out of the Ruins

[1] Richard N. Gardner, *Sterling-Dollar Diplomacy in Current Perspective: The Origins and Prospects of Our International Economic Order*, rev. ed. (New York: Columbia University Press, 1980), xiii.

[2] John Maynard Keynes, *The Collected Writings of John Maynard Keynes*, vol. 7: *The General Theory of Employment, Interest and Money* (London: Macmillan, 1973), 383.

[3] Keynes, *The Collected Writings*, vol. 9: *Essays in Persuasion* (London: Macmillan, 1972), 311.

[4] David W. Ellwood, *Rebuilding Europe: Western Europe, America, and Postwar Reconstruction* (London: Longman, 1992), 21–22.

[5] John W. Dower, *Embracing Defeat: Japan in the Wake of World War II* (New York: Norton, 1999), 60.

[6] Ibid., 550.

[7] Charles S. Maier, "The Politics of Productivity: The Foundations of American International Economic Activity after World War II," in *The Cold War in Europe: Era of a Divided Continent*, ed. Maier (New York: Markus Wiener, 1991), 180.

[8] Eleanor M. Hadley, "The Diffusion of Keynsian Ideas in Japan," in *The Political Power of Economic Ideas*, ed. Peter A. Hall (Princeton: Princeton University Press, 1989), 298n.

[9] Ellwood, *Rebuilding Europe*, 31; Victor Klemperer, *I Will Bear Witness: A Diary of the Nazi Years, 1942–1945*, trans. Martin Chalmers (New York: Random House, 1999), 434, 494.

[10] Claire Duchen, *Women's Rights and Women's Lives in France, 1944–1968* (London: Routledge, 1994), 9; Ellwood, *Rebuilding Europe*, 55–56.

[11] Ellwood, *Rebuilding Europe*, 62.

[12] Ibid., 167.

[13] Ibid., 118.

[14] These advertisements, all from 1949, can be found at <http://www.adflip.com>.

[15] Bob Thomas, *Walt Disney: An American Original* (New York: Simon & Schuster, 1976), 277.

[16] Richard Kuisel, *Seducing the French: The Dilemma of Americanization* (Berkeley: University of California Press, 1993), 52.

[17] Ibid., 65.

[18] Ibid., 55.

[19] Ibid., 63.

Chapter 3   The Third World: First Tremors in Asia

[1] Edgar Snow, *Red Star over China* (originally published 1938; New York: Grove Press, 1961), 131.

[2] Michael H. Hunt, *The Genesis of Chinese Communist Foreign Policy* (New York: Columbia University Press, 1996), 77.

[3] Stuart R. Schram, *The Political Thought of Mao Tse-tung*, rev. ed. (New York: Praeger, 1969) 250.

[4] Peter J. Seybolt, *Throwing the Emperor from His Horse: Portrait of a Village Leader in China, 1923–1995* (Boulder, Colo.: Westview, 1996), 7.

[5] Schram, *Political Thought*, 167, 350.

[6] Ibid., 405.

[7] Chen Jian, *Mao's China and the Cold War* (Chapel Hill: University of North Carolina Press, 2001), 315n14.

[8] Schram, *Political Thought*, 235.

[9] Ho Chi Minh, *Selected Writings (1920–1969)* (Hanoi: Foreign Languages Publishing House, 1973), 251.

[10] *Vietnam: A History in Documents*, ed. Gareth Porter (New York: New American Library, 1981), 29, 30.

[11] Truong Buu Lam, ed. and trans., *Patterns of Vietnamese Response to Foreign Intervention, 1858–1900* (New Haven, Conn.: Yale Southeast Asia Studies, 1967), 79; Huynh Kim Khanh, *Vietnamese Communism, 1925–1945* (Ithaca: Cornell University Press, 1982), 29–30n.

[12] Gérard Chaliand, *The Peasants of North Vietnam*, trans. Peter Wiles (Baltimore: Penguin, 1969), 74, 143.

[13] Nguyen Thi Dinh, *No Other Road to Take: Memoir of Mrs. Nguyen Thi Dinh*, trans. Mai V. Elliott (Ithaca: Cornell University Southeast Asia Program, Department of Asian Studies, 1976), 25, 27, 28.

[14] *The Indian Nationalist Movement, 1885–1947: Select Documents*, ed. B. N. Padney (London: Macmillan, 1979), 142.

[15] Lionel Hastings Ismay, *Memoirs* (New York: Viking Press, 1960), 417.

[16] *Hind Swaraj and Other Writings*, ed. Anthony J. Parel (Cambridge, Eng.: Cambridge University Press, 1997), 150–51.

[17] Bina Agarwal, *A Field of One's Own: Gender and Land Rights in South Asia* (Cambridge, Eng.: Cambridge University Press, 1994), 431.

[18] Judith M. Brown, *Modern India: The Origins of an Asian Democracy*, 2nd ed. (Oxford, Eng. Oxford University Press, 1994), 350.

[19] Judith M. Brown, *Nehru* (London: Longman, 1999), 36.

[20] Data from Angus Maddison, *Monitoring the World Economy, 1820–1992* (Paris: Development Centre of the Organisation for Economic Co-operation and Development, 1995), 24, 63.

[21] David Joel Steinberg et al., *In Search of Southeast Asia: A Modern History*, rev. ed. (Honolulu: University of Hawaii Press, 1987), 277.

[22] Benedict J. Kerkvliet, *The Huk Rebellion: A Study of Peasant Revolt in the Philippines* (Berkeley: University of California Press, 1977), 11.

[23] Ibid., 51.

[24] Ibid., 164, 269.

Part Two   The Cold War System under Stress, 1953–1968

[1] Marika Sherwood, *Kwame Nkrumah: The Years Abroad, 1935–1947* (Legon, Accra, Ghana: Freedom Publications, 1996), 98, 141.

[2] Kwame Nkrumah, *Revolutionary Path* (New York: International Publishers, 1973), 426.

Chapter 4   The Cold War: A Tenuous Accommodation

[1] Amy W. Knight, *Beria: Stalin's First Lieutenant* (Princeton: Princeton University Press, 1993), 209.

[2] Nikita Khrushchev address reproduced in U.S. Senate, *Congressional Record,* 84th Cong., 2nd Sess., (Washington D.C.: U.S. Government Printing Office, 1956), vol. 102, pt. 7, pp. 9391, 9395.

[3] Stephen F. Cohen and Katrina vanden Heuvel, *Voices of Glasnost: Interviews with Gorbachev's Reformers* (New York: Norton, 1989), 262.

[4] Elena Zubkova, *Russia after the War: Hopes, Illusions, and Disappointments, 1945–1957,* trans. and ed. Hugh Ragsdale (Armonk, N.Y.: M. E. Sharpe, 1998), 185, 188.

[5] William J. Tompson, *Khrushchev: A Political Life* (New York: St. Martin's, 1995), 246.

[6] Ibid., 257, 258.

[7] Richard Stites, *Russian Popular Culture: Entertainment and Society since 1900* (Cambridge, Eng.: Cambridge University Press, 1992), 133.

[8] The notion of "bread-and-butter" socialism is central to Tompson's interpretation in *Khrushchev.*

[9] Zubkova, *Russia after the War,* 162.

[10] David Holloway, *Stalin and the Bomb: The Soviet Union and Atomic Energy, 1939–1956* (New Haven: Yale University Press, 1994), 339, 343.

[11] Robert V. Daniels, ed., *A Documentary History of Communism and the World: From Revolution to Collapse,* 3rd ed. (Hanover, N.H.: University Press of New England, 1994), 124.

[12] Ibid., 170, 171; *New York Times,* November 5, 1956, p. 22.

[13] Daniels, *A Documentary History of Communism and the World,* 166.

[14] Michael H. Hunt, *Crises in U.S. Foreign Policy: An International History Reader* (New Haven: Yale University Press, 1996), 169.

[15] Ibid., 274.

[16] Ibid., 294.

[17] David Nordlander, "Khruschchev's Image," *Russian Review* 52 (April 1993): 262; Cohen and vanden Heuvel, *Voices of Glasnost,* 264.

[18] Raymond L. Garthoff, *Reflections on the Cuban Missile Crisis,* rev. ed. (Washington D.C.: Brookings Institution, 1989), 133–34.

[19] Michael H. Hunt, *Lyndon Johnson's War: America's Cold War Crusade in Vietnam* (New York: Hill and Wang, 1996), viii, 60.

[20] Hunt, *Crises in U.S. Foreign Policy,* 361.

[21] Robert McNamara with Brian VanDeMark, *In Retrospect: The Tragedy and Lessons of Vietnam* (New York: Times Books, 1995), 190–91; The Senator Gravel Edition, *The Pentagon Papers: The Defense Department History of United States Decisionmaking in Vietnam* (5 vols.; Boston: Beacon Press, 1971–72), 4: 616.

[22] Data from *UN Demographic Yearbook,* U.S. Department of Commerce's Bureau of the Census, and National Center for Educational Statistics.

[23] William H. Chafe, *The Unfinished Journey: America since World War II,* 3rd ed. (New York: Oxford University Press, 1995), 152.

[24] Ibid., 317; Rhodri Jeffreys-Jones, *Peace Now! American Society and the Ending of the Vietnam War* (New Haven: Yale University Press, 1999), 104; Alexander Bloom and Wini Breines, eds., *"Takin' it to the streets": A Sixties Reader* (New York: Oxford University Press, 1995), 232.

[25] Terry H. Anderson, *The Movement and the Sixties: Protest in America from Greensboro to Wounded Knee* (New York: Oxford University Press, 1995), 138.

[26] Bloom and Breines, *"Takin' it to the streets,"* 62, 68.

[27] Todd Gitlin, *The Sixties: Years of Hope, Days of Rage*, rev. ed. (New York: Bantam Books, 1993), 206.

[28] Data from the Organisation for Economic Co-operation and Development (OECD).

[29] Ronald Fraser et al., *1968: A Student Generation in Revolt* (New York: Pantheon, 1988), 213.

[30] Thomas R. H. Havens, *Fire across the Sea: The Vietnam War and Japan, 1965–1975* (Princeton: Princeton Univerity Press, 1987), 205.

[31] Ibid., 58.

[32] Ibid., 186.

[33] Elena Poniatowska, *Massacre in Mexico*, trans. Helen R. Lane (New York: Viking Press, 1975), 218.

[34] Gale Stokes, ed., *From Stalinism to Pluralism: A Documentary History of Eastern Europe since 1945*, 2nd ed. (New York: Oxford University Press, 1996), 126.

[35] Jerzy Eisler, "March 1968 in Poland," in *1968: The World Transformed,* ed. Carole Fink et al. (Cambridge, Eng.: Cambridge University Press, 1998), 245.

[36] Mark Kramer, "The Czechoslovak Crisis and the Brezhnev Doctrine," in *1968: The World Transformed*, 127.

[37] Robert V. Daniels, *Year of the Heroic Guerrilla: World Revolution and Counterrevolution in 1968* (New York: Basic Books, 1989), 164.

Chapter 5   Abundance and Discontent in the Developed World

[1] Data from Louis Johnston and Samuel H. Willamson, "The Annual Real and Nominal GDP for the United States, 1789–Present," Economic History Services, April 2002, <http://www.eh.net/hmit/gdp/>.

[2] Richard M. Nixon, *Six Crises* (Garden City, N.Y.: Doubleday, 1962), 253, 259–60; *Khrushchev Remembers: The Last Testament*, ed. and trans. Strobe Talbott (Boston: Little, Brown, 1974), 366.

[3] Robert M. Collins, "The Economic Crisis of 1968 and the Waning of the 'American Century'," *American Historical Review* 101 (April 1996): 416.

[4] Data from Angus Maddison, *Monitoring the World Economy, 1820–1992* (Paris: Development Centre of the Organisation for Economic Co-operation and Development, 1995), 83; and Vera Zamagni, *The Economic History of Italy, 1860–1990* (New York: Oxford University Press, 1993), 40.

[5] This notion is central to the interpretation in Alan S. Milward with the assistance of George Brennan and Federico Romero, *The European Rescue of the Nation-State*, 2nd ed. (London: Routledge, 2000).

[6] This encyclical, issued on May 5, 1961, can be found in the archives in the Vatican website at <http://www.vatican.va>.

[7] Data from Angus Maddison, *The World Economy: A Millenial Perspective* (Paris: Development Centre of the Organisation for Economic Co-operation and Development, 2001), 135.

[8] Milward, *The European Rescue*, 208.

[9] Ibid., 390.

[10] Morita Akio with Edwin M. Reingold and Mitsuko Shimomura, *Made in Japan: Akio Morita and Sony* (New York: E. P. Dutton, 1986), 79, 82.

[11] Ibid., 189.

[12] Ibid., 180.

[13] *New York Times Magazine,* July 13, 1969, p. 10.

[14] Mary A. McCay, *Rachel Carson* (New York: Twayne, 1993), 23–24.

[15] Ibid., 64.

[16] Rachel Carson, *Silent Spring* (Boston: Houghton Mifflin, 1962), 99, 297.

[17] Betty Friedan, *Life So Far* (New York: Simon & Schuster, 2000), 133.

[18] NOW statement of purpose, adopted at the founding conference in Washington, D.C., on October 29, 1966, at <http://www.feminist.org/chronicles/early1.html>.

[19] Claire Duchen, *Women's Rights and Women's Lives in France, 1944–1968* (London: Routledge, 1994), 91.

[20] Organisation for Economic Co-operation and Development (OECD) data.

[21] Duchen, *Women's Rights,* 185.

[22] Kathleen S. Uno, "The Death of 'Good Wife, Wise Mother'?" in *Postwar Japan as History,* ed. Andrew Gordon (Berkeley: University of California Press, 1993), 313.

[23] Gabriel Almond quoted in Tony Smith, "Requiem or New Agenda for Third World Studies?" *World Politics* 37 (July 1985): 537.

Chapter 6   Third-World Hopes At High Tide

[1] Stuart R. Schram, *The Political Thought of Mao Tse-tung* (New York: Praeger, 1963), 247.

[2] Stuart R. Schram, ed., *Chairman Mao Talks to the People: Talks and Letters, 1956–1971,* trans. John Chinnery and Tieyun (New York: Pantheon Books, 1975), 92.

[3] Ibid., 142.

[4] Ibid., 184; Sidney Rittenberg and Amanda Bennett, *The Man Who Stayed Behind* (New York: Simon & Schuster, 1993), 272.

[5] Huang Shu-min, *The Spiral Road: Change in a Chinese Village through the Eyes of a Communist Party Leader,* 2nd ed. (Boulder, Colo.: Westview, 1998), 61–62.

[6] Peter J. Seybolt, *Throwing the Emperor from His Horse: Portrait of a Village Leader in China, 1923–1995* (Boulder, Colo.: Westview, 1996), 75.

[7] Meiczyslaw Maneli, *War of the Vanquished,* trans. Maria de Görgey (New York: Harper & Row, 1971), 154.

[8] Gareth Porter, ed., *Vietnam: The Definitive Documentation of Human Decisions,* 2 vols. (Stanfordville, N.Y.: Earl M. Coleman Enterprises, 1979), 2: 383–84.

[9] Ibid., 2: 477–78.

[10] Ho Chi Minh, *Selected Writings (1920–1969)* (Hanoi: Foreign Languages Publishing House, 1973), 361.

[11] Richard H. Immerman, *The CIA in Guatemala: The Foreign Policy of Intervention* (Austin: University of Texas Press, 1982), 102.

[12] Jim Handy, *Revolution in the Countryside: Rural Conflict and Agrarian Reform in Guatemala, 1944–1954* (Chapel Hill: University of North Carolina Press, 1994), 175.

[13] Ibid., 4; Piero Gleijeses, *Shattered Hope: The Guatemalan Revolution and the United States, 1944–1954* (Princeton: Princeton University Press, 1991), 369.

[14] Piero Gleijeses, *Politics and Culture in Guatemala* (Ann Arbor: Center for Political Studies, Institute for Social Research, University of Michigan, 1988), 7.

[15] Pablo Neruda, "In Guatemala," in *Song of Protest,* trans. Miguel Algarín (New York: William Morrow, 1976), 59.

[16] Peter G. Bourne, *Fidel: A Biography of Fidel Castro* (New York: Dodd, Mead and Co., 1986), 230.

[17] Lee Lockwood, *Castro's Cuba, Cuba's Fidel* (New York: Macmillan Company, 1967), 42.

[18] Bourne, *Fidel*, 119.

[19] Data from Tim Golden, "Castro's People Try to Absorb 'Terrible Blows'," *New York Times*, January 11, 1993, pp. A1, A6, supplemented by literacy figures from CIA's *World Factbook*, 1991.

[20] Kwame Nkrumah, *Revolutionary Path* (New York: International Publishers, 1973), 240.

[21] Ayi Kwei Armah, *The Beautyful Ones Are Not Yet Born* (New York: Collier Books, 1969), 104.

[22] Baffour Ankomah and Mike Afrani, "'If I Fall, Fall as a Man': Kwame Nkrumah 25 Years after his Death," *New African*, no. 351 (April 1997): p14.

[23] Tony Smith, *The Pattern of Imperialism: The United States, Great Britain, and the Late-Industrializing World since 1815* (Cambridge, Eng.: Cambridge University Press, 1981), 131.

[24] Mohammad Musaddiq, *Musaddiq's Memoir: The End of the British Empire in Iran*, ed. Homa Katouzian and trans. Katouzian and S. H. Amin (London: JEBHE, National Movement of Iran, 1988), 74.

[25] Asadollah Alam, *The Shah and I: The Confidential Diary of Iran's Royal Court, 1969–1977*, ed. Alinaghi Alikhani and trans. Alikhani and Nicholas Vincent (New York: St. Martin's Press, 1992), 323, 360.

[26] P. J. Vatikiotis, *Nasser and His Generation* (London: Croom Helm, 1978), 145.

[27] Gamal Abdel Nasser, *Nasser Speaks: Basic Documents*, trans. E. S. Farag (London: Morssett Press, 1972), 29.

[28] J. R. McNeill, *Something New under the Sun: An Environmental History of the Twentieth-Century World* (New York: Norton, 2000), 168–69.

[29] *Umm Kulthun: A Voice Like Egypt* (dir. Michal Goldman; 1996; 67 min.).

[30] Vatikiotis, *Nasser and His Generation*, 266.

[31] Gilles Kepel, "Islamists versus the State in Egypt and Algeria," *Daedalus* 124 (Summer 1995): 121.

[32] The Atlantic Charter text is available at <http://www.yale.edu/lawweb/avalon/wwii/atlantic/at10.htm#1>.

Part Three   From Cold War to Globalization, 1968–1991

[1] Ray Kroc with Robert Anderson, *Grinding It Out: The Making of McDonald's* (Chicago: Henry Regnery, 1977), 9.

[2] Ibid., 15.

[3] John F. Love, *McDonald's: Behind the Arches*, rev. ed. (New York: Bantam Books, 1995), 464.

[4] From "McDonald's Reports Global Results for 2002," released January 23, 2003, available at <http://www.mcdonalds.com/corporate/press/financial/2003/01232003/index.html>.

[5] "McAtlas Shrugged," *Foreign Policy* 124 (May/June 2001): 26.

Chapter 7   The Cold War Comes to a Close

[1] Stephen J. Whitfield, *The Culture of the Cold War*, 2nd ed. (Baltimore: Johns Hopkins University Press, 1996), 19.

[2] Nixon remarks to White House staff, July 19, 1971, available at <http://www.gwu.edu/~nsarchiv/NSAEBB/NSAEBB66/ch-41.pdf>; Nixon speech, July 6, 1971, *Public Papers of the Presidents of the United States: Richard Nixon, 1971* (Washington D.C.: Government Printing Office, 1972), 804.

[3] Stephen E. Ambrose, *Nixon*, vol. 2: *The Triumph of a Politician, 1962–1972* (New York: Simon & Schuster, 1989), 660.

[4] H. R. Haldeman, *The Haldeman Diaries: Inside the Nixon White House* (New York: G. P. Putnam's Sons, 1994), 322.

[5] Robert V. Daniels, ed. and trans., *A Documentary History of Communism in Russia: From Lenin to Gorbachev*, 3rd ed. (Hanover, N.H.: University Press of New England, 1993), 295, 297.

[6] Lawrence S. Wittner, "The Nuclear Threat Ignored," in *1968: The World Transformed*, eds. Carole Fink et al. (Cambridge, Eng.: Cambridge University Press, 1998), 455.

[7] Stephen White, *Russia Goes Dry: Alcohol, State, and Society* (Cambridge; Eng.: Cambridge University Press, 1996), 40.

[8] Isaac J. Tarasulo, ed., *Perils of Perestroika: Viewpoints of the Soviet Press, 1989–1991* (Wilmington, Del.: Scholarly Resources, 1992), 182; White, *Russia Goes Dry*, 172.

[9] Hedrick Smith, *The New Russians* (New York: Random House, 1990), 25.

[10] Mark Kramer, "The Czechoslovak Crisis and the Brezhnev Doctrine," in *1968: The World Transformed*, 168.

[11] Raymond L. Garthoff, *Détente and Confrontation: American-Soviet Relations from Nixon to Reagan*, rev. ed. (Washington D.C.: Brookings Institution, 1994), 40, 114–15.

[12] Gottfried Niedhart, "Ostpolitik: The Role of the Federal Republic of Germany in the Process of Détente," in *1968: The World Transformed*, 181.

[13] *New York Times*, February 19, 1993, p. A4.

[14] *Cold War International History Project Bulletin*, 8–9 (Winter 1996/1997): 120.

[15] Odd Arne Westad, ed., *The Fall of Détente: Soviet-American Relations during the Carter Years* (Oslo: Scandinavian University Press, 1997), 301.

[16] Frances Fitzgerald, *Way Out There in the Blue: Reagan, Star Wars and the End of the Cold War* (New York: Simon & Schuster, 2000), 31.

[17] Jeane Kirkpatrick, "Dictatorships and Double Standards," *Commentary* 68 (November 1979): 44.

[18] Garthoff, *Détente and Confrontation*, 70, 860.

[19] Archie Brown, *The Gorbachev Factor* (New York: Oxford University Press, 1996), 39.

[20] Ibid., 336n152.

[21] Ibid., 94.

[22] Don Oberdorfer, *From the Cold War to a New Era: The United States and the Soviet Union, 1983–1991*, 2nd ed. (Baltimore: Johns Hopkins University Press, 1998), 381, 383.

[23] Timothy Garton Ash, *The Magic Lantern: The Revolution of '89 Witnessed in Warsaw, Budapest, Berlin and Prague*, 3rd ed. (New York: Vintage, 1999), 16.

[24] Gale Stokes, *The Walls Came Tumbling Down: The Collapse of Communism in Eastern Europe* (New York: Oxford University Press, 1993), 139, 140.

[25] Oberdorfer, *From the Cold War to a New Era*, 460, 465.

[26] Daniels, *A Documentary History of Communism in Russia*, 392.

[27] Brown, *The Gorbachev Factor*, 88.

[28] Data from Natural Resources Defense Council Archive at <http://www.nrdc.org/nuclear/nudb/datab9.asp and /datab10.asp>.

[29] Allan M. Winkler, *Life under a Cloud: American Anxiety about the Atom* (New York: Oxford University Press, 1993), 212; George F. Kennan, *The Nuclear Delusion: Soviet-American Relations in the Atomic Age* (New York: Pantheon Books, 1983), 176.

[30] Jonathan Schell, *Fate of the Earth* (New York: Knopf, 1982), 182.

[31] Data from Angus Maddison, *Monitoring the World Economy, 1820–1992* (Paris: Development Centre of the Organisation for Economic Co-operation and Development, 1995), 186–87.

Chapter 8   Global Markets: One System, Three Centers

[1] Data from Angus Maddison, *The World Economy: A Millennial Perspective* (Paris: Development Centre of the Organisation for Economic Co-operation and Development, 2001), 272, 275, 284, 298.

[2] Data from the *New York Times*, January 27, 1992, p. C5.

[3] David A. Stockman, *The Triumph of Politics: How the Reagan Revolution Failed* (New York: Harper & Row, 1987), 429.

[4] Robert M. Collins, *More: The Politics of Economic Growth in Postwar America* (New York: Oxford University Press, 2000), 216.

[5] This Springsteen song is from his album *Born in the U.S.A.* (Sony; originally released 1984).

[6] Studs Terkel, *The Great Divide: Second Thoughts on the American Dream* (New York: Pantheon Books, 1988), 175, 197.

[7] Milton Friedman with the assistance of Rose D. Friedman, *Capitalism and Freedom* (Chicago: University of Chicago Press, 1962), 5.

[8] Ibid., 15, 16.

[9] Data from Louis Johnston and Samuel H. Williamson, "The Annual Real and Nominal GDP for the United States, 1789–Present," Economic History Services, April 2002, <http://www.eh.net/hmit/gdp/>.

[10] Terkel, *The Great Divide*, 381.

[11] Ibid., 352.

[12] *New York Times*, January 3, 1995, p. A4.

[13] Ibid., August 4, 1989, p. A7.

[14] Ibid., February 17, 1998, p. A4.

[15] *Khrushchev Remembers: The Last Testament*, ed. and trans. Strobe Talbott (Boston: Little, Brown, 1974), 253; David S. G. Goodman, *Deng Xiaoping and the Chinese Revolution: A Political Biography* (London: Routledge, 1994), 35.

[16] Han Minzhu, ed., *Cries for Democracy: Writings and Speeches from the 1989 Chinese Democracy Movement* (Princeton: Princeton University Press, 1990), 221.

[17] Derek W. Urwin, *The Community of Europe: A History of European Integration since 1945*, 2nd ed. (London: Longman, 1995), 111.

[18] Data from Vera Zamagni, *The Economic History of Italy, 1860–1990* (New York: Oxford University Press, 1993), 40.

[19] James H. Mittelman, *The Globalization Syndrome: Transformation and Resistance* (Princeton: Princeton University Press, 2000), 223.

[20] Data in Sheldon M. Garon, *Molding Japanese Minds: The State in Everyday Life* (Princeton: Princeton University Press, 1997), 216.

[21] *New York Times*, February 20, 1990, p. A6.

[22] Gale Stokes, *The Walls Came Tumbling Down: The Collapse of Communism in Eastern Europe* (New York: Oxford University Press, 1993), 233.

Chapter 9   Divergent Paths in the Third World

[1] Niccolò Machiavelli, *The Prince*, trans. Luigi Ricci and E. R. P. Vincent (New York: Random House, 1950), 21.

[2] Ben Kiernan, *The Pol Pot Regime: Race, Power, and Genocide in Cambodia under the Khmer Rouge, 1975–79* (New Haven: Yale University Press, 1996), 11.

[3] Ibid., 247; Alexander L. Hinton, "Why Did You Kill? The Cambodian Genocide and the Dark Side of Face and Honor," *Journal of Asian Studies* 57 (February 1998): 93.

[4] Kiernan, *The Pol Pot Regime*, 111.

[5] Hamid Algar, ed. and trans., *Islam and Revolution: Writings and Declarations of Imam Khomeini* (Berkeley: Mizan Press, 1981), 21.

[6] Ibid., 182.

[7] Ibid., 132.

[8] This reading follows Michael M. J. Fischer, *Iran: From Religious Dispute to Revolution* (Cambridge, Mass.: Harvard University Press, 1980), 182, 354–55.

[9] Quote from the documentary, *Iran: Adrift in a Sea of Blood* (writ. and dir. Ron Hallis; 1986; 27 min.).

[10] Mark Mathabane, *Kaffir Boy* (New York: Macmillan, 1986), 33.

[11] Sheridan Johns and R. Hunt Davis Jr., eds., *Mandela, Tambo, and the African National Congress: The Struggle against Apartheid, 1948–1990, A Documentary Survey* (New York: Oxford University Press, 1991), 138.

[12] Ibid., 133.

[13] Ibid., 172.

[14] Martin Gilbert, *Exile and Return: The Emergence of Jewish Statehood* (London: Weidenfield and Nicolson, 1978), 39.

[15] Charles D. Smith, *Palestine and the Arab-Israeli Conflict: A History with Documents*, 4th ed. (Boston: Bedford/St. Martin's, 2001), 75.

[16] Ibid., 121.

[17] Helena Cobban, *The Palestine Liberation Organization: People, Power and Politics* (Cambridge, Eng.: Cambridge University Press, 1984), 246.

[18] Data from Joshua Teitelbaum and Joseph Kostiner, "The West Bank and Gaza: The PLO and the *Intifada*," in *Revolutions of the Late Twentieth Century*, ed. Jack A. Goldstone et al. (Boulder, Colo.: Westview Press, 1991), 302, and from CIA World Factbook 2000.

[19] Smith, *Palestine and the Arab-Israeli Conflict*, 342, 344.

[20] Shaul Mishal and Reuben Aharoni, eds., *Speaking Stones: Communiqués from the Intifada Underground* (Syracuse, N.Y.: Syracuse University Press, 1994), 58.

[21] Hanan Ashrawi, *This Side of Peace: A Personal Account* (New York: Simon & Schuster, 1995), 89.

[22] Walter LaFeber, *Inevitable Revolutions: The United States in Central America*, rev. ed. (New York: Norton, 1993), 256.

[23] Piero Gleijeses, *Politics and Culture in Guatemala* (Ann Arbor: Center for Political Studies, Institute for Social Research, University of Michigan, 1988), 9.

[24] Margaret Hooks, *Guatemalan Women Speak* (London: Catholic Institute for International Relations, 1991), 125.

[25] Data from Angus Maddison, *The World Economy: A Millennial Perspective* (Paris: Development Centre of the Organisation for Economic Co-operation and Development, 2001), 288, 304, 307, 323, 325–26.

[26] Kevin Shillington, *Ghana and the Rawlings Factor* (New York: St. Martin's Press, 1992), 33.

[27] James E. Mahon Jr., "Economic Crisis in Latin America: Global Contagion, Local Pain," *Current History* 98 (March 1999): 109.

[28] Data from Maddison, *The World Economy*, 30.

[29] Bina Agarwal, *A Field of One's Own: Gender and Land Rights in South Asia* (Cambridge, Eng.: Cambridge University Press, 1994), 263.

[30] Erika Friedl, *Women of Deh Koh: Lives in an Iranian Village* (New York: Penguin, 1991), 10.

Conclusion   Globalization Ascendant: The 1990s and Beyond

[1] J. R. McNeill, *Something New under the Sun: An Environmental History of the Twentieth-Century World* (New York: Norton, 2000), 3.

[2] Kirkpatrick Sale, *The Green Revolution: The American Environmental Movement, 1962–1992* (New York: Hill and Wang, 1993), 83.

[3] Ibid., 77.

[4] Norman Myers, *Ultimate Security: The Environmental Basis of Political Stability* (New York: Norton, 1993), 25.

[5] *New York Times*, September 9, 1997, p. B7.

[6] *Selected Speeches of Indira Gandhi*, vol. 2 (New Delhi: Ministry of Information and Broadcasting, 1975), 448.

[7] Data from Angus Maddison, *The World Economy: A Millennial Perspective* (Paris: Development Centre of the Organisation for Economic Co-operation and Development, 2001), 46, 127, 241.

[8] "The Siena Declaration," September 1998, printed as an advertisement in the *New York Times*, November 24, 1998, p. A7, and also available at <http://www.twnside.org.sg/title/siena-cn.htm>.

[9] *New York Times*, April 13, 2000, p. A12.

[10] Julie Mertus et al., eds., *The Suitcase: Refugee Voices from Bosnia and Croatia*, trans. Jelica Todosijevic et al. (Berkeley: University of California Press, 1997), 153.

[11] The Universal Declaration of Human Rights, adopted by the UN General Assembly in December 1948, available at <http://www.un.org/rights/50/decla.htm>; Paul Gordon Lauren, *The Evolution of International Human Rights: Visions Seen* (Philadelphia: University of Pennsylvania Press, 1998), 223.

[12] Lauren, *The Evolution of International Human Rights*, 199.

[13] Clinton in *New York Times*, November 28, 1995, p. A6; George H. W. Bush in *Public Papers of the Presidents of the United States: George Bush, 1991*, book 1 (Washington, D.C.: Government Printing Office, 1992), 74; George W. Bush address, September 20, 2001, available at <http://www.whitehouse.gov/news/releases/2001/09/20010920-8.html>.

[14] Henry R. Luce, "The American Century," *Life* 10 (February 17, 1941): 65.

[15] Graph from the Center for Defense Information <http://www.cdi.org/issues/wme> (July 6, 2002).

[16] David Halberstam, *War in a Time of Peace: Bush, Clinton, and the Generals* (New York: Scribners, 2001), 230, 308.

[17] Bush's remark captured on camera in *The Gulf War* (writ. and prod. Eamonn Matthews; 1996; 232 min.); Mark Bowden, "Tales of the Tyrant," *Atlantic Monthly* 289 (May 2002): 50.

[18] *Public Papers of the Presidents of the United States: George Bush, 1991*, book 1 (Washington, D.C.: Government Printing Office, 1992), 197.

[19] Susan A. Aaronson, *Trade and the American Dream: A Social History of Postwar Trade Policy* (Lexington: University Press of Kentucky, 1996), 147.

[20] Philip H. Gordon and Sophie Meunier, *The French Challenge: Adapting to Globalization* (Washington, D.C.: Brookings Institution Press, 2001), 89.

[21] Stephen F. Cohen, "Endangering U.S. Security," *The Nation* 274 (April 15, 2002): 6; *New York Times*, December 13, 1993, p. A6.

[22] *New York Times*, April 13, 1999, p. A6.

INDEX

Pages in italics followed by a letter refer to: *f* figures, including charts and graphs; *i* illustrations, including photographs; *m* maps; and *t* tables.

ARCTIC OCEAN

Greenland
(Den.)

Alaska
(U.S.)

ICELAND

See inset

CANADA

ATLANTIC OCEAN

UNITED STATES

Azores
(Port.)

Madeira Is.
(Port.)

TUNISI

MOROCCO

Hawaii
(U.S.)

BAHAMAS

MEXICO

CUBA

DOMINICAN
REPUBLIC

Canary Is.
(Sp.)

ALGERI

JAMAICA

BELIZE

HAITI

Western Sahara
(Mor.)

MAURITANIA

MALI

NIG

GUATEMALA
EL SALVADOR

HONDURAS

NICARAGUA

See inset

CAPE
VERDE

SENEGAL

BURKINA
FASO

PACIFIC OCEAN

COSTA RICA

GUYANA

SURINAME

GAMBIA

GHANA

PANAMA

VENEZUELA

French Guiana (Fr.)

GUINEA-BISSAU

GUINEA

CÔTE
D'IVOIRE

COLOMBIA

SIERRA LEONE

BENIN

TOGO
EQ.

Galápagos Is.
(Ec.)

ECUADOR

LIBERIA

GUINEA

SÃO TOMÉ
& PRÍNCIPE

SAMOA

Am. Samoa

PERU

BRAZIL

GABON

TONGA

BOLIVIA

PARAGUAY

Puerto Rico
(U.S.)

ANTIGUA
AND BARBUDA

Virgin Islands
(U.S. & Br.)

ST. KITTS
& NEVIS

URUGUAY

ATLANTIC OCEAN

Montserrat
(Br.)

Guadeloupe
(Fr.)

CHILE ARGENTINA

DOMINICA

Martinique
(Fr.)

ST. LUCIA

BARBADOS

ST. VINCENT &
THE GRENADINES

GRENADA

Falkland Is.
(Br.)

TRINIDAD AND
TOBAGO

ARCTIC OCEAN

SOVIET UNION

MONGOLIA

CHINA

KOREA

JAPAN

PACIFIC OCEAN

NORWAY
FINLAND
N. IRELAND
SWEDEN
IRELAND
BRITAIN
DENMARK
NETHERLANDS
GERMANY
POLAND
SOVIET
UNION
BELGIUM
LUX.
CZECHOSLOVAKIA
FRANCE
AUSTRIA
HUNGARY
SWITZ.
ROMANIA
PORTUGAL
YUGOSLAVIA
BULGARIA
SPAIN
ITALY
ALBANIA
TURKEY
GREECE
Gibraltar (Br.)

TURKEY
Cyprus (Br.)
SYRIA
IRAQ
KUWAIT
(Br.)
IRAN
AFGHANISTAN
Malta
(Br.)
LEBANON
BAHRAIN (Br.)
PALESTINE
(Fr./Br.)
TRANS-
JORDAN
(Br.)
QATAR (Br.)
LIBYA
EGYPT
TRUCIAL
STATES (Br.)
FRENCH
EQ.
AFRICA
ANGLO-
EGYPTIAN
SUDAN
SAUDI
ARABIA
MUSCAT
AND OMAN
(Br.)
CAMEROONS (Br.)
ERITREA
(Br.)
YEMEN
ADEN
(Br.)
CAMEROONS (Fr.)
FR. SOMALILAND
ETHIOPIA
BR. SOMALILAND
UGANDA
(Br.)
ITALIAN
SOMALILAND
BELGIAN
CONGO
KENYA
(Br.)
RUANDA-
URUNDI
(Bel.)
TANGANYIKA
(Br.)
Zanzibar (Br.)
NYASALAND
(Br.)
Seychelles (Br.)
NGOLA
(Port.)
Comoro Arch. (Fr.)
N. RHODESIA
(Br.)
Madagascar (Fr.)
W. AFR.
(S.A.)
S. RHODESIA
(Br.)
MOZAMBIQUE
(Port.)
Mauritius (Br.)
Réunion (Fr.)
BECHUANALAND
(Br.)
SWAZILAND (Br.)
UNION OF
SOUTH
AFRICA
BASUTOLAND
(Br.)

INDIA
(Br.)
SIKKIM
(Br.)
BHUTAN
(Br.)
NEPAL
Damão
(Port.)
Diu
(Port.)
Goa
(Port.)
FR. ESTABL.
IN INDIA
Ceylon
(Br.)
Maldive Is.
(Br.)
BURMA
(Br.)
LAOS (Fr.)
THAILAND
VIETNAM
CAMBODIA
(Fr.)
MALAY
STATES
(Br.)
Singapore
(Br.)
Macau
(Port.)
Hong
Kong
(Br.)
PHILIPPINES
(U.S.)
Borneo
(Br.)
Brunei
(Br.)
Sarawak
(Br.)
NETHERLANDS INDIES
Christmas I.
(Br.)
Port. Timor

Mariana
Islands
Guam
(U.S.)
Marshall
Islands
TRUST TERR. OF
THE PACIFIC ISLANDS
(U.S.)
Caroline
Islands
Nauru
(Austr.)
TRUST TERR.
OF NEW GUINEA
(Austr.)
Gilbert &
Elice Is.
(Br.)
Papua
(Austr.)
Solomon
Is. (Br.)
New Hebrides
(Fr./Br.)
Fiji
(Br.)
New Caledonia
(Fr.)

AUSTRALIA

NEW
ZEALAND

INDIAN OCEAN

	Independent states as of August 1945
	Dependent and colonial territories
(Br.)	State in control
	Occupied territories at the end of World War II